KEEPERS OF THE KEYS

*A History of the Popes
from St. Peter to John Paul II*

KEEPERS OF THE KEYS

A History of the Popes
from St. Peter to John Paul II

NICOLAS CHEETHAM

Charles Scribner's Sons
New York

First Published by Charles Scribner's Sons 1983
Copyright © 1982 Sir Nicolas Cheetham

Library of Congress Cataloging in Publication Data

Cheetham, Nicolas, Sir, 1910-
  Keepers of the keys.

  Bibliography: p.
  Includes index.
  1. Papacy—History. I. Title.
BX955.2.C465 1983   282′.09   82-16950
ISBN 0-684-17863-X

1 3 5 7 9 11 13 15 17 19 H/C 20 18 16 14 12 10 8 6 4 2

Printed in the United States of America.

Contents

Part Six: The Popes at Bay

Part Seven: Modern Times

Epilogue: John Paul II

Illustrations

THE EARLY CHURCH

Roman religion in the first century of our era was a bewildering mixture of cults subsisting side by side and not intolerant of each other. It was hardly strange that this should be so in an empire stretching from the Atlantic to the Euphrates. The Greek world of the Mediterranean, the ancient civilizations of the Near East, the mosaic of people which divided Italy between them before the Romans ruled it and even the less evolved and recently conquered societies of Western and Balkan Europe all contributed their quota of deities claiming worshippers in the capital, Rome.

Before Italy was dominated by the Roman Republic the north was settled by Celtic-speaking Gauls. To the south of them lived the Etruscans with their own peculiar language and religion. The centre and south of the peninsula were occupied by numerous Italic peoples speaking Latin and other related tongues, while the coastal areas from north of Naples down to the toe and heel were studded with the cities of immigrant Greek colonists.

The old Italic religion which the Roman 'religion of Numa' resembled in its essentials was the worship of innumerable little local gods, gods of the family and the hearth, of the powers of nature and rural pursuits, of the genii of the fields, hills, woods and streams. It has been perpetuated in the devotion paid to the minor Saints of the Christian calendar and to many who have no right to figure in the calendars at all. A shadowy but omnipresent goddess, the Bona Dea, guided the lives of women. On this dense substratum there was imposed at an early date the classic Hellenic pantheon of major gods and goddesses. Zeus, Hera, Poseidon, Athena and the rest, all identified exactly or approximately with Latin equivalents, Jupiter, Juno, Neptune, Minerva and so forth. Presiding over these Olympians was Zeus–Jupiter, the Indo-European sky-god common to both Greeks and Italians. The identifications were painstakingly established but lower down in the scale they can appear rather doubtful. Take for example Heracles–Hercules. Although he was revered widely throughout Italy, the immortal Greek hero tended to be confused with the earthy Italian patron of cattle-sheds and pigsties with a like-sounding name.

In the steps of the Greek gods came Greek philosophy, expounded to the Roman upper clan by Greek professors. The aristocrats who conquered the whole Mediterranean basin in the last two centuries before the Christian era were looking for something more intellectually satisfying than the formal call by the Olympians, now the official patrons of the Roman state, and the rustic and domestic rituals of the Latin countryside. It mattered little whether these philosophies tended to dispense with the gods altogether or to divorce them from the mortal order. General suspicion about religion did not prevent the patricians from respecting the traditional observances in the temples made in their own homes. In the first century AD the fashionable philosophy was Stoicism. For the upper class and the intellectuals it had many advantages. It offered to its followers a rule for living in accordance with virtue and reason, a sense of moral freedom and a means of consolation for the tyranny of bad emperors. It appealed to the element of gravity and devotion to duty in the old Roman character. The stoic God was a vague universal spirit or soul of the world underlying the moral and natural order with which the Stoic aspired to live in harmony. As for the Olympians, they could be ignored or allegorized. Some eminent Stoics hankered after a refined form of immortality. Such, for instance, was the statesman Seneca who, like the Christian apostles, perished under Nero.

Philosophic ideas, however, had little effect on popular belief. Nor were the philosophers and mundane sceptics by any means free from the superstitions to which the Romans, high and low, were always addicted. They were all fascinated by signs and omens, ghosts and portents, augury and divination. Astrology, although officially discouraged, was the rage. These practices flourished all the more strongly while the old religion decayed; the temples were deserted and the ancient traditional rites, many of which had become almost meaningless, were no longer celebrated. The longest period of neglect began after the Punic Wars (about 200 BC) and reached its lowest point in the civil wars preceding the reign of Augustus (29 BC–14 AD). It was he, the first Emperor of Rome, who initiated, for reasons of state policy, a great religious and antiquarian revival, suitably hymned by Virgil and other court poets. If the gods were no longer objects of belief they must be revered as symbols of Empire. It says much for Augustus's foresight that the policy was highly successful. Without arousing religious fervour it gave a new and lasting impulse to the state cults. Scores of the musty temples were restored and re-endorsed. Their half-forgotten ceremonies were again enacted by the sacred colleges, priesthoods staffed by eligible aristocrats under imperial sponsorship. These men exercised no sacerdotal functions; they were simply guardians of the state shrines and members of bodies resembling exclusive clubs or companies. Places in them were eagerly prized. Presiding over the most important college of all, that of the pontifices, was the Emperor himself in his capacity of Pontifex Maximus, the Supreme Bridge-Builder or secular patriarch of the State Church. Patrician ladies had their own college of the Vestal Virgins.

But in the two centuries before Augustus oriental religions had moved into Rome to fill the spiritual vacuum. The two most persuasive were those of Cybele, the Great Mother Goddess of Asia Minor, and of Isis and Serapis from Egypt. The cult of the former reached Rome from Galatia in 204 BC, during the second Punic War, and it hung on there so tenaciously that it was still being attacked by St Augustine in the late fourth century AD. Livy tells us how the Senate, in accordance with a verse discovered in the Sybilline Books, sent to fetch her image at a time of great danger to the Republic. Soon she was installed in her own temple on the Palatine, an exotic among Olympians. So exotic indeed that no Roman citizen was permitted to serve as her priest for over a century. In time, however, she became extremely popular, not so much with the patricians who had imported her as with the masses, especially the freedmen and slaves of whom so many hailed from her own Asia. To be sure her cult and that of her son Attis was essentially un-Roman and orgiastic its priests and votaries practised self-mutilation and emasculation. At some festivals long-haired eunuchs, bizarrely costumed, pranced through the streets to the sound of flutes, cymbals and tambourines, shrieking ecstatically and slashing themselves with knives. Not all its rites were so extravagant. In its calmer manifestations it struck deep roots, especially in the family life, and its colleges were more lively and widely diffused than those of the official gods. It had little moral appeal, its mysteries were not profound and the satirists made fun of it. Nevertheless it had become familiar and respectable and not easy to displace.

Nor was the worship of Isis and Serapis, the official religion of Ptolemaic Egypt. Isis was the age-old goddess of the Nile, originally associated with Osiris and the child Horus. But when the Macedonian Ptolemies established their capital at Alexandria she was linked with Serapis, a new composite god with both Hellenic and Egyptian attributes, and the infant was Hellenized as Harpocrates. The cult of the trinity to which the jackal-headed Anerbis was sometimes added, was brought to Greece in the fourth century BC and in the second century to Rome via the Greek cities of southern Italy. By that time it had shed its more outlandish Egyptian characteristics. Periodically frowned on under the later Republic, and especially when Anthony and Cleopatra were arrayed against Rome, it was not only tolerated but encouraged by the Emperor of the first century. The temple of Isis stood prominently at the Campus Martius.

The Isiac religion was less Corybantic and revivalist than that of the Great Mother. Indeed it resembled in many respects our own conception of an organized church complete with hierarchy and professional clergy, and well endowed. Regular and elaborate services quite unlike the formal honours paid to the Olympians, were conducted by robed and tonsured priests passing in and out of the sanctuary where stood the image of the goddess. Besides the daily sacrifice the liturgy included prayers, hymns and sermons. Holy Water from the Nile was available. Major festivals were celebrated by splendid processions in the open air. It was inevitable that many of these outward features should have been reproduced in the future rituals of the Christian Church.

Penitence and purification were required of the faithful, and if the priests were satisfied eligible votaries could be initiated into the various degrees of Isiac mysteries. From these they derived inner enlightenment and glimpses of immortality. Although Roman satirists were apt to deride the more freakish aspects of the cult as lurid and corrupt, it certainly inspired genuine devotion among all classes, achieving its widest influence in the second century AD.

One Oriental religion which the Romans of the early Empire neither understood nor tried to understand was that of the Jews, although there were already Jewish colonies living in every Roman city of consequence. They could not imagine anything more irrational than Jewish monotheism. When Pompey, full of curiosity, walked into the Holy of Holies in the Temple at Jerusalem in 63 BC, he could not conceive why a shudder of disgust ran through the Jewish world. However, the Jews of Palestine, fanatical and bellicose, behaved very differently from those of the Dispersion, who were on the whole peaceful and industrious contributors to the stability of the Empire. Men like St Paul's father no doubt fully merited their Roman citizenship. The Palestinian Jews had been kept quiet for many years by their Arab King, Herod the Great, the friend of Augustus, but ten years after his death in 4 BC the Emperor felt it safer to make Judaea a minor Roman province under direct rule. The rest of Palestine continued to be ruled by princelings of Herod's house, and the whole country was carefully watched by the Governor of Syria and the four legions under his command. The largest Jewish community outside Palestine was that of Alexandria, which in turn maintained close commercial touch with much smaller communities in southern Italy including that of Rome. Largely hellenized, it had adapted itself to life in a non-Jewish environment, but in times of unrest such as the reign of Caligula (37–41) AD ugly racial riots were apt to break out between Jews and Graeco-Egyptians. The Jews of Rome necessarily kept a low profile. They did not even suffer seriously as a result of the ghastly war waged in 66–70 AD between the Romans and the Jewish nationalists in Palestine.

It may be assumed that the Crucifixion took place during the reign of Tiberius and about half way through Pontius Pilate's term of office (27–36 AD) in Judaea. How soon the first Christian convert or missionary reached Rome from Asia is a matter of pure conjecture. From the Acts of the Apostles and the Pauline Epistles we learn or can deduce a great deal about the spread of Christianity in Syria, Asia Minor and Greece during the forties and fifties of the first century. We can trace St Paul's journeys in detail and particularly his voyage under guard to Rome. The Acts leave Paul in his rented house at Rome in about the year 58 AD, surrounded by a circle of believers and in touch with similar circles of 'churches' in Greece and Asia. He may have written his Epistle to the Romans about four years before his arrival in the capital. We may also guess that if his case even came up in a Roman court the charges against him were dismissed as invalid. He would then have been perfectly free to travel wherever he chose and indeed there is a tradition that he visited Spain and Provence before his death in Nero's persecution of 64 AD. But as regards the date and circumstances of St Peter's arrival in Rome our information is a blank. It is known that in 48 AD the former Galilean fisherman was arrested by Herod Agrippa in Jerusalem, that he escaped from prison, that he conducted his own missions in Asia and disagreed to some extent with St Paul about the conversion of the Gentiles. They debated the matter in Jerusalem in about 49 AD. Peter then disappears into a mist of surmise. We have little or no idea of his whereabouts and movements during the years preceding the Neronian persecution. Apart from the mysterious reference to Babylon (usually taken to mean Rome) at the end of the first Epistle of Peter there is no reference in any strictly contemporary writings to his presence in the capital. The lack of any concrete evidence of the later stage of his life and of his relationship with Paul at the time of the latter's residence at Rome is very puzzling. Many scholars, from Marsilius of Padua (1326) onwards, have questioned whether he was in Rome at all; others, such as the Protestant Harnack and the unbeliever Renan, have seen no reason to deny his presence there. If it was just a legend, along with the story of his martyrdom, the origin and meaning of the papacy would of course be invalidated. What surely matters is the strength of the tradition, handed down from the early days of Christianity in Rome and fortified rather than weakened by modern scholarship and archaeology, that both the Apostles lived and were martyred in the city. It is irrelevant that the tradition later became encrusted with legend. In its original and simple form it leaves no room for doubt that the leaders of the early Roman Christians were Peter and Paul and that they both lost their lives, the former by crucifixion and the latter, as befitted a Roman Citizen, by decapitation, in the reign of Nero. Thirty or forty years afterwards there were plenty of Christians alive who had seen and spoken with the Apostles. They did not bother however, to record facts and dates for a posterity they did not believe would ever exist.

Nor do we find any reference to Christians in general in Rome in non-Christian literature of the mid-first century. They only begin to crop up towards its end. What Tacitus, a high official and eminent historian, wrote forty or fifty years after Nero's persecution is worth quoting in full, but the background to this passage (*Annals* xv 44) demands a brief explanation.

By 64 AD the Romans had become disillusioned by their young Emperor, who had ruled them for ten years. His first five years, the *Quinquennium Neronis*, had been full of promise. The Roman world was on the whole peaceful and prosperous; it was well governed by serious administrators. At home the record was stained only when, a year after Nero's accession, Britannicus, the son of his predecessor Claudius and his only rival in the imperial house, died suddenly and prematurely. It was assumed, no doubt correctly, that the Emperor had had him poisoned. Apart from that flaw, there seemed to be no reason why Rome should not look forward to an untroubled if not a golden age.

But as from 59 AD matters took a turn for the worse. Shaking off the control of his competent ministers, Seneca and Burrus, Nero began to indulge his extravagant and vicious tastes to the full. Having disposed of his mother and his wife, he attacked the aristocrats, the rich, the intellectuals and all those whom he suspected of disloyalty to his arbitrary and eccentric rule. He outraged Roman public opinion of all classes by his acts of cruelty, his vain artistic pretentions and his addiction to Greek and oriental favourites. The general feeling of nervous discontent was intensified when half the city was devastated by a huge fire.

Such conflagrations were no novelty. Fifty years earlier it was claimed that Augustus had found Rome a city of brick and left it a city of marble. In fact it was still in Nero's time a mostly jerry-built mass of ramshackle tenements, overcrowded by a constantly increasing stream of indigent immigrants, mostly from the eastern provinces of the empire. After serious fires in 23 BC and 6 AD Augustus had formed a corps of 700 *vigiles* (watchmen and firemen). It signally failed, however, to cope with the disaster of 64 AD, which reduced Rome to a state of shock. This is how Tacitus introduced the Christian community in classical literature as the scapegoats on whom Nero tried to pin the blame for the catastrophe.

They were called Christians. The Christus from whom the name was derived had been put to death in the reign of Tiberius by the Procurator Pontius Pilate, and the pestilent superstition was checked for a while; but it began to break out again, not only in Judaea, the birthplace of the evil thing, but also in Rome, where everything that is horrible and shameless flows together and becomes fashionable. In the first place, then, some were arrested and confessed. On their testimony a vast magnitude was convicted, not so much of responsibility for the fire as for hatred of the human race. They were put to death with mockery and insult. They were dressed in the skins of wild animals to be torn to death by dogs; they were fixed to crosses or condemned to the flames; and when the daylight failed they were burned to give light by night. Nero had granted the use of his gardens for that display, and gave a circus performance, mixing with the common people in the dress of a charioteer seated in his chariot; and so a feeling of compassion arose (though it was for guilty persons who deserved severe punishment), since they were being done to death not for the public good, but to satisfy the cruelty of a single individual.

The above passage is one of the two earliest extant mentions of the Christians in Rome by a non-Christian or non-Jewish writer. Tacitus probably composed it at the same time as Pliny the younger, Governor of Bithynia in northern Asia Minor, was conducting his famous correspondence with the Emperor Trajan about the problems of dealing with the flourishing Christian sect in his province. What is crucial in the record of Tacitus is that as early as 64 AD the Christians in Rome were so numerous, identified as such and differentiated from the Jews, that Nero should have thought it worth while to deflect on to them the fury and frustration of the Roman mob. The evidence of the Pauline Epistles might, on the other hand, only suggest the existence of a small and struggling minority leading an obscure if not underground life of its own. So would an isolated remark by a third Roman,

Suetonius. This confectioner of highly flavoured and selective prose, also writing in the second century and muddled about Christian origins, ignores the events of 64 AD so far as the Christians were concerned and confines himself to blaming one 'Chrestus' for causing a riot among the Jewish colony in 49 AD. Quite obviously he did not think of the Christians as a 'vast multitude'. Nor did Flavius Josephus, the Jewish Historian of the destruction of Jerusalem in 70 AD. Writing in about 93 AD and referring, like Tacitus, to the condemnation of Jesus by Pilate, he casually mentions the 'tribe of Christians' as 'even now not extinct' (*Antiquities* XVIII 3.3). He knew more than any Roman about the Christian background in Palestine but clearly thought that the Roman Christians had not recovered from their horrifying ordeal under Nero. Yet the truth was that they were very much alive and flourishing a quarter of a century after the catastrophe.

PART ONE

THE
FOUNDATIONS

HEIRS OF THE APOSTLES
(64–335)

According to the list of early leaders of the Roman Church compiled in the third century, the successors of St Peter were Linus and Cletus (or Anencletus), shadowy figures who are each allotted twelve years of office. While it may be convenient to describe them as 'Popes', it must be kept in mind that this title did not exclusively designate the heads of the Roman Church until the ninth century at the earliest. The Greek word *papas* which was merely the popular diminitive of *pater* (father), was applicable to any senior or leading member of a local Christian Community; in the Greek Orthodox Church of today it means village priest. Linus and Cletus no doubt had difficulty in rallying the much reduced body of the faithful, and at that period the Eastern churches of Syria, Asia Minor and Greece were making a larger contribution than Rome's to the development of Christianity. But with the third 'Pope', Clement, we are on firmer ground. He emerges as a strong personality infusing vigour and courage into an expanding community drawn from more than one social class.

It would be a mistake to picture these early Christians as belonging exclusively to the lowest stratum of the population. Ancient society at that time was in any case complex and fluid. In the capital of the Empire Roman citizens, rich and poor, mingled with free immigrants from the Greek-speaking East and the Latin-speaking West and with a vast slave element of very diverse origins. The line between slave and free was easily crossed. Labourers and craftsmen could be found in either category, and the slaves in a great Roman household would include not only menials and domestics but also educated persons, stewards, secretaries, tutors and even tame philosophers. Once a new religion had penetrated an establishment of this kind, it would affect all its members, high and low, and especially the women. The numerous class of freedmen, too, was peculiarly susceptible to the influence of Oriental cults. Clement was possibly a freedman or client of a family very closely related to the imperial house. To judge from his writings, he was of Jewish descent.

The Roman aristocrat connected by Christian tradition with Pope Clement was Titus Flavius Clement, first cousin to the Emperor Domitian (81–96 AD) and husband of Flavia Domitilla, the Emperor's niece. He held the consulship in 95 AD but was executed, shortly after laying down his office, for alleged treason. Suetonius accused him of 'contemptible inertia'; which was perhaps one way of saying that he found the secret or overt practice of the Christian religion, absorbed through his household, incompatible with his consular functions. Dio Cassius, the third-century historian, added for good measure that the consul was guilty of 'atheism', which he equates with Judaism. It does look as if Christianity had seeped into the highest circles, for another victim of Domitian connected by tradition with the new religion was Manius Acilius Glabrio, consul in 91 AD and also executed in 95 AD. At that time the Emperor, soon to be assassinated himself, allegedly by one of Domitilla's freedmen, was lashing out not only against Christians but against all other real and fancied opponents of his tyranny.

The Christians' dead were already beginning to be interred in cemeteries identified with prominent families attracted by or adhering to the new cult. Evidently they had regained confidence in the early part of Domitian's reign and were making many converts. Despite Domitian's persecution Clement asserted the primacy of the Roman church in no uncertain tones when he rebuked the Christians of Corinth for lapsing into dissidence or schism. The Epistle chiding them for their quarrels and usually attributed to him has the authentic papal ring, both authoritative and paternal. Clement invokes the example of the Apostles, whom he had almost surely known in his youth, describing them as 'athletes of our own time' and 'glorious examples of our generation'. 'Peter', he continues, 'endured not one or two but many labours . . . and went his way to the place of glory which was his due,' while 'Paul . . . seven times in chains . . . became a herald both in the east and in the west . . . and went his way to the holy place, having become the greatest pattern of endurance.' 'Along with those great men,' Clement adds, 'there was associated a great multitude of the elect, who endured many indignities and tortures.'

We do not know how Clement, a man of high character and culture, ended his life. The story is that he was exiled to the far Crimea, where he either died or was executed. His successors in the second century were not particularly eminent men. They were outshone in intellect, if not in faith and pertinacity, by their great contemporaries in the eastern churches, such as Polycarp, Ignatius and Irenaeus, as well as by the leaders of the dangerous heresies that cropped up in those years. Nevertheless the bishops of Rome, as the heads of the church in the imperial capital, were consulted and listened to with respect by all the influential Christians who came to visit them from other important centres, from Alexandria and Antioch, Ephesus and Smyrna. At that time there was still nothing very awe-inspiring or hierarchical about the title of bishop (*episkopos*); the Roman bishops regarded themselves neither as the vicars of Christ nor as the exclusive wielders of apostolic authority. The word *episkopos* had originally no priestly significance; it was used in a purely administrative context and meant 'supervisor' or 'steward'. The *episkopos* of an early Christian community seems normally to have been assisted by a council of 'presbyters' or elders, a small group of older and experienced men. They too exercised no priestly functions in the modern sense but served as advisers or teachers. Lesser administrative, social and charitable tasks were entrusted to the *diakonoi* (literally 'servants') or deacons. Some scholars hold that in the early days there were several elders holding the title of bishop in Rome, though only one is mentioned in the official list drawn up at a later date. However that may be, we can be sure that as the church drew away from Jewish practice, evolving its own liturgy, sacraments and observances, the administrators soon developed the characteristics of priests of the new religion. But so far there was no recognized canon of scripture; nor had the simple language of faith and inspiration been elaborated, under the influence of Greek philosophical ideas, into a formal theology.

Most of the second-century bishops seem to have been unassuming folk. However there were plenty of rich Christians in the booming, populous Rome of the period; it was in their homes that Christian communal worship took place, as no regular church buildings yet existed. The bishops, like their flocks, were normally Greek-speaking and bore Greek names. Xystus (116–125) is recorded as having united with his community the colony of Asiatic Greek Christians resident in Rome, and the common language of their liturgy and intercourse must have been Greek. Pius (140–155), once a slave, had a Latin name but his brother Hermas, also a freed slave, was an imaginative writer of great power. His work, *The Shepherd*, was composed in Greek and translated into Latin. It is a visionary masterpiece, abounding in symbol and allegory, and its author inaugurated a long tradition of Christian literature exemplified in the Middle Ages by Dante and in Protestant England by Milton and Bunyan.

Between the reigns of Nerva and Antoninus Pius (96–161) there was little or no indiscriminate harrying of Christians in Rome itself. The Emperors, particularly Hadrian and Antoninus, tended to discourage popular agitation against them. Nevertheless martyrdoms occurred from time to time. One of the victims was Telesphorus, bishop from 125 to 136, who was put to death during the destructive Second Jewish War in the Middle East. No doubt the Christians, whom pagan prejudice barely distinguished from Jews, were made to suffer on that account. But on the whole the period was one of continuous and rapid growth for the church. In fact what endangered its survival was not persecution but disruption and threatened loss of identity.

The Christians in Rome were still 'largely a foreign community' and Christianity an oriental religion. During the first half of the second century Orientals were flooding into Rome in unprecedented numbers, chiefly from Syria, Asia Minor and Egypt. These people were only partly hellenized; they might speak Greek but their behaviour and inclinations were oriental. And they introduced into Rome the confused religious ferment that was seething and spilling over in their countries of origin.

The bishops of Rome were glad to receive visits from such pillars of the eastern churches as Ignatius of Antioch and Polycarp of Smyrna, the representatives of Christian congregations far larger and more solid than those of Italy and the whole western part of the Empire. Their beliefs and observances varied little from those of the Roman Christians. Less welcome was the host of deviants, the founders and adherents of dozens of sects that selected or rejected whatever ingredients of the Christian faith they liked or disliked, while adding to it exotic features of their own. At that time the Christians had not worked out a dogmatic theology. There was no such thing as strict orthodoxy and no clear line was drawn between Catholic (the Greek word means 'universal' and was first used in its Christian sense by Ignatius early in the second century) and heretic. It was hard for the Roman bishops, confronted by a jungle of strange cults and disputatious personalities, to stick to the straight road trodden by the Apostles. At the same time the propounders of those cults could count on recruiting followers in the rootless eastern proletariat of Rome, and among the intellectuals as well.

The most notorious of the so-called 'heresiarchs' who established themselves in Rome under the nose of its bishops were Valentinus from Alexandria, Cerdo from Syria and Marcion from Pontus on the Black Sea. Others, such as the Alexandrian Basilides, operated no less effectively from a distance. Each propagated his own version of the 'gnosis' or esoteric interpretation of the Christian message, a fatally distorted one. What they had in common was a decided aversion for Christianity's Jewish origins and a tendency to construct, with perverse ingenuity, elaborate theological systems incorporating elements from Egyptian magic and Persian myth as well as from Pythagoras and Plato. Among other doctrines they taught that only the initiated or elect had access to the inner knowledge of religious truth, that matter was evil and conventional morality unimportant. The gospel story and the personality of Jesus were variously accounted for and explained away, while the most complicated cosmologies were invented to fit in God (or gods), higher and lower universes and hierarchies of angels and powers. When the heresiarchs set up their schools and founded their rival churches in Rome the contemporary bishops and especially Pius and his successor Anicetus, were faced with a dangerous challenge. Indeed if they had not overcome it Christianity might easily have been dissolved into a multitude of ephemeral sects and superstitions and failed to survive in any recognizable form.

The bishops were campaigning on two fronts: against pagan hostility and internal disruption, and against intimidation and secession. While organizing and stimulating their community they seem to have left the task of controversy to others. Brilliant Christian writers, the 'apologists', like Aristides and Justin, presented to the educated public reasoned defences of their religion, using the philosophic language which pagan critics would understand. From time to time they were encouraged by visits from grand old figures from the Seven Churches of Asia. Polycarp of Smyrna, shortly before he was martyred in his homeland, came to Rome in support of Anicetus (155–66), when the latter's election was being contested by heretics. The bishop was chosen by the whole community, but this was split by dissension.

Anicetus was still in charge when the church was struck by a fierce renewal of persecution. Under the mild rule of the Emperor Antoninus Pius (138–61) martyrdoms were usually the result of popular clamour in the provinces, but when Marcus Aurelius succeeded him the Christians were subjected to the full weight of official displeasure. A hard doctrinaire under his philosophic trappings, the Emperor regarded Christianity as a repugnant superstition and a source of political disloyalty. Any believer who, when questioned, confessed to being a Christian and refused to make the formal gesture of sacrifice to the Emperor, exposed himself to execution. Roman citizens were normally beheaded; humbler persons might be condemned, along with criminals, to fight with wild beasts in the amphitheatre. Curiously enough no bishop was put to the test, and the real horrors of mass persecution were perpetrated far from Rome, in Asia Minor and in Gaul. No attempt was made to cripple Christianity by first striking at its centre, Rome. Fortunately Anicetus and his successors, Soter and Eleutherus, were able to weather the storm.

Consequently the position of the Roman bishop was much strengthened in those difficult years and his prestige enhanced. Irenaeus, another Smyrniot who had accompanied Polycarp on his mission to Rome and subsequently became bishop of Lyons in the years following the savage persecution of Christians in that city, produced a slashing denunciation of the heretics in five books. Although himself an Asiatic, he asserted the primacy of Rome over the other churches. His Latin phrase (translated from the original Greek) '*potentiorem principalitatem*', echoed endlessly throughout successive ages of the papacy. He was writing in the time of Eleutherus (174–89), a greatly respected bishop during whose term of office the pace of persecution slackened. For his benefit Irenaeus defined what was to become the Roman claim of centralism. The Christians of Asia might be much more numerous than those of the West, but the Roman church had been founded by the two great Apostles. All roads led to the city, the centre of the Empire; it was there that all the traditions and experiences of the church were gathered, examined and reconciled.

Stability in doctrine and practice came from Rome, which opposed its steadying influence to unsettling currents from the East, to Greek intellectualism and the emotionalism of Asia. Only Rome could impose unity on a universal church.

The next bishop, Victor (189–98), was an African by birth; that is to say, he hailed from the province of Africa (Tunisia and part of Algeria) and thus from the Latin-speaking half of the Empire. His own native language might have been Punic or Berber. When he succeeded Eleutherus, Commodus (180–192) had been reigning for nearly ten years. He figures in Roman history as the classic 'bad' Emperor, notorious for his cruelty and frivolity by contrast with his wise father Marcus Aurelius whose policies he reversed. But one of those policies, the stern enforcement of law against the Christians, was much relaxed, and the Roman bishops even established a foothold in the palace. Moreover Victor also enjoyed the protection of Marcia, the Emperor's favourite mistress, and of the eunuch Hyacinthus, who combined his duties towards the three hundred inmates of the gynaeceum with those of a Christian presbyter. On one occasion he intervened to rescue a batch of Christians condemned to forced labour in the Sardinian mines.

Apart from such salutary intrigues, Victor was chiefly concerned with asserting the growing authority of Rome in matters of doctrine and discipline. As before, the threat to unity came from the East. Over the last thirty years Montanism, a revivalist movement deriving from the upland villages of Phrygia, had made disquieting progress in Asia Minor and beyond. Montanus, its founder, had once been a priest of the goddess Cybele, with whose cymbal-clashing cult the Romans had been familiar since republican times. His followers resembled some modern sectaries in the United States and elsewhere, running wild in their ecstatic 'prophesying' and outpourings of the spirit by which they claimed to be possessed. For Victor their practices were of dubious morality and their claims to sanctity savoured at least of heresy. He equally disapproved of two other deviations stemming from Asia. These were 'Monarchianism', which failed to distinguish between the Father and the Son, and 'Adoptionism', which maintained that Jesus was a man who became God by successive accretions of divine power. In addition there was a tiresome controversy about the date of Easter, which some Asiatics insisted on celebrating on the fourteenth day of the Jewish month Nisan.

However, for all his energy and strong-mindedness Victor did not succeed in imposing uniformity on the overseas churches. His rebukes were much resented and even Irenaeus, hitherto an advocate of Roman leadership, thought that he was being too dictatorial. In a lively exchange of letters Polycrates, the venerable bishop of Ephesus, defended the ancient traditions and local usages of Asia as equally valid with those of Rome. He refused to submit to Victor, whose subsequent attempt to excommunicate him (that is, to exclude him from the Christian fellowship and from the sacraments) proved a damp squib. It was the first use of that weapon of doubtful efficacy. On the other hand the objectionable movements lost ground, and the Roman custom at Easter eventually prevailed. More important for the future was Victor's suggestion, in writing to Polycrates, that the latter should convoke a synod of local bishops to consider the issues. Polycrates duly complied, and although his synod supported him against Rome, Victor's initiative sparked off an explosion of synodical meetings dealing with Montanism and Easter. Later writers mention synods held in Gaul, Italy, Asia Minor, Syria, Mesopotamia, Palestine and Egypt. Thus began the conciliar system which has played, and is still playing to an increasing extent, so significant a part in the activity of the Catholic Church.

The government of the church in Rome had been monarchical, as opposed to collective, since its earliest days. Whether or not the famous 'Tu es Petrus' text (*Matthew* xvi. 18) was in fact introduced into the Gospel during the third century, the tradition of Peter and Paul was radiating from its Roman centre with increasing strength. Nevertheless, under the long government of Zephyrinus (198–217), the Roman church showed signs of faltering. Weak and indecisive, the new bishop leaned heavily on his able deacon Callistus, a former slave in the imperial household, for guidance in both management and theology. His term was troubled by a sharp renewal of persecution under Septimus Severus (193–211) and by the 'adoptionists' in Rome, who set up a rival bishop in the shape of one Natalius, an obscure individual whose only distinction was to head the long line of historical anti-popes, and who soon lost courage and begged for forgiveness.

A more serious schism followed the death of Zephyrinus. After a disputed election Callistus and Hippolytus each claimed to be the legitimate bishop of Rome, and each had a strong body of supporters. Only Callistus figured eventually in the official list of Popes, but both ended as martyrs and are revered as such. (Callistus was much mourned when, in 222, he lost his life in a mysterious riot, possibly between Jews and Christians, in the Transtiberine quarter of Rome.) Quite apart from theological differences there was evidently a strong personal antipathy between the rivals. To judge by their names, they were both of Greek or oriental descent, but Hippolytus, who was a man of property and an intolerant intellectual, affected to despise the ex-slave Callistus. They and their factions were probably divided by their social origins more than by their doctrinal opinions; the well-to-do took a less strict view of their Christian duties than did the slaves or the poor artisans dependent on the state '*sportula*'—the dole.

Christians were no longer leading a subterranean existence, creeping furtively in and out of the catacombs; they were already more numerous than the devotees of other eastern cults and, given their numbers and ubiquity, the nature of their religion was in no sense secret. They had no temples, but everyone knew that they met for worship in private houses or chapels in their catacombs. Their bishops were already prominent personalities. From time to time they underwent grisly penalties enjoined by the law, the severity of which was tightened or tempered by imperial whim. The threat was never far removed, but they were not the only sufferers from the tyranny of a Commodus or a Caracalla.

The year 217, when Callistus succeeded Zephyrinus, also marked the accession to power of the short-lived Syrian dynasty of Roman Emperors, descendants of the second wife of Septimus Severus the African. In their native country they were the hereditary priests of the Ball or sun-god of Emesa, monotheists by tradition but cosmopolitans by inclination. The first of them, Elagabalus, was a debauchee interested only in the fertility aspect of his cult; however, he had no prejudice against the Christians. His cousin and successor, Severus Alexander (222–35), was very different—honest, sober and well-meaning. He welcomed all religions that worshipped a most high god, and installed in his private chapel statues of their originators and prophets, including Orpheus, Abraham and Jesus. He and his mother encouraged Christian thinkers such as Hippolytus and the Egyptian Origen. The Roman church basked in this unprecedented atmosphere of toleration; Christians were able to take their place unhindered in business and government and their individual prosperity enriched a growing community. A good example of their adaptation to changing times was one Julius Africanus, a Palestinian who was successively a cavalry officer, a municipal leader in his own country and the Emperor's librarian in the Pantheon at Rome. The two bishops who spanned this period, Urbanus and Pontianus, were in no way remarkable, but it is of interest that they both bore Latin names. Now that the city was receiving fewer immigrants from the East the Greek-speaking element was on the decline.

The Christians were sharply reminded that they had not fully fitted into the Roman scheme of things when, in 235, Severus was murdered by his troops, who raised to the purple a competent but unsubtle Thracian soldier called Maximinus. As protégés of the former regime, the Christians were made to pay the penalty; Bishop Pontianus and Hippolytus were both despatched to martyrdom in the Sardinian mines. There followed twenty-five years of uncertainty and tribulation. The Empire was entering a period of crisis which was to last for the next half-century. While the Roman state celebrated its thousandth anniversary in 248, Goths from the north and Persians from the east, soon to be joined by Germans from across the Rhine, were battering at its frontiers. Suddenly it was engaged in a dour battle for survival. Military disasters and the prevailing insecurity caused a loss of nerve, which in turn exposed the Christians to a new and intense series of persecutions. These sprang from a certain feeling of revulsion against a huge body of citizens whose allegiance to Rome was regarded as suspect, or at least as passive and unenthusiastic. In particular there were doubts about the loyalty of the many Christians serving in the army.

In an effort to strengthen morale the Emperor Decius (249–51) decided that citizens must, if required, obtain a certificate of loyalty to the state religion by making a formal sacrifice to its ancient gods. This requirement was not new, but had been many years in abeyance. Now Valerian, a future Emperor, was appointed to supervise its application. Evidently it was felt that while the Emperor was absent from Rome fighting barbarians, the Christian bishop was challenging his own and the Senate's authority in the capital. Indeed according to Bishop Cyprian of Carthage, Decius declared that he would prefer to hear of the rise of a rival Emperor than of the election of a new bishop of Rome. Accordingly he put to death Bishop Fabian (236–50), a wise administrator who had held the church together for many difficult years. His two successors, Cornelius and Lucius, lasted only two years each and both died in exile.

In the face of this official campaign huge numbers of Christians took the easy way out; they either made the sacrifice or bribed state officials to grant the necessary certificate. Most of them abjured in order to save their lives and had no real intention of abandoning their religion, but a fierce controversy arose within the church as to whether such persons could be readmitted to communion. Whereas Cornelius advocated leniency towards those who had lapsed, subject to their submitting to the prescribed penances, the stricter Christians who insisted on their exclusion refused to recognize him and chose Novatian as their anti-bishop. The schism lasted for seven years and plunged the weakened church into confusion. Bishop Stephen (254–57) avoided his predecessors' fate, but persecution flared up even more dangerously in the later years of the Emperor Valerian (253–60). In consequence of an edict requiring sacrifice to the gods and aimed specifically at the Christian clergy, Bishop Xystus II (257–58) was condemned to death along with his deacon Laurentius, victim of the gridiron. Finally all Christian meetings were officially banned.

Relief came at last when, in 260, Valerian was taken prisoner by the Persian King Shapur and failed to return from captivity. (Decius, the former persecuting emperor, had in his time met a violent death at the hands of the Goths.) Valerian's successor, Gallienus, at once reversed his father's policy towards the Christians, issuing an edict of toleration which abolished all the penalties and disabilities from which they had been suffering. A ruler of great fortitude and intelligence who saved the empire from collapse, he must have realized that the Christians were not a divisive element or fifth column. On the contrary, the state had gained nothing from the deliberate alienation of so large a body of citizens over the last decade. Persecution had caused social unrest, lowered the morale of the population as a whole and weakened its spirit of resistance to the barbarian invasions.

So Christianity was no longer an illicit religion. For the next forty years the church enjoyed immunity from official interference and freedom to proselytize. Its membership greatly expanded, and it became 'prosperous, dignified and wordly'. Roomy places of worship distinct from private houses and underground chapels came into existence at this time, although no churches in anything like the magnificent style of the pagan temples appear to have been built in Rome before the reign of Constantine in the next century. Benefactions flowed in from the rich members of a community in which the sense of unity was still strong.

Christians by this time exceeded in number the adherents of any other religion but the old official paganism. They had long outstripped their former oriental rivals such as the once-popular cult of Egyptian Isis; nor were they yet seriously challenged by the devotees of the god Mithras, later a favourite with the soldiery, nor by those of Mani, author of the dualist doctrine that the universe is the scene of an endless struggle between the powers of light and darkness. Both these movements, which were to gain strength in the fourth century, sprang from the soil of Rome's chief enemy, Persia.

For the moment, the bishops were important persons in Roman society, yet they remain insubstantial figures. From 260 to 296 we have the names of Dionysius, Felix, Eutychianus—but no significant record of their lives or individual contributions to the Church's development. The primacy of the Roman Church, by comparison with those of Antioch, Jerusalem, Alexandria and evan Carthage, was by no means taken for granted, while the colloquial appellation of 'Papa' might be accorded to any popular bishop anywhere. The prestige and importance of the city of Rome itself were in decline; at the end of the century Rome was no longer the administrative capital of the empire or the normal seat of the emperors. Diocletian, the Dalmatian who ruled from 284 to 305, visited the city for the first time in 303. Previous emperors had spent more and more of their time away from Rome, busy with repelling barbarian invasions of the frontier provinces. Now Diocletian met the requirements of defence by dividing the imperial functions among two senior Augusti and two junior Caesars, each of whom was entrusted with the protection of a vast area of the Roman world. The West was to be governed from Trier on the Moselle, the Balkan peninsula from Sirmium on the river Save and the all important East from Nicomedia, a small city just south of the Bosporus. Even Italy was to be administered not from Rome but from Milan.

Rome's prestige naturally suffered as a result of this rearrangement. Its atmosphere was becoming almost provincial. It was no longer attracting immigrants from the lively, rich and intellectual East, and any fresh newcomers tended to come from the West and from north Africa. Rome was consequently re-latinized. The Greek language went out of common use, especially among the poorer class and increasingly too among the educated, and had ceased to be the basic language of the Church. Consequently the latter became less responsive to the ideological stimulus of Greek-speaking Asia. But the ground was being slowly prepared for the day when the greatest man in Rome would be not the non-resident emperor but the pope as father of the Roman people.

Not content with reforming the government, the army and the currency, Diocletian introduced a new concept of the imperial office. As senior Augustus, he was anxious to establish a religious as well as a political basis for his absolutism. He wished to be adored by his subjects as the representative of Jupiter on earth, or, in the Persian style, as the living manifestation of the Sun-god. Obviously it was a claim that no Christian could accept if challenged to make a formal act of acquiescence. Diocletian only moved against the Christians when urged to do so by his son-in-law Galerius, first Caesar and then, after Diocletian's abdication in 305, Augustus of the eastern half of the empire. Like Decius and Valerian, Galerius regarded the Christians as a weak and uncooperative element that could be dragooned into whole-hearted obedience. They were weeded out of the army and civil service, and once Diocletian retired to his palace on the Adriatic coast Galerius increased the pressure. Tortures and executions were renewed, property destroyed or confiscated, the sacred books and vessels burned and profaned. Even so the pace and extent of the persecution varied from one sector of the empire to another. Not all the Augusti and Caesars were persecutors; more especially Constantine, promoted an Augustus in 305 and stationed for military reasons in Britain, and himself the husband of a Christian, Helena, applied the official edicts with all possible leniency. As had happened fifty years earlier, the harsh policy caused great social disruption. So in 309 Galerius was compelled, a year before his death, to publish an edict of partial toleration. Meanwhile countless Christians, including Bishop Marcellinus of Rome (296–304), had perished, while the empire itself was shaken by conflicts between its monarchs and semi-monarchs. Marcellinus was reputed to have faltered at one stage and burned incense to the Emperor, but later to have regained courage and invited execution. His two ephemeral successors, Marcellus and Eusebius, were lucky to be banished and thus escape with their lives.

Diocletian's over-ingenious system by which two Caesars were automatically to replace two Augusti and were themselves to be replaced by two new Caesars had hopelessly broken down. In the struggle among the surviving dynasts Constantine triumphed because he outclassed his rivals in military skill, political imagination and sheer nerve. In 312 he crushed Maxentius, ruler of Italy and Africa and an active enemy of Christianity, at the very gates of Rome, and his soldiers entered the city with the emblem of the cross displayed on their shields.

In the following year he invited Licinius, ruler of the East, to meet him at Milan and there persuaded his co-emperor to subscribe to a further edict confirming and extending that of Galerius. So far as Constantine was concerned, the Christians were now favoured as well as tolerated, and there was no longer any question of their being obliged to perform an act of acceptance of a non-Christian state religion. Moreover Christianity was recognized as a 'religio licita' without any disabilities. The Christians had their property restored to them for the second time and once again enjoyed equal rights with the still pagan majority of their fellow citizens. This great triumph was accompanied by a series of significant concessions: all privileges previously enjoyed by pagan priesthoods were extended to the Christian clergy, pagan symbols were removed from the coinage, and Sunday was recognized as a public holiday. While this revolution was under way Constantine was preparing his stroke against Licinius, whose distaste for Christianity was taking the form of renewed discrimination against it in the East. That was ended in 323 when Constantine overwhelmed his rival in a ferociously successful campaign.

Constantine was not by temperament a religious man. His aim, which he pushed persistently and passionately, was the unity and stability of the Roman state, ruled not by Diocletian's committee of emperors but by himself as sole autocrat. But he was sensitive to the religious feelings of others, and saw that the religion of the future was bound to be some form of monotheism. What suited him personally would have been an official cult of the 'Unconquered Sun', over which the deity would have presided like a glorified terrestrial monarch. He perceived, however, that such a religion would be too formal and frigid for popular appeal in an age when people were looking for a combination of the emotional and the intellectual. More and more of them were turning towards Christian monotheism because it exactly satisfied that urge. He therefore intended that the state should take a benevolent interest in Christianity, help it to resolve its internal differences and enlist its energies in the imperial interest.

In this momentous change of policy the Roman bishop Miltiades (310–14) played a curiously passive role. Clearly he earned the Emperor's esteem, for one of Constantine's first acts was to present him with the Lateran Palace, a fine aristocratic mansion, as his official residence. Miltiades is also thought to have been the first pope to receive an official letter from an Emperor. The purpose of this missive was to invite him to bring calm to a dangerous dispute between two parties in the North African church, which was soon to develop into a so-called Donatist Schism. The Donatist movement arose out of the bitter division between those who had stood fast against persecution and those who were suspected of compounding with the imperial authorities under pressure. Its adherents did not differ in doctrine from the Catholics, but were distinguished by their puritanical outlook and their racial and class origin; they drew their strength from the poorer, Berber-speaking element of the population. Not that the Emperor was personally concerned with such nuances. What troubled him was that Africa was in a ferment because two factions were at loggerheads among the Christians to whom he had accorded his favours.

Miltiades responded by calling a synod in his Lateran Palace at which a selection of bishops from Italy and Gaul confronted representatives of the two African parties. Although it pronounced against the Donatists, its decision signally failed to resolve the dispute, which continued to reverberate for another two centuries. In a second and equally unsuccessful effort to find a solution, Constantine himself convoked a second and much larger synod at Arles where he did not ask Miltiades to preside. The bishop of Rome had to be content with being represented by two presbyters and two deacons, and by the time it was over he had been succeeded by Silvester (314–35).

Silvester's personality is still a great enigma. The first bishop to be regularly accorded the title of pope, he survived until two years before the death of Constantine, and the Roman church prospered under his leadership. Yet it is hard to credit him with any social talents or achievements. In later centuries people failed to understand how it was that he apparently accomplished so little of note. They felt that the contemporary head of the Church must have played just as eminent a part as the head of the state in the founding of the Christian Empire. Was it really conceivable that Silvester had been so colourless and retiring a character as the silence of history suggested? Surely the pope who stood shoulder to shoulder with the great Emperor in carrying out so vast a design must have been equally, if not more, famous. Indeed it must have been he who provided Constantine with the necessary inspiration.

Thus, for the benefit of the simple-minded, legend gradually encircled Silvester with a halo of wonder. Alerted by a vision of the Apostles, he had granted the Emperor baptism, thus curing him of a fit of insanity before extracting from him an order of deliverance for the Christians. Subsequently he had rescued Rome from the ravages of a poison-puffing dragon. The official legend of Silvester took a long time to mature. Starting as a medley of folk-lore, it developed towards the end of the fifth century into an imaginary account, deliberately prepared in the papal chancery, of Constantine's conversion to Christianity by Silvester, of his recognition of the Bishop of Rome as the head of the Church throughout the Roman Empire and of his surrender to him of the supreme jurisdiction in the city and the western provinces. As we shall see in the context of the eighth century, it formed in turn the basis of a more famous papal forgery, the so-called 'Donation of Constantine' framed in order to validate the theory of papal supremacy and the exercise of temporal power. The Emperor was represented as having written a letter to Silvester in 315 acknowledging the latter's precedence over the other four great episcopal sees of the Empire – Antioch, Jerusalem, Alexandria and Constantinople – and bequeathing to him and his successors 'Rome and all the provinces, districts and cities of Italy and the West as subject to the Roman church for ever'. It went on to explain that Constantine had decided to build his own capital in the East because it would not be right for him to hold sway in the city where the head of the Christian faith, the 'universal Pope', was reigning. It also went into elaborate detail about the Pope's right to wear imperial insignia (with the exception of the crown) and to have the Emperor ceremonially hold his horse's bridle.

The blatantly unhistorical nature of the document was not seriously questioned until the renaissance. The truth is that the Emperor never became a Christian, except possibly on his death-bed. In 315 he was totally occupied with the consolidation of his dominions in the West and with his rivalry with Licinius in the East. He never dreamed of surrendering his sovereignty over any city or province and it was not until 326 that he founded Constantinople. During these years Silvester was a strictly secondary figure in Constantine's scheme of things. Their relationship was one of master and servant. Silvester was very useful to him in Rome as an intermediary between the Church and himself, a combination of administrator and high priest, but less so in the western provinces and in the eastern hardly at all. But if he regarded the Pope primarily as an instrument for directing the allegiance of Roman Christians towards himself, he proved also to be a constant and generous patron of the Church. Spurred on by his Christian mother, as well as by reasons of policy, he lavishly subsidized its institutions and buildings. He financed the construction of the first two great Roman basilicas, the Pope's own church adjoining the Lateran Palace and the one that arose on the traditional site of St Peter's grave in the Vatican Cemetery. Full of new worshippers, these and other edifices confronted the still magnificent but dusty temples of the ancient gods, the shrines of formal and increasingly unreal cults. Silvester had to welcome a great influx of converts, not all of whom were joining the Church for the worthiest of reasons. Opportunists were taking full advantage of the Emperor's hint that advancement would not pass by new adherents to Christianity. Installed in some state in his rambling old patrician residence he led a life not much different from that of an influential Senator at the height of the pagan empire, characterized by dignity rather than by ease. The anterooms of the Lateran would have been crowded by clients and church members seeking favours and charity, and when he went out, dressed as any Roman nobleman of the time, he would have been attended by the same obsequious throng.

In future centuries the Roman Church failed to understand why Constantine chose to desert Rome, the city of the Apostles, in order to build a new capital on the site of the little Greek town of Byzantium. Hence, in part, its urge to invent, by way of consolation, the legend of Silvester and the Donation of Constantine. But at the time the reasons were obvious enough. The East was by far the richest, the most populous, intellectually the most active and socially the unruliest half of the empire. From a strategic point of view, its exposure to attack by the Goths on the lower Danube and the Persians on the Syrian frontier demanded the Emperor's close attention. Constantine had hardly overcome Licinius and released eastern Christians from the disabilities they had suffered under his rule, when the religious harmony of this vital region was threatened by the Arian controversy, the crucial issue of the status of the second person of the Trinity. Arius, a popular priest of Alexandria, thought that Christ was not God in the fullest sense; he was not co-eternal with the Father but had been created by him out of nothing. For preaching this doctrine Arius was expelled from the Church by his bishop, but he commanded much sympathy among the Christians of Syria and Asia Minor.

The Emperor sought to stifle the dispute by summoning the first General Council of the Church. But when more than three hundred bishops met at Nicaea under his presidency in 325 Silvester was not invited to attend, and Constantine chose as his adviser on dogmatic questions not the Pope of Rome but the Spaniard Hosius, bishop of Cordova. His dramatic intervention and imposing presence prevailed over the Arians and ensured the adoption by a large majority of the Nicene Creed. In the long term, however, he was no more successful in reconciling Catholics with Arians than with Donatists. The Council was followed by a strong reaction in favour of Arianism throughout the whole East. The Emperor, perplexed and distracted by theological arguments, began to doubt whether he had been unwise to favour the Catholics.

At his death in 337 the controversy was raging with redoubled fury but fortunately it hardly affected Rome and the West in Silvester's time. Constantine's last visit to Rome, on which he was accompanied by the imperial family, took place in 326, between the Council of Nicaea and the foundation of Constantinople. He was made welcome by neither Christians nor pagans, both of whom resented his decision to reside permanently in the East. Moreover his visit coincided with a double tragedy of intrigue within his family involving the successive executions of his son Crispus by his first wife and of his second wife, Fausta, who was convicted of slandering her son-in-law. It gave Constantine a distaste for Rome which was heartily reciprocated by the Romans. For the rest of his life he ruled from the Bosporus and Silvester was left in peace.

2

THE LAST YEARS OF ANCIENT ROME
(335–526)

In the period following Constantine's death his sons, Constantius and Constans, who inherited his empire became more personally and deeply concerned with religious matters. Constantius, his successor in the East, was an open and intolerant Arian. He deprived Athanasius, the fiery anti-heretical bishop of Alexandria, of his see and replaced both him and his colleagues by Arian nominees. His championship of heresy brought the contemporary bishops of Rome, Julius I (337–52) and Liberius (352–6), to the defence of Catholicism. Luckily for them, the Christians of Italy and the West were in general stoutly catholic; so was populous Egypt, so long as Athanasius was there, between successive expulsions, to uphold the cause. But the East was predominantly Arian and outside the empire's boundaries the Goths were in the process of conversion to that form of Christianity. The principal missionary to their nation was their compatriot Uefilas, who was trained at Constantinople in the heyday of Arianism and translated the Bible into Gothic. From the Danube basin the new faith spread northwards and won over other Germanic tribes which were eventually to invade the Roman Empire.

The Emperor's brother Constans, who controlled the West, was more sympathetic to the Catholics but did not rule from Rome; he was usually to be found at Trier on the Moselle. But separation from court and government worked to the advantage of Pope Julius. He also happened to be a personality of commanding stature, cast in the old Roman mould and quite the opposite of the meek Silvester. He was not afraid to wield authority and launch initiatives. Nor did he hesitate to oppose Constantius and the massed forces of ecclesiastical Arianism.

When Athanasius had to flee from Alexandria and took refuge at Rome Julius convoked a synod of fifty bishops who gave him their full support. They pronounced him to have been uncanonically deposed. In announcing the synod's decision to his colleagues in the East Julius reminded them in no uncertain terms of the primacy of the Roman see. He insisted that no ecclesiastical body in the East was justified in condemning Athanasius or any other prelate without the charges having previously been referred to Rome for judgement by its bishop. So uncompromising a claim was contested by a counter-synod at Antioch presided over by Constantius himself. Tension was high when Julius, choosing his moment carefully, begged Constans to intervene. The result was that the two co-emperors agreed to call a general synod at Serdica (Sofia), which happened to lie just on the western side of the administrative boundary between the brothers' dominions. It was to be held under the chairmanship of Constantine's former adviser, the Spaniard Hosius.

In the event no discussion took place. The eastern delegates, finding themselves outnumbered and outwitted, walked out amid an exchange of anathemas and excommunications as soon as they learned that Athanasius had been invited to participate. But the westerners continued in session, again rejected the accusations against Athanasius and confirmed the jurisdiction of the Bishop of Rome in the sphere of appeals. Julius, who did not himself attend the Council, certainly had the best of the encounter. Arian pretensions suffered a setback. Constantius backed down and, among other concessions to the Catholics, restored Athanasius to his see. For the first time the Pope emerged as an international figure, with his prestige in the whole Roman world immensely enhanced. Unfortunately his discreet protector, Constans, was assassinated in 350 and he himself died two years later. Constantius, now ruler of the whole empire, returned to the fray.

The new Pope, Liberius, was also a man of courage, but he had little room to manoeuvre. He saw all too clearly that Constantius, a disagreeable and suspicious monarch, was now determined to impose his will. The Emperor's idea of the Church was that it should preferably be Arian, and that it should obey him in matters of doctrine as well as of organization. As for his bishops, they should be as subservient as his civil servants. He, rather than his father, was the inventor of what was later termed 'Caesaropapism'. It was an uninviting prospect for Liberius, who had nothing to sustain him but the Catholic loyalty of his Christian Romans and the strong dislike of all Romans for the arbitrary methods of Constantinople.

When Constantius came to the West, Liberius first tried conciliation, without yielding on principle. Synods were duly held at Arles and Milan, but it became clear at once that it was the Emperor's aim to secure not merely a final condemnation of Athanasius but a uniform extension of Arian doctrine throughout the western church. At Milan he succeeded in browbeating the Italian bishops; the only three who resisted were displaced by Arians. Such action posed a direct threat to the Pope, who was not present at the Synod. When he refused to give way to intimidation by the Emperor's emissary, the eunuch Eusebius, he was forcibly removed from Rome by night, in case his arrest by day might provoke a riot, hustled over the Apennines and brought face to face with Constantius at Milan. Convinced that he was now the sole effective champion of Catholicism, he bravely stood his ground in defence of the Nicene Creed. No doubt he was relieved to escape a worse punishment than deportation to Beroea in Macedonia (355).

Worse still, the Romans had an anti-pope foisted on them in the person of a certain Archdeacon Felix, who was promptly ordained by three Arian bishops. When Constantius at last visited Rome in 357 the Christians clamoured for the return of Liberius. To their surprise he was restored to them, but under the bizarre condition that he should share his see with Felix. Obviously such an arrangement would not work; street fighting broke out and the unpopular Felix was chased from the city. It is uncertain what price Liberius had to pay for his permission to return. Although it may well have been a far-reaching compromise it did not affect his standing with his own people. The later years of Constantius were full of synodical activity; reflecting the malaise felt by all Christians on account of the prevailing disunion. Indeed the air was thick with formulae aiming at compromise between the extreme Arian and the orthodox Nicene views of the relationship between the Father and the Son, but according to Jerome, writing a generation later, the world seemed on the point of being the Arians' when Constantius died in 361. For all his zeal in promoting a form of Christianity, he delayed his own baptism until the last moment.

To add to the confusion of minds, this obstinate Arian was succeeded by a romantically-minded philosophic pagan, his cousin Julian (361–3). Paradoxically enough his attempt to revive the cult of the old gods resulted in a truce between the Christian factions. All bishops removed by Constantius were restored to their sees. In the new atmosphere of reconciliation Roman Christians saw little objection to formal honours being paid to the ancient pantheon. Although the mass of the population was already Christian, it was not fanatically prejudiced against the survival of traditional practices. Liberius was rewarded for his constancy, or rather his flexibility, by three quiet years at the end of his pontificate. After Julian had been killed in battle against the Persians the new Emperor in the West, Valentinian (364–75), was disposed to favour the Catholics, but preferred to avoid religious controversy altogether.

Damasus (366–84) was the last and most remarkable of a trio of great fourth-century Popes. Taking advantage of a decisive revulsion against Arianism throughout the whole Roman sphere, he proclaimed in the firmest of terms the primacy of his apostolic see at the precise moment when the Catholic faith became indisputably the empire's official religion.

Portuguese by birth, he was chosen bishop by a majority among the Roman clergy and people but opposed by a group of unruly zealots, led by one Ursinus, who objected to the policy of reconciliation inherited from his predecessor. Rioting broke out and, to the disgust of the inhabitants of a conservative and well-ordered city, wild excesses, of a kind that was to become familiar in later ages, were committed on both sides. Many lives were lost when the supporters of Damasus stormed the Basilica of Liberius (now Santa Maria Maggiore), in which the partisans of Ursinus had barricaded themselves. In the end the Prefect of the city restored order and expelled Ursinus. That did not prevent him from bringing a criminal action against the Pope in the courts. Damasus was acquitted, but he remained subject to imperial jurisdiction in such matters.

In the religious field, however, Damasus enlisted powerful allies. Among them were two of the most illustrious Saints of the Church. Ambrose, a former civil servant who was elected bishop of Milan in 373, worked closely with him to extinguish the remnants of Arianism in Italy. In the East Basil, the great doctor and bishop of Caesarea in Cappadocia, was leading a hard struggle against the official Arianism still upheld by the Emperor Valens (364–78). Basil had his differences with Damasus, whom he regarded as arrogant and unappreciative of the subtler nuances of eastern Christianity. But they were striving towards the same goal. The turning-point came when Valens and his whole army were overwhelmed and slaughtered by the Goths (also Arians) at the battle of Adrianople. The way was then clear for three new co-emperors, Valentinian II, Gratian and Theodosius, to issue a decree requiring 'all nations' subject to Rome to adhere to the religion that St Peter had bequeathed to the Romans and was now professed by Damasus and Peter of Alexandria, the successor of Athanasius. In the same year, 380, Theodosius expelled the Arians from all the churches in Constantinople.

So far Damasus had obtained all he could desire. But he scented danger when Theodosius went on to call a general Council of the eastern Church at Constantinople. When Arianism had been condemned he directed the Council to establish an order of precedence among the principle sees of the empire. Rome was accorded the primacy of honour, but Constantinople, as the New Rome and seat of the eastern Emperor, was elevated to second place. Damasus feared that it would soon present a more direct challenge. Summoning a Council of his own, he issued the clearest and most uncompromising claim for the primacy of the Holy Roman Church. It did not, he announced, rest on any synodical decisions but on Christ's own promise to Peter, the famous: 'Thou art Peter and on this rock I will build my Church.' For that reason, and also because Paul had met his death there on the same day as Peter, Rome had precedence over all other cities. Second to it in the Apostolic order came Alexandria, because it was Peter who had sent Mark there, and third came Antioch, because Peter had lived there before moving to Rome. Of upstart Constantinople there was no mention.

It is not recorded what impression, if any, the Pope's sharp snub made on Theodosius. But meanwhile, at Rome, his colleague Gratian was striking a succession of hard blows at official paganism. Temples were closed, priestly colleges lost their revenues, sacrifices were forbidden and the statue and altar of Victory removed from the Senate House. At the instance of Damasus and Ambrose all appeals and protests from prominent pagan Senators were dismissed. When Damasus died in 384 it seemed that Catholic Christianity had won a complete triumph. Paganism still had its deep roots among the country folk, but in the city it became before long the preserve of upper-class and antiquarian conservatism. While pagan magnates fought a stubborn rearguard action the Christian Pope was already integrated into the Roman system. He was an essential component of the governing caste, while the whole of society was permeated by the host of clerics under his control. Indeed one of his most highly-placed pagan friends, the praetorian prefect Praetextatus, used to say to him: 'Make me a bishop of the Roman Church and I shall be a Christian at once.'

In his later years Damasus largely relied on the recorder of that remark as his adviser and private secretary. He was called Eusebius Hieronymus Sophronius (Jerome), doctor of the Church and man of the world. Born in Dalmatia, he learned his letters at Rome from Donatus, the most eminent scholar of the day. Having become a Christian he travelled widely throughout the empire, residing for various periods in Germany, Asia Minor and Syria. He was ordained priest at Antioch and studied theology at Constantinople. On his return to Rome his combination of deep piety, intellectual brilliance and social charm soon won him a high reputation. He became spiritual director to a group of influential noble ladies, some of whose husbands and sons were pagans. More importantly, the Pope entrusted him with the work for which he is most famous, the revision of the Latin text of the Bible. His attainments would certainly have qualified him to succeed Damasus had it not been for the animosity which he had inspired among the higher clergy by his scathing criticism of their laxity and worldliness. He reserved his strongest denunciations for the new breed of opportunist ecclesiastics. His descriptions of perfumed deacons dancing attendance on ladies of fashion, legacy-hunting monks and other clerical parasites suggest that early Christianity in its hour of success had lost little time in producing the types whom we usually associate with Renaissance Italy and eighteenth-century France, the tonsured sceptic and the drawing-room Abbé. He wrote of one such:

Anyone seeing this man would take him for a bridegroom instead of a cleric. He drives up in a smart carriage, dressed in scented silks, his hair carefully curled. He is everywhere and nowhere to be met with; nothing happens that he is not the first to know; there is no city gossip that he has not heard nor exaggerated. He has become a priest in order to have access to beautiful women.

Whenever he finds anything beautiful in a house he admires it until it is presented to him.

However that may be, the Roman Church was steadily accumulating power and wealth. Pope Siricius (384–99) was a worthy successor of Damasus, but as a Christian leader was overshadowed by Ambrose. It was he, not the Pope, who forced the Emperor Theodosius I to do penance for the massacre by his troops of the citizens of Thessalonea. But the Church as a whole benefited greatly from the unrelenting pressure Theodosius exerted on the remaining institutions of paganism. Unfortunately for both Church and Empire, he was the last strong ruler capable of keeping the imperial fabric from falling apart.

The quarter-century following the death of Damasus was the Indian summer of old Rome. There was as yet no sense of impending catastrophe. The poet Claudian was still celebrating the victories of imperial generals. Barbarian invasions had by no means ceased, but they were almost invariably repelled with vast loss to the invaders. Internal struggles between emperor and usurpers were the concern of professional armies and minimally affected the smooth functioning of the civil government. Communications by road, river and sea were excellent. The rich enjoyed their immense estates dotted all over Italy and the provinces, and the poor enjoyed many material facilities, free distribution of foodstuffs, chariot races, gladiatorial combats (not yet suppressed by Christian sentiment) and massacres of wild beasts.

Yet the fancied immunity of the ancient world was almost at an end. The small, compact nation of West Goths was already settled within the empire's Balkan frontiers, acknowledging imperial sovereignty but still plundering the provinces at will. In 408 they migrated to Italy and two years later looted Rome itself, causing little material damage but inflicting a moral shock on the old order from which it never recovered. These Arian Goths eventually set up their own kingdom in the south of Gaul (419) and in Spain. Meanwhile another Germanic nation, the Arian Vandals, were beginning their long trek from Germany through Gaul and Spain which ended in their occupying the province of Africa. The result of these movements was the political disintegration of the empire in the West and the subjugation of vast Catholic areas by a ruling Arian minority. The Vandals were especially dangerous because they threatened Rome's food supplies and interrupted traffic by sea through the Mediterranean; in the religious sphere they tolerated, if they did not actively encourage, various forms of heresy.

Innocent I (402–17) was Pope when Alaric and his Goths plundered the undefended city. Since the civic authorities were helpless and the Emperor Honorius remained passively entrenched behind the marshes of Ravenna, only the Church could offer the population a measure of protection. Innocent personally interceded with Alaric to the best of his ability and with some effect. There was no bloodbath, and the Goths respected the Church's buildings and treasures; after three days they moved out. Alaric may also have been the more inclined to listen to the Pope's pleas because Innocent had recently visited Ravenna in a vain attempt to induce Honorius to come to terms with the Gothic leader.

Innocent's energy was spent in trying to widen the influence of the Roman see as far as possible. His letters to other bishops are full of purposeful reminders of the status and prerogatives of the Roman bishop, of his right as St Peter's successor to issue directives and to act as the highest instance of appeal. We hear in them the authentic voice of Roman discipline. He was also imbued with a deep sense of Rome's universal mission. This led him, in the earlier years of his pontificate, to

respond to appeals from the popular bishop of Constantinople, Jo.
for support in his struggle against pressure from the eastern Em
hostility of ecclesiastical rivals. Despite the inherent Roman suspicion o
nople, Innocent had the vision to recognize in John an enthusiast for chur
opposed to an instrument of Byzantine autocracy. In the event he failed to
John's banishment, but it is no mere coincidence that both these kindred spir
subsequently canonized. Innocent, however, was successful – in association wi
even more renowed Saint, Augustine – in dealing with the Pelagian heresy, wh
denied Original Sin and the necessity of Grace. Its author, Pelagius, was a mor
from Britain who settled in Rome about the year 400 and moved on to Africa ten
years later. His errors were castigated at Jerusalem and Carthage, but it was not
until the Pope had solemnly endorsed a further denunciation, composed by Augustine as bishop of Hippo, that they were finally condemned.

Innocent's firm grip on affairs gave place in his successors to a certain lack of
nerve. The Gothic presence in Gaul and Spain, together with the Vandal domination of Africa, loosened the ties that bound the bishoprics of those countries to Rome;
there was recurrent friction with Constantinople about the line of demarcation in the
Balkans between the two sees; and the Church as a whole was convulsed by the bitter
theological dispute concerning the nature of Christ that initially opposed Cyril,
Patriarch of Alexandria, to Nestorius, Patriarch of Constantinople. Rome for its part
was not free from personal animosities; these flared up in fierce fighting between
rival church factions in 418, when the election of Boniface I (418–22) was challenged
and Symmachus, the last great pagan Prefect of the city, took grim pleasure in
quelling the disturbances. But in another important respect, the development of
Christian art, the period was important. It produced, for instance, the brilliant series
of mosaics in the churches of Santa Pudenziana and Santa Maria Maggiore. Apart
from their aesthetic value they are of especial interest as depicting, in the Apostles
and figures from the Old Testament whom they represent, contemporary clerics and
Christian worthies wearing the costume of the time, as yet no different from that of
the secular Romans.

The first round of the Christological controversy was decided in favour of Cyril at
the third ecumenical Council, which took place at Ephesus in 431, but the strong
resentments it aroused were never to be appeased. Against Cyril's doctrine of the
perfect union of the divine and the human in Christ, Nestorius maintained that they
were essentially separate, and that the divine element had been, as it were,
superimposed on the human. It followed from his view that Mary was not the
Mother of God but only of the man Jesus, a conclusion that profoundly offended
ordinary Christians in the West and many in the East as well. The other extreme was
represented by Eutyches, who took a simpler and more radical view than Cyril.
According to him Christ has only one nature, the divine, after his incarnation. This
was the heresy known as Monophysitism which was to gain the passionate allegiance of the people in Syria and Egypt and nearly became predominant in
Constantinople. It appealed to an austere monotheism for which the West had no
feeling at all. The opposing theses, together with numerous nuances expressed in a
wealth of Greek philosophical verbiage, were to reverberate throughout the fifth and
sixth centuries. The Roman Church, however, had no use for such subtleties. It
opposed with equal clarity of thought both Nestorianism and Monophysitism. The
delegates whom Pope Celestine I (422–32) sent to Ephesus gave powerful support to
Cyril, but the firmest and most effective champion of Catholicism in its Roman guise
proved to be Leo I (440–61). The first of only two Popes to whom history has

...e of Great, he towers up like a second rock of St Peter in the midst c
...nt with dread and disaster.

... Tuscan, the native of a country that had given Rome its ancient religion
... in future be the nursery of many celebrated Popes. His personal origins
...ure, and we do not even know his full names. Probably he sprang from a
...of Etrurian landowners or city magistrates. What is certain is that at the time
...s election he was already an outstanding figure among the Roman clergy,
...l-educated, highly competent, fully conscious of the majesty of his future office
...nd eager to assert it in the most authoritative fashion. At the same time he was
aware of the limits of his power in those troubled years when the Bishop of Rome
needed to be a resilient and cool-headed diplomat as well as the spiritual leader to
whom vast regions looked for guidance and comfort. In fact he turned out to be the
perfect Pope in an era of adversity.

When elected by clergy and people he was on a political mission to Gaul, where
the Emperor Valentinian III (425–55) had asked him to compose the differences
between his military commander, Aetius, and the chief civil functionary, the
Praetorian Prefect Albinus. With half Gaul in the hands of Visigoths, Burgundians
and Franks, and with Spain disputed between Visigoths and another Germanic
tribe, the Sueves, this was obviously a matter of crucial importance for both State
and Church. On his return to Rome Leo spent the first ten years of his pontificate
grappling with the problems created for the Church by the rise of barbarian
kingdoms within the empire's boundaries. It was vital for him to keep his bishops on
a tight rein. As his 150 surviving letters show, he insistently reminded them of their
dependence on the see of St Peter as the fount of all authority, of their duty of
obedience to it and of its own duty of caring for them. When Hilarius, bishop of
Arles, tried to assert the independence of the Gallican church against Rome, Leo
obtained from the pliant Valentinian a decree confirming the absolute primacy of
the Apostolic See and forbidding the bishops of Gaul or any other imperial province,
under threat of legal penalities, to contravene its ordinances.

At the same time he was working out a theory of papal monarchy. He wished to
establish that the powers conferred on St Peter by Christ himself were automatically
handed down to the Apostle's successors and all the future Bishops of Rome who
were, at least in principle, elected by the city's clergy and laity. He described himself
as the 'unworthy heir of St Peter', meaning that he and all other Popes, while
inheriting the Apostle's powers to the fullest degree, did not presume to possess his
virtues. In other words any Pope, whatever his personal failings, was as legitimately
entitled to perform his functions and govern the Church as the most morally and
intellectually perfect individual. The theory implied that in the exercise of his
inherited powers a Pope could not be judged by any outside authority; he was, in
effect, infallible. Leo's claim stemmed not only from the Text in *Matthew* xvi but from
an utterly spurious letter from the first century Pope Clement informing James, the
brother of Jesus, at Jerusalem, that St Peter had passed on his powers to Clement
and his successors in the presence of the Christian community at Rome. For all its
apparent flimsiness it was not questioned by Leo's contemporaries.

While Leo was imposing and justifying his authority in the West heresy was once
more active in the East, where the reaction led by the Monophysite Eutyches against
the official doctrines of the two natures of Christ had gained momentum and
attracted the sympathy of the Emperor Theodosius II (408–50). It was opposed by
Flavian, the Patriarch of Constantinople, who had remained loyal to the decisions of
the Council of Ephesus. Such was Leo's reputation that both these irreconcilable

contenders invoked his support. The Pope, in a magisterial exposition of orthodox doctrine known as the 'dogmatic epistle', pronounced in favour of Flavian. In 449 his envoys (legates) brought this document to Ephesus, where Theodosius had convoked another council (the so called 'robber' synod) packed with Monophysite fanatics, with the object of deposing Flavian and condemning the doctrine of the two natures. Leo's legates were not even permitted to present his letter, and their oral protests, which were ineffective because they were unable to express themselves intelligibly in Greek, were rudely ignored. The unfortunate Flavian was so severely manhandled that he died of shock three days afterwards.

It seemed as if Monophysitism had won the day and that a fatal schism had opened between the two halves of Christendom. Fortunately Theodosius died in the following year and the religious policy of the court of Constantinople was reversed under his successor Marcian (450–57). It was he who assembled, in 451, the fourth General Council of the Church at Chalcedon on the Bosporus, which the Pope was invited to attend. He replied that neither past custom nor present political anxieties (the invasion of Europe by the Huns) would permit his absenting himself from Rome, but he sent an impressive band of legates to represent him. Thanks largely to their intervention, and to the respectful attention that the Council paid to Leo's views, the doctrine of the two natures in one Person was triumphantly upheld and the Pope's stand vindicated. When his letter was at last expounded, the members of the Council rose to their feet exclaiming that St Peter had spoken through Leo. Although Monophysitism remained a strong force in the East, it was for the moment sharply checked. Leo's satisfaction was diluted, however, by the Council's decision, against the objections of his legates, to declare the see of Constantinople to be equal in status to that of Rome itself and superior to those of Alexandria and Antioch. In effect it was accorded the same position in the East that Rome enjoyed in the West, and this was regarded by the Pope as a potential threat to the primacy of St Peter.

But Leo had more pressing worries at home. In the second half of his pontificate Roman political power in the West was crumbling without much hope of recovery. Britain, Spain and Africa had already been lost, and now in Gaul the Gallo-Romans who still formed the majority of the population were deciding to compound with the Germanic invaders rather than preserve a tenuous political connexion with Italy. The interests of indigenous Italians were best served by the Church, which not only held their spiritual allegiance but was also becoming the greatest property owner in the peninsula. Quite apart from his religious influence over a much wider sphere, the Pope was the foremost Italian, and it was to him that the Italians looked for their salvation from the barbarian menace.

The Huns, a nomadic people of Central Asian origin, had been encamped on the Danubian frontier of the empire since the beginning of the fifth century. As from about 440 their king, Attila, invaded the Balkan provinces, threatening communications by road between Rome and Constantinople at the same time as the Vandals were blocking the sea routes. It was no longer easy, as it had been in the previous century, for Christian bishops to circulate freely from one synod to another at different ends of the Mediterranean. In 451 Attila, at the head of a vast Asiatic horde swelled by satellite Germanic tribes, burst into Gaul. He had formed an alliance with the Vandal king Genseric, who was on the worst possible terms with Theodoric, the King of the Visigoths in Southern Gaul. Attila had also received an offer of marriage from Honoria, the wayward sister of Valentinian, the western emperor. He was in fact attempting to grab, in Honoria's name, the largest and most productive provinces of Valentinian's shaky realm, within which the Visigoths, by arrangement with the western emperors, had made their home.

As it happened the Huns were fought to a standstill on the Catalaunian plain, a battlefield situated near Chalons-sur-Seine, or possibly Troyes, by the combined forces of the Roman general Aetius and of the Visigoth Theodoric. They retreated eastwards but in 452 made a sudden incursion into northern Italy. They devastated Liguria and Venetia, destroying the flourishing city of Aquileia. Terrified by the prospect of a Hun descent as far as Rome, Valentinian despatched an embassy headed by the Pope to Attila's camp near Mantua. Leo was accompanied by a Consul and a former Praetorian Prefect, but there is no doubt that he was the most influential of the trio. We have no idea what arguments he used to dissuade Attila from penetrating further into Italy. Centuries later, writers and artists, including Raphael, made great play with the picture of a venerable Pope threatening the savage chieftain with divine retribution if he should pursue his raid southwards. No doubt Leo impressed Attila with his fearlessness and eloquence. But Idatius, a contemporary chronicler and Spanish bishop, was probably nearer the mark in attributing Attila's moderation and retreat from Italy to shortage of supplies, together with the fear of being cut off in the peninsula by the troops of Aetius and the Emperor Marcian. Christians, however, inevitably saw the hand of God in Attila's death, which occurred the following year.

Leo had to endure an equally dangerous ordeal three years later. By then Aetius, the last effective champion of Roman rule in the West, had been murdered by his jealous master Valentinian, and the latter had been assassinated in his turn. The new Emperor was an insignificant nobleman named Petronius Maximus. It was then that Genseric, a ruthless and dynamic ruler whose career in the Mediterranean strangely anticipated that of the eleventh-century Norman princes, saw his opportunity. When in the year 455 his powerful fleet, manned by Vandal warriors and their Moorish auxiliaries, arrived off Portus, Rome's harbour, he found the city once again undefended. There were no troops to man the Aurelian Wall, the civil authorities were impotent, and Maximus was killed by one of his own men. The Roman people's only protector was again the Pope, but this time there was little that Leo could do. When he met Genseric at the city gates he was told that while the Vandals had no intention of burning down Rome or of massacring its inhabitants, they were determined to humiliate it and to collect the maximum amount of booty. Theirs was to be no random pillage like that of the Goths. Thus Rome was methodically sacked for a fortnight. Some churches were looted and profaned, but the chief victims of this 'vandalism' were the ancient public buildings and temples. These were systematically stripped of their accumulated treasures, their historic relics such as the Jewish spoil removed by Titus from Jerusalem, their works of art, their bronze and gilded roof tiles, in short everything of permanent or saleable value. The same fate befell the private houses of the rich, while as many of their owners as had not fled were shipped to Carthage to await ransom. While the physical structure of Rome and the general apparatus of civilized life remained intact, the resulting social disruption and impoverishment were considerable. Thus for the rest of his life Leo played no further part in politics but devoted himself to the encouragement and relief of his people. The charitable function of the Church was becoming of equal importance to that of the State.

For the next seventy-five years and the duration of a dozen pontificates the real power in Italy was wielded by three military leaders, each belonging to a different Germanic tribe, Ricimer the Sueve, Odovacer the Herulian and Theodoric, King of the Ostrogoths. The chief distinction between them was that whereas the first two commanded barbarian troops nominally in the Roman service, Theodoric was the ruler of a small nation in arms that settled in Italy just as the Visigoths had previously settled in Gaul. At the same time the Italians continued to acknowledge an Emperor, although from 476 there was no longer one reigning in the West but only in remote Constantinople. Italy and Rome were administered by the same bureaucratic machine as before, by their traditional Senate and by magistrates whose offices in some cases traced their origins back to the Roman Republic. Lastly the Church, with the Pope at its head, was strengthening its hold on men's minds and acquiring in the process a great deal of property. Despite the conflicts of loyalties inherent in the system, it extended the life of the ancient world for another short but useful span, and allowed the papacy to operate in relatively peaceful circumstances. Ricimer set up various puppet emperors but did not hesitate to depose or execute them if he found them inadequate. Odovacer, for his part, forced the last of them to abdicate and ruled by formal appointment by the eastern emperor as 'Patrician'. Theodoric, who reigned for thirty-three years after disposing of Odovacer, keenly admired Roman civilization. His policy was to interfere as seldom as possible with either the civil institutions or with the Catholic Church (although he himself was a strict Arian). Such favourable conditions did not save the Church from grave dissensions. Between 484 and 519 Rome and Constantinople were in schism, while from 498 to 506 the papacy itself was in dispute between two obstinate rivals, each supported by a vigorous faction in Rome and the whole of Italy.

The so-called 'Acacian' schism was provoked by a revival of Monophysitism in the East. Faced by the dangerous political implications of a division within his empire between Monophysite Egypt and Syria on the one side and orthodox Asia Minor and the Balkans on the other, The Emperor Zeno (474-91) sought a compromise. In 482 he promulgated his *Henotikon*, a declaration of Union to which he hoped that both Monophysites and Orthodox Christians would be able to subscribe. The leading spirit in its compilation was the Patriarch of Constantinople, Acacius. The *Henotikon*, while ostensibly basing its doctrine on the first three General Councils of the Church, said nothing about that of Chalcedon, which it neither invoked nor controverted. The East was ready enough to accept it as putting an end to unnecessary strife, but it encountered the most strenuous opposition in Rome, where unequivocal submission to the doctrine of Chalcedon was considered as vital as acceptance of the primacy of St Peter. In addition Rome was shocked because the Emperor was intervening in doctrinal issues that only a Council of the Church could properly settle.

The publication of the *Henotikon* coincided with the death of Pope Simplicius (468-83) and the election of Felix III (483-92), a strong-minded Roman aristrocrat. He took alarm at once, but with diplomatic caution sent two bishops to Constantinople to find out exactly what was happening. If necessary they were to remonstrate with Zeno and his Patriarch. These clerics, however, were sufficiently dazzled by Byzantine eloquence, or seduced by Byzantine gold, to do exactly the opposite and take the Patriarch's side. On their return Felix had them excommunicated by a specially convened synod, which for good measure excommunicated Acacius as well. To make matters worse, the envoy whom he despatched with the relevant decree was corrupted in the same way as the bishops, and Acacius replied by excommunicating the Pope.

The rift took long to mend, though the Popes continued to address the Emperor in terms of respectful loyalty. Unfortunately Anastasius (491–518), the elderly bureaucrat and financial genius who came after Zeno, was also a stubborn Monophysite with a taste for theology, while Pope Gelasius (492–8) was an even more uncompromising champion of the spiritual supremacy of his office. An African refugee from Vandal rule, like St Augustine, he had a passionate Punic temperament as well as a remarkable command of the Latin language. It was he who, as Felix's secretary, drafted the papal missives to the court of Constantinople. His own warnings to Anastasius against the imperial tendency to encroach on the Pope's spiritual domain were even more trenchant. All would be well, he told the Emperor, if he would only stick to his secular role and not play the priest as well. His short-lived successor, Pope Anastasius II (496–8), took an easier line and offered Roman acquiescence in the *Henotikon* in return for a formal condemnation of Acacius by the eastern church, but the deal was unpopular with his own clergy and unacceptable to the Emperor. Pope Symmachus (498–514), on the other hand, swung back to the Gelasian position, and what seemed to be complete deadlock ensued.

Symmachus won in a struggle for the papal chair which began in 498. A backwoodsman from Sardinia and a pagan in childhood, he seems a surprising choice for the Roman clergy and people to have made. Opposition to his candidacy had been building up even before Pope Anastasius died, and the opposing party had decided to back the Archpriest Laurentius. The result was that separate elections were held on the same day by rival groups of partisans, those of Symmachus in the Lateran basilica and those of Laurentius in Santa Maria Maggiore. Each claimed to have been regularly elected and refused to yield to the other.

The causes of this sudden split seem to have been political and social rather than religious. Senators intervened in the elections on both sides, for the influence of the Senate had been revived since the disappearance of the western emperor and the establishment of Theodoric's kingdom. While Italy's frontiers were secured by the Gothic army, aristocrats drawn from the Senate ran the King's civil administration on Roman lines. Its chiefs, such as the Praetorian Prefect and the Prefect of the city, were powerful men. Despite Vandal depredations these magnates were still very rich, and many had a vested interest in the survival of Theodoric's regime. Others found the barbarians' presence distasteful and hankered after the direct rule of the Emperor at Constantinople. Most of them would also have welcomed a reconciliation with the eastern church. But all were intensely concerned with securing the election of a Pope who would be certain to cherish the interests of the senatorial class, preferably someone like Felix who was one of themselves. Although their way of life had not changed much since pagan times, they were by now virtually all Christians.

As Symmachus was not a Roman and his origins were plebeian, he was personally less sympathetic to the Senators than was Laurentius. Nevertheless he was upheld by a strong faction among them, as well as by a majority of his fellow clerics. To clinch the matter the King ruled in his favour. The ruling was confirmed by an Italian synod and Laurentius was consoled with a bishopric. The King himself visited Rome, addressed the Senate and people and appealed for calm. But the deep feeling aroused by the quarrel failed to subside. The Pope's highly-placed enemies, led by Faustus, the head of the Senate, concocted a charge that he had celebrated Easter on the wrong date. When summoned to Theodoric's court at Ariminum to answer it, and other accusations of immoral behaviour, Symmachus lost his nerve. He rushed back to Rome and took refuge in St Peter's. Laurentius promptly returned too and put himself at the head of his partisans.

From then on the pendulum swung violently between Pope and anti-pope. As a concession to Laurentius Theodoric appointed a visitor to investigate the complaints against the Pope and convened a fresh synod at Rome. The bishops were terrified by rioting mobs in the streets, and the Roman populace, enthusiastically in favour of the Pope, clashed with the armed slaves and clients of his senatorial opponents. The latter prevented Symmachus from leaving St Peter's in order to attend the synod and murdered two of his senior priests. Meanwhile Laurentius installed himself in the Lateran Palace and was soon controlling the greater part of the city. Strife and anarchy lasted intermittently for four years, in a scenario typical of the more unruly Middle Ages. Eventually the King was induced to intervene. When he pronounced in favour of Symmachus Laurentius gave up the struggle and retired to a senatorial estate, where he died from the effects of an excessively severe fast.

Symmachus had won his long-drawn-out battle at home, but his abrasive style precluded all reconciliation with the eastern church during his lifetime. That task he bequeathed to Hormisdas (514–23), the wise and patient Pope who succeeded him and devoted himself to repairing the breach. A number of embassies passed between Rome and Constantinople before any result was achieved, but the path to reunion was smoothed by the growing influence and eventual ascendancy of the orthodox party on the Bosporus. When Justin I (518–27), an old soldier from the Balkans, replaced the intransigent Anastasius, his government immediately disavowed Monophysitism. Orthodoxy was restored at a Council held in the presence of the Pope's legates, Acacius and other eastern prelates were branded as heretics, and the names of the Emperors Zeno and Anastasius were for good measure equally condemned. So far Rome had scored a complete success, and Hormisdas had been careful to secure King Theodoric's acquiescence in the rapprochement with Constantinople. Nevertheless, the delicate new equilibrium between East and West was almost immediately upset. Soon Justin's nephew Justinian (527–65) was to launch his grandiose attempt to wrest the western provinces from their barbarian overlords. His enterprise was to impoverish and depopulate Italy, to open the way for a new wave of more primitive and destructive barbarians and virtually to bring civilized life to an end in the peninsula. Moreover the Emperor's absolutism, manifested in his insistence on dictating to the papacy on religious as well as all other issues, was to precipitate an acute crisis between the Empire and the Church in the West.

3

ROME AND BYZANTIUM

(526–590)

In 526 Pope John I (523–26) broke precedent and paid a formal visit to Constantinople. He did not go there of his own volition but at the instance of King Theodoric and as leader of a large delegation comprising Senators and clerics. Disturbed by the Emperor Justin's persecution of the Arians, the King had entrusted the Pope with the delicate mission of persuading the Emperor to abate his zeal. John was received with pomp and deference at Constantinople. Justin accorded him the place of honour, higher than that of the Patriarch, at public ceremonies, invited him to celebrate the eastern Mass according to the Roman rite and arranged that John should re-crown him. The Emperor was also, for political reasons, disposed to relax his anti-Arian measures. He refused only Theodoric's demand that those Arians who had been converted to Catholicism should be allowed to return to their faith. But when John reappeared at Ravenna to report the success of his diplomacy he was surprised to find the King highly displeased. He and his fellow delegates were arrested and he himself very soon died, elderly and exhausted, in detention.

No doubt the King was irritated by the honours lavished on the Pope by Justin, who had indeed treated him as the chief priest of his own empire with scant regard for Theodoric's feelings. But the major ground for his action was political. In his old age the King was becoming extremely intolerant of opposition and suspicious of disloyalty among his Italian subjects. His relations with other Germanic rulers in the West, to whom he had been dynastically connected, had deteriorated. His sister, married to a former King of the Vandals, had been put to death by his successor, while the Frankish and Burgundian monarchs had both shocked him by turning Catholic. Worse still, he was convinced that distinguished Romans in his own service were plotting against him.

The most eminent of these were Boethius, philosopher, poet, consul, higher civil servant and encylopaedic scholar, the latter's father-in-law Symmachus (no relation of the Pope of that name), consul, former Prefect of the city and historian, and Faustus Albissus, also a former consul and Praetorian Prefect. They were all pillars of the King's own administration and the cream of the intellectual Roman aristocracy. During the Acacian schisms they had with Theodoric's approval faithfully supported Pope Symmachus. But since the reconciliation with Constantinople and Justin's assumption of power they had evidently developed strong imperial sympathies regarded by Theodoric as subverse. Most probably they were in correspondence with the eastern court. Moreover they and their considerable following were very close to the learned theologian Pope John, who was well known for his connections with the East. It was precisely for this reason that Theodoric had sent him to plead the Arians' case before Justin. By the time the Pope returned all three grandees were under arrest or confined to their properties, and it is not surprising that John was similarly treated. There was far too much potentially treasonable unity among influential Romans for the King's liking. But he was soon to find that John, intimate as he was with the aristocrats, was also highly popular with the Roman people, who mourned for him as a martyr to Arian intolerance. His body was carried in solemn state from Ravenna to Rome for burial, under the inscription, 'Victim of Christ', in the porch of St Peter's.

The King himself on the brink of death but undeterred by the odium he had incurred, gave orders for the execution of Boethius and Symmachus and for the election, if it could be arranged, of a Pope whom the Goths could trust. Such a person was found in Felix IV (526–30), but for the next ten years the papacy was in disarray. The tendency to elect elderly deacons or persons ordained late in life, produced five Popes during the period and hardly contributed to its stability. There was a divided election in 530 when the pro-eastern candidate, Dioscarus, a Greek from Alexandria, was opposed to Boniface II (530–32), the first Pope of Germanic descent, the son of one Sigibold. All the elections were tarnished by bribery and intimidation, against which the Senate was obliged to pass a decree.

The Gothic monarchy, however, was in still worse confusion. Theodoric who died shortly after the election of Felix, was succeeded by his young grandson Athalaric, at first under the regency of his Roman-educated mother Amalasuntha. Her very upbringing made her suspect to her own countrymen. While their own government was paralysed at the top and the climate of confidence which had at one time prevailed between them and the Italians had been spoiled, the Goths were deeply disturbed by the successful execution of the first stage of the new Emperor Justin's plan for the reconquest of the western Mediterranean. By the spring of 534 his general Belisarius had destroyed the powerful Vandal kingdom in a single six-month campaign, thus restoring the whole of North Africa, together with Corsica, Sardinia and the Balearics, to imperial rule. The Mediterranean had become a Byzantine lake and the Gothic Kingdom was practically encircled. On Athalaric's death from drink later in the same year his mother was imprisoned and then strangled. Her cousin, Theodahad, who then acceded to the Gothic throne, did not have long to wait, for in 535 Belisarius opened hostilities by seizing Sicily.

The Pope at that moment was Agapetus I (535–6), another elderly cleric but one of interesting antecedents and undoubted courage. He was a member of the same family as Felix III and of the future Pope Gregory the Great. A noted scholar, he had founded a library of the Church Fathers in his house on the slopes of the Caelian Hill, and it seems that he and the Gothic King's minister Cassiodorus were planning to expand it into a sort of Christian University. Suddenly he was bidden by the stricken Theodahad to go to Constantinople and beg Justinian to call off his forces. This political mission met with no success. In the religious field, however, he convinced the Emperor that the Patriarch Anthimos was tainted with the Monophysite heresy. Having secured the Patriarch's condemnation and presided over the consecration of his successor, Agapetus died before he could return to Italy. His action, like that of John, demonstrated how authoritative was the papacy's mystique so long as it was not expected to prevail in straightforward power politics. In his place the King procured the election of Silverius, an obscure sub-deacon who was the son of Pope Hormisdas. Six months after his consecration Belisarius made an unopposed and triumphal entry into Rome.

This event was the first of a chain leading to the ruin of the city and of Italy as a whole. It marked the end of a civilized way of life that had subsisted in its essentials since the Roman Republic and that no one expected to be so abruptly extinguished. There seemed no reason why its main features in the metropolis – the Senate, the public offices, the law courts, the markets, the public baths, the race courses, the theatre – should not last indefinitely. The immediate sequel to the Byzantine invasion was a rally by the Goths, who killed the feckless Theodahad and chose the warrior Vitigis as their leader. Soon they invested Rome with superior forces and besieged Belisarius for a year and nine months. Silverius, as a Gothic nominee, was in a weak position. However, as he had helped Belisarius to take over the city without bloodshed he might well have remained unmolested but for an imperial intervention. According to the story current at the time it was the Empress Theodora, herself a Monophysite and a former patroness of Anthimos, who had made up her mind to install a Pope who might compromise with Monophysitism. To that end she had been working on the deacon Vigilius, a Roman occupying the key post of *apokrisiarios*, or nuncio, at the imperial court. Vigilius was duly despatched to Rome, but as there was no way of getting rid of Silverius except by deposition Belisarius summoned him, had him stripped of his papal robes and ordered the Romans to elect a new pope. This they obediently did, and the wretched Silverius was shipped into exile in Asia Minor. Subsequently he was sent back to Italy by Justinian's command, only to be consigned on arrival to the Island of Ponza and left to die there by privation. The whole affair was sad and sordid, but the tale of feminine intrigue was conceivably exaggerated in order to present a purely political operation in suitably lurid colours. In other words Belisarius, at the height of the siege, caught the Pope in correspondence with the besiegers and acted accordingly.

If Vigilius (537–55) did not connive at the abasement of the papal office, he was cast first as the instrument and later as the victim of blatant imperial interference in church affairs. When his pontificate ended Rome was a wreck, Italy had been devastated by war and plague and its society was in dissolution. He himself had been removed to Constantinople and reduced to misery by imperial bullying over a seemingly insoluble religious dilemma.

The horrors of the Gothic war have often been described. Sufficient to say here that by 552, when the main Gothic army was at last crushed by Justinian's eunuch general Narses, Rome had stood three sieges and had been taken and retaken four times. It had been plundered from end to end and its citizens sucked dry by the exactions of both sides. The historic system of social aid by which the poor received free rations from the authorities had broken down and the corn supplies were no longer arriving regularly from Sicily and Africa. The cutting of the great aqueducts caused a shortage of drinking water besides putting the public baths out of action. Whenever there was a break in the fighting the inhabitants abandoned the city *en masse*. The rich fled to their estates but found no security there, for apart from the passage of armies Totila, the Gothic king who brilliantly sustained the struggle for ten years after the capture of Vitigis, deliberately stirred up a popular revolution in the countryside that attracted slaves and peasants to his banner. The slaughter of many landowners and the flight of many more overseas effectively broke up the old senatorial and administrative class. Meanwhile the bubonic plague ravaging the Mediterranean area swept through the cities. Many of them, too, were stormed and sacked during the war years; the second capital of Italy, Milan, was totally ruined amid the massacre of most of its 300,000 inhabitants. Although bishops and clergy stood by their flocks there was little that the best organized church could do in mitigation, and when the worst crisis struck Rome Vigilius was not there to meet it.

It is a far cry from this scene of apocalyptic disaster to the theological arena on the Bosporus. As if he was not already preoccupied by his wars, Justinian was being prodded by Theodora to bring about a reconciliation between Catholics and Monophysites. The latter were becoming bolder and more vocal, especially in Syria. In 543 the Emperor's religious adviser Theodore Ascidas, Bishop of Caesarea, suggested that a basis for harmony might be found in an official condemnation of those works of three fifth century theologians known as the 'Three Chapters'. While accepted as orthodox by the Council of Chalcedon, they seemed to the Monophysites to savour of Nestorianism. Ascidas assured the Emperor that the Monophysites would be sufficiently appeased if the Three Chapters were jettisoned by the Catholics as unsound. They were not, after all, major works of Christian Doctrine.

In accordance with this advice Justinian issued in 544 an edict condemning the Chapters and obliged the principal eastern prelates, including the Patriarch of Constantinople, to subscribe to it. The Church in the West, however, repudiated any claim by an Emperor to lay down the law on an issue of doctrine, and Vigilius, for all his close ties with the imperial court, was consequently bound to resist the edicts and to uphold the orthodoxy of the Chapters. Justinian decided that the only effective means of putting pressure on him would be to abduct him from Rome. On 22 November 545, he was hustled on board a warship in the Tiber and taken first to Sicily and thence by easy stages to Constantinople. When he arrived there in 547 he was treated to alternate doses of cajolery and intimidation, an exhausting ordeal which lasted for another eight years. For a long time he succeeded in keeping the Emperor at bay by a mixture of obstinacy and indecision and avoided committing himself to an unconditional condemnation of the Chapters. He knew that many easterners sympathized with him and were distressed to see the senior bishop of Christendom held in constraint.

But Justinian was losing patience. He ordered Ascidas to draft a second and more drastic edict and began to prepare a general Council to endorse it. The Pope, in a rare display of resolution, reacted by excommunicating Ascidas. This gesture of defiance infuriated Justinian and Vigilius sought sanctuary in the basilica of St Peter. When imperial agents forced their way into the church to lay hands on him an undignified brawl ensued, culminating in the collapse of the altar to which he was desperately clinging. At that stage a crowd of outraged supporters obliged the assailants to retreat. This was the first, if not the most dramatic, of the frequent occasions when a Pope was to suffer physical injury at the hands of a Christian ruler or his minions. Recognizing that he had gone too far, the Emperor sent a high-level delegation, led by Belisarius, to apologize and escort the Pope back to the palace where he was lodged, but Vigilius soon eluded his guards, had himself rowed across the Bosporus and took refuge in another church. This time Justinian left him alone, but his attempts to hold out gradually weakened. He was unable to prevent the Emperor from rigging a Council and obtaining from it the necessary condemnation of the Chapters. Isolated and kept under close watch, he lost his capacity for resistance. Only when his spirit was effectively broken did Justinian grant permission for him to return to Rome. Vigilius embarked on the long sea voyage, but died from kidney trouble when his ship reached Syracuse.

Among the western clerics confined at Constantinople was the deacon Pelagius. After winning great respect by his conduct during the siege of Rome by Totila, he joined Vigilius in exile and had been foremost in encouraging him to withstand imperial pressures. He belonged to a distinguished Roman family and was a talented diplomat and administrator. It occurred to the astute Justinian, who knew him well,

that his ambition to become Pope might perhaps be found to outweigh his devotion
to the Three Chapters. He therefore offered him the papal office on condition that he
should publicly denounce those works. The Emperor had not misjudged his man,
because Pelagius immediately swallowed his previous convictions and accepted. He
had probably made up his mind that after two successive Popes had fallen foul of
Justinian's conception of imperial primacy in the sphere of religion further opposition would be pointless. It would be preferable that he, a loyal and competent
Roman, should succeed to the see than some unworthy creature of the eastern court.

His election, on reaching Rome, was a formality. Indeed, although the papacy
would not henceforth be exactly in the Emperor's gift, every election between 556
and 741 would have to be referred for confirmation to Constantinople. In Italy, as a
result of twenty years of war, famine and pestilence, the senatorial hierarchy, the old
Roman officialdom and municipal institutions had vanished, to be replaced by the
Byzantine Military Administration of the victorious general Narses. Italy had
become a derelict second-class province run as the colony of an empire centred in
Asia Minor. The sole native institution to survive, with its structure battered but
essentially unaltered, was the Roman Church, with its central and episcopal
apparatus ministering to the people's needs.

Early in his term of office Pelagius I (556–61) was intensely unpopular in Italy,
especially among churchmen scandalized by his apparently cynical volte-face over
the Three Chapters. He was boycotted by the bishops and it was some months before
a quorum could be found to consecrate him. Even in Rome, where his pastoral
record had been exemplary, people believed that he had caused the death of Vigilius.
The hard-headed Pope did not allow himself to be disturbed by this hostility, but
calmly went about restoring the Church's revenues, renewing its personnel and
bringing its neglected properties back to production. He ransomed prisoners and fed
the poor, as he had done in Totila's time, at the expense of his private fortune. He
calculated correctly that the pragmatic Italians would soon become more interested
in his work for their welfare rather than his attitude towards the orthodoxy or
otherwise of three obscure Greek Doctors. Before long even the bishops were
shedding their reservations about his theology. More importantly, he laid – in five
years of intense effort – the foundations of the order on which, at the end of the
century, a much greater Pope was to build.

John III (561–74), a senator's son, carried on the work of retrenchment as best he
could, but in the second half of his pontificate the unity and security of Italy were
fatally shattered by the Lombard invasion. The Lombards, a Germanic people
converted to Arianism but scarcely touched by Roman civilization, had for some
time been settled in what is now Western Hungary. Feeling themselves threatened
by their neighbours to the east, the Turkic Avars, they decided to move further afield
and in 568 broke into Northern Italy. They were formidable warriors and the
Byzantine garrisons were too weak to repel them. In a very short time they occupied
Venetia, the Po Valley and Tuscany, and fixed their capital at Pavia. Meanwhile,
their spearheads probed southwards and established semi-independent duchies at
Spoleto and Benevento, threatening Rome from both sides. On the other hand they
were not numerous or powerful enough to subjugate the whole peninsula. The
Byzantine governor, or Exarch, secured himself in Ravenna, which was virtually
impregnable, and from there retained a hold over Emilia, Romagna and a thin belt
of territory stretching as far as Rome and Naples, which were each defended by a
Duke or military commander. The north-south corridor could of course be severed
at any moment during the endemic hostilities which were waged between Lombards

and Byzantines to the detriment of the Italian population. In the south, Apulia and Calabria remained under Byzantine control, but their frontiers and those of the Lombard duchy of Benevento were constantly shifting.

For the Roman church, whose spiritual domain included all Italy, the prospect was dour. It lost its landed estates in Lombard territory and had to suffer continual depredations from Lombard raiders on the Roman side of a very imprecise boundary. Rome itself was from time to time besieged but never taken. To this awkward state of affairs, which was to last for some two centuries, the Popes adapted themselves with surprising coolness and skill, for the imperial authorities could give them scant effective aid. After the failure of their sole serious attempt, in 575, to crush the Lombards, the rulers at Constantinople were too heavily engaged with Persians in the east, and with Avars and Slavs in the Balkans, to spare troops and funds for the defence of Italy.

4

GREGORY THE GREAT
(590–604)

It was in these harsh conditions that Gregory I, the Great, began his career. Strange as it may seem, the papacy had already exceeded one quarter of its total span to date by the time that he entered on his pontificate (590–604), yet his is the first papal personality of which we possess, largely through his own writings, more than a sketchy knowledge. He was born about 540 into a rich patrician family that had already produced two popes, Felix III and Agapetus I. The former was his great-grandfather. His kinsmen formed a closely knit group of pious aristocrats, some of whom took orders at an early age. His father, though a layman, held an administrative office in the Church; his mother, Silvia, was renowned for her saintliness and become a nun after her husband's death.

Gregory's childhood was spent in the family palace on the Caelian Hill. Despite the hardships of the Gothic War he was given the conventional education in grammar, rhetoric and dialectic, and perhaps in law as well. Although he was to complain that 'all the pomp of secular dignities' had vanished, that the Senate had been dissolved and Rome was tumbling into decay, he initially chose a civil career. Indeed he proved so efficient an administrator that by his early thirties he had risen to be Prefect of the City, a post inherited from the imperial past and still surviving under the Byzantine regime. It was he who was responsible for providing the much reduced population of Rome with bare necessities and whatever social services could still be made available. After 573, however, he abruptly abandoned the secular life and became a monk according to the rule of St Benedict.

Monasticism had reached Italy in the mid-fourth century, but Benedict of Nursia, who was born about 480, first gave it coherence and discipline. As a young man with a social background and traditional education similar to Gregory's he became an ascetic recluse and went on to found the monastery of Monte Cassino on one of his family's estates. He established it in accordance with his 'Rule', a code of conduct which forbade excessive austerities and sensibly divided the life of its inmates between prayer, manual labour and the pursuit of learning. He died when Gregory was still a child. Years later, when Monte Cassino was sacked by the Lombards, its monks fled to Rome, and Gregory, then at the height of his official career, became powerfully attracted by their way of life. Besides founding six monasteries in his lands in Sicily, he turned his palace on the Caelian Hill into a Benedictine community where he retired as a simple brother, devoting himself to religious exercise, study and works of charity. Subsequently, in his biography of St Benedict, he exalted both the virtues of the latter's 'Rule' and of his model who 'with a realistic mind only to serve God . . . sought some place where he might fulfil his holy purpose'.

He was not destined to stay there long. After about three years Pope Benedict I (575–9) ordained him deacon and put him in charge of one of the city's seven ecclesiastical regions, thus returning him to administrative duties at the time of plague, floods and Lombard incursions. Then Pelagius II (579–90), the son of a Goth, despatched him to Constantinople as his nuncio (*apokrisarios*) in the hope of convincing the Emperor of the need to rescue the city from the Lombards. Perhaps the choice of Gregory for the job was not entirely happy, for he neither spoke nor condescended to learn Greek. Nevertheless, lodged in the same palace as that once occupied by the hapless Vigilius, he made himself deeply respected by the Patriarchs and by the Emperors. His relationship with Maurice (582–602) is particularly interesting. Personally they got on well together. But whereas Maurice saw his task as wholly that of a stern soldier dedicated to the defence of a sprawling empire, Gregory conceived it as his duty to concentrate his sovereign's attention on Italy, which in the Byzantine scheme of things could only be considered as a secondary sector. They were to have many clashes after Gregory became Pope, but his communications with the Emperor were always couched in terms of genuine deference and admiration. He returned to Rome in 585 with an intimate knowledge of the workings of the imperial court and government.

For the next five years he settled down to literary work and biblical teachings in his monastery of St Andrew. As a writer he was tireless and voluminous; as regards style, he once asserted that 'the word of God should not be bound by the rule of Donatus the grammarian' but he also wrote that 'ignorant of profane literature, we cannot penetrate the depths of sacred learning'. In fact his Latin was supple and pithy; he was a master of the language as spoken in his own age. In particular, his 800 or more letters, a selection of which was compiled for Charlemagne by Pope Hadrian I, are of inestimable value for the historian.

When Pelagius died of the plague there was no doubt at Rome as to who should succeed him. Gregory made a show of reluctance, which gave rise to the legend that he ran away and hid in the woods, but as he explained to various great personages at Constaninople he was genuinely appalled by the tasks which awaited him. Irresistibly drawn towards an ascetic life he was still too much of a Roman to avoid the worldly responsibilities of his class. In theory he held that the service of God in the cloister was superior to the service of God's creatures on earth, but in practice he was forced to lead a thoroughly unsequestered existence, behaving more like a proconsul than a prophet and spiritual mentor. This is how he himself expressed his dilemma:

How can I think what my brethren need and see that the city is guarded against the swords of the enemy and take care lest the people be destroyed by a sudden attack, and yet at the same time deliver the word of exhortation fully and effectively for the salvation of souls. To speak of God we need a mind thoroughly at peace and free from care.

On his election as Pope, Gregory found himself carrying out much the same functions as when he was Prefect. Natural disasters had been aggravated by the flight to Rome of thousands of destitute refugees from Lombard raids, and one of his first tasks was to ensure the regular arrival of corn supplies from Sicily. But he was soon involved in the day to day conduct of diplomacy and war. He would have preferred an arrangement by which the barbarians and the imperial authorities might have agreed to respect each other's preserves, for it was only in such conditions that the former could be converted from Arianism and the church properties, scattered throughout Italy, safeguarded. In fact the Head of the Church had a more real interest in keeping the peace than Romanus, the Byzantine Exarch at Ravenna. But in view of the latter's sluggishness and jealousy of papal prestige Gregory was forced to assume responsibility for the defence of Rome and Naples against attacks from Ariulf and Arichis the Lombard Dukes of Spoleto and Benevento. Soon he was acting as civil and military governor of the whole area, paying the imperial troops, appointing their officers, directing their movements, negotiating with the Lombards, 'men whose promises are swords and whose grace a punishment', and buying them off if necessary with the Church's money. When the truce he had concluded with Duke Ariulf was disowned by the Exarch, who resented the Pope's independent initiatives, the Lombard King Agilulf, who reigned at Pavia, reacted by besieging Rome. Again Gregory fended him off by tactful handling and a bribe of five hundred pounds of gold. Such direct dealings with the Lombards displeased both Romanus and the Emperor Maurice, who accused him of political naïveté. He refuted this charge with force and dignity, praying that 'God would rule with his own hand our most pious Lord the Emperor and in his terrible judgment would find him free from all offence'. And in protesting against Maurice's decree that no civil servant nor soldier should be permitted to turn priest or monk, he declared that while submitting to the imperial command he must make it quite clear that it offended against God's wishes. This was bold language to use to the Emperor, but in writing to other correspondents, he was even franker. 'We cannot describe', he protested, 'what we suffer at the hands of your friend the Lord Romanus. I will only say that his malice towards us is worse than the swords of the Lombards.' Fortunately, a new Exarch, Callinicus, proved more co-operative; by 600 the worst of the Lombard menace had been averted.

Gregory's role as statesman imposed a huge burden on the papal treasury and his administrative talent was hard put to replenish its reserves. The latter were chiefly derived from the patrimony of St Peter, a wide network of landed estates spread over Italy, Gaul, Dalmatia, Africa, Sicily, Sardinia and Corsica. These properties had been accumulating through pious donations and endowments ever since the reign of Constantine, and during the disruption of the sixth century much land abandoned by its owners had been hurriedly bequeathed to the Church. But as much or more had been grabbed by barbarian invaders or had simply passed out of cultivation. Concurrently an elaborate organization had grown up for the management of the Church's estates. Gregory brought it to a high pitch of efficiency, thus ensuring that the lands should remain as productive as the hard times allowed. The whole heritage was divided into fifteen separate patrimonies, each controlled by a rector nominated by the Pope. This official was responsible for the choice of leaseholders (*conductores*), the collection of rents, transport and sale of produce, and above all the rendering of exact accounts. His duties also included the care of the poor, the development of charitable institutions and the upkeep of churches and monasteries. The rectors were powerful men, and as their operations were open to abuse, the Pope kept them on a tight rein and was swift to check any misconduct. He paid particular attention to Sicily, Rome's granary and the island where his own former estates were situated. It was unravaged by war and so productive that he split it into two patrimonies.

The farms were worked either by slaves or by *coloni*, legally freemen but bound to the soil. Gregory's attitude to slavery rural and domestic, was that although it was an evil it must be eliminated gradually because sudden and universal manumission would only cause social chaos. As for the *colonus*, he was paid a fixed price for his produce, and his rent, calculated in accordance with his means, was specified by written agreement; he was also allowed to work for pay, in his own time, off the estate. Evidently slaves were scarce and there was competition between the Church and private landowners to acquire them.

Much of the income accruing from the patrimony was expended on the upkeep of the Pope's central government and of the clerical bureaucracy that had so largely taken the place of imperial officialdom. The priests and deacons of the early church were now organized in colleges, headed respectively by the archpriest and the archdeacon. Originally, the distinction was between the priests who were concerned with the sacraments and the deacons who ran the social services, but the growing importance of the administrative branch led to the creation of a new category of sub-deacons and of two further colleges, the notaries and the *defensores*, each headed by a *primicerius* or chief secretary. As their names imply, the notaries dealt with the whole secretarial, diplomatic and legal business of the papal chancery, kept the archives and listed decrees and precedents. The volume of correspondence that they handled could be compared only with that which passed through the government offices of Constantinople. The *defensores* were a body of executive officers who could be switched from one mission to another as occasion demanded, and many served as rectors of the patrimony. Lastly, the office of *arcarius*, or treasurer, was assuming prime importance. No very accurate assessment can be formed of the number of clerics working in the central Roman organization, but the deacons were the élite element. When Gregory became pope there were only nineteen of them, seven of whom corresponded to the seven regions of the city, and the popes were usually elected from among them. The priests could have numbered between a hundred and two hundred; Gregory ordained thirty-nine in the course of his pontificate.

The Pope's authority over the bishops of Italy, other parts of western Europe and north Africa was at that period not absolute. Its strength varied according to the proximity of their diocese to Rome. Once elected by the local clergy, notables and people and ordained by the Pope, the bishop was vested with wide powers and responsibilities, both ecclesiastical and civil. It was therefore important for the Pope to make sure, if possible, that only the candidates whom he considered most suitable should be selected. On the whole Gregory preferred local to Roman clerics, although the latter were no doubt easier for him to control. In central and southern Italy and other regions where he had metropolitan authority or his influence was paramount, he did not hesitate to exercise patronage, while doing so discreetly and without resorting to the veto or to direct intervention. In the north, where the bishoprics covered both Lombard territory and that governed by the Exarch, the position was more difficult, especially as strong feeling persisted there among Catholics against the papacy's condemnation of the Three Chapters. The important See of Aquileia went into schism on that issue and stayed in schism for 150 years. On the other hand Gregory managed to block the Exarch's candidate for the See of Ravenna and get his own elected.

While forced to assume diverse non-ecclesiastical roles, those of diplomat, civil and economic administrator, military organizer and territorial landlord, Gregory never lost sight of his conception of the papacy as headship of a universal church, of a union of all Christians both within and outside the Roman Empire. His ideal was of course incompatible with Justinian's 'Caesaropapism', the theory that the Emperor was divinely endowed with authority in matters of faith, as well as with secular sovereignty, within the empire's boundaries. It was succinctly expressed by his

Council of Constantinople in the phrase 'nothing should be done in the church against the command and will of the Emperor.' During the reign of Justinian, when imperial power was being reasserted and lost territory regained, the Popes contested this scheme of things at their peril. In Maurice's time the Empire was on the defensive, battered by Lombards, Slavs and Persians, and his predecessor's claims looked less convincing. Nevertheless he was by no means disposed to abate them, and Gregory, while prepared to argue strongly with the Emperor on individual issues, always did so in respectful terms, as befitted a loyal subject, and with a manifest desire to avoid dangerous confrontations. A serious cause of friction between them was Maurice's compliance with the assumption of the title of 'Oecumenical' by John IV 'the Faster', Patriarch of Constantinople. Both Pelagius II and Gregory regarded it as a challenge to the primacy of the Roman bishop and refused to recognize it, but the Emperor dismissed their complaints as frivolous and allowed John's successor to inherit the title. Even if the Patriarchs meant the word 'Oecumenical', implying as it did a universal jurisdiction, to refer solely to the eastern or Greek-speaking world and were not trying to usurp the Pope's position in the West, their behaviour was at least tactless. Gregory, for whom it was outrageously provocative, redoubled his protests. Their total rejection by the Emperor ruined the personal friendship between those two gifted men. When the military situation led to a mutiny of his army in the Balkans, followed by the Emperor's murder and the slaughter of his whole family, Gregory so far forgot his customary prudence and charity as to offer fulsome congratulations to the brutal and vulgar centurion, Phocas, who had seized his throne. 'Let the heavens rejoice and let the earth be glad,' he wrote, 'and may all the people of the Empire exalt in your kindly deeds.'

Yet it was his own dynamism, rather than the frustrations of his relationship with the imperial government, that impelled him to pursue the expansion and consolidation of the Church, outside the imperial framework, in the former Roman Provinces now ruled by the barbarian kings of Germanic origin. It is unlikely that he consciously formed a grand design for a new European order not based on the Roman Empire. On the other hand Catholic Christianity could not hope to flourish in the barbarian kingdoms unless its development was fostered and guided by Papal influence. Papal supervision was needed to improve the standard of Christian behaviour among rulers, clergy and laity, to keep local churches in contact with the Holy See and to convert Arians and pagans. Hence the concern felt by Gregory for the future of Lombard North Italy, Frankish Gaul, Visigothic Spain and Anglo-Saxon Britain. The results he achieved in the course of his agitated pontificate were not uniformly impressive, and it was not until the eighth century that Western Catholicism acquired a new shape and strength through the alliance between the papacy and the Frankish monarchy. Nevertheless his activity demonstrated the resilience of the Holy See, its unifying power and its ability to repair the division and confusion caused by the barbarian invasions.

When Gregory became pope Arianism was still entrenched in the Lombard Kingdom. In Spain, however, the Visigothic King Reccared had recently abjured the heresy and embraced the religion of the vast majority of his subjects, who were Roman provincials by origin and therefore Catholic. This shrewd political move was backed by the Pope's close friend Leander, bishop of Seville. As a sign of his delight Gregory presented the King with two very holy relics, a key made from St Peter's

Chains and a cross containing wood from the Cross of Christ and hairs of St John the Baptist. To Leander he sent a pallium, the band of white wool that popes from the sixth century onwards conferred on bishops as a mark of special favour, or of their new status of metropolitan archbishops. Spain was now securely Catholic, but the conversion of the Lombards was a more complex and difficult matter. They were more numerous than the Visigoths, more obstinately devoted to their Arian faith and only recently exposed to the influence of the Latin culture. There was no likelihood of their being rapidly submerged in the mass of Italians, much less of vanishing, like the Ostrogoths earlier in the century, from the scene of history.

But Gregory was not only faced with the prickly Germanic tribalism of the Lombards. He also had to reckon with the jealousy of the principal Catholic bishoprics of north Italy, in imperial as well as Lombard territory, for the Roman See. Even when withdrawn to imperially held Genoa so as to be out of reach of the Lombards, the metropolitan archbishopric of Milan tended to resent papal super-vision, which had to be exercised with tact and restraint. Fortunately, the wife of two successive Lombard Kings, Autharis and Agilulf, was Theodolinda, a Frankish Catholic Princess from Bavaria. This lady, although opposed to the Pope on the Three Chapters issue, intervened vigorously in favour of Catholicism at the Lombard Court and had her son baptized as a Catholic. From then on Arianism was on the decline. Although some of the seventh-century kings were staunch heretics Catholicism gradually gained ground and by 700 Arianism was virtually extinct in the kingdom and the outlying duchies of Spoleto and Benevento.

To the north the huge amorphous realm of the Franks, divided into three kingdoms and extending over France, the Netherlands, part of Western Germany and Switzerland, offered a dismal spectacle to papal eyes. Nominally the whole region was Catholic and had been so since the Franks had adopted the faith early in the sixth century, but in the interval the standard of civilization had decayed disastrously. Royal authority was weak, Kings and great nobles ruling precariously amid barbaric ostentation, fought and intrigued against each other, economic and cultural progress was at a standstill and the general climate of violence and insecurity rivalled that of Italy. To judge from the blood-curdling stories of atrocities and betrayals related by Gregory, bishop of Tours, in his history of the Franks, public and private conduct was at its lowest ebb. The prevailing demoralization of society also affected the Church. Some of the bishops, recruited like Gregory of Tours from the descendants of the Gallo-Roman governing class, still clung to their Latin, Christian traditions; others allowed themselves to be corrupted and brutal-ized. Simony, the traffic in ecclesiastical offices, was universal and laymen were commonly promoted by royal favours to the most lucrative sees. In his numerous letters to the bishops the Pope strenuously condemned these abuses, but those who profited from them were seldom inclined to heed his remonstrances. When they were ignored Gregory turned to Brunhilde, the formidable Queen-Regent of Austrasia, the eastern Frankish Kingdom, and of Burgundy, exhorting her to summon a synod which would enforce the necessary prohibitions.

Brunhilde was a princess of Visigothic Spain, a convert from Arianism, superior in education and accomplishments to her contemporaries at the Frankish Courts. Her life was spent in trying to create order out of the surrounding anarchy. At a distance she got on very well with the Pope, with whom she corresponded amiably on questions of religion and politics. In the interests of enlisting royal aid in his efforts to reform the Church of Frankish Gaul, Gregory found it advisable to turn a blind eye to the cruelties and treacheries with which the Queen countered the similar crimes of her dynastic rivals. He even commended her for her 'admirable and God-pleasing goodness'. She, for her part, while grateful for papal support for her conception of a centralized Catholic monarchy, was not prepared to apply pressure on the rich and powerful episcopate. It was more than her life was worth in an age when she was eventually to lose it, after a palace revolution, by being dragged at the tail of a wild horse. Indifferent as she was to Gregory's insistence on Church reform, she understood the advantage of a firm link between the papacy and a united Frankish monarchy. In particular, she supported Gregory's policy of fostering monasticism as a spiritual and civilizing influence. The Romano-Frankish episcopate, on the other hand, while treating the Pope with formal deference preferred to keep him at arm's length in matters of internal organization and discipline.

Gregory successfully invoked help from Brunhilde and the Gallican church in his project for the conversion of the English. Whatever truth there may be in the story of his chance encounter with fair-haired Anglo-Saxons in the slave market, there is nothing strange in his ambition to roll back the frontier of paganism and reclaim for Christianity a former Roman province. In any event we find him in 595 instructing the rector of the Gallic patrimony to buy up Anglo-Saxon youths so that they may be prepared in monasteries for God's service. Possibly he thought of using them as interpreters for the mission of forty monks he was to despatch to England in the following years. It was headed by Augustine, prior of his own monastery of St Andrew. In the event, however, the interpreters whom Augustine took with him were Frankish priests, proficient in both Latin and Anglo-Saxon, found for him by Brunhilde, whose Catholic niece Bertha was married to the Heathen king Ethelbert of Kent.

The conversion was planned on a grand scale, with metropolitan archbishoprics at London and York and a dozen suffragan sees. Full of optimism, Gregory evidently had in mind the conditions prevailing in Christian Britain two centuries earlier. He was imperfectly informed about the nature of the Anglo-Saxon conquest and about the activity and characteristics of the Celtic Church, which from its flourishing base in Ireland was itself sending out missionaries to convert the Picts of Scotland and the northern English and even to found monasteries on the continent. When Augustine and his monks reached southern Gaul they were so horrified by the tales they heard of English barbarism that Augustine returned to Rome and asked Gregory to cancel the mission. The Pope would have none of it. He firmly told Augustine to persevere and equipped him with more letters of recommendation to eminent persons in the Frankish realm. His onward journey was made easier for him, and when the mission crossed the Channel it met with unexpected success. The ground had indeed been well prepared. On 1 June 597 King Ethelbert consented to be baptized and thousands of his subjects followed his example. Consequently Augustine rushed back to Gaul and had himself consecrated 'Archbishop of the English' by Virgilius, Archbishop of Arles and the Pope's Vicar, or spiritual representative, for Gaul. The procedure followed was hierarchical and correct. On receiving his pallium from Rome Augustine set up a more modest ecclesiastical establishment than Gregory had envisaged, with himself as Archbishop of Canterbury and subordinate sees at London and Rochester. Nevertheless the Pope was overjoyed. 'By the shining miracles of his preachers,' he declared,

God has brought to the faith even the ends of the earth. He has linked in one faith the limits of East and West. Behold, the tongue of Britain which could only utter Barbaric sounds has lately learned to make the Hebrew Alleluia ring in God's praise.

He had not much longer to live. Apart from his eminence as a statesman and his promotion of missions and monasteries, his great achievement was to organize the papal government as an elaborate, smoothly functioning and purposeful machine in a period when society in Italy and the West in general was falling irretrievably into decay. We can form a fairly convincing picture of the ancient world and of the middle ages, but it is much harder to understand the Dark Age that was then beginning. On the one side we watch the decline of culture and technology (as represented by the once brilliant Roman engineering), the disappearance of time-honoured institutions and physical dilapidation of Rome's fabric, the prevalence of famine, disease, poverty and insecurity. Outside the city walls the country is terrorized by bands of uncouth and expertly warlike barbarians on domestic forays, plundering property and snatching people for ransome.

But this state of affairs is not incompatible with the orderly rise of so confident and sophisticated an entity as the Roman Church. In Gregory's Rome, where material existence is so bleak, there is still a feeling that the city is part of a great empire, subject to one Emperor and guided by one Church, and that the barbarians are an intrusive nuisance that will not last for ever. Squalor and demolition are not yet universal. Some public baths are fitfully operating, so is the slavemarket, so are the granaries stocked by the Pope. There are occasional races in the Circus Maximus. While a few Patricians linger in their tottering houses, the Pope lives in the Lateran Palace, and the Byzantine Exarch, if he ever comes to Rome, is lodged in a still habitable part of the Palace of the Caesars. The churches blaze with gold and mosaic. At the end of a century of bizarre contrasts, the transition to the middle-ages is far from complete.

PART TWO

TRIUMPHS
AND
DECADENCE

5

FROM GREEKS TO FRANKS

(604–772)

After Gregory's death the development of the papacy, as well as the destinies of individual popes, became even more closely bound up with their relationship to the eastern empire, now battling for its very existence. The condition of Italy, divided between Byzantium and the Lombards, remained relatively stable throughout the seventh century, but the empire as a whole was saved from extinction only by the exertions of a dynasty of talented but wilful autocrats. Constantinople was beset by invaders, first by Avars and Persians and then by Arabs. The great Christian strongholds of Syria, Egypt and (more gradually) north Africa as far as the Atlantic, fell to the Arabs, while the once universal Roman Empire was confined to Asia Minor and to insecure footholds in Italy and the Balkans. Once again the Mediterranean was made unsafe for peaceful maritime traffic.

Gregory's five successors were uniformly undistinguished and lasted for only twenty-one years. The first two, Sabinian (604–6) and Boniface III (607), who had both served as *apokrisiarios* under Phocas, worked so successfully on that incompetent tyrant that he issued a decree deciding in the Pope's favour the outstanding dispute over the oecumenical title. In return he was honoured by the erection in the Roman forum of a column surmounted by a gilded statue, and the compliment was repaid when Phocas presented the Pantheon to Boniface IV (606–15) for conversion into the church of Santa Maria ad Martyres. The same pope held a synod that was attended by Mellitus, the first Bishop of London and a future Archbishop of Canterbury.

In 610 Heraclius, son of the Exarch of Africa and founder of the new imperial dynasty, removed the tyrant and set about the task of expelling the Persians from Byzantine territory. It took twenty years to accomplish, during which one Exarch of Italy lost his life in a revolt and another, appointed by the Emperor to restore order, rebelled himself, only to be executed by his own troops. The Popes wisely held aloof from these disturbances and were careful not to offend Constantinople, but their humdrum conduct of church affairs was suddenly invigorated by the accession of Honorius I (625–38).

The new pope's father, Petronius, had owned land in Campania and a mansion in Rome, which his son, following Gregory's example, turned over to his monks. Described as a 'consul' he was a survivor of the old governing class from which Gregory sprang. Honorius himself showed the same confident touch, genius for administration and authority over men as his great forerunner, combined with the same energy and an eagerness to assert himself in all fields open to him. Like Gregory too he cultivated good relations with the Lombard court while discreetly encouraging the spread of Catholicism in the kingdom. He severely repressed the Istrian schism and sent Birinus, a future Saint, to set up the bishopric of Dorchester among the still heathen West Saxons.

His care for Rome and its inhabitants earned him the title of *Dux Plebis* ('Leader of the People'), as attested by an inscription in St Peter's, and he is especially remembered for his efforts to arrest the decay of the city. Besides putting back into operation the aqueduct which until the Gothic war supplied water from Lake Bracciano, he built or refurbished countless Roman churches. He used a vast quantity of silver in the decoration of St Peter's and, with the Emperor's permission, the bronze tiles were stripped from the temple of Rome and Venus to cover its roof. His lavish expenditure for these purposes suggests that the finances of the patrimony were in good order.

Unfortunately for his future reputation, Honorius had little interest in theological intricacies, and before he had scented the danger he was enmeshed in the new doctrinal dispute that fatally weakened the empire on the eve of the Arab onslaught. As in the case of the Three Chapters, the matter now at issue was of vital significance in the East but of no direct import to the West. Having reconquered the full extent of his eastern domains from the Persians, Heraclius was naturally concerned with retaining their allegiance, and that was still placed in doubt by the stubborn preference of their peoples for Monophysitism. It was the Patriarch Sergius of Constantinople, the hero of the defence of that city against the Avars, who thought up a fresh compromise designed to ensure their loyalty. While insisting that Christ possessed two natures, as laid down at Chalcedon, he was ready to agree, if it would help the Monophysites, that he could only have one 'energy' (a very tricky word in the Greek philosophic vocabulary). When asked for his opinion, Honorius replied testily that though the new definition seemed to him unexceptionable he had no patience with theoreticians who persisted, like a lot of 'croaking frogs' in re-opening old quarrels. He had not apparently grasped either the theological or the political aspects of the controversy. No doubt he then dismissed the matter from his mind.

At first it looked as if the Emperor and Sergius had succeeded in building a bridge between Chalcedonians and Monophysites in the East. 'Monoenergism' was welcomed by the heads of the Church in Syria, Armenia and Egypt. But it was not long before the Orthodox faithful, led by the Patriarch of Jerusalem, were objecting that the new doctrine was simply Monophysitism under another name and must therefore be rejected. In response to appeals from Heraclius, Sergius obliged with a new formula in which 'will' was substituted for 'energy' and in 638, the year of Honorius's death, an edict known as the *Ecthesis* commanded the Emperor's subjects to forget about energies and to conform to the doctrine of one will, or Monotheletism. By that time however, theological distinctions were looking less important. Two years before the issue of the *Ecthesis* and only four years after the death in 632 of the hitherto obscure prophet Mohammed, the Arabs had swept out of their deserts, defeated the imperial army and occupied Palestine and Syria. Egypt proved a harder nut to crack, but by 646 the whole country had fallen into Arab hands. Thus three of the four eastern Patriarchates – Antioch, Jerusalem and Alexandria – had been lost to the Empire along with its most prosperous, but Monophysite, provinces. It began to appear as if the religious balance between eastern and western Christendom might in future cease to be tipped in favour of Constantinople. But for the moment the orthodox in the East, contemptuous of the new formulas as mere exercises in word-chopping, were angry because Honorius had cut the ground from under their feet by his apparent approval of Monoenergism. In fact he considered himself to be perfectly orthodox and was accepted as such in Rome, but the Monotheletes were only too keen to quote his rash statement as supporting their case. The result was that the Pope, who could not have been more staunch in promoting the Church's true interests, was to be condemned for heresy by a General Council and indefinitely marked by that stigma. If it had not been for one unguarded letter, he might easily have been canonized instead. Luckily for him, he did not survive to weigh the consequences of his indiscretion, and three years later Heraclius died too. There followed nearly forty years of great trial for the papacy.

Under the new Emperor, Constans, who succeeded as a boy of eleven, both government and Church at Constantinople were Monothelete and the popes were at first under heavy pressure to accept the *Ecthesis*. Severinus (639–40), John IV (640–2) and Theodore I (642–9) staved it off by an adroit mixture of firmness and procrastination, but the former was unable to prevent the Exarch from seizing the contents of Honorius's well stocked treasury and carrying them off to Ravenna. During the pontificate of Theodore, not a Roman but a Palestinian Greek and a refugee from the Arabs, the Orthodox rallied their forces and the imperial government, while unwilling to abandon its official Monotheletism, decided that something must be done to prevent them from becoming as disaffected as the Monophysites (now mostly under Moslem rule) had previously been. Constans therefore annulled the *Ecthesis* and replaced it with a fresh edict known as the *Typos* which arbitrarily prohibited all discussion of the subject of wills and energies. If its purpose was to stifle religious controversy altogether, in practice it had precisely the opposite effect. Its implication that one doctrine was theologically as valid as the other was found particularly shocking at the Lateran, where the Greek Theodore was soon succeeded by Martin I (649–54), a bold and vigorous Roman cleric.

At Constantinople the papal *apokrisiarios* refused to submit to the *Typos* and was promptly banished; his mission was closed down and many orthodox protesters were savagely punished. However, Martin refused to be intimidated. Without waiting for his consecration to be confirmed by the Emperor, he called a synod of 105 western bishops who, enthused by the presence of orthodox fugitives from the East and Africa, roundly condemned the *Ecthesis*, the *Typos*, Monotheletism in general and the Monothelete Patriarchs. They then forwarded their conclusions to the Emperor and invited him to endorse them. Constans was of course incensed by such impertinent defiance and repudiation of his religious policy. He commanded his new Exarch, Olympius, to enforce observance of the *Typos* in Italy and to arrest the Pope if he persisted in his opposition to it. But Olympius soon found that support for Martin was so solid among clergy, people and army that he did not dare to carry out his master's orders. After an abortive attempt to have the Pope murdered in church he confessed his intended crime, was forgiven and set out for Sicily to deal with an Arab raid. There he took the opportunity to revolt against Constans, but almost immediately died of disease.

The Emperor waited for three years before trying again. This time his instructions to the Exarch, Theodore Calliopas, were to treat Martin in the same way as Justinian had treated Vigilius a hundred years earlier. When he entered Rome on a Saturday with a strong body of troops, Martin withdrew to the Lateran basilica. The Exarch prudently left him to celebrate Mass there on Sunday undisturbed, but on the Monday he entered the church and placed the Pope under arrest. He found him lying ill in bed, like a sacrificial victim, before the altar. Nevertheless he dragged him away and launched him, like Vigilius on the long sea voyage to Constantinople. But whereas Vigilius had received all due honours and attentions, Martin's health and comforts were studiously neglected. True, he was accompanied by a valet and six minor servants, but he was only permitted to land once, in the island of Naxos, there to have a bath. All the time he was liable to be captured by the Arab warships already ranging the Aegean. On reaching Constantinople he was a physical wreck and could hardly stand on his feet. After a day's deliberate exposure to the insults of the mob he was shut up in prison for a further three months.

His sufferings and humiliations were intensified when he was brought to trial, charged not with religious contumacy but with conspiracy. He faced his accusers valiantly, held up by court officials because he was not allowed to sit down. The result was a foregone conclusion. He was condemned to death, publicly flogged and returned to prison to await execution. At that point the Monothelete Patriarch was seized with remorse and pleaded with the Emperor for Martin's life. Eventually Martin was sent into exile at Cherson, the remote Byzantine outpost in the Crimea. There he died in 655, just two years after his arrival at Constantinople, worn out by his tribulations. Only a man of exceptional toughness, both physical and moral, could have outlasted such ordeals, which are well attested by his own surviving letters and by an account written by a contemporary sympathizer.

The Emperor's brutality was inexcusable by any standards. Nevertheless it is hard not to have some regard for Constans, a courageous and imaginative ruler whose character was vitiated by a strain of eccentricity, if not madness, in his family and by the intolerable burden of an empire apparently on the brink of collapse. It was largely due to his exertions that it did not break up. Unlike Justinian and his grandfather Heraclius, he was interested in religious questions not for their own sake, but only in so far as they affected the safety and unity of the state. If these were threatened by an insubordinate Pope's flouting of his *Typos*, no punishment was severe enough for the Pope. He was an autocrat whose remedy for the empire's ills was the exercise of his own untrammelled power.

His cruelty to the Pope horrified and cowed the Roman clergy. They hastened to recognize Martin's deposition and would not even send any material assistance to him in his exile. As regards the *Typos*, Pope Eugenius I (654–7) tried to temporize, only to be menaced by Constans with 'roasting' if he failed to toe the line. Vitalian (657–74) was more pliant, but it turned out that both Emperor and Pope were now disposed to put aside doctrinal differences. The reason was that Constans, after several years of ding-dong struggle against the Arabs, had managed to stabilize his eastern frontiers. He had concluded a treaty with the Caliph Muaviah and beaten off the Balkan Slavs. He now proposed to turn his attention to the West and even to reside there for a while. He wished to chastise the Lombards and, if possible, to prevent the Arabs from eating their way further west across north Africa. Possibly, too, he foresaw the threat they were soon to pose to southern Europe. It was therefore necessary for him to conciliate his Orthodox subjects in Italy and elsewhere.

Constans landed at Tarentum in 664 and marched against the Lombards, who offered such stiff resistance that he was glad to bring the campaign to an end through a treaty. At Rome the arrival of the first Roman emperor to visit the city for two and a half centuries – and incidentally the last to do so before Rome was lost to the eastern Empire – was awaited with excitement tinged with misgiving. The Pope greeted him at the sixth milestone on the road to Naples and escorted him in procession to his quarters on the Palatine. To general relief he stayed for only twelve days and on the whole behaved graciously, praying in the churches and distributing gifts. However he also removed the roof tiles from the Pantheon, so recently donated to the Church by Phocas, together with such works of art that caught his fancy for the adornment of Constantinople. These he shipped to Syracuse, where he established his base of operations against the Arabs. Four years later he was assassinated there in his bath, the victim of an obscure military plot. It was promptly suppressed by his son Constantine IV, who set sail for Sicily with an overwhelming armada. He was grateful to the Pope for disowning the rebels and encouraging the imperial troops in Italy to contribute to their defeat.

There is no doubt that Vitalian, a quietly effective Pope, handled both Emperors with consummate skill. At the same time he was very active in a quite different sphere, the Roman mission to England launched by Gregory the Great. The conflict in the island between the usages of the Celtic and Roman churches was settled during his pontificate in favour of the latter, and he was about to consecrate an Englishman, Wighard, as Archbishop of Canterbury, when he died at Rome and the Pope had to find a successor. His first choice, Hadrian, a learned African, suggested that Theodore, a Greek monk from Tarsus in Asia Minor, would be more suitable, and Vitalian persuaded him to fill the office. In the event Hadrian accompanied Theodore to barbarous England, and so did Benedict Biscop, the pious Northumbrian nobleman who founded monasteries at Wearmouth and Jarrow and visited Rome on five occasions during his lifetime, thus revealing that travel across Europe in the Dark Ages was not so difficult as one might suppose. Whatever the importance accorded by the Pope to the English mission, no more brilliant churchman could have been found for it than Theodore, primate of England for twenty years, and Hadrian who exchanged his monastery near Naples for that of St Peter and St Paul at Canterbury, opening a school where Latin and Greek was taught as well as mathematics, astronomy, music and medicine. The consequent flowering of English Christianity, shortly to evangelize Germany, was due to the vision and energy of this cosmopolitan, expansionist and flexibly minded pope.

His successors Adeodatus (672–6) and Donus (676–8) remained loyal to Constanine while rejecting the credentials of his still Monothelete Patriarchs. They were anxious spectators of the Emperor's prolonged and eventually triumphant conflict with the Arabs, which ended in 678 with the utter defeat of their two grand assaults on Constantinople. His successes earned him enormous prestige and the congratulations of the whole western world, including the Spanish Visigoths, the Franks and the Lombards. They also stimulated him to put an end to Monotheletism, which was no longer acceptable to the majority of his subjects. He therefore appointed an Orthodox Patriarch and invited the Pope, whom he addressed as 'oecumenical', to participate in a Council at Constantinople which would redefine the position of the universal Church. Pope Agatho (678–81) responded with enthusiasm, nominating a strong team of legates and fortifying them with the decisions of synods meeting at Milan and at Heathfield in England. The sixth General Council of the Church lasted for ten months in 680 and 681, with Constantine presiding but not intervening in its debates, and ended with the acclamation, in that order, of the Emperor, the Pope, the Patriarch and the Senate. Its conclusions amounted to as great a victory for the Orthodox in the religious field as for the Byzantine armies in their fight against the infidels.

The aftermath of reconciliation between East and West was a marked increase in Greek influence at Rome. Of the ten Popes who reigned between 680 and 715 only one was a Roman. All the others hailed originally from Greek-speaking lands, chiefly Syria and Sicily. Most of them were elderly deacons or priests who lasted no more than a year or two; only Sergius I (687–701) and Constantine (708–15) survived long enough to make their mark. One reason for the election of Greek clerics was the low standard of education in Italy where knowledge of the Greek language, so necessary for dealing with the eastern Church and the imperial government, had well nigh vanished. Also the Greek colony in Rome had been greatly augmented by refugees from regions dominated by heretics or Saracens. They lived in a distinct quarter of the city, permeated the Roman clergy and provided a supply of suitable candidates for the papacy.

At the same time a new native element, the Roman militia, was making its voice heard in the papal elections. Locally recruited, it tended, at the height of the empire's duel with the Arabs, to replace regiments drawn from outside Italy. It intervened in two disputed elections and, more significantly, when Pope Sergius clashed with Justinian II (685–95 and 705–11). This Emperor, the last and most unbalanced member of the house of Heraclius, held a Council, which he wished to be regarded as oecumenical, in order to regulate questions of discipline and morals which had not been properly covered by the last two General Councils. He omitted, however, to invite legates from Rome, and when the decrees were forwarded for the Pope's signature, they were found to contain such objectionable features as permission for priests to marry. Though they had been approved by all the eastern Patriarchs, and even by his own *apokrisarios*, Sergius refused his signature, especially as he noticed a clause specifically granting the Patriarch of Constantinople equal rights with the Pope. Like the first Justinian and his grandfather Constans, the Emperor decided to enforce compliance. He first had the Pope's principal advisers arrested, and when that had no effect on Sergius, he sent a high official, the *protospatharios* Zacharias, to bring him to Constantinople. But such arbitrary behaviour could no longer be tolerated in Italy. The Exarch's own troops from Ravenna joined with the Roman garrison and populace in rescuing Sergius from arrest, and Zacharias, who had arrived without a military escort, was in turn so frightened that he hid under the Pope's bed in the Lateran Palace. He barely escaped with his life and had to return empty-handed to the Bosporus. There he found that Justinian himself had been dethroned by a revolution and packed off, with his nose slit, into exile at Cherson. To all appearances the Pope had won a resounding triumph.

It so happened that after ten years Justinian was restored to his throne by another *coup d'état* and again pressed for endorsement of his Council's decrees. Curiously enough he now seemed disposed to compromise as regards those to which Rome had taken exception, while Pope John VII (705–7), the son of a Byzantine official, was so scared that he was ready to concede all the Emperor's original demands. The matter was not settled until the next Pope, Constantine, was invited to Constantinople. After the usual leisurely coasting voyage, which included a winter spent at Otranto, he reached the capital and met the Emperor at Nicomedia. This time Justinian treated him with almost exaggerated deference, kissing his feet and embracing him in public. No further difficulty was experienced over the decrees, and the Emperor ratified the privileged status of the Roman Church.

The Byzantine atmosphere of Rome was enhanced in many ways during this period, when the administration, commerce and the Church were largely staffed by Greeks or Greek-speakers. The old Latin culture, still alive in the days of Gregory the Great, had been superseded by something more exotic. While its doctrine remained impeccably Roman, the Church was enriched by Greek monasticism, learning, art, music and ritual. Many new churches were built, especially in the pontificate of Sergius I, and often dedicated to eastern saints. It is true that church-building and decoration had never been suspended, even in the most troubled times, but in the seventh and eighth centuries it was intensified. The interiors were embellished with columns and marbles torn from ancient edifices, with contemporary paintings and mosaics and a profusion of gold and silver ornaments. Despite the gradual ruin of temples and former public buildings for which there was no longer any use, the external aspect of the city had to some extent recovered from the desolation of the Gothic and Lombard wars. Rome was once more lively and thriving, and even epidemics and famines had become less frequent. Pilgrims from England and the Frankish realm were overwhelmingly impressed by its faded magnificence and new religious pomps. Meanwhile the splendour of the papal establishment recalled the era of Damasus rather than that of Gregory, as its ceremonial and administrative apparatus was increasingly modelled on that of the Byzantine court. Elaboration in externals was introducing more than a touch of luxury into the Pope's personal life, and John VII, dissatisfied with the old Lateran, built himself a second palace below the Palatine hill.

The uneasy partnership between the head of the universal Church and the monarch claiming to rule the whole civilized world had now lasted for four centuries. Since their remaining differences had been settled, there seemed to be no reason why the newly restored harmony should not endure indefinitely. It could hardly have been predicted that within fifty years the link between Rome and Constantinople would be virtually severed and the papacy's connexions reoriented. This revolution was to occur during the reigns of two remarkable Emperors and three equally outstanding Popes.

Pope Constantine had hardly returned to Rome when the murder of Justinian threw the empire into chaos. It only ended when Leo III (717–41), a stalwart Syrian soldier, was chosen Emperor and, in 718, utterly destroyed the Saracen army and fleet, which had beleaguered Constantinople for a whole year. By that time Constantine had been succeeded by Gregory II (715–31), a native Roman who had distinguished himself as administrator and diplomat since the pontificate of Sergius. Trouble began when the Byzantine government levied heavy taxation on Italy in order to help pay for the war in Asia. The Pope encouraged resistance to these exactions and the Roman militia prevented their enforcement by the Exarch's troops. But Byzantine fiscality had long been a cause for complaint, if only because Italians failed to understand to what desperate straits the empire was periodically reduced in the East, and the Pope's disapproval of it did not imply disloyalty. It was only when Leo proclaimed Iconoclasm, or the prohibition of the cult of images, to be the official policy of the empire that Gregory was reluctantly pushed, for religious reasons alone, into uncompromising opposition. Even so he carefully distinguished between abhorrence of what he regarded as heresy and rebellion against the legitimate sovereign.

Leo himself did not consider Iconoclasm to be unorthodox. However, as an Asiatic and a native of puritan Syria, where the bulk of the population had embraced first Monophysitism and then Islam, he was naturally inclined towards a simple form of Christianity as a more effective barrier against further Saracen advance. He distrusted some Orthodox practices as idolatrous and characteristic of a too independent monkish establishment which he would like to see disciplined. For the Italians, on the other hand, icons, that is to say representations of Christ, the Virgin

Mary and the Saints in painting, mosaic and any other media, were an indispensable element in their religion. Nor, unless they were acute theologians, did they differentiate between the mere veneration of an image and the worship of its prototype. They were simply outraged, and though they did not go so far as the inhabitants of Greece, who equipped a fleet to attack Constantinople, they burst everywhere into revolt, killing the Exarch, Paul, and other imperial officers. The Pope disapproved of such exercises but was unable to stop them. He was engaged in the almost impossible task of holding the Italians to their allegiance while at the same time scolding the Emperor, in vigorous and undiplomatic language, for his arrogance in laying down the law in religious issues that were not his business.

If this dilemma were not daunting enough, the Lombard King Liutprand was trying to exploit the disarray of imperial Italy in order to extend his rule over the whole peninsula, including the Byzantine exarchate and the more or less independent duchies of Spoleto and Benevento. Though the Lombards had turned Catholic and assimilated Italian ways, they were still a rough lot and Gregory was dismayed by the prospect of their holding Rome at their mercy. There followed a complicated round of political and military manoeuvres, involving the new Exarch, Eutychius, the Pope, the King and the two Lombard Dukes. Alliances shifted with bewildering rapidity. At one point Liutprand invested Rome in force and only retired when Gregory, meeting him in solemn state at the approaches to the city, persuaded him that his interests as a Catholic ruler could not be served by violence against the papacy. At his death in 731 he had been successful in holding the ring and preventing either King or Exarch from dictating to the Holy See. He had demonstrated that no secular power could hope to assert its supremacy in Italy if its policy ran contrary to the interests of the Church.

Gregory shared his predecessor's interest in the English Church and particularly in its missionary activities on the continent. Just as Sergius I had ordained one Englishman, Willibrord, as Bishop of Utrecht among the pagan Frisians, conferring on him the Roman name of Clement, so Gregory entrusted a second, the Benedictine monk Winfrith, or Boniface, from Crediton in Devon, with the vaster task of converting the whole of western and southern Germany and thus of strengthening Frankish rule over that region. A frequent visitor to Rome, he was consecrated Archbishop and Primate of Germany by the next Pope, Gregory III. The importance to the papacy of this extension of the Christian faith must be judged in relation to its contemporary eclipse in Africa and Spain, both now dominated by Islam.

The new Gregory (731-41) was a Syrian like the Emperor Leo but, in his strict orthodoxy, even more hostile to that heretical monarch than the Roman Gregory II. He began his reign by calling an Italian synod to anathematize Iconoclasm and by formally denouncing it in letters to the Emperor. Leo retaliated by sending war galleys to arrest the Pope and, when they were providentially wrecked by a storm in the Adriatic, by appropriating the revenues of the papal patrimonies in southern Italy and Sicily and by placing those provinces under the ecclesiastical control of Constantinople. In Gregory's eyes, however, Liutprand's ambitions were more immediately dangerous, especially as he had for a short time succeeded in wresting Ravenna from the Exarch. Gregory tried to counter his progress by repairing the walls of Rome and enlisting the alliance of Trasamund, the Lombard Duke of Spoleto, but the King had much the best of the subsequent campaign and seized four towns uncomfortably near to Rome. The Pope was now in a serious predicament, although he can hardly be blamed for falling out with the Emperor and the King at the same time; he was bound to oppose the former's hard-line Iconoclasm and the latter's territorial aggression. In despair he appealed for help to Charles Martel, the powerful Frankish Mayor of the Palace, who had recently won immense prestige in Christian Europe by his crushing defeat of its Saracen invaders at the battle of Poitiers. But Charles had no desire to quarrel with the Lombard Kingdom, on whose support he was relying in the event of the Saracens' renewing their attacks.

The situation was no less tense after Gregory III, Leo and Charles Martel all died in the same year, 741. Fortunately the new Pope Zacharias (741–52), a Greek from Calabria, was not only a scholar (he translated Gregory I's *Dialogues* into his own language) but a statesman whose skill as a negotiator was matched by his personal charm. His abilities were taxed to the full in warding off Lombard pressure on Rome and its surrounding territory. With Byzantium, however, he maintained peaceful if distant relations. Though a fervent Iconoclast, the Emperor Constantine (741–5) was too much involved with Arab wars and devastating outbreaks of plague in his dominions to wish to bully the Pope or pursue his ideological quarrel with him to the bitter end. In short they agreed to differ, and Zacharias never renounced his formal loyalty to the Emperor.

Zacharias began by a neat reversal of the papal alliances, transferring his support from Duke Trasamund to King Liutprand in return for the latter's promise to give back the four lost towns. But with Trasamund out of the way and shut up in a monastery, the Pope could obtain no satisfaction from the King until, at a carefully staged personal interview with him at Terni, he persuaded him to restore not only the towns but a whole row of patrimonial territories that the Lombards had seized long before. A twenty-year treaty of peace was signed between the Kingdom and the papal duchy of Rome (the word 'duchy' connoting a military district), and the meeting ended with a banquet at which, as he confessed later, the King was vastly diverted by the Pope's company.

But the treaty did not cover the exarchate, which the Emperor, for his part, now regarded as hardly worth defending. When Liutprand attacked it in 743, the Exarch begged Zacharias to intervene on his behalf. A mere embassy was unsuccessful, so the Pope decided once more to try his personal influence. He set out for Ravenna, where he did his best to reassure the Exarch, and from there sent a second embassy to the King. Again it was turned away, as if Liutprand was insisting on treating the Pope as a suitor at his feet, and Zacharias, not to be deterred by considerations of prestige, bearded him at his own capital, Pavia. Again he yielded, after some hesitation, to the peculiar combination of authority and charm that the Pope's personality always seemed to radiate, consenting to quit most of the territory he had already overrun pending direct negotiations with Constantinople. In his later years his Catholicism seemed to outweigh his regal ambition. If his object was the extinction of the exarchate he never achieved it, for he died in the following year.

The next Lombard sovereign, Ratchis, was pious and peace-loving and for a few years left the Pope undisturbed. Zacharias employed his energies in developing the Church's properties in the duchy of Rome. These estates, acquired by bequest or purchase and known as *domuscultae*, were remodelled as ecclesiastical collective farms, each with a newly built church as its nucleus. The desolate lands of the Campagna, once the source of private wealth for the Roman patriciate, were thus brought back into cultivation, their revenues partly compensating the Church for the loss of its Sicilian patrimony. But in 749 Ratchis was forced by his own nobles to renew operations against the exarchate. He besieged Perugia, a fortress controlling

Leo the Great meeting Attila outside Rome

Attila, 'Scourge of God'

Gregory I, the Great

Gregory the Great

S·LEO·MAGNVS·I·PAPA·ROMA

Leo the Great

Gregory the Great with *left* his father
Cordianus and *right* his mother Sylvia

Two versions of the coronation of Charlemagne

the road linking Ravenna with Rome. For the last time Zacharias came to the rescue and by the sheer force of his character stopped the Lombard invasion in its tracks. In 751, however, Ratchis was displaced by his brother Aistulf, who quietly but finally put an end to the Byzantine presence in north Italy.

Circumstances had compelled Zacharias to act as a secular ruler, bargaining with the Lombards and directing the government, army and economy of the Roman duchy. So far the magic of his personality had prevailed over Liutprand and Ratchis, but there was no guarantee that it would be equally potent in handling Aistulf, who promised to be much more aggressive and unscrupulous. Now that Byzantium's interest was confined to south Italy and Sicily, it was imperative for the papacy to find a champion elsewhere, and as Gregory III had realized when he approached Charles Martel, that protector could only be the Frankish Mayor of the Palace. It must be kept in mind that in the eighth century the Christian world had notably shrunk. The conquests of Islam had enormously reduced the area of the eastern empire, the Balkan peninsula was swamped by heathen Slavs and Bulgarians and the Arabs from Spain had crossed the Pyrenees. The British Isles were Christian but remote. Thus only the vigorous and expanding Frankish realm remained to provide the Pope with the support he needed.

Zacharias had in fact been discreetly cultivating the Frankish rulers for some years, using Boniface, the English Archbishop of Mainz, as his intermediary. After Charles Martel's death his sons, Pippin and Carloman, had divided the kingdom between them, with the latter taking the Germanic half, but in 747 Carloman suddenly abdicated, travelled to Rome and received a monk's habit from the Pope. Like the Lombard Ratchis, he chose Monte Cassino as his place of retreat. Rome's glamour was such that some years earlier two successive kings of the English West Saxons, Ine and Caedwalla, had elected to retire there, though not as monks. Carloman's departure left his brother in sole control of territories stretching from Aquitaine to Bavaria, the only snag being that he was not their legitimate sovereign. The title of King of the Franks nominally belonged to Childeric, the last representative of the old Merovingian dynasty, still leading a fossilized existence quite removed from the conduct of affairs. It was not until 751 that Pippin sent the Bishop of Würzburg, a protégé of Boniface, and the Abbot of St Denis to Rome in order to obtain a formal reply from the Pope to the question whether the royal title should not be held by the man who exercised the real power. Predictably Zacharias supplied the desired answer, and in 752 Boniface anointed Pippin King at Soissons.

It is remarkable that the Pope, at the moment when his position in Italy seemed most vulnerable, should have figured as arbiter of sovereignty in the most powerful of Christian monarchies. His decision in favour of Pippin was to have momentous consequences in the future, though its implications were not immediately apparent to Aistulf. In the spiritual field the papacy was abruptly brought up against the deplorable condition of the Frankish Church. As Boniface was only too well aware, its morality and discipline were at the lowest ebb. In the past the bishops of Gaul, drawn exclusively from the cultured Gallo-Roman aristocracy, had governed the Church wisely and in harmony with Rome. But as barbarism gradually took over, the Gallo-Romans had merged with the Frankish warrior class and no longer produced clerics of the stamp of St Remy (Remigius), St Eloi (Eligius) and Gregory of Tours. Corruption and simony were even more rampant than in Brunhilde's day, with the Kings rewarding their lay supporters with lucrative bishoprics and abbeys. Pluralists abounded and according to a letter from Boniface to the Pope, 'although they say they do not commit fornication or adultery, some bishops are nevertheless drunken and unreliable, or go hunting or fight in the army.' As for the lower clergy, 'as deacons they have had four or five or more concubines at night in bed and are yet not ashamed to read the gospel.' While the Franks were proud of their Catholicism, the behaviour of their clergy had slipped to an extent inconceivable to a pontiff accustomed to the well ordered ecclesiastical life of Italy. No wonder that Boniface, a proper Englishman, ended by exchanging his archbishopric for martyrdom, as a simple missionary, at pagan hands. The peculiar problems of the Gallican Church were to haunt the papacy for centuries, just as the election of French popes was to arouse resentment in Italy. It was France, the Church's favourite daughter, that in time inflicted on the papacy its worst humiliations.

Zacharias was dead before Pippin could repay his debt, but the opportunity to do so arose at once in the short but fateful pontificate of Stephen II (752–7). This capable and resolute Roman was confronted by the Lombard menace in its most acute form. Disregarding the Pope's friendly overtures, Aistulf claimed sovereignty over the duchy and demanded a capitation tax of one gold *solidus* (the basic Byzantine currency) per inhabitant. Clearly the only alternative to submission was to invoke Frankish help, and it seemed to Stephen that the surest way to obtain it would be for him to appear personally as a suppliant at Pippin's court. But first he managed to convey to the King a secret message, carried by a returning pilgrim, asking whether this dramatic gesture would be well received, and in that event whether the King would provide him with an escort through Lombard territory. To his delight Pippin agreed to both proposals, and in October 753 the Pope set out for France, accompanied by two high Frankish notables. Aistulf did not dare dispute his passage and indeed welcomed him in state at Pavia. As an act of formal politeness towards Constantinople he demanded the return of the exarchate to the Emperor and, having received the expected refusal, proceeded on his journey. Travelling conditions in the Dark Ages had starkly deteriorated, and even for a Pope attended by a large retinue and greeted with every honour on Frankish soil, the winter crossing of the Alps on horseback was an arduous ordeal. When he eventually met Pippin at Ponthion, near Chalons sur Marne, the King dismounted, prostrated himself and led the Pope's horse by the bridle. According to another account it was the Pope who knelt to Pippin with ashes on his head, but in whatever way the encounter was staged, the occasion called for a piece of theatre.

Ill and exhausted by the rigours of the journey, the Pope spent the rest of the winter quietly at the Abbey at St Denis outside Paris. The negotiations that followed were not easy. The Frankish nobles did not at first take kindly to their King's abandonment of his family's traditional friendship with the Lombards. Even Boniface advised against his new policy. His brother Carloman, who may have been got at by Aistulf, left Monte Cassino in order to protest but was confined for his pains in another monastery at Vienna. However the king was determined to bring about a general settlement with the papacy for the advantage of both parties. He was proud to undertake the duty of defending the heirs of St Peter and to guarantee their territorial rights.

So far as Italy was concerned the highlight of the deal was the so-called 'Donation of Pippin'. The document embodying it has not survived, but it seems to have defined the obligations assumed by the Pope's protector and to have listed the lands and cities Pippin undertook to recover for the 'Church of the Republic of the

Romans'. These included the ex-imperial territories, that were to be restored not to the Emperor but to the Pope. The agreement was apparently modelled on the 'Donation of Constantine', reputed to have been fabricated in the papal Chancery during the feverish weeks when Stephen was preparing to leave for France. In the eighth century it would have been regarded not so much as the arrant forgery it undoubtedly was but as an excusable and symbolic justification of the steps the papacy had to take to safeguard its future existence.

When the agreement had been concluded the Pope solemnized it by re-anointing Pippin, together with his wife and two sons, at St Denis. He also conferred on him the title of Patrician of the Romans. It was of course understood that the Franks would have to force the Lombards to give up their conquests, so Pippin invaded Lombardy in the autumn of 754, laid siege to Pavia and extracted an undertaking from Aistulf to quit the territories involved. Thereupon the Pope re-entered Rome in triumph, but no sooner had the Frankish host marched home than Aistulf reneged on his promises. Far from giving up the lands he mounted a grand assault on the city. The siege had already lasted two months when a new despairing appeal from Stephen, prefaced by the words 'I, Peter' reached France by the sea route. With some reluctance Pippin was obliged to organize a second punitive expedition. This time Aistulf was reduced to vassalage and compelled to pay a heavy indemnity. Pippin also rejected a Byzantine request for the restitution of the exarchate, thus confirming, for all practical purposes, the Pope's status as an independent territorial ruler. Nevertheless the fiction of Byzantine overlordship was not formally discarded.

It would be an exaggeration to claim that all the Popes of that era were paragons of virtue and wisdom, but they did set consistently high standards of piety, moral courage, personal conduct and practical intelligence. When the external threat had been removed and Stephen reinstalled in Rome the papacy's prestige and authority, fortified by Frankish power, seemed unassailable. Paradoxically, however, morale began to falter as soon as that high point had been reached, and there ensued a short period of decadence and confusion.

Stephen's brother and successor Paul I (757–67) was not an effective ruler of the new papal state. He proved unable either to control the quarrelling factions that were springing up among the Roman notables or to stem encroachments by Desiderius, the new King of the Lombards. He complained nervously to his Frankish protectors about the Lombard's intrigues with the Byzantine Emperor, his seizure of the duchies of Spoleto and Benevento and his continued occupation of towns in the former exarchate which he refused to surrender to the Pope. But Pippin made light of his fears and declined to intervene for the third time. How unsteady the papal position had become was only revealed when on Paul's death Rome suddenly lapsed into anarchy and the most barbarous party strife.

It seemed as if the Holy See, in assuming a secular role, had lost its moral standing in Rome. The new nobles, a raw and unruly lot sporting a bizarre mixture of Greek and Germanic names, showed an unhealthy interest in the papal election. One of them, Toto of Nepi, descended on the city with his armed retainers and scared the electors into elevating his brother Constantine, who was a layman and had first to be ordained bishop. It was a sad departure from the ordered dignity that had formerly graced the Lateran. Luckily this mock Pope lasted for only a year before the Roman clergy, led by the Archdeacon Christopher, called on Desiderius to help depose him. For the first time Lombard troops penetrated into the city. They killed Toto in the subsequent street fighting and clapped Constantine into gaol. The King's agent, the Lombard priest Waldipert, then proceeded to rig the election of his own puppet,

Philip, regardless of Christopher's wishes. But that was too much for clergy and people; they lost patience and elected, in proper form, the candidate proposed by Christopher, a Sicilian who was consecrated as Stephen III (767–72).

Nevertheless, his was a miserable pontificate, the climax of excitable barbarism and political ineptitude. A weak and shifty character, the Pope was at first manipulated by Christopher and his son Sergius, who unleashed a rancorous and savage persecution against all possible rivals. Constantine, Waldipert and many others were blinded and mutilated. Sergius was hurriedly despatch to the Frankish court in order to obtain approval for Stephen's election. On arrival there in 768 he found that Pippin was dead and that his sons Charles (Charlemagne) and Carloman were sharing the royal power. He persuaded them to send a number of Frankish bishops to a synod in Rome which formally confirmed the deposition of the wretched Constantine. Stephen now felt secure, but his confidence was soon upset by a change in Frankish policy involving reconciliation with the Lombards and the marriage of Charles to the daughter of Desiderius. Suspecting that he might no longer be able to count on Frankish help against Lombard pretentions, and in the knowledge that Desiderius was furious with Christopher over his inhuman punishment of Waldipert, the Pope resolved to ditch his former sponsors in favour of a pro-Lombard clique. On the advice of the foremost Lombard partisan, Paul Afiarta, he invited the King to Rome, ostensibly as a pilgrim, in Lent of 771. Christopher and Sergius were now doomed; they tried to resist by force of arms and attacked the Pope in the Lateran, but he got away in time to St Peter's and the two clerics fell into Afiarta's hands. He treated them with the same ferocious cruelty as they themselves had practised. Torn from sanctuary and blinded, Christopher soon succumbed to his injuries, while Sergius was strangled in prison.

From these atrocities and intrigues the Pope derived no benefit at all. A few months after the latest bloodbath Charles, now sole King of the Franks, put away his Lombard wife and reverted to his father Pippin's Italian policy. Early in 772 the Pope died, having disgraced his office and plunged Rome into shameful confusion.

6

A CENTURY OF
GRANDEUR
(772–882)

The pontificates of Hadrian I (772–95) and Leo III (795–816) mark the climax of the papacy's involvement with the Frankish monarchy. Although this connexion rescued the papacy from its immediate dangers, it was by no means uniformly harmonious and demanded from the popes new qualities of adaptation. Iconoclast Constantinople, from which Rome had recently emancipated itself, was far away across the sea; on the other hand military access to Italy from France, so long as the Alpine passes were open, was relatively easy, as the Franks found when they first intervened. They could therefore impose on Italy and Rome a degree of subordination and control of which Byzantium was no longer capable. Moreover the new type of European kingship represented by Pippin and Charles did not resemble the remote Byzantine sovereignty to which the popes had long been accustomed. If they no longer needed to profess even formal loyalty to a Roman Emperor in the East, they had to work out and define a new kind of relationship to their transalpine protectors. The Frankish conception of monarchy had changed greatly since its original establishment in Gaul and the ruler owed his election to the Germanic tribal warriors who raised him on a shield. Now, under the influence of biblical portrayals of Hebrew kingship, the ruler of a great nation of mixed origins saw himself as king by Grace of God, an autocrat whose power was derived from above, with or without a sacramental act of anointing or crowning performed by a pope or any other bishop.

Charles had a great respect for Hadrian and Hadrian, in spite of the inherent weakness of his position, showed much ability in handling Charles. A strong-minded administrator, he was not at all disposed, once elected, to become the tool of the pro-Lombard party. His first step was to get rid of its leader, Paul Afiarta. This he accomplished by a neat piece of trickery worthy of a Renaissance Pope. He sent the unsuspecting Afiarta on a mission to his patron, King Desiderius, but arranged that on his return journey he should be arrested and held prisoner by the Archbishop of Ravenna. Meanwhile he ordered the rehabilitation of Afiarta's victims, Christopher and Sergius, and the solemn reinterment of their remains in St Peter's. Those considered responsible for their deaths were put on trial and condemned, together with Afiarta in his absence, to death or banishment. Afiarta's place of exile was still being debated when the Archbishop conveniently had him executed in his Ravenna prison.

Desiderius could hardly have been expected to ignore the downfall of his trusted agent. He at once moved on Rome, mopping up various papal possessions on the way. As was equally certain, Hadrian hastily appealed for Frankish aid, and the promptitude with which it was granted suggests that the sequence of events had been foreseen at the Frankish court. However that may be, the events of 753 repeated themselves twenty years later, with Charles playing the role of his father Pippin, Desiderius that of Aistulf and Hadrian that of Stephen II, the only difference being that Charles, on invading Italy, decided to put an end to the Lombard Kingdom altogether. Even so there were hesitations on both the Lombard and the Frankish side. When threatened by papal anathemas, Desiderius seemed reluctant to press home his attack. Nevertheless he rejected the enormous bribe, 14,000 gold pieces, offered him by Charles for surrendering the Church's territories that he had occupied. In the end he shut himself up in Pavia, where he was prepared to withstand a long siege. The city had held out for six months when Charles, leaving his army to reduce it, visited Rome in state at Easter 774.

As a young boy, Charles had been deputed by his father to greet Stephen II on his way to Ponthion. He had doubtless been impressed by the significance of the occasion and by the Pope's dignity as a suppliant. Now, when he himself came to Rome as its protector and conqueror of the Church's enemy, he knew perfectly well that he had more to give Hadrian than Hadrian had to offer him. For that reason alone he was scrupulous in his devotion to the Holy See and in his deference to the Pope's person. He was received with the theatrical pomp with which the papal court, against a background of decayed magnificence, was always ready to welcome an illustrious visitor. The show began on Easter Eve at the 24th milestone, just south of Lake Bracciano, where the civic magistrates and guards of honour from the army of the Roman duchy were waiting to escort the King on the last stage of his journey. At the city limits he found the bulk of the army drawn up, together with bands of school children carrying branches of palm and olive. An excited and well drilled populace provided ample applause. There Charles dismounted and walked with his nobles to the atrium of St Peter's. According to Hadrian's biographer, the honours paid to him were those laid down in the papal protocol as suitable for an Exarch or Patricius. Very probably they resembled those accorded more than a century earlier to the Emperor Constans, but whereas the latter accepted them with grudging condescension, Charles seems to have entered whole-heartedly into the spirit of the spectacles in which he was in fact the principal actor.

Hadrian, the stage manager, was waiting in the porch of the basilica. As the massed clergy intoned the 'Blessed is he who cometh in the name of the Lord', the King climbed the steps on his knees. When he reached the top he embraced the Pope and they entered the church together. Having prayed at the Apostle's tomb, they went down into the crypt to take an oath of peace and loyalty to one another. There followed three days of carefully programmed devotions and ceremonies, with the Frankish troops encamped outside the walls. The King formally begged leave to enter the city proper in order to visit the Lateran and other churches, but he too spent his nights outside. It was not until the Wednesday after Easter that he and the Pope got down to political business. Their talks, held in St Peter's, did not last long. As previously understood between the parties, their purpose was to confirm the Donation of Pippin, in other words to restore to papal sovereignty and jurisdiction the territory of the Exarchate and other lands usurped by Desiderius. As soon as they were over Charles hastened north in order to receive the capitulation of Pavia and to relegate Desiderius to a monastery. From that moment he adopted the title 'King of the Franks and Lombards, Patrician and Defender of the Romans'. In fact he dominated all Italy except the Byzantine provinces in the toe and heel of the peninsula. The powers he now wielded exceeded those of the Exarch and the

Lombard King put together, and while guaranteeing the Pope's political and territorial rights, he really put him in the shade.

Moreover Hadrian did not find the royal protection quite as effective as he had hoped. To his bitter disappointment, the terms of the Donation were not being properly fulfilled. The Duke of Spoleto refused to acknowledge his overlordship; the Archbishop of Ravenna proclaimed his independence and appropriated the rich cities of the Romagna; the Duke of Benevento was nibbling at the Patrimony from the south. Though the Pope bombarded Charles with complaints, he got no satisfaction until Easter 781, when the King again appeared in Rome and stopped any further frittering away of papal territory. The northern cities were handed back and the boundaries generally redrawn, but six years later Charles was obliged to mount a special campaign to bring the Duke of Benevento to order. As a quid pro quo for his first intervention he required Hadrian to anoint his son Pippin as King of Italy, a pointed reminder that the King of the Franks had finally displaced the Byzantine Emperor as the Pope's political patron. Indeed it was in the same year that papal documents ceased to be dated by imperial reigns.

In the Frankish kingdom bishops were regarded as royal servants, and it was not surprising that when Frankish rule embraced Italy the greatest bishop in Christendom should sometimes feel the King's heavy hand, especially over political issues. But it was more grievous for Hadrian that Charles should interfere in what was basically a religious matter. This is what occurred in 787 when Iconoclasm, which had been the rule at Constantinople throughout the century, was condemned by the synod of Nicaea, the seventh General Council of the Church. That the veneration of images had been restored in the East was largely the work of the Empress-Mother Irene, a native of Athens, but it also conformed to popular sentiment and to a desire for reconciliation with the West, as a result of which Irene had succeeded in betrothing her son, Constantine VI, to a daughter of Charles. Such developments could only meet with the Pope's approval, and his delegates had been duly invited to attend the Council. Unfortunately no such invitation had been extended to King Charles, who regarded himself as the foremost sovereign of the Christian world. If Frankish bishops had been present at the Council, all might have been well, but in their absence the King chose to take offence. Not only did he annul his daughter's betrothal, but he challenged on religious grounds the Council's decisions which had already received the Pope's eager approval. Believing, or professing to believe, that the Council had called on Christians to worship, and not merely to venerate, images, he set his own theologians to work to fight its conclusions. This they did, in the most trenchant and sarcastic manner, by a treatise known as the *Libri Carolini*. In vain Hadrian tried to explain that the fuss was due to a mistranslation from the Greek into Latin, and that veneration did not imply worship. Charles insisted on assembling his own Frankish synod at Frankfurt for the purpose of denouncing the Nicaean decisions, and the papal envoys were obliged to toe the line.

This quite undeserved humiliation soured the Pope's relations with Charles during the last year of his life. Accustomed as he was to getting his own way, the King was probably unaware of the offence he was causing. He had always regarded Hadrian as an ally and found him personally sympathetic. He was genuinely grieved by his death and mourned him, we are told, like a brother or one of his children. Hadrian certainly ranks among the most able pontiffs. As he soon realized, it was no easy task for him to reconcile his role as Holy Father, head of the universal Church, with that of secular ruler of a satellite principality within a huge empire, but he performed it skilfully and on the whole with success. It was not his fault that he is remembered for his political talents rather than for his priestly virtues, and if his repeated appeals to Charles smack of subservience and flattery, it is only because they were couched in the inflated diplomatic jargon of his age.

Hadrian was untiringly diligent in his care for Rome and its people. While the city enjoyed unusual peace and quiet he employed the expanding revenues from the papal state to carry out a vast programme of much needed public works. He mobilized labour from the whole patrimony to restore the city walls, crowned with 387 towers, the quays of the Tiber and the four principal aqueducts of ancient Rome. He revived the agricultural colonies (*domuscultae*) in the Campagna. He also rebuilt or redecorated many churches, the most lavish outlay, including generous contributions from Charles, being devoted to St Peter's. The Pope's biography gives an exact account of the gold and silver plating that covered the walls and floor of the Apostle's shrine, of the gold and silver statues representing Christ, the Virgin and the Apostles, the mosaics, the gold and purple tapestries and the enormous chandelier known as the 'lighthouse' (*pharos*) with its 1370 candles. Ancient buildings were unmercifully plundered of the cut stones needed for the colonnades, forecourts and staircases of St Peter's, St John Lateran and many other churches.

Such new splendour, conspicuous among the contemporary slums and the battered monuments of antiquity, excited the admiration of the increasing throngs of northern pilgrims who braved the horrors of the journey to Rome. They were cared for in the hostels set up by the resident foreign communities (*scholae*) the most notable of which was the Schola of the Anglo-Saxons. Originally founded in 727 by King Ine of Wessex, it was enlarged and enriched by King Offa of Mercia, the overlord of all England, who paid his respects to St Peter in the year preceding Hadrian's death.

There was no trouble over the election of Leo III (795–816), but he was hardly a brilliant choice. A south Italian Greek by descent, he lacked the sterling qualities of his predecessor, a Roman of the old commanding breed. It is ironical that so second-rate a personality should have performed an act that influenced the course of history for the next thousand years.

His election, though unopposed, soon aroused resentment among a group of prominent churchmen closely connected with the late Pope, including his nephew, the *primicerius* Paschalis and another relative, the treasurer Campulus. They were angry at having fallen out of favour and disturbed by what seemed to them to be Leo's unnecessarily sycophantic attitude towards King Charles, to whom his legate had presented, after his consecration, the Keys of St Peter's tomb and the banner of the city of Rome. At the same time he caused symbolic mosaics to be set up in a Roman church, as well as in a magnificent new hall that he built in the Lateran palace, depicting Charles and himself bound together in close alliance under the aegis of St Peter. In their view, this was going too far in self-advertising and in stressing the Pope's dependence on his patron. To reinforce their case they sent messengers to Charles accusing Leo of immorality and perjury.

When these charges were understandably ignored, Paschalis and his friends resorted to crude violence. On 25 April (St Mark's Day) 799 the conspirators waylaid the Pope as he took part in the procession of the greater Litany from the Lateran to the church of St Laurence. Their hired bravos knocked him off his horse and as he lay on the ground, made as to blind him and cut out his tongue. Somehow, however, he avoided mutilation and was carried, wounded and under guard, into the Greek monastery on the Caelian hill. Whatever his enemies intended to do with him, he was then rescued by his supporters and brought first to St Peter's and subsequently to greater safety at Spoleto. At that stage the royal authorities took over and transported him swiftly to the King's headquarters, which happened to be at Paderborn in distant Germany.

Charles received the Pope with due honours but did not keep him long. He knew exactly what to do and sent him back to Rome with such despatch that he arrived there on 29 November, attended by a formidable retinue of Frankish prelates and notables. For the early Middle Ages the speed of travel both ways had been remarkable. Clearly Charles could not let the Pope down; he had to restore his authority and see that it was not again flouted. On the other hand his principal adviser, the Englishman Alcuin of York, had warned him that the moral charges levelled at Leo were not unfounded; he was so shocked that he had burned a detailed account of them. Consequently the King ordered an investigation, and while the authors of the outrage were removed to Frankish territory a commission of enquiry was set up at Rome. As was perhaps inevitable when a body of northerners was dealing with a typically Italian situation, it reached no clear cut conclusions, but it was sufficiently embarrassing for the Pope to have to wait another whole year before Charles had time to come to Rome and personally consider them at a meeting with the commissioners and representatives of the Roman clergy and people. After three weeks of discussion, the principle that a Vicar of Christ could not be judged by his fellow men was held to prevail; all the same Leo was required to mount the pulpit of St Peter's and to read, under oath, a statement formally exculpating himself from the accusations brought against him. The mere fact that he should have been so obliged meant that he was not altogether free from discredit.

On Christmas Day, two days after the exculpation ceremony, a much more remarkable scene was enacted in St Peter's when the King attended Mass. As he rose from his knees before the crypt of St Peter, the Pope suddenly placed a crown on his head and the whole assembly in the packed Church burst into the declaration 'Life and Victory to Charles the most pious Augustus, crowned by God, the great and pacific Emperor', which was solemnly repeated three times.

There is no doubt whatever about what happened on that day, but historians have never been able to agree about the inspiration and significance of the event. Obviously it was carefully planned in advance by Leo; the select Roman congregation knew what he was going to do and what they were meant to shout. But had it been concerted between Leo and Charles? Certainly they had had plenty of time to prepare it at Paderborn and afterwards. On the other hand, Einhard, Charles's biographer, may have truthfully recorded that the King was taken by surprise and would never have entered the Church if he could have foreseen what would occur. As the master of most of western Europe, the conqueror of the barbarian Saxons and Avars, he had nothing substantial to gain by exchanging the Roman title of Patricius for the equally honorific title of Emperor. To do so was likely to cause embarrassing complications with the Byzantine empire, with which he was anxious to remain on good terms; indeed he was contemplating a marriage with the Empress Irene. He had no interest in either taking territory from the eastern empire or claiming the title of universal Roman Emperor.

Leo, for his part, needed to refurbish his own tarnished reputation. For that purpose it was important for him to figure as the man who had the power to bestow an imperial crown on Europe's mightiest prince. His motive also corresponded with the permanent policy of the Roman curia to exalt the popes in relation to all purely temporal rulers. Finally his new status as an Emperor's sponsor gave him the right to expect that his local enemies, past and future, would be indicted for treason against the highest secular authority.

Once the crown had been clapped on his head, Charles accepted it with a good grace. His new title was a sign that he had the upper hand in his partnership with the papacy and that so far as Italy was concerned, he would have no trouble in maintaining political control. In the ecclesiastical sphere as well he could call the tune so long as he could count on so compliant a pontiff, a weak though ingenious man who could never stand up to his own masterful personality. Within the Frankish system the Pope had simply become the senior of the twenty-one Metropolitans of the realm whose appointments were in the King's gift, just as the patriarchate of Constantinople was in the gift of a strong Emperor at Byzantium. Charles's protective function had developed into a power to dominate, and subordination to his will was now the price of the Pope's security. Even in doctrinal matters Charles did not hesitate to impose his preference and that of his Gallican Church. He pressed the reluctant Leo to add the famous '*Filioque*' clause to the Nicene Creed in order to provide for the Procession of the Holy Spirit from the Son as well as from the Father. To his credit Leo refused to be moved, but he was unable to prevent the new usage from becoming normal in the West, and thus a major source of disagreement between Rome and Constantinople.

Charles the Great, the new-style Roman Emperor, left the city at Easter 801. He never came back to it and, when he made his only surviving son Lewis co-Emperor in 813, he conspicuously failed to invite the Pope to crown him at Aachen. Leo, however had found it politic to visit Charles at Reims in 804, and from there accompanied him to Aachen before returning to Italy. Apart from that exhausting expedition he spent the rest of his pontificate quietly enough at Rome, where he continued Hadrian's programme of rebuilding and adornment. But when Charles died in 814 he again faced dissidence on the part of sympathizers with his old enemies Paschalis and Campulus and had to call on Frankish help to quell it.

Whereas the central problem for both Hadrian and Leo had been to adjust to the realities and demands of Frankish power, their successors in the ninth century had to adapt the papacy to the disintegration of the Carolingian empire and the loss of its effective protection. Fortunately most of those who reigned throughout the critical years were steady, competent men, deeply conscious of their responsibilities and not frightened by dangerous situations.

Nevertheless the Popes first displayed an utmost anxiety to placate the Emperor Lewis the Pious and his sons. At his own request and without any summons, Stephen IV (816–17) also hurried across the Alps to Reims in order to anoint Lewis and his wife, and had hardly returned to Rome before he died of his exertions. Paschal I (819–24) obtained from the Emperor the '*Pactum Ludovicianum*', a confirmation of previous Carolingian donations and of papal rights more valuable in a legal context than as a guarantee that these rights would in practice be respected. He also strengthened his personal position by crowning Lewis's eldest son Lothar as co-Emperor at Easter 823. But in the last year of his reign he was involved, directly or indirectly, in the murkiest of criminal affairs. All Rome was shocked to hear that two high officials of his court, well known for their pro-Frankish sentiments, had been found blinded and beheaded in the precincts of the Lateran. Some said that he had connived treacherously in their death, others that he was the victim of a plant.

Although Paschal's legates promptly dissociated him from the outrage, Lewis ordered an inquiry on the spot. However, when the imperial commissioners reached Rome they found that the Pope had eluded them by taking the oath of purgation, just like Leo III, in the presence of 34 bishops. While avoiding more disagreeable consequences, he made himself so obnoxious to the Romans that they refused to bury him in St Peter's, and his reign ended in popular tumults.

It was hardly surprising that the Emperors should now decide to put an end to scandal and disorder in what they now regarded as their city of Rome. Thus the pontificate of Eugenius II (824–7) was the high-water mark of Carolingian interference with the papal government. Lothar returned in person and proceeded to dictate a 'Constitution' to the Pope and Rome generally. It laid down in detail a new administrative and judicial system and defined the relations that should in future prevail between the Emperor, the Pope and the Romans. Papal government and justice in the temporal sphere were firmly subjected to imperial supervision. The Romans were allowed to choose the legal code under which they might be judged, Roman, Frankish or Lombard, but while the Pope held immediate jurisdiction in all temporal cases the Emperor reserved for himself the ultimate decision on appeal. Papal elections were to be the province of the Romans to the exclusion of all outside influence, but clergy and people were required to swear to the Emperors that they would allow an election to proceed in accordance with canon law. As for the elected candidate, he might not be consecrated before taking a similar oath before the resident imperial envoy and the people.

To all appearances the papacy was becoming a docile appendage of the Frankish monarchy, with the Pope's personality reduced to a secondary importance. But the Constitution had hardly been imposed when the pendulum started to swing the other way. From a coherent whole the Carolingian realm fell rapidly to pieces during the pontificate of Gregory IV (827–44). Elected strictly according to Lothar's Constitution, he did all he possibly could to arrest its collapse as the result of dissensions between members of the dynasty. Lewis himself was a man of principle. His ideals were the unity of the realm, the disciplined unity of the Church within the realm and the uniformity, so far as that might be possible, of ecclesiastical and civil institutions. Unfortunately none of them could be realized in conditions that were still partly barbaric, the chief obstacle being the persistence of the old Frankish custom that a King must divide his territory between his sons. It was incompatible with any theory of empire, and Lewis was therefore in a hopeless position from the start to compose his differences with them and theirs with each other. As from 830 the Frankish empire was the scene of endemic warfare and shifting alliances between Carolingian princes.

In such circumstances Gregory displayed courage and a sense of duty in quitting Rome and offering himself as a negotiator between Lewis and his sons. The journey accomplished, he found the rich and lordly Frankish prelates politically split. They were also inclined to look askance at the Italian whom they treated as a fellow archbishop rather than as the Holy Father. They also accused him of bias in favour of Lothar, without whose help he would never have reached the scene of conflict. Defending his impartiality, he reminded the bishops, in lofty Roman style, of the supreme status of the Apostolic See, whose authority in spiritual matters transcended that of any prince in secular affairs. His was the only mediation that could hope to bring the contenders to their senses. Unhappily, when that assumption was tested in 833 at Colmar, where the armies of Lewis and his sons were ranged against each other, the Pope's influence on the probable field of battle was exposed as non-existent, for while he was still shuttling from one camp to the other in order to negotiate a peace, the issue was decided by Lewis's whole army deserting to the other side. Nevertheless we have here the only example in history of a pope throwing himself between armies apparently preparing to fight.

Gregory's mission had been an honourable failure of which he had no reason to feel ashamed. On re-entering Rome, he remained a passive spectator of the great civil war between Lewis's sons that ended in the partition of his empire between them into three virtually separate kingdoms. Meanwhile he was himself confronted by a very real threat from a different quarter. Saracen raids on the Italian coasts had multiplied since Arabs from Tunisia had begun, in 827, their conquest of Byzantine Sicily, an enterprise that took them fifty years to complete. They took Palermo in 831 and nine years later both Bari and Taranto on the mainland. Thus Rome and all papal territory were dangerously exposed to attack. The city, packed with treasures accumulated during many decades of peace and with wealthy pilgrims suitable for ransom, was a tempting target but relatively immune behind its strong walls. So the Pope contented himself with refounding and fortifying the old harbour of Ostia, with the object of keeping the Saracen ships out of the Tiber.

Such limited precautions proved inadequate, for the Saracens were preparing a *razzia* on a vast scale. It was no more a piratical escapade, but a venture as coldly planned as the Vandal expedition of 455. Gregory's successor Sergius II (844–7) was taken by surprise when 75 ships landed 10,000 men at the mouth of the Tiber. The late Pope's fortress (pompously christened *Gregoriopolis*) was stormed at once and the Saracens swept on to sack everything of value outside the stout city walls. That meant the whole open quarter lying on the right bank of the river, including the Basilica of St Peter and the Basilica of St Paul on the left bank. The shrines of both Princes of the Apostles were thoroughly profaned and plundered by the Moslems without the Franks, nominal protectors of the Holy See, being able to lift a finger in their defence.

The chroniclers are understandably reticent about the extent of the damage. The churches themselves were not torn down but stripped at leisure of their entire riches, the offerings of eastern and western rulers over a period of five centuries and countless private dedications. Statues, altars, candelabra, gold and silver plating, all was carried off. The destruction of objects of pure sanctity and veneration must also have been enormous. What happened after the sack is also uncertain. There was apparently some sporadic fighting on the right bank and in the Campagna as Frankish, Lombard and other troops rallied and closed in. It ended, however, in a tame armistice that permitted the raiders to re-embark with their booty. Many of the ships, we are assured, were lost in a storm with all their treasure.

The blow to Christian pride and Frankish self-esteem was naturally immense. It was all the more galling that Lothar's son, Lewis II, titular King of Italy, had spent much time the year before at Rome not providing for its security but quarrelling pointlessly with the Pope about the latter's non-compliance with the Constitution of Lothar. Evidently, Sergius felt, a little prematurely, that the divisions in the Carolingian empire gave him a chance to reassert himself in his own city and patrimony. Shamed into action, Lewis undertook a not unsuccessful campaign against the Saracens in south Italy, but the Pope failed to survive the shock of the sack.

The next 35 years, comprising five pontificates, were critical and dramatic. The problem for the Popes, all men of talent, was to prise themselves loose from the faltering but still irksome grip of the later Carolingians in order to establish their own independent authority. Crippled by their own divisions and bothered by Viking attacks, the Franks were now an encumbrance rather than a help for the papacy. Whether it would be able to hold its own was another matter; happily the ninth-century Popes believed that it could and acted in that spirit.

Leo IV (847–55) made it his first task to repair the damaged caused by the Saracens and to guard against future raids. Besides strengthening the old defences of Rome, he protected St Peter's by building a new rampart round what is now the Vatican quarter and was then named the Leonine city. St Peter's and other churches that had suffered pillage were redecorated with even greater brilliance than before, the cost being shared between the church's reserves, Frankish contributions and special levies from papal territory. Meanwhile Portus, the older of the two Roman harbours, and that of Civita Vecchia to the north-west, were rebuilt and repopulated, the former with refugees from Corsica. Before these works were complete, another Saracen fleet appeared off the Tiber's mouth, only to be decisively repulsed by the united squadrons of Naples, Amalfi and Gaeta, cities nominally subject to Byzantium but in practice autonomous. The work of rebuilding took 5 years, and was a very considerable achievement.

But the Pope's relations with Lewis II were uneasy. In the knowledge that the latter's power was limited to north Italy and his title had therefore little significance, he had no objection to crowning him Emperor without necessarily accepting his directions. Lewis, for his part, was irritated by Leo's independent airs and suspected him of intrigues with Byzantium. In any case he wished the next pope to be a more pliable instrument. His eye lit on one Anastasius, the learned and clever Cardinal-priest of St Marcellus, who did not get on with Leo and had found it advisable on that account to remove himself to Ravenna. There the pro-Frankish kept him, though excommunicated, carefully in reserve until the Pope's death. It thus happened that the accession of Benedict III (855–8) brought an immediate trial of strength between the imperial and papal parties. The legates sent to announce his election to Lewis were intercepted by Anastasius and his supporters and either bullied or cajoled into accepting the excommunicated priest as anti-pope. Anastasius then hastened to Rome, escorted by imperial officers and a large body of armed Franks.

There ensued another of those sudden outbreaks of violence, typical of the times, in which a Pope is exposed to outrage and insult. Brushing aside the pontiff's representatives who went to meet him, Anastasius led his partisans to St Peter's, where they tore down the notice of his excommunication affixed to the doors and, it was alleged, damaged some very holy icons. They then forced their way into the Lateran Basilica, pulled the Pope off his throne and placed him under guard. But when the Emperor's men urged the clergy to consecrate Anastasius in his stead they firmly refused, in face of all threats, to do anything so uncanonical. On the contrary, they and the people unanimously confirmed Benedict's election and obliged the Frankish envoys to back down. It was now the turn of Anastasius to be arrested, but with admirable moderation the Pope merely consigned him to a monastery in Trastevere of which he was soon made Abbot. We shall hear more of him.

This victory paved the way for the reign of Nicholas I (858–67, the most vital of all Popes between Gregory I and Gregory VII. Outstanding in his intelligence and strength of character, he was eminently a man of ideas who held the loftiest conception of his spiritual mission. He saw himself simply as Christ's representative on earth, guardian of the true faith, the unquestioned superior of all Patriarchs and Metropolitans of East and West and as the spiritual father of all Christian princes, whose first duty it was to protect the Church and uphold its moral authority. He was the unbending enemy of all lay encroachments on the Church's sphere and of the corresponding tendency of prelates, especially in the lands north of the Alps, to engage in worldly affairs. He enjoyed controversy and never shirked a fight with the great when principle required.

At the start he had no differences with Lewis II. Indeed the Emperor, who had been visiting Rome just before Benedict's death, turned back to attend his consecration. Another sign that he was not prejudiced was that he chose his predecessor's rival, Anastasius, as his intimate adviser. It was he who in the guise of *Bibliotecarius*, the Librarian, supervised the Lateran archives and the official papal biographies, the *Liber Pontificalis*. But he was also the Pope's right-hand man, his *éminence grise* in important affairs. He drafted his correspondence, much of which has survived, and is thought to have drawn his attention to the 'false Decretals', an ingenious mixture of genuine and spurious decrees of early Councils and Popes concocted by a group of forgers in the diocese of Reims and attributed to the seventh-century Spanish bishop Isidore of Seville. Originally designed to reinforce the Frankish bishops against their own Metropolitans, it proved, when adroitly used, an ideal weapon for asserting papal supremacy over the same Metropolitans. Thus armed, Nicholas first crushed the pretentions of the Archbishop of Ravenna, whom he excommunicated in person in his own city. He then successfully overrode the most independent prelate of all, Hincmar, the Archbishop of Reims, by reinstating in his See the bishop of Soissons whom he considered Hincmar had unfairly deposed. It was high time that the church of the western Franks, long notorious for its indiscipline, worldliness and lack of deference towards Rome, should be sharply brought to heel.

Nicholas was involved in two major controversies, from both of which he emerged with greatly enhanced prestige. The first of these opposed him to both the Carolingians and the powerful transalpine hierarchy. It arose out of the matrimonial difficulties of Lothar II, brother of Lewis and King of Lotharingia (the middle Kingdom of the three into which the Frankish monarchy had split). Lothar was anxious to get rid of his wife in order to marry his mistress, by whom he had already had three children. His spiritual advisers, the Archbishops of Cologne and Trier, were perfectly well disposed to find excuses for an annulment, and whatever hesitations were felt locally were dismissed by a synod of all the Lotharingian bishops. But the Pope, to whom this sort of moral issue, as deployed on a broad stage, was all important, objected very strongly indeed, remitting the matter to a wider Council drawn from the whole episcopate of the western and eastern Franks. Perhaps he was not surprised when threats and bribery produced the same result as before. The Council pronounced in favour of annulment and sent the same two Archbishops to convey its findings to the Pope.

Nicholas welcomed the challenge as a test of his authority. When the prelates reported to him he declared the Council's decisions null and void and themselves to be deposed and excommunicated. Thereupon they rushed home to denounce him to the royal brothers as 'Lord Nicholas who calls himself Pope, accounts himself as an apostle among the apostles and would like to make himself emperor of the whole world'. Moreover they persuaded Lewis to put pressure on the Pope in Rome. When he entered the city early in 864 Nicholas ordered fasts and ceremonies of intercession, one of which was rudely broken up by the Emperor's troops. As usual on such occasions the Pope barricaded himself in St Peter's and settled down to a contest of wills. Luckily the Romans were on his side and, with the Empress acting as mediator, Nicholas argued his way to total success. Lothar's union with his mistress was not legitimized and the ban on the Archbishops was not lifted. Nicholas's only failure was in his attempt to put the seal on his success by holding a grand Council of the Frankish Churches at Rome under his own presidency. The northern hierarchy would go no further in acknowledging its defeat.

Nicholas had proved that a strong pope was fully capable of standing up to the weakened Carolingians and the ecclesiastical magnates in their kingdoms. Simultaneously he found time to engage in a nagging dispute with the Patriarch of Constantinople. There was no doctrinal reason for such a quarrel, especially as the East had repudiated Iconoclasm several years before. But Nicholas chose to take offence when the Emperor Michael III dismissed his Patriarch, Ignatius, and nominated in his stead Photius, the empire's most distinguished layman. He refused to accept the formal letter in which Photius announced his appointment. The new Patriarch, an easy-going man of the world as well as a portentously learned classical scholar, had no wish to clash with the Pope; so far as he was concerned, East and West could live and let live. Unfortunately the two men were in temperament poles apart, for whereas Photius might have been at home in the twentieth century the Pope's sternly mediaeval spirit was devoted to the single aim of establishing the supremacy of the Roman Church, and—in this instance—at Byzantium's expense. It was probably Anastasius who induced him to propose a deal to Photius, offering to recognize him in return for handing over Illyricum to the ecclesiastical jurisdiction of Rome. By Illyricum was meant the vast territory occupied by the Danubian and Balkan Slavs, who by now had become ripe for conversion to Christianity.

The bargain, obviously unacceptable to Constantinople, was rejected without ado. Thenceforth relations between Pope and Patriarch petered out in a slanging match, with the latter sneering at the Latin language as 'barbarian and Scythian'. A Lateran synod of 863 declared Photius excommunicated and Ignatius restored, and four years later a Byzantine synod excommunicated the Pope, after which there was no doubt that the two Churches were in schism. Meanwhile a lively struggle had been taking place for the souls of the Bulgarians. Their czar Boris, baptized at Constantinople in 864, first invited Greek missionaries to his country, but changed his mind two years later and applied to Rome. To the discomfiture of Byzantium Nicholas immediately sent him two trusted bishops, who taught the Bulgarians western usages and the addition of the *Filioque* to the Creed.

Nicholas's energy and self-confidence had raised papal prestige to an unprecedented height. Yet the Pope's position remained essentially fragile; as soon as a firm hand was thought to be lacking, local anarchy raised its head. Hadrian II, who succeeded Nicholas in 867, was an elderly cleric of the same family as Stephen IV and Sergius II, and before he was even consecrated, Duke Lambert of Spoleto raided Rome and retired with a load of loot. Lewis II restored order and demonstrated his support for Hadrian by attending his consecration, but the old man's authority was soon shaken by an affront to his personal honour that also compromised Romans in high places. Hadrian had been married before he took orders and when he became Pope his daughter by that marriage was betrothed to a noble Roman. However, a certain Eleutherius, a cousin of Anastasius the Librarian and member of the pro-Frankish faction in the city, ran off with the girl and when pursued at Hadrian's request by imperial officers, stabbed her and her mother to death. This Borgiaesque episode resulted in the disgrace of the murderer's family, including the Librarian. He was excommunicated for the second time in his career, but soon rehabilitated, and in 869 we hear of him attending the eighth General Council of the Church at Constantinople as personal representative of Lewis II.

After this shaky start Hadrian governed prudently and moderately. A less combative character than Nicholas, he declared a local amnesty and re-admitted the erring King Lothar to communion. When Lothar died he strove unsuccessfully to prevent Lewis the German and Charles the Bald, Kings of the east and west Franks respectively, from dividing Lotharingia between them. In his eastern policy he had two strokes of luck. The first was a dynastic revolution at Constantinople that replaced Photius by Ignatius and enabled the breach between the Churches to be patched up at the General Council. The second was the decision by Cyril and Methodius, the Greek apostles of the Moravians, to seek papal endorsement of their mission, with the eventual result that the Slavs of the Danube basin chose obedience to Rome. Bulgaria, on the other hand, had to be abandoned to Byzantium.

Thanks to a series of talented Popes, the Church was more than holding its own in an increasingly chaotic Europe. Yet the political dangers showed no signs of abating. Indeed they crowded in on Hadrian's successor in even more daunting forms. Appropriately John VIII (872–82) proved to be a political Pope on the grand scale. After 20 years as Archdeacon and experienced Church administrator he emerged as a bold and resourceful statesman. He may have modelled himself on Hadrian I and Nicholas I, but his life soon came to resemble that of a Renaissance pontiff. If it seemed to lack spiritual content, it was only because politics thrust themselves inexorably upon him. In reality he never lost sight of the Church's universal mission or of his own pastoral duties. It was manifestly unjust of the German historian Gregorovius to stigmatize him as 'ambitious, intriguing, sophistic and unscrupulous' in his struggle to keep the papacy afloat. Tenacious and versatile, he made the most skilful use of his abilities in the Church's cause.

The Saracens were the immediate and continuously destructive menace; at any moment they might mount a new assault by land or sea. To do him credit Lewis II, the crowned Emperor, was tireless in repelling them; he retook Bari, won a Battle at Capua and relieved Salerno. But after his death in 875 the Moslem raiders pillaged at will up to the gates of Rome. John exhorted the maritime cities (Naples, Amalfi, Salerno and Gaeta) to combine with the dukedoms of Spoleto and Benevento, nominally feudatories of the Holy See, and with the Byzantines against the infidels. When local jealousies frustrated his plan, he fitted out a pontifical squadron and took command of it himself. Encountering off Monte Circeo the Saracen fleet that had been plundering Latium, he engaged it and took 18 of its ships. It was the first and only time that a Pope has figured as a victorious admiral. Yet he failed to promote a permanent alliance against the Arabs and was reduced to buying them off.

In the absence of a Carolingian residing, like Lewis II, in Italy, John had to find a protector north of the Alps. He needed a shield against the Saracens, the minor Italian rulers who were reluctant to treat either Emperor or Pope as overlord, and the upstart Roman nobles who flouted the Pope's authority in his own city. The choice lay between Lewis's uncles Charles the Bald of the west Franks and Lewis the German, but the mere existence of an alternative divided the unruly Romans, nobles and clerics, into two camps. When John preferred Charles the Bald, who was crowned Emperor at Rome and King of Italy at Pavia, the German faction plotted a revolt. Although the Pope succeeded in stifling it, he was soon disappointed in Charles as protector. On the first occasion that his help was invoked it only needed the appearance of Carloman, son of Lewis the German, at the head of a German army to send him scuttling back through the Alps, and he died on the journey.

Entering Italy unopposed, Carloman got himself proclaimed King, but the Pope, who still preferred the French to the German connexion, declined to crown him Emperor. Nor would he yield to the dukes of Tuscany and Spoleto, whom Carloman deputed to occupy Rome. They held John in custody for a month without affecting his resolution. Finally he passed to the offensive, excommunicated the dukes and, having closed St Peter's to worship and pilgrimage, took ship for France. Braving the Saracen sea-rovers, he crossed to Provence and took refuge with its Count Boso, Charles the Bald's brother-in-law.

John stayed away from Rome for a whole year; strangely enough the German party made no move to unseat him. During 878 and 879 he experimented with every possible political combination in the West that might save Rome from the Saracens. First he tried Lewis 'the Stammerer', son of Charles the Bald, whom he crowned King at Troyes, but soon discarded as manifestly incapable. Count Boso also failed the test, and John began to think that the Italians might rather have a German Carolingian as their overload, real or nominal. So he reversed his position and chose Charles 'the Fat', Carloman's brother; he even crowned him Emperor at Rome. However he had at last come to the conclusion that he was wasting his time in crowning this succession of fainéant sovereigns, and was already negotiating with Constantinople. As a result of his approach he obtained from the Greek Emperor Basil I, who was vigorously regaining Byzantium's hold on south Italy, the military help the Carolingians could no longer provide. With Greek help the Saracens were trounced by land and sea. The change of policy also brought an adjustment of the never very steady relationship between papacy and patriarchate. By a switch of imperial favour the latter's incumbent was once again Photius, with whom John could feel an affinity that had been entirely lacking between Photius and Nicholas I. Thus the eastern and western Churches were for once on good terms, each satisfied with its sphere of influence and with the other's orthodoxy.

It would be pleasant to record that the old Pope died in peace. Certainly he had done everything that his diplomatic energy and the force of his personality could accomplish to sustain the papacy's existence and unifying power. Yet doubt obscures the circumstances of his death. A solitary German annalist maintained that a jealous relative tried to poison him and, when the draught failed to work, smashed his skull with a hammer. Scurrilous Roman gossip perhaps, but if true a fitting start to the squalor and horrors of the succeeding age.

7

THE PAPACY IN THE DOLDRUMS
(882–1046)

The century following the death of John VIII is not one of which the Roman Church can be proud. It offers a lamentable record of weakness, corruption and violence, a catalogue of squalid and almost unbelieved decadence. During the early Carolingian period the Popes had sustained a generally high standard of personal morality, intelligence and ability. Some were inspiring leaders of men; others displayed outstanding qualities of mind and spirit. All of a sudden there occurs a catastrophic decline. We now see many pontiffs leading openly disreputable lives. Not all of them were of course vicious and incapable, but the pious and well-intentioned were in a minority. Even those personally respected were insignificant, the prisoners of their own debility and of a harsh environment. They no longer influenced great events on the European scene. Obsessed by parochial matters, they were reduced to puppets manipulated by Roman 'nobles', robber barons of uncertain origin, or by whichever dynast happened to hold the upper hand in northern and central Italy. Their pontificates were uniformly ephemeral; whereas eleven popes reigned in the eighth century and as many in the ninth, up to and including John VIII, no fewer than thirty-five flitted in and out of the Lateran between 882 and 998. From 896 to 904 ten individuals occupied the Holy See, of whom at least one was strangled and two died or were murdered in prison. Cardinal Baronio, the church historian of the Counter-Reformation, rightly described it as the 'obscure century', but the darkness was from time to time illuminated by extremely lurid flashes.

The wider background to this depressing local picture was the disintegration of the Carolingian empire in the second half of the ninth century. A realm so large and amorphous could only be held together by an exceptional personality. There was no strong central authority in western Europe capable of repelling the devastating incursions of the Vikings, which apart from their political and economic effects were inflicting enormous damage on monasteries and church property in general. At the same time the Moslems, masters of Spain, north Africa and Sicily, dominated the western Mediterranean and continuously raided the coasts of Italy and southern France. Entrenched in a permanent camp at the mouth of the River Garigliano, between Rome and Naples, they sallied forth year by year to ravage papal territory. The worst plague was the Magyar horde that occupied the Danube basin shortly before 900 and terrorized Germany, France and Italy with its sporadic but destructive forays for the next half century. When the Hungarians first raided Italy in 899 several Lombard cities went up in flames. Nor did European princes scruple to make use of them as mercenaries. Conspicuous among the latter was the Frank Arnulf, Duke of Bavaria and King of Germany, who after fighting the intruders entered into an alliance with them. Only the church's inherent vitality enabled it to survive the abject condition into which the papacy had fallen amid the apparently total insecurity that had enveloped western Christendom. The tide began at last to turn when Henry 'the Fowler', the first King of the new Saxon dynasty in Germany, defeated a Magyar host in 932. Happily eastern Christendom was being simultaneously upheld by a powerful Byzantine dynasty, the Basilian, which also kept a firm hold on Apulia and Calabria.

Papal elections at the end of the ninth century were rigged by the stronger of the two main factions fighting for power in the city. The old German party looked for support to Duke Berengar of Friuli, who in turn depended on Arnulf. Opposed to it were the adherents of Guido, Duke of Spoleto, who held the advantage of being closer to the scene. The Popes oscillated uncertainly from one side to the other, from time to time conferring a meaningless imperial crown on their patron of the moment. Formosus (891–6) started by re-crowning Guido (already crowned by his predecessor Stephen V), then crowned Guido's son Lambert and ended by crowning Arnulf, thus making a complete mockery of the imperial title. This Pope was an able, ambitious opportunist. Nicholas I had entrusted him, as bishop of Portus, with an important mission to Bulgaria. But John VIII, suspecting him of intrigues against himself on behalf of the German party, had him excommunicated and deposed from his see. Reinstated after John's death, he lay low until his own election permitted him, while at first pretending to favour the Spoletans, to promote the German interest. In doing so, however, he was running against a nascent Italian feeling. The Romans frankly preferred Guido; even after his death they reacted so strongly against Formosus that when Arnulf came to Rome for his coronation in 896, he was first obliged to take the city by storm and liberate the Pope. His enemies were holding him prisoner in the Castel Sant' Angelo, the former mausoleum of the Emperor Hadrian.

Formosus died in the same year, possibly from an unnatural cause. In view of his unpopularity in Rome he was lucky to escape a worse end. His successor, Boniface VI, died of gout within a fortnight. The short reign of Stephen VI (896–7) was remarkable for a piece of grisly play-acting in which the Holy See, blinded by party fanaticism, lost all sense of religious decency and moderation. It was resolved to hold a trial of the dead Pope before a Synod acting as a tribunal. The corpse was accordingly exhumed, dressed in pontifical vestments and seated on the pontifical throne. After a travesty of legal proceedings Formosus was condemned for uncanonical conduct and struck from the roll of heirs of St Peter. His body was then stripped of its robes, the fingers of his right hand that had given the pontifical blessing were hacked off, and the remains flung into the Tiber. But within a few months popular sentiment swung violently the other way. Stephen was deposed and throttled without any kind of formality, and what passed for the corpse of Formosus was retrieved from the river and entombed in St Peter's.

Political feuding and personal animosities were combining to reduce the shrunken papal state to near-anarchy. While various short-lived Popes vainly sought help from neighbouring Spoleto or remote Germany, religious and civic discipline had all but collapsed. Partisan outrages were met with equally savage reprisals. Sergius III (904–11), formerly a bitter enemy of Formosus and elected through Spoletan influence, again caused his memory to be condemned, his acts to be annulled and his nominees evicted. Ruthless, power-loving and lacking all spiritual authority, he ruled by terror, starting with the murder in prison of both his predecessors, Leo V (903) and Christopher (904). He managed to restore some sort of order, but his sole really laudable act was to rebuild the Lateran Basilica which, with appropriate symbolism, had fallen down during the trial of the corpse of Formosus.

Sergius could also rely on the support of the most powerful clan among the Roman nobility. Its head was a certain Theophylactus. This personage first figures as a city magistrate (*judex*) in 901. Subsequently he is described as a *vestararius* ('papal treasurer'), *dux*, *magister militum*, 'consul' and 'senator', a long list of titles, honorary or otherwise, indicating that he was a very considerable magnate. His wife Theodora struck their contemporaries as being an even more forceful character and devoid of all moral scruples. Liutprand of Cremona, a Lombard bishop and diplomatist of the mid-tenth century and the wielder of a peculiarly scurrilous pen, called her an 'impudent whore who in not unvirile fashion held the mastery of the city of Rome. She had two daughters, Marozia and Theodora, not only equal to herself but readier in the pursuit of love (*veneris exercitio*).' Indeed, Marozia was destined for a brilliant career, both in love and in politics, and it was assumed, correctly or incorrectly, that Pope Sergius had been one of her earlier lovers. It was also believed that they were the parents of a later Pope, John XI. Whether we accept or reject the testimony of contemporary scandalmongers, the facts suggest that in this age of violence and extravagance they hardly needed to exaggerate. Another Lombard writer, Ratherius of Verona, depicts the bishops of Italy as wallowing in more than Byzantine luxury and at the same time devoted to more strenuous pleasures in the hunting field. Among other bizarre practices, whenever a pope or prelate died, the populace exercised the privilege of looting his palace from top to bottom. No wonder that with the frequent changes of pontiff few of the Lateran treasures survived.

At all events the papacy was now unavoidably in the gift of the family of Theophylactus, or of its ladies, the so-called pornocracy. They did however make a good choice in John X (914–28), formerly for nine years Archbishop of Ravenna. Rumour had it that when a young priest he had been the lover of the elder Theodora; what is certain is that he had developed into an energetic churchman who took his duties seriously. Within a year he succeeded in forming a league of Italian princes and cities, together with the governor of Byzantine Apulia and Calabria, in order to root out the Saracen pirates' nest on the Garigliano. The campaign, in which the Pope himself took command, was brilliantly successful, and he returned to Rome in triumph. Yet he was acting under tutelage, for the leaders of the Roman contingent in the allied army were the Senator Theophylactus and an adventurer from Spoleto named Alberic, Marozia's first husband.

Even before the campaign, John had been chasing the old illusion of a prince capable of protecting the Pope from his own Romans as well as from external dangers. Apparently with the consent of the Theophylactus clan, he invited Berengar of Friuli, the then ruler of Lombardy, to Rome and crowned him Emperor. But it was noticeable that Berengar did not stay to take part in the extirpation of the Saracens; nor did he prove more effective as defender of the papacy. By 924 he was dead, the victim of revolts by his own vassals and of his own error in summoning the wild Hungarians to his aid. Rudolf of Burgundy, the next wearer of the iron Lombard crown, held no interest for John, but Hugh of Provence, who soon supplanted him, seemed the right man to help the Pope escape from the toils of Marozia and her relatives. By that time the lady had lost Alberic and acquired her second husband, the Margrave Guido of Tuscany. It did not at all suit her that the Pope should assert his independence, and when she knew that he was making overtures to King Hugh and had actually travelled to meet him at Mantua, she took drastic action on his return to Rome. His brother, Peter, was slaughtered in his presence by Guido's man; he himself was thrown into a dungeon in Sant' Angelo from which he never emerged.

Such was the end of John's rash attempt to put the papacy back on its feet. In 928 Marozia was the unchallenged mistress of Rome. Assuming the titles of Patricia and Senatrix, she sponsored in succession two shadowy Popes in three years. She then conceived two bold ideas, both of which she proceeded to put into execution. The first was to make her own son pope as John XI (931–6); this colourless young man, probably a layman and probably though not certainly the son of Pope Sergius, could be relied upon to do as he was told. The second was for herself to marry King Hugh, for Guido of Tuscany had conveniently died. Hugh hastened to accept the offer of her hand; it would make him ruler of Rome and two-thirds of Italy, besides opening the way to his becoming Emperor. He came to Rome in 932 with the utmost eagerness and not, as Liutprand later wrote, 'like an ox dragged to the altar', and was married to Marozia in Sant' Angelo. Presumably it was the bride's son who officiated.

The pair's plans for the future were, however, suddenly and unexpectedly upset. They had failed to reckon with the youth Alberic, Marozia's son by her first husband, who had taken a violent dislike to his new stepfather. According to the current story he was obliged to act as a page during the festivities that followed the wedding and was smacked on the face by the King for his clumsiness. Infuriated by the insult, he incited the Roman nobles and people to attack Sant' Angelo. Apart from the personal aspect of the affair, the Romans needed no encouragement; they were tired of Marozia and had no wish to be ruled by her northern husband, who was notoriously self-seeking and tyrannical. At all events they reacted so furiously that Hugh took fright. He escaped from the fortress by sliding down a rope at night, leaving his wife at her son's mercy. Alberic locked her up for the rest of her life; as for his reputed half-brother the Pope, he kept him under close watch in the Lateran.

As a result of this strange revolution Alberic was appointed 'Prince and Senator of all the Romans' and as such governed the papal domain until his death in 954. His regime took the form of a personal dictatorship resting solidly on the support of the nobility, clergy and people. Essentially it was an oligarchy controlled by a prince-president. But it would never have lasted so long if it had not been for his own exceptional qualities. Despite his extreme youth when he assumed power his authority was undisputed from the first. Under his military leadership the Romans successfully repelled three attempts by King Hugh to upset their republic; finally they composed their differences and Alberic married Alda, the King's daughter. His administration was a welcome change from the former insecurity and bloodstained confusion, for he was moderate and sensible in his internal policy, a shrewd diplomatist and curiously modern and pragmatic in his general outlook.

At the same time he put the papacy respectfully but firmly in the shade. So far as its temporal powers were concerned, he took them over completely. The four pontiffs who reigned between 936 and 955 were strictly confined to their religious functions. He ensured, too, that they were all pious and worthy men. If only for political reasons he promoted a measure of Church reform, beginning prudently with the monasteries. Here he found an invaluable ally in Abbot Odo of Cluny. This famous Benedictine reformer visited Rome several times during Alberic's tenure of power. Besides reconciling him with King Hugh, he helped in the restoration of many monastic houses deserted during the period of chaos or ruined by the Saracens. In short, while the papacy was politically in eclipse, the demoralization of the Church was at least temporarily checked.

Alberic's virtue, after he had settled with King Hugh, was to have kept Rome and the papacy out of north Italian politics. After 950, however, that was no longer possible, for Otto the Great, the second King of the Saxon Dynasty in Germany and by far the most powerful prince in Europe, had become closely involved in Italian affairs. Having succeeded his father, Henry the Fowler, in 936, he had spent the first fourteen years of his reign in arresting predominance in Germany, keeping the Hungarians at bay and pressing back the Slavs on the eastern borders. In 951, when he intervened in Italy, it was to rescue Adelaide, daughter-in-law of King Hugh and heiress of Lombardy, from imprisonment by a usurper, Berengar of Ivrea. This done, he married the lady as his second wife (the first was the English princess Edith), had himself crowned King of Italy and sent two German bishops to Rome to propose his coronation as Emperor. However, Agapetus II (946–55), the last of the four Popes already sponsored and directed by Alberic, rejected his request. For a few years, preoccupied by a rebellion of his principal feudatories and by new Hungarian inroads, he was unable to enforce it.

Meanwhile, Alberic, just before his death in 954, took an uncharacteristically foolish step. It was already understood that he was to be succeeded as Prince of the Romans by his teenage son Octavian, but he also induced the magnates to swear that this imperially named youth should be elected pope on the demise of Agapetus. This occurred in the following year and the Romans duly carried out his wishes. Octavian became pope as John XII (955–64). The result was that the papacy relapsed into the disrepute from which Alberic had temporarily extracted it. Octavian's private tastes inclined towards horses and girls. According to a contemporary chronicler, he was addicted to hunting 'not like an apostolic but a wild man; he adored his collection of women . . . hateful to the church, beloved of violent youth'. Many tales were told of his excesses: he consecrated a ten-year-old boy bishop; he ordained a deacon in his stables; he had a cardinal-deacon castrated; he called upon the old Gods to help him at dice. In other words he had a riotously good time and did not care whom he shocked. His political touch was equally erratic. Having fallen out with Berengar, Otto's former enemy but now his viceroy in northern Italy, whom he accused of filching papal territory, he besought the King to intervene again with all urgency. His appeal exactly suited Otto's book. He crossed the Alps with a large army, reduced Lombardy to obedience and on the last day of January 962 presented himself expectantly at the gates of Rome.

This time he came invested with even greater power and prestige. Since his crushing victory over the Hungarians at the battle of Lechfeld (955) he had been revered as the Saviour of Europe, and in the narrower Italian context he was regarded as the pacifier of Lombardy and as a deterrent to any expansion of the Byzantine province in the south. Once invited to Rome he easily obtained what he wanted, the imperial title to which he had perhaps aspired ever since he was acclaimed King of the Franks and Saxons in Charlemagne's church at Aachen. On Candlemas Day the Pope crowned him and Adelaide Emperor and Empress. Unwittingly enough, the irresponsible Octavian had entangled the papacy in an interminable love-hate relationship with the rulers of Germany, a close interaction and clash of interests that was to last for the next three hundred years.

Otto ratified all the rights accorded to the Holy See by his Carolingian predecessors, and in return the Pope sanctioned the creation of an archbishopric at Magdeburg for the purpose of converting the recently conquered Slavs. On the surface it was a satisfactory quid pro quo, but John soon found that the new Emperor's idea of sovereignty was very different from his own. In Otto's eyes the imperial function was not simply that of a protector or guarantor; he himself was the ultimate sovereign and the Pope exercised his temporal power by imperial favour. When John belatedly realized how badly he had misjudged matters, he swung to the other extreme and began to intrigue rashly with Berengar, the Byzantines and any other real or fancied enemies of the Emperor. This brought Otto back to Rome in a fury. John escaped just in time, carrying the treasures of St Peter with him to Tivoli, but he had to look on while Otto convoked a synod that deposed him in his absence for immoral conduct and treason. In his place the Romans were forced to elect, in the presence of the Emperor, the blameless papal archivist, a layman who was un-canonically consecrated as Leo VIII (963–5). But they were in a thoroughly recalcitrant mood. However strongly they may have disapproved of John's morals, they preferred Alberic's son to anyone imposed upon them by a German tyrant. So as soon as Otto's back was turned they restored him. While simply excommunicating Leo, he punished some of his clerical critics with revolting cruelty. One had his nose, tongue and two fingers cut off, another lost his hand. On that note Octavian died, either of a stroke or, as it was rumoured, knocked on the head by a husband whom he had cuckolded.

This was by no means the end of Otto's duel with the Romans, with the Popes as passive victims of the struggle. Instead of reinstating Leo, the Romans elected another learned and unexceptional cleric, the Cardinal-deacon Benedict. Otto, however, was adamant that no pope might be elected or ordained without his consent; he marched on the city and subjected it to a regular siege. When it surrendered he brought Leo back and sent the innocent Benedict into exile at Hamburg.

Leo's successor John XIII (965–72) belonged to a well-known Roman family, the Crescentii, and no fault could be found with him as a churchman. On the other hand he was frankly the Saxon Emperor's nominee and as such was damned in the eyes of his compatriots. After two months they mounted a rebellion against him under the leadership of their city prefect and removed him to a castle in Campania. Nevertheless their coup was somewhat half-hearted, for no attempt was made to find a substitute pope and John was allowed to escape from his prison. Thereupon the Romans, hearing that Otto was once again on his way to Italy, changed their minds and recalled him. But this tardy repentance failed to save them from Otto's anger. This time he decided to teach them a real lesson. Many of their leaders, civic and military, were executed, blinded or banished. As for Peter, the City Prefect, he was reserved for one of those semi-brutal, semi-carnivalesque displays that have never ceased to delight an Italian mob. First he was hanged by his hair from the statue of Marcus Aurelius on the Capitol; then he was paraded through the streets sitting naked and facing backwards on an ass. After the show he joined other Romans in their German exile.

There was now no further question of resistance to Otto. He spent the remaining six years of his reign, from 966 to 972, in Italy. He took his role of Emperor of the Romans much more seriously than any Carolingian, regarding himself as the effective and legitimate successor of Constantine and the western Caesars. By contrast the Pope, though in principle head of the universal Church, had in reality declined to the status of the Saxon Caesar's chaplain-in-chief. 'Woe to Rome,' lamented a monk of Latium, 'thou art crushed and trodden down by so many peoples; made captive by a Saxon king, thy folk subdued by the sword and thy strength brought to naught. . . . Thou who wast a mother art now become a daughter.' In order to leave no doubt that he was an effective Caesar and Augustus,

Otto staged three great ceremonies. The first was a synod at Ravenna, where the Pope played a strictly subordinate part, the second the coronation of his son Otto at Rome and the third, the grandest of them all, the wedding of Otto the younger, aged 17, to the 16-year-old Byzantine princess Theophano, at which the Pope officiated. It was the measure of his persistence and confidence that Otto overcame the initial revulsion that he first encountered at Constantinople to his request for Theophano's hand.

Before he died in 973 he procured the election of another nominee, Benedict VI (972–4), but as soon as his stern hand was removed Rome slid back into the only too familiar anarchy. Assuming the leadership of the national party, one of the Crescentii deposed Benedict and replaced him with an obscure deacon named Franco, who became Boniface VIII. This person turned out to be, in the words of a future pontiff, a 'horrendous monster, surpassing all men in wickedness'. He had his predecessor strangled, but on the approach of an imperial commander decamped to Constantinople with all the valuable objects he could lay his hands on. Unfortunately Rome had not seen the last of him. In despair of finding a suitable Roman the 18-year-old Emperor Otto II offered the papal chair to Maiolus, the saintly Abbot of Cluny. He wisely refused but recommended the bishop of Sutri in Latium, who was elected as Benedict VII (974–83).

We know little about this would-be reformer, the modest forerunner of a great movement, but he must have possessed remarkable qualities to hold his own during Otto's absence from Italy in the early part of his reign. The national party remained quiet and Crescentius even retired into a monastery. No scandals nor uprising are recorded. When Otto did come, it was to launch a campaign to expel both Byzantines and Arabs from south Italy and Sicily. Disastrously defeated by the latter, he retreated to Rome in 982 and died in the following year. To replace the Pope, who predeceased him by two months, he picked on Peter, his chancellor for Italy and bishop of Pavia. As John XIV (983–4), his first duty was to bury Otto in St Peter's, the only Emperor ever to be interred there.

The events of the next two years showed that the degradation of the papal office had not yet reached its limit. Very soon after Otto's death the unspeakable Boniface reappeared in the guise of a Byzantine agent. Although the Empress-mother Theophano was a Greek princess, the government at Constantinople had not forgiven her late husband for his attempt to end Byzantine rule in south Italy; it was alarmed by the Saxon ruler's preoccupation with Italian affairs and irritated by their pose as rival Roman emperors. It therefore subsidized Boniface to bribe his way back to Rome and engineer a coup that deposed the ex-Chancellor. John XVI was consigned to Sant' Angelo, where he was poisoned or possibly left to die of hunger. But even the Romans could not for long stomach a pope who had done away with two previous popes. Within a year, Boniface fell victim to a counter-coup by the Crescentii; he was summarily slaughtered and his body dragged through the streets. John Crescentius, head of the dominant family, secured the election of a Roman archdeacon as John XV (985–96). The latter was a cautious man who succeeded in conciliating both Crescentius and the Empress Theophano, guardian of the infant Otto III.

By this time the reputation of the papal office had sunk so low, and its tenure had become so precarious, that it is a wonder that anyone could be found to fill it. While the tradition of St Peter remained potent throughout Christendom, his heirs were apt to inspire either horror or contempt. Those who suspected that the world might anyhow be coming to an end at the first millennium after Christ may not have been surprised, but responsible churchmen, especially outside Italy, were pinning their faith on reform. In the French kingdom the influence radiating from Cluny and its daughter monasteries had ended by affecting an episcopate too long characterized by its worldliness. In Germany as well as France clerics and monks had woken up to the fact that even if their own standards were far from perfect they were greatly superior to those observed at the papal court. They were disgusted and exasperated by what they heard of atrocities, corruption, impotence and cynicism at the Church's centre. Even the level of general culture was higher north of the Alps; in central and southern Italy few clerics were still capable of writing respectable Latin. There were few facilities, and little desire, to study the arts and sciences.

Outspoken criticism of the Holy See boiled over at synods held in France during the pontificate of John XV. The most notable of these was that of Reims in 991 when Gerbert of Aurillac, the foremost scholar of the age, was elected Archbishop to the exclusion of Arnulf, a descendant of the Carolingians whom the synod deprived of his see for treason against the king, Hugh Capet. Its decision was immediately contested by John's legate, who argued that only a Pope had the right to depose a consecrated Archbishop. In the ensuing wrangle between the Pope and the French bishops, which lasted for five years, the latter let themselves go in scathing attacks on the papacy's moral failings, but in the end Gerbert, when faced with excommunication, gave up the struggle and accepted the young Otto III's invitation to join his court. It was this apparently downward turn in his fortunes that elevated him in 999 to the papal chair.

It is worthwhile to trace the steps by which this intellectual prodigy made his way, if only to show how a humble but intelligent boy could arrive at the top in the early Middle Ages. Born somewhere in Aquitaine about 950, Gerbert was educated in the Benedictine monastery at Aurillac and later sent to study mathematics at Vich in Catalonia, under the patronage of the local count and bishop. Impressed by his talents, his sponsors passed him on to Rome, where he was brought to the notice of Pope John XIII and Otto I. At his own request the Emperor despatched him to learn logic at Reims, where he was soon appointed head of the cathedral school. In 982 Otto II made him Abbot and Count of Bobbio, the famous monastery near Genoa founded by the Irishman St Columban, but he found the monks there so troublesome that within a year he was back at Reims. It was there that he established his European reputation. To his all round learning, embracing Latin, Greek, philosophy, mathematics, astronomy and music, he added a keen practical intelligence and a marked capacity for political intrigue. Such were the qualifications of the former archbishop whom Otto III, at the age of 15, summoned 'to rid him of his Saxon rusticity and stimulate his Greek subtlety'.

It was natural that Otto should take his grandfather's and father's protégé as his intimate adviser, but the time had not yet come to make him pope. In 996 Otto personally took over the government of his realm. By that time John XV was quarrelling with Crescentius and entreating the young Graeco-German monarch to come to Rome. Otto readily complied, but on reaching Pavia he learned that the Pope was dead. Acting on an impulse that was approved by his German prelates, he chose his own cousin to succeed him. Thus Bruno, son of the duke of Carinthia and one of Otto's chaplains, became the first non-Italian Pope for 250 years; his election, of course, was purely nominal.

Gregory V (996–9) was a learned and estimable young man, but only 24 years of age. Otto's coronation at his hands left papacy and empire in the hands of juvenile Saxon idealists, eager for church reform and the 'renovation' of Rome in the fancied style of the first Augustus. They were also so benevolent that they failed to take any sanctions against Crescentius and his party who, as Gregorovius remarked, 'would rather have seen a monster of Roman birth seated on the sacred chair than a saint of Saxon origin'. As had been demonstrated so many times, no foreign ruler could control Rome without a permanent foreign garrison, a solution that was impossible in tenth-century conditions. No sooner had Otto's army quitted the city than Crescentius expelled Gregory and began to look for an anti-pope. The man who was so unwary as to accept this hazardous role was a careerist Calabrian Greek called Philagathus. Originally patronized by Theophano and made bishop of Piacenza, he had recently returned from Constantinople, where he had unsuccessfully sought a Greek bride for Otto III, and was ready to try his luck. But if Crescentius and his anti-pope had been gambling on Otto's previous mildness they were rudely undeceived. On his second expedition to Rome (998) the exasperated Emperor indulged in a very considerable bloodbath. Philagathus was caught hiding in the Campagna, blinded, mutilated, paraded through the city on the traditional ass and left to die in a monastery. Then it was the turn of Crescentius, who tried to defend himself in Sant' Angelo. The castle was taken by assault and he and all twelve legionary captains of Rome were hanged or beheaded.

The Emperor was accompanied by his cousin Gregory, who had meanwhile been quietly reforming the Church from the safety of Pavia. He also brought Gerbert to Italy, presenting him with the see of Ravenna and the rich abbey of Nonantula. It was inevitable that on Gregory's sudden death in 999 Gerbert should succeed him, but equally significant that the Abbot of Cluny, the power-house of reform, should have urged his election. That event coincided with Otto's decision to make Rome his principal residence and to emphasize the Roman origin and character of his empire. Gerbert fully sympathized with his ambition to figure as a second Constantine and to that end himself adopted the name of Constantine's pope Silvester. Steeped though he was in the Latin classics, the writer of elegant Ciceronian prose, his conception of imperial Romanism was to encourage Otto to model his court closely on that of Constantinople. Thus the Emperor built himself a Byzantine-style palace on the Aventine hill and dignified his entourage, both German and local, with resounding Byzantine titles. Etiquette was strictly based on the *Book of Ceremonies* written by the tenth-century Emperor Constantine VII Porphyrogenitus. It is hard to judge just how seriously Gerbert could have taken these antics, some of which could not have failed to strike him as faintly ludicrous, but they suited Otto's romantic temperament and could be useful in flattering the Romans.

In fact Gerbert spent barely half of his four-year pontificate (999–1003) in the city itself. As teacher and prelate in France he had strenuously opposed the pretentions of unworthy Italian pontiffs, but as pope he behaved as a thoroughly authoritarian reformist, castigating simony and misconduct among the clergy and forcing King Robert of France to get rid of his wife. Much of his energy was devoted to the expansion of the Church in eastern Europe, and particularly to the creation of the archbishoprics of Griezno in Poland and Esztergom in Hungary. It was he who sent the original Holy Crown, symbol of the admission of Hungary to the Christian community of peoples, to King Vajk, now baptized as Stephen and afterwards canonized. But Rome proved obstinately unsuitable either as the capital of a revived western Roman empire or as the fount of the Church's universal mission. In the absence of a permanent foreign military force all authority, spiritual and political, was at the mercy of petty but heavily armed local magnates and of a wildly excitable populace, and there could have been no starker contrast between the respect accorded to the Pope in Christendom as a whole and the factious disregard with which he was treated at the centre of Christianity. In 1001 the delicate balance between Rome and both its overlords was upset by an apparently minor incident, a rebellion by the citizens of Tibur (Tivoli) and its suppression by imperial troops. What the Romans were objecting to was not the crushing of the revolt but the lack of severity with which Otto punished the rebels, for whom the former nourished an ancestral antipathy. Led by the Count of Tusculum (Frascati), a descendant of Theophylactus, they raised an uproar sufficient to send Pope and Emperor scuttling from the Lateran and the Aventine, to which neither ever returned. For a time Otto planned a third occupation of Rome, but eventually renounced it as impracticable. He died in 1002 and Silvester a year later.

Otto's two non-Italian Popes, the first German and the first Frenchman, were after all a mere flash in the pan. For the next forty years or so papal elections were controlled by one or the other of two rival Roman clans, the Crescentii and the Counts of Tusculum. Strangely enough this period was one of calm, unmarred by bloody revolutions and atrocious acts of vengeance. One reason for this change was that a peaceful modus vivendi existed between the German Emperors, the Roman Popes and the latter's local patrons; they had learned to respect each other's spheres of authority and to avoid clashes. The second and more potent influence for good was the steadily increasing strength of the reform movement in Europe as a whole.

John Crescentius, son of the Patricius executed by Otto, dominated the scene for nine years, during which he sponsored three insignificant Popes. It was then the turn of the Tusculans. Their leader, another Alberic, put up his own brother Theophylac-tus, who reigned until 1024 as Benedict VIII. In Church matters he turned out to be a vigorous, reformist and outward looking Pope, capable of working in close harmony with the Emperor Henry II and Abbot Odilo of Cluny. He crowned Henry at Rome and they presided jointly over an important reforming synod at Pavia. At the same time he showed a marked penchant for warfare against both infidels and Christians. He personally led the papal forces which, in alliance with the Pisans and Genoese, reconquered Sardinia from the Spanish Moslems. His other enemy, the Byzantine governor in south Italy, proved tougher; although he journeyed as far as Bamberg to persuade the Emperor to join him in a campaign, it had little success.

A second Tusculan, John XIX (1024–32), and yet a third, Benedict IX (1032–1044), followed the first. The former, originally called Romanus, was Benedict VIII's brother, and the latter, son of Alberic, was the nephew of both his predecessors. Thus the papacy seemed to have become anchored, with imperial consent, within this powerful and prolific clan. John had been a layman, described as consul, dux and senator, before his election and during his pontificate the civic and spiritual functions were combined in one man. The best that can be said of him is that he was an efficient administrator and committed no enormities. He kept the peace in the city and stayed on good terms with Conrad II, the first Emperor of the new Salian or Franconian dynasty, whom he crowned in the presence of a dis-tinguished pilgrim, King Canute of England and Denmark. But he was a bad churchman, quite unspiritual, notoriously corrupt and indifferent to the freedom with which the strong-willed Conrad made and unmade bishops and abbots without bothering about papal rights.

On John XIX's death the family conclave decided on a separation of powers. The civil government was delegated to Gregory, one of Alberic's numerous sons, and the papal chair to another Theophylactus, an immature boy of fifteen or so. The latter's elevation appears to us even less comprehensible than that of John XII (Octavian), the earlier juvenile pontiff from the same family. It was certainly an insensitive act and a cynical affront to all enlightened opinion in the Church outside Rome. Even so, in the circumstances of the eleventh century, it might have escaped heavy censure if the conduct of the new Pope, Benedict IX, had been less crassly irresponsible. He was no less materially minded than his uncle but also, at least in the early years of his reign, unblushingly and arrogantly dissolute. Naturally the spectacle of the Pope carousing and whoring his way around Rome aroused chroniclers to heights of indignation; they accused him of every vice and crime in their repertory of abuse. But the scandals, sexual and otherwise, that they described with such relish were heightened in the telling and may not have amounted to much more than an immoderate taste for enjoyment. He had a bad name for corruption and violence, but was obviously no Caligula or Nero, still less a Borgia. The Emperor tolerated him because he found him useful and subservient. He twice met Conrad outside Rome and once travelled as far as Marseilles, where he consecrated the abbey church of St Victor and presided over the synod that proclaimed the Truce of God, a system by which the endemic hostilities of the age were in theory suspended between Wednesday evening and Monday morning.

Perhaps he was becoming more responsible as he grew older, but in 1044 his enemies in Rome, of whom there were plenty, forced him to quit the city for one of his family's castles. He was swiftly replaced by Bishop John of the Sabina (the preserve of the Crescentii), under the name of Silvester III. There ensued an interval of intense confusion. While Silvester, unable to maintain himself in the Lateran, retired to the Sabina, but without renouncing the papacy Benedict thought it more prudent to resign his rights in favour of the Archpriest John Gratian, who happened to be his godfather. Subsequently, however, he denied that he had abdicated. Thus in 1045 and 1046 there were three Popes, each claiming legitimacy, in the Roman field. It was a ludicrous situation that could not last long.

Of the three contenders the only worthy one was John Gratian (Gregory VI). He is thought to have been a descendant of the Pierleoni, a family of rich Jews from the Transtiberine quarter. He was a serious cleric and a keen reformist, but unhappily for himself it was believed that he had accepted the papacy in return for guaranteeing to his godson an annual sum equivalent to the 'Peter's pence' received by the Holy See from the pious realm of England. This allegation of simony may well have been a calumny but it stuck. At the time Gregory's pontificate was greeted with joy by the Cluniacs and other reformers, and it was later remembered that Hildebrand, later to be Gregory VII, the greatest of all reforming Popes, was then serving as his chaplain. Nevertheless he found it increasingly hard to survive amid the local chaos. He was still struggling when the crisis was resolved by the new German King, Henry III.

It is uncertain from what quarter Henry received the appeal that moved him to intervene, but his quick response to it undoubtedly stemmed from his deeply religious sense of duty as well as from his political absolutism. On his way to Rome in the autumn of 1046 he interviewed Gregory at Piacenza and heard his side of the story. However he soon came to the conclusion that all three Popes must be deposed and had it endorsed by synods held successively at Sutri and in St Peter's. Some clerics thought that Gregory, who was banished to Germany, had been unfairly treated, but no sympathy was wasted on Benedict or Silvester. Peter Damiani, the famous hermit from Ravenna and a future Cardinal-bishop, had no doubt about the matter; he praised Henry for 'snatching us from the jaws of the insatiable dragon and striking off the heads of the many-headed hydra that is the heresy of simony'. Nor did Henry hesitate to choose a new pontiff and have him elected on the spot. As might have been expected he was a German, Suidger, bishop of Bamberg. On Christmas day, immediately after his consecration as Clement II, he crowned Henry Emperor and conferred on him the dignity of Patricius of Rome. But Henry's first German nominee lasted for only ten months and his second, Bishop Poppo of Brixen (Damasus II) for only forty days. Both were swept away by malaria, the 'Roman fever' to which northerners were fatally susceptible.

Bryce, in his history of the Holy Roman Empire, remarked that it was under Henry III that the empire 'attained the meridian of its power'. 'The Roman priesthood', he wrote, 'were forced to receive German after German as their bishop at the bidding of a ruler so powerful, so severe and so pious.' That statement may suggest that the whole Roman clergy shared in the moral and intellectual unworthiness of individual Popes over the last century and a half and was equally responsible for the papal office's loss of prestige and dignity. The charge is only partly justified. It is true that reformers of the Cluniac school who inveighed against the immorality and inadequacy of the pontiffs themselves were equally shocked by the general laxity and venality of clerical Rome, by the marriage and concubinage of ordained persons and the thriving traffic in offices and church property. Such abuses, which they had to some extent checked in their own countries, were peculiarly rampant at the heart of Christendom. But there was another side to the picture. The papal government in the Lateran continued to operate, even in the most tumultuous times, with a smoothness and competence derived from 600 years of experience, and it can almost be said that the further its influence radiated from Rome the more effective it became. Directions issuing from the central chancery might be flouted by the barons of the Campagna, but they were faithfully carried out by the hierarchies of France, England and Germany. The privileges, exemptions and favours emanating from the Lateran were eagerly awaited and welcomed in countless sees and abbeys. As for the remoter regions, missionary activity in northern and eastern Europe had never been so vigorously prosecuted as in the depressing tenth century. Nor did the atmosphere of Rome, with all its corruption and unruliness, arouse any significant feelings of scepticism or discouragement among the flocks of pilgrims who came to worship at the shrines of the Apostles, to venerate relics and enjoy the colourful ceremonies of the papal year. Their piety and loyalty to the Church were minimally affected by the misbehaviour of Popes and the shortcomings of the papacy's servants.

Rome, then, was the unchanged source of faith and doctrine. The Church possessed an admirably disciplined machine and an incomparable network of communication and control. It only needed a revival of its spirit, as evoked by a series of active and devoted Popes, to accomplish its reform and assert its independence.

8

GREGORY VII
(1046–1085)

The reform movement in the church gathered strength as Europe was gradually emerging from the confusion of the Dark Ages and regaining some degree of order and prosperity. Reference has already been made to the impulse given to it by the remarkable revival of monasticism centred on the Burgundian abbey of Cluny, founded in 910 by Duke William of Aquitaine. At that moment monastic life was at a low ebb. Many monasteries had been destroyed in Viking or other raids, while the remaining houses were suffering from control by powerful laymen and from laxity by the monks themselves in the observance of the strict Benedictine rule. In order to safeguard the independence of Cluny from local pressures its founder placed it under papal protection, a measure that proved effective despite the impotence of individual Popes. From their base at Cluny successive Abbots, all of the highest quality, undertook the reform of monasteries in various parts of Euorpe. We have seen how Odo (916–42) went to Italy, where with Alberic's support he tackled four houses in Rome, the Abbey of Farfa in Latium and even Monte Cassino itself, the birthplace of western monasticism. A similar campaign, encouraged by the Saxon monarchs, spread from Lorraine to the Rhineland and beyond. Novices poured into the reformed houses and the new foundations alike and as from 950 the Cluniac Order, while not officially recognized as such by the papacy until over a century later, expanded with spectacular success. By 1100 Cluny ruled nearly 1,500 separate priories. Their priors all acknowledged its Abbot as their head and were personally appointed by him. He was the apex of a huge monastic hierarchy dedicated to the reform and glory of the Church. One mark of its success was its building programme; as a monk of Cluny, Raoul Glaber, wrote shortly after the year 1000, 'it was as if the whole earth were clothing itself anew in a white mantle of churches.'

The secular clergy lagged behind the monks. Nevertheless the Ottonian episcopacy was in general an improvement on the Carolingian. An outstanding example of the former was Bruno, the first Otto's younger brother, Archbishop of Cologne, director of the royal chancery and governor of the duchy of Lorraine. Himself a scholar in both Latin and Greek, he founded a school for the formation of churchmen who would also be competent to serve as royal administrators. The class of bishops that he represented owed scant allegiance to the pope. Nevertheless they were profoundly influenced by Clunian reformism. Such a one was another Bruno, bishop of Toul in Lorraine, whom the Emperor Henry III chose to be his third non-Italian pope. By origin a nobleman from Alsace, he had governed his bishopric for twenty-two years and won a high reputation for reforming zeal. He was just the man to infuse the necessary spirit into the church from the centre.

Arriving in Rome dressed as a pilgrim, he made it known that although he had been nominated by the Emperor he would return to his diocese unless convinced of his unanimous approval by the Roman clergy and people. Needless to say he was acclaimed on the spot. Two months after his ordination as Leo IX (1049–54) he held his first reforming synod at the Lateran, which was chiefly concerned with clerical abuses. It was on that occasion that he was warned that if he acted too strictly the Roman churches would be left without priests, and received a memorandum from Peter Damiani luridly entitled 'Gomorrhianus, or a Diversity of Crimes against Nature'. However rife these crimes and other offences may have been, the severe disciplines he imposed in order to prevent them met with surprisingly little opposition. There was no question of a revolt by the usually unamenable nobles or people, and the clergy had no alternative but to submit.

The new broom was already at work as the Pope gathered round him a group of trusted collaborators who were to form a kind of papal cabinet. Among them was Hildebrand, who after accompanying his master Gregory VI into exile had retired as a monk to Cluny. Leo ordained him sub-deacon and appointed him rector of the monastery of St Paul Without the Walls, but his primary job was to rebuild the Church's shattered finances. Humbert, a clever monk from Moyenmoutier near Toul, was made bishop of Silva Candida, one of the seven so-called 'suburbicarian' sees surrounding the city; he became the effective head of the Lateran chancery and fulfilled vital missions as legate. In both those functions he worked in close harness with Frederick of Liège, brother of the Duke of Lorraine; starting as papal librarian, he became Abbot of Monte Cassino and eventually Pope Stephen IX. Peter Damiani, Prior of Gubbio and later Cardinal-bishop of Ostia, was also an intimate adviser, especially as regards monastic reform. All these were men of the highest intellectual and administrative calibre; they were also non-Romans.

Leo did not spare himself. He was almost always on the move, spending only the Easter season at Rome where, unlike his predecessors, he was certain of his authority. He rushed from synod to synod, from Pavia and Vercelli to Reims and Mainz and back to Salerno and Siponto in southern Italy. He had to be seen as widely as possible exercising his leadership of the universal Church and enforcing a uniform reformist discipline. Everywhere he went he imposed his personality, preaching eloquently to huge crowds and officiating at solemn and striking cere-monies. On the whole he created the desired impression, but he ran occasionally into trouble. When he consecrated the new basilica of St Remigius (Remy) at Reims he staged a very special show. Placing the Saint's shrine on the altar, he called upon all the bishops and abbots present to stand up in public and declare that they had obtained their offices without recourse to simony. That was far from being always the case and many senior clerics, perhaps suspecting a trap, had therefore absented themselves from the synod. Their Gallican tradition made them anyhow wary of papal pressure and they knew that their King, often the accomplice of simony, had likewise refused to attend. Those with a guilty conscience were caught at a disadvantage; some confessed and were excommunicated or otherwise punished. In that important confrontation the Pope clearly triumphed; at Mainz, in the Em-peror's presence, he had it all his own way; only at Mantua, where he was barracked and threatened by bishops hostile to reform was he compelled temporarily to back down.

Leo came unhappily to grief when he turned his attention to the tricky field of south Italian politics. The position in what is now known as the Mezzogiorno was then complicated by the intrusion of a considerable body of adventurers from

Normandy. Originally enlisted by Apulian rebels against the government of the Byzantine province, these mercenaries from the north had settled down there and struck out on their own at the expense of both Byzantium and the small Lombard principalities south of Rome. Their leaders were the Hauteville family and Rainulf of Aversa. By 1050 they were the principal power in the southern half of the peninsula, and in extending their conquests they had ruthlessly exploited the country and appropriated the Church's patrimony. In that year Leo, on visits to the shrine of St Michael on Mt Gargano and to the monastery of Monte Cassino, had been startled by the evidence he saw of Norman excesses. He accepted the petition of the inhabitants of Benevento for the Church to assume the overlordship of their duchy, and in 1052 travelled to Germany in order to seek the Emperor's help in repelling the Normans. Owing to other commitments Henry could only spare a modest German force, but with that at his disposal and the prospect of help from the Byzantine governor Leo decided to launch a campaign. He personally led the papal army and proclaimed a holy war against the spoilers of the Church. That was unwise because the Normans, for all their destructive and acquisitive habits, were no heretics and protested their devotion to the Holy See. It was equally rash for the Pope to engage them on the battlefield before he had time to link up with the Byzantines. The result was that he was decisively beaten and taken prisoner. The Normans treated him with exaggerated respect, and once they had obtained his confirmation of their conquests and their release from excommunication, escorted him back to the Lateran. A few months later he died exhausted.

The year of Leo's death was also that of the final schism between the eastern and western Churches. The Pope himself was a spectator rather than an actor in the crisis leading up to that event. Most of the time he was a captive of the Normans; he was a sick and tired man and the chief part on the Latin side was consequently played by the Lombard Cardinal Humbert. The latter's opponent on the Greek side was the Patriarch, Michael Cerularius. That the quarrel should have come to a head in so acute a form was largely due to the clash between these two irreconcilable personalities.

Political and doctrinal factors were of course also involved. Cerularius, a stiff bureaucrat who had become a churchman only in later life, was deeply worried by the progress of the Normans. Whether or not they fell out with the Pope they were Latins in religion; if they succeeded in dominating southern Italy they were sure to put an end to the ecclesiastical supremacy of Constantinople in that region. Nor would the western reform movement, which the Pope had been busily promoting through his southern synods, permit the survival of Greek rites and usages. The Patriarch even distrusted the anti-Norman military alliance which the local Byzantine commander, who happened to be a Lombard and a Catholic, had formed with the Pope. It was only too likely, he thought, that all these western elements would soon unite against the Byzantine State and the Greek Church. His reaction was both clumsy and provocative. Besides closing the Latin churches in Constantinople, he arranged for the Greek Archbishop of Ochrida in Macedonia to address a letter to the patriarchal representative in Italy, for transmission to the Pope, violently attacking Latin customs such as fasting on Saturdays and the use of unleavened bread for the Sacrament.

If Leo had not responded to this immoderate missive he might have avoided both controversy and schism. In the event, however, it sparked off a correspondence replete with misunderstandings and culminating in angry recrimination. Unfortunately Humbert loathed the Greeks as much as Cerularius hated the Latins. The

The Second Council of Nicaea, convened in 787 by the Empress Irene, at which
iconoclasm was rejected: sacred images should be venerated, though not worshipped

Leo III, who laid the basis of the Holy Roman
Empire when he crowned Charlemagne in 800

Theodore I, a Greek pope
who reigned from 642 to 649

LEO · III · PAPA · ROMANVS

SCS
PE
·T·R
VS

✠ S C̄SSIMVS
DNE
LO
PP

DN CARVLO REGI

BEATE PETRE DONA

VITA LEONI PPÆ BTCTO

RĪA CARVLO RFGI DONA

From Leo III's triclinium, a mosaic now in the Lateran, showing Saint Peter *seated* with *left* Leo and *right* Charlemagne

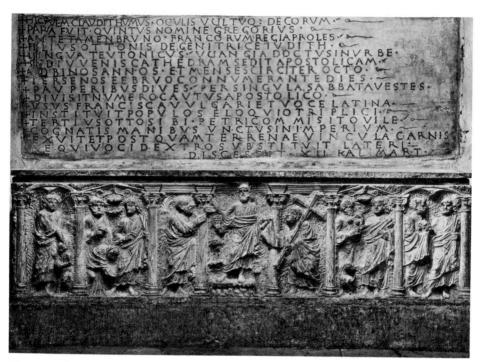

The sarcophagus of Pope Gregory V in the crypt of the Vatican

The sarcophagus of Otto II, only Roman Emperor to be buried in St Peter's

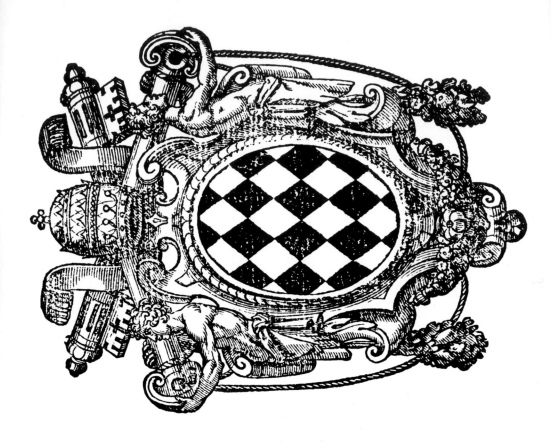

Damasus II, whose brief reign lasted only a few weeks in 1048

tone of the Latin letters that he composed for the Pope was needlessly offensive and his translations of the Patriarch's Greek letters were inaccurate. On the other hand Cerularius outraged Leo by calling him 'Brother' instead of the protocolar 'Father' and above all by terming himself 'oecumenical'. So far as the Pope was concerned, the concept of universality belonged to Rome alone. These echoes of ancient disputes created a thoroughly bad atmosphere even before the ailing Leo decided to send legates to thrash the matter out at Constantinople. For that duty he nominated Humbert, Frederick of Liège, and the Archbishop of the Italo-Greek diocese of Amalfi. Humbert, for all his brilliance in law and administration, was no diplomatist; a fiery soul, he had no interest in compromise and little charity of spirit. Among the Greeks the only compromiser was the Emperor, Constantine IX, and he knew well that popular sentiment in his capital favoured the Patriarch's extremism. After the legates arrived in the month of the Pope's death relations went from bad to worse. Humbert, entirely losing his sense of balance, unnecessarily raised the dormant issue of the *Filioque* and finally wrecked all chances of concord by mounting in St Sophia the same sort of demonstration that the Pope had found so effective at Reims. He marched into the church and slapped on the altar a Bull of excommunication against the Patriarch and other eminent Greeks. Horrified, the Emperor tried to persuade the legates, who had precipitately left Constantinople, to return and make it up, but they refused and continued on their journey. Even then the fence could have been mended if there had been a wise pope at Rome; it happened that there was no pope there at all and the fence still remains unrepaired.

The years 1055–72 cover five pontificates, or six if an anti-pope is included. They were vital for the internal development of the papacy and at the same time prepared the way for the progressive assertion of its authority in the affairs of western Europe. Above all it began to shake off the excessive, if initially beneficial, influence exercised over it by imperial Germany during the reign of Henry III. While four of the pontiffs were in themselves notable figures, papal policy became almost exclusively the province of Hildebrand, archdeacon of Rome as from 1059. He guided the Church through many moments of turbulence and danger.

Victor II (1055–7) was Henry's last direct nominee. As Bishop Gebhard of Eichstatt he had served as imperial chancellor and as pope he continued to act as the Emperor's closest adviser. Henry attended a grand synod that he held at Florence on his accession and in the next year summoned him for consultation to his court at Goslar. The link between empire and papacy seemed unbreakable. Victor was still at Gosler when Henry died that autumn, and he himself succumbed to the dreaded Italian fever in the following summer. Their demise overturned the existing system. To succeed Victor the inner circle at Rome, the leading members of which were Hildebrand and Humbert, quickly pushed through the election of their colleague Cardinal Frederick of Lorraine. The opportunity was too good to miss; the new German King, Henry IV, was a small boy and it was considered sufficient to send Hildebrand to announce the result of the election to his mother, the regent. This was the first and crucial step in the papacy's emancipation.

Most unfortunately Cardinal Frederick (Stephen XX) lasted for only eight months. He died while visiting his brother, the Margrave of Tuscany, at Florence and before Hilderbrand had returned from Germany. In the ensuing vacuum the Roman magnates made what proved to be their final bid to recover their grip on the papacy. Led by Count Gregory of Tusculum, brother of Benedict IX, they suddenly seized the city and proclaimed the election of John, bishop of Velletri. This person, who reigned throughout 1058 as Benedict X, was a perfectly respectable cleric, and Leo IX had thought him suitable enough to create him a Cardinal. However Peter Damiani, who with other friends of Hildebrand was forced to leave Rome in a hurry, denounced him as 'dull, indolent and lacking in intelligence'. Obviously neither he nor his Tusculan sponsors could be tolerated by the reformers. Gathering at Florence under the protection of the Margrave of Tuscany, they decided that the bishop of that city, the Burgundian Gerhard, would make the best Pope, and with the added support of the Empress-regent of Germany the Cardinals duly declared him elected. As the Roman clergy and people had not been consulted, the election was technically invalid, but not more so than that carried out through the Tusculan coup.

Once elected on 6 December, Gerhard took the appropriate name of Nicholas II (1058–61). After holding a synod for the deposition of his rival, he was installed in the Lateran without much difficulty. The ground had been already well prepared by Hildebrand's agents with help of funds provided lavishly by a mysterious figure from the Trastevere. This was Leo, the son of a converted Jew named Benedict, formerly Baruch. It is intriguing that Hildebrand, the son of a poor Tuscan carpenter of Lombard descent, should have formed connexions in the ghetto, the history of which stretches as far back as the early Roman empire; it is suggested that he may have been related to Leo on his mother's side, and we may also remember his former attachment to Gregory VI, who is supposed to have been descended from the Jewish Pierleoni. However that may be his measures were effective; the Tusculans were brushed aside and Benedict fled from the city.

The highlight of Nicholas's short but fruitful pontificate was the electoral decree adopted by his Lateran synod of 1059. The need for regularizing the procedure in papal elections was only too urgent, for the theory of the free choice of a pope by clergy and people was a fiction that had long become ridiculous. It was also clear that if the Church was to regain its independence and to retain the allegiance of Christians no laymen, whether they were local magnates or foreign rulers, should be allowed to dictate the appointment of its Head. The decision should lie purely and simply with the Church itself. The decree, mainly the work of Cardinal Humbert, specified that the initial choice of candidates for the papal chair should be made by the seven original Cardinal-bishops (Ostia, Porto, Albano, Silva Candida, Palestrina, Sabina and Tusculum). The final selection from among them would be entrusted to the whole body of Cardinals, the Cardinal-bishops (7), the Cardinal-priests (28) and the Cardinal-deacons (18), plus those clerics outside those categories who had been specially created Cardinals by papal nomination. When the whole assembly had made up its mind, the presentation of the selected candidate for approval by clergy and people in general would be purely a matter of form. So would its approval by the German King and his successors, to whom proper honour and respect were due, but who held no right of veto. It was further intended that the Cardinals, acting as a college or, as Peter Damiani termed it, the Pope's Senate, should not only conduct elections but serve corporately as the government of the Church, taking charge through its individual members of the various branches of the long existent Lateran officialdom. Together they would form what is still known as the Curia. In addition, the Lateran synod drew up, and issued to the western Church, a series of stringent canons, or ecclesiastical rules, the chief of which—soon to have resounding implications—was that no ordained person might accept an office, free or for money, from the hands of a layman.

Nicholas had a strong mind of his own but luckily saw eye to eye with his two principal advisers, Hildebrand and Humbert. A good example of their collaboration was their handling of the Norman problem. The Norman princes, Richard of Capua and Robert Guiscard, had grown even more powerful since their humiliation of Leo IX and Nicholas was convinced that it would now be wise to drop the quarrel and enlist them as allies. For that purpose he visited Guiscard at his Apulian capital, Melfi, shortly after the issue of the electoral decree, and negotiated a treaty that satisfied the interests of both sides. What was original about it was that the Norman princes thereby agreed not only to protect the papacy against its enemies, and in particular to help the Cardinals to carry out future elections, but also to acknowledge the Pope as their feudal overlord. As his vassals, Richard was enfeoffed with Capua and Guiscard with the former Byzantine provinces of Apulia and Calabria which the Normans had conquered. Guiscard also received Sicily, which was yet unconquered from the Saracens. It was a bold stroke of policy, for it committed the Normans to defend the Pope against both dissident Romans and, by implication at least, imperial German pressure. It was also a challenge to the empire's current claim to treat all Italian territories as its fiefs. Lastly, in the religious context, it permanently removed southern Italy from the control of the Byzantine patriarchate. As for the Normans, the advantage they gained from the arrangement was enormous; it converted them from a band of rapacious adventurers into the shield, and on occasion the sword, of St Peter. They could be reasonably sure that any further enterprise in which they might engage could be launched under the papal banner. Before long they were to embark on the recovery of Sicily, which though not perhaps ranking as a Crusade, was a significant prelude to the crusading era.

The electoral decree and the Norman treaty were of course both regarded by the German court as infringements of imperial rights. But although the 'union of perfect charity', which Peter Damiani had once advocated as the right relationship between papacy and empire, had failed to become a reality, the breach between the two powers was slow to open. It needed a third cause of tension to produce the confrontation that occurred between them in the next pontificate. This was the papacy's interference in the affairs of the Lombard cities. Milan in particular, controlled by nobles and prelates, was like a stronghold of imperial authority and the centre of obstinate resistance to the reforming activity of Rome; its higher clergy were notorious for the simony, moral laxity and all the short-comings combated by the followers of Leo IX. On the other hand reform was enthusiastically welcomed by the rising merchant and artisan classes opposed to the ruling oligarchy and organized in a political movement known as the 'Patarini' (the word means dealers in old junk). The Pope hurried to the latter's support; high-level legates, including Hildebrand and Peter Damiani, were despatched to put pressure on the Archbishop and for a time reduced him to obedience. But the German court was alarmed and German bishops were siding with the Lombard hierarchy. When Nicholas died suddenly in 1061 a crisis was building up between the Roman reformers and their opponents in Italy and beyond.

Spurred on by Hildebrand, the Cardinals lost no time in electing, under the new procedure, a man who had been an ardent reformer and supporter of the Patarini, Bishop Anselm of Lucca. He also owed his bishopric to Henry III, had often served as legate in Germany and was consequently regarded as having a foot in both camps. He was duly enthroned as Alexander II (1061–72). However the imperialists and anti-reformers, both Germans and Lombards, would have none of him, and even at Rome opposition from the nobility was only quelled by Norman troops. A council, hastily assembled at Basle in the presence of the boy-King Henry IV and presided over by his chancellors for Germany and Italy, proclaimed Cadalus, bishop of Parma, as Honorius II, thus creating a serious schism in the Church. It set a baneful precedent for future years. There had indeed been anti-popes in the past, but in the ensuing century they were to become far too numerous.

Neither Pope nor anti-Pope was of the highest calibre, but Alexander was the more sensible and reputable of the two. He was not easily discouraged and he had Hildebrand at his elbow. The early years of his pontificate were confused if not chaotic; until 1064 it was touch and go as to whether he would win. The battle, which was waged on all fronts, military, political and ecclesiastical, convulsed all central Italy. There was much marching and counter-marching, but such fighting as took place was indecisive, because neither the German court, which favoured Cadalus in a somewhat lukewarm fashion, nor the Normans who were Alexander's declared protectors, cared to commit themselves to a serious struggle. When Cadalus advanced on Rome for the first time it was with Lombard help alone. After defeating local troops whom Hildebrand had scraped together he managed to occupy the Leonine quarter, while Alexander maintained himself in the city proper. The deadlock was resolved by Duke Godfrey of Lorraine, the husband of the Margravine of Tuscany, who then appeared before Rome with a large force. Having first persuaded the rival Popes to retire to their former dioceses, he suggested that the new Regent of Germany, the Archbishop of Cologne, should appoint an arbitrator to decide between their claims. The result was that in 1062 the German court reversed its attitude and pronounced that Alexander had been legitimately elected.

Cadalus, however, refused to give in. His adherents still held the Leonina and he was also supported by most of the nobility of Rome and the Campagna. In 1063 he again attacked Rome. For a time Alexander and Hildebrand were hard pressed, but they resisted with some Norman help and a second stalemate ensued, punctuated by bloody skirmishes and heated exchanges of excommunications. Cadalus was entrenched in Sant' Angelo facing Alexander on the other side of the Tiber in the Lateran. With further assistance from Duke Godfrey and the Normans, Alexander gradually gained the upper hand and the discomfited Cadalus again retreated to Parma. The next step was taken by Peter Damiani, who was at the time acting as Alexander's legate in France. From there he got into touch with the Regent in Germany and arranged that the papal dispute should be settled once and for all by a synod of German and Italian bishops meeting at Mantua, before which both contenders would be invited to appear. In the event Cadalus declined to attend; Alexander took the chair and the synod decided in his favour. Cadalus was deposed from the papacy, though not from his bishopric, and Alexander, after narrowly escaping an attempt to assassinate him, re-entered the Lateran in triumph.

After these years of uncertainty the rest of Alexander's pontificate was spent, with Hildebrand as the moving spirit, in untiring efforts to strengthen the papacy's influence in Europe. Its most striking success was achieved at Milan, where the Pope's support enabled Erlembald, the leader of the popular party, to unseat the anti-reformist Archbishop Guido. As a symbol of his attachment to the Holy See Erlembald was presented with a papal banner, white with a red cross. A second was awarded to William of Normandy on his invasion of England and a third to another Norman, Roger the brother of Robert Guiscard, for his venture in Sicily. He was already a vassal of the Holy See, and the Curia was soon to advance a similar claim in respect of England. Meanwhile the King of Aragon, also involved in war against the Moslems, visited Rome and voluntarily declared himself a vassal of St Peter. A final assertion of authority, which was to have dubious consequences, was that which prevented the young Henry IV from divorcing his wife. Again acting as legate, Peter Damiani warned the King that if he persisted the Pope would refuse to crown him Emperor.

Twenty-five years after Henry III had rescued the Holy See from apparent disintegration, it had reformed itself and emerged as the most potent moral and political force in Europe. Instead of representing a moribund and discredited tradition, it had once more become a source of inspiration and leadership. But Hildebrand's circle was shrinking fast. Of the paladins of reform, Humbert died in 1061 and Peter Damiani in 1072, shortly after he had attended the Pope's consecration, amid splendid ceremonial, of the new abbey church at Monte Cassino. When Alexander himself disappeared from the scene a year later, there was no question that anyone but Hildebrand might succeed him.

Strangely enough his election failed to conform with the procedure laid down in 1059. According to contemporary narratives he was caught up on a sudden tide of popular enthusiasm and swept, protesting his unworthiness, into the church of St Peter in Vincoli, where he was declared elected by acclamation and immediately enthroned by the assembled Cardinals. Although the event was no doubt pre-arranged, it certainly met the wishes of clergy and people. He took the name of Gregory in memory of the first and greatest of the line, but he may also have borne in mind Gregory VI, the Pope whom he had not deserted in adversity.

Hildebrand was born about 1020. As we have seen his origins are obscure, and his undoubted connexions with the Jews of the Trastevere equally enigmatic. His father may have been a Tuscan but his own upbringing was thoroughly Roman. As a young Benedictine in the monastery of Santa Maria on the Aventine he was less conspicuous for learning than for steadfastness of character, devotion to principle and practical intelligence. His monastic life ended in 1049 when Leo IX, recognizing his ability, brought him back to Rome from Cluny and ordained him sub-deacon. Since that time he had been absorbed first in the administration of the Church and more recently as its chief policy-maker and power behind the throne. Although Alexander's pontificate had enormously enhanced papal prestige, the work of reform, as Hildebrand saw it, remained incomplete. Its pace must not be allowed to slacken; above all it would be vital to establish the absolute and transcendental nature of papal authority and of the prerogatives that stemmed from it. If his programme entailed a head-on collision with the German conception of empire and monarchical privilege, he was prepared for it.

The clash did not occur immediately. The first year of Gregory VII's pontificate was anyhow largely occupied by a grandiose but abortive project for a crusade in the east, the double aim of which would be the repulse of the Turks, who had broken into the heartland of the Byzantine empire in Asia Minor, and the reunion of the Churches under papal supremacy. But at his first synod on 1074 he alarmed the German bishops by his uncompromising denunciation of simony and clerical marriage, which they knew was aimed principally at them, and by his proposal that the enforcement of his reform decrees in Germany should be entrusted to Cardinal-legates from Rome. When they proved recalcitrant he attacked them again at his lenten synod in 1075, threatening to deprive offenders of their sees or offices and to forbid the faithful to attend their Masses. What was of greater significance, he issued his first decree prohibiting lay investiture; it declared roundly that in future no cleric, high or low, was to accept an ecclesiastical office from any layman, however exalted.

It is doubtful whether people thought at the time that the prohibition would be enforceable against the German King or any other powerful prince, or whether the Pope would be so bold as to try to enforce it. Gregory, however, was in dead earnest. During or immediately after the synod he set out, in 27 sentences or brief statements of principle, the papal claims to primacy in relation to secular rulers. This list of prerogatives, collectively termed the *Dictatus Papae*, constituted the theoretical and legal justification of the policy Gregory intended to pursue to its logical end. To cite some of its claims, the Roman Church had never erred and would never err; the Bishop of Rome has the sole right to be called 'universal'; he is the sole judge of all matters, both spiritual and secular, in the Christian world that he considers to be 'major causes'; he himself may be judged by no one; he has the power to depose emperors, kings and their servants; he alone can depose bishops; no decrees of a synod are valid without his approval; he can release subjects from allegiance to their sovereign. Although lay investitures are not explicitly mentioned, they are obviously incompatible with the sweeping powers claimed.

The ideology underlying the papal claim to supreme and universal jurisdiction had taken centuries to mature, and its formulation had been less the work of individual Popes than that of industrious clerks in the papal chancery. It was they who had fabricated the 'Donation of Constantine' at short notice for the visit of Stephen II to the court of King Pippin. So long as Byzantine ascendancy lasted in Italy it would hardly have been possible for the Holy See to assert papal supremacy as opposed to merely ecclesiastical primacy. But in the mid-eighth century it had shaken itself free from Byzantium and was looking for a protector who might more readily fall in with its theoretical claims in return for papal support for his rise to hegemony in Europe. As it happened Pippin and Charles were wary of papal sponsorship. The latter never intended to be labelled 'Roman Emperor'; nor did he wish to appear in any way indebted to the Pope or dependent on him for the exercise of his imperial authority. In simple terms Charles's position was that the Pope's function was to give spiritual sanction to his own absolute government over church and state within the confines of his empire. The papal idea of theocracy, on the other hand, was that the Emperor was required to act as the secular arm of the papal monarchy, the executor of St Peter's decisions. Subsequent Carolingians were less careful than Charles. They allowed their coronation ceremonies to be conducted in so symbolic a fashion as to leave no doubt that the Frankish monarch was being created a Roman Emperor by virtue of being chosen and appointed to rule by the Roman Pope. Besides crowning and anointing him, the Pope girded him with a sword, the symbol of delegated authority in worldly affairs, and expected him, as a gesture of respect, to lead his horse by the bridle.

In the mid-ninth century the papal thesis was strengthened and advertised by the False Decretals. As already mentioned, these were collections of partly genuine but mostly forged decrees, both papal and imperial, and decisions and synods dating back to pre-Constantinian times. The most important of them, the Pseudo-Isidore, was attributed to the seventh-century Bishop of Seville and commanded wide but entirely uncritical respect. Compiled by Frankish clerics and monks, their purpose and effect was nevertheless to exalt the papacy at the expense of the later Carolingians. They entirely suited the book of the theorists in the papal chancery, and Pope Nicholas I and Hadrian II made full use of them, insisting in a series of unequivocal declarations on the subordination of all royal and imperial power to the authority of the pope. But the collapse of Carolingian power later in the century, together with the accompanying decline in the quality of the papacy, postponed a series of confrontations of papal and imperial personalities. And when Otto I, the saviour and master of Europe, had been crowned at Rome he was not disposed to tolerate papal assumptions of superiority. If he and his successors were Emperor by the grace of God, the Popes of the Ottonian period frankly owed their election and confirmation in their office to imperial favour. Finally, under Henry III, they were simply being nominated by the Emperor. This was not a humiliation to which a Church in the full swing of self-reform was prepared to submit indefinitely. It was already armed with an ideology elaborated with dogged consistency and single-mindedness from one century to another. It was staffed with keen reformist figures and only required a leader of exceptional stature who, like Gregory, was ready to offer or accept a challenge. What was uncertain was the reaction of the young King Henry IV to claims calculated to subvert his authority over Germany and Italy.

Henry's reaction was not immediate, as he was engaged in a war with rebellious Saxony, but he continued to appoint his own nominees to high ecclesiastical offices. These included the key archbishopric of Milan, the possession of which had been for some years strenuously disputed between the royal and papal candidates. In view of his evident determination to retain the right of investiture, Gregory decided to bring matters to a head. In December 1075 he sent the King the sternest possible message of admonishment, summoning him to conform under pain of excommunication, deposition or even the fate of Saul. The confrontation had now become critical.

In the same month as he launched his ultimatum the Pope was kidnapped. The reasons for this extraordinary occurrence are not clear, but it certainly demonstrated that no mediaeval pontiff, however popular at the moment, was immune from local violence. While he was celebrating midnight Mass in Santa Maria Maggiore on Christmas Eve armed men rushed into the church and snatched him from the altar. They were led by Cencius, a nobleman whom he had already had punished for unruly behaviour. Either he was simply nourishing a personal grudge, or he represented an element in the city still opposed to reform and in touch with the German court. Slightly wounded, Gregory was held prisoner in a fortified tower and a large ransom in the form of church property was demanded from him. But he resisted all threats with characteristic firmness and within a few hours the tower was besieged by infuriated crowds seeking his release. This was speedily obtained; moreover he kept his promise that his captor would come to no harm. When the incident was over he calmly resumed his Mass at the point where it had been broken off.

After this trying interlude Gregory was faced by Henry's counterblast to his letter. Disturbed, as he might well be, by the Pope's move to undermine the whole concept of Christian kingship, he called a council of German princes and bishops at Worms in order to consider his riposte. Unwisely influenced by Hugh Candidus, a Cardinal whose services Gregory had often used but with whom he had later quarrelled for personal reasons, the council decided to attack the Pope not on basic issues but on the ground that he had been uncanonically elected and that his subsequent actions had therefore been illegal. It summoned the 'false monk Hildebrand' to resign, and couched the demand in downright if not injurious terms. This was a mistake, for when the communication reached the Pope's Lenten synod in 1076, the latter retaliated promptly by 'depriving King Henry, for his rebellion against the Church, of the government of the whole kingdom of Germany and Italy', and by 'releasing all Christian men from the allegiance they had sworn or might swear to him'. The King was also 'bound in the bonds of anathema', while the bishops who had subscribed to the summons from Worms were excommunicated or suspended unless they retracted.

The papal thunderbolt had a shattering effect. In the past Emperors had deposed unsatisfactory popes, but no pope in the exercise of his spiritual authority had even attempted to remove a German monarch. At Easter Henry indeed pronounced the Pope deposed, but this empty gesture failed to prevent a strong revulsion in Gregory's favour. Many bishops took fright and the princes exploited Henry's quarrel with him for their own political purposes. After a meeting with papal legates they went so far as to threaten their own King with dethronement. He had no choice but to capitulate; he declared himself willing to annul the decisions of Worms and to obey the Holy See. Nevertheless they decided to proceed to the election of a new king unless Henry were freed from his excommunication by February 1077. Meanwhile they invited the Pope to meet them at Augsburg for the Feast of Candlemas.

Henry was sufficiently alarmed by this development to send an envoy to Rome in order to seek release from the ban. However, he failed to obtain it because he called on the Pope to reciprocate by defending himself against accusations of arbitrary behaviour. Thereupon Gregory resolved to accept the invitation to Augsburg; he set out for his first stopping-place, Mantua, where he expected to find an escort from the princes.

At that point Henry realized that unless he acted very quickly he was almost sure to lose his throne. His only hope was to intercept the Pope before he could join the princes and make an unequivocal submission. That was not an easy proposition in an exceptionally harsh winter and when the passes leading more directly from Germany to Italy were blocked by his opponents. He was therefore obliged to go round by Burgundy and the Mont Cenis, which he crossed with a small retinue in appalling conditions. On January 25 he caught up with the Pope at Canossa, a castle in the Apennines belonging to the Countess Matilda of Tuscany, the papacy's most fervent supporter. Fortunately for the King, Gregory had returned there from Mantua when he found that his escort had not arrived.

The stage was thus set for the famous scene of royal humiliation that has so often been inaccurately described. In fact there was no question of self-abasement on Henry's part. He was on record as willing to submit and was hardly in danger of losing more prestige than he had forfeited already. He did not stand, as the romantically but adversely minded chronicler pretended, bare-footed in the snow for three successive days as a suppliant before the castle gates. As a gesture he wore a penitential dress, but he was happy to have gained the opportunity of foiling his enemies' intentions during three days' negotiations with the pontiff. Nor was Gregory disinclined for negotiation; at the risk of ditching his allies of the moment, he preferred in the last resort to deal directly with a German King than through a host of unsteady German princes and churchmen. In view of Henry's public repentance he could hardly refuse to readmit him to communion, and although he did not explicitly withdraw his sentence of deposition, he continued to address him, and to treat him in practice, as King. The future was so uncertain that his best tactic was to gain time. He did not therefore intervene when the German princes elected Rudolf of Sabia, Henry's brother-in-law, as anti-King. For the next three years he remained neutral between them as they contended for supremacy, hoping that he might be invited to adjudicate between them.

The question of lay investiture was not thrashed out at Canossa, but Gregory's conviction that Henry would never yield on that issue brought him down eventually on Rudolf's side. At his Lenten synod of 1080 he renewed Henry's excommunication and deposition. But he had chosen the wrong moment; Henry's fortunes in Germany were improving and there was no longer any need for him to temporize. Having for the second time declared the Pope deposed, he assembled at Brixen in the Tyrol a synod of German and Italian bishops which obediently elected Wibert, Archbishop of Ravenna, anti-Pope as Clement III. In doing so it opened a new schism which was to last for 20 years.

Wibert was a shrewd choice. He was an experienced cleric who excelled as both politician and intellectual. Like Cadalus he was a native of Parma and had supported his compatriot against Alexander II. As imperial chancellor of Italy and archbishop he became leader and spokesman of the conservative churchmen who opposed the Hildebrandine reforms and defended the German King's rights. For the time being he remained quietly at Ravenna, and an attempt by Gregory's ally the Countess Matilda to evict him by force was foiled by the King's Lombard partisans. Meanwhile, with Rudolf killed in battle, Henry felt strong enough to move against Rome.

In the spring of 1081 and again a year later he marched up to the city and tried unsuccessfully to persuade the Romans to accept Clement instead of Gregory. However they were not so willing; nor were the King's forces powerful enough to storm the Aurelian walls. Persevering in 1083, he took the Leonine city but got no further. Negotiations for having a synod to resolve his differences with the Pope were nullified because he prevented bishops known to be unfavourable to his cause from entering Rome. The long duel was therefore prolonged for yet another year, by which time Roman support for Gregory was weakening. He had always had enemies among the nobles and the people were sick of war. It had also become clear that the Pope could expect no effective help from Robert Guiscard, his official protector, locked as the latter was in conflict with the Byzantine Emperor Alexios Comnenos, whose Balkan provinces he had invaded. As for Alexios, he had enlisted the aid of Venice, already a rising maritime power, and of King Henry whom he could count on for hostility against the Normans.

By reason of that alliance Henry was campaigning in Apulia early in 1084. While so engaged he received a message urgently recalling him to Rome. He was assured that besides nobles and populace thirteen Cardinals were on his side and that he would encounter no resistance. He immediately turned back and entered the city unopposed just before Palm Sunday. His first act was to have Wibert re-elected and enthroned. Then, on Easter Sunday, he and his wife were crowned by the anti-Pope.

But while these ceremonies were proceeding in St Peter's and the Lateran, Gregory was still holding out in Sant' Angelo. His supporters were also defending themselves on the Capitol and in the Septizonium, the ruinous but immensely solid palace of Septimus Severus on the Palatine. This great monument of imperial Rome was battered down by Henry's siege engines, but as usual Sant' Angelo proved inexpugnable. It was then learned that Robert Guiscard, hitherto so remiss in coming to Gregory's aid, was at last approaching with an army considerably outnumbering the Emperor's. There was nothing the latter could do but retire, taking his Pope and the dissident Cardinals with him, and in the last week of May the Normans marched in.

Gregory was liberated and all might have been well if uncontrollable fighting had not broken out between his liberators and the Romans. In later days, as the Byzantine Greeks and others were to discover, the Southern Normans became specialists in the sack of cities, but their operations were usually carried out with cold and businesslike efficiency. In view of the sanctity of Rome it may be doubted whether Guiscard intended to plunder it systematically. What happened was that his troops got out of hand. Indeed they can hardly have been expected to abstain from looting. The city's accumulated riches were very tempting; the churches in particular were vast storehouses of wealth, hardly diminished by the tumults that disturbed the papacy. Moreover, apart from the disciplined Norman knights, Guiscard's army was largely composed of wild Calabrian mountaineers and Saracens from Sicily whose atrocities excited reprisals from the infuriated towns-people. Over and above the robbery and massacre the city was swept by devastating fires. Whole quarters of ramshackle houses crowded among the remains of antiquity were consumed and remained desolate; twelfth-century travellers were horrified by the persistent evidence of destruction. The districts around the Lateran and the Coliseum seem to have been particularly affected.

For the Pope, watching impotently from Sant' Angelo, this fortuitous and un-necessary disaster must have seemed more grievous than Henry's occupation of Rome and the challenge to his own position from Clement III. What ended in calamity might so easily have turned out a triumph. As it was, Rome was clearly untenable, not only because the Lateran was damaged but because the Romans held the Pope responsible for their plight. He had never been universally popular there, and his kidnapping in 1075 coincided with the period when his international prestige was at its highest. After the sack he left the city in company with Guiscard and was given shelter by Desiderius, the sage Abbot of Monte Cassino who made it his business not to fall out with any of the contemporary dynasts. Under his protection Gregory settled at Salerno where he died, a spent force, a year later. His last words are said to have been 'I have loved justice and hated iniquity; that is why I am dying in exile.'

His final tragic disappointment may well have obscured for him how far he had gone towards achieving his aims, the centralization of authority in the Church, its purification from abuses and its liberation from control by laymen. Not all his battles were won, but more were won than lost. He left behind him the impression of a phenomenal personality, equally capable of attracting or repelling; Peter Damiani summed him up neatly as a 'holy Satan'. He was distinguished not by intellect but by his exceptional steadfastness of purpose, by intense energy and a burning confidence in his mission as Vicar of Christ. His enemies condemned him for pride and ruthlessness, while unable to find fault in his piety and the monastic simplicity of his personal life. He was without doubt the greatest Pope since Gregory I, and the obstacles he had to overcome were just as formidable as those confronting his namesake five centuries earlier.

PART THREE

MEDIAEVAL APOGEE

9

CRUSADES AND INVESTITURES
(1085–1154)

Gregory's departure left Rome a fire-scarred no-man's-land in which neither the survivors of the reform party nor the adherents of the anti-Pope could gain the upper hand. Each faction had its own strongholds and conducted a desultory guerrilla war with its opponents. While there was no question of the reformist Cardinals deserting to Clement, they had difficulty in finding a successor to Gregory; for material chaos and political uncertainty had deprived the pontificate of much of its attraction. A whole year passed while they tried to persuade Abbot Desiderius to accept his candidature. This descendant of the Lombard dukes of Benevento was perfectly happy at Monte Cassino, which he had much embellished and turned into a centre of cultural, economic and social activity where political opponents could come together on neutral ground. He had no desire to exchange its amenities for the perils of the papacy and it was with the utmost reluctance that he consented to be elevated as Victor III. Only four days after his election grave disorders in the city obliged him to leave the field to his rival. On returning to his abbey he hopefully discarded the papal insignia.

But his supporters would not let him enjoy his library and good company at Monte Cassino. In May 1087, after Norman soldiers had evicted Clement from the Leonine city, he was escorted back and consecrated in St Peter's. Eight days later he had had enough; again he bolted and had to be restored with the aid of the Countess Matilda. However he still held only the Leonina, Sant' Angelo and the Trastevere, while Clement ruled opposite him from the Pantheon. Victor was no fighter, and rightly judging his position to be undignified and dangerous he retired to his monastery for the third and last time and died there in September.

So the reformers had to think again. Still united in opposition to the anti-Pope, they assembled at Terracina and chose a pontiff utterly unlike the elderly and ailing abbot. This time it was a Frenchman, Odo of Châtillon-sur-Marne, a former Prior of Cluny whom Gregory had appointed Cardinal-bishop of Ostia and employed as legate in Germany where Henry IV had kept him in prison for some time. On the day after his elevation he sent a circular to all the bishops of that country announcing his intention of following faithfully in Gregory's footsteps. Fortunately he was a man of wide views, an experienced organizer and a diplomat of uncommon ability. Barred for most of his pontificate from the Roman headquarters of the Curia, always on the move and working in difficult conditions, Urban II (1088–99) adapted himself to circumstances with such skill that he completely regained the leadership in Europe which Gregory had disputed with the Emperor. Without being a passionate and combative character, he knew exactly where and when to seize the initiative.

In the first place he was not at all mesmerized by Rome. Very wisely he absented himself from the city, refrained from useless skirmishing with Wibert and allowed him or his followers to maintain themselves there, however precariously, for the whole of his reign. What mattered to him was the papacy's primacy in Christendom as a whole. So far as Italy was concerned, he contented himself with strengthening the papacy's existing alliances with the Normans and Matilda of Tuscany. He formed a close understanding with the Great Count Roger, Guiscard's youngest brother and the conqueror of Sicily, whom he rewarded with far-reaching privileges in connexion with the new Church established in the island. As for Matilda, now a widow of 42, he found her a martial husband, twenty years younger than herself, in the shape of Welf, a son of the Duke of Bavaria, also called Welf and a life-long enemy of Henry IV. The marriage was arranged, as a chronicler remarked, 'not so much to prevent incontinence as for the sake of obedience to the Roman pontiff'. The result was that the Emperor became bogged down in unprofitable campaigns in northern Italy. At first it looked as if he would prevail; Matilda was hard pressed and was losing her fortresses one by one. Then came a reversal of fortune. Suddenly Henry's heir Conrad, his viceroy in Italy, defected to Matilda and the Lombard cities followed suit. By 1095 the Emperor was helpless and immobilized, but for the Pope that year was to be filled with intense and fruitful activity.

While holding Henry and the anti-Pope at bay Urban had been striving busily but quietly to assert his influence in the other Kingdoms of western Europe. He was particularly successful in Spain, where the process of reconquest from the Moslems was gathering pace. At Toledo, captured from the Moors in 1085, he founded a new archbishopric, the holder of which he designated Primate of Spain, and a second was established at Tarragona. All Spain was bonded closely to the Holy See, the King of Aragon and the Count of Barcelona declaring themselves its vassals and faithful adherents of Urban. The situation in France, however, was not so easy and in England it was exceedingly difficult. In both countries the investitures problem was potentially as explosive as in Germany, but Urban knew how to handle his own compatriots and in dealing with the spiky and anti-clerical William Rufus he drew to the full on his reserve of tact and patience. His method was to apply Gregory's principles firmly but with discretion and above all to shun dramatic confrontations. In the long term he was working towards a solution by which, to put it as simply as possible, the Pope would invest a bishop with the symbols of his purely religious functions while the King would be free to confer on him those of his non-ecclesiastical duties and rights—judicial, economic and military—that a high cleric was expected to exercise in mediaeval society. That aim was perhaps easier to achieve in France when the Pope was French and the French king was as weak as he was in the eleventh century. In England the conflict that centred around the appointment of Anselm as Archbishop of Canterbury outlasted both Urban and William II. The Pope did his best to defuse it, but his task was complicated by Anselm's high-minded intransigence and by the traditional tolerance by the English episcopate of the practice of royal investiture.

What Urban chiefly gained by his diplomacy in the western kingdoms was their firm acknowledgement of his legitimacy as opposed to Clement's and of the validity of Gregorian reform. But as he shifted his residence from one place to another in Norman territory he was also making overtures to Byzantium. He had viewed Guiscard's attacks on the eastern empire without enthusiasm and saw no reason for quarrelling with it on either political or religious grounds. His first move was to release the Emperor Alexios from the excommunication pronounced against him by Gregory VII. It was favourably received and in subsequent exchanges the differences of doctrine and usage between Rome and Constantinople were carefully played down. It was a far cry from the days of Cardinal Humbert and the Patriarch Cerularius. Alexios believed that he had much to gain from good relations with the papacy. He was still in grievous straits, although he had with much difficulty fended off the Normans in Epirus and later annihilated a vast horde of Pecheneg nomads from the northern steppes at the approaches to his capital. Nearly all Asia Minor was in the power of the Seljuq Turks and he had neither sufficient nor good enough troops to expel them. He badly needed trained and disciplined mercenaries, and those could only be hired in the west. In the hope of obtaining them he despatched ambassadors to explain his predicament at the synod which the Pope had convoked at Piacenza in March 1095. No doubt they urged that it was the bounden duty of Christians to throw back the Moslems in Asia, just as had been recently accomplished with such success in Sicily and Spain.

The council was very well attended. One of the spectacles it offered was that of the Emperor Henry's second wife, the Russian princess Praxedis of Kiev, who had run away from her husband's camp at Verona, complaining in public of her husband's sexual practices. Altogether it was a slap in the face for Henry and his anti-Pope and a striking demonstration of Urban's capacity for leadership. Whether or not the idea of a Crusade in the east had already occurred to him, it was no doubt stimulated by the envoy's persuasiveness. In order to launch it, however, he waited until he was on his own ground. From Piacenza he went on to Cremona, where Henry's son Conrad paid him homage, and then to France. At Le Puy in Auvergne he held a conference with its bishop Adhemar, who was to become one of the most inspiring and effective leaders of the First Crusade, and sent out a summons for a synod at Clermont in November. In the interval he toured around Provence and Burgundy, talking to princes and clerics, showing himself in public and watching how men's minds were moving. He decided that the asmosphere was propitious for a grand gesture.

The synod opened with routine denunciations of simony, clerical immorality and lay investiture. It continued by excommunicating King Philip of France for adultery, a measure that may not seem to have been a happy prelude to exhorting Frenchmen to join in a Crusade. But Philip was not the most powerful of the princes then ruling in what is now France, even if he happened to be their feudal superior, and it was thought that by appropriating the wife of Count Fulk of Anjou he deserved the papal sanction. When such local business had been disposed of Urban delivered his flaming appeal to princes and people to rescue Byzantium and to liberate all eastern Christians and the Holy Places from Moslem domination. It was the moment his hearers, well primed as regards his intention, had been impatiently awaiting. Although it was late in November, huge crowds had assembled in the open air to hear him speak. They knew more or less what he was going to say but were not prepared for the emotional impact of his address. Carried away by mass fervour, they fell on their knees and cried *Deus le volt* (God wills it).

When Urban was speaking as a Frenchman to Frenchman his eloquence was no doubt irresistible. He had chosen the right moment and the right audience for an appeal that would surely have fallen flat in cynical and divided Italy. His success stemmed largely from his personal charm. Unlike Gregory VII, the small insistent, restless plebeian whose magnetism was judged either superhuman or inhuman, he was supremely human, tall, handsome, outwardly easy and aristocratically distinguished. He rubbed no one up the wrong way. But he had not reckoned on the speed with which his popularity and the enthusiasm generated at the synod would spread. He could hardly have foreseen that in addition to the magnates who responded to his call it would attract so great a multitude of lesser knights and of poor, ordinary folk from France, the Rhineland and other parts of western Europe. Nor could he have guessed how eagerly it would be repeated by popular preachers of the type of Peter the Hermit. It is hard to believe that his persuasive power alone inspired at least 100,000 men to quit their homes and suddenly set out for the unknown east. Few of them could have understood what might be involved in driving the Turks from Asia Minor and delivering the Holy Places. They had no idea how remote these places were. The economic and social reasons for seeking an outlet from contemporary miseries—over-population, poverty, lack of cultivable land, subjection to oppressive lords and the general drabness of life—were probably as potent as religious idealism, but it was the Pope's visionary exhortation that first pointed the way of escape and the opportunity of adventure. However the first Crusade proved impossible to co-ordinate. Urban tried unsuccessfully to ensure that it should take the form of a single expeditionary force under competent and preferably princely leadership, which would proceed to Constantinople and there concert its further progress with the Greek Emperor. When events eluded his control he returned to Rome, where he found conditions much improved, and settled down to watch developments. In the end several separate expeditions were to make their way towards the Bosporus in the course of 1096 and 1097.

The first expedition, led by Peter the Hermit, an unkempt, fiery little monk from Picardy and a spell-binding orator, numbered about 20,000 persons. Although it included some heavily mailed knights of the type led by William the Conqeror at Hastings, it was of small military value. Most of its members were not soldiers but peasants and humble townspeople imbued with genuine religious fervour. They were encumbered by women and children and useless camp-followers. Starting from Cologne, they followed the Rhine and Danube as far as the Byzantine frontiers at Belgrade. By that time their discipline was breaking down and the onward march to Constantinople was marked by endless looting and at least one pitched battle with imperial forces appointed to guide them and keep them in order. When they arrived near the capital the Emperor shipped them as soon as possible over to the Asiatic shore, where they were joined by an Italian contingent that had arrived by sea. They established a fortified camp in territory adjoining that occupied by the Turks, but employed their time in plundering the Greek Christian countryside. Soon they were attacked and virtually annihilated by the army of the Turkish Sultan. Peter, who happened to be in Constantinople at the time, was one of the few survivors of the catastrophe.

The second expedition was an even more shameful fiasco. It was composed mainly of Rhineland Germans and its leaders were minor German and French nobles. As a prelude to their march they perpetrated horrifying massacres of Jews in the principal towns of the Rhine and Moselle valleys. The efforts of the local episcopate to prevent these excesses were largely unavailing. At last the expedition set out for the east in three columns. On entering the Hungarian kingdom they behaved like brigands and marauders and were deservedly slaughtered by the royal troops.

The western princes and their armies, the real backbone of the crusade, reached the Bosporus by different routes. Hugh of the Vermandois, brother of King Philip of France, travelled through Rome and crossed the Adriatic from Bari. He was wrecked on the Albanian coast but arrived safely at Constantinople. A second and greater army from northern France, headed by Robert of Normandy, the eldest son of William the Conqeror, Stephen of Blois and Robert of Flanders, followed Hugh's example and, like Hugh, the leaders received the Pope's blessing. They too embarked at Bari. The important contingent from Lorraine and the Low countries, commanded by the brothers Godfrey of Bouillon and Eustace and Baldwin of Boulogne, chose the land route via Hungary. The southern French, under Raymond of Toulouse, undertook an appallingly rough journey through northern Italy and down through Dalmatia. Lastly the Normans of southern Italy, under Bohemond of Taranto, crossed from Bari and marched through Macedonia and Thrace. The successive arrival of these proud and quarrelsome magnates and their unruly troops taxed the diplomatic and other resources of the Byzantine Empire to the utmost. There were plenty of disagreements and armed clashes, but the whole crusading host of perhaps 30–40,000 men was eventually transported across the Bosporus to Asia.

The Crusaders' first task was to reduce the ancient Christian city of Nicaea, now occupied by a Turkish garrison. After its surrender, not to them but to the Emperor, they started their epic march to Jerusalem. First on 1 July 1097, they routed the Turkish Sultan's army at Dorylaeum. Then, having traversed the Anatolian plateau, they descended into the plain of Cilicia and in October stood before Antioch, another great Christian city in infidel hands. There they suffered a long check. They took fifteen months to capture the city and to defeat successive attempts by Moslem rulers to relieve or recover it. When they resumed their march in January 1099, Raymond of Toulouse was in command; Bohemond stayed in Antioch and Baldwin of Boulogne further east in Edersa. Far away in Rome, the Pope could do little to direct the course of events, but he was normally concerned with regulating the future status of the catholic church in any conquered countries and its relations with their existing Orthodox or Armenian or Christian population, more numerous at that time than the Moslem, and with the Orthodox hierarchy, which included the Patriarchs of Antioch and Jerusalem. Urban's legate with the army was his friend Adhemar, Bishop of Le Puy, whose martial ability rivalled his spiritual virtues. He was sensible enough to work in concord with the Orthodox clergy and particularly with Symeon, the Patriarch of Jerusalem, who happened to be living in exile in Byzantine Cyprus. It was also still an open question how far the Emperor Alexios would try to press his claim to the Syrian lands that had belonged to Byzantium as recently as 1085. There was all to be said for conciliating the Greeks. Unfortunately, Adhemar died at Antioch. On learning of his death the Pope appointed Archbishop Daimbert of Pisa to succeed him, but the new legate did not arrive in the east until after the Crusaders had stormed Jerusalem, massacred its Moslem and Jewish inhabitants and consolidated their triumph by destroying the Sultan of Egypt's army at Ascalon. He found that the victors had also installed an obscure sub-deacon, Arnulf, as Latin Patriarch of Jerusalem, thus barring the way to a satisfactory accommodation with the Orthodox Christians of Palestine. Later he was deposed and Daimbert, no friend of the Orthodox and lacking Adhemar's political flair, took his place. These development, however, were hidden from Urban. He died on 29 July, in ignorance that Jerusalem had fallen two weeks earlier.

Urban's successor, Paschal II (1099–1118) was troubled by the frequent revolts of the Roman nobility and was more than once obliged to quit the city until they could be quelled. He also had three anti-popes to contend with after Clement's death in 1100. By 1106 he had chased them all away, only to be plunged for the rest of his pontificate into an intense conflict over investitures with the new German King Henry V, the second son of Henry IV and an equally if not more formidable antagonist. Paschal was another Tuscan and Cluniac. A staunch Gregorian by conviction, he was temperamentally inclined to search for a compromise that might end this wearisome controversy. Henry too expressed his willingness to negotiate. Having deposed and imprisoned his father, he was anxious to confirm his legitimacy through an imperial coronation. Nevertheless Paschal was not contemplating a surrender of Gregory's basic principle. He repeatedly took his stand on it at synods held in Italy and France and a meeting with Henry's envoys at Châlons-sur-Marne. Since no progress was made in the first four years of his reign Henry decided to force the Pope's hand. In the autumn of 1110 he swept through Lombardy at the head of a huge array, subduing all opposition and giving notice that he expected to be crowned at Rome and to receive satisfaction as regards investitures. In the knowledge that he would now be negotiating under duress, Paschal made a last moment attempt to reach an acceptable agreement. Unfortunately his proposal, though idealistic in appearance, was quite impracticable.

In essence it was that in return for the King's renunciation of his right of investiture the Church, as instructed by the Pope, would surrender to the Crown all the rights, properties and functions—the so-called regalia—not pertaining to the sphere of religion; in future it would support itself purely by tithes and contributions from the faithful. Henry was of course delighted, at least in principle, by the prospect of acquiring, at the cost of a simple gesture, the vast possessions of the German bishoprics and abbeys. He hastened to accept the Pope's proposal and arrived at Rome for his coronation. At the same time he could hardly have seriously believed that the great ecclesiastical princes of his realm would tamely allow themselves to be deprived of the powers, lands and riches. The date fixed for the ceremony was 12 February 1111. As a prelude to the actual crowning Paschal read out the text of the agreement. As soon as the prelates and lay princes (mostly Germans) assembled in St Peter's grasped its terms they exploded with indignation, causing such a tumult that it was impossible to proceed with the coronation. The Pope refused to perform it, while Henry declared that as the Church was obviously not in a position to carry out its part of the bargain he for his part could not think of renouncing the right of investiture. The argument went on all day and as tempers became further inflamed he placed Paschal and most of his Cardinals under arrest. On the next day the Roman populace attacked the Germans and there was furious street fighting in the course of which Henry was wounded. Eventually he withdrew his army from the Leonine city, taking the Pope and Curia with him. They were confined in various castles and the current anti-Pope, Silvester IV, was invited to the royal camp.

Paschal's imprisonment lasted for two months. By that time his never very courageous spirit was broken, and in a document known as the *Privilegium* he conceded unconditionally the right that Gregory VII and Urban II had consistently withheld. He also promised that the King would never in future be harassed or excommunicated over investitures. All he got in return was a general assurance of protection and the dismissal of the anti-Pope. Thereupon he was brought back to Rome and compelled to go through with the imperial coronation. His humiliation was indeed complete.

The rest of his pontificate was spent in wriggling out of the consequences of his own weakness. All western churchmen (except in Germany) were aghast at the extent of his betrayal of the principle that he had previously championed. The French bishops were especially aroused. Some wished to indict him for heresy, but the wiser realized that he was the victim of blackmail. A circular that he issued in self-justification was ill received. Therefore, now that the Emperor had returned to Germany, he started to back down. At his spring synod of 1112 he was already proclaiming his mistake. Referring to Gregory and Urban he announced that 'whatever they have condemned I condemn; whatever they have rejected I reject.' In view of his specific promise he was chary of excommunicating the Emperor, but he did not rebuke a French synod that did that very thing, nor his own legate to the crusading kingdom of Jerusalem, a German who was Cardinal-bishop of Palestrina. As was so often the case, papal authority was less potent at the centre than when exercised vicariously at the extremities. But although so many churchmen were on his side it was not until 1116 that he gathered courage to denounce his own *Privilegium* as heretical and once more to forbid lay investiture. Even so, while approving his legate's action, he did not dare personally to pronounce a ban on the Emperor, with whom he now maintained an uneasy armistice.

The last two years of his very agitated reign were bedevilled by typically Roman strife. His own candidate for the prefecture of the city, a Pierleone, was rejected in favour of a young Tusculan noble who provoked what virtually amounted to a civil war. He was twice obliged to leave the city and on the second occasion the Emperor slipped in behind him, accompanied by his young wife Matilda, daughter of Henry I of England. Henry V took the opportunity to have himself recrowned, but as neither the Pope nor any Cardinal would consent to officiate, he had recourse to an ambitious southern Frenchman, the archbishop of Braga in Portugal. After his departure Paschal forced his way back with Norman help, but only in time to die. He was no hero; however, his reign had at least proved how hard it was for any potentate to have his way against the prevailing will of the Church.

The short reign of Gelasius II (1118–19) is remarkable only as illustrating even more clearly the fact that whatever influence the papacy might be exerting in an outside world stretching as far as Constantinople and Jerusalem, an individual Pope was physically at the mercy of the Roman mob or robber barons, especially when the latter was operating as the Emperor's agents. The Cardinal-deacon John of Gaeta was a Benedictine by training and had served as chancellor to Urban II. That is to say he headed the papal administration at a peculiarly difficult period, when the pontiff was often absent from Rome and an anti-pope disputing his control of the chancery. He had also shared Paschal's imprisonment by Henry V. He had hardly been elected when he was seized by Cencius Frangipani, leader of the imperialist faction of Roman nobles, severely mishandled and locked up in a tower belonging to his captor. According to an eye-witness Cencius 'hissing like a huge snake . . . grabbed the Pope by the throat . . . struck him with his fists, kicked him and drew blood with his spurs . . . dragged him off by the hair and arms.' Although he was immediately liberated by the city Prefect and his own supporters the Pierleoni, the Frangipani incited the Emperor to make a sudden raid on Rome and catch Gelasius by surprise. Warned just in time and narrowly avoiding the experience of his predecessor, the Pope and his suite hurried on board two galleys in the Tiber and landed at his birthplace, Gaeta. Henry countered by sponsoring the election of the complacent Mauritius, archbishop of Braga, as Gregory VIII. Gelasius, now sheltering with the Norman prince of Capua, promptly excommunicated them both.

The factions at Rome were evenly balanced, and as soon as Henry marched away the anti-Pope was not strong enough to prevent Gelasius from re-occupying the city. But he clung to the Leonina, and a few weeks later, while Gelasius was celebrating Mass in Santa Prassede, the Frangipani again fell upon him. Again he barely got away, this time on a horse and still wearing his vestments. He rode as far as his mount would carry him and was found by his followers sitting quietly in a field outside the walls. For a while he hung on in Rome, but only in order to organize his departure for a more hospitable France. In company with six Cardinals and a large retinue, he made a dignified progress to Pisa and Genoa and so on, by Montpellier and Avignon, to Vienne. His last destination was Cluny, where on his deathbed he named Guido, archbishop of Vienne, as his most suitable successor.

Surprisingly enough, his wishes were carried out without any trouble. Guido's election by the small minority of Cardinals present at Cluny was unanimously confirmed at Rome. Calixtus II (1119-24), a Burgundian nobleman by birth and related to the Kings of France and England, was a capable and strong-minded Frenchman of the same stamp as Urban II. An enthusiastic fighter for reform and no respecter of lay personages, it was he who had presumed to excommunicate Henry V on his own account as 'a second Judas'. On the other hand he was no fanatic. He rightly sensed that the combatants in the investitures dispute had reached the point of exhaustion and that the Emperor in particular was disposed to discuss a compromise. He also wisely decided to open negotiations from France, where he enjoyed solid support, rather than from insecure Rome.

Following Urban's train of thought, he saw a good prospect of agreement in the distinction, already adopted as the basis for settlements of the investitures problem in France and England, between the consecration of a bishop—a sacramental act—and his investiture—a non-sacramental act, relating solely to his feudal duties as a holder of royal fiefs and properties. He set his legates to work at the Emperor's court and obtained approval for his policy from a council at Reims attended by over 400 bishops. The negotiations were going so well that he prepared to conclude them at a personal meeting with Henry, but at the last moment full agreement could not be reached and the talks were broken off. The Pope took this rebuff calmly; he was sure that they would be resumed sooner or later. After a prolonged stay in his native country he travelled to Italy in the spring of 1120.

His journey was a triumphal procession. In June he entered Rome and subsequently made a leisurely progress through southern Italy. The time had now come to dispose of the anti-Pope Gregory, who had fled to the fortress of Sutri. It fell after a week's siege and the ex-archbishop of Braga, after being exhibited to the Romans on the back of a baggage camel, was confined for the rest of his life to an abbey. Soon afterwards Calixtus received the gratifying news that the Emperor was again ready to negotiate and had appointed a committee of twelve princes for the purpose. He despatched three Cardinals, equipped with full powers, to meet them at Worms in the Rhineland. There the wearisome bargaining continued for some months until on 23 September 1122, it resulted in the famous 'Concordat'. The agreement was enshrined in two documents. In the first the Emperor finally renounced his right to invest with ring and staff and guaranteed to the higher clergy their freedom of election and consecration; in the second the Pope conceded to the Emperor or his representative the right to be present at an election, but in the event of the latter being disputed the Emperor undertook to respect the decision of the most authoritative section of the electors, defined as the metropolitan and bishops of the province in question. The investiture of a bishop with crown fiefs and properties was to take place in Germany between his election and his consecration, and was to be symbolized by the conferment of a sceptre. This complicated procedure, while admittedly giving the Emperor some chance of influencing the electors by his mere presence, was an undeniable victory for the Church. Its spiritual functions were now safeguarded from lay interference, and the powers of the ruler in respect of ecclesiastical properties were exactly delimited.

Both sides were reasonably satisfied by this pragmatic compromise. It was accepted without demur in Germany. As for Calixtus, his personal prestige was immensely enhanced in the whole of Europe by the outcome of the negotiations and the skill with which he had managed them. He was especially prudent to have worked through trusted legates while staying calmly in Rome, safe from the pressures that might have been applied to him had he himself gone to Worms. He celebrated his success by holding a general council at the Lateran in the spring of 1123. It set the seal on his main achievement, but a no less remarkable feat was that of reigning in Rome, untroubled and in full control, from 1120 until his premature death at the end of 1124.

After more than a thousand years the uncongenial atmosphere of Rome continued to hamper the Pope in his role as the heir of St Peter and the Christian Caesars. The thirty years period between the death of Calixtus II and the accession of Hadrian IV (1154–9) was peculiarly troubled by disputed elections and rivalries between Roman factions. The feud between the Frangipani, the most prominent noble clan, and the Pierleoni, the money-lending house of Jewish descent that had enjoyed a special relationship with popes since the days of Leo IX and Gregory VII, was responsible for a disputed election in 1124 and for a serious schism lasting from 1130 till 1138. Each party had its adherents in the College of Cardinals. On the first occasion the Frangipani got their way easily. Although the College had already unanimously elected the Cardinal-priest Theobald (Celestine II), they frightened him into resignation in favour of Lambert, Cardinal-bishop of Ostia, who then succeeded as Honorius II (1124–30). In fact he was an excellent choice, for he had been the chief negotiator of the 'Concordat'. Of humble origin, he was able and learned. As the Abbot of Monte Cassino remarked, 'I do not know whose son His Holiness is; all I know is that he is filled with letters from head to foot.' His pontificate was uneventful and marred only by an ill-judged attempt to stop Roger II, the powerful King of Sicily, from extending his dominion over Apulia and Calabria and thus founding what was to become the historic kingdom of Naples and Sicily.

In 1130 the Frangipani also planned to manoeuvre their candidate into the papal chair. Again he was a suitable and morally unimpeachable figure; as the Cardinal-deacon Gregory, Papareschi too had taken part in the talks at Worms and possessed the necessary international experience. His sponsors took charge of Honorius on his deathbed and mobilized sixteen Cardinals to proclaim Gregory as Innocent II (1130–43). But this time the Pierleoni were better prepared. Their opponents' procedure was blatantly uncanonical and their own lavish use of funds had assured them the support of the Romans in general. Almost immediately enough Cardinals came over to their side to give them a majority, to nullify Gregory's election and to legalize that of their own candidate. Above all he himself was a Pierleone, son of a Roman magnate and grandson of the converted Jewish banker who had established the family's fortunes in the preceding century. But Peter Pierleone, Cardinal-priest of Santa Maria in Trastevere (his family's stronghold), had been given the most careful of Christian educations. After studying theology and philosophy in the schools of Paris he had entered Cluny as a monk. Ordained Cardinal-deacon by Pope Paschal, he had carried out important legations in Fance and England. He was no less capable and distinguished than his rival, but the manner of his election did not help his reputation away from Rome. In the outside world only Sicily and Scotland were for Anacletus II, as he styled himself; France (except Aquitaine), England and Christian Spain were for Innocent. So was Lothar III, King of Germany, and most significantly of all Bernard of Clairvaux, the acknowledged spiritual leader of western Europe. The future Saint campaigned energetically against Anacletus, not hesitating to cast the most insulting aspersions on his Jewish origin.

The odds were therefore against Anacletus, who would hardly have survived for eight years without the backing of Roger of Sicily. Meanwhile Innocent, with Bernard at his elbow, was seeking support in France and Germany. Synods acclaimed him in both countries. Meeting King Lothar at Liège, he persuaded him to mount an expedition to Rome for the purpose of expelling the rival Pope and receiving the imperial crown. In the autumn of 1132 he returned to Italy and joined the King of Piacenza. Lothar's army was very small, but Innocent had employed his time well in reconciling the maritime republics of Genoa and Pisa and hiring ships from them to take Rome from the seaward side. During the spring of 1133 their forces converged cautiously on the city, unopposed because Roger was occupied in dealing with a critical rebellion in Apulia. On the other hand Lothar was too weak to storm Sant' Angelo and the Leonina. The result was the familiar deadlock, with one pope watching from his ramparts while the other crowned an Emperor in the Lateran. Proposals for an arbitration, to which Anacletus declared himself ready to submit, were rejected by Innocent. So in the absence of any solution, ecclesiastical or military, Lothar retired tamely a few days after his coronation while Innocent, threatened by the hostility of the Romans and the advance of Roger's troops, followed him two months later.

Undeterred by this ignominious failure, Bernard and Innocent worked hard to organize a second venture. The former's eloquence, religious fervour and practical talent were deployed not only in upholding Innocent's supremacy in the Church but in meeting the expenses of an itinerant Curia and of the whole papal apparatus outside central Italy. Lothar, for his part, was anxious to try again so long as he was able to assemble an army capable of overcoming Roger on his own ground. This condition was fulfilled when he reached, with Bernard's help, an agreement with his Hohenstaufen opponents in Germany. Then Bernard proceeded to Italy, stood behind Innocent when he held a council at Pisa and made a great impression by winning over the key city of Milan, formerly an Anacletan stronghold, to the side of his protégé. It took three years to prepare the ground, but in the autumn of 1136 Lothar entered Italy in apparently overwhelming force. One column advanced through Tuscany to Capua, the other down the Adriatic as far as Bari. But both by-passed Rome, and with Roger prudently avoiding battle, Innocent and the Emperor began to quarrel about feudal rights in south Italy. Also the hot summer of 1137 had a fatal effect on the morale of the German army. Soon it was streaming back across the Alps, and it was there that Lothar died in the following winter.

Bernard, in company with the disappointed Innocent, was left in Italy to pick up the pieces. Finding Roger in an accommodating mood, he arranged a new arbitration between the Popes by a committee of three Cardinals from each side. It broke down because Roger, to whom it was really quite indifferent who held the papacy, failed to make up his mind, but the difficulty was removed by the death of Anacletus. Although he was at once replaced as anti-Pope by Cardinal Gregorio Conti, who took the name of Victor IV, Bernard's talents had already been exercised on the Romans with such good effect that they let him drop after two months, thus putting an end to what had been a very damaging schism. Thus re-established in the Lateran, Innocent lasted for another four years. Instead of leaving Italian politics well alone, he plunged into a rash and unnecessary war with Roger on behalf of Robert of Capua, the only independent principality still existing south of Rome. He even took the field himself, but like Leo IX on a similar occasion, was easily defeated and captured in an ambush. He was treated with courtesy, but the price of his release was the recognition of Roger as King of the great unitary realm of the two Sicilies. It was only a partial consolation that he and his sons formally held these territories as papal fiefs.

It is refreshing to pass from this succession of dreary pontificates to that of Eugenius III (1145–53), which although quite as insecure and restless as Innocent's, was enlivened by the sudden rise of republicanism at Rome and by the Second Crusade in the Orient. Innocent's last months had already been unsettled by a dispute with the Romans over the fate of Tivoli, the little town guarding the city's approaches that had always obstinately defended its identity. As in the time of Silvester II, the Pope had reduced it to obedience but subsequently treated it leniently whereas the Romans were demanding its destruction. Like Silvester, Innocent refused to act so brutally, and was consequently threatened by popular dissidence quite distinct from the familiar squabbling between factions. Now it took the form of a full-scale republican movement posing a very real challenge to papal authority. Taking root among the new middle class modelled on the society of the north Italian cities, it grew apace during the ephemeral pontificates of Celestine II (six months in 1143 and 1144) and Lucius (eleven months in 1144 and 1145). Moreover, it drew its inspiration from radical ideas stemming from Abelard, the philosophic rebel of the schools of Paris, and from Arnold, the Augustinian canon from Brescia who was loudly proclaiming his distate for the hierarchy of the church.

An ascetic in religion, Arnold was also a gifted demagogue. His early training with Abelard in Paris had stimulated his scepticism about the quality of Church leadership, and as Augustinian prior in his own city he had got into trouble through his outspoken criticism of the higher Lombard clergy. Condemned as a schismatic by Innocent II and expelled from Italy, he wandered back to Paris, taught there in the schools and thus incurred the emnity of Bernard of Clairvaux. Outlawed in turn from France by the latter's agency, he went to Zurich and then to Prague, where he was protected by the legate and even recommended by him to the Pope. In 1146 Eugenius released him from excommunication and summoned him to Rome to lead a life of penance.

This was a bad mistake on the part of Eugenius. When Arnold arrived in Rome he found it under the sway of a republican commune dominated by enthusiasm for the antique by a recrudescence of pride in the clerical past. Mediaeval Romans always liked to style themselves Senators and Consuls, but the new commune set up while Lucius was pope went further and restored the Senate as a working body, sitting on the Capitol, electing magistrates and issuing a coinage. Under the leadership of Jordan Pierleone, a brother of Anacletus II, it displaced the Pope's government and announced the end of his temporal power. When the adherents of Pope Lucius attempted to oppose it fighting broke out and according to an account written some forty years later, Lucius was mortally wounded by 'great stones,' presumably launched from a catapult while he was directing an assault on the Capitol.

Although the commune had the best of this encounter, the Cardinals managed to elect Eugenius. He was Bernard of Pisa, Abbot of a Christian Monastery at Rome and a pupil of Bernard of Claivaux. For two years, amid a host of difficulties, he strove to come to terms with a hostile and truculent republic, which even denied him consecration in St Peter's. His negotiations with the Senators were conducted from friendly Viterbo, where he retired three days after his election with his Curia and Chancery. He did indeed obtain a pact whereby the republic recognized his sovereignty over Rome and the patrimony in return for his acceptance of the Senate's authority to govern, subject only to his confirmation of the Senator's election by the people. This arrangement however, while sounding admirably democratic, did not work. Under Arnold's influence the commune was becoming more and more anti-papal, or at least anti-curial. He railed with increasing violence against the bishops and the whole principle of authority in the Gregorian Church. Soon Eugenius found it impossible to sustain the responsibilities of the papacy in so uncongenial an atmosphere. After spending one Christmas in Rome he returned to Viterbo and finally, in the spring of 1147, travelled by way of his native Pisa to France, accompanied by his cardinals and secretariat. As we shall see, his presence was very urgently required north of the Alps, and for the moment he was content to leave Arnold and the commune to stew in their own juice. Arnold is a curious figure. In other circumstances he might have developed into a reformer on the grand scale, a precursor of Martin Luther and his peers of the sixteenth century. But the times were not ripe for such an enterprise and he was not of a calibre to measure himself against St Bernard. Primarily his protest was a personal one. He bitterly hated the worldliness of the higher clergy, their preoccupation with politics and property. But after he came to Rome he allowed himself to be absorbed in the Roman atmosphere, its visionary republican ideals and the secular purposes of ousting the temporal government of the Pope by one based on the popular will. He no longer pressed his ambition to reform the church from the top.

Meanwhile Eugenius was engaged with a wider and more urgent problem for Christendom as a whole, the seemingly imminent collapse of the Crusading states in Syria and Palestine. It was high time that he shook himself free of Rome and personally associated himself with the preparations for the second Crusade. The immediate cause of the crisis was the loss to the Moslems of the county of Edersa, the eastermost of the Christian states and a vitally important bastion. On hearing the news at Viterbo in 1145, the Pope decided that a new crusading effort must be launched.

In December of that year he addressed a fervent appeal to the King, princes and people of France to take up the Cross. Although the pious Louis VII needed no urging, his vassals and advisers were at first unresponsive. It was only when he and the Pope entrusted the preaching of the Crusade to Bernard of Clairvaux that French enthusiasm was aroused. Bernard's speech at Vezelay, where the King publicly took the Cross at Easter 1146, had the same electrifying effect as that of Urban II at Clermont fifty years earlier, and from that moment French support for the Crusade was whole-hearted.

The Pope was delighted, but he became anxious when he heard that Bernard was extending his mission to Germany. Eugenius was only aiming for French Crusaders;

he had no wish to involve the Germans and least of all Conrad III, the first King of the Hohenstaufen dynasty. He would have much preferred Conrad to stay in Europe. He was counting on his help to restore him to Rome at an opportune moment and to act as a counter-weight to Roger of Sicily, nominally a papal vassal and ally but an uncomfortably powerful neighbour. He may also have suspected that the two crusading Kings would fall out between themselves. Bernard was inclined to underestimate his former pupil, to patronize him and even to regard him as slightly simple-minded. In reality Eugenius was much shrewder than he affected, and had plenty of expert advisers in his Curia. But he himself had underestimated the effects of his master's zeal, which infected the Germans as it had the French. Only Conrad was reluctant, and Bernard had to beard him twice before he consented to take part in the expedition. However, once he had given in, the Pope could not expect to reverse his decision. When he journeyed to France in 1147 he could only hope for the best and give his blessing to the Crusade as it had developed. He had long interviews with Louis and held synods at Paris and Reims. But he made no move to see Conrad, and it was long after both monarchs had left for the east that he and the Curia spent the winter months of 1147–48 at Trier on German soil. He did not return to Italy until the summer of 1148. His sojourn in the north had been very fruitful. He had been received in France, the centre of European affairs, with all possible honours, and gratifying tokens of respect had reached him from Germany, England and Spain. The further the Pope moved from Rome, the greater, it seemed, was the prestige that he accumulated.

Eugenius cannot be held responsible for the disasters that befell the Crusade of the two Kings. The German expedition began inauspiciously with another massacre of Rhineland Jews. Then during the summer of 1147, Conrad's undisciplined host moved slowly across Europe to Constantinople. On crossing the Byzantine frontier the Germans behaved just as badly as their predecessors of the first Crusade and continued to cause trouble after the Emperor, Manuel Comnenos, had encamped them outside the walls of his capital. In the early autumn, just as the French contingent began to arrive, he persuaded Conrad to cross the Bosporus. The unruliness of the Germans alarmed the Byzantines and disgusted the French to the point that relations between the two western armies were thoroughly strained before campaigning began. As for the emperor, he was deeply embarrassed by the presence of the westerners. Although prepared to provide them with guides and military advice, he would have much preferred them to stay at home and leave him to deal with the Turks by his own methods. Furthermore, King Roger of Sicily, a cynical opportunist whom neither the Pope nor his fellow sovereigns could trust and who was not adverse to extending his power at the expense of Moslems and Christians alike, had chosen the moment to attack Byzantine territories in the peninsula of Greece.

Such was the atmosphere in which the Crusaders started their blundering march across Asia Minor. Starting first, the Germans under Conrad were immediately mauled by the Turks and fled back to Nicaea. The survivors were joined by the French and the Kings rode on together as far as Ephesus, where Conrad fell seriously ill and had to return to Constantinople. He was nursed back to health by the Emperor and eventually taken direct to Palestine aboard an imperial vessel.

Meanwhile the Franco-German force pressed unsteadily on, suffering heavy losses in combat and grevious privations. Somehow it maintained its cohesion, but it was only with extreme difficulty that Louis, his queen Eleanor of Aquitaine and a much reduced army won through to Palestine by sea and land.

In the summer of 1148 they regrouped their forces. Conrad rejoined them and their host Baldwin, the Latin King of Jerusalem, found himself at the head of a splendid array of western Princes. Despite the setbacks sustained by the Crusaders they were still very formidable; all seemed set for a grand campaign that would recover all the ground recently lost to the Moslems. But they proceeded to squander their resources on an ill-conceived attack on Damascus, which met with an ignominious repulse, and the whole enterprise promptly evaporated. The Kings went their separate ways, Conrad back to Constantinople, where he cemented a firm alliance with Manuel Comnenos, and Louis, who was determined to make Byzantium the scapegoat for his own failure, to France by way of the Sicilian kingdom. In the course of his journey Roger tried to enlist him as an active ally against Manuel, and even St Bernard was willing to preach an anti-Greek crusade. Fortunately, and to the Pope's relief, the scheme was scotched by a firm veto from Conrad.

Back in Italy and saddened by the frustration of his hopes for the east, Eugenius was forced to pursue with some loss of face, an accommodation with the Roman Republic. A settlement was indeed patched up and in 1149 he returned to the Lateran for six months. However Arnold made life so difficult for him, denouncing him as a man of blood, that he again retired to Latium, wandering from one small town to another almost in sight of the hostile city. Conrad's return from Constantinople revived his hopes; he invited the King to come to Rome for his imperial coronation and was glad when he snubbed a vital suggestion from the commune that he should take it under his protection as the capital of a new-style Roman empire. He sent Eugenius a cordial acceptance but died in 1152 before he could fulfil his wish.

The Pope's local prospects now depended on Conrad's nephew and heir Frederick I of Hohenstaufen ('Barbarossa'). He too received an approach from the commune. He was told that the Romans proposed to adopt a new constitution; it would provide for an emperor, two consuls and 100 senators, all to be elected annually; the former would owe his office to the city of Rome, mistress of the world, instead of to heretical priests and false monks. While paying no attention to this impertinent rigmarole, Frederick sent envoys to Italy to discuss the future political relations between papacy and empire and to insist that they should be regularized by a formal treaty. Their meeting with a commission of Cardinals scared the commune into inviting Eugenius to return to Rome while the negotiations were renewed at Constance. They resulted in an agreement by which the Emperor promised to respect the 'honour' of the Church and the Pope the 'honour' of the empire, in other words the other's exclusive rights. More specifically, Frederick undertook to subject the Romans to papal control and not to make peace with the Normans of Sicily without the Pope's consent. The Pope undertook to crown Frederick whenever he might appear and although the point was not at the moment relevant, both agreed to oppose any revival of Byzantine territorial claims in southern Italy. Altogether the treaty was a holding operation. It concealed Frederick's far-reaching ambitions for German imperial ascendancy and gave the papacy time to assess how the new Hohenstaufen would behave. No date for a coronation had been fixed when Eugenius died at Tivoli in July of the same year. Thus Hadrian IV (1154-9) was the first pope to experience the full force of Barbarossa's personality and to defend the papal position in a struggle that was to last for twenty-three years.

10

FROM HADRIAN TO
INNOCENT
(1154–1198)

Hadrian's pontificate may justly be regarded as ushering in the High Middle Ages, the period when a distinctive civilization reached its zenith in Catholic Europe, a brilliant synthesis of intellectual and material achievements. The Church in particular produced enduring masterpieces of theology and philosophy, besides inspiring the finest flowering of art and architecture. Society seemed to have assumed a settled if rigid form. The dominant and sometimes overpowering personalities of secular rulers—Frederick I Barbarossa, Henry II Plantagenet, Philip II Augustus of France and finally Frederick II ('Stupor Mundi')—were matched by a succession of imposing and versatile pontiffs.

The first of his line was Hadrian, the sole English pope of history. For a year and a half before his accession the Lateran was occupied by the aged Cardinal-bishop of Sabrina, reigning as Anastasius IV, and on the latter's death the Sacred College unanimously elected Nicolas Brakespeare, Cardinal-bishop of Albano. The Englishman had reached high rank in the Church from humble beginnings. His father was a poor priest and then a monk of St Albans. Educated by his own efforts in the schools of France, he eventually became head of the Augustinian house of St Rufus near Avignon. When he visited Rome Eugenius III was so impressed by his learning and zeal that he made him a Cardinal and sent him as legate to Scandinavia. He worked there very effectively for four years, returning to Rome just in time to be chosen pope.

Hadrian was a bold and forceful character who knew what he wanted. His first move was to get rid of the intolerable Arnold, by whom he found himself confined to the Leonina and St Peter's. Outraged by an assault by Arnold's men on one of his Cardinals, he reacted, shortly before Easter 1155, by using the most potent weapon in his spiritual armoury, the interdict, thereby withholding all religious services and consolations from the people of Rome. So drastic a measure, to which no pope had previously resorted, proved entirely effective. In return for the lifting of the interdict the Senate gave in and banished Arnold for good, while Hadrian triumphantly took possession of the Lateran. A year later, by arrangement with Frederick, Arnold was arrested by the latter's officers and handed over to the city Prefect. He had done too much harm to the papacy to expect mercy; he was hanged, burned and his ashes thrown into the Tiber.

With his standing fortified in Rome, Hadrian rather rashly took a high line with William I of Sicily, who had succeeded his father in 1154. William had been crowned King in Roger's time without any consultation with the Pope, his feudal superior, and for that reason Hadrian refused to accord him the royal title. William responded by an invasion of papal territory and was therefore excommunicated. But the Pope's future relations with the Sicilian ruler depended on the extent to which he might be able to play Frederick off against him or vice versa, and Frederick's attitude was still an unknown factor. After his accession Hadrian had twice sent a deputation of Cardinals to obtain an assurance that the King would abide by the treaty of Constance, but had received no clear reply. Now, in the summer of 1155, Frederick was on the way to his coronation and a crucial discussion could not be long delayed.

Before they met at Sutri Hadrian must have had a fairly clear notion of what to expect. His legates had no doubt warned him that Frederick was full of inflated ideas about the historical and mystical significance of the Roman imperial office as held by German Kings. For him it was not merely formal and decorative. He shared contemporary interest in the classical and post-classical empire and eagerly imbibed what his advisers, steeped in the revived study of Roman law in the university of Bologna, told him about the absolute nature of an emperor's authority, which was as valid in religion as it was in law. As had been recognized in the days of the Christian emperors Constantine, Justinian and Charles, the ruler's power was derived from God and his will had the force of law. Such heady doctrine, contrary to what was being taught by the equally active exponents of Canon Law, the law of the Church, was of course anathema to Hadrian, who maintained that divine sanction for the imperial Office must be transmitted to its holder by the pope.

A clash was therefore inevitable, although neither party yet wished to pursue disagreement to its logical extreme. At Sutri it took the form of an unseemly squabble about symbols. Frederick caused a great flurry when he purposely omitted to lead Hadrian's horse and to hold his stirrup, thus indicating that he considered himself to be in no respect subordinate to the Pope. The difference was patched up when it was explained to the King that the custom of holding reins and stirrups was an ancient tradition without ulterior meaning, but it prevented any real concord between them. As they rode on to Rome in an atmosphere of mutual distrust they were met by a deputation from the Senate demanding that the King should receive his imperial crown not from the Pope in St Peter's but from the city's magistrates on the Capitol and for a fee of 5,000 pounds of gold. Frederick, already at loggerheads with the communes of Lombardy, would have no truck with this piece of Roman insolence, but in dismissing it he insisted that in wielding his *imperium* he was in any event the rightful lord of the imperial capital and as such superior to both the republican commune and the Pope.

Frederick's rejection of the Senate's requirements was ill received by the Romans. His coronation duly took place but was followed by a furious attack by the city militia and mob on the Leonina, where the Emperor and Pope were guarded by German troops. The latter repelled them with great carnage, but as they were themselves incapable of besieging Rome Frederick withdrew them into the surrounding Campagna, taking the Pope with him. Hadrian still hoped that in accordance with the treaty of Constance the Emperor might agree to take the field against William of Sicily, but here again he was disappointed. Frederick himself was willing enough, but the German lords in his army were not prepared to risk a summer campaign against the redoubtable Normans. They argued that quite enough trials awaited the Emperor in Lombardy. Thereupon he marched northwards, leaving the Pope in the lurch and the difficulties of their future relationship unresolved.

At this point a streak of impatience in his character drove Hadrian to play dangerously high politics. If he could not induce Frederick to help him against

William, he would try Manuel Comnenos instead. The Byzantine government, with its long view of history, had not given up hope of recovering its lost provinces in southern Italy, and the Emperor had appointed for that purpose two enterprising commanders, Michael Palaeologus and John Ducas. At the same time the Norman barons of Apulia were in full revolt against their King. It seemed to Hadrian that a combination of the rebels, papal troops and the Byzantine expeditionary force might very well suffice to strike a decisive blow against the arrogant Sicilian monarchy. All the same his policy was a gamble, and one that did not come off. The coalition won early success and at the end of 1155 William had all but lost control of the mainland. Six months later however, the position was entirely reversed. The Greek fleet and army had been crushed at Brindisi, rebellious Bari had been razed to the ground and William's army was marching towards the papal frontier. There was nothing the Pope could do but submit and seek the best possible terms. With that object he sent his chancellor, Cardinal Roland, to negotiate with William's delegates at Benevento.

It was not in William's interest to humiliate the Pope, but he exacted from him the recognition of all his family's previous claims and conquests on the mainland—Apulia, Calabria, Capua, Naples, Salerno, Amalfi, the Abruzzi—in return for an annual rent of 1,000 gold pieces. The Treaty of Benevento confirmed him as the undisputed monarch of the united kingdom of Sicily and South Italy. In Church matters he retained the privileges previously conferred on Count Roger by Urban II, while conceding to the Pope a greater measure of control over the clergy in the mainland territories. But the chief import of the treaty was that the papacy once again reverted to the policy of dependence on the Normans that had been initiated by Nicholas II in 1059; and if it had not constantly been adhered to that was hardly the papacy's fault. But its latest renewal involved an obvious disregard of the Treaty of Constance which in other contexts Hadrian had been exhorting the Emperor to respect, and his alliance with the Byzantines had of course been an equally blatant violation of the same agreement. Some of the Cardinals were unhappy with these developments. Nevertheless Hadrian's prestige emerged with little damage. In November 1156 he returned tranquilly to Rome, commissioning his English nephew, the Cardinal-deacon Boso, to enforce his authority throughout the papal state.

Grievances were not lacking on either side. Nevertheless relations between Pope and Emperor, though strained, were not broken. In 1157 Hadrian despatched Cardinal Roland on a probing mission to the German court. When he arrived Frederick was holding a grand imperial Diet at Besançon in Upper Burgundy. If Roland's approach was meant to be conciliatory, it had precisely the opposite effect. He began by demanding an apology for injuries suffered in the preceding years by the aged Archbishop of Lund, primate of Sweden, on his passage through German territory. He went on to remind the Emperor of past benefits received from the Pope. Unfortunately, the language he used suggested to the assembly that the Pope was not merely talking about favours such as the coronation but was claiming to have bestowed the empire on Frederick as a papal fief. Whether their indignation was genuine or feigned, the German magnates could hardly be restrained from assaulting the legate, who had to quit Besançon in a hurry. Worse still, papers found in the baggage that he left behind him indicated that the Holy See was contemplating a radical reform of the German Church. This awkward discovery united all Germans, churchmen and laymen, with their Emperor in opposition to the Pope.

Some months later Hadrian sent two more Cardinals to Frederick in order to clear up the misunderstanding over the use of language. The Emperor accepted their explanation without further argument, but his attention was by then fixed on his imminent invasion of Lombardy. His object was to reduce its recalcitrant cities to obedience and to reassert his traditional imperial rights. He was determined to crush by force of arms these rich trading communes with their republican governments and pretentions to independence. At first he was overwhelmingly successful. The cities were frightened into temporary submission and he imposed on them a new definition of his rights involving heavy financial burdens. His demands covered certain lands, especially in Tuscany, considered as belonging to the states of the Church. These and other differences were lengthily but fruitlessly wrangled over at further meetings between legates and imperial representatives. Hadrian himself prudently retired to Anagni, which adjoined his frontier with the Sicilian kingdom. It appeared to him that Frederick's subjugation of the Lombard communes was only a step in a more grandiose programme of refashioning the empire as he imagined that it had been conceived by Charlemagne or Otto I. It was a process which if pursued to its logical conclusion would reduce the Holy See to the status of one major bishopric among others. So without rejecting the Emperor's final embassy, which was headed by the Count Palatine Otto of Wittelsbach, he entered into a secret pact with a number of still dissident Lombard cities. It provided that they should not make peace with Frederick without the Pope's consent and that he would excommunicate the Emperor within forty days. That period had not expired when Hadrian died, utterly worn out. As he told his distinguished countryman, John of Salisbury, he wished he had never left England or his priory in Provence. He had suffered so many hardships on the papal throne that all previous bitterness seemed to him sweet by comparison. A strong man operating from a weak base, he left an even grimmer conflict to be waged by his own Chancellor and right-hand man.

Most of the Cardinals who had gathered in St Peter's to elect a successor to Hadrian had supported his anti-imperial policy, and although there was also a strong minority who felt that he had been taking the wrong course they had apparently agreed not to oppose Roland's election. But neither side trusted the other. Hadrian's nephew Cardinal Boso took the precaution of securing the fortified tower adjoining the church, while the imperialist sympathizers worked out a theatrical plot of their own. The ceremony of election proceeded without incident until the moment when Roland was due to be vested with the scarlet mantle of his office. It was then suddenly interrupted by Cardinal Octavian, the leader of the imperialists, who grabbed the mantle and tried to assume it himself. The confusion was such that he put it on back to front and presented an absurd spectacle as he fumbled to arrange it. The ceremony at once dissolved into a ludicrous brawl. Exactly what happened is not clear, but the result of the very Italian scuffle was that Octavian and not Roland took his seat on the papal throne, protected by a troop of armed bullies. After a *Te Deum* had been somehow sung he was escorted to the Lateran and there acclaimed as Victor IV. Meanwhile Roland and his Cardinals had escaped to the refuge Boso had so thoughtfully provided.

There ensued further scenes of second rate opera. The Romans on the whole preferred Roland and clamoured for his release. This he obtained and after a few days sojourn in Trastevere he was led round the city amid delirious applause. Octavian found it safer to retire from it altogether. His example was soon followed by Roland, to whom the Roman chaos was equally distasteful. Within a few weeks the former was consecrated at the abbey of Farfa and the latter at Ninfa, a domain of the

Frangipani. The schism had now hardened and was to last, as three more anti-popes came and went, for the next twenty-one years.

Roland (who took the papal title Alexander III), a Bandinetti from Siena, possessed the highest qualities as well as remarkable stamina. He was an experienced statesman and diplomat, not easily rattled by the ups and downs of his fortunes. A jurist who had once taught in the schools of Bologna, he was fully capable of refuting the host of lawyers from the same university employed by Frederick to substantiate his claims. His rival Octavian, Cardinal-priest of Santa Cecilia, was a lesser figure. A Monticelli from the Sabina and a descendant of the Counts of Tusculum, he was well connected locally and with families in the north of Europe, but in intellect and character he was no match for Alexander.

The rivals confronted each other at a distance of a few miles in their different headquarters in Latium. The Emperor, campaigning in Lombardy, called a synod at Pavia which pronounced Victor to be the lawful Pope, and Alexander countered by excommunicating him and releasing his subjects from their oath of allegiance. Such gestures had little effect, but it was gratifying for Alexander to be recognized by the Kings and Bishops of France and England, as well as by the Sicilian and Spanish Kingdoms, Byzantium and the Latin Kingdom of Jerusalem. Despite this impressive show of support his position in Italy was precarious. Frederick was bludgeoning the northern cities into submission, Sicily was racked by an internal crisis and Rome, as usual, was untenable for more than a few weeks at a time. At the end of 1161 he decided, like Innocent II, that he would be safer and able to work more effectively in France. A Sicilian galley took him from Terracina to Genoa, where he stayed for two months. By April he had reached Montpellier and for the next four years he moved from one place to another in France. Once again the long-suffering Curia had to resign itself to a peripatetic existence. Nevertheless it was easier for the Pope and his chancery to control the Church and transact its multifarious business from a French base than from unreliable Rome. In France he was treated with the deep respect of which he could never be sure in Italy, and he was provided with all the necessary facilities. It was some consolation that as the anti-Pope also shunned Rome the Lateran archives remained in the charge of his own Cardinal-vicar.

But France was the centre of intense diplomatic and ecclesiastical activity, and Alexander did not lead an easy life there. King Louis in particular hankered after an accommodation with the Emperor. He floated a plan for the two monarchs to meet on a bridge over the Saône, at the border between their realms, where the two Popes would be summoned to argue their claims. Wisely Alexander would have nothing to do with it. He sharply rejected the idea of arbitration, sticking to the principle that the Apostolic See cannot be judged by any human agency. The danger was thus averted; the Emperor failed to turn up for his meeting with the King and Alexander arranged a much more satisfactory interview for himself by the Loire with Louis and Henry II. On the other hand he did send two embassies of his own to see if he could wean Frederick away from Victor IV. The latter died in 1164, but the imperial chancellor, Rainald of Dassel, promptly contrived the election by schismatic Cardinals of a second anti-pope, Paschal III (1164–8). He then sought to exploit Henry's celebrated quarrel with Thomas à Becket in the hope of detaching him from the Pope and Louis. This intrigue, however, also came to nothing. The dispute itself acutely embarrassed Alexander, for if he failed to rebuke Henry he risked compromising the rights of the Church, while a too zealous championship of Becket might well have driven the King to desert him for the anti-Pope. It was not surprising that he was unable to resolve it.

Amid these anxieties Alexander was unexpectedly recalled to Rome. In the absence of either Pope it had been governed by the Senate, but the Romans were sadly missing their accustomed profits from the pilgrim trade and the presence of the papal court. They therefore begged the Cardinal-vicar to invite Alexander to return. He set out at once on what was a hazardous voyage. Ships from imperialist Pisa, and even hired corsairs, were waiting to intercept him, but he eluded them all and sailed to Messina, where William I provided him with money and an escort to Ostia. On 23 November 1165 the rejoicing Romans led him in triumph to the Lateran.

Possibly Alexander had no illusions about how precarious his position might at any moment become. The anti-Pope was established at Viterbo and the imperial troops upholding him had recently ravaged the Campagna. Frederick, who three years earlier had razed Milan to the ground, seemed implacably hostile; the western Kings were too far away to help. Within six months his friend King William of Sicily was dead, but not before sending him a large subvention. One of his difficulties was that a major source of his income, the revenues from the papal state, had greatly dwindled, and he was largely dependent on such foreign subsidies. However the Sicilian Kingdom was now controlled by a regency which might not prove so reliable in a crisis. Ominously enough that was also Frederick's opinion. In the autumn of 1166 he began to prepare for an ambitious campaign in Italy. Its object was threefold. First came the reduction of Ancona, the Adriatic city which to his annoyance had placed itself under the protection of Byzantium; secondly the expulsion of Alexander from Rome and his replacement by Paschal, and thirdly, if those operations succeeded, the destruction of the Sicilian Kingdom itself.

In the event Frederick failed to take Ancona, although he laid siege to it in person. The capture of Rome he left initially to two martial German archbishops, Rainald of Cologne and Christian of Mainz. The Pope had collected a large army to oppose them, but it was unprofessional and unable to withstand German knights and mercenaries from Brabant. It was routed on 29 May 1167 outside Tusculum and the Germans encamped before Rome. Before attacking it they waited for the Emperor and the anti-Pope to join them. As in the case of previous sieges, the first line of defence was the wall of the Leonina, and within that enceinte the basilica of St Peter's and neighbouring structures had been fortified and equipped with catapults. Alexander, who refused to negotiate, stayed in the main city. The assault began on 21 July. The wall of the Leonina was easily breached, but the improvised citadel in the Vatican held out for eight days. The Romans fought with fanatical courage, their enemies with brutal savagery. Vast damage was inflicted on the complex of sacred buildings. The monumental portico, recently restored by Innocent II, was wrecked, the chapel of Santa Maria in Turri above the atrium, with its splendid mosaic depicting Christ and Peter, was entirely destroyed, and finally the bronze doors of the basilica itself were broken down with axes. The shrine was heaped with corpses before the remnants of the garrison laid down their arms. Undismayed by this unparalleled desecration of St Peter's, the anti-Pope celebrated Mass there on the following day, and on 1 August he crowned the Empress Beatrice in the presence of her husband.

A very short pause followed. The Romans, secure behind their city walls and holding a bridgehead in Sant' Angelo, were inclined to parley with Frederick, who proposed that both Popes should abdicate and agree to a fresh election. Alexander, sheltering in a Frangipani tower by the Arch of Titus, suspected a trap. As the

Romans were wavering he decided on flight. Disguised as a pilgrim, he slipped out of the city and made his way to the coast, where he was spotted three days later waiting for a ship while enjoying a forlorn beach picnic. He was duly rescued and soon arrived safely at Benevento.

In the normal course of events Barbarossa might have made his peace quickly with the Romans and proceeded with his campaign as planned. Although he was not admitted into the city he received assurances of its future loyalty and all was ready for his march into Apulia. Twelve years earlier his vassals had refused to face the risks of a southern summer, but now they were hardly prepared for the ghastly revenge the climate was about to exact. The weather was freakish. On the day after Beatrice's coronation an appalling deluge broke over Rome, followed by hothouse heat. These conditions, combined with lack of hygiene in the German camp, immediately produced a devasting epidemic, probably malarial but with other complications. Within a few days the soldiers were dying in thousands; so were the Romans. Frederick's chief advisers and warriors, including his chancellor Rainald, perished by the score. As early as 6 August it had become obvious that the expedition was doomed, and the decimated German army trailed away despondently towards Lombardy. The Italians thought that their fate was a striking manifestation of God's judgment on sacrilegious barbarians.

The immediate result of this extraordinary turn of affairs was the revolt of northern Italy. Sixteen, and eventually twenty-two, cities joined the Lombard League against the Emperor, who barely escaped across the Alps. They expelled his nominees, civil and ecclesiastical, and replaced them with persons acceptable to the Pope. Indeed Alexander became so popular in the north that a new city, Alexandria, was founded and named after him. He watched these developments with satisfaction, but nothing would induce him to try his luck once more in Rome. Whereas the anti-Popes Paschal III and Calixtus III (1168–79) led an obscure and harassed existence in the city (in which his own Cardinal-vicar still looked after his interests), he found it safer to reside with his Curia either at Benevento or at various little towns in Latium and Campagna such as Sagni and Veroli. It was also more convenient for the tranquil conduct of international business. The nearest he came to Rome was Tusculum (Frascati), where he received envoys from England at the height of the crisis between Henry II and Thomas à Becket. Negotiations also continued, fitfully and with little prospect of success, for a reconciliation with the Emperor and the end of the schism. Alexander was in no particular hurry. While never entirely severing his relations with the German court, he waited for a decisive moment in the long struggle between Barbarossa and the Lombards. It came in May 1176, when the Milanese and their allies heavily defeated the Emperor at the battle of Legnano.

The exemplary patience exhibited by the Pope since his flight from Rome was now ripe for rewards. If Frederick was to make peace with his Italian enemies he had no choice but to seek a preliminary settlement with the Holy See, and for that purpose a great imperial embassy, headed by the archbishops of Cologne, Mainz and Magdeburg, made its way in October 1176 to Anagni. It took only a fortnight for the parties to reach an agreement based on recognition of each other's rights. In particular Alexander was acknowledged as the only lawful Pope; he regained his supremacy in Rome and all the Italian lands and revenues of which the papacy had been wrongly deprived. Imperial pretentions to overlordship were tacitly dropped. In return the Pope undertook to release Frederick from excommunication and to mediate in his disputes with the Lombards and others. In general the terms were framed so as not to cause the Emperor unnecessary humiliation, and for that reason they were not

Gregory VII, Benedictine, reformer, canonized in 1728

Gregory VII

Hadrianus 4ᵗʰ

Hadrian IV, the only English Pope

Henry IV abasing himself before a haughty Gregory VII at Canossa (1077)

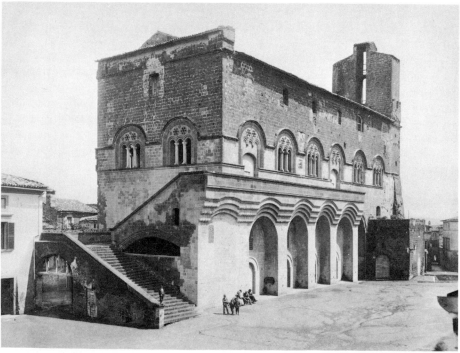

The Palace of the 'Captain of the People', Orvieto

very agreeable to the Lombards. Nevertheless the way was clear for a full peace conference, which was held at Venice in the summer of 1177. Alexander sailed up the Adriatic from Siponto in a Sicilian vessel. However, four months of hard argument, in which he played a conciliatory part, were to elapse before the Emperor was ready to join the negotiators for the final symbolic ceremony. On 25 July Alexander took his seat on a throne in front of St Mark's. Approaching him in solemn procession, the Emperor took off his purple cloak, prostrated himself and kissed the Pope's feet. Alexander raised him up, embraced him and gave him his blessing.

After eighteen years of war and schism the Pope's triumph was complete. It only remained for him to consummate it in Rome. Accompanied by an imperial escort, he entered the city on 12 March 1178 and in August the anti-Pope, who first made a show of defying him, submitted and was graciously appointed Rector of Benevento. In the following spring Rome was the scene of the third Lateran Oeucumenical Council, attended by some 300 bishops. It is chiefly remarkable for its decision providing that popes must in future be elected by a two-thirds majority in the College of Cardinals; it failed to mention either any imperial rights on such occasions or the right of confirmation by the Roman clergy and people.

It is impossible not to admire Alexander's achievement in withstanding for so many years, and finally frustrating, the aims of the mightiest ruler of the age. Nor does it detract from his success that Frederick was at the same time contending with the Lombards and hampered by the enmity of the Guelfs in Germany. The Pope's strategy was based on his cool appraisal of political realities and his tactics, if unspectacular, were perfectly effective. He never lost his head or his nerve. 'Tenacious' and 'resilient' are the epithets historians have rightly applied to his character. Above all he was a superb administrator, and he was in consequence well served by his Curia, his legates and the whole ecclesiastical machinery. It functioned with such smoothness and efficiency that the papacy emerged from the long conflict with its dignity greatly enhanced, but with depleted finances and, as was to prove more serious, at the cost of a marked neglect of its spiritual mission. Corruption in the overgrown clerical bureaucracy was rife and sarcastically criticized. Alexander's personal establishment, however, seems to have been modest enough. After the Lateran Council he again withdrew from Rome until his death two years later at Civita Castellana, from where he continued to direct diplomatic activities ranging from Spain to Sweden and from Ireland to Constantinople. The sheer volume of business transacted by his chancery exceeded that dealt with by any contemporary court. A more lasting result of his pontificate, and especially of his residence in Latium, was his contribution to the build-up of canon law. His own eminence as a jurist inspired a vast output of decrees and decisions on every conceivable detail of church organization, discipline, ownership and finance. One disadvantage, his unpopularity with the Romans, he never overcame. All the respect owed to him in the wider Christian world could not prevent his funeral procession from being pelted with stones and filth.

Seventeen crowded years separate the reign of Alexander III from that of Innocent III, the most famous of mediaeval Popes. Of the five men who filled the office during that period all were Italians and all were engaged to a varying extent in a prolonged sparring match with the Hohenstaufen emperors. The Third Crusade (1187–92), although the outstanding international event of the time, was perhaps of less direct concern to the Holy See. The most notable of these pontiffs was Celestine III (1191–8), who died at the age of 92 after a very active pontificate.

Lucius III (1181–5) was also an elderly man, a Cistercian who had been promoted by Bernard of Clairvaux. Hadrian IV had made the monk Ubalde Allucingoli Cardinal-bishop of Ostia; as a member of the Curia he had helped to negotiate the Treaty of Benevento and the Peace of Venice. He was celebrated for his rectitude and pacific dispostion, and like his precedessors he soon found life in Rome impossible. The Romans were angry with him for refusing their demands for money, and persecuted him by harassing his loyal towns in Latium. Most of his time was spent at Segni discussing with imperial envoys the old vexed question of the Tuscan lands and revenues bequeathed by the Countess Matilda to the papacy but appropriated by the Emperors. In 1184 he went to meet Frederick at Verona, but although their interviews were friendly there was not much give and take. In particular Lucius refused to crown Barbarossa's son Henry as co-emperor, but while they were still talking Frederick posed a new threat to the papacy as an Italian power by betrothing Henry to Constance of Sicily, daughter of Roger II and heiress of the childless William II. This meant that Henry would become the effective ruler of the Sicilian Kingdom and that the papal state would be hemmed in on both sides by Hohenstaufen territory.

At this point Lucius died at Verona and the Cardinals, thoroughly alarmed, elected as Urban III (1185–7) a Milanese who could be relied upon for his hostility to the Hohenstaufens. He was Umberto Crivelli, who had very recently been appointed archbishop of his native city. He was also a man of sharp temperament. He could not avoid sending his legates to the wedding in Milan cathedral, but at the same time he launched a bitter attack on imperial claims to regalian rights in Italy and encroachments on papal preserves. Lucius had held the same views on the subject but had been at pains to avoid an open breach. Frederick's reaction was to order his son to invade and occupy the whole state of the Church, with devastating effect on its already shaky finances. Deprived of Rome, from which he was completely estranged, and of all other papal territory, and also expelled from Verona, Urban died sadly at Ferrara and was buried there in exile.

The College of Cardinals, accustomed to the perambulating life, had already caught up with the Pope at Ferrara and were ready to elect in his place Cardinal Alberto of Morra, Chancellor of the Church since 1178. He took the name of Gregory VIII (1187). He was a good example of the cosmopolitan curial churchman. Born at Benevento, he became an Augustinian canon at Laon in France, gained the degree of Master of Law at Bologna and carried out an important legation in England. An ascetic by nature and a strict disciplinarian, he was an excellent choice, but he only lasted for 8 weeks. He found time, however, to make peace with Henry by promising to crown him at the first opportunity, and to issue an urgent appeal to the Western Kingdoms to mount the third Crusade.

In 1187 the Latin states of the East were in a desperate predicament. They had managed to hold their own after the collapse of the Second Crusade and in 1169 had even joined the Byzantines in an expedition against Egypt. But five years later the Moslem East, Syria and Egypt, was united under one ruler, the great Saladin, who posed a growing threat to their existence. King Baldwin IV of Jerusalem defended Saladin's Egyptian army in 1177 and there followed ten years of sporadic campaigning and uneasy truce, with the westerners avoiding unnecessary provocation. Yet the balance was precarious. When Baldwin died of leprosy in 1185 his successor, Guy of Lusignan, reversed the previous policy of caution, with the result that the Christian army was annihilated by Saladin at the battle of Hatium. Three months later, in October 1187, he recaptured Jerusalem and it looked as if the remaining Christian stronghold would soon fall into his hands.

Gregory VIII did what he could. Having issued his appeal, he travelled to Pisa in order to mediate between it and its inveterate enemy Genoa, for the fleets of both cities would be indispensable in any properly organized crusade. But he died there before he could give any further impulse to the preparations. The Roman Paolo Scolari, Cardinal-bishop of Palestrina, who succeeded him as Clement III (1187 –1191), took up the task and found little difficulty in stirring up the princes of Europe. Even so they wasted much time in composing their own quarrels and the movement of their forces to Palestine was poorly co-ordinated. Contingents from England, Flanders and Denmark made their way separately to the Levant and it was not until the spring of 1191 that King Richard of England and King Philip of France disembarked at the fortress-port of Acre. As they were on good terms with the Sicilian monarchy, the leading maritime power in the Mediterranean, it was safer and more practical to travel by sea. Frederick Barbarossa, on the other hand, chose the land route through the Balkans that the Germans had followed on the two previous Crusades, with fatal results to their discipline and cohesions.

The third expedition was no exception to the pattern of former disasters. The old Emperor, approaching his seventieth year, started in 1189 at the head of a powerful army. Like its predecessors it had a stormy passage through Byzantine territory and there were sharp differences between Barbarossa and the Emperor Isaac Angelus. The march through Asia Minor, harassed by Turkish bowmen, was equally gruelling. And no sooner had Frederick surmounted the worst obstacles and descended into the coastal plain of Cilicia than he fell from his horse into the swift flowing River Calycadrus and was swept to his death. This disaster wrecked the army's morale; by the time it struggled into Christian territory at Antioch it had ceased to count as an effective fighting force.

Pope Clement did not live to hear of the subsequent triumphs and disappoint-ments of the Crusade, of Richard's epic duel with Saladin and his treaty that left the Moslems in possession of Jerusalem. At home his objectives had been to reconcile the papacy with his own fellow citizens and to persuade the Hohenstaufens to evacuate the Church's domains in Italy. He was reasonably successful on both counts. While no one expected that his pact with the Romans would last, it was at least a sincere effort to find a basis for co-operation between Pope and commune. The Pope was thereby acknowledged as overlord and the Senators were to take their oath to him. He received the right to coin money, a third of which was to be remitted to the Senate, and was authorized to use the city militia for the defence of the patrimony so long as he paid for its services. He further undertook to compensate the Romans for any war damage, to contribute a yearly sum for the upkeep of the walls and to continue the customary 'presents' to individual Senators and municipal offices. Clement was prepared to pay a stiff price for the privilege of living quietly in his native city.

At the time of Barbarossa's death Clement was preoccupied by the Sicilian question. William II was now dead, but the claims of Henry and Constance to the succession were being challenged by Tancred of Lecce, an illegitimate grandson of King Roger. The Pope was in a dilemma; he would have preferred to recognize Tancred but could hardly dare to alienate Henry whom he in fact undertook to crown as emperor in the spring of 1191. However he too died before the ceremony took place and his problem was inherited by Celestine III (1191–8).

It is not clear why the Cardinals so promptly elected a man of 85, but Celestine, the doyen of the College, was both universally respected and immensely experienced in legations and other curial affairs. He was also a Roman. Hyacinth was his name and his family, the Boboni, were shortly to adopt the surname of Orsini. He had been a Cardinal for nearly half a century and took his pontifical name from Celestine II, the Pope who had originally appointed him. He was a distinguished theologian and renowned for his personal probity.

Such was the man who was called on to confront Henry VI, a young man of boundless ambition and, as the unhappy Sicilians later became aware, capable of the most inhuman ferocity against all who opposed him. He saw himself as emperor of Germany and all Italy, and a future conqueror of what remained of the Byzantine empire. Despite the ignominious collapse of the German Crusade he conceived the German emperor as altogether superior to the Kings of England and France who at least had got as far as fighting in Palestine. If Celestine was to baffle him as Alexander III had baffled Frederick, and to prevent the union of the empire with the Sicilian Kingdom, he could only hope to do so by temporizing, and he was a masterly temporizer. After crowning Henry he warned him against the risks of campaigning against Tancred and besought him to leave Sicily alone. He was proved right; the campaign failed and Henry had to hasten home to deal with disaffection among the German princes. As Celestine understood very well, Germany was a weak point in Henry's position and without provoking an open clash with the Hohenstaufen emperor, he did nothing to discourage the rival house of Guelf. In 1192, when Henry's difficulties in Germany were at their worst, he went so far as to recognize Tancred as King.

There things might have remained had it not been for two unforeseen developments. First Richard of England, Tancred's ally and brother-in-law of Henry the Lion, head of the Guelfs, fell into the Emperor's hands on his way back from the Crusade and only purchased his liberty by paying an enormous ransom and helping to reconcile Henry with his opponents in Germany. Secondly Tancred died in 1194 and Henry was able to take possession of Sicily. What the papacy had most feared had now come about. Nevertheless Henry still needed papal approval for the Sicilian succession, for the crowning of his infant son, Frederick Roger, as King of the Romans, for the assertion of his supremacy in Germany and for his plans for expansion in the eastern Mediterranean. For the next three years he pursued tortuous negotiations with the Holy See which Celestine spun out for as long as possible. He offered a yearly proportion of imperial revenue to be earmarked for papal expenses, but the Pope was too astute to fall into a trap which could have fatally compromised the papacy's independence. Talks were still in progress when Henry unexpectedly succumbed, at the age of 32, to the ever-present threat of malaria. Celestine, aged 92, survived him by just over three months.

INNOCENT III AND HIS SUCCESSORS
(1198–1254)

Henry's disappearance from the scene presaged an immediate upturn in the papacy's fortunes, and it speaks much for the sagacity of the sacred college that it elected the right man to extract the fullest advantage from it. It unhesitatingly elevated the 37-year-old Lothario, Cardinal-deacon of St Sergius and St Bacchus and son of the Count of Segni, a feudal lord of Lombard descent. Although he had not yet made his mark in the service of the Church, his talents had not remained undetected, and he had received the best possible clerical education in Paris and Bologna.

Innocent III (1198–1216) was determined from the start to be master in his own house. His own strong Roman connexions, as well as the power vacuum in Italy resulting from Henry's death, helped him to impose his authority in the city. He had no trouble in removing the prefect, an imperial nominee, and the senior Senator representing the Roman people, together with a number of judges, and replacing them with papal officials responsible to himself. At the same time he was thoroughly purging and reorganizing the curial bureaucracy. A more lengthy and difficult task was the so-called 'recuperation' of the numerous Italian territories forfeited through the weakness of the papacy, which the German emperors, despite repeated assurances and agreements, had failed to return. Now, in the wake of the reaction that had set in against the imperial system and German rule in general, the Pope re-established direct control over the Duchy of Spoleto and the March of Ancona. He was less successful in the Romagna, where the Archbishop of Ravenna refused to relinquish his rights, and in Tuscany, the papacy's inheritance from the Countess Matilda, where great communes like Florence and Siena emancipated themselves from either imperial or papal control. Nevertheless, by the time of Innocent's death in 1216, the area of the papal state had been more than doubled, forming a compact block in central Italy.

It is important not to ignore the reverse of the medal. Even in the heyday of the mediaeval papacy the Holy See was powerless to stop petty wars between the Roman commune and small towns in the patrimony of St Peter. The Romans were intensely jealous of any privileges the Pope might confer on the latter. For instance Celestine III failed to prevent the total destruction of Tusculum and the dispersal of its inhabitants, and Innocent barely averted the same fate from Viterbo. A pope who successfully composed disputes between the Kings of Europe was unable to check the sordid and bloody feuds on his own doorstep.

In Sicily the prospects also seemed favourable at first. The Empress Constance, on assuming the regency, hastened to get rid of her husband's German advisers and to have her 3-year-old son proclaimed King. She also asked Innocent to accept the kingdom as a papal fief and to act as the boy's guardian. To this he agreed, while withdrawing all the rights in church matters conceded by former popes to the Sicilian monarchs. But when Constance almost immediately died he was faced with responsibilities which he was unfit to fulfil. Papal rule was no substitute for strong Norman government. Sicily soon dissolved into anarchy and there was nothing that Innocent could do to stop it. It was only in 1208, when Frederick attained his majority at the age of 14, and the Sicilians rallied to him, that order could be restored. From the Pope's point of view, however, Sicily proved more a burden than a threat.

In Germany the picture was more confused. With the young Frederick at least temporarily out of the running, a double election produced two German Kings, the Hohenstaufen Philip of Swabia, Henry's brother, and the Guelf Otto of Brunswick, the first supported by the King of France and the second by his nephew the King of England. Neither would step down and both angled for papal approval. While naturally preferring a Guelf to a Hohenstaufen, Innocent was initially inclined to remain neutral and to discourage the rivals from fighting one another. In 1201, however, he recognized Otto as King of Germany and potential emperor, subject to his solemn promise to respect papal sovereignty in central Italy. After a time Otto's fortunes declined and the Pope welcomed overtures from Philip. But just as he was about to switch his sympathies Philip was assassinated and there seemed to be no further point in keeping Otto at arm's length, especially as he had promptly married his dead rival's daughter. So in 1209 he invited him to assume the imperial crown at Rome.

As it turned out, that was a bad mistake. When he met Otto at Viterbo he found him vain, obstinate and disposed to ignore his former engagements. However, he swallowed his misgivings to the extent of escorting Otto to Rome and crowning him in due form. Then everything went wrong. After the almost ritual fight between the Roman mob and the imperial troops the Emperor ignored the Pope's protests and began calmly to re-annex the Church's territories. Acting just like his Hohenstaufen predecessors, he next proceeded to invade southern Italy and Sicily. Innocent was deeply shocked and grieved. 'It repenteth me', he exclaimed in the words of *I Samuel* 15:2, 'that I have set up Saul to be King, for he is turned back from following me', but the counter-measures that he took were remarkably effective. He excommunicated the newly-crowned monarch, absolved the German princes and bishops from their allegiance and incited the King of France against him. Faced with unrest at home, Otto called off his Sicilian enterprise and hurried back to Germany, only to find that his supremacy there was being more seriously undermined than he thought. The fact was that Innocent had finally reversed his pro-Guelf policy and switched back to the Hohenstaufens. Otto had hardly reached his own country when the young Frederick, summoned by the Pope and already conscious of the welcome he might expect from the German supporters of his house, arrived at Rome on the first stage of an adventurous journey to the north.

The meeting was of crucial importance. Innocent knew perfectly well that he was taking a great risk in sponsoring yet another Hohenstaufen, the grandson and son of two rulers whose conception of empire had in the past so disastrously clashed with the papacy's traditional theory of the proper relationship between the spiritual and secular powers in the Christian world. Was it not inevitable that if Frederick succeeded in establishing himself as King of Germany he would inherit all his predecessors' aspirations, and especially those concerned with Italy? Was it not clear that whatever guarantees might at that stage be extracted from him, they would eventually not prevent the union of the German and Sicilian realms under one King-Emperor? Would he not immediately revive the former Hohenstaufens' claim that their election as Kings of Germany and their simultaneous assumption of the misleading title of 'King of the Romans' automatically led to their coronation as emperors and their overlordship of all Italy, including the papal state and the city of Rome? Like Celestine before him, but even more emphatically, Innocent was determined to rebut that contention. For him there was no doubt at all that only a pope could choose and make an emperor; the latter was simply the sworded arm of the universal Church; the Pope was the sun and the Emperor, shining with reflected light, the moon.

The dangers were obvious. All the same there was no other suitable prince whom Innocent could at that time have opposed to Otto. Moreover Frederick's bid for the German crown was also a gamble and nobody could have foretold that the untried (but already married) youth of 18 would grow into a 'Stupor Mundi' and cause unparalleled anxieties to future pontiffs. So Innocent had to be content with his formal renunciation of the Sicilian throne in favour of his infant son Henry, together with the tight renewal of the engagements regarding Sicily as a papal fief entered into by his mother Constance.

However, as soon as Frederick had vanished over the Alps, the Hohenstaufen threat lay dormant until the next pontificate. The issue of his subsequent contest with Otto was not decided until the summer of 1214, when the latter was routed by the King of France, Frederick's ally, at the battle of Bouvines. A year later the papal legate crowned him King of Germany on Charlemagne's throne at Aachen. But at that moment Innocent was already preparing for the impressive climax of his reign, the Lateran Council of November 1215, and was not unduly preoccupied by Frederick and the future evolution of the empire. Indeed this massive and mainly political problem had for many years claimed rather less of his attention than other matters of more vital import for the Catholic religion and the development of the Church. These were the Fourth Crusade, the rise of heresy and the foundation of the Mendicant Orders.

From the start of his reign the Pope had been anxious to inspire a fresh attempt to recover the Holy Places, and when he heard that a number of influential lords in France, Flanders, Germany and north Italy were planning an expedition he gave them every encouragement. It was, he thought, essential to avoid the mistakes of the Third Crusade and particularly the quarrels between royal leaders that had nullified its victories. Therefore he was glad that the new venture was being promoted not by kings but by senior vassals. Once it was launched Innocent was not personally involved in the preparations. In principle the leaders decided to attack Egypt, the centre of Moslem power in the Near East, but many of the Crusaders would have preferred to sail straight to Palestine. In any case only the Venetians could provide the necessary shipping which, together with their own participation, they offered at the immense price of 85,000 pounds of silver and the promise of a half share of any land and booty that the expedition might acquire. A further and more sinister complication was that the Crusade became entangled, against the Pope's wishes and even without his knowledge, in the dynastic affairs of Byzantium.

The Pope had already been in touch with the eastern emperor, Alexius III Angelus, about a possible reunion of the Churches. But Alexius's hold on the empire was precarious. He had lately usurped it by dethroning and blinding his elder brother Isaac, and Isaac's daughter was married to the Hohenstaufen Philip of

Swabia, the King of Germany. Isaac's son, also called Alexius, had escaped to the west and concerted with Philip and Boniface of Montferrat, the prospective military leader of the Crusade, a plan by which the Crusading fleet, instead of attacking Egypt directly across the Mediterranean, would first proceed to Constantinople and help the young Alexius to displace his uncle. They tried to persuade the Pope that this would be the best way of achieving the acceptance of papal supremacy by the eastern church. But Innocent was suspicious of their motives and would have nothing to do with any project to divert the Crusade, even temporarily, to Constantinople. He knew that Boniface and the Doge of Venice, Enrico Dandolo, both nursed personal grudges against the Greeks; Dandolo had lost an eye in a riot at Constantinople thirty years earlier and Boniface's brother, married to a Byzantine princess, had perished there in a popular massacre of westerners in 1182. Moreover, compared with a hazardous campaign against the Sultan of Egypt, the conquest of the shaky Greek empire looked like an easy option. Nevertheless it is unlikely that Boniface's project had yet matured to that extent. What was quite certain was that the Crusaders, by now (1202) encamped outside Venice, were unable to produce half the sum demanded by the Republic. But the Doge then offered to let them off the deficit if they would help him to recapture the Dalmatian city of Zara (Zadar), which had fallen into the hands of the King of Hungary. They all too readily agreed, and Zara was duly stormed and sacked in November.

Innocent was indignant. He excommunicated the Venetians, as mainly responsible for this piece of trickery, and would have extended his ban to the others if he had not considered them to be a degree less guilty. No notice, however, was taken of his fulminations. As they wintered on the Dalmatian coast, the leaders of the expedition received from the young Alexius further promises of military and financial support for the Crusade, provided that they helped him to win the Byzantine throne. He also specifically undertook to bring the eastern Church over to Rome. When the latter message was relayed to Innocent, he merely repeated that Jerusalem, not Constantinople, was the Crusaders' proper target and exhorted them to abstain from further aggression against Christians. Venetian influence ensured that this admonition was also ignored. In June 1203 the fleet finally reached Constantinople; after some not very serious fighting Alexius III fled from the city and his nephew was installed as Alexius IV with his father, blind Isaac, as his colleague. But that was by no means the end of the affair. The Crusaders soon discovered that Alexius IV, a foolish and unpopular ruler, was incapable of redeeming his promises. Moreover the Byzantines, intolerant of his western leanings, rose against him; he was deposed and murdered and a son-in-law of Alexius III was raised to the purple as Alexius V, a champion of Greek nationalism. Thereupon the western leaders lost patience. Again stimulated by the Doge, they decided to seize the city and put an end to Greek rule. There was no further thought of going on to Palestine or Egypt. On 12 April, after one unsuccessful effort, Constantinople was taken and for the next three days given over to the ultimate humiliations of atrocity, desecration and pillage.

The first intimation of this horrific event reached the Pope in the form of a glowing report from Baldwin, Count of Flanders, whom the conquerors had proclaimed as Latin emperor of the former Byzantine realm. Though shrunken it was still an impressive inheritance. While dividing up the enormous booty from the sack, and without bothering to consult the Holy See, the Latin Crusaders were calmly carving up the Orthodox Christian territories among themselves. As envisaged Venice obtained the lion's share, Crete and all the valuable islands and trading stations of the Aegean. Boniface was enfeoffed with Thessalonica and northern Greece, and the rest of Hellas was waiting to be appropriated by Frenchmen. Baldwin, as emperor, was left with Constantinople, Thrace (menaced by the Bulgarians) and western Asia Minor (bordered by the Turks and still in the possession of the Greeks). On the ecclesiastical side a Venetian had been consecrated, also without papal sanction, as Latin patriarch of the whole region.

At first Innocent was delighted to hear of this revolution. The Crusade might not have done its straightforward duty, but at last and at one stroke eastern Christendom had been reduced to the Roman obedience; the schism was no more and a reformed Byzantium would surely serve as a base for the recovery of the Holy Sepulchre. But when he realized the full extent of the excesses committed, his reaction was one of utter revulsion against those who had defiled religion and outraged humanity. He condemned the sack as 'an example of perdition and the works of darkness' and excoriated the leaders of the Latins for not heeding papal advice in sharing out their conquered estate. However there could be no reversing of what had been done. A new Latin-ruled Orient had come into being and there was no knowing how it might develop. Meanwhile, although no elaborate western hierarchy was established in the Aegean world and the orthodox bishops were expelled from their sees, the people unanimously rejected Roman Christianity and followed their village priests who celebrated the old cult. The achievement of real unity between the two halves of Christendom had been made more difficult than ever, if not frankly impossible.

Thus in the East the Papacy was outwardly victorious, but its gains were counterbalanced by the ominous spread of heresy in its Western heartlands, Italy and France. Catharism, the dualist religion of the heretics, derived its name from the Greek word meaning 'pure'. Its eastern origins can be traced back to the Gnostic doctrines current in the Roman Empire in the second century and to those propagated by the Persian prophet Mani in the third. These teachings sought to give an explanation of the eternal conflict between light and darkness, good and evil, and to account for the apparent equivalence of the two opposing principles. In the process they developed a fantastic theology, in which Christian and magical elements were inextricably confused, and what was more significant, an ascetic morality to be observed strictly by the elect but not compulsorily for the common run of believers.

The heresy was tough and resilient. Having survived, not without difficulty, the triumphs of Catholicism in the Roman Empire, it took deep root in the highlands of Armenia where its adherents, known as Paulicians, long defied the efforts of the Byzantine rulers to suppress it. Indeed they established an independent state which was only destroyed, after a series of stiff campaigns, by the Emperor Basil I in 872.

A century later many thousands of the remaining heretics were transplanted to the Balkans in order to defend the Byzantine frontiers. The result was that the Balkan Slavs became infected with dualism. The numerous heretics in Bulgaria and Bosnia were known as Bogomils. From the Balkans the movement spread westwards, as early as the eleventh century, to northern Italy and France. Throughout the twelfth century it was already supplanting Catholicism as a popular cult with alarming speed and thoroughness.

Catharism was not, as is still widely assumed, simply an early and abominable form of Protestantism, although it owed most of its success to popular dissatisfaction with abuses in the Catholic Church and social conditions in the mediaeval world, the shabby realities behind the resplendent façade of the High Middle Ages. Its trappings, literature and nomenclature were largely borrowed from Catholic Christianity, but its basic tenets amounted to a denial of the Christian faith. As Steven Runciman succinctly puts it, 'there is no room for Christ in a truly dualist religion', 'all good Christians must necessarily fight against dualism.' Other sects too were active, such as the Waldenses of Lyon and the Humiliates of Milan, but these, although anti-clerical and non-conformist, were strictly Christian and conspicuous for their simple piety. They did not believe, like the Cathars, that the world about us had been created by Satan.

Languedoc was the region most deeply permeated by Catharism. As early and 1119 we find Calixtus II condemning it at Toulouse and in 1147 Eugenius III was sufficiently alarmed by its progress to send the great Bernard of Clairvaux to preach against it. Alexander III denounced it in 1163 at the Council of Tours and later despatched two separate missions, each headed by a Cardinal, to combat it in Languedoc. But none of these measures had any lasting effect. By the end of the century Catharism had become the dominant religion and Catholic Christianity had been left high and dry. Catharism catered for all tastes, for the most rigorous asceticism as practised by its own élite, the 'Perfects', and for the permissive morality better suited to the courtly culture of southern France. It appealed both to the people, who preferred the fervent exponents of heresy to the worldly prelacy, to the lazy or discouraged Catholic priesthood, and to the princes and nobles with their pleasures and refinements. In Italy the situation was less desperate, but an attempt by Lucius III to break up the well-organized Cathar communities in Lombardy and Tuscany was equally unsuccessful.

Innocent was determined to stop the rot. He immediately appointed a mission, staffed by Cistercians, to replace unworthy Catholic clerics and to put pressure on the princes. It was headed by a legate, Peter de Castelnau, and by the Abbot of Citeaux himself. Soon it was reinforced by two stalwart Spaniards, Bishop Diego of Osma and his sub-prior Domingo de Guzman, the future St Dominic, who struggled to regain the allegiance of the masses in the guise of bare-footed itinerant preachers. But neither approach availed, for Catharism had taken a firm hold of all sections of society. In 1208 a crisis flared up when the legate was assassinated by a henchman of Count Raymond VI of Toulouse, the most powerful of the feudal magnates concerned and notorious for his indulgence towards the heretics. It seemed to the Pope that further efforts to convert them by peaceful means would be useless; the time had come to call on the secular arm. But when he applied to Philip of France, the Count's feudal superior, the King answered that he was too busy with wars against England and the Emperor Otto. Nothing daunted, Innocent appealed to the royal vassals over his head, proclaimed a Crusade against the Cathars and obtained an eager response. The indignant northern barons, avid for loot and lands in the rich south, ranged themselves under the banner of Simon de Montfort and in the next year a bitter and merciless war began. The southerners were crushed at the battle of Muret (1213), but it took another full scale invasion by Louis VIII of France (1226) and another half century of steady persecution by papal inquisitors before Catharism was extirpated.

The Cathar crisis was at its height and the issue still in doubt when, in 1210, Cardinal John Colonna brought Francis of Assisi, accompanied by his first eleven followers, to see the Pope. It was only the second year of his mission as wandering preacher and exponent of the virtues of apostolic poverty. Greatly to his credit, Innocent at once accepted these ragged ascetics as his allies in the fight against heresy and in his insistence that prelates and minor clergy should lead simpler and more diligent lives. He did not regard them as a threat to his own conception of a hierarchically ordered Church. In their externals they may have resembled the Cathar 'Perfects' and some contemporary Protestant sectarians, but he was convinced by their profession of total obedience to the Pope and his bishops. Therefore he gave them his blessing and orally approved their primitive rule. He did not however formally recognize the Franciscans as an Order. He could hardly have foreseen the phenomenal expansion of a movement which in the next decade was to recruit 5,000 members in Italy alone. It was already well under way, and the subject of much controversy within the Church, when Innocent convoked his great Council of 1215.

Mediaeval Rome had never witnessed so magnificent a spectacle. It far surpassed imperial coronations, which were usually confined to the Leonina and marred by bloody clashes between Romans and Germans. The citizens were now treated to a dazzling display of the Church's power and wealth. The 2,283 representatives of the Catholic world included the Latin patriarchs of Constantinople and Jerusalem, 71 archbishops, over 400 bishops, 800 abbots and envoys from all the feudal states and cities of Europe. In his opening address Innocent took as his text *Luke* 22:15, 'With desire I have desired to eat this passover with you before I suffer.' He was interpreted both as foretelling his own early death (he was only 56), which was to occur six months later, and as pointing towards the fulfilment of two major goals or transitions of his pontificate, the launching of a new Crusade and the reform of a Church united and delivered from heresy. He was encouraged because Frederick, when crowned King of the Romans earlier in the year, had taken the Cross, and the Cathar cause in Languedoc looked desperate. But the main achievement of the Council was strictly practical. It adopted 70 magisterial and carefully drafted canons for inclusion in the papal law-book, mostly dealing with Church discipline and Christian duties in thorough detail. The first of them, however, approved for the first time the doctrine of transubstantiation, the conversion of the bread and wine of the Eucharist into the body and blood of Christ. Apart from the deposition of the unfortunate Otto, purely political matters were hardly touched on.

Innocent designed the Council as an exaltation of the Church in all its glory. He was not a vain man and there was no arrogance in his stands at the apex of the pyramid. But in his conception the office of Vicar of Christ was supremely grand, indeed grander than it had appeared to any of his predecessors. He also had confidence in his own abilities and a deep sense of mission. Despite very real disappointments he was convinced by results that he was following the right path. Certainly his blend of authority, piety and efficiency had raised the papacy's prestige to unexampled heights within a very few years. At the same time his ideas were not unboundedly theocratic. He did not pose as a super-sovereign in the style of a Justinian or even of a Frederick Barbarossa. When he spoke, echoing Leo I, of exercising the 'plenitude of power' it was strictly as the spiritual head of Christendom; it did not mean that he aspired to control the secular affairs of the Christian kingdoms even when their rulers held them as papal fiefs. As a temporal ruler himself he was content with the State of the Church. He did however both claim and exercise the absolute right to exhort and reprove, as well as to foil any attempt by a prince to infringe the Church's rights or to offend against the order of Christian morality and justice. He did not, for instance, flinch from excommunicating King John for his flagrant interference with ecclesiastical appointments or even from placing England under an interdict lasting five years. He imposed similar penalties on King Philip and France for the sovereign's personal misbehaviour as a husband, and in both cases brought the monarchs to heel.

Historians have rightly lavished praise on Innocent's virtues—the nobility of his character, his firmness of purpose, the lucidity and flexibility of his mind, his courage, integrity and common sense, his legal acumen, his capacity for work and grasp of detail, the simplicity of his personal life. Both intellectually and morally he towered over his contemporaries. Furthermore, his predominance was universally accepted and respectfully admired. He had no enemies and no rivals. There was clearly something particularly captivating as well as imposing in his appearance, voice and manner, something that daunted opposition and disarmed criticism. We are told that he was a small man with a 'pale oval face, long dominating nose, oblique eyes, tiny ascetic mouth and forceful chin'. He has been accused of lack of imagination, but it is hard to see how any further endowment of that kind could have produced better results in action. He may too, have misjudged personalities, at least in the sense that they failed to live up to his exacting standards, and did not appreciate the inevitable limitations of papal authority. However that may be, he left the papacy in a more flourishing condition than either of his two predecessors, Gregory I and Gregory VII, who have an equal claim to greatness.

To Innocent there succeeded as Honorius III (1216–27) the elderly Cardinal Cencio Savelli, a native of Latium and for many years a diligent and efficient member of the Curia. As Vice-Chancellor and Chamberlain of the Church he had controlled its finances and compiled the *Liber Censuum*, the official register of its revenues and properties. By disposition he was mild and patient. Hardly an inspiring figure, he was yet quick to discern threats to papal interests and obstinate, if not always successful, in their defence. His pontificate began calmly enough but the clouds soon gathered about it.

He conceived it his prime duty to persevere with Innocent's plans for a new Crusade which would atone for past disappointments and disasters. One of these had been the ghastly farce of the childrens' Crusade; only in Spain, after the decisive Christian victory of Las Navas de Tolosa, had the Moslems lost ground. The Fifth Crusade, busily sponsored and partly financed by Honorius, lasted from 1217 till 1221 and was in some respects more hopeful than any of its predecessors since the First, but it was an ill co-ordinated affair and the leadership was both divided and incompetent. At one time or another the Kings of Hungary and Cyprus, the titular King of Jerusalem, the Dukes of Austria and Bavaria and the Grand Masters of three Military Orders were all engaged in the expedition, which was composed of contingents from many European countries. However its operations in Syria were quite ineffective, and it was only when they were switched to Egypt that it posed a serious threat to Moslem supremacy in the Near East. The Crusaders captured Damietta in the Nile delta but failed to advance much further towards Cairo. Fighting was very stiff and the issue long remained undecided. Incongruously enough, Francis of Assisi turned up in the Christian camp and during a truce interviewed the Sultan al-Kamil. In order to resolve differences among the princely generals the Pope appointed his own legate as commander. He was Cardinal Pelagius, a keen but intransigent Spaniard whose presence had the opposite effect. He did his best but in the end the Crusaders succumbed to Moslem numbers and strategy. In September 1221 they capitulated and were permitted to sail away.

The collapse of this great enterprise, in which tens of thousands of western troops were employed, deeply saddened the Pope. What grieved him most was that Frederick II, who had taken the Cross at his coronation as King of Germany, had persistently shirked his manifest obligation to assume the command. The whole of his pontificate, both before and after the failure of the Crusade, was spent in strenuous efforts to persuade Frederick to join it or to lead yet another host to the reconquest of Jerusalem. But the Hohenstaufen had other ideas. While never saying no he fobbed off Honorius with excuse after excuse until he had carried out his own design. This was to take back Sicily into his own hands and to induce the German princes to elect his son Henry as their King, thus reversing his solemn undertaking to Innocent III that Henry would have Sicily while he reigned in Germany and north Italy. By 1220, the year fixed for his coronation at Rome, his preparations were complete. He correctly judged that he would be able to overcome the Pope's misgivings by giving him to understand that as soon as he was crowned he would commit himself to a Crusade. Honorius was of course not duped, but he could not help being outmanoeuvred by a negotiator in a stronger position.

First, at the cost of wide concessions to the German princes, Henry was duly elected. Then, in the summer and autumn of 1220, Frederick made a slow and stately progress through Italy towards Rome. Before he was crowned on 22 November he again assured Honorius that the only link between the German and Sicilian kingdoms would be his own personal sovereignty and their administrations would be kept quite separate. After the ceremony in St Peter's he again took the Cross and undertook to start his Crusade by August 1221. He took great pains to appear dutiful and conciliatory. As custom demanded he held the Pope's stirrup and bridle. He announced additional privileges for the Church throughout the empire and stern measures against heretics. He sensibly went out of his way to be generous to the Romans, distributing ample largesse and providing them with a gorgeous show. Outwardly his relations with the papacy could not have been more cordial when he continued on his way to Sicily.

As the years passed, however, the irritations grew. It is true that Frederick was not entirely to blame for his reluctance to leave for the east. He did send a small fleet to Egypt in 1221, though when it arrived the Crusaders had already surrendered. But he found the Sicilian realm, incidentally a papal fief, in chaos and needed several years of hard work to put things right. Among other difficulties he faced a serious revolt by the Moslem population in the island itself. During this period he twice held conferences with the Pope and obtained his unwilling consent to successive postponements of his Crusade. Honorius was obliged to reproach him for allowing his subordinates to grab Spoleto and Ancona from the papal state; it was the old story but this time the Emperor intervened in the Pope's favour. Honorius, with his usual exemplary patience, reciprocated when Frederick's bid to reassert his power in north Italy alarmed the Lombard cities. They revived their League in order to resist him and blocked the Alpine passes so as to prevent the young King Henry from joining his father. The Pope's mediation, however, resulted in a temporary compromise. Meanwhile in 1225, Frederick entered into yet another engagement to start the Crusade two years later, promising to fit out a very large fleet and to pay a huge sum into a special fund for the purpose. He accepted that failure to carry out his obligations would result in his excommunication. Such was the position when Honorius died in March 1227.

The gradual decadence that the papacy underwent throughout the thirteenth-century, that eventually led to schism and disruption, stemmed from the irreparable nature of the breach between the Emperor and Gregory IX (1227–41), a feud prosecuted with increasing violence during the pontificate of Innocent IV (1234 –1254). It is ironical that while the energies of these talented Popes were almost totally absorbed in this barren and frequently barbaric conflict, the mediaeval civilization around them was reaching its zenith. Catholicism was graced and enriched by saintly figures and outstanding intellects, by a galaxy of philosophers, mystics and poets. It was the century of Albertus Magnus, Bonaventura and Thomas Aquinas. Gothic architecture was at its peak and there were signs of a great revival in the visual arts.

The successor of Honorius, Ugolino, Cardinal-bishop of Ostia, was a very old man. Matthew Paris, the contemporary English chronicler, says that he was nearly 100 when he died. He was the son of a Count of Segni and thus closely related to Innocent III, many of whose finer characteristics he shared, but he was more rigidly resolute, sterner and more passionately uncompromising. His presence, both venerable and dominant, caused Honorius to describe him as a 'Cedar of Lebanon in the Church's park'. Educated at Paris and Bologna, he was a brilliant theologian and canonist. At the same time his personal piety was deeply inspired by the mysticism typified by his friend Abbot Joachim of Flora, whose prophetic utterances were sometimes regarded as bordering on heresy. Above all he was the sponsor of both the booming Mendicant Orders. In 1217 Honorius had wisely appointed him official protector of the Franciscans, with a mission to bring their activities into line with the Church. To Francis all such organization was anathema, but he trusted Ugolino, who was more tactful in religion than he could ever be in politics, and together they worked out a definitive Rule for the Order which took effect in 1223. Five years later it fell to him to canonize his saintly friend. Owing to his efforts the Franciscans evolved swiftly from a swarm of ascetics into the intellectual and moral workforce of the Church, competing in those functions with the Dominicans in whose development Gregory was equally concerned. For better or for worse he sanctioned according to strict procedures their operations as papal inquisitors, which originated from their founder's combat with heresy.

Gregory knew Frederick well enough to distrust him from the start. He suspected that the Emperor was as insincere in his religious beliefs as he was determined to construct a secular Roman empire in the Mediterranean free of any dependence on the papacy. He was therefore not surprised to hear that Frederick, having assembled a vast Crusading force at Brindisi in August 1227 and actually embarked for Palestine, had turned back and landed at Otranto. He refused to credit what was in fact true, that the host had been decimated by a fearful epidemic of dysentery, to which Frederick himself was lucky not to succumb, and excommunicated him without further ado. Although he had correctly summed up Frederick's character and aims, his action was a tactical error. The Emperor had firmly decided to go to the east, not only to rescue the Holy Places but to assert his rights in Cyprus (an imperial fief) and as regent (on behalf of his second wife Yolanda de Brienne) of the Latin Kingdom of Jerusalem. Undeterred by the papal ban and bitter anti-imperial propaganda, he resolved to leave in the summer of 1228. Meanwhile he defiantly countered the Pope's recriminations. He also instigated a revolt against him in Rome, headed by the Frangipani, thus causing Gregory to retire to Perugia. After this parting shot he at last set sail for Cyprus and Palestine.

Not even the old Pope, with his long experience of wordly affairs, could have guessed how the excommunicated Emperor would conduct his Crusade, that he would recover Jerusalem without fighting but by means of a peaceful though tricky negotiation with the Sultan al-Kamil. It seemed almost sacrilegious to him that no infidel blood had been shed and that the Moslems had even been permitted to retain their own shrines in the Holy City. It was infuriating that Frederick, celebrating his triumph without benefit of clergy in the church of the Holy Sepulchre, should have calmly clapped the crown of Jerusalem on his own head. Gregory's reaction was to release the Emperor's Sicilian subjects from their allegiance. Meanwhile open warfare blazed up in Italy with Frederick's general invading the papal state and papal troops, the 'Soldiers of the Keep', attacking Campagna and Apulia. It ended when the Emperor, after nearly a year's absence from Europe, returned and routed the papal forces in a rapid campaign.

Both sides now needed a respite. Frederick wished to be absolved from the ban, to enjoy his prestige as liberator of Jerusalem and to develop his beloved Sicilian realm. The Pope desired to return to Rome and, while he had no illusions about Frederick's future behaviour, to restore so far as possible the harmony that had prevailed between papacy and empire under his two predecessors. Moreover there was much pressure in favour of reconciliation from the princes of Europe and from inside the College of Cardinals. Thus, in 1230, an accommodation was reached by the Peace of Ceprano. Frederick in particular was not disposed to haggle. He rescinded the counter-measures that he had taken against the Church after his excommunication and the frontiers of the papal state remained intact. After the treaty had released him from the ban he paid a private and amicable visit to Gregory at Anagni. To all appearances they had composed their quarrel and the Pope ratified all the arrangements Frederick had concluded for Palestine.

Nevertheless Gregory's pontificate was to become even stormier. While completing his monumental codification of canon law (1234) he faced a real revolution at Rome. This had been brewing for some time and seems to have been one of those outbursts of aggressive independence to which the Romans were periodically addicted. Led by the Senator Lucas Savelli, a nephew of Honorius III, they made sweeping demands, including the right to elect Senators, to raise taxes and to issue a coinage. They pressed for the abolition of clerical immunities and the exemption of all Romans from excommunication. They also threatened the very existence of the papal state, declaring its cities and provinces to be the property of the Roman people and extending their claims as far afield as Tuscany. But they had chosen to defy the wrong man and at the wrong moment. Retreating with his Curia to Rieti, Gregory encouraged the smaller cities to resist Roman pretentions. He also called on Frederick for aid, which in the new climate was promptly supplied. The Emperor intervened in person and the Romans, crushed in battle at Viterbo, were compelled to submit.

In return for this very substantial aid Frederick invoked the Pope's support in his current difficulties with the Lombards, but Gregory's attempts at mediation were at best half-hearted. He obliged the Emperor by excommunicating his hapless son the King of Germany, who was conspiring with the Lombard League against his father, but became deeply alarmed when Frederick persuaded his German vassals to join him in subjugating the north Italian cities by force of arms. He seemed determined to impose on them the same absolutist system as prevailed in the Sicilian Kingdom, which in Gregory's view would inevitably lead to the establishment of a unitary Italian realm with Frederick as its unchallenged autocrat and himself reduced to the status of a regional bishop. The state of the Church would disappear and Rome would become the capital of a secular empire. He began actively to encourage the cities in their resistance. He was appalled when, in 1237, Frederick overwhelmed the

Milanese at Cortenuova and, with sardonic humour, presented the captured *carroccio*, their ceremonial war chariot, to the Roman people.

By 1239 Pope and Emperor were ranged in open opposition to each other. Papal legates were active in sowing dissension in Germany and stiffening the Lombards, while a defensive alliance was negotiated with Venice and Genoa. Meanwhile Frederick was secretly trying to suborn the Cardinals. When Gregory found out what was happening he riposted with a new sentence of excommunication. This was a blunt weapon but its employment at that instant amounted to a declaration of war. Hostilities began by an exchange of virulent abuse in the form of well publicized manifestos. Imperial propaganda belaboured the Pope as a veritable Antichrist, and unworthy false prophet who had dared to slander the legitimate Roman emperor and deserved to be deposed by a General Council. Gregory's countering encyclical denounced Frederick as the monster of the Apocalypse, the 'furious beast from the sea', the fount of blasphemy and unbelief. From words the Emperor passed swiftly to deeds. His forces isolated Rome and the Curia from the rest of the world and in February 1240 he invested the city. It was touch and go whether his partisans would take it over and admit him, but the centenarian Pope refused to be intimidated. He paraded the Church's most sacred relics, including the heads of the Apostles, from the Lateran to St Peter's laid his mitre on them and exclaimed 'May the Saints defend Rome if the Romans will not defend themselves.' Thus he rallied them to his side. In any case the defences were too well manned by his supporters to make an assault worthwhile and the exasperated Emperor was forced to sheer off.

Gregory's next move was to summon his own General Council for Easter 1241. Since all roads to Rome were blocked, he arranged for the Genoese to transport the foreign prelates by sea. However Frederick got wind of the plan and had them intercepted by his Sicilian fleet. Over 100 were made prisoners. Worn out by this fiasco and ravaged by kidney disease, the implacable old man died in the heat of August. The imperial army, encamped in Latium, still shrank from attacking the Roman walls.

If the Emperor remained baffled, the Curia was in chaos. Only ten Cardinals were available to elect a new Pope. Half of them had been devoted to Gregory while the others favoured a compromise with Frederick. In the hope of forcing a quick decision the Senator of Rome, Matteo Orsini, herded them into one dilapidated room in the Septizonium and kept them deprived of servants, doctors and proper food. Their guards mishandled them horribly, amusing themselves by defecating on them through holes in the roof. In such nightmarish conditions one Cardinal, an Englishman, died during the conclave and all fell ill. It was a marvel that they stuck it out for two whole months before electing Godfrey, Cardinal of Sabina, as Celestine IV, but after sixteen days he too perished from exhaustion. The survivors scattered and nothing would induce them to risk another such ordeal.

There followed an interregnum of nearly two years. Eventually, after the demise of one more Cardinal and the release of two whom the Emperor had held captive, the nine remaining members of the battered College assembled at Anagni. Their choice fell on the Genoese Cardinal Sinibaldo Fieschi, who assumed the name of Innocent IV. A curial jurist of high distinction, he was inclined to neutrality in politics, but his family, the Counts of Lavagna, were zealous imperialists. Frederick was therefore well satisfied and saluted him as a 'noble son of the empire'. Very soon, however, he was to revise his opinion and to observe ruefully that 'no Pope can be Ghibelline' (a term derived from the ancestral Hohenstaufen domain of Waiblingen in Franconia). Once installed in Rome, Innocent began to fight the Church's battle with the same energy and obstinacy as his predecessor. But he did so with weapons that suited his own sophisticated temperament. His frigid subtlety ended by disconcerting the Emperor much more effectively than Gregory's passionate straightforwardness. There is no reason to doubt his sincere devotion to the Church's ideals, but it was not marked by conspicuous piety or spiritual charisma. He was a master of political manoeuvre.

However unpromising the prospects, Innocent was bound to try for a general settlement in Italy, of which he held nothing outside the walls of Rome. He therefore spent several months negotiating with imperial envoys. In order to release Frederick from the ban the Pope required him to evacuate the papal state, but even if a deal could have been concluded on that basis Innocent was unwilling to give him carte blanche to subdue the Lombards. Were he to get his way in Lombardy, no guarantee of the papal state would be valid. It dawned on the Pope, while keeping the Emperor at arm's length, that he might be wiser to pursue the struggle from outside Rome and perhaps away from Italy. So long as he remained in the Lateran he would necessarily be negotiating under duress.

Therefore he decided to break out. His escape, less romantic than that of Alexander III, was planned in great secrecy with the help of his Genoese connexions. Having arranged to meet Frederick at Narni, he travelled as far as Civita Castellana and thence made an excursion to Sutri. In the middle of the night he rode over the hills with a small escort to the port of Civita Vecchia, where Genoese galleys were awaiting him. But Genoa was only the first stage of his journey, for he felt that his future campaign would be more safely launched from beyond the Alps. The devout King of France, Louis IX, had no wish to irritate the Emperor by receiving the Pope in his own kingdom. However he had no objection to his residing at Lyons, nominally an imperial city but in fact governed independently by its archbishop. It was there that the Pope and his Curia, enriched by twelve recently appointed Cardinals, established themselves in the winter of 1244. From that moment it was again war to the knife between Pope and Emperor. Nevertheless Innocent did not find it easy to whip up enthusiasm in northern Europe, where kings and bishops failed to understand the intense enmity that had divided Italy into two irreconcilable camps. All Italians had become embittered Guelfs (papalists) or Ghibellines (imperialists); city was pitted against city, ruler against ruler and family against family. The genuine ideological differences between the two sides were accentuated by unrestrained and often vicious propaganda to which the Emperor, with his notorious scepticism and oriental propensities, was more vulnerable than his opponent. The Pope's cause was effectively served by the Mendicant Orders, whose influence had become as powerful in intellectual circles as among the populace, and benefited from the waves of revivalist enthusiasm that from time to time swept over Italy during the thirteenth century. Moreover the whole Church apparatus in the peninsula, though weakened by the absence of its head, was still in being and ably directed by the capable and unscrupulous Cardinal Rainer of Viterbo.

Innocent's relentless campaign lasted until Frederick's death in 1250. He started by summoning a General Council at Lyons (1245) which, if poorly attended, pronounced the Emperor to be both excommunicated and deposed. Then, ignoring offers of mediation from Louis IX, he mobilized all available resources to undermine Frederick's position in Germany and Italy. Unfortunately the papacy was very short of money; on his accession he had been obliged to hide in a corner of the Lateran from a mob of creditors demanding the repayment of debts contracted by Gregory IX. To the despair of King Louis, who was trying to finance his coming Crusade, vast sums were levied from the faithful in France while indulgence and marriage dispensations were hawked freely around. In Germany the Pope's efforts set up two successive anti-kings, Henry Raspe of Thuringia and William of Holland, neither of whom lasted for very long, but the blows he struck in Italy proved more deadly. The first took the form of a widespread Guelph conspiracy aiming at the murder of Frederick and a general uprising against Hohenstaufen rule. There can be no doubt that Innocent personally sanctioned the proposed assassination, for his own brother-in-law, Bernardo Orlando di Rossi, thitherto a trusted imperial official, was its prime mover. It was discovered and ferociously suppressed, but Orlando escaped to organize a coup which fatally damaged the whole structure of imperial power in Italy.

In 1247 Frederick prepared to march north. His intention was to reduce Germany to obedience and to chase the Pope from Lyons. But before he could start the Guelfs seized by a bold stroke the key city of Parma. He turned back, built an elaborate fortified camp and sat down to invest it. He was still doing so in February 1248 when the garrison and citizens turned the tables on him, storming and burning his camp. This defeat was the signal for many papalist commanders to take the field; bloody battles and sieges took the place of intrigue and propaganda. Depressed by the treason of his favourite counsellor, Piero della Vigna, and by the capture of Enzio, his favourite illegitimate son, by the papalist Bolognese, Frederick fought bravely on and by 1250 it looked as if he had the upper hand. The Pope, threatened by bankruptcy, gloomily watched the Ghibellines, stiffened by Frederick's Saracens and mercenary German Knights, regaining the lost ground. Suddenly he was saved by an undreamed-of reversal of fortune. On 13 December 1250 the Emperor, who had seemed perfectly healthy, died of dysentery while on a hunting trip in Apulia.

Innocent lost no time in returning to Italy, where he was received with enthusiasm in Milan and other Guelf cities. For the time being he avoided Rome, that source of endless trouble and embarrassing demands for cash, and settled at Perugia or Viterbo. He was anxious to press his advantage by wresting control of the Sicilian kingdom from the Hohenstaufens. The latter were now represented by Conrad, King of Germany, Frederick's son by his second wife, and his bastard Manfred who was acting as the King's regent. The Pope's object was to substitute for them a ruler willing and pliant enough to accept Sicily as a papal fief. He tried Richard of Cornwall, brother of Henry III of England, Henry himself on behalf of his son Edmund, and Charles of Anjou the brother of King Louis, but all three cautiously refused so tricky an honour or posed too many conditions. Meanwhile Conrad, who had reached Italy shortly after Innocent, took over the Kingdom and it appeared that Germany and Italy were again united under one monarch. But Innocent's hopes revived when Conrad died in 1254 and Manfred felt constrained to conclude a treaty by which he was to govern a papal vicar on terms very unfavourable to himself. Innocent seemed to have achieved his purpose. With Manfred holding his bridle he entered the Kingdom in state and proceeded through Capua to Naples. Total triumph, however, still eluded him. Disgusted by his humiliation at the hands of the Guelfs, Manfred broke away from the cortège, rallied his father's Saracen regiments and inflicted a resounding defeat on the papal forces. When Innocent heard the news he was already dying at Naples. He was buried there and the inscription on his tomb read 'he destroyed the snake Frederick, Christ's enemy.'

12

THE SLOPE TO EXILE

(1254–1305)

Under Innocent IV the papacy took a downward turn from the high peak attained under Innocent III and Gregory IX. The entire energies of the Church had been devoted to political objectives. It had slipped from the position of impartial judge of disputes in Christendom as a whole to that of one of two contestants fighting furiously for power in the Italian peninsula. Absorbed in diplomatic, juridical and financial activities, the Curia neglected its religious functions. Even the friars, bursting with spiritual zeal, had been diverted to mundane ends, and the huge material resources of the Church had been squandered for political and military purposes. The moral decline of the papacy and its instability as an institution are illustrated by the short pontificates of the second half of the thirteenth century, during which no fewer than thirteen Popes came and went. Without regaining moral stature they lost their grip on political affairs and became virtually appendages of French royal hegemony. Some of them were pious, energetic and well-meaning but none lasted long enough to make their mark. Political dissensions in the Sacred College and among the Romans caused long and damaging interregnums and absences of the Popes from the city.

The Guelf-Ghibelline conflict formed the background to the first three of these pontificates. Alexander IV (1254–61), an unassuming cleric who had served for 23 years as Cardinal-bishop of Ostia, could do nothing to stop a Ghibelline revival. Manfred, now crowned King of Sicily at Palermo, occupied much of the papal state and the army of stoutly papalist Florence was routed at Montaperti in 1260. Factional strife and social revolution had already driven Alexander out of Rome. The governing Senator, Brancaleone degli Andalo, was a Bolognese who had been called in by the merchant guilds and the rising artisan class, whereas the Pope, a nephew of Gregory IX, belonged to the nobility. Not wishing to be personally involved in civic feuds, the easy-going Alexander chose to retire to Viterbo and Anagni while the parties fought it out. First the democrats prevailed; it is recorded that Brancaleone demolished 140 fortified towers belonging to the nobles. In the end the latter restored the situation, but the Pope prudently stayed where he was. Besides, he loved a quiet life and indeed seems to have been a rather lovable character; one chronicler, free with his epithets, called him 'placid, sanguine, plump, humble, pleasant and risible'. However, he was interested in things of the mind and made his influence felt at a distance. A keen patron of the Mendicant Orders, he upheld their claims to teach at the University of Paris and thus helped them build their great edifice of mediaeval theology and scholastic philosophy.

Urban IV (1261-4) avoided Rome altogether. Jacques Pantaleon was a Frenchman, the son of a poor shoemaker of Troyes, who owed his advancement in the Church to his own abilities. Most of his career had been spent in legations and in the bishopric of Verdun. Alexander IV had appointed him Patriarch of Jerusalem, a city again in Moslem hands although the Crusaders still held a diminishing foothold in Palestine. He owed his election to the fact that he happened to be visiting Viterbo at the time of the conclave.

Not only was Jerusalem irrecoverable but in 1261 the Greeks re-took Constantinople and expelled its Latin Patriarch. However, Urban was gratified by a message from the Byzantine emperor, Michael VIII Palaeologus, suggesting that the moment had come to discuss the reunion of the Churches. Nothing came of the approach because Urban's attention was wholly focused on the Sicilian question. Manfred was eager for a settlement. For his enfeoffment with the Kingdom he made a straight offer of cash – 300,000 ounces of gold down and 10,000 yearly thereafter. It was tempting enough for a papacy so deeply sunk in debt but the Curia's innate hostility to the Hohenstaufens ensured its rejection. The French Pope's thoughts were fixed on the French prince Charles of Anjou, Count of Provence. Before negotiations with the latter could begin it was necessary to persuade the conscientious King Louis that the rights of Conradin, King Conrad's son and the only surviving legitimate Hohenstaufen, could be overriden and the still extant candidature of Edmund of England withdrawn. When that was done papal envoys were despatched to discuss with Charles the territorial and financial details of the proposed settlement. While they were still talking the Romans took it upon themselves to elect Charles as Senator of Rome for life. Whether or not the Pope was forewarned of this move it embarrassed him exceedingly; as he himself put it, he had no wish to exchange Scylla for Charybdis. With difficulty the agreement was rehashed to provide that Charles, who had already installed a Provençal garrison in Rome, should give up his Senatorship as soon as he had conquered Sicily, but the agreement was still unsigned when Urban died at Perugia. It was left to his successor to apply the finishing touches.

He, Clement IV (1265-8), by name Guy Fulquois, came from Saint Gilles on the border between Provence and Languedoc. As a lay jurist, married and the father of two children, he had served as adviser to Louis IX. After his wife's death he took orders and rose to become bishop of Le Puy and archbishop of Narbonne. Urban made him a Cardinal and sent him as legate to England, where he upheld Henry III against Simon de Montfort. Elected Pope in his absence, he made his way through Italy disguised as a simple monk, for fear of interception by the Ghibellines, and was consecrated at Perugia. He too never went near Rome.

Like most of his compatriots he personally disliked Charles of Anjou, that cold, hard and overwhelmingly ambitious northern Frenchman. At the same time he fully accepted the curial view that the Church's supreme interest was to get rid of the Hohenstaufens, and by underwriting Urban's settlement he effectively delivered the papacy into French hands. He watched passively from Viterbo while Charles marched to Rome, where he was enfeoffed and crowned King of Sicily, but with characteristic caution he left these offices to be performed by a committee of Cardinals. He protested angrily when Charles occupied the empty Lateran palace and his troops bullied the Roman populace. Later he remained an unenthusiastic spectator of the epic campaigns in which Charles successively vanquished and killed Manfred at Benevenuto (1267) and overcame the hapless young Conradin at Tagliacozza (1268), taking him prisoner and subsequently executing him. This cruel act was neither inspired nor condoned by the Pope, who barely survived to witness Charles's triumph.

He had not been alone in his misgivings about Charles. By no means all the Cardinals were reconciled to the prospect of an Italy controlled by the Angevins, and the College was also divided by national and personal differences. It was in total disarray and in the end took nearly three years to elect a new Pope. While the headless Curia functioned by its own resources and the longest conclave in papal history dragged on at Viterbo, Charles was busy developing his plans to reconquer Constantinople and to build up for himself a Mediterranean dominion as originally conceived by the Hohenstaufen Henry VI. The execution of his project was however delayed by the need to support his brother's crusading attack on Tunis, in the course of which Louis IX died of typhoid and the expedition had to be rescued by the Sicilian fleet and army. In 1271 he and the new King of France, Philip III, went together to Viterbo and pressed the Cardinals to reach a decision. At last they compromised on a comparatively obscure cleric, Teobaldo Visconti, a native of Piacenza and archdeacon of Liège. When the news of his election reached him he was crusading in Palestine and did not reach Viterbo until early in 1272. But he insisted on being consecrated in Rome. Charles, in his capacity of Senator of the city, ensured that the ceremony in St Peter's was conducted without a hitch.

As Gregory X (1271-6) Teobaldo was by far the most effective Pope of the period, very religious minded and quietly determined to pursue church policies independently of royal ambitions. He wanted a Crusade against the infidel but no repetition by Charles of the dreadful events of 1204; in no event must the venture be turned against Christians. If there was to be a new Crusade he needed Byzantium as an ally and accordingly responded to the overtures already made by the Emperor Michael to Alexander IV and Clement IV. He immediately decided to convoke another General Council, the main purpose of which would be to pursue the issue of Church reunion. Later he announced that it would be held in 1274 at Lyons, well away from Charles's reach. If reunion could be achieved and a Crusade mounted with Byzantine co-operation Charles's designs would clearly be thwarted. He was anyhow involved in a war with Genoa, which had gone over to the Ghibellines, and with other Ghibelline cities in north Italy.

So far as ecclesiastics were concerned the Council was more fully attended than Innocent IV's, but the Pope was disappointed when only one of the fourteen kings he had invited consented to turn up. Thus no practical steps could be taken towards a Crusade. On the other hand negotiations for union were deceptively successful. The Byzantine envoys, two prelates and George Acropolita, the diplomatist and historian, made no serious objection to Gregory's terms for ending the schism of 1054. They acknowledged the primacy of Rome and joined in singing the Creed in Latin and Greek with the addition of the *Filioque*. But troubles began when they returned to Constantinople. Despite the Emperor's sponsorship of the act of union the Patriarch refused to accept it and was consequently deposed, and it was either denounced or ignored by the Orthodox clergy and people. Yet so long as it was formally valid it prevented any direct aggression by Charles against the eastern empire.

The Council also adopted thirty reform decrees. The most interesting of these, the Constitution '*Ubi periculum*', was designed to avoid interminable delays in papal elections. It specified that the Cardinals already present at the Curia should wait only ten days for their absent colleagues to join them; they should then be segregated from the outer world in conclave (literally under lock and key) and treated to a gradually austerer diet as time passed; nor should they receive any revenues. These prudent regulations were not always observed in practice, but in its essentials Gregory's Constitution is still in force.

But the most constructive and lasting achievement of this all too brief pontificate was the Pope's promotion of Rudolf of Habsburg as King of Germany. The title had been held since 1257 by the English Richard of Cornwall, but never effectively exercised. After his death the most insistent candidates for the throne were Alfonso of Castille, grandson of a Hohenstaufen, and Ottokar the powerful King of Bohemia. But Gregory, an excellent judge of character and prospects, firmly favoured the election of Rudolf, the rich and uncontroversial Landgrave of Alsace. He got his way and had this newcomer to empire proclaimed King of the Romans at the Lyons Council. One of the last acts of his reign was to meet Rudolf at Lausanne and to invite him to be crowned Emperor at Rome. Before this could happen he himself died at Arezzo (1276), but the vigorous and intelligent Rudolf was a perfect counterweight to Angevin pretensions.

Three ephemeral pontificates followed in less than eighteen months. Both Innocent V (Peter of Tarentaise, Archbishop of Lyons) and Hadrian V (Ottobuono dei Fieschi) were fervent partisans of Charles of Anjou, who also governed Rome in virtue of his office as Senator. The King was much irked by their premature deaths just when it looked as if the Church was falling altogether under French influence. The third of these popes, John XXI, was a more unusual figure. He owed his election to the small group of anti-Angevin Cardinals, headed by the Roman John Gaetani Orsini, who were looking for a candidate likely to be less subservient to Charles. They found him in Peter Juliano, Cardinal-bishop of Tusculum, a Portuguese with no marked political leanings. He was in fact a polymath of vast intellectual attainments. While master of the Faculty of Arts at Paris he wrote a handbook of logic which remained in academic use for 200 years, as well as a long psychological treatise on the Soul. He also produced works on theology and medicine. The superstitious Italians inevitably regarded him as a magician. But although by nature an unworldly scholar, he held the political ring with sensible impartiality. Unfortunately he died of his injuries when the ceiling of his newly built residence at Viterbo fell in and crushed him in his bed.

One of his decisions had been to suspend Gregory X's strict rules for the conclave. Consequently the College, split equally between Italians and Frenchmen, wrangled for six months before electing John Orsini as Nicholas III (1277–80). The son of the Senator Matteo Rubeo Orsini, he was first and foremost a Roman noble with a deep attachment to his native city. Secondly he was the doyen of the Cardinals, a statesman with 30 years experience in the College, a masterful character devoted to the freedom and independence of the Holy See. The policy of his brief but dynamic reign was based on the firm possession of Rome and the papal state, the existence of which was threatened by the Angevins just as it had been by the Hohenstaufens. Fortunately for him Charles's ten-year tenure of the Senatorship expired in 1278 and Nicholas, in a Constitution beginning with the splendid words 'Fundamenta militantis ecclesiae', decreed that in future no Senator should be appointed without the Pope's permission; only Roman citizens were eligible and the office was restricted to one year. For a start he nominated his own brother, a favour which, among others, earned him a place among the famous simoniacs, upside down in the eighth circle of Dante's Hell.

So long as he lived he successfully kept the balance between Charles and Rudolf. He persuaded the former to renounce the imperial vicariate of Tuscany and the latter to surrender all his rights in Romagna to the Holy See. He further sought to promote a lasting settlement between the two potentates. Rudolf was to receive the imperial crown and to guarantee not to attack the Sicilian kingdom. The Angevins were to continue to hold Provence, but as an imperial fief, and would gain in addition the so-called kingdom of Arbo which adjoined it. Finally Rudolf's daughter was to marry Charles's grandson. Although these plans were not fully realized, their negotiation kept the peace and gave a much needed boost to papal prestige. While strongly discouraging Charles's eastern projects, Nicholas was also pressing the Byzantine Emperor hard to enforce conformity with the Union on his recalcitrant subjects.

He liked to live in a grand style that matched his self-confidence and family pride; in that respect he may be regarded as a forerunner of the Renaissance Popes. He built a country mansion for himself and his kinsman near Viterbo, but his principal care was for Rome. There he restored the basilicas of St Peter and the Lateran, founded a new residence at the Vatican and embellished it with gardens.

It is hard to conjure up the outward appearance of Rome at this period. Essentially the city had never recovered from the Norman sack of 1084 and the endless tumults of the succeeding age. Some new churches had indeed been built, and old ones repaired and adorned, by twelfth- and thirteenth-century popes and certain ancient monuments, such as the Pantheon and Trajan's column, had been preserved by the Church or the authorities of the commune. Many more, however, had been disfigured by transformation into fortified dwellings or simply fallen into shapeless ruin. The populace lived in closely packed and tumbledown slums and the whole townscape was dominated, as in other Italian cities, by the tall but jerry-built brick towers of the nobles. Nevertheless enough wonders, both classical and Christian, remained to be listed in the mediaeval guide-book entitled the *'Mirabilia Urbis Romas'*, which was compiled and frequently re-edited, with more imagination than accuracy, for the edification of pilgrims and distinguished visitors. There was also a processional route, the *Via Papalis*, which was regularly used on ceremonial occasions, winding its way past sacred sites and traversing the triumphal arches of antiquity.

The lack of continuity in papal affairs was graphically demonstrated when Nicholas died of a stroke in his new country house on 22 August 1280. With Gregory X's rules in abeyance the Sacred College was as evenly divided as it had been before his election. Once again the Cardinals argued fruitlessly for six months. The deadlock was broken only by pressure from King Charles and by a strong local reaction at Viterbo, where the conclave took place, against the house of Orsini. The new pro-Angevin *podestá* of the town burst into the conclave and arrested the two Cardinals belonging to that clan, whereupon the rest of the College hastily gave its votes to Simon de Brie, who succeeded as Martin IV (1281–5). A former Chancellor of Louis IX and created Cardinal of Santa Cecilia by the French Pope Urban IV, he was an unashamed promoter of French interests, and as such completely reversed his predecessor's policy in favour of Charles. All Nicholas's careful plans for papal independence and political equilibrium went by the board and Angevin garrisons moved into the papal state. In Rome, where the Orsini were also in eclipse, the Pope assumed the Senatorship but promptly handed it over to the King. He himself was consecrated at Orvieto and stayed there, stocking the Sacred College with French Cardinals.

As Martin was well aware, no further obstacle remained to the realization of Charles's long contemplated attack on Byzantium. Throughout 1281 huge armaments were built up in the ports of south Italy and Sicily. Martin eagerly treated the aggression as a Crusade and contributed thereto the proceeds of six years' tithes from Sardinia and Hungary. At the same time he contemptuously rebuffed further assurances from the Emperor Michael regarding Union. But neither he, nor surprisingly enough the Curia, had apparently sensed that secret diplomacy was working hard to thwart the enterprise. For some time an anti-Angevin conspiracy of formidable dimensions had been spreading its web from one end of the Mediterranean to the other, uniting the Byzantine Emperor to Peter III of Aragon, the husband of Manfred's daughter Constance and sole heiress of the Hohenstaufen claims. It was largely run by exiles from the Sicilian kingdom and the chief of these, John of Procida, a medical doctor from Salerno, had been appointed Chancellor of Aragon. In earlier days he had attended Nicholas III (then Cardinal Orsini) and according to stories current at the time Nicholas was privy to the plot before he died. However that may be, the inhabitants of Sicily were already sick of the arrogance and rapacity of Charles's frenchified government, as well as incited by John's agents, when the rebellion of the Sicilian Vespers on 30 March 1282 destroyed Angevin rule in the island and confined it, after wars which involved all the western Mediterranean kingdoms and rumbled on well into the next century, to the south Italian mainland. The Pope and his immediate successors, grimly clinging to the Angevin connexion, redoubled their excommunications and interdicts against rebels and Aragonese, but without any lasting success.

There is no need to go into the details of these interminable hostilities. By the end of 1285 all the principal actors – Charles of Anjou, Peter of Aragon and Pope Martin – were dead, the last, it was said, after dining too well on milk-fed eels from Lake Bolsena cooked in wine. During the pontificates of Honorius IV (1285–7) and Nicholas IV (1288–92) the political exertions of the papacy became more and more ineffectual. All attempts to dislodge the Aragonese from Sicily failed disastrously and proposals for mediation proved equally unpromising. Honorius, Cardinal-deacon of Santa Maria in Cosmedin, a member of the Roman house of Savelli and nephew of Honorius III, was an elderly valetudinarian who lived quietly at Rome in a palace which he had built on the Aventine. He was crippled by gout, as also was his brother the Senator Randulf, but their short government was remarkable for the good order that reigned in the city. Unhappily his invitation to Rudolf of Habsburg to come there for his long-delayed coronation foundered when the German bishops refused to raise a special tax to finance the German King's journey.

After Honorius's death the chair remained vacant for eleven months. Although the conclave was held peacefully in the Aventine palace, the mortality among the participating Cardinals was unusually fearsome; no fewer than six succumbed during the summer heat of 1287 and the rest broke up in confusion. When they reassembled in the winter they elected Jerome of Ascoli, Cardinal-bishop of Praeneste (Palestrina) and a former General of the Franciscans. Unlike Honorius he was not at his ease in Rome. According to one account he was 'violently ejected' from the city and retired to Rieti early in his reign. Apparently his partiality for the Colonna family, which had dominated his former bishopric, was resented by the Orsini and other nobles. Later he returned, and in the tradition of Nicholas III distinguished himself as a restorer of churches and a patron of artists such as the mosaicist Torriti and the painter Cavallini. He lived in a palace adjoining Santa Maria Maggiore in which the former did some of his best work. In Rome there was a faint glimmer of cultural revival. The Pope was also active in the missionary field, using as his agents friars from his own order. To one of them, John of Monte Corvino, he entrusted letters to remote eastern potentates, beginning with the Mongol Great Khan of Persia. An indefatigable traveller, John went on to India and even to China, where a subsequent Pope, Clement V, optimistically appointed him Archbishop of Peking.

But something was clearly wrong with an electoral system which produced either an elderly and ephemeral stop-gap or no Pope at all. What should always have been a choice from among the élite of Christendom had been reduced to the result of trafficking between two rival Roman clans, the Orsini and the Colonna. For over two years the twelve Cardinals concerned failed to reach a two-thirds majority for any one candidate; at first they could not even decide where the conclave should be held. They met finally at Perugia under pressure from Charles II of Anjou and plumped in desperation for an entirely neutral figure, the holy Calabrian hermit Peter of Morone. They did not all do so cynically, or because they assumed that so simple-minded a person could easy be manipulated by the Curia. Some of them, including the Dominican Cardinal Malabranca, were deeply impressed by his spiritual qualities and genuinely desired a break with the past. Malabranca spoke mysteriously of a vision in which the hermit had foreseen calamity for the Church if the vacancy were allowed to continue. Certainly the College was not unaffected by the contemporary current of mysticism, which contrasted so sharply with its own crass politicking. Peter's personality had anyhow been familiar to Popes and people for many years. Originally a Benedictine, he left his monastery for the solitude of a cell on Monte Marone near Sulmona. So many followed his example that over thirty communities of hermits sprang up in the papal state and southern Italy. Together they formed a Congregation which Urban IV affiliated to the Benedictine Order. Peter, however, continued to live as a solitary and gained a wide reputation for sanctity. Many Italians believed that he was destined to reign as the 'Angelic Pope' of whom there was much talk in mystical circles.

King Charles's attitude was equivocal. He too was personally impressed by Peter but also attracted by the prospect of keeping a popular pope under his thumb. When the hermit rejected the first overtures from the College, he summoned both him and the Cardinals to meet him at Aquila. Peter rode into the town on an ass, accompanied by the King and his son and acclaimed by excited crowds. He was immediately consecrated as Celestine V in a church belonging to his own Congregation. Many members of the Curia must have regarded the elevation of this octogenarian anchorite as an elaborate farce; there could have been no doubt that it was yet another temporary expedient and no answer to the problem of papal continuity. After procuring from him the nomination of twelve new Cardinals, seven of whom were French, Charles hustled him off to his capital, Naples, where he and the harassed Curia were installed in the Castelnuovo. But the whole bizarre experiment ended abruptly, after less than five months, in December 1294. Celestine had shown no disposition to attend to public affairs, even at the King's dictation, and confined himself as before to private devotions. He was thoroughly unhappy with his lot and there was no alternative to letting him abdicate at his own piteous request. The College, meeting under Gregory X's rules, elected Cardinal Benedict Gaetani in his stead.

The abdication raised a storm. It was a shock to popular hopes and some ecclesiastics argued that the Vicar of Christ had no right to step down. Dante, scornfully misjudging Celestine's character, branded *'il gran rifiuto'* as an act of cowardice while Petrarch, many years afterwards, praised it for its exemplary humility. Other contemporaries saw in it a plot by Gaetani. It would not be fair to blame the new Pope overmuch for smoothing the way to his own elevation, but he can be justly reproached for his subsequent treatment of Celestine. The wretched old man longed for nothing better than to return to his old cell. When he was told that he would not be permitted to stay there he ran away and tried to escape over the Adriatic to Dalmatia, but he was driven ashore and apprehended. Two years later he died under strict guard in a castle at Farentino. It is hard to believe that if left alone he would have allowed himself, as Gaetani feared, to be exploited as an anti-Pope. In 1313 he was canonized by Clement V.

Few could have predicted that as Boniface VIII (1294–1303) Gaetani, a worldly-wise prelate in his late seventies, was about to plunge the papacy into the worst and longest crisis of its history. He was the son of Loffred, a Knight of Anagni, and a nephew on his mother's side of Alexander IV. An outstanding jurist and experienced legate, he had been appointed to the Sacred College by the Frenchman Martin IV and had consistently supported the Angevin cause in Sicily. Yet by a strange paradox he was to meet his downfall in a combat *à outrance* with the French King Philip IV, the Fair.

Without possessing any of the spiritual gifts of a Gregory VII or an Innocent III, Boniface was passionately determined to reassert just as forcefully the universal authority of the Apostolic See in the face of its increasing usurpation by the national monarchies of Europe. He was a political extremist, pathologically power-conscious and impelled into dramatic confrontations by his imperious pugnacity and an arrogant confidence in his own intellect and abilities. He had no feeling for conciliation and compromise and no regard for the dangers of causing offence. With ferocious intransigence he rushed into conflicts he could not win. Quite apart from his main quarrel with France, his political touch was apt to be unsure. Despite all his efforts an Aragonese prince was eventually confirmed as King in the island of Sicily, and the Pope was forced to acknowledge Albert of Habsburg, of whom he first keenly disapproved, as King of Germany and future emperor.

The fight with King Philip started in 1296. War between France and England had resulted in heavy taxes and contributions being levied from the clergy by the royal treasuries of both sides. The Pope, who might have been wiser to accept these demands as inevitable, chose to challenge them on the question of principle. Did any King have the independent right to tax ecclesiastical institutions the ultimate ownership of which was vested in the papacy? It was by no means a new issue, but it came sharply to a head when Boniface published his Bull *'Clericis Laicos'* formally forbidding the taxation of clergy and Church property without express permission from Rome. In the event no breach with England was involved, if only because Parliament took the papal side, but in France, where the taxation had been much more onerous, the Crown retaliated by forbidding the export of currency and the entry of papal collectors into the country. Here Philip held the whip hand; Boniface had to back down and publish a further Bull restoring the royal right 'in case of need'.

Before the battle was resumed Boniface became involved in furious local strife with Colonna. This arose from the Pope's intervention in a family dispute regarding property by which he antagonized the two powerful Cardinals belonging to the clan. They also disliked his autocratic style of ruling and canvassed sympathy from all those who thought that Celestine had been unlawfully deposed. Boniface for his part suspected the Colonna of intriguing against him in the interests of King Philip. An open conflict broke out when two Colonna laymen pilfered a load of bullion (extracted, according to themselves, by papal agents 'from the tears of the poor') on its way to the papal treasury. Boniface's reaction was to order the Colonna to admit papal garrisons to Palestrina and other strongholds and when the demand was refused to expel both Cardinals from the College. A violent war of words followed. Two thunderous papal Bulls were countered by a manifesto denouncing Boniface for every conceivable malpractice and calling for a General Council to judge him. The Pope then proceeded to act. He declared all Colonna properties forfeited, mostly in favour of his own relatives, and all members of the clan excluded from ecclesiastical and wordly offices. Meanwhile his mercenaries methodically destroyed their numerous castles and razed their town of Palestrina to the ground. To such relentless bludgeoning they could offer no resistance; they either surrendered or dispersed in flight. The two Cardinals begged the King of France to intervene, but as he had recently wrung from the Pope the withdrawal of 'Clericis Laicos' he preferred to let matters rest for the present.

Well pleased with his victory, Boniface arranged to celebrate 1300 as a Jubilee year. It turned out a great success. Pilgrims converged on Rome in vast numbers and their offerings replenished the papal finances. Pomps and ceremonies were brilliantly staged. Perfect order prevailed, the Romans discarded for the moment their habitual aversion to foreigners and the city was kept well supplied. One visitor recorded that bread, meat, fish, wine and oats were plentiful and cheap in the markets; only lodging, stabling and hay were expensive. The general euphoria tempted the Pope to reopen his feud with Philip the Fair. The occasion was the arrest and trial of an obscure French bishop charged with treason and insulting behaviour in the royal Chancellor's court. When his demand for this cleric's release was ignored Boniface followed it up by another Bull repeating the provisions of 'Clericis Laicos'. It sparked off a bitter war of bulls and propaganda which continued with increasing intensity throughout the next two years and into 1303. The Pope, with an overweening sense of his own superiority, convoked the whole French episcopate for a Council in November 1302. Then, in 'Ausculta fili', he loftily summoned the King in person, rehearsing all the familiar grudges and exalting the primacy of the Holy See over all secular powers. Whether Boniface was suffering from megalomania, was living in a world of his own imagination or was simply enjoying the combat, the King, on his side, had his feet firmly planted on the ground. He eagerly took up the challenge, convinced that he could call the Pope's bluff. His astute and unscrupulous Chancellor, Pierre Flotte, together with all the nationally-minded theologians and lawyers France could produce, would be more than a match for the Curia, which was merely harking back to the past. So far as scurrility was concerned the French certainly won the day. They even circulated a forged version of the latest Bull accompanied by an imaginary royal reply with the delightful title of 'Sciat maxima tua fatuitas' ('Your utter stupidity should know'). On a more serious note the King assembled the three Estates of the realm in April 1302 to compose a formal remonstrance to the Holy See. Two months later the Pope called a Consistory of Cardinals and made a speech comparing Flotte with Achitophel and menacing Philip with deposition.

In the circumstances it was remarkable that as many as thirty-nine French bishops turned up at the Council where Boniface published his last Bull, the famous *'Unam Sanctam'*. It contained the starkest exposition of the papal claim to universality ever advanced in the Middle Ages, insisting that the spiritual power wielded by the Pope, as opposed to the secondary and secular power exercised by a King under papal licence, is absolute and can be employed at any time to override royal initiatives. Conscious of the strength of national feeling in France, the King saw no point in continuing the argument in terms of religious or political theory. It was clear that Boniface was incapable of enforcing by precept the principles formulated by Leo I, Gregory I and VII and Innocent III. As recommended by his new adviser Guillaume de Nogaret (Flotte having been killed in battle with the Flemings), Philip concentrated on attacking the Pope's character. So when Boniface excommunicated him he retaliated by calling another Council of senior clerics and lay magnates, at which the royal spokesman indicted the pontiff under twenty-nine heads, *inter alia* as a sodomite and simoniac and disbeliever in the immortality of the soul. In conclusion he repeated and broadcast throughout Europe the call for a General Council to pronounce on the Pope's record.

The struggle was now approaching its climax. Boniface prepared a new Bull to rebut the French charges and announced that it would be published on 8 September, but in the meantime Nogaret decided to take violent action against his person. His intention was either to place the Pope in custody or at least to frighten him into inaction. He had already arrived in Italy and was plotting with the Colonna and others whom Boniface had offended by his high-handedness and nepotism. Their leader was Sciarra Colonna. The conspiracy was planned in great secrecy and the Pope, who was holding court at Anagni, suspected nothing. He was taken by surprise when Sciarra's bravos stormed his palace on 7 September. For three days Sciarra and Nogaret tried to bully him into submission, but he held out and defied them to kill him. The former was for executing him on the spot, the latter for sending him to France. While they were still disputing the citizens of Anagni rallied and drove them out, leaving the Pope uninjured but very severely shaken. The Orsini escorted him back to Rome and lodged him in the Vatican, but after a month he died, aged 86, from the effects of his ordeal. Obsessed by the majesty of his office, he had consistently failed to grasp its limitations or to live up to its moral responsibilities. For that reason Dante unerringly placed him with Nicholas III in Hell.

On the day of his death Charles II of Naples appeared in Rome. Through his influence and in the absence of the Colonna Cardinals the College elected the pious Dominican Nicholas Boccasini, one of the only two who had stood by Boniface at Anagni. As Benedict XI (1303–4) he strove to calm the Roman factions and to keep the French at arm's length. He excommunicated all those responsible for the outrage but released King Philip from his ban. However he found his task impossible and died after eight months at Perugia, which thus became the scene of the next conclave.

The papacy was once more in serious disarray, and the College took eleven months to find a new pontiff. It was inevitable that whoever was chosen would have to enjoy favour with the French Crown and in general conform to its policies. But the participants in the Conclave could not have guessed that the next seven Popes would be Frenchmen and that they would all reside on the French side of the Alps. Severed from its traditional, though often uncomfortable, seat at Rome the papacy would have to function in the shadow of the strongest national monarchy in Europe. Moreover its very *raison d'être* as an institution of universal scope and validity was about to be called in question by skilled publicists. There was a real danger that as a dependency of France it might lose its paramount character or even disappear altogether, leaving the Church leaderless.

PART FOUR

SCHISM
AND
RECOVERY

13

AVIGNON AND THE GREAT SCHISM
(1305–1389)

It was at Avignon that the papacy made its new home under successive French pontiffs. They found in this delightful little city by the Rhône, formerly a possession of Charles II of Naples, the peace, stability and ease that they could not have hoped to enjoy by the Tiber. In the two centuries preceding their move the Popes had spent as many as 122 years out of Rome and it can hardly be denied that its atmosphere had exercised a stultifying influence on all but the most spiritual or strong-minded occupants of the Holy See. Internal unrest, varied by destructive interference from outside, had kept them perpetually on the move, even when they did not leave Italy, and deeply unsettled the operations of the Curia. It is indeed a wonder, only to be explained by a thousand years of experience, that it succeeded under such conditions in operating as efficiently as it did.

Avignon, on the other hand, offered few drawbacks and many advantages. It was tranquil, compact and well fortified; its population, numbering about five thousand, was not inclined to turbulence; the high countryside of the adjoining Comtat Venaissin provided healthy summer retreats. There would be no more endless traipsing between Viterbo and Anagni. Moreover the new papal residence was centrally sited in Western Christendom with excellent communications by road, river and sea. A French historian of the Avignon papacy points out that a messenger would have taken five days to Paris, ten to London and thirteen to Rome. And no sooner had the Popes established themselves than Italian bankers and merchants hastened to make Avignon a flourishing focus of financial and commercial activity.

Clement V (1305–14) was the first pope of the not very aptly named 'Babylonish Captivity'. He was Bertrand de Got, Archbishop of Bordeaux, and as a Gascon technically a subject of Edward I of England. Once selected by the Sacred College, he preferred not to travel to Rome for his coronation, which accordingly took place at Lyons in the presence of King Philip and an imposing assembly of French magnates. The ceremonies were marred by a serious accident. A wall collapsed and knocked the Pope off his horse; other notables in the procession were hurt and the Duke of Brittany died of his injuries. After this inauspicious start Clement could not make up his mind where to settle down. He roamed indecisively between Poitiers, Lyons and Bordeaux before finally coming to rest at Avignon in 1309. Apparently he selected it as being conveniently close to Vienne, where he was to hold a General Council two years later. Clement revoked all Boniface's anti-French bills and created several more French Cardinals; in all 23 out of his 24 new appointments were Frenchmen. But the King, now that he had him under his power, was insatiable in his demands.

The Papal Lodge at Viterbo

Alexander III pardons King Frederick 'Barbarossa'

CLEMEN∂:P: QIIII

KAROLVS IIIPRIMЪREX

Above: Clement IV assigning to
Charles d'Anjou, by Bull, the
crown of the Kingdom
of the Two Scicilies

Left: Innocent III, a thirteenth-
century painting

Above: Boniface VIII,
by Giotto, in the
Basilica of St John
Lateran

Left: Innocent III,
who put England
under the interdict
and formally deposed
King John in 1212

INNOCENTIVS · III · PONT MAX·ANAGNIN

Urban IV, who reigned from 1261 to 1264

Boniface VIII – who knew the publicity value of this sort of display – receiving a lowly novice

Amongst these were the public condemnation of Boniface, the release of Nogaret from the ban, the permanent establishment of the Curia in France, the convocation of a General Council and, most important of all, the proscription of the Order of the Templars. For nearly two centuries these knights, drawn chiefly from France, had formed the military and financial mainstay of the crusading states in the east, but since the latters' extinction their original role had lapsed. In short, the King's reasons for dissolving the Order were two-fold; it formed a state within a state, and it was extremely rich. The Templars were great landowners and international bankers, and the royal treasury was itching to lay its hands on their resources. In 1307, without informing the Pope, the King had them arraigned for heresy and immorality. Neither Clement nor his Curia seriously believed these charges, which, if not entirely unfounded, were such as could easily be cooked up against an exclusive and secretive organization. They would rather have dealt leniently with the Order and, if possible, diverted part of its wealth into the Church's coffers. But Clement, while well aware where the best interests of the papacy lay, did not have the courage to defend them. Egged on by Nogaret, the royal inquisitors pursued the Templars with relentless savagery. Their Grand Master, Jacques de Molay, was brutally tortured and burned, while the Archbishop of Sens sent 54 Knights to the stake on the same day. The papacy did nothing to mitigate the severity of one of the nastiest judicial crimes in history. Nor did the Council of Vienne, which was largely concerned with the affair and approved the Bull that finally extinguished the Order. All that the papacy gained in return for its abject behaviour and a catastrophic loss of prestige was the King's agreement that the memory of Boniface, that staunch but rash champion of its independence, would not be publicly condemned. At the same time, the assembly denounced the demoralized Curia for incompetence and corruption, and the Pope, who had raised five members of his family to the Cardinalate, for crass nepotism.

So far as Italy was concerned, neither Clement nor the vicars he appointed to safeguard his interests were capable of controlling events. North of the kingdom of Naples conditions were chaotic, with Guelfs fighting Ghibellines and the Colonna feuding with the Orsini in Rome. Revenue from the papal state was not reaching the Curia in France. The Pope would have liked to strengthen his authority by reaching an understanding with the German King, Henry of Luxemburg, but was forced by France and Naples into taking an anti-German line. Determined to be crowned in Rome, Henry had to fight his way into the city in the teeth of an Angevin garrison. The ceremony was performed by a Cardinal in what remained of the old Lateran Basilica, which had been ruined by fire in 1308. Henry's ambitious plans for the restoration of imperial and Ghibelline power in Italy were nullified by his death on campaign in 1313.

The Holy See was vacant from 1314 to 1316. The French members of the college now out-numbered the Italians but were unable to agree amongst themselves. A first conclave, held at Carpentras, was broken up by unruly Gascon adherents of the late Pope. The cardinals then moved to Lyons, where King Philip V confined them to the Dominican convent until they elected Jacques Drèze of Cahous, the candidate of the French and Neopolitan courts and a former Chancellor of the Angevin Charles II, who reigned as John XXII from 1316 to 1334. He was already 72 when he returned to Avignon, of which he had once been bishop.

John was a hard man, obstinate and combative, lacking tact, charity and insight. While remodelling the curial administration in its new home he strove to reassert the damaged papal authority over as wide a sphere as possible. If the French kings who came after Philip IV had been of the same overbearing type he might have found this an impossible task, but the monarchs' three sons and successors were fortunately not of the same calibre. Also France was soon to be plunged into the Hundred Years' War with England and the re-organized papacy, while careful not to offend France, became free to pursue independent policies. In Italy, still the main source of the Church's revenue, conditions were less propitious for any effective restoration of papal influence.

The whole north and centre was distracted by internecine quarrels between communes and local despots. The only hope for the re-establishment of peace and order lay in a harmonious understanding between the Pope and the King of Germany, but that solution was perversely ruled out by the former. John's election had coincided with a double election in Germany, where Lewis of Bavaria faced a rival in Frederick of Habsburg. For some unclear reason John conceived an intense dislike of the former, rebuffed his overtures and determined to prevent him from assuming the leadership of the Italian Ghibellines. This policy turned out to be grievously mistaken. It was Lewis who won the day. Having worsted Frederick in battle he descended into Lombardy and relieved Milan from investment by a papal army under Cardinal Bertrand du Poujet, another churchman from Cahors. The Pope sternly summoned him to withdraw and after some fruitless exchanges excommunicated him in the following year.

As background to these events a furious ideological conflict had already been raging for some years. In 1317, while trying to invalidate Lewis's election as King of Germany and to block his claim to the Empire, John had proclaimed that the Pope alone possessed the right to appoint imperial vicars in Italy, and indeed over the whole Empire in the event of a vacancy. In support of that contention all the old arguments for papal primacy were duly deployed. But in the course of centuries they had lost their credibility, except perhaps in logic, and were promptly and damagingly challenged by eloquent propagandists on the other side. Lewis himself replied to the papal ban in a manifesto addressed to 'John, who calls himself Pope'; it accused the pontiff of heresy, denied the validity of his election and demanded a General Council. But in order to refute the Pope's jurists he also recruited some of the ablest intellectuals of the age.

By far the most eminent of these was Marsilius of Padua, formerly rector of the University of Paris. In 1324, when the controversy between Pope and King was at its height, he published his famous book *Defensor Pacis*, the purpose of which was to exalt the role of the Emperor in Christendom and to call in question the whole theory of the plenitude of papal power. He not only impugned the Roman pontiff's pretensions to govern and legislate for all Christians but also implied that they were the real cause of dissensions between them. According to him the Church did not need a pope. As there was no firm evidence that St Peter, as opposed to St Paul, had ever lived in Rome, the bishop of that city could not claim primacy over other bishops; they all possessed equal rights as successors of the Apostles. These heady radical opinions, which were widely diffused, threatened to sap the very foundations of the hierarchy. In some respects, however, they were not entirely novel. Using more dignified but just as direct language, Dante had already asserted in his *De Monarchia* that the Pope had no right to exercise universal government or to dictate to the Emperor, who received his authority not from him but directly from God. It followed that in the last resort the State was above the Church, and if the Church still required a titular head neither he nor the institution any longer deserved excessive veneration.

Similar scathing attacks on the papacy and the Pope's person were made in more theological terms by the English Franciscan philosopher William of Ockham. It was unfortunate that John, a too rigid disciplinarian, had come to antagonize the whole Franciscan Order. For many years it had been split between the Conventuals, who freely accepted Church discipline and observed a rule resembling those of other religious Orders, and the Spirituals who hankered after absolute poverty and mystical perfection in accordance with their founder's principles. The differences between the two groups came to a head in 1318, when the Pope condemned the Spirituals on the ground that obedience was a greater virtue than either poverty or chastity, and unleashed a vicious persecution against them. Many were sent to the stake for their ascetic aspirations. Scandalized by such brutality, the Conventuals too, headed by the General of the Order, resolved to adhere to the principle of poverty, only to be convicted by the Pope of heresy. From 1323 the whole Order was in a state of rebellion. Its General, Michael of Cesena, was imprisoned at Avignon until he escaped to Germany, where he joined William of Ockham at Lewis's court. John's unnecessary vendetta against the Franciscan and all other mystical movements of the period alienated many churchmen and lost him the sympathy of simple Catholics. For all his intelligence, ability and courage he was utterly unspiritual and incapable of understanding the yearnings of others.

As the verbal wrangling continued the Ghibellines gained ground in Italy. In 1327 Lewis took the iron crown of Lombardy at Milan and marched southwards, brushing aside opposition from the Guelfs. Meanwhile a popular revolution at Rome, headed by the Ghibelline veteran Sciarra Colonna, had driven out the supporters of King Robert of Naples, whom the Pope had designated as his Vicar-General. Lewis was consequently made welcome in the city and had himself crowned Emperor by Sciarra and two excommunicated bishops. His next step was to mount a theatrical 'trial' of the Pope by the Roman people and to arrange for his deposition as a heretic and offender against the majesty of Christ. Effigies of the 'fake priest Jacques of Cahors' were burned in the streets. This led in turn to the elevation of an obscure Franciscan friar, Peter Rainaldusci, as the anti-Pope Nicholas V (1328-39). His election was entrusted to a commission of the terrorized Roman clergy and confirmed by the Emperor, who himself placed the tiara on the anti-Pope's head. The procedure was of course entirely irregular and uncanonical and soon produced a reaction in John's favour. It was felt that Lewis's assumption of the role of an Otto I or Frederick Barbarossa was an absurd piece of play-acting. He had in fact overreached himself, and as so often had happened to German Kings in Italy, his early successes went sour on him. He was not strong enough to tackle Robert of Naples and when the latter moved troops into Latium he ignominiously abandoned Rome in company with his anti-Pope. Their departure was followed by a counter-revolution; Sciarra Colonna was expelled and the former regime restored.

By the end of 1329 Lewis was back in Germany. The Pope had after all won the duel without stirring from Avignon and the prestige of St Peter had once again overcome imperial aggression as well as a concerted intellectual assault. Obviously the papal cause was not lost in Italy. Nevertheless the victory was a barren one, if only because Italian allegiances were irreconcilably divided. There would have been no point for John to return to Rome and thus to become immersed in local squabbles. Many Italians, however, hurried to Avignon to make their peace with him. In their train Nicholas V made him humble submission and was placed in confinement until his death three years later.

John's personality was unattractive. He did not try to endear himself to his contemporaries and made himself unpopular, especially among churchmen, by his autocratic behaviour, the tight centralism of his government, his nepotism and his harsh preoccupation with fiscal matters. In his private life he was frugal and studious. He undeniably hauled the papacy out of the abyss into which it had sunk under Clement V and set it once more on an even course. When nearing 90 years of age and perhaps slightly in his dotage, he shocked the theologians by propounding publicly in his sermons that the souls of the Just do not obtain a beatific vision of God before the Day of Judgment. While repeating that it was only an opinion which he was anxious to have discussed, he was induced to recant it on his death bed for fear of further charges of heresy.

Jacques Fournier, who reigned as Benedict XII (1334–42) was the son of a miller in the County of Foix. He entered the Cistercian Order, obtained a doctorate of theology at Paris and succeeded a Cistercian uncle as Abbot of Fontfroide near Narbonne. His whole career before his election was spent in Languedoc. As Bishop of Pamiers, one of the last Cathar strongholds, he mercilessly stamped out the heresy. A big man with a plebeian aspect and loud voice, he lived modestly and continued to wear his monk's habit, but when occasion demanded he appeared in the full pomp and showy magnificence for which the Avignon Popes were celebrated. He was calm, honest and conscientious, and his only and perhaps venial weakness sprang from his huge appetite for food and drink. His pontificate was free from nepotism; as he himself observed, 'the Pope must resemble Melchizedek who had neither father nor mother, nor a family tree.'

A dedicated reformer, he insisted on probity and economy in the papal administration. Above all he set out to prune the overgrown curial bureaucracy. This had multiplied since the move to Avignon and although greared to the collection of Church revenues, had itself become extravagant and corrupt. Its proliferation had been encouraged in the peaceful surroundings of the Rhône valley. The poet and scholar Petrarch, whom Benedict patronized and presented with a canonry, sneered at the cramped and dirty state of Avignon, but we may be sure that conditions of work and recruitment there compared very favourably with those prevailing in anarchic Rome and the small Italian towns where the Popes were used to seeking refuge. Avignon offered a reasonable degree of security and stability. It is easy to understand, even without exploring the intricacies of papal finance and the system of benefices, that the centralized Curia could not hope to carry out its tasks without a host of notaries, clerks, registrars, accountants and mere copyists engaged in financial matters, ecclesiastical administration and diplomatic exchanges. However, it had become far too cumbersome and rotten with abuses. Benedict slashed both numbers and expenditure. He sent back to their dioceses all clerics whom he saw hanging uselessly about the Curia in search of pickings, sharply checked corruption and tightened discipline in the religious Orders. The troops of begging monks who infested the streets were firmly packed off to their monasteries. Whereas his predecessor had spent two thirds of his revenues for military purposes in Italy, he reduced the figure to about five per cent. Such stringent economy refilled the treasury, but his pontificate was too short for the reforms to take full effect.

Benedict showed little zest or aptitude for high politics. He tried to woo the Italian Ghibellines instead of making war on them, but by doing so lost control of most of the papal state. He also sought unsuccessfully to mend his fences with the Emperor and to mediate between France and England at the start of the Hundred Years' War. He sensibly ignored a flowery appeal from Petrarch, the friend of the Colonna, to rescue Rome from its chronic civil war, for he was quite rightly convinced that it would be madness to retransfer the reformed Curia to Italy. In that spirit he pulled down the old episcopal residence at Avignon and began to build the present Palace of the Popes, designed by its architect, Pierre Poisson de Mirepoix, for spacious comfort as well as for defence. It could also accommodate the most important sections of the Curia and the papal archives, which Benedict managed to bring from Assisi where they had been placed in store. For its embellishment he employed the best French and Italian artists, including the great Sienese painter Simone Martini. At the same time, however, he paid for repairs at St Peter's and the Lateran.

Under Clement VI (1342–52) the atmosphere of the papal court changed abruptly. Reform and careful management gave way to easy-going attitudes and a confident, even ostentatious, splendour. The new style reflected the personality of the Pope, the son of a Limousin nobleman. Trained and educated as a Benedictine, Pierre Roger developed into an excellent theologian and an eloquent preacher, but in later life learning and monastic discipline sat lightly on his shoulders. His talents earned him one distinguished office after another in Church and State, two archbishoprics, the chancellorship of France and membership of the Sacred College. At the time of his election he was the ablest prelate-statesman in Western Europe, an intelligent, lucid and versatile man of the world. He was devoted to French interests and increased the proportion of Frenchmen in the Cardinalate. Indeed his capital resembled that of an independent prince in southern France rather than that of the spiritual head of Christendom. In 1348 he bought Avignon outright from the Queen of Naples (and Countess of Provence) for 80,000 gold florins, which amounted to at least a quarter of the papacy's annual expenditure. His palace, enlarged and further adorned, was the scene of lavish entertainments. His love of horses was satirized by Petrarch, who sarcastically called him Nimrod, the 'mighty hunter before the Lord', while his niece and hostess, Cecile de Turenne, was labelled Semiramis. Naturally every kind of innuendo circulated about the lady's role and the Pope's alleged fondness for women in general. But while he enjoyed courtly and civilized pleasures, he was no idle voluptuary, nor was Avignon a worse sink of iniquity than Rome. Petrarch's scurrilous invective on that subject is thoroughly untrustworthy. Clement's weak point was an uncontrollable generosity of which his kinsmen and an army of hangers-on took full advantage. His brilliant and extravagant court was an island of elegance and culture, fostering the values which in the French Kingdom were being submerged by the war with England. However overspending on inessentials soon depleted the reserves accumulated by his two predecessors.

Clement's better qualities came to the fore in 1348 when the Black Death struck Avignon with devastating force. Three quarters of the population of the over-crowded city died, 11,000 in a single month. Among its victims were seven Cardinals. But it was remarked that the Curia worked on amid mortality and social confusion, while the Pope was praised for his calm courage, his efforts to provide relief and the openhandedness with which, as usual, he spent his funds. When the populace turned on the Jews, accusing them of having poisoned the wells, he sternly quelled its excesses. He also suppressed the Flagellants, bands of fanatical penitents who roamed the country proclaiming that the plague was a divine punishment for sin and lacerating themselves by way of expiation.

A little surprisingly for a man of his equable temperament, Clement pressed to its conclusion the papal feud with the Emperor Lewis that had been more or less dormant under Benedict XII. In 1338 and the following year, however, Lewis, the German Diets and the electoral princes had all issued a series of declarations repeating that the imperial office stemmed from God alone and that electors' choice required no papal confirmation. Benedict had failed to react to these provocations, but Clement brought matters swiftly to a head. Germany was already subject to an interdict. He now renewed the Emperor's excommunication, summoning him to lay down his title and submit to papal jurisdiction. At the same time he was assuring the German princes and prelates that his quarrel was with Lewis personally; he had no intention of infringing the rights and customs of the empire as such. These intrigues proved effective, especially as some of the princes had become dissatisfied with Lewis. In 1346 the majority of the electors set up Charles of Luxemburg, grandson of Henry VII, as anti-king. He received full support from Clement, although the crucial question of papal confirmation was studiously left undecided. Civil war in Germany was fortunately averted by the death of Lewis on a bear hunt. Thus, by dint of persistence, the Pope had won what was virtually the last round of a useless and exhausting struggle.

What was happening at Rome was calculated to puzzle a French Pope and his expatriate Curia. At the start of his pontificate Clement had understandably rejected another plea for his return to the city. He did however agree to an alternative request that he should decree another Jubilee Year in 1350. It was represented to him that a man's lifetime was so short that it would be desirable to hold a Jubilee every 50 years; moreover it was immediately essential to boost the city's flagging morale and depressed economy. In a Bull of 1343 he promised full indulgence to all who visited the tombs of the Apostles. The trouble with Rome was that, under the nominal direction of a papal vicar, local power fluctuated between representatives of the people and the nobility, which was itself racked by family animosities. While the Roman delegation was still at the papal court the popular party gained the ascendancy and despatched as its envoy to Avignon, in the hope of winning Clement's favour, a clever young notary named Cola di Rienzo ('Nicholas, son of Laurence'). It was his destiny to provoke a revolution at Rome to rival that of Arnold of Brescia two centuries earlier.

In fact Cola had little in common with Arnold, the Augustinian who became the dedicated enemy of the Church hierarchy. He sprang from the Roman proletariat which was glad, whenever possible, to have the Pope on its side against the Roman nobility. His father kept a wineshop by the Tiber, where his mother also worked as a washerwoman. When she died he was sent to live with peasant relatives at Anagni. Returning to Rome as a young man, he somehow acquired an excellent education, and particularly a deep knowledge of the Latin classics. Through his fluency in the language he developed a passionate interest in the Roman past and a longing to restore its glories. He married the daughter of a notary and adopted the same profession. At Avignon he made the best of his opportunities. Petrarch appreciated his scholarship and enthusiasm for antiquity, while the Pope himself was impressed by an eloquent oration which he delivered on the desolation of Rome and its oppression by the nobles. In doing so he greatly offended Giovanni Colonna, the senior Italian Cardinal, but Petrarch intervened in his favour and Clement ended by appointing him an apostolic notary at five gold florins a month.

Back in Rome, where the nobles again dominated the government, he devoted his considerable talents to political agitation. He preached a doctrine of popular sovereignty derived from his own vision of republican Rome in ancient times, with himself as a mediaeval Gracchus defying a brutal and corrupt oligarchy. The condition of Rome under noble rule was indeed so wretched that he had no difficulty at all in persuading the commons, the commercial class and the lower clergy that peace and prosperity could only be achieved by a democratic revolution. Within three years he had so thoroughly prepared the ground as to be able to mount a successful *coup d'état*, and he did it so adroitly that the Colonna and other noble clans suspected no danger, regarding him as a harmless and rather ludicrous fanatic. But at Whitsun of 1347, with the papal vicar at his side, he ascended the Capitol with his supporters and took over the city without encountering any resistance from the thoroughly disconcerted nobles. Proclaiming himself 'Tribune of liberty, peace and justice, liberator of the Roman republic', he proceeded to assume the fullest dictatorial powers.

The reforms, some of them very sensible, that he initially instituted might have had a salutary effect if his regime had not dissolved into absurdity. As it happened too much power and ill-digested learning went to his head. He began to suffer from delusions of grandeur, one of which was that he was the son of Henry VII. In his public declarations he revealed an ambition to unite all Italy under Roman leadership; he claimed that the choice of a Roman emperor should in future rest with the Roman people alone and that the title ought to be borne by an Italian, a clear hint that it should be himself. For his own exaltation he devised a series of showy and tasteless ceremonies. Settling in the Lateran palace, he had himself dubbed 'White-clothed Knight of the Holy Spirit, Liberator of the City, Champion of Italy, Friend of the World, August Tribune', and took a ritual bath in the porphyry basin in which, according to the legend, Pope Silvester had baptized the Emperor Constantine. Finally he was crowned with six separate crowns and presented with an imperial orb. The papal vicar, who was in attendance, tried in vain to check these mummeries.

On hearing the news the Pope sent his Cardinal-legate from Naples to find out how it was that the promising young man whom he had admired at Avignon had degenerated into a pathological case. He was to make it clear that unless Cola behaved moderately he would forfeit papal support. His report was adverse, but the Pope was spared the trouble of getting rid of Cola by the Romans themselves. The nobles pulled themselves together and the people tired of his arrogance and eccentricity. Although his soldiers caught the Colonna in an ambush and cut down the leading members of the clan, he suddenly lost heart and ran away after only seven months of power. Excommunicated by the legate and deprived of all his offices, he wandered off into the wilds of the Abruzzi, where the Fraticelli (the hermit community founded by Celestine V) gave him shelter. In 1350, Jubilee Year, one of them advised him to seek out Charles IV, the King of Germany, at his capital, Prague, and to try to enlist his aid. The King, however, summed him up as a dangerous madman and kept him in custody for two years before handing him over to the Pope. Clement, who always had a sneaking sympathy for Cola, had him tried for heresy while arranging for his acquittal. He was still living in honourable captivity at Avignon when the Pope died.

In the ensuing conclave the Cardinals drew up a 'capitulation' designed to restrict the powers of the Pope and subject them in important respects to a two-thirds majority of the College, which would be limited to twenty members. Once elected Innocent VI (1352–62) vetoed these dispositions, but at the cost of 75,000 gold florins distributed to the Cardinals. Etienne Aubert was another Limousin and his episcopal career had been limited to France, but he conceived it his duty to reconquer the state of the Church in Italy as an essential preliminary to the papacy's re-occupation of Rome. He knew that it would be a long and costly task. The hire of the indispensable mercenaries would require strict economy in the Curia, the drastic curtailment of his predecessor's spending spree and more unpopular exactions by papal tax-gatherers. But Innocent was dour and determined. He also, by a stroke of genius, found the right instrument for the purpose in Cardinal Egidio de Albornoz, a Spaniard free from any previous Italian influence or prejudice. As Archbishop of Toledo and Chancellor of Castile he had campaigned successfully against the Moors of Andalusia, but after falling out with his King, Pedro the Cruel, he made his way to Avignon and placed himself at the Pope's disposition. Innocent appointed him his legate and Vicar General for Italy. This true representative of the church militant took thirteen years to complete his work but he did it very thoroughly, not only by military means but by putting into force the *Aegidian Constitutions*, a legal and administrative code which remained in force throughout the papal state until 1816.

Meanwhile Rome, where neither the noble nor the democratic faction could prevail for long, had relapsed into near-anarchy. Pilgrims arriving in Jubilee Year were dismayed by the spectacle of disorder and decay. The most eminent of them, Petrarch, had been alternately fascinated and repelled by the city since his first visit to the city thirteen years earlier. Before Cola came on the scene he had been duly flattered by an elaborate pseudo-classical ceremony of coronation as poet-laureate staged in his honour on the Capitol by his patrons, King Robert and the Colonna, but even then he had been exasperated by the lack of real interest shown by the Romans in their antique traditions and monuments. 'Who are today more ignorant of Roman matters', he complained, 'than the citizens of Rome? I hate to say so, but Rome is nowhere less appreciated than at Rome itself.' So much for the antique, but in 1350 he was also denouncing the neglect of their Christian past. The Lateran Palace, he wrote, had collapsed and St Peter's was reduced to a 'formless heap of ruins'. No doubt he was rhetorically exaggerating, but it was true that the Jubilee was a miserable failure. The despairing Pope sought a remedy by releasing Cola and sending him back to Rome as Senator. At first the Romans received him with joy, but soon they perceived that he had lost his glamour; they found him cruel, greedy and incompetent. After nine weeks in 1354 they had had enough of him. Hemmed in by rioters on the Capitol, he tried to escape disguised but was recognized and slaughtered. Subsequently, while the papal state was being gradually pacified, the city too became sufficiently quiet for Charles IV to pay it a fleeting visit in 1355 to be crowned emperor by the Cardinal-bishop of Ostia. His relations with the Pope were friendly enough, but in his Golden Bull of 1356, which minutely laid down the procedure for future German elections, he effectively excluded all papal claims to control them at any stage, and the King's right to coronation as emperor was held to stem from the fact of his election and not from papal favour.

Innocent wisely refrained from useless protests. Charles was his sole ally. Otherwise he was in a shaky position, both politically and financially. His offers to mediate between warring France and England had been rejected by both sides, and France in its exhausted condition violently resented the efforts of the papal collectors to raise revenue for Albornoz's campaigns in Italy. Even after the Treaty of Brétigny (1360) brought respite, the security of Avignon was threatened by bands of unemployed mercenaries. The most dangerous of these had to be bought off for

14,500 gold florins. When Innocent died the papacy was both unpopular and insolvent, and he had acquired a somewhat undeserved personal reputation for avarice. It was unjust of St Bridget of Sweden, no enemy of the Church and the founder of a flourishing Order of nuns, to castigate him as 'more abominable than the Jewish usurers'. He had in fact done his best to uphold the Holy See in very adverse circumstances.

Pressures were increasing for a return to Rome. They were not unwelcome to Guillaume de Grimoard, the Benedictine abbot and canon lawyer who succeeded as Urban V (1362–70). Indeed they corresponded with his own strongly felt inclinations. Like Benedict XII and Innocent VI he was a pious and well-intentioned reformist who tolerated neither extravagance nor abuses, but the sweetness of his character, and his simple and scholarly way of life, disarmed criticism of his strictness. Opposed to a move were the French King and not unnaturally the French Cardinals, who were in no way disposed to exchange their familiar comforts for the uncertainties of derelict Rome. On the other hand Charles IV paid a surprise visit to Avignon to strengthen Urban's resolve and in 1367 he decided to take the plunge. Leaving only five irreconcilable Cardinals behind, he embarked on 20 May with his whole Curia at Marseilles in a fleet of sixty vessels provided by the Italian maritime cities. After putting in at Genoa and Pisa he landed at Corneto. There Albornoz met him and accompanied him to Viterbo, but his sudden death in August prevented the bellicose old Cardinal from escorting his master to Rome. So when Urban entered the city on 16 October he lacked his most reliable defender and counsellor.

As a former legate at Naples he was no stranger to Italy and for a time all went well. The Romans were glad to see their Pope living in the Vatican and engaged in restoring the Lateran and other dilapidated Christian monuments. In 1368 the ever-solicitous Charles IV paid him a visit and had his Empress crowned in St Peter's. Another visitor was the Byzantine Emperor John V Palaeologus who, pressed to extremity by the Turks, came to beg for aid from the West and to offer submission to the Holy See, an act promptly disavowed by his own clergy and subjects. Urban seemed to be thinking in terms of a Crusade in which the numerous mercenary companies then infesting Europe might be employed, but the idea was plainly chimerical. Nor did he realize how unstable his own position in Italy was becoming. His appointment of only one Roman among eight new Cardinals caused local irritation, while the loss of Albornoz exposed the newly regained papal territory to encroachments by Barnabo Visconti, the aggressive tyrant of Milan, who threatened Bologna and other cities. Finally Perugia revolted, hiring the famous English *condottiere*, Sir John Hawkwood, to drive out the papal troops. As disaffection spread farther Urban suddenly lost heart; he felt that his dearest aspirations had been frustrated and betrayed. Just as firmly as he had resolved to quit Avignon he now announced his decision to return there, to the delight of the French Cardinals. In his farewell letter to the Romans, however, he carefully absolved them from blame for his withdrawal, which he attributed to external forces beyond his control. In September 1370 he re-entered Avignon. But he was already tired and ailing, and within three months he was dead.

It was clear that whoever was Pope would have to make up his mind whether the Church could more appropriately be governed from provincial and comfortable Avignon or from hallowed but incurably agitated Rome. From the point of view of the Curia it was probably easier to deal from Avignon with the problems arising from the endless Hundred Years' War and the difficulty of raising revenue from the territories of the exhausted belligerents. The same applied to Church interests in

Germany, Scandinavia and the Iberian peninsula. Yet Rome, notwithstanding its appalling defects, was the spiritual heart of Christendom and it was there that Christians expected the succesors of St Peter to reign. Such was the dilemma facing the new Pope Pierre Roger de Beaufort, a nephew of Clement VI, who was elected as Gregory XI (1370–78). He was a highly educated, clear-sighted man in delicate health, animated by good intentions but fatally slow in putting them into effect.

He was personally convinced that his right place was in Rome. His legates advised him that the sooner he came the better; so did St Catherine of Siena, with an urgency rivalling that of her contemporary St Bridget. Although there were obvious practical objections to uprooting the Curia for the third time in a few years, Gregory hesitated unduly. In his absence the officers administering the state of the Church, most of whom hailed from France of Provence, made themselves thoroughly disliked. Neither the papal cities nor the free communes of Tuscany trusted them to respect their liberties or protect their interests against the Visconti of Milan. The crisis of confidence was aggravated by a resurgence of national feeling. In 1375 Florence renounced its traditional alliance with the papacy and changed sides, followed by Bologna and most of the cities of central Italy. From that moment there was no averting a disastrous war. On the papal side it was waged with dull ferocity by mercenaries, Bretons and Gascons under Cardinal Robert of Geneva and Hawkwood's English company, which horrified all Italy by a massacre of 4,000 innocent people at Cesena. The outrage coincided with the Pope's arrival early in 1377, when St Catherine was urging him to stretch out the 'hand of love' to the rebels. Rome, which had not joined the revolt, received him calmly but without enthusiasm, and for the remainder of the year he watched the restoration of his temporal power by ruthless military repression. The cities yielded one by one, while Florence accepted an offer of mediation from Bernabo Visconti. In March 1378 a congress, reinforced by envoys from several kingdoms, met at Sarzana and negotiated a settlement entirely favourable to the Holy See. Its conclusion, however, was immediately followed by Gregory's death.

In his last days Gregory had been much distressed by the atmosphere of despair, cynicism and lack of faith prevailing at Rome. He was also preoccupied by the problem of the succession. He correctly foresaw that the unity of the Church would be endangered unless the excessive French influence in the Sacred College could be reconciled with the very understandable clamour in Italy that the next Pope should be an Italian. Somehow the French grip would have to be loosened and Avignon renounced for good. For the first time in 75 years the conclave was held at Rome and under pressure from the Roman mob. Some French Cardinals did not attend and those who were present were divided, with the result that the whole College, including the Italians, was looking for a compromise candidate. What seemed to be the ideal one was Bartolomeo Prignano, Archbishop of Bari. He was an Italian but not a Roman, a senior and experienced churchman but not a Cardinal. As a Neapolitan he was a subject of the French House of Anjou, and as vice-Chancellor of the Church he had directed the operations of the Curia both at Avignon and at Rome. In short he was known as a hard-working and competent administrator who could be relied upon to hold a middle course. All the same the Cardinals were so nervous that in order to forestall a popular tumult they went through the farce of publicly enthroning their elderly colleague, the Roman Tebaldeschi, as if he were the elected pontiff. On the following day they were obliged to confess in some embarrassment that their choice had in fact been Prignano, who was then enthroned in his turn without trouble. The actual course of events on that occasion was obscured by later contradictory statements, but the most probable explanation is that he was canonically elected as a suitable and uncontroversial head of the Church. The Holy See needed above all peace and quiet and an opportunity to allow wounds to heal. What it got, quite unexpectedly, was the great Schism.

In the event Urban VI (1378–89) confounded all hopes. His failure sprang not from his convictions and policy but from a basic instability of character and the explosions of a violent temperament which he proved unable to keep in check. The discreet and efficient bureaucrat turned overnight into an overbearing despot. His treatment of the Cardinals was offensive in the extreme. On the excuse of chiding them for simony and luxury he hurled abuse at them during his consistories and could hardly be restrained from striking them. It seemed that he was obsessed with getting his own back on his former ecclesiastical superiors. Robert of Geneva, the warrior-prelate who had recently battered the papal state into submission, protested in vain that he was 'diminishing their honour' by such conduct and threatened reprisals if he went too far. During the summer of 1378 they began to slip quietly out of the city in twos and threes until all the French, or 'ultramontane', members of the College were assembled at Anagni. There, after unsuccessfully summoning Urban to resign or to accept the judgment of a General Council they debated how they might get rid of him and replace him by a Pope who would be willing to lead them back to Avignon. Since there were no legal grounds for deposing a pontiff for eccentric or even mentally unbalanced behaviour, they questioned the validity of the election, maintaining that it had been obtained through intimidation. Finally they lost patience. Moving to Fondi, nearer to the Neapolitan border, the thirteen rebellious Cardinals declared Urban's elevation to have been uncanonical and elected Robert of Geneva as Clement VII (1378–94). Each Pope thereupon formally excommunicated the other, a procedure repeated many times before the Schism was over, while Urban countered the secession of the Cardinals by appointing twenty-nine of his own.

Clement's position was precarious. The Italians loathed him for his brutality and Urban had no difficulty in raising Italian troops to fight his foreign mercenaries. The castle of Sant' Angelo at Rome, held for him by a Provençal captain, was taken and partly demolished. He himself fled to Queen Joanna at Naples. Her subjects, however, favoured their compatriot, Urban, and Clement soon found it safer to quit Naples for Avignon. There he settled under the benevolent eye of the French monarchy, supported by his Cardinals and a strong nucleus of curial officials who had never left the city for Rome. For the whole of his long pontificate (if it can be properly called such) he was free to indulge his princely tastes. A younger son of the Count of Geneva and a kinsman of the King of France, he automatically adopted the Church as a career; he had no religious vocation nor sense of mission. Although he had formerly enjoyed soldiering, he showed no further desire to campaign in Italy, which he expected to fall into his hands without any effort on his part. Still in his late thirties, he preferred to lead an easy life, generously dispensing hospitality and rewarding poets, artists and musicians. Critics inevitably denounced his court as wallowing in luxury and vice; it was certainly brilliant and blatantly expensive. Clement lived on credit and the proceeds of his taxgatherer's exactions in France. Fortunately for him the Apostolic Camera, or fiscal department, had not been dismantled when Gregory XI left for Rome and the King was prepared to ignore the sufferings inflicted on his subjects. He was content to keep one Pope under his control while contriving the downfall of the other.

In the event Urban, though reduced to the most desperate straits, was not to be dislodged. His personal shortcomings were not entirely to blame for the outbreak of another lengthy and ruinous war in Italy, which was provoked both by his rivalry with Clement and by dynastic conflicts involving the throne of Naples. It was important for him to retain, if possible, the support of the southern kingdom. Consequently, having fallen out with Queen Joanna, he helped to supplant her by the young Angevin prince Charles of Durazzo. But Clement and Charles V of France had other ideas. They were that the king's brother, Louis of Anjou, should first conquer the papal state and turn it into a new kingdom of 'Adria'; he would then take over Naples as Joanna's heir and in the process Urban would be squeezed out of Rome. The plan was neat enough but did not work. Charles of Durazzo, crowned King of Naples by the Pope, imprisoned Joanna and probably had her murdered. He was a much better general than Louis and signally defeated his attempts at invasion. When he was killed in 1384 there should have been no real obstacle to concord between Charles and Urban and to the consolidation of the latter's authority in Italy. However they were already at odds over Charles's refusal to reward the Pope's nephew with several important fiefs. Urban left Naples, where he had been temporarily residing with the Curia, and secluded himself in the castle of Nocera.

At this point his temper became so savage and unpredictable that the Cardinals in his suite began to intrigue against him. When he got wind of the plot he flung six of them into the dungeons and subjected them to torture. He also excommunicated the King, whom he suspected of being privy to the conspiracy. His subsequent adventures were nightmarish. Besieged in Nocera, he was rescued by mercenaries hostile to Charles, hurried across the peninsula to the Adriatic coast, embarked on a Genoese galley and conveyed to Genoa by way of Messina. The captive Cardinals went too and were put to death on arrival. Only one of them, the Englishman Adam Easton, was released at the request of his sovereign, Richard II. For the next three years the Pope, discredited and half-crazy, was the unwelcome guest of the Republic. Still dallying with impracticable schemes for the recovery of Naples, he returned in 1386 to Rome, only to die peacefully there in the following year. The best that could be said of him by a contemporary was that, unlike Clement, he put more money into the treasury than he took out of it.

Europe had not absorbed the shock of the Schism. There had been plenty of anti-popes in the past, but the divisions they caused had been transitory and far from fatal. What had now occurred quickly acquired an air of permanence. The Church had two Popes, two papal capitals, two Colleges and two curial system, both fully staffed and furiously competing with each other. Moreover Europe had split into two political camps, each supporting a different pontiff. France, the Spanish kingdoms, Scotland and Cyprus adhered to Clement, while Urban retained Germany (though not Austria), England, Scandinavia, Hungary and Poland. North Italy and Portugal wavered between the two. Of Christian personalities, St Catherine declared for Urban, St Vincent Ferrer for Clement. The universities took sides; the monastic and mendicant orders were all internally divided.

The resultant disarray among the laity was even more grievous. How could it be otherwise when one claimant to the throne of St Peter was behaving like a bloodthirsty lunatic and the other was openly obsessed by secular aims and the systematic extortion of money from the faithful? Uncertain where their loyalties should lie and disillusioned with a papacy which had devalued itself as a spiritually and morally credible institution, Christians were turning for guidance to their individual consciences. In England Wyclif was voicing the popular dissatisfaction in a very radical form and it was soon to be echoed in Bohemia by his pupil John Hus. But less revolutionary spirits, doctors and jurists of many countries, were at the same time urgently examining ways by which the Schism might be ended and the Church fortified against its recurrence. In particular they were studying how its constitution might be modified by according a decisive role to its General Council.

14

THE GREAT
COUNCILS
(1389–1447)

The learned doctors were agreed in principle that the General Council, not the Pope, should be the supreme authority in the Church as representing the whole body of Christians. As early as 1380 theologians at the university of Paris were propounding that view, which in fact reflected the previous teachings of Marsilius and William of Ockham. Their difficulty, however, was that a Council could only be convoked by the Pope, and neither of the two existing and equally balanced rivals was willing to forgo what he regarded as his lawful right. Various remedies were suggested and vehemently argued. One was for an arbitral body to decide which was the rightful Pope; a second for the supporters of both to renounce their allegiance and a third, which eventually found the most favour, for both to abdicate simultaneously and permit a new election. But neither showed the slightest disposition to step down. When Urban died his remaining Cardinals at once elected another Neapolitan, Pietro Tomacelli, as Boniface IX (1389–1404), thus disappointing all who expected that Clement would be left alone in the field.

Boniface was young, affable and an unashamed simoniac, in all respects the antithesis of his predecessor. He worked hard, however, to conciliate and control the Romans and to stabilize the papal state, where he took the easier line of appointing as his vicars local dynasts such as the Malatesta at Rimini, the Este at Ferrara and the Montefeltri at Urbino. His homeland, the Kingdom of Naples, was still distracted by war between the heirs of the former contenders, Louis II of Anjou and Ladislas the son of Charles of Durazzo. He sided with the latter but it was not until 1400 that his protégé was finally established at Naples. All in all his reign was calm and brought much needed relief to the Italian faithful. His chief weakness was his pre-occupation with money. He held a profitable Jubilee in 1390, when the traffic in indulgences and benefices reached an unexpected height. Indeed he was later obliged by protests to revoke the indulgences already granted.

He did nothing positive to end the Schism, insisting that the only possible solution was the unconditional abdication of his rival at Avignon. Strong hopes were entertained on Clement's death in 1394 that the Avignon Cardinals would refrain from electing a successor, but they too were frustrated when the schismatic College hastened to elevate the Aragonese Pedro de Luna as Benedict XIII (1394–1417). This they did in defiance of the King of France, Charles VI, who had been convinced by the Paris theologians, Pierre d'Ailly and Jean Gerson, that the most suitable method of ending the Schism would be by abdication, the 'way of cession'. But his urgent plea to the Cardinals that they should conform to this advice was pointedly unheeded, and it was clear that heavier pressure would have to be applied to break the deadlock.

Benedict was not the kind of man who could easily be shifted once his mind was made up. By birth a nobleman, he had taught canon law at Montpellier. As a young Cardinal he had voted for Urban VI and had been one of the last of the ultramontane members of the College to desert him for Clement. Subsequently, while acting as the latter's legate for the Iberian Kingdoms, he had rallied them to Avignon. He had also served as legate for France and Scotland. When the conclave was held at Avignon he and each of his colleagues promised that in the event of their election they would be prepared to resign, if called upon to do so, in the interests of terminating the Schism, but as soon as he had been unanimously chosen his attitude hardened. From that moment no pressure would compel him to abdicate voluntarily. A proud and obstinate Spaniard, he formed an unshakeable belief that he was the only rightful Pope and stuck to it uncompromisingly for the rest of his life.

For more than a decade he withstood all efforts by the French Crown and its allies to remove him. In 1395, after a Council of the French Church had pronounced in favour of cession, an imposing delegation led by three royal dukes (Berry, Burgundy and Orleans) presented itself at Avignon in an attempt to win him over. It was courteously received but dismissed with a firm rebuff. During the next three years the French court worked tirelessly to enlist the support of other European monarchies in order to redouble the pressure on both Popes, but the envoys despatched to Rome and Avignon in 1398 had to report that they had made no progress with either Boniface or Benedict. A second national Council was then held at Paris in the King's presence. Spurred on by the doctors of the university, Crown and Church decided to proceed against Benedict by the 'way of subtraction'; in other words they withdrew obedience to the Pope on the ground that his refusal to abdicate made him guilty of schism and heresy. The result was that all papal revenues and prerogatives were taken over by the national Church, which was for all practical purposes subordinate to the Crown.

These far-reaching measures, foreshadowing as they did future movements towards an independent Gallican Church, caused little concern to Boniface in Rome. Benedict's position was of course seriously threatened. Most of his Cardinals seceded from him in a panic, but he himself was not dismayed. He put his palace in a state of defence and gambled on disunity among his opponenets. It turned out that his estimate was correct. The French faithful soon discovered that under the new dispensation the taxes formerly due to the papacy were passing into the Crown's coffers and had become more onerous than ever. Many ecclesiastics were uneasy about the whole concept of a national Church. Other kingdoms, notably in the Iberian peninsula, openly took Benedict's side; so, in France itself, did the powerful Duke of Orleans. Blockaded in his palace, he waited calmly until, in 1403, he judged that public opinion had swung sufficiently in his favour for him to break out and challenge the opposition. Then, with the Duke's aid, he escaped into friendly Provence.

What began as a flight ended in a triumph. Almost at once Benedict's Cardinals returned to him and the embarrassed Crown acknowledged defeat. It agreed to drop its 'subtraction' on the understanding that he would at least start a dialogue with his rival about ways of repairing the Schism. In 1404 he duly sent an embassy to Rome proposing that they should meet for the purpose. The timing, however, was unpropitious, for Boniface had never felt more secure. In the latter part of his pontificate he had dissolved the Roman commune and replaced it with his own direct administration; he had inflicted a very sharp check on the rebellious Colonna and refortified Sant' Angelo and the Vatican. Consequently he felt disinclined to consider any form of compromise that might upset his rule. The argument was still raging when he died and the situation again became fluid.

The next Roman Pope, Innocent VII (1404–6), was the Archbishop of Ravenna, Cardinal Cosimo dei Miliorati from Sulmona. A serious and unassuming scholar, he is chiefly remembered for his intention, if he had lived, to found a university at Rome with a chair for the study of Greek. Since he had no talent for politics or administration, the city again dissolved into a welter of warring factions. In order to quell them he called on Ladislas of Naples, but further disturbances flared up when eleven prominent Romans deputed to negotiate with the Pope were brutally murdered by his nephew and commander of his troops. Innocent was forced to leave the Vatican and was only brought back by his partisans six months before his death. There was no question of his accepting Benedict's proposal for a meeting. In the hope of taking advantage of his less sophisticated rival Benedict travelled as far as Genoa, where he was enthusiastically acclaimed and tempted to advance further into Italy. However unfavourable developments in France caused him to hurry back to Avignon. His protector, the Duke of Orleans, had lost influence at the French court and the University of Paris was once more pressing for 'subtraction of obedience'. Moreover the national Church was forbidding the payment of taxes and tithes to the Curia and the conferment of benefices by the Pope. Now that his prospects were again becoming uncertain he anxiously watched the election of his third successive rival.

Gregory XII (1406–15), the Cardinal of San Marco, was a Venetian nobleman named Angelo Correr. Over 80 years of age, he was learned, conscientious and known to be devoted to mending the Schism. He and his electors had also bound themselves by strict conditions. Whoever was chosen must undertake to abdicate in the event of the death or resignation of the anti-Pope, in which case the two sets of Cardinals would combine for a fresh election; he must advertise his acceptance of the conditions in a circular and approach the anti-Pope within three months with a view to arranging a conference. Gregory duly complied. He announced that he would hasten to the meeting-place by sea in a fishing boat or by land holding a pilgrim's staff; he was ready to give up his child, the Church, rather than see it rent asunder. He received an apparently forthcoming reply. It was decided that he and the anti-Pope should come together at Savona, a small town on the Ligurian coast to the west of Genoa, on 29 September 1407. In the event, however, they never met. Benedict, under heavy French pressure, arrived at Savona on the agreed date but in the meantime Gregory had only reached Siena. For all his public willingness to proceed he was being discouraged by his political backers—among them Ladislas of Naples, the future emperor Sigismund of Luxemburg and the Republic of Venice— all of whom profoundly distrusted France and were determined that the eventual sole Pope should not be a French puppet. Benedict for his part had no illusions about the French but saw no harm in putting Gregory in the wrong. He therefore went on to Portovenere, near La Spezia, but nothing could move Gregory further than Lucca. What is more he went back on his previous undertakings, refusing flatly to meet the anti-Pope or even to contemplate abdication in any circumstances.

At this juncture the Cardinals began, at first rather hesitantly, to take matters into their own hands. The majority of Gregory's College left him and put themselves in touch with the members of Benedict's. Before they could reach any joint decision the French Crown intervened forcefully; it renewed the withdrawal of obedience, issued a declaration defining the freedoms of the Gallican Church and announced that it would henceforth adopt a policy of neutrality towards both Popes. It also ordered the arrest of Benedict, who was then at Genoa, but he eluded the royal officers and made for Perpignan, just outside the frontier of the French Kingdom, where he set up a much reduced court. Meanwhile the Cardinals of both obediencies, meeting at Leghorn in June 1408, launched an appeal to all senior churchmen, including Benedict and Gregory, and representatives of lay rulers to join with them in a General Council at Pisa on 25 March of the following year. The Popes' reaction was for each to summon a council of his own, one at Perpignan and the other at Cividale in Friuli. Both eventually took place but were total failures, poorly attended and unhelpful to their conveners. While the delegates streamed towards Pisa Benedict, deprived of his revenues, was immobilized at Perpignan and Gregory, in scarcely better shape, moved from the protection of the Malatesta at Rimini to that of the King of Naples at Gaeta. By then Ladislas was in occupation of Rome and most of the papal state.

The size of the attendance at Pisa was a striking proof of the strength of the conciliar idea. It comprised 24 Cardinals, 4 patriarchs, 80 bishops and the nominees of 102 others, the heads of 4 religious orders, many dozens of abbots and priors and numerous contingents of theologians and jurists from the universities and cathedral chapters. It was an extremely impressive gathering and very largely representative of the Catholic Church as a whole. Not all the princely embassies supported conciliarism, and Gregory, as the legally elected Roman Pope, could still count on the allegiance of such powerful rulers as the Kings of Germany and Naples, though no longer of his native Venice. Benedict's adherents, on the other hand, were restricted to Spain and their voice was not heard at Pisa.

The Council lasted from 25 March until 5 June. On its opening day the presiding Cardinal called upon the absent Pedro de Luna and Angelo Correr to give an account of themselves, and at its conclusion they were both condemned and deposed as 'notorious schismatics and heretics'. There followed throughout its fifteen sessions much anguished debate about the validity of its proceedings. Some speakers doubted whether the Council, having been irregularly convoked, had the right to call itself a General Council. Others, upholding the traditional view that a pope could not be judged, except on the ground of heresy, by any human agency, pointedly enquired of what heresy either Benedict or Gregory had been guilty. The somewhat disingenuous answer was that schism was in itself tantamount to heresy. As regards legality, the Council contented itself with declaring that it was indeed a General Council of the whole Catholic Church, and as such fully justified in arraigning the Popes. The envoys of the King of Germany, Rupert of the Palatinate, lodged their protest and withdrew. The sentence of deposition, however, was overwhelmingly confirmed by the churchmen present. After the closure the Cardinals went into conclave and elected Cardinal Pietro Philargi, Archbishop of Milan, who assumed the name of Alexander V (1409-10).

The conciliar Pope was not an Italian but a Cretan, and consequently the first Greek to occupy the papal chair for 700 years. Crete had been a Venetian colony since the thirteenth century, and it was the Venetian Franciscans who plucked him, a starving orphan, from the streets of its capital, Candia. They educated him and sent him for further study to Oxford and Paris. Subsequently he held several Italian bishoprics. An accomplished scholar with a mind of his own, he might well have made an excellent Head of the Church. Unfortunately he lacked a solid political base in Italy and Gregory's sponsor, King Ladislas, was in possession of Rome. With the aid of Louis II of Anjou, still pursuing his claim to the southern Kingdom, and of the warlike Cardinal Cossa, legate in the papal state, the Neapolitans were driven out of Rome, but before Alexander could take control of the city he died at Bologna. The Italians believed that he had been poisoned by Cossa, who was disappointed by not having been chosen Pope at the last conclave. In any case his ambition was promptly satisfied through his election by the same Cardinals.

Events had made the Council of Pisa look foolish, for its only apparent result was that there were now three Popes in the field instead of two. Confusion was absolute. Moreover Baldassare Cossa, who succeeded as John XXIII (1410–15) was a thoroughly unsuitable choice. The son of a minor Neapolitan nobleman, he began his career as a soldier or, so his enemies alleged, a pirate. He then took minor orders and entered the service of the Curia under Boniface IX. Intelligent, resourceful and unscrupulous, he rose to be papal chamberlain and Cardinal-deacon. His talents, however, were chiefly administrative and military. He had no religious feeling, no conscience and no principles and was in consequence generally feared and distrusted. His contemporaries tended to regard him not as a Holy Father but as a swashbuckling and immoral *condottiere*. They accused him of every kind of turpitude, of violence, extortion and sexual outrage.

While Louis of Anjou marched against Naples John installed himself unopposed at Rome. But after some early successes the campaign fizzled out, Louis returned to France and John was left to face Ladislas alone. Quite unexpectedly that erratic prince decided that his interests would be better served by dropping Gregory and recognizing John as lawful Pope. An arrangement was soon concluded. In return for a large subsidy Ladislas became John's protector and the unhappy Gregory again took refuge with his staunch friend Carlo Malatesta.

So things stood at the end of 1412. John's position, however, was not as secure as it might have seemed. It was not only that he was afraid of Ladislas. His trouble was that he had failed to establish his authority and credibility in Rome or Christendom as a whole. A man with his record could simply not be taken seriously as a spiritual leader. His first attempt to hold a Synod ended in farce; it was sparsely attended and several writers recorded that the opening Mass was interrupted by an owl which glared and screeched at the Pope. But he still saw himself as presiding over a Council which would deal with pressing Church problems like the heresy of Wyclif and Hus. Thus, with the double object of reinforcing his prestige and finding a reliable patron, he turned to Sigismund of Luxemburg son of the Emperor Charles IV, King of Hungary and as from 1410 also King of Germany.

Sigismund was a towering figure, outstandingly gifted and resolute, keen to restore Church unity and to promote it through another and more effective General Council. He was also an inveterate enemy of the Neapolitan House of Durazzo. It was therefore not surprising that as soon as Ladislas got wind of the Pope's approach he would proceed against him. In June 1413 he seized Rome and sent John in flight to Florence. That autumn Sigismund himself came to north Italy and discussed the holding of a Council with the Pope's envoys, making it quite clear that he expected to supervise it himself. Furthermore, before meeting John personally at Lodi before Christmas, he announced that it would open at Constance on 1 November 1414. John had no alternative but to accept his relegation to a secondary role. He waited at

Bologna, only too aware that his waning authority in the Church now hardly exceeded that of the other two papal exiles at Rimini and Perpignan.

In October he set out on his journey to Constance. He had few illusions about its outcome; as he put it, the trap was ready for the fox. From Meran onwards the Duke of Austria, Frederick of Habsburg, escorted him and was rewarded with the title of Captain-General of the papal forces. The delegates were slow in arriving but in the end numbered between six and seven hundred churchmen and laymen, including 29 Cardinals. It was an even more representative array than the Council of Pisa. The champions of conciliarism, headed by Cardinal d'Ailly and Jean Gerson, were there in force and both Gregory and Benedict were represented, the former by the able Cardinal Dominici of Ragusa. John Hus, protected as he thought by a safe-conduct from King Sigismund, appeared to defend himself against charges of heresy but was placed under arrest by the Pope's orders after preliminary examination. This was virtually the last act of authority that John was permitted to perform. When Sigismund himself arrived in time for Christmas he took charge of the Council and removed Hus into his own custody. He also postponed the discussion of vital issues until the settlement of a crucial question of procedure. Should the delegates vote as individuals or by nations? For John, who had tried to pack the Council with the holders of small Italian bishoprics, it was important that the former system should be adopted, and it was therefore a fatal setback to him that it was decided to vote by 'national' blocks—French, Italian, English and German, the latter including the Scandinavians and eastern Europeans. Spain, which still acknowledged Benedict, was not represented as a nation. Within the blocks all delegates, from Cardinals downwards, enjoyed equal voting rights.

John's position therefore became untenable. What the Council required was the abdication of all three Popes and particularly his own. There was also a loud clamour for him to be put on trial for manifold misdeeds. He consequently offered to resign, but while the conditions of his resignation were under discussion he was secretly planning flight with the connivance of Frederick of Austria. On 20 March the Duke arranged a grand tournament in Sigismund's honour under cover of which John, although he was being watched, was helped to escape during the night, disguised as a stable boy, to the sanctuary of Frederick's castle at Schaffhausen.

The Council was momentarily thrown into confusion and several Cardinals defected to John. Sigismund, however, soon pulled it together. On 6 April it pronounced that for the purpose of ending the Schism, its collective authority must override that of the Pope. Its more radical members would have liked to establish that principle on a general and permanent basis, but the majority were against it. Further measures followed. John, who was now at Freiburg and hoping to find refuge across the Rhine with the Duke of Burgundy, was peremptorily summoned to abdicate without conditions. On his refusal to do so the King's officers were sent to apprehend him. As no minor prince any longer dared to offer him shelter he was incarcerated in a series of German strongholds. Meanwhile the Council tried and condemned him in his absence. On 29 May he was convicted of 'obdurate schism', 'notorious simony' and 'detestable and dishonourable morals', and sentenced to be confined by the King at the Council's pleasure.

John's deposition was only the first of the tasks the Council had set itself. It continued its work until 1418 and held in all 45 formal sessions. During the summer of 1415 when John Hus was condemned for heresy and burned at the stake, the delegates also addressed themselves to the problem of getting rid of the two anti-Popes. They had already agreed that neither would be eligible for re-election.

In the event Gregory, now a very old man, gave little trouble and in return was treated with deference. His advocates, Carlo Malatesta and Cardinal Dominici, explained that his only wish was that his canonical acts should not be disavowed. After receiving that assurance he abdicated and was at once appointed Cardinal-bishop of Porto and legate for the March of Ancona, where he died in 1417 at the age of 90.

It proved much harder to dispose of the intransigent Benedict, especially as he was backed by the Iberian Kingdoms. In an attempt to secure his resignation Sigismund travelled all the way to Perpignan, but after two months' haggling no agreement could be reached on conditions. Having rebuffed the King, Benedict retreated to the greater safety of Peñiscola, his family's coastal fastness south of Tortosa and remained there, clinging to all his pretensions, until his death six years later. Sigismund then resorted to more general diplomacy, but it took months of hard work before the rulers of Aragon, Castile and other states could be induced to abandon Benedict and despatch a Spanish national delegation to the Council. Discussions of his case did not even begin till November 1416, and when a summons for him to appear at Constance was delivered at Peñiscola it merely elicited the reply 'Here is the Ark of Noah'. Finally, on 17 July 1417, the Council condemned Pedro de Luna and deposed him as a breaker of oaths, a notorious heretic and a promoter of schism.

Officially the Great Schism was at an end, but the Council was still locked in controversy about reforms and the election of a pope. There was general agreement on the necessity of reforms based on a conciliar system, but not on the latitude, if any, that should be left to the new Pope in putting them into effect. After much debate between the out-and-out conciliarists and those inclined towards a return to papalism a number of important decrees were promulgated, all imposing restrictions on the rights and powers of future pontiffs. It was unambiguously declared that the General Council was the supreme authority in the universal Church, deriving its powers directly from Christ, and that the Pope must obey its decisions. Briefly, its function was the continuous reform and supervision of the Church 'in its head and members'. To that effect Councils were to be held regularly, the first five years after that of Constance, the second after another seven years and subsequently every ten years. Provisions were laid down to forestall a new schism, to limit papal taxation and to prevent the arbitrary appointment and transfer of bishops. It was also stipulated that the new Pope should undertake, at least in principle, to carry out these and other measures.

It only remained to draw up rules for the election. In order to guard against the preponderant influence of the Italian Cardinals (15 out of 23) the Council decided to co-opt six representatives from each of its five 'nations' and to require two-thirds majorities from both the College and the whole conclave. Nevertheless it was an Italian who was elected, and once more a Roman of the Romans, Odo Colonna, Cardinal-deacon of San Giorgio in Velabro. Elected on St Martin's day, he chose to be named Martin V (1417–31).

The Council, by virtue of its collective strength, had saved the Church from Schism and possibly from disintegration. That it also succeeded in rescuing the papacy from the impotence and disrepute into which it had so deservedly fallen was due to the exceptional talents of the Pope it had caused to be elected. The grandson of a Roman Senator, Martin was deeply versed in curial affairs and legations. Raised to the Cardinalate by Innocent VII, he had steered his way skilfully through the shoals of the Schism and the early conciliar period, enjoying the special favours of John XXIII. Unlike most members of his family, who had in the past given more trouble than comfort to the Holy See, he took the highest view of the dignity and indispensability of his office. Indeed he was hailed on his accession as the 'column that held up the tottering Church'. At the same time he was no Innocent III. Neither was his approach to his mission theoretical, nor did he claim a universal supremacy for the Holy See transcending and overriding the authority of secular rulers. As envisaged by the Council of Constance, he proceeded to negotiate separate Concordats with individual sovereigns, thus conceding that, at least in temporal matters, he treated them as his peers. These agreements were subject in principle to endorsement by a Council, but in practice there was now nothing to prevent a prince from asserting control of his own national church and from curtailing any papal taxes that competed with his own revenue demands.

The veteran Cardinal John of Ragusa remarked that the very word 'Council' filled the Pope with horror. Such a judgement, however, was hardly fair to Martin. Certainly he was no enthusiast for the conciliar system, which he operated sceptically but correctly. However, he had no objection to reforms, and especially curial reforms, so long as he was given a free hand to apply them and was not subjected to irresponsible frustration by dedicated anti-papalists. He was rightly convinced that for all practical purposes the affairs of the Church must be directed by a single consistent head and not left to the whims of quarrelsome and not necessarily representative assemblies, incapable of taking rapid and firm decisions on pressing issues of doctrine, discipline, policy and administration.

In that spirit Martin addressed himself to the heavy task of reconstituting the papal government, but nearly three years passed before he found it safe to move it back to Rome. The reason was that two rival *condottieri* were fighting for the possession of the city. One of them, Sforza of Attendolo, commanded for Queen Joanna II of Naples, while the second, Braccio of Montone, had taken advantage of papal weakness to carve out a principality of his own within the State of the Church. Martin was therefore obliged to wait at Mantua and Florence until, by clever and patient diplomacy, he had reached agreement with the Queen and induced Braccio to serve as his own Vicar at Perugia. At last, on 30 September 1420, he entered Rome and took up residence in a house belonging to his family, pending the restoration of the derelict Vatican. The environment in which he had chosen to work was indeed dispiriting. The city was more ruinous than ever, the people were starving and the streets choked with rubbish. Even the great basilicas were roofless and crumbling; some churches were being used as stables and wolves howled nightly in the Vatican gardens. If Martin had not been a Roman himself he might well have been tempted by suggestions made to him by Kings Charles VI and Sigismund that he should transfer the Holy See permanently to France or Germany. As it was he politely rejected both invitations.

A brilliant and determined administrator, Martin soon brought an apparently hopeless situation under control. He reimposed civic order and initiated a vast programme of rebuilding and repair. Artists from Florence and the north— Masaccio, Pisanello and Gentile da Fabriano—were brought in to decorate the Lateran basilica and other churches. At the same time he remodelled the Curia out of the separate elements left behind by the three former Popes and, with an eye on the Councils, very carefully selected recruits for the Sacred College without giving preponderance to any one nation. Italians, Frenchmen, Englishmen, Germans and

Spaniards were all included in the 19 Cardinals comprising the College at his death in 1431, and they were mostly outstanding personalities. The restoration of his authority in the papal state brought a welcome improvement in the finances; within a few years two-thirds of the papal revenue was forthcoming from that source, as opposed to taxes squeezed from reluctant foreigners. The Curia also benefited from the income derived from the Colonna estates, which by now covered the greater part of Latium, while a policy of unashamed nepotism enriched the Pope's family with fiefs and offices.

The process of consolidation was in full swing when Martin, punctiliously, and in conformity with the decisions of Constance, issued invitations to a General Council at Pavia in the spring of 1423. He did not, however, undertake to attend it himself; the representatives of the nations were merely asked to meet his legates. As he had no doubt calculated, the Council was a fiasco from the start. Europe was so deeply embroiled in the Anglo-French conflict, the Hussite war in Bohemia and other turmoils that very few national delegates appeared, and when plague broke out at Pavia the assembly was hurriedly shifted to Siena. But it was still very thinly attended and as it could hardly claim to represent the Church as a whole Martin wisely stayed at Rome. In the event there was little business to occupy the delegates and after a quorum (fewer than 30 prelates) had been barely achieved, his legates had no difficulty in staving off the efforts of a few bitter French anti-papalists to impose further restrictions on the pontiff's authority. All that could be agreed was to hold the next Council at Basle in 1431. To all appearances Martin's aloof though formally dutiful attitude towards conciliarism had been vindicated. He was entitled to assume that if he had so easily weathered Pavia and Siena he would be able to weather Basle as well when the time came. Before he died he had already appointed Cardinal Giuliano Cesarini to represent him there.

A further cause for anxiety was the behaviour of the King of Aragon, Alfonso V, who also ruled Sicily and Sardinia and claimed the throne of Naples. Martin had no wish to have this powerful monarch as his neighbour, especially as Alfonso had never entirely regulated the tenacious old anti-pople Benedict XIII, still ensconced in the Aragonese fortress of Peñiscola. And when Benedict died in 1423 he raised no objection to the election by the latter's remaining adherents of the Provost of Valencia, Gil Sanchez Muñoz, as Clement VIII (1423–9). To make things worse Queen Joanna proceeded to adopt Alfonso as her successor and to enlist the Pope's old enemy, Braccio of Montone, as her general. In order to counter this formidable combination Martin called to his aid the alternative pretender to the Neapolitan throne, Louis III of Anjou, supported by Joanna's former commander Sforza. The result was a spirited war in the course of which Joanna confused the issue by repudiating Alfonso and adopting Louis in his stead. However, after four years of conflict and tortuous intrigue both the generals were dead and Alfonso's Italian ambitions had been frustrated. Nevertheless he continued to recognize Clement VIII until 1429 when, at the cost of 150,000 gold florins, Martin persuaded him to abandon the anti-Pope. The latter thereupon resigned and was consoled with the bishopric of Majorca. Even so the Great Schism continued to cast a faint and ridiculous shadow in the person of one Bernard Garnier, who was proclaimed as Benedict XIV by Jean Carrier, Benedict's Vicar General for the County of Armagnac. What eventually happened to this individual cannot be ascertained; what is certain is that by 1430 the division that had once threatened to rend the

Church fatally asunder had disappeared in a mixture of bribery and farce.

Martin was undoubtedly a very able man, and his natural gifts were matched by his good fortune. The words *Temperum suorum felicitas* inscribed on his monument (the work of Donatello and Michaelozzo) in St John Lateran reflect his popularity with the Romans, to whom he had brought peace and order. His sudden death spared him the long and exhausting struggles with both the conciliarists of Basle and the recalcitrant Romans who were to afflict his successor.

Gabriel Condulmer, who took the name of Eugenius IV (1431–47), was a Venetian and a new phew of Gregory XII. As befitted a former Augustinian hermit, he was a man of austere habits, pious and upright. He was also prepared to fight for the Church's cause with the same obstinacy as his compatriots displayed in the defence of their maritime empire. His uncle had made him a Cardinal in 1408 at the age of 25. Before electing him the conclave, under the influence of the conciliarist Cesarini, committed the next Pope to continuing and vigorous reform of the Church through the Council's machinery. For the moment Eugenius seemed to accept its decision by confirming Cesarini's appointment to preside at Basle, but he was too much of a realist tamely to abandon Martin's policy of re-asserting papal independence. After the Council's formal opening in July 1431 the delegates responded very slowly to the call. In fact attendance was initially so poor that the Pope was emboldened to dissolve it, announcing that he would personally preside over a fresh meeting at Bologna in 1433. He was suspicious of conciliar radicalism and disturbed by the news that without his permission the Council had invited representatives of the Hussite heresy to Basle. But the delegates, now more numerous and plucking up courage, refused to be dissolved and their defiance of papal decrees provoked an angry tussle from which the Council emerged apparently victorious.

Headed by Nicholas of Cusa, a fisherman's son from the Moselle valley but an outstanding theologian, the extreme conciliarists insisted that the Council, deriving directly from Christ, was the supreme body in the Church. The Pope had no authority to dismiss it; on the contrary it was entitled to depose him for heresy or for not carrying out the proper duties of his office. In this case it threatened to arraign him for contumacy unless he appeared in Basle to answer the charges against him and withdraw his Bull of dissolution. As Eugenius refused to move and was equally adamant about the paramountcy of the Holy See a complete break was avoided only by the intervention of the King of Germany. Sigismund was well cast as a mediator because he needed the support of both Council and Pope in his war with the Hussites and the establishment of his rights in north Italy, where he had difficulties with Venice and the Visconti of Milan. Persevering throughout a mass of misunderstandings and backed by the Crowns of France and England, he persuaded Eugenius to be less intransigent while damping down the Council's more irresponsible attacks on the papacy. At the end of May 1433 he came to Rome and was crowned Emperor. Nevertheless he found it hard enough, on assuming the presidency of the Council a few months later, to moderate its anti-papal stand, and the resultant settlement was less of a compromise than a papal surrender. Menaced with invasion by the Visconti, Eugenius signed a document withdrawing all previous anti-conciliar Bulls and recognizing the Council's primacy in three spheres, the suppression of heresy, the restoration of peace in Christendom (i.e. with the Greek Church) and the far-reaching reform of the Church in the West. At the same time, however, he was assuring the Dog of Venice that he would rather forfeit his life than allow his authority to be usurped by the Council.

During these anxious years the Pope's base had become insecure; in fact he was fighting the Council with one hand behind his back. As so often happened in papal history, his efforts to cope with vast problems of ecclesiastical principle on an international scale were constantly hampered by local disturbances. His pontificate had scarcely begun when the Colonna and their partisans, loth to give up the advantages they had enjoyed under the previous regime, sought to intimidate him by a display of armed force. Eugenius quelled their revolt with help from Florence and Venice, but his health was much impaired by the strain and he nearly lost his grip of affairs. Worse trouble assailed him in the critical months following Sigismund's coronation when the Council's pressure on him was at its strongest. *Condottieri* in the pay of Filippo Maria Visconti, the pro-conciliar Duke of Milan, twice invaded Latium and blockaded the Pope in the city. Their second attack in May 1434 touched off a revolt by the Romans. Convinced that Eugenius had lost his battle with the Council, they turned against him and restored a republican form of government. They failed, however, to lay hands on the pontiff himself, whose escape from Rome counts among the most melodramatic in the long annals of papal flights. Disguised as a monk, he boarded a small boat from the Trastevere riverside and was rowed to a galley waiting at Ostia. Although he was soon spotted, pursued and bombarded with stones and arrows from the banks as he crouched under a shield at the bottom of the boat, he somehow managed to get through and was safely carried to Pisa. By the end of June he had reached Florence, where he was joined in due course by the Sacred College and the Curia.

His host in papalist Florence was the famous Cosimo de Medici, under whose protection he set up his government for the next nine years. Freed from Roman tumults, he found it an ideal centre from which to renew his duel with the Council. While not even trying to return to Rome, he determined to reduce it to obedience. For that purpose he selected a certain Giovanni Vitelleschi, nominally a papal official in minor orders but in reality a military commander of more than ordinary competence and ruthlessness. He made him a bishop and gave him carte blanche. In a remarkably short space of time he had subdued Rome, crushed the barons of Latium and dealt severely with any dissident communes in the papal state. For those services he was rewarded with a Cardinal's hat, the Archbishopric of Florence and the honorary Patriarchate of Alexandria.

Eugenius did not lack Venetian subtlety. Watching the Council's progress from his vantage point at Florence, he soon discerned signs of disunity in its ranks. At first it was riding very high. Swollen by large numbers of middle and lower clergy, university doctors and canon lawyers, it was becoming more and more radical and in some sense democratic. For the purpose of its work it divided itself into four deputations or main committees, each voting by simple majority. Thus constituted it poured out a stream of increasingly anti-papal and anti-curial decrees, arrogating to itself the powers and functions of the Holy See. As relations between Basle and Florence steadily deteriorated senior churchmen became alarmed; they felt that the conciliar process was being pushed too far. When the question of reunion with the Greek Church again arose in an acute form Eugenius found the chink he was looking for in the Council's armour.

The Byzantine empire was at its last gasp, restricted as it was to Constantinople and the southern part of the Greek peninsula. The Emperor John VIII Palaeologus knew that it was bound to succumb very soon to the Turks unless the West mounted a new and successful Crusade on a grand scale, and he also knew that a Crusade was unlikely to be set in motion unless the union of the Churches, involving a measure of submission by the Greek Church to Rome, could be quickly achieved. In 1434 envoys from Constantinople appeared in Basle. They perceived, however, that the Council was so busy with its own affairs that it was not primarily interested in either the fate of Byzantium or even in the prospect of union itself. They therefore indicated that they would prefer to meet the Pope, together with representatives of the Council, in some Italian city. They relied on a sympathetic hearing from a Venetian sensitive to the danger posed by the Turks to the Republic's outposts in the eastern Mediterranean. The matter came to a head in 1437 when the Council, by majority decision, proposed Avignon as a meeting place. Meanwhile the Pope quietly despatched a legate to Constantinople in order to invite the Emperor to Italy. This done, he issued a Bull ordering the dissolution of the Council and its re-assembly at Ferrara.

His action threw the conciliarists of Basle into disarray. Their immediate and petulant answer was to summon him to their presence in order to indict him, and to menace him with deposition if he ignored their behest. But this new display of radical offensiveness deflated its object. Many influential clerics, among them Cesarini and Nicolas of Cusa, left Basle to join the Pope. Early in 1438 the Emperor and his Patriarch landed at Venice and went on to Ferrara. Their suite, totalling 700 persons, included numerous eminent clerics and scholars, the cream of Byzantine intellect, but just as many leading churchmen in the East remained distrustfully aloof, firm in their traditional hostility to Rome. Even so discussions were lengthy and difficult. After a year the delegates moved to Florence, but it was not until 6 July 1439 that the act of union was signed there and promulgated in the Bull *Laetentur Caeli*. The text was solemnly read out in Latin by Cesarini and in Greek by Bessarion, Metropolitan of Trebizond and a future Roman Cardinal.

This result was of course a triumph for the Pope and a heavy blow for the radicals of Basle. At the moment it was not realized, at least in the West, that the agreement so painfully reached merely papered over the cracks in doctrine and practice and would soon be repudiated by the Greek Church and people as a whole. Its exaltation of the Pope's primacy was as displeasing to Basle as it was to public opinion in Constantinople. Almost simultaneously with the signature of the act the rump of the Council, including only seven bishops, pronounced the deposition of Eugenius as a schismatic and heretic and reconfirmed the doctrine of the Council's supremacy over the Pope. It then set up its own electoral college, which proceeded to make itself ridiculous by creating a new schism. Its choice of the last anti-Pope of history was indeed curious. In the absence of a suitable prelate it elevated Amadeus, Count of Savoy, as Felix V (1439–49). He was a devout and worthy layman and grand seigneur, dean of a Knightly Order, that of St Maurice, founded by himself on the Lake of Geneva. Needless to say the influence of this blameless old gentleman was limited and his obedience embraced only the fringe countries of Europe such as Switzerland, Austria and Denmark. For Eugenius he represented only a nuisance value. In the ensuing years, as the Council gradually melted away, the principle rulers, most of whom had taken the conciliarist side, made their peace with the Pope. Such were Charles VII of France and the King of Germany, Frederick III of Habsburg. In both their realms, however, conciliar decrees weakening papal authority were already enforced by law, thus strengthening royal powers over the national Churches.

In 1443 Eugenius re-entered Rome, which in his absence had relapsed into its former forlorn condition. While engaged in putting things right he received the homage of Europe, the reward of his perseverance in adversity. When he died four years later, his prestige was enormously enhanced, for he had achieved more than any pope since the thirteenth century. Enea Sylvio Piccolomini, the humanist who later become Pope Pius II and had once been his severe critic, summed him up as follows: 'He was a quiet and glorious pope; he despised money, loved virtue, was neither arrogant in fortune nor dispirited in adversity. He knew no fear; his resolute soul always bore the same aspect; stern and hard towards enemies, he was benign towards those whom he took into his confidence. Tall of figure and of handsome countenance, his old age was full of majesty.' His last years were however clouded by the failure of the Crusade launched in 1444 to save eastern Christendom. After splendid victories in the Balkans won by the Hungarian John Hunyadi, it was finally smashed by the Sultan Murad at the battle of Varna where the indefatigable Cardinal Cesarini, acting as the Pope's legate with the army, met his end.

15

THE RENAISSANCE PAPACY

(1447–1521)

The revival of learning, the rapid development of an intense and methodical curiosity about the culture of the classical antiquity profoundly affected the fifteenth-century Popes. The conditions prevailing in Rome during the period of exile and schism had hindered it from sharing the intellectual and artistic activity, the prelude to the Renaissance, which had flowered in northern Italy, and particularly in Florence, during the preceding century. Rome produced neither a Dante, nor a Petrarch, nor a Bocaccio. Painters and mosaicists had disappeared from the scene and the general atmosphere was one of stagnation. While the Avignonese Popes readily patronized writers and artists, no such encouragement was forthcoming on the banks of the Tiber. It is true that Cola di Rienzo and his friends were genuinely fascinated by the remains and traditions of the remote past, but their enthusiasm was quite unsophisticated. No facilities existed in Rome, as they did in the northern cities, for higher studies in law, theology, philosophy or any other discipline. In 1303 Boniface III had endeavoured to found a university, but the project lapsed after his downfall; so did Innocent VII's attempt to resuscitate it in 1406.

Nevertheless it was inevitable that despite the troubles of the Great Schism and the Council of Constance the Popes and their entourage should feel the influence of the new climate of humanism. This was particularly strong in the Curia, which was largely recruited from outside Rome. Some of its members had been coached in Greek and classical studies by the Byzantine scholar Manual Chrysoloras, who was teaching at Florence towards the turn of the century. He also visited Rome and enthused over its shattered monuments. One of his Italian pupils was Leonardo Bruni, an Apostolic secretary under John XXIII and Martin V, Chancellor of Florence and translator of the Greek classics. Another was Poggio Bracciolini, perhaps the most notable of the early Italian Humanists. These are only two prominent examples of the erudite company that staffed the Curia in the first half of the fifteenth century and helped the papacy to outclass all its opponents, both within and outside the church, in political and diplomatic skills. Meanwhile young Italian students were being trained at Constantinople, and the influx of Greek intellectuals at the Councils of Ferrara and Florence, as well as after the fall of the Byzantine capital, increased the general hunger for a liberal education.

The employment of humanists in the Curia was proof of the broadmindedness of the pontiffs, for these scholars were frequently touchy and quarrelsome, while their copious literary output, in Latin and Italian, varied between the most polished essays in philosophy, history and poetry and the most scabrous satires and squibs.

Even Eugenius IV, who was not temperamentally sympathetic to humanism, tolerated the sarcasm lavished by Poggio on the Minorites, his favourite order of Friars. Immediately after his accession he re-established and endowed the neglected university. Later he turned his attentions to restoration and new building. He had not much time left, but work was started on the city walls and gates. St Peter's, the Vatican and the Lateran basilica and palace streets were widened, squares paved and the Pantheon cleared of the rubbish of centuries. One of his humanist secretaries, Flavio Biondo, dedicated to him a topography of the ancient city entitled *Roma instaurata*, 'Rome Restored'.

Despite the promising start made by Eugenius, his successor Nicholas V (1447 –1455) is more widely regarded as the first true Renaissance Pope. Tomasso Parentuccelli, the son of a modest physician from Liguria, earned his living as a tutor in Florence and as such became acquainted with the principal scholars at the Medici Court. Subsequently, as a Curial officer and legate he displayed a talent for concilatory statesmanship. He used it to good effect with Frederick of Habsburg, whom he crowned with much pomp at Rome in 1452. It was in fact the last papal coronation of a German Emperor. He was on equally good terms with his neighbour Alfonso of Aragon, now finally in possession of Naples, and with Francesco Sforza of Milan. The only saddening feature of the external scene was his inability to prevent the fall of Constantinople to the Turks in 1453, or to stir the western sovereigns to attempt another rescue.

In the same year Nicholas, whose mild rule and care for their city had generally endeared him to the Romans, was threatened by a conspiracy. Its author, Stefano Porcaro, was a Roman knight who had held many positions of trust under the papacy since the reign of Martin V. He was also an accomplished humanist, but his love of classical antiquity took the form of an urge to restore the Roman republic and emulate Cola de Rienzo. When Eugenius died he made an inflammatory public speech exhorting the Romans to rebel against priestly government. They failed to respond and the Pope, treating him as a harmless lunatic, sent him into honourable exile at Bologna. There, however, he continued to plot in concert with kindred spirits in Rome; they collected arms and planned to kidnap the Pope at the feast of the Epiphany. Fortunately his legate in Romagna, the Greek Cardinal Bessarion, got wind of what was impending and warned Nicholas, with the result that Porcaro was apprehended and put to death. This was the only violent incident of a peaceful but strenuous reign.

Buildings and books were the Pope's two greatest passions, and the company of learned men was his only relaxation. With restless energy and a sense of fighting against time he turned Rome into a vast construction site. The scale on which he strengthened its fortifications had been criticized but is perfectly understandable in the light of the occupation of the lands across the Adriatic by the aggressive Ottoman Turks, playing the same role as the Arab corsairs of the ninth century. For the spiritual needs of the Romans he built or repaired nearly 50 churches. Moreover he conceived a grandiose transformation of St Peter's, the Vatican and the whole Leonine city in accordance with plans worked out by the most original of all Renaissance architects, Leo Battista Alberti. It was this genius who wrote of the Pope's regime: 'The city had become a city of gold through the Jubilee; the dignity of the citizens was respected; all reasonable petitions were granted by the pontiff. There were no exactions, no new taxes. It was the whole care of the pontiff to adorn the city.' The execution of Alberti's designs for a neo-classical Rome of more than imperial dimensions was halted by the death of Nicholas, but their spirit remained to influence future Popes. Nicholas also called in famous artists, Fra Angelico, Piero della Francesca and Benozzo Gozzoli, to decorate both new and existing buildings.

His love of letters was manifested in many ways. He continued to enjoy the friendship of eminent writers and patronized them liberally. He also keenly promoted the search for ancient manuscripts and the production and collection of books of all ages. One of his intimates was Vespasiano da Bisticci, the greatest bookseller of the period when printing had hardly begun; his 45 copyists turned out about 1,000 volumes a year. But the Vatican itself employed numerous *scriptores* and subsidized translations of Greek and Latin classics by well-known scholars. Above all he spent 30,000 gold florins in restocking the papal library, which had virtually ceased to exist since the volumes previously stored at the Lateran had been removed to Avignon and thence to Peñiscola. While supervising these intense activities he lived quietly and soberly, eschewing personal extravagances. In all modesty he remarked to Vespasiano that the Florentines he had known could never have believed that he, 'mere bell-ringing priest', could ever have risen to be Pope. He was a small ugly man and study had worn down his health, but he could sparkle with wit and as Aeneas Sylvius used to say, what he did not know was outside the scope of human knowledge. His memory and eloquence were alike prodigious; it was recalled that on his election he sat out a congratulatory speech for an hour and a quarter, apparently in a deep slumber, but promptly replied at equal length and with the same wealth of language. Like Eugenius, he put up with the foibles of the humanists at his court, even when Lorenzo Valla denounced the Donation of Constantine as a forgery. His contemporaries agreed that he was a noble figure, dedicated to glorifying the papacy and not himself, but there was nothing democratic or conciliar about his government. We see in him a rounded personality; in other words there was no contradiction between Nicholas as humanist and Nicholas as Pope.

The same cannot be said of Pope Pius II (1458–64), whom history has somewhat unfairly allowed to outshine Nicholas V as the model Pope of Humanism. Between them came Calixtus III (1455–8), a dry old Spanish jurist whose only claim to be remembered is that he was called Alonso Borja and became the founder of the Borgia family fortunes. His energies were in fact wholly devoted to the advancement of his kinsmen. He raised two nephews, sons of his sisters, to the Cardinalate and made them assume his own name, italianized as Borgia. One of them, Rodrigo, was to become Alexander VI, the Borgia Pope. A third, Pedro, was enfeoffed with Benevento and destined, so it was thought, for the throne of Naples and in succession to King Alfonso. But the Pope's plans were frustrated by Pedro's death. When his own shortly followed the whole swarm of needy Aragonese whom he had installed in lucrative posts was expelled from Rome and the papal state.

Although his pontificate was so short Pius II (1458–64) is certainly the most fascinating Pope of the high Renaissance. His complex and adaptable personality, the versatility of his talent, his practical ability and not least his human qualities can only excite our sympathy and admiration. Enea Silvio Piccolomini was a self-made man, descended from a Sienese family which had come down in the world. Nevertheless he managed to obtain the best possible education from the early Florentine humanists and soon established his own reputation as a literary stylist. As such he was appointed private secretary to Cardinal Capranica and accompanied him to the Council of Basle. Since Capranica was no friend of Eugenius IV, Enea's fortunes were at first linked to the conciliar cause. For a time he was employed in the Council Secretariat. Frederick of Habsburg, who appreciated his competence in affairs as well as his literary gifts, gave him a job in the Chancery at Vienna and sent him on confidential missions abroad. In those years he thus acquired an extensive knowledge of countries as far afield as Scotland. But he was also busily writing poetry, much of it frivolous or erotic, and various forms of prose, dialogues, letters and historical studies. By 1445 he had returned to the papal camp, and Eugenius IV rewarded him, after he had at last taken orders, with the bishopric of Trent. In 1450 he was transferred to Siena, while continuing to undertake diplomatic missions for Nicholas V, and was taken into the Sacred College two years before his election as Pope.

His change of allegiance also involved a change of outlook amounting to a genuine conversion. He need not be accused of cynicism. Together with a growing religious awareness he acquired a clear sense of responsibility for the welfare of Christendom and the grandeur of the Church. Perhaps he was anyhow less frivolously inclined than his writings suggested. It seems that even before he was chosen pontiff he was resolved to give up his old habits and pursuits. He was no longer interested in captivating his contemporaries by sheer intellectual vivacity. Thus he disappointed the humanists who were expecting to greet a Maecenas eager to outdo Eugenius and Nicholas in his munificence. Instead they encountered a Pope earnestly dedicated to the Church's cause. He had not of course become a Philistine overnight, but the humanists were outraged and vented their spite against him in mordant epigrams. Filelfo, the most waspish of them all, went so far as to condemn the 'Stygian darkness' of his mind. Pius, though unmoved by that sort of nonsense, composed an eloquent 'retractation' in which he confessed his former errors. He neatly summed up his attitude in the words *Aeneam rejicite, Pium recipite*—reject Aeneas (the classical devotee and man of the world) and accept Pius (the man of the Church). At the same time he had an easy touch with the Romans, who were charmed by his mildness and geniality. A single minor conspiracy by republican zealots was easily squashed.

As agreed in the conclave, he committed himself to war against the Turks, the reform of the Curia and a measure of control of his actions by the Sacred College. But the last of these obligations he could safely ignore once elected. Irritated by complainants who persisted in demanding the right of appeal to a General Council he issued a Bull condemning such appeals as heretical and deserving of ban and interdict. For a former conciliarist this was a remarkable evolution. In defence of his own primacy he also manoeuvred Louis XI of France into repealing the so-called Pragmatic Sanction by which the monarchy had deprived the Holy See of its rights in respect of appointments and taxation. But this was merely a formal gesture and the Crown's control of the French Church remained for all practical purposes absolute.

Pius was only 53 when he acceded but his wandering and semi-bohemian life had undermined his health. He further wore himself out in his unavailing efforts to raise a Crusade, which in his new idealism he regarded as his prime duty. His diplomatic experience should have taught him that the venture was hopeless, but he persisted all the same. In 1458 he invited the western sovereigns to a congress at Mantua. The replies he received were uniformly evasive. Nevertheless he made a solemn progress, lasting 5 months, to Mantua by way of Perugia, Siena, Florence and Ferrara. In all those cities he was welcomed with elaborate ceremonial, but was dismayed to find on arrival at his destination that there was nobody there to discuss business. It was only in September that he was able to open the proceedings in the presence of a few stray delegates from eastern Europe and the Greek islands. But despite the failure of the

Congress and of his further attempts to stir the French and German courts into action, Pius did not abandon hope. His legates sent encouraging reports from Venice and from the courts of Burgundy and Hungary.

Meanwhile Rome was edified by his reception, with much pomp and rejoicing, of the head of St Andrew, a relic brought from Turkish-occupied Patras in the Morea, and the prospects of financing the campaign were increased by the discovery at Tolfa in Latium of rich deposits of alum, the material used in dyeing and a valuable source of revenue. The Pope also composed, but probably never despatched, an eloquent letter to Sultan Mehmet demonstrating the errors of Islam and adjuring him to adopt the Christian faith. Finally he announced that he would head the Crusade in person; the soldiers were to assemble at Ancona where the Venetian fleet would pick them up. Although the Duke of Burgundy backed out at the last moment, the ailing Pius left Rome for Ancona on 18 June 1464, after taking the Cross in St Peter's. With the utmost difficulty he survived the journey, which took a whole month, but was distressed to discover on his arrival that the army, such as it was, lacked leadership, organization and equipment. He lingered on until 12 August when the Doge, Cristoforo Moro, sailed into the harbour with only 12 galleys. Two days later he died exhausted and heartbroken.

At the next conclave the 22 Cardinals constituting the Sacred College sought to bind the future Pope by a set of 'capitulations' circumscribing his powers and controlling his decisions. However this fresh attempt to turn the papacy into a Venetian oligarchy, with the pontiff filling the restricted role of Doge, was frustrated by the College's own choice of another Venetian Pope, who happened to be one of its least distinguished members. Pietro Barbo, a nephew of Eugenius IV, had been destined to become a merchant, but on his uncle's elevation he forsook commerce for the priesthood and was duly made a Cardinal in 1440 at the age of 22. His lack of ambition or ability kept him in the background until the election, at which he was clearly regarded as a compromise candidate.

This hard-headed Venetian had a streak of vanity. He wished to take the name of Formosus, an obvious reference to his handsome appearance, but was persuaded to alter it to Paul. As Paul II (1464–71) he promptly declined to endorse the agreed capitulations and bullied the Cardinals into signing a watered down version which in any case remained a dead letter. He went on to reshape the Curia in his own way by drastically cutting down the number of clerks his predecessor had recruited from his native Siena or from the ranks of the humanists. The latter violently assailed him as a tyrant and barbarian and their leader, a certain Bartolomeo Sacchi who liked to call himself Platina, unwisely threatened him with the prospect of a Council. Paul threw him into the dungeons of Sant' Angelo and let him cool his head for 4 months. The same punishment was inflicted on members of the Roman Academy headed by the self-styled Pomponius Laetus, a brave but pretentious intellectual who paraded an exaggerated affection for antiquity and an indifference towards the Catholic religion. Their supporters raised a tremendous outcry, alleging that they were being inhumanly tortured. Nevertheless they were acquitted of conspiring and heresy and released when Bessarion, the Greek Cardinal, intervened in their favour.

If the Pope had no taste for letters, and was indeed derided by the humanists because he could not express himself properly in Latin, he was no enemy of Renaissance culture. He assiduously collected works of art, jewellery and valuable objects of all kinds. He restored the arches of Titus and Septimus Severus, built the splendid Palazzo Venezia and encouraged two Germans to set up the first Roman printing press. He was inconsistently criticized for hoarding as well as for extravagance. Undoubtedly he was a self-indulgent hedonist, delighting in banquets and gorgeous displays, horse-racing and other diversions of the Carnival. According to current gossip he was 'prone to lust'. He sumptuously entertained Frederick III on his visit to Rome in 1468, but was in general quite uninterested in world politics and war. He was by no means an ideal pontiff, but his easy-going nature and lack of spiritual gifts did not prejudice his practical concern for the welfare of the Roman people, on whose behalf he undertook a salutary reform of the city's administration, finances and judicial system. Characteristically he died from a stroke brought on by a surfeit of melons.

Under Sixtus IV (1471–84) the defects of the Renaissance papacy were for the first time glaringly revealed. Its vices were seen to have outstripped its virtues and the pontiff's own development provides a striking example of the corrupting influence of high office. Francesco della Rovere, the son of poor parents at Savona, entered the Franciscan Order at an early age. As a teacher at various Italian universities he was highly esteemed by Bessarion and other serious churchmen for his learning, skill in controversy and apparent zeal for reform. In 1467, aged 53, he was General of his Order and Cardinal of San Pietro in Vincoli. So unimpeachable a record fully justified his election. Nevertheless such expectations as he had aroused were belied from the start. It was as if a mass of purely secular tastes and ambitions pent up within him for years suddenly burst out with uncontrollable force. The key-notes of his reign were lavish grandeur at Rome and unscrupulous political initiatives in the rest of Italy.

The extent of his nepotism scandalized even the least sensitive of his contemporaries. Of his six young nephews two, the future pope Giuliano della Rovere and Pietro Riario, were immediately made Cardinals and a third, Girolamo Basso, was similarly promoted a few years later. A shower of offices and favours descended on other members of his family. Pietro's career was bizarre in the extreme. He was endowed with no fewer than four bishoprics or archbishoprics (Spoleto, Seville, Valencia and Florence), which, together with a few abbeys, brought him an income of 60,000 gold florins, and dignified with the empty title of Patriarch of Constantinople. Thus provided he ran riot for two years, spending 200,000 gold florins on every kind of extravagance and debauchery, as chronicled in dry or salacious detail by writers of the time. He died, worn out by his excesses, in 1474 at the age of 28. He was not a monster but a thoroughly spoiled and self-indulgent young man. His brother, Girolamo Riario, was married to Caterina Sforza, a daughter of the Duke of Milan, and invested with valuable fiefs in the Romagna. Yet another nephew, Leonardo della Rovere, was made Prefect of Rome and married to a daughter of the King of Naples. On the youngest of the brood, Giovanni, he bestowed the daughter of the last Montefeltro Duke of Urbino and the succession to the duchy. Unbelievably good fortune had descended upon the grandsons of a humbe Ligurian sailor.

Early in his pontificate Sixtus sent his most eminent Cardinals to the European courts in order to whip up support for a campaign against the Turks. They mostly failed in their mission, but Venice and Naples, the powers whose interests were most in danger, helped him to equip a fleet. Under the command of the Neapolitan Cardinal Carafa, it ravaged the coast of Asia Minor. By way of retaliation the Turks caused a real flurry by landing on the heel of Italy and seizing Otranto. It was however soon retaken and Turkish pressure was generally relaxed after the death in 1481 of the formidable Mehmet the Conqueror. Opposition to the Ottoman advance was at least a laudable activity for any pope. The same could not be said for Sixtus's other political adventures. He was unable to resist an urge to involve the papal state in a dreary power game with the other major Italian states, Venice, Milan, Florence and Naples. It would be a waste of space to sort out the shifting alliances or to follow the course of the numerous petty campaigns of his pontificate. The papacy gained nothing from these sterile and expensive manoeuvres. As Geoffrey Barraclough points out, it 'thereby lost its universal pretensions and position . . . ceased effectively to be the head of Christendom and became instead one of the Italian powers', with the Pope just another Italian despot. It sacrificed what Eugenius and his immediate successors had regained in terms of moral prestige since the end of the schism.

The most unsavoury incident was the Pope's embroilment in the conspiracy of the Pazzi at Florence against the brothers Lorenzo and Giuliano de' Medici. Sixtus had fallen out with the Medici, who at first acted as his bankers, because they opposed Girolamo Riario's encroachments on their borders and the territorial expansion of the papal state. He replaced them by their political and financial rivals, the Pazzi, and was certainly privy to the plot they were hatching to bring down Lorenzo and his brother. It is doubtful whether he was prepared to condone their assassination, but when Giuliano was stabbed to death at High Mass in the cathedral of Florence (Lorenzo escaping with a slight wound) everyone assumed his connivance. The chief conspirators, who included an Archbishop of Pisa recently appointed by the Pope, were promptly hanged and Raffaelle Riario, a great-nephew whom Sixtus had made a Cardinal at 17 years of age and sent to Florence as his legate, was lucky to escape with temporary imprisonment. In return the Medici were excommunicated and Florence laid under an interdict, a sentence which led to general and indecisive war in Italy. It rumbled on for two years until the Turkish seizure of Otranto frightened the combatants into making peace.

The Pope's obsession with politics and war depleted his coffers and devalued his claim to spiritual authority, but the sheer magnificence of his reign still prevented his office from sinking into disrepute. As a Maecenas, the patron of literati, artists and architects, as builder and town-planner, the '*instaurator urbis*', he was incomparable. The humanists were recalled to favour, the Roman Academy was revived and the formerly disgraced Platina appointed prefect of a splendidly enriched and adorned Vatican library. Sixtus will always be remembered as the creator of the Sistine Chapel, but he was also the restorer and rebuilder of innumerable churches. For their decoration he summoned the most renowned masters of painting and sculpture, Botticelli, Ghirlandajo, Perugino, Pinturicchio, Signorelli, Melozzo da Forli, Mino da Fiesole, Giovanni Dalmata—the list of famous names is endless. At the same time he was the first Pope to tackle the problem of urban renewal on a large scale. After a thousand years of dereliction Rome at last emerged from its rut. Hovels were demolished, more streets and piazzas were widened and paved. The Hospital of San Spirito and a new bridge over the Tiber, the Ponte Sisto, are the most notable of his public monuments. Nevertheless the Renaissance city did not achieve as an ensemble the measured order of the baroque age. It remained until then a jumble of ramshackle houses traversed by labyrinthine streets, among which the glittering palaces of the rich Cardinals confronted the ever diminishing vestiges of ancient Rome. The almost religious respect for antiquity professed by the educated contrasted oddly with their frantic wrecking and pillaging of classical buildings, many of which disappeared for ever during this period. The Pope's restoration of the bronze equestrian statue of Marcus Aurelius on the Capitol is a rare example of a more enlightened attitude towards the past.

The various operations of the papacy, in some respects meritorious but for the most part unspiritual, put a heavy strain on the treasury. The Holy See was soon deeply in debt to its bankers. In order to devise new ways of raising money a second financial department, the Datary, was set up alongside the Apostolic Camera. Its main function was to receive the proceeds of a greatly increased issue of plenary indulgences during and after the Jubilee in 1475. Heavier taxes were exacted from the papal state, within which the Pope established a lucrative monopoly in grain. Offices and sinecures, many of them newly invented, were freely put up for sale. According to the Venetian ambassador, Sixtus used to say that he only needed a pen and ink to raise any sum he wished. In fact venality knew no bounds; a Carmelite from Mantua, author of a poem entitled *De Calamitatibus Temporum*, wrote 'your temples, priests, altars, rites . . . prayers, heaven and God too are for sale.' Although many such protests were voiced, especially from abroad where it was suspected that contributions for the Turkish war were being diverted to other purposes, the Pope could safely ignore them. In Italy at least he was regarded with a mixture of tolerant cynicism and admiration of his panache. Men were not inclined to be censorious when, in spite of intermittent warfare, culture and the economy were booming and all classes sensed that they were living in a vivid world of change and renovation.

But whereas the times were not conducive to pessimism the unrestrained behaviour of his nephews and the venality of his court exposed Sixtus to scurrilous personal attacks. Contemporary writers accused him of every possible enormity. One of them, Stefano Infessura, depicts him as gloating over a stabbing duel to the death between members of his bodyguard, and alleges that 'as experience showed, he was a lover of boys and a sodomite.' There is no reason to believe or disbelieve such calumnies, which were perhaps inevitable in the general atmosphere of his reign. It is equally impossible to judge whether, as rumoured, he had in fact fathered one or more of his nephews, a suspicion hardly supported by the quite different reputation he enjoyed at the time of their births.

The best that could be said of Innocent VIII (1484–92), the Genoese Giovanni Battista Cibo, is that his pontificate was uneventful. Neither his personality nor his record justified his elevation and the papacy suffered a sharp decline through his lack of character and leadership. By contrast with his predecessor and his successor he was a nonentity. The conclave that elected him was divided into two groups headed respectively by Cardinals Giuliano della Rovere and Rodrigo Borgia, but as neither of these vigorous and ruthless prelates could command the requisite majority they compromised on a colourless figure. As it happened it was the former who succeeded in manipulating the Pope for his own ends. His Angevin sympathies involved the Pope in sporadic hostilities with the Aragonese King of Naples which lasted throughout his reign but ended in a marriage between the King's grandson and the Pope's grand-daughter. Innocent had no compunction in acknowledging his children by a Neapolitan mistress and in advancing their fortunes. He even managed to betroth his son Franceschetto, an undistinguished parasite, to Madalena, the daughter of Lorenzo de' Medici of Florence, at the price of a Cardinalate for Giovanni, Lorenzo's 13-year-old son. Both these weddings, and that of a second grand-daughter, were celebrated with the utmost ostentation in the Vatican.

Innocent had no coherent foreign policy and lost his grip on Rome and the papal state. The Colonna again fought with the Orsini while the city, which had been well policed under Sixtus IV, was infested by bandits and distracted by brawls between the retinues of rival Cardinals. The shaky finances were only maintained by an ever-increasing traffic in offices and indulgences. However they were to a certain extent replenished from an unsuspected source, the Turkish Sultan. On the death of Mehmet the Conqeror the Ottoman succession was disputed between his sons Bayezit and Jem. When the latter lost the contest he took refuge in good faith at Rhodes with Pierre d'Aubusson, Grand Master of the Order of St John, who then dishonestly agreed with Bayezit to keep him under guard in return for a subsidy of 40,000 ducats a year. For greater safety he sent him to France, but always in the Order's custody. There Jem stayed until 1489 when the King, Charles VIII, arranged his transfer to Rome in exchange for concessions in other fields and a red hat for d'Aubusson. His arrival with his turbaned suite naturally caused a sensation, but what mattered most to the Pope was that in the following year a Turkish embassy presented him with 120,000 ducats, totalling three year's subsidy, for Jem's maintenance and an assurance that there would be no war between Christendom and the Ottoman empire. This payment, which amounted to 60 per cent of the revenue from the papal state, helped save the Holy See from utter bankruptcy, but the Vatican, in so far as it housed a Moslem prince and a Pope's progeny, offered a strange spectacle to pious pilgrims.

During the second half of the fifteenth century the papal state, as a member of the group of middle-sized Italian powers, wasted its energies and substance on petty combinations and manoeuvres in the peninsula. Europe on the whole, however, was undergoing a process of monumental change. In the west the familiar world of small units loosely linked to their superiors by feudal ties was rapidly giving way to a system dominated by three, powerful, centralized and highly competitive monarchies: France, Spain and England. The French Valois kings, after expelling the English from France, proceeded to absorb, by a mixture of warfare and dynastic accident, their principal feudatories, the duchy of Brittany and the heartland of the duchy of Burgundy; and they rounded off their national kingdom by inheriting Provence and grabbing the whole of Languedoc up to the Pyrenees. At the same time Spain, by virtue of the Aragonese and Castilian crowns under Ferdinand and Isabella, emerged as a second great power. It soon justified its claim to be regarded as such by the double triumph it celebrated in 1492, the conquest of Granada, the last Moslem outpost in the Iberian Peninsula, and the discovery of the Caribbean Islands, soon to be followed by Spanish settlement in the western hemisphere. To the north England, although excluded from the continent, was recovering its strength and influence as a maritime nation under Edward IV and the Tudor Henry VII. In central Europe the sprawling Holy Roman Empire ruled by Maximilian of Habsburg might appear ramsachkle and amorphous, but it had been fortified by his marriage to Mary, the heiress of Burgundy, and his consequent acquisition of the Low Countries, the part of the former duchy which had not fallen to France. Furthermore his more easterly dominions were for the moment well protected from aggression by the Ottoman Turks, masters of the Balkans, by the continued existence of a strong Hungarian Monarchy in the Danube basin. Such was the new alignment in Europe when Alexander VI, the second Borgia Pope, acceded in 1492. Four years later even wider political horizons were opened by the marriage of Juana, sole heiress of Aragon and Castille, with Philip, sole heir to the Empire of Maximilian.

The Pope who first had to deal with this revolution in European affairs, and who reigned from 1492-1503, was Rodrigo Borgia, the sexagenarian Vice-Chancellor of the Church and Bishop of Valencia and Porto. Essentially he was an Italianized

Spaniard who combined Iberian toughness with a totally non-Iberian lack of principle. His ecclesiastical career had been more personally lucrative than rich in achievement, but he had used the personal wealth he had amassed to extend his influence and had not dissipated it in needless extravagance. His early private life was relatively discreet, though Pius II had to admonish him for unpriestly behaviour. About 1470 he began to live with Vanozza de Cataneis, a Roman lady who while married to two other men in succession bore him four children, Juan, Caesar, Lucrezia and Jofre. It was recognized that as Cardinal Borgia's mistress she led an unassuming life and after he became Pope she was married off to a third husband.

Alexander's reputation as a shrewd politician and administrator had convinced the Romans that he was the right man to succeed the feeble Innocent VIII. He was handsome, eloquent and wielded an insidious charm; few cavilled at his lack of religious feeling and neglect of his churchly duties. He at once betrayed his inordinate passion for the advancement of his family. His second son, Caesar, was made Archbishop at 17 and Cardinal at 18, while the eldest, Juan Duke of Gandia, was destined to become a secular prince. Lucrezia was affianced to Giovanni Sforza, Lord of Pesaro. In all, five members of the family were to receive the red hat.

For some years, however, Alexander's projects for the aggrandizement of the Borgias were interrupted by the shattering irruption of French arms into Italy. Even if the Pope had been able to foresee this danger there is little he could have done to ward it off. Opinions differ as to the motives of the King of France, Charles VIII, in invading the peninsula. He probably did so simply because he was young, headstrong and avid for personal glory, possessed an overwhelmingly powerful army itching to be used, and was egged on by a bevy of discontented and persuasive Italians. At all events he decided to make good the long-standing Angevin claim to the Kingdom of Naples, then ruled by a branch of the House of Aragon, and prepared the ground by an alliance with Ludovico Sforza, the regent and future Duke of Milan. It was a bad sign for the Pope when his old rival in the Sacred College, Cardinal della Rovere, absconded to the French court. Really frightened, he entered into a tortuous but fruitless negotiation for an alliance with Sultan Bayezit against the Christian monarch.

In September 1494 Charles crossed the Alps. There was no concerted opposition to his advance southwards. Venice refused to stir, Florence expelled the Medici and came to terms with the French, and the Neapolitan troops were easily brushed aside. Rome and the Papal states were obviously defenceless; indeed the Pope begged Alfonso II, the King of Naples, not to make a fight of it at the approaches to the City. On the last day of the year Charles made his triumphant entry. While Alexander retired behind the bulwarks of Sant' Angelo the thickly armoured French Knights, the ponderous artillery and the terrifying regiments of Swiss and German mercenaries paraded unopposed and were applauded by the populace.

They stayed for one month only, but it was sufficient for Alexander to display his negotiating skill. His enemies among the Cardinals were already urging Charles to summon a Council with the object of either deposing the Pope or forcing him to submit to reforms. What interested the King, however, was an assurance of papal backing for his misty projects of conquest, and particularly the seizure of Naples as a base for aggression against the Ottoman empire. At the price of a Cardinal's hat Alexander won over or suborned Briçonnet, Charles's confidential adviser. As a result of their parleys the King received the Pope's blessing for his plans; the idea of a Council was dropped and the papal state remained inviolate except for a few strongpoints. When Charles marched on to Naples he took with him Caesar Borgia as a hostage for his father's behaviour and Prince Jem as a bargaining counter in his future dealings with the east. But within a few weeks the Sultan's brother died with suspicious suddenness.

As Alexander had suspected, the French expedition was doomed to failure. It was well equipped for a blitzkrieg but not for a continuing programme of occupation and conquest. Charles's army was immobilized in Naples, a prey to fever and syphilis; the Aragonese princes eluded him and the people resorted to guerrilla warfare. Caesar Borgia escaped from supervision and went into hiding. Meanwhile Alexander was helping to organize a general anti-French alliance, the so-called Holy League, with which Maximilian of Habsburg, Ferdinand of Spain, Milan and Venice were all associated. Faced with this threat Charles decided on retreat. In May 1495 he abandoned Naples and withdrew slowly northwards, passing through Rome on the way. But the Pope had already removed himself to Perugia, leaving Cardinal Morton, the Archbishop of Canterbury, to represent him in the city. After fighting a stiff battle at Fornavo with an all-Italian force commanded by the Marquis of Mantua, the depleted French host struggled back to its own country.

Alexander had won a tactical success. He now believed that he would be free to pursue his own policy of driving out the numerous petty tyrants from the papal state and of converting it into an appendage ruled directly by one or more members of the house of Borgia. But in concentrating on this limited aim he overlooked the danger that Italy would be helplessly vulnerable to intervention by the great European powers. In fact it was fated to be ravaged, impoverished, humiliated and reduced to despair during the next three decades and more by the passage of destructive foreign armies. The French claim to Naples was sustained by Charles VIII's successor, Louis XII, and strongly countered by Spain. Southern Italy became a battlefield between the two powers in which King Ferdinand's General, Gonçalvo de Cordova, eventually gained the upper hand, and the Neopolitan kingdom became a province of the Spanish monarchy.

Alexander had first intended that his favourite son, Juan Duke of Gandia, should become a great territorial prince and even aspire to the throne of Naples. However, his hopes were dashed when Juan disappeared one night after dining with his brother Caesar and his body was hauled out of the Tiber on the next day pierced with nine wounds. While the Romans exchanged witticisms about the Pope's role of fisher of men, suspicion inevitably fell on Caesar. The most scurrilous of the rumours circulating was that the brothers had been rivals for the love of their sister Lucrezia, but a more likely explanation is that Caesar had become jealous of Juan's worldly prospects. As a mere Cardinal-deacon he seemed destined for a secondary part. However that may be, he was almost certainly the murderer, and in the next few years he was to do away with a host of real or fancied enemies. The Pope himself appeared to go in awe of him and soon suspended the official enquiry into Juan's death. He then devoted himself whole-heartedly to Caesar's advancement. This involved the latter's resignation from the Sacred College, his promotion to secular prince and a reversal of the papacy's previous anti-French stance. Alexander proceeded to negotiate an arrangement with the French crown by which Louis XII obtained Papal consent for the annulment of his marriage and an assurance that the Holy See would no longer oppose his claims to Milan and Naples. In return he invited Caesar to visit him in great state, vested him with the dukedom of Valence and married him to the sister of the King of Navarre.

The way was thus opened for further French campaigns in Italy and for others in which Caesar methodically ousted the feudal dynasts of Romagna and the Marches,

Umbria and Latium. One by one they were expelled or assassinated until by 1503, the year of Alexander's death, the whole papal state had passed into the personal possession of the Borgias. Caesar, the unchallenged tyrant of central Italy, was threatening the independence of Florence. There is no reason to suppose that Alexander was unduly perturbed because the real power in the Papal state belonged to his son. Family pride was his dominant passion. Moreover Caesar had no interest in poisoning his father, if only because he himself could never, even in the corrupt condition of the papacy, have aspired to become Pope.

Tradition demands that Alexander's pontificate should be depicted in the most lurid of colours. Nevertheless the truth is elusive and cannot easily be disentangled from the effusions of contemporary scandalmongers and latter day moralists. Was the papal court really so depraved as it has been represented in so many columns of purple prose? Did fifty Roman whores really couple at the same time with fifty palace servants for the Pope's entertainment? How high a degree of credence can be given to the oft-repeated tales of incest and poisoning? The reign cannot be dismissed as a catalogue of tyrannical violence and sensual success. Rather it was remarkable for its absorption in narrow and selfish ends against a background of sweeping international and dynastic change. At its conclusion Alexander, although seventy years of age, was by no means sunk in dotage, surviving, as gossip would have it, through his delight in vicarious orgies and exhibitions and sadistic cruelty. On the contrary he remained remarkably spry. After pensioning off Vanozza he acquired a new mistress, Giulia Farnese, and he was not troubled by twinges of remorse or anxiety. In 1500 he held a successful and profitable Jubilee. At the moment when the most scabrous stories were circulating in Rome about his personal habits, his addiction to his own daughter and his alleged maintenance of a seraglio of girls and boys in the Vatican, he was blessing in his spiritual capacity a crowd of 200,000 pilgrims in St Peter's Square. There could not have been a more complete divorce between the papacy as the font of christian faith and the condemnation of the reigning pontiff's personal behaviour.

In a carefully balanced estimate of Alexander's character the Florentine historian Guicciardini stated that he was 'most sensual towards both sexes', but judged by the lay standards of his time his habits differed little from those of an Ottoman Sultan, to say nothing of Christian monarchs such as François I of France. He was never besotted by his pleasures, unforgivable as they were in a priest. Again according to Guicciardini, he was guilty of avarice, cruelty, injustice and duplicity, vices common to most Renaissance sovereigns but spotlighted by his relationship to Caesar, in whom they assumed an exaggerated form. Lacking as he was in any spark of religious feeling, he took a perversely short-sighted view of his office, and though a man 'of the utmost power and of great judgement and spirit' he dissipated and misused his qualities. In other words, as the Florentine sums up, 'he was more evil and more lucky than, perhaps, any Pope before.' His sudden death was attributed by many to his having drunk poisoned wine at a dinner party given by one of his Cardinals, but it is more probable that the fever that struck him and from which Caesar, who was also present, recovered was caused by a bacterial infection at the height of an unhealthy summer. His German master of ceremonies, who recorded the enormities of Alexander's reign, in a deadpan diary, attached no sinister significance to his demise.

The pontificates of Julius II (1503–13) and Leo X (1513–23) marked the culmination of the renaissance papacy and combined its best with its worst features. Each was splendid in its own way but considered together they were the swan song of the long era before western Christendom was divided between those who accepted and those who rejected Rome. The condition of Italy deteriorated sadly around them, for the background to their magnificence was one of political confusion, shifting alliances, unceasing domestic warfare and the devastating incursions of foreign armies.

Alexander's death took Rome by surprise. The Cardinals were terrified of Caesar and waited to see how he would react, but he was still prostrated by the illness that killed his father and incapable of resolute action. Meanwhile his little empire quickly dissolved as the papal state threw off his authority. In order to be on the safe side, the College hurriedly elected the old and feeble Francisco Piccolomini, Cardinal of Siena, as Pius III. However, he lasted for only 26 days and the Cardinals then turned to the dynamic Giuiliano della Rovere, Alexander's former rival but his supporter in his pro-French policies. For a short time after his election as Julius II he temporized, detaining Caesar in Rome until he was satisfied that Borgia power was broken for good. Then he let him escape to Gonçalvo de Cordova at Naples. The Spanish Commander, after promising him his liberty, packed him off to Spain, where he remained until 1506. In the following year he was killed fighting as a minor captain in the service of the King of Navarre.

Like his uncle Sixtus IV, Julius was a born ruler and politician. Known to the Italians as 'il Terribile', he possessed an iron will and a resolution undaunted by setbacks. His lively career had involved him in more than one change of front, but as Pope he pursued only one object, the temporal grandeur of the papacy. Whereas Alexander had used the papacy to further his own family ends, Julius, though by no means indifferent to the fortunes of his relatives, used them to further the interests of the Holy See. Those he saw as identical with Italian patriotism. As soon as he could reassert and consolidate papal power, as opposed to Borgia power, in the state of the Church, he conceived it his duty to rid north and central Italy of the 'barbarians', that is of his former friends the French, now holding Milan, and their Teutonic mercenaries. As for the south, he was realistic enough to admit that the Spaniards were likely to be its masters for the foreseeable future. For the time being it would be advisable to have them on his side. His efforts earned him the title of liberator of Italy; nevertheless their success was ephemeral and caused infinite bloodshed and distress.

He began by leading his own troops to recover Perugia and Bologna, cities which had again fallen into the hands of local despots, the Baglioni and the Bentivogli. Then he joined the League of Cambrai which Louis XII and Maximilian of Habsburg had formed to check Venetian expansion in north Italy and the Adriatic. Thus threatened and defeated in the field by the French, Venice surrendered to the Pope several important towns of the Romagna which it had occupied after the fall of the Borgias. But having once restored the boundaries of the papal state, Julius saw no reason to prolong hostilities with the Republic, whose co-operation was indispensable for defence against the Turks. During the last three years of his reign he embarked on a much more risky enterprise against the French and their Italian satellites. He insisted on taking the field in person although, at 67, he had to be carried on an oxcart or in a litter. His first campaigns, however, ended in defeat and the loss of Bologna. Nothing daunted, he fell back on diplomacy and soon succeeded in organizing yet another Holy League, this time consisting of Venice and Spain, to which Henry VIII of England also adhered. Maximilian remained neutral for the moment but was preparing to join the allies. War convulsed the whole of north Italy. On 11 April 1512, a tremendous battle was fought at Ravenna between the French and the forces of the League, among which Spaniards predominated. The French won a crushing victory but their commander, Gaston de Foix, lost his life and in the following months the whole structure of French power in Italy collapsed. Maximilian openly joined the League and withdrew the German mercenaries in Louis's service, while a large corps of Swiss in papal pay descended on Milan. At the cost of enormous suffering among the wretched Italians Julius had attained his object. The French retreated across the Alps and, by agreement between the allies, the Sforza returned to Milan and the Medici to Florence. To complete his triumph, Julius annexed Reggio, Parma and Piacenza to the papal domain.

While the fighting continued he also foiled an attack on his authority as head of the Church. In 1510 King Louis summoned a national synod at Tours to condemn papal aggression for political ends and to confirm the right of national Churches to withhold obedience in such cases. He also prevailed on a group of dissident Cardinals to convoke a schismatic Council at Pisa on the ground that the Pope had not done his duty to call a General Council in accordance with decisions of Constancce. As might have been expected the meeting at Pisa made no impact. Julius countered it by summoning his own Council to the Lateran in May 1512, proclaiming it to be the eighteenth General Council of the Church. It accomplished little but remained in session under Leo X until 1517.

Julius was undeniably a most formidable personality. It is held against him that he exhausted and demoralized Italy by his wars, that he betrayed his spiritual trust by his extreme concentration on secular affairs and that he thus opened the way for a movement to abolish the papacy altogether. According to the contrary thesis, the spiritual revival of the papacy in the sixteenth century could not have taken place unless its secular authority had been previously fortified. In other words, the spiritual base and the territorial power base were inseparable in the circumstances of the time. If Julius had not asserted himself as he did, papal prestige could not have been upheld against the great European monarchies of the age. Rome might have been reduced to a simple bishopric or the Church again driven into the catacombs.

Whichever conclusion we may prefer, Julius's nature would not have allowed him to behave otherwise. He acted from conviction and not as a selfish opportunist. He loved display but his public and private life was dignified and free of scandal. The venality of the hierarchy and the Curia was less obvious. He kept good order at Rome and the scale on which he planned its development and adornment exceeded anything contemplated by his predecessors. Bramante, Michelangelo, Raphael, Perugini, Sansovino, Sangallo all worked for him. To him we owe the new basilica of St Peter, the foundation stone of which was laid in 1506, the *Last Judgment* in the Sistine Chapel, the frescos of the Stanze della Segnatura and the Vatican Museum's collection of ancient sculpture. Michelangelo's *Moses*, created for the Pope's funeral monument but only set up many years later in his titular church of San Pietro in Vincoli, may be regarded as a fit expression of his masterful presence.

The heroic flavour of his pontificate was conspicuously lacking in that of his successor, Leo X. The electors, who were perhaps instinctively seeking a pope who would be the antithesis of Julius, found him in Giovanni de' Medici. This was the son of Lorenzo the Magnificent whom Innocent VIII had made a Cardinal at 13. In the intervening period, during which his family had been expelled and then restored to Florence, he had done his best to avoid trouble and had not been deeply involved in political or ecclesiastical affairs. He was however present as Julius's legate at the battle of Ravenna, where he was taken prisoner by the French. He was known to be amiable and unambitious, generous and cultivated, a keen patron of art and learning. Although still only 38, he suffered from poor health and was not expected to live for very long. Finally, his peaceful disposition seemed to rule out the possibility of any serious crisis.

Certainly few of his contemporaries could foresee the danger to which the Church would be exposed by his insouciance and failure to grasp realities. He himself viewed his function in terms of secular splendour and the furtherance of humanist culture. He is often quoted to have remarked to his brother Giuliano, 'Let us enjoy the papacy which God has given us.' His gorgeous inaugural pageant alone cost 100,000 ducats, and his court life was a continuous round of festivities, banquets, carnivals, theatrical shows, balls and hunting parties. Nevertheless its ostentatious extravagance was not incompatible with his open-handed liberality towards artists and scholars and his critical appreciation of their work. His biographer, the Latinist and historian Paolo Giovio, described his reign as the golden age of Italian culture: according to an epigram Rome, which had belonged successively to Venus (under Alexander) and to Mars (under Julius), was now Minerva's domain. As men of genius flocked to Rome in an extraordinary concentration of talent, the rich Cardinals and bankers who were adorning the city with new palaces vied with the Pope in sponsoring them.

Papal finances were more badly damaged by Leo's lavishness than by the warlike operations of Julius, who in fact left a reserve of 700,000 ducats in the treasury. It was quickly dissipated and the Holy See lived from hand to mouth off credit from Roman and Florentine bankers, the Gaddi, Bini, Salviati, and the greatest of them all, Agostino Chigi. Although they charged him 40 per cent, they themselves were seriously embarrassed by the Pope's demands. In order to recoup his losses Leo multiplied the sale of offices and indulgences. He also milked the Cardinals, many of whom could of course very well afford to pay up. His mass creation of 31 new members of the College in 1517 netted him half a million ducats. It followed the discovery of a mysterious plot to poison him, engineered for personal reasons by a Cardinal Petrucci, but in which some of the latter's colleagues were believed to be implicated. Petrucci was executed by strangulation while the others were pardoned on payment of sums varying between 5,000 and 50,000 ducats. Not all the new creations were unworthy, but they included three professional financiers.

Leo had little flair for politics. His waverings irritated the two imposing rivals who assumed power during his pontificate, François I of France and Charles, the future Emperor and ruler of Spain, Naples and vast territories in the Americas. The Pope first joined the league opposing the French King's successful attempt to recover Milan, but after François's crushing victory over the League's army at Marignano (1515) he rushed out to greet him at Bologna. Their discussion resulted in a treaty in which the papacy gave up Parma and Piacenza but safeguarded Medici rule at Florence, and in a Concordat which guaranteed to the French Crown full control of appointments in the Gallican Church. Rightly or wrongly Leo judged France to be a lesser threat to the survival of the papal state than an all-enveloping Habsburg monarchy. It was only when he began very belatedly to grasp how badly he might need Charles's help in combating the Lutheran movement that he again changed sides, supported Charles's election as Emperor by the German princes and concluded with him, shortly before his own death, a new anti-French alliance. Even more insensitive in religious than in political matters, he had failed to take heed of the warning signs that the spiritual authority of the church was in mortal danger.

PART FIVE

DEFENCE
AND
REFORM

16

THE REFORMATION
(1521–1549)

To all appearances the fifteenth-century papacy had successfully withstood the shocks of exiles and schism. Thanks to its timely but not very sincere acceptance of conciliarism it had recovered its unity and repelled, not without difficulty, the attacks of radical reformers of the type of Hus and Wyclif. Yet the ease with which these individuals had been able to launch mass movements had disquieted the Church, and it was hardly to be expected that similar voices of protest would remain indefinitely stilled. At the same time the humanism which had permeated Rome itself, and which was encouraged to a varying extent by all the Renaissance Popes, freely paraded its scepticism and indifference to dogmatic religion. Finally the increasingly unabashed secularism of the Pontiffs, their blatant disregard of common morality and their preoccupation with politics, war, their pleasures and the amassment and dissipation of wealth, were bound to provoke a revolution sooner or later.

An ominous indication of the form dissent might take was provided at Florence by Girolamo Savonarola. Whether this Dominican friar can properly be regarded as a precursor of Martin Luther is a matter of argument between specialists, but it is difficult not to draw a parallel between the Italian Dominican and the Augustinian monk from Germany. Savonarola, who came from Ferrara, was received into the Dominican Order in 1475. His early aspiration to become a popular revivalist preacher in the cities of north Italy was disappointed; few were disposed to listen very seriously to his message until 1490 when Lorenzo the Magnificent, scenting that he was a potential genius whom the Medici would be well advised to have on their side, summoned him to Florence. In the following year he was made prior of the Dominican convent of St Mark and Pope Alexander VI even appointed him Vicar General with the task of reforming all the houses of his order in Tuscany. Thus established he won an immediate mass response to his talent for vivid oratory. His prophetic sermons, in which he accurately foretold the ruin of Italy, spared neither the ruler of Florence nor the Pope. Earlier in his life, during the pontificate of Sixtus IV, he had denounced Rome as a 'deceitful, proud, harlot'; now, in equally scathing language, he castigated Alexander as Antichrist. In 1495, after the death of Lorenzo, the expulsion of the Medici from Florence and the passage southwards of the French army, he assumed both the political and the religious leadership of the new republican regime, on which he imposed a strong theocratic and puritanical stamp, not only anti-papal but hostile to the whole spirit of the renaissance. But he failed to sustain his role of prophet-administrator. At first his attacks on Roman corruption and Alexander's personality were widely welcomed, and he was careful to insist that in his zeal for reform he was trying neither to impugn Catholic doctrine nor even to undermine the authority of pope and hierarchy so long as they were willing to reform themselves. Later, however, the arbitrary nature of his government, and especially his rigorous censorship of morals and manners, drove the Florentines to repudiate him. It seemed that, intoxicated by his own eloquence, he had lost control of himself and was behaving like a crazy fanatic. Excommunicated by the Pope, disavowed by the Florentines whose city had been laid under an interdict, he was eventually removed from power, tried, defrocked and publicly executed.

But a sounder and broader conception of Church reforms from within was already occupying some of the best minds in Europe. During the second half of the fifteenth century Christian humanists in Italy and elsewhere had been busily and critically examining the established Hebrew, Greek and Latin texts of the scriptures and fathers of the church in the light of the sudden availability of new manuscripts brought to the West by refugees from the extinct Byzantine empire. Thus the output of revised texts and commentaries grew rapidly and was everywhere diffused by that new invention, printing. By the turn of the century tens of thousands of literate clerks in holy orders, to say nothing of laymen, were absorbing these products of Renaissance scholarship and questioning assumptions on which the teachings and practices of the church were currently based. The flood of publications had become so ample that the organs of supervision and censorship at Rome's disposal were swamped, to the consternation of those for whom any amendment or reinterpretation of scriptural and patristic texts were equivalent to heresy.

The foremost and most articulate of these would-be reformers was Erasmus of Rotterdam, whose authority at its peak almost attained that of a rival Pope. His most important works, culminating in his edition of the Greek New Testament, appeared during the pontificates of Julius II and Leo X. He was in correspondence with every distinguished scholar in Europe and on intimate terms with such liberal-minded Catholics as Thomas More and John Colet in England. He pleaded earnestly for simplicity in doctrine, the reduction of theology to a minimum, the revival of biblical study and a thorough purge of the institutional church. There was little savour of revolt in his message, still less of heresy, but it inevitably filled his hearers with deep distate for the sloth, ignorance and corruption prevailing in the Church, as well as with contempt for a ruling hierarchy whose idea of religion was a frozen theology, a dull outward conformity and the performance of meaningless propitiations.

The contemporary Popes seemed little aware of this intellectual ferment. They did not grasp that their inability to reform was endangering their own position and even undermining the church's foundations. At Julius's own Lateran Council of 1512 two Venetian monks submitted to him a full reforming programme, but he could not be bothered with it. To Erasmus, who visited Rome at about that time, he appeared absorbed by his own folly and by a domestic urge to harass his fellow men. Obviously the Papacy under Julius was irredeemable, but Erasmus still hesitated to say so in so many words. On the contrary, a few months before Martin Luther burst upon the world with his famous act of defiance at Wittenburg, we find Erasmus assuring Leo X that his reign will turn out an age of gold. In return the cultured pope did not fail to compliment him on the success of his newly published Greek Testament.

Erasmus described Luther as a 'Goth'. What he meant was that the German monk was not one of his own moderate and polished company who longed for reform to be thorough but above all peaceful. He recognized Luther's honesty of purpose and did not shrink from arguing with him, much as he disliked his violent temper, rough manners and coarse language. He had quickly foreseen how effective the monk's message was likely to be in terms of popular appeal and that it threatened to bring about the worst schism that the Church had ever suffered.

Of course Luther, for all his addiction to the language of the gutter, was no mere boor, but a genius of compelling power. Born in 1483, the son of a miner, he had received an excellent education at the university of Erfurt and a thorough spiritual and theological training with the Augustinians. When he was 25 he was already lecturing on the scriptures at the University of Wittenburg and making a name for himself. In 1511 he went to Rome and was confronted with the system of Julius II at its worst. What shocked him especially was its venality, although he was wrong in assuming that at that moment the Holy See was vastly rich instead of deeply in debt. He returned to Germany aflame with indignation. Nevertheless he might never have found an opportunity to proclaim his protest with such resounding force if it had not been fortuitously afforded him by a quarrel between two German grandees, the Archbishop of Mainz and the Elector Frederick of Saxony, over the sale of indulgences, a papal device for raising money which Luther naturally abominated. In this case the transaction was particularly sordid. The Archbishop who had recently paid the Pope a stiff price for the privilege of holding more than one see, was authorized to recoup his losses by promoting a sale of indulgences over the whole of Germany for the alleged purpose of rebuilding St Peter's. Frederick, however, refused to allow the traffic to take place within his own electoral territory. Luther cleverly chose this moment to turn the squabble into an issue of high principle. When he directly assailed papal prerogative by affixing his ninety-five theses against indulgences to the church door at Wittenberg, he was assured not only of maximum publicity, but of the support of his prince, the Elector, of the German humanists and of the German people.

If his action was instantly acclaimed by the exasperated Germans, it caused little alarm at Rome. The Pope's advisers had no reason to fear that this gesture of indiscipline by an apparently unimportant monk might herald a religious revolution. Nor was Leo so warned by his legates in Germany, who were confident that the dissenter would promptly be silenced by means of persuasion or punishment. They could not have made a worse judgement. Far from recanting, Luther became more assertive. In 1518, at the Imperial Diet of Augsburg, he made his first appearance on a wider political stage in the presence of the Emperor Maximilian, from whom he had received a safe-conduct, and of his protector Frederick of Saxony. His meeting there with the pope's legate, the Cardinal of Gaeta, came to nothing, as did similar disputations with other emissaries from Rome during the next two years. Although given every chance to yield gracefully, he grew more radical and anti-papist. When Leo eventually condemned him in his Bull *'Exsurge Domine'* of 15 June 1520 such action was too late to be effective. It only stimulated him to produce the astonishing sequences of writings that were to build the foundations of Lutheran Protestantism and exclude millions of Christians from the Roman Church. Similarly, when the new Emperor, Charles V, summoned him to his first Diet at Worms in 1521, he emerged unharmed. It was inevitable that Charles, the ruler of so many Catholic Lands should yield to Papal pressure to the extent of formally placing Luther under the ban of the empire, but German sympathizers were so strongly in the reformer's favour that the sentence had no practical effect. His life was not endangered nor his freedom of action compromised. In the castle of Wartburg, where Frederick of Saxony prudently confined him, he continued to write voluminously and shape the progress of Protestantism.

Leo X died in December 1520, leaving a legacy of discord within the Church and of hostilities in Italy between the rulers of France and the Empire. The 39 members of the Sacred College, 36 of whom were Italians, were evenly divided between the partisans of the two rival monarchs, Charles and Francis. Finally their choice fell, for the last time until 1978, on a non-Italian, Cardinal Hadrian of Utrecht, bishop of Tortosa in Spain, who assumed his own name as Hadrian VI (1522–3). It was a clear victory for the imperial interest, for Hadrian, a Fleming, was a subject of Charles and his former tutor. More lately he had acted as regent in Spain during the Emperor's absence in Germany. He was not present at the conclave and was dismayed by the news of his election. He knew that his reputation for devout simplicity was not likely to endear him to the Romans in general, while they too could hardly believe that the College had foisted on them this obscure 'barbarian' who could not even speak Italian. Their worst fears were justified when he introduced a regime of rigid economy and arid austerity. The luxurious court was virtually liquidated, the curial bureaucracy was pursued and traffic in offices ceased abruptly. So did the favours formerly showered on artists and intellectuals. The Pope made do with three personal servants, all Flemings, and as head of the Datary, or financial department, he appointed another compatriot. Naturally, he encountered obstructions and scorn. No Cardinal imitated his way of life. His stinginess and assumed lack of culture was savagely satirized, but it was remarked that he stayed quietly in the city when it was ravaged by plague.

He had very little time to make his influence felt outside Rome. While instructing his legate in Germany to enforce the ban imposed on Luther he freely acknowledged that the responsibility for the latter's errors and the threatened secession of Germany from the Church rested on the papacy itself and the evils it had so long tolerated and encouraged. He had no intention of widening the rift and stressed his own determination to introduce the necessary reforms as soon as he could bring Rome under control. At the same time he was trying to reconcile Charles and François with a view to forming a new alliance against the Turks, who had captured Rhodes from the Templars and were threatening Hungary. The French king, however, understandably suspected him of partiality for the Habsburgs and was bent on another campaign of conquest in Italy. When Hadrian discovered that François had suborned one of the senior Cardinals he reluctantly resigned himself to joining the Emperor, England and Venice in an anti-French coalition, and died of fatigue and disappointment just as the French invasion was beginning.

A feature of his brief reign which should not be overlooked is his concern with the mass conversion of the Indians in Charles's newly acquired realm of Mexico. The first transatlantic bishoprics had been set up by Julius II in the Antilles and Panama, but it was Cortés, the conqueror of Mexico, who proposed to the Emperor that the conversion should be entrusted to Spanish Mendicant friars. While Hadrian issued the Bull authorizing the initiative it is significant that even before the arrival of the Spanish mission the gap was filled by three friars from the Pope's Flemish homeland, one of whom, Peter of Ghent, was reputed to be a Habsburg bastard, probably the Emperor's uncle.

Ranke, the most eminent German historian of the sixteenth-century papacy, dismissed Clement VII (1523–34) as the most disastrous of all pontiffs. During his reign Rome was brutally sacked by the imperial troops who should have been its protectors, the English church broke with the papacy and the Protestant tide in Germany and the Nordic countries was shown to be irreversible. With the firm support of powerful princes, Lutheranism established itself as a separate Christian cult with its own distinctive doctrine and practices, while there were signs that other Protestant sects were about to emerge under the influences of individual reformers. Yet it might be more charitable to blame those calamities and setbacks on Clement's entanglement, as Gregorovius put it, 'in the labyrinth of inherited evils' than on his own personal shortcomings. An illegitimate Medici, he had been advanced in the Church by his cousin Leo X, who made him Cardinal-Archbishop of Florence. He was regarded as a friend of the Habsburgs and a reliable foe of French aggression. Unfortunately his preoccupation with politics and war fatally prevented him from attending to the vital religious issues of reform and schism. To put it bluntly, he was quite unequal to the task of healing the new division in Christendom.

He also proved incapable of holding the balance between the two great European powers. By trying to be too clever in his diplomacy he appeared untrustworthy to both. As the fortunes of war varied in north Italy, the wavering Pope chose to desert Charles and to conclude an alliance with François. He could not have made a worse decision, for in February 1525 the imperialists overwhelmed the French at the battle of Pavia and took their King prisoner. Faced with the consequences of Charles's anger and mistrust, Clement foolishly continued to play the Machiavellian game. While openly negotiating an arrangement by which the Emperor would take the Papal State under his shield, thus rounding off his domination of Italy, he began covertly to stir up a national uprising. Such was the situation when Charles released his prisoner, whom he had bound by the crippling Treaty of Madrid (1526). But as soon as he was free François repudiated his engagements and the Pope hastened to join him, together with Venice and Florence, in a renewal of the anti-Habsburg alliance. This time it was called the Holy League of Cognac.

It was of course a capital misjudgement. Even if Clement was right in thinking that the Habsburgs in Milan and Naples were a greater threat to Italian liberty than possible French conquests, Habsburg supremacy in Europe was obviously more favourable than detrimental to the cause of the church. Moreover, from the secular point of view which was of undue concern to a Medici Pope, the Habsburgs were more powerful than the Valois. But Clement maintained a defiant posture. As he continued to reject Charles's overtures for a reconciliation the traditionally Ghibelline Colonna staged an anti-papal revolution in Rome which was very nearly successful. The insurgents plundered the Vatican quarters and only withdrew because the Emperor still hoped to bring the Pope to reason.

However a very much worse fate was impending. When Charles realized that the Pope had no intention of abandoning the League of Cognac, he decided to strike directly at Rome. Absorbed in futile intrigue, Clement, his Cardinals and the Curia seem to have had no premonition of what might occur. Nor indeed did the Emperor. His army which marched on Rome, like most armies of the time, was cosmopolitan, undisciplined and underpaid. Under the command of a renegade Frenchman, the Constable de Bourbon, it included Italian adventurers, tough Spanish infantry who despised the Italians and grimly professional German *landsknechts* who, if they had any religion at all, were infected with Lutheranism. All were avid for loot and destruction. Nevertheless the Pope foresaw no serious danger and even dismissed many of his own mercenaries. When the attack was launched on 7 May 1527 there were not enough defenders to man the walls. When Bourbon was killed by a random shot, which the rapscallion writer Benvenuto Cellini claimed to have fired, the last hope vanished of maintaining order in the imperial army. While the city was stormed and the Pope fled to Sant' Angelo, the Swiss guards in the Vatican were cut down to the last man. As from midnight on the day of the assault Rome was given over to sack at the hands of 30,000 soldiers. The atrocities and profanations they committed far exceeded those inflicted in the past by Goths or Vandals, Saracens or Normans, and were only paralleled by the outrages suffered by the Greeks of Constantinople at the hands of the so-called Crusaders in 1204. The horrors continued in full spate for eight days and sporadically for several months. The loss of life, property and works was immense. Rome was left a shell from which half the inhabitants had fled, but the damage to its major monuments was happily not irreparable.

After a month's battering by the besiegers' artillery the Pope surrendered Sant' Angelo and threw himself on the Emperor's mercy. In far away Madrid Charles was genuinely horrified by the news of the sack and not disposed to persecute him unnecessarily. As soon as he had promised his neutrality, provided hostages and paid an indemnity he was allowed to leave for Orvieto and Viterbo, those traditional retreats of fugitive pontiffs, pending his return to the shattered city. Meanwhile a ruinous war continued in Italy until the final discomfiture of the French. Charles's triumph was then consummated by two treaties, one imposing terms on the French and ensuring their definitive exclusion from Italy, the other with the Pope who was treated more than leniently. Charles insisted only on safe-guarding such essential interests as his hold on Naples. For the rest, the papal state was to remain intact and the Medici were once again to be restored to Florence. The conclusion of these settlements was to be celebrated by Charles's double coronation as King of Italy and Emperor. Attended by an impressive suite of Spanish grandees, he landed at Genoa and proceeded to Bologna, where the Pope had been summoned to meet him and perform the ceremonies.

No effort had been spared to mark the significance of the occasion. The iron crown of Lombardy was brought from Monza, the gold imperial crown, with the other insignia which the sack had fortunately spared, from Rome. The Italian princes, now satellites of the empire, were present in force, as well as the dignitaries of the Church. Such humanists and artists as had survived the sack put on as brave a show as possible. The time-honoured courtesies were observed, with the Emperor holding the Pope's stirrup. The proceedings were terminated on 24 February 1530 (Charles's birthday and the anniverary of the battle of Pavia) by his imperial coronation in the cathedral of San Petronio. But as a background to these pomps tense discussions had taken place on matters of Church and state. Before holding a German Diet at Augsburg Charles was anxious to agree with the Pope on a programme for the containment of Lutheranism and action against the Turks, whose advance had swamped Hungary and reached the walls of Vienna. Clement, however, was in his most evasive mood. He failed entirely to respond to the Emperor's suggestion that the Lutherans might most easily be brought back to the Catholic fold by means of a General Council. He shrank from reform in general and in particular from a conciliar solution which might, in the climate of Lutheranism, very gravely impair papal authority. From a political point of view it also occurred to him, as it did to the King of France, that the chief obstacle to Charles's hegemony in Europe might be the rise of a politically independent Protestantism in Germany. So when the Emperor left for Augsburg his chances of either compromising with the Lutherans or enforcing the decrees of the Diet of Worms were very slender. Clement's delaying tactics fended off renewed pressure from the Emperor at a second meeting in Bologna in 1532, and in the next year he reckoned that he had brought off a striking coup by marrying Catherine de' Medici, sister of Alessandro Duke of Florence, to the French King's second son Henri d' Orleans. Their wedding was celebrated with ostentatious pomp, at Marseilles, where the Pope arrived escorted by ten Cardinals. Simultaneously Margaret, a natural daughter of the Emperor, was betrothed to Alessandro. By this means he enhanced the prestige of his family and performed, in his own estimation, a successful balancing act. It was no substitute, however, for constructive statesmanship.

As might have been expected, indecision marred his handling of the King of England's request for the dissolution of his marriage to the Emperor's aunt Catherine of Aragon. When Henry's VIII's envoys first approached him at Orvieto they received an apparently unfavourable reply, and Clement then sent an experienced legate, Cardinal Campeggio, to see Cardinal Wolsey and discuss with him on what grounds the marriage might be declared invalid. This step predictably drew a protest from the Emperor, whereupon the Pope withdrew his legate and referred the case to the leisurely processes of the Curia. He was admittedly in a dilemma from which it was hard to devise an escape. For obvious reasons he could not afford to offend the Emperor; nor did he wish to alienate Henry, whose anti-Lutheran zeal Leo X had rewarded with the title of Defender of the Faith. He therefore temporized, thus losing the initiative and control over events. If he had taken a firmly negative line with Henry at an early stage, instead of prevaricating until it was too late, he might conceivably have retained papal authority over the Church of England, saved the lives of many eminent English Christians, of whom Sir Thomas More and Bishop Thomas Fisher were among the first, and arrested the country's subsequent slide into Protestantism. As it was his death narrowly preceded the passing of the Act of Supremacy by which Henry assumed the leadership of the English Church.

Political manoeuvring would not rescue the church from its predicament. The need was for a pope with sufficient insight and courage to renew the reforming process that had been in abeyance since the Councils of the preceding century. It hardly seemed that Alessandro Farnese, who succeeded as Paul III (1534–9) possessed the right qualities to carry out a counter-reformation. Sixty-seven years of age, the brother of Alexander IV's mistress, he belonged to the same milieu as the Medici Popes and shared their tastes and habits. As soon as Rome began to recover from the sack the Vatican was enlivened by the same festivities. Paul was intelligent and cultured, a pupil of the humanist Pomponio Leto and a friend of Ariosto the poet. Under him Michelangelo painted the *Last Judgment* and assumed, after Sangallo's death, full responsibility for the completion of the Vatican Palace and the new St Peter's. He also finished the Farnese Palace, which Sangallo designed. For many years Paul had led a free and easy life. A Cardinal at 25, he had reached his fifties before he was ordained priest. He had fathered several children, all legitimized by his predecessors, and showed no scruples about nepotism. Two of his grandsons became Cardinals at 16 and 14. His favourite son, Pierluigi, was created Duke of Parma and founded a famous dynasty.

Basically, however, Paul was serious and capable. Unlike the Medici he grasped the significance of Protestantism. Hence his persistence in promoting the reform movement, which resulted in the Council of Trent. In organizing it he encountered formidable difficulties and delays which took him more than ten years of strenuous effort to overcome. His objectives were threefold, a General Council, a reconciliation of the two great powers and a common front against the Turks. All were bedevilled, though by no means totally thwarted, by the lasting antagonism between the Emperor and François I. Fortunately he survived long enough to give the Church a new sense of purpose.

To some extent the urge to reform was spontaneous. It was especially strong among certain religious Orders, the Augustinians, the strict Capuchin branch of the Franciscans, new groups such as the Theatines and Barnabites and of course the Jesuits, who received the papal licence in 1540. At the same time the Curia, stimulated by several new and zealous members of the Sacred College, was directed to prepare for a Council. In 1537 a committee of nine Cardinals submitted its report to the Pope. It contained a frank confession of the abuses that had so long disgraced the Holy See; in fact its tone was so radical that when it leaked and was printed in Germany Luther took alarm and denounced it for stealing his thunder. Many of its proposals affecting the hierarchy and administration of the Church were at once put into effect. Paul also sent nuncios to France, Germany and Spain announcing his intention to hold a Council at Mantua in the same year as he received the Committee's report. The Emperor's response was not whole-hearted; he doubted whether a Council would be effective and still aspired to compose religious differences in Germany by his own efforts. The Protestant princes were of course opposed to the idea; so was Henry VIII, while François was glad to see Charles's empire weakened by religious strife. The Pope then proposed Trent for 1542, but met with an equal lack of enthusiasm from all concerned.

To reform the Roman Church would be an arduous task; to reclaim it for the German and Nordic lands which had seceded to Lutheranism was beyond the power of Paul or any other pope. Less than twenty years after Luther's appearance the schism was already too wide to be mended; the only question was whether it would not grow wider still. At all events there was no longer any practical prospect of restoring papal supremacy and of re-erecting the ecclesiastical and monastic structure which Luther had dismantled. Moreover his religious revolution had been complemented and buttressed by powerful secular forces. The princes of northern and central Germany had repaid the moral encouragement which he gave them in 1524 to suppress large scale desperate peasant uprisings by forming a solid Protestant political and military bloc to uphold him, and if necessary themselves, against a Catholic revival.

The position of the Emperor, their sovereign, was indeed delicate. As it seemed to him, the empire would lose its meaning and would be incapable of defending Europe against the Turks if it were disunited in both religion and politics. Since a council summoned by the Pope did not, in his opinion, offer the prospect of a useful dialogue between Catholics and Protestants, he himself sponsored in 1540-41 a series of discussions between churchmen and humanists on both sides in the hope of finding common ground. The participants included, on Charles's side, his own Chancellor Granvelle, a Burgundian from Franche-Comté, and for the Pope, the experienced and open-minded legate Cardinal Contarini. But despite their evident goodwill and lack of fanaticism, they failed to agree. Apart from the question of papal supremacy, they had not grasped how far Catholics and Protestants had drifted apart in theology and practice. Luther's Augustinian doctrine of justification by faith and not by works, the uncertainty as to where the Protestants stood with regard to the real presence in the Communion and the Protestant insistence of biblical foundations all proved to be very real stumbling-blocks to reconciliation and the talks broke up without any kind of consensus being reached.

The Pope's Council finally met at Trent in December 1545, during a period of temporary peace between Charles and François. It was ill-attended and got off to a sluggish start in an atmosphere of general scepticism. Nevertheless it slowly gathered momentum. Its proceedings, conducted by three Cardinals, one of whom was the Englishman Reginald Pole, continued for fifteen months until it was decided to adjourn to Bologna, that is to a papal city outside imperial jurisdiction. The issues to be discussed were so vital, and the obstacles to success so numerous, that it is a wonder that it eventually accomplished so much. Two distinct tendencies became apparent from the start. Should the Council concern itself primarily with detailed reforms or with a re-statement of those doctrines which were under Lutheran attack? The Pope thought that the latter should have precedence, especially as administrative reform was already well under way. It was the basic tenets of the Church that Lutheranism was undermining. Moreover the process of reform should not be allowed to threaten, as at previous Councils, the personal authority of the pontiff. The Emperor, on the other hand, was afraid lest the Council, by taking a too rigidly dogmatic stand, might rule out any hope of a religious compromise in Germany. The delegates sensibly decided that they must deal with both tasks concurrently; they must tackle both fundamental problems of theology (the meaning of the Sacraments, grace, human freedom and justification) and practical questions of Church discipline.

Progress was being made in both spheres when the move to Bologna took place. The ostensible reason for the adjournment was an outbreak of typhus in Trent, but the Emperor interpreted it as implying that the Pope had given up hope of rescuing Germany and wished to concentrate on strengthening the Catholic hold on the rest of Europe. While his suspicions were perhaps ill-founded, the timing of the move was unfortunate because Charles, with the help of papal troops, seemed to be winning the war he was now fighting against the Protestant League of Schmalkalde. He believed that if the Protestants could be decisively beaten in the field it might be possible to bring them to the Council, but not if it was transferred to Italy. He was accordingly much annoyed, and in order to avoid further misunderstandings the Pope suspended the Council's sessions in 1548. A year later, shortly before his death, he wound it up altogether. That decision too was premature, for much business remained unfinished, but Paul was 82 and ailing.

A more questionable weapon which he brought into action against heresy was the Holy Office. The inquisition had ceased to operate, so far as Rome and Italy were concerned, since the suppression of the Cathars in the thirteenth century. Lately, however, it had been very active in Spain, where Moorish and Jewish heretics abounded and the Church, for good measure, stood in less need of reformist attention than in the rest of Europe. The Pope was moved to revive it in Rome by the alarming influence of Protestant ideas among Italian churchmen. Lutheranism even raised its head in Naples, where curiously enough it was propagated by a Spaniard, Luis Valdés, and there was a great scandal when the respected Vicar-General of the Capuchins deserted the Church. Possibly encouraged by Ignatius of Loyola and his Jesuits, the Pope re-established the 'Holy Roman and General Inquisition' by a Bull of 1542. It took the form of a committee of six Cardinals, headed by the Neapolitan Carafa, a stern fanatic, but so long as Paul reigned its activities were kept strictly under control and no excesses could be charged to it.

Apart from the steady extension of German Lutheranism, the secession of England and the rise of Calvinism, an even less palatable form of Protestantism, in Switzerland, Paul's worst worry, which he shared with the Emperor, was the inability of Christendom to organize a concerted resistance to the Turks. Whether or not the Ottomans were on the offensive, most of his predecessors had proclaimed their devotion to the idea of a Crusade, but during the reign of Suleiman the Magnificent (1520–66) the danger to Christian Europe was a very real one. The Turks were not only raiding Italy and Spain from their naval bases in the Aegean and North Africa but penetrating in force into the Danube lands. The Pope's command to his architect Sangallo to refortify the Leonine city was no formal gesture. So he was delighted when, in the first year of his reign Charles sent an armada against Tunis. But he was shocked to hear, in 1536, that His Most Catholic Majesty, the King of France, had actually entered into an alliance with the Sultan against the Habsburgs. He sought out François at Nice and remonstrated with him, but all he could obtain was a promise of an armistice between France and the Empire. The King still declined to join the Empire, Venice and the Pope in hostilities against the Ottomans, who after destroying a Christian fleet off the coast of Epirus continued their attacks on the Danube. Meeting the Emperor at Lucca, Paul pleaded for a counter-campaign in Hungary, but Charles insisted on mounting an expedition against Algiers, which turned out a complete failure.

Charles could not understand why, in face of French provocations, the Pope so carefully preserved an attitude of neutrality as between the two great monarchies. In 1536 he made an Easter visit to Rome and in a public speech addressed to the embarrassed Paul and his Cardinals, pleaded for him to break with France. He tried again at a meeting near Parma in 1542. But the Pope was not to be moved. Mindful of his predecessor's mistakes, he refused to join, either openly or covertly, the Emperor against the King or the King against the Emperor. Grieved as he was by the King's behaviour, he disliked the oppressive Habsburg presence in Italy; it was, he felt, calculated to reduce any pontiff of weaker fibre than himself to the status of a puppet. Memories of the sack were still vivid. On the other hand he was wise enough to avoid serious quarrels with the principal Catholic sovereign who, among other things, was engaged in spreading the Catholic faith throughout his vast overseas possessions.

Unfortunately there was little or no personal sympathy between the two men. In Church matters they never saw eye to eye on the tactics of combating Protestantism and were unnecessarily distrustful of each other's motives. Before the Council opened Charles failed to appreciate how sincerely the Pope's legates were seeking a way to reconciliation with the Lutherans. When he blamed them for their lack of success it was the Pope's turn to protest against the doctrinal concessions the Emperor was advocating. Indeed, after the Council's adjournment to Bologna Charles tried to impose a provisional solution, the so-called 'Augsburg Interim', by means of a formula which would permit clerical marriage and the use of wine in the Communion by the laity.

Paul was upset by this purely administrative intrusion into the religious sphere. He had already withdrawn the papal contingent from the Emperor's campaign against the League of Schmalkalde because he judged that Charles, who had at least one Protestant leader fighting on his side, was pursing political rather than religious ends of Germany. Again he was mortified because the imperial governor of Milan had, as he suspected, connived at the murder of his son Pierluigi and invaded the Farnese duchy of Parma and Piacenza. When he died in November 1549, old and worn out, his relations with the Empire had gravely deteriorated. Nevertheless his achievements had been impressive. In the teeth of the most daunting difficulties and dangers he had rescued the papacy from decadence, preserved its independence, restored its morale and set it again on the right path.

What the Church of the Renaissance had lost was irrecoverable, but Paul, who was himself a man of the Renaissance, had endowed that Church with a new confidence and vitality.

17

THE COUNTER-REFORMATION
(1549–1621)

The remaining Popes of the sixteenth century, the age of Tridentine reform and of the Counter-Reformation, were for the most part striking and original personalities with widely differing temperaments and talents. With the exception of Gregory XIII (1572–85) and Clement VIII (1592–1605) none of them enjoyed a long reign. But they all made their mark and were in general distinguished by their zeal and devotion to the faith.

In the earlier years of the period the papacy was on the defensive. Lutheranism had come to stay; it was penetrating eastwards into Poland and southwards into Bohemia. England, after returning to the Catholic fold under Mary Tudor, fell away again and, what was even more alarming, France, the favourite daughter of the church, became infected with Calvinism. Calvin, himself a Frenchman, had picked up much of his theology from a Swiss, Zwingli, and it was at Geneva that he had established a theocratic community dedicated to the doctrine of predestination and governed by a repressive social discipline. It was hardly a regime calculated to appeal to Frenchmen. Nevertheless the very novelty and radicalism of the heresy attracted followers. By the mid-century the Calvinists, or Huguenots, comprised a substantial minority of the population, including the influential nobles and the junior Bourbon branch of the royal house. Scotland, and shortly afterwards the Netherlands, embraced Calvinism as the dominant religion. Western Christianity thus assumed three main distinct forms, apart from a welter of small deviant Protestant sects. The Catholic Church reacted positively to the challenge by renewing its fervours, tightening its discipline and proclaiming ever more emphatically its identity as the only true universal church of Christ. The reformed papacy recovered its confidence and braced itself to withstand the shocks of the last and most destructive phase of the wars of religion.

The first of the Popes of the Counter-Reformation, Paul's immediate successor Julius III (1550–55) has been undeservedly reproached for frivolity and ineffectiveness. In his own time Giovanni Maria del Monte was esteemed as a lawyer and administrator and for that reason had been appointed one of the three presidents of the Council of Trent. During a three months conclave the College was divided along familiar lines between the German and French parties. Eventually del Monte prevailed over the other most promising candidate, Cardinal Pole, who was thus narrowly prevented from becoming the second English Pope. Like Paul III's, Julius's private tastes were those of a typical Renaissance grandee; he enjoyed banquets, spectacles and hunting; he liked country life and built for his relaxation a splendid villa outside the Porta del Popolo. He was unconventional and possessed a peculiar sense of humour which seems to have puzzled his contemporaries. He kept a troop of buffoons. His favourite, a 15-year-old boy called Innocenzo, he raised to the Cardinalate. He caused his brother to adopt him and even appointed him to the Secretariat of State, happily without executive functions. The wits maintained that his real job was to look after the Pope's pet monkey. Such eccentricities may have been quite harmless, but they did his fame no good.

On the other hand he was undoubtedly clear-sighted and conscientious in the performance of his duties. He followed the same neutral policy as Paul without nourishing any territorial ambitions on behalf of his own family. He recalled the Council of Trent for May 1551. Although the French stayed obstinately aloof, representatives came from both Catholic and Protestant Germany. Debates continued for about a year until the incalculable Protestant Elector, Maurice of Saxony, suddenly left the Council to join Henri II of France in a war against the Emperor. The Pope was forced to suspend the Council for two years, but nearly ten passed before it could again be assembled. This was a painful setback for Julius. He also suffered a political rebuff when, at the Emperor's insistence, he attempted to dislodge the Farnese from Parma. The campaign had to be called off through lack of effective aid from Charles and French threats to help the Farnese. But he was amply consoled by the return of England to the Catholic fold under Mary Tudor. The Roman Curia was overjoyed by this unexpected triumph. It seemed that the Protestant tide had been checked for the first time since Luther's dramatic appearance at Wittenberg. After Mary's marriage to Philip, the Emperor's son, Cardinal Pole was sent back to his own country as legate and was later made Archbishop of Canterbury. The Pope also strengthened the Catholic reaction elsewhere by encouraging the expansion of the Jesuit Order.

He did not live to witness England's prompt relapse into Protestantism. Nor did his successor Marcellus II, who died after a pontificate of three weeks. He was the Marcello Cervini who had formerly presided at Trent in company with Julius and Reginald Pole. His loss was a tragedy because he was acknowledged to be the most competent, zealous and morally unimpeachable of the reformist Cardinals. He took his own name (and that of the obscure fourth-century bishop of Rome), and his only enduring monument is Palestrina's masterpiece of Church music, the Mass of Pope Marcellus.

Paul III had pulled the papacy together. Under Paul IV (1555–9) it passed to the offensive; indeed, in accordance with the Pope's character, it became almost fiercely combatant. Gian Putro Carafa was a stern, austere, domineering and unmerciful champion of the Catholic faith, the implacable enemy of heresy, impiety, corruption and vice. As a patriotic Neapolitan he detested the Spanish regime in the southern kingdom and disliked the Habsburg hegemony in general. When legate in Spain under Leo X he had quitted the royal court in a huff; later he had suffered injury in the sack of Rome. All his life he had been an ardent reformer. Under Paul III, who made him a Cardinal, he had been the moving spirit of the Pope's committee of 1537 and the director of the revived Holy Office. Now aged 79 he burned, in the short time left to him, to intensify his work.

His anger was especially aroused by the two major events of 1555. The first was the abdication of Charles, which meant that his brother Ferdinand took over the Empire, with the Kingdoms of Bohemia and Hungary, while his son Philip had Spain, the Indies, the Netherlands, Naples and Milan, in fact a stranglehold on

Italy. The Pope did not care for Charles but denied his right to lay down his responsibilities. Secondly he was incensed by the Augsburg settlement, which the Habsburgs had promoted between German Catholics and Protestants. It amounted to an agreement to differ peacefully, with each side adhering to its own form of religion pending an eventual reconciliation between divergent doctrines and practices. Paul regarded it as a betrayal of the faith and proclaimed it as such. Heretics and schismatics, he insisted, should not be cajoled; they should be fought to the bitter end. As his Cardinal Secretary of State he appointed his nephew Carlo, a rough soldier who shared his defects but not his finer qualities. The Colonna and other imperialist sympathizers were persecuted and their lands confiscated. As for the Spaniards, he denounced them as the offspring of Jews and Moors; he found it offensive, he said, that people who in former times had only been known to the Italians as cooks and grooms should now presume to lord it over them. Not content with words, he secretly concluded an anti-Spanish pact with Henry II. When the King promptly double-crossed him by negotiating with Spain he sent Carlo to incite him to break the truce and even to suggest that the Sultan should be urged to attack Naples. The upshot of these rash intrigues was that King Philip ordered his general, the Duke of Alba, to invade the papal state. The Pope's troops, supported by a French corps under the Duke of Guise, were roundly defeated. Consequently he was obliged to renounce the French alliance and declare himself reconciled with the King in a reluctant acceptance of Spanish supremacy.

The atmosphere was obviously not conducive to a further recall of the Council. In any case Paul preferred direct reform on his own initiative to the inconclusive discussion of conciliar programmes. What distinguished his measures from the numerous essays in reform undertaken by previous Popes was the thorough-going severity with which they were applied. Past attempts had failed because they were half-hearted, introduced for the sake of appearances or of expediency, or because they were frustrated by obstruction and inertia. Clerical, and especially curial, abuses had flourished because they had profited the papal treasury. Paul enforced his policy by the weight of his personal authority and by ruthless sanctions. Heavy penalties were inflicted for contumacy and evasion. Discipline was strictly tightened at the top, notably in the case of Cardinals owing their appointments to foreign influence and of bishops absenting themselves from their sees. Dispensations were reduced and curial offices drastically pruned. Simony was treated as heresy and punished accordingly. Such reform of the Church at its centre was salutary and lasting, but it involved a serious shrinkage of revenue already reduced by the defection of large areas of Europe, and a much heavier burden was laid on the inhabitants of the papal state.

By temperament Paul was a mediaeval absolutist, and he was the master of Rome, where independent institutions no longer existed, as no mediaeval Pope could have hoped to be. Intolerant and incapable of moderation (in that respect he resembled the hated Spaniards), he used the Holy Office not only to ensure conformity of doctrine but to curb by intimidation and censorship the easy-going morals and intellectual freedom of the Romans. The powers and activity of the Inquisition were greatly extended. It exercised, if not a classic reign of terror, at the very least a numbing and frightening influence. Rome had been inured at various times to arbitrary arrests, tortures and executions, but not to a regime of such cold suspicion, espionage and delation. Heretical writings had often been condemned in the past, but it was Paul who first drew up a systematic Index of forbidden books. Thousands were burned and the director of the Holy Office, Cardinal Ghislieri, had to warn the

Pope not to exaggerate by trying to ban famous works like Ariosto's *Orlando Furioso*. The trouble was that he could not rest content with his own remarkable work of reform. His preoccupation with safe-guarding it turned him into a harsh bigot. His pathological tendency to distrust and persecute shocked his own Cardinals; one, Seripando, condemned his use of the Inquisition as inhuman; a second, Morone, was locked up for indiscipline in Sant' Angelo; a third, Pole himself, was summoned from England to answer a charge of heresy. In his defence he wrote a dignified denunciation of papal unreasonableness, but died before he could be exonerated. At the end of his life Paul seemed to feel remorse for his relentless behaviour. To the general relief his nephew Carlo was dismissed from office. He subjected himself to penances which undermined his health. When he died, aged 83, the mob burned down the Inquisition's headquarters, knocked the head off the Pope's marble statue on the Capitol and threw it into the river.

There followed four months of intense political lobbying before some forty Cardinals meeting in Conclave elected Gian Angelo de' Medici as Pius IV (1559–65). A Milanese and unconnected with the Medici of Florence, he was known as *il Medichino* (the little Medici). His career in the Church had not been particularly distinguished. Besides holding various administrative posts he had twice accompanied papal forces in campaigns against Turks and German Protestants. He was neither a fanatic nor an ascetic, but a shrewd and level-headed man of the world. At the same time he was sincerely devoted to the Church's cause. Without dismantling his predecessor's reforms, he at once put an end to harshness and persecution. His mission as he saw it, was to restart the Council of Trent and to complete its work in the fields of doctrine and reform. For that purpose and for the general welfare of the Church he needed to sustain good relations with the two Habsburg rulers, Philip II and Ferdinand I. Indeed he had withdrawn from working in the Curia because he disapproved of Paul IV's anti-Spanish posture. As his Secretary of State he chose a nephew, but that nephew was Carlo Borromeo, Archbishop of Milan and future Saint, renowned for his piety and ability.

His Bull convoking the Council was issued in November 1560. He did not however hurry over the preparations, for there were many preliminary difficulties to be overcome. The Protestant princes refused flatly to be represented, maintaining that a Pope had no right to call a Council. Among the nations that promised attendance there were serious differences of principle. Should the Council, for instance, be regarded as a new one or simply as a prolongation of that which had been suspended in 1552? In other words were decisions already adopted susceptible of revision in the hope that the Protestants might be persuaded to accept amended versions? Ferdinand and the French advocated a flexible approach; King Philip, predictably, insisted that previous decisions must stand. Ferdinand pressed for reform to be debated before doctrine; discussion of the latter should await the delayed arrival of the French delegates headed by the Cardinal of Lorraine, Charles de Guise. The Pope was alarmed because the French were thought to be resigned to concessions being made to the Huguenots, who by now had multiplied and enjoyed a measure of toleration; they also were known to favour the old theory of papal subordination to a General Council. All the non-Italians were ill-disposed towards the Roman Curia; for example when the Italians argued that the Pope had power to dispense a bishop from residing in his see (a provision which mainly benefited Italian bishops), the Spaniards replied that the obligation of residence was imposed by divine law and could not be modified by the Pope. Ferdinand was so suspicious of the Curia that he established his court at Innsbruck, within easy distance of Trent, in order to apply pressure if necessary.

Not all these matters, nor many others, could be resolved before the Council opened in January 1562. From then until the final session of 4 December 1563 the papal legates manoeuvred with superb skill. One by one the crises were surmounted. When the French at last arrived, nine months late, formal sessions were suspended until harmony could be restored behind the scenes. At the final session the 250 delegates (many more than had attended under Paul III or Julius III) could hardly believe that they had reached full agreement on all the questions of doctrine and reform submitted to them. No one expected at that stage that they would be able to heal the rift in western Christendom, but they had in fact renewed the fabric and strengthened the foundations of the Catholic faith. Furthermore, in doing so, they had reasserted the Pope's predominance over the Council and any that might follow. It was he who was entrusted with the confirmation and execution of its decrees. Modestly he refrained from crowing over what was certainly a personal triumph, but worked even harder for the two remaining years of his reign. He appointed a special committee of Cardinals to put the decrees into effect, refashioned the Curia, abolished all clerical privileges incompatible with the Tridentine reform, cut the Index down to size and dismissed 400 superfluous members of the papal household. At the same time he pleased the Romans by his liberality and affable manner. Architects, artists and writers were again in favour. But when occasion demanded he could act very sternly, as in the murky cause célèbre involving the Carafa family. The Duke of Paliano, brother of Carlo Carafa, had his wife strangled on suspicion of adultery and stabbed her presumed lover to death with his own hand. The Pope put both Duke and Cardinal on trial, and when the court established the wife's innocence he had them both executed. A younger Carafa Cardinal, Archbishop of Naples, shared in their disgrace and died of chagrin.

It seemed almost a rule that the personalities of successive Popes should show up in sharp contrast to one another. Indeed their only common characteristic at this period was their advanced age. Pius V (1566–72) was the Michele Ghislieri who had served as the Carafa Pope's Grand Inquisitor. The son of poor parents at Alessandria, he had entered the Dominican Order at the age of 14. He became famous for his deep piety and strenuous asceticism. As Pope he continued to wear his friar's habit under his pontifical robes; he sported a long white beard and liked to walk barefoot and bareheaded in penitential processions. Not unnaturally the Romans were afraid that he might turn out another Paul IV. In so far as heretics were harshly repressed and many of them sentenced to death, their fears were largely realized, but the persecution was neither arbitrary nor carried to excessive lengths. The Pope, who personally attended inquisitorial sessions, was determined to prevent the seepage of Protestantism into Italy and the consequent extension to the peninsula of the religious strife that was tearing apart the countries north of the Alps. In that aim he was conspicuously successful. In an atmosphere of enforced piety, clergy and laity were subjected to an increasingly stringent discipline; for their edification the Roman Breviary and Catechism were re-edited. Pius also embarked, with less felicitous results, on the moral regeneration of Rome. Beggars and prostitutes were proscribed; the luxuries of the rich and the carnivalesque distractions of the poor were equally penalized. Fasts and feasts had to be strictly observed. Doctors were told to insist on their patients confessing and receiving the Sacraments. Women were not admitted to view the papal collections of classical sculpture. Pius would have liked to dispense with them altogether, but had to content himself with ordering the nudities in the *Last Judgment* to be chastely disguised by overpainting.

Internally the Church was regaining strength and acquiring a new spirit. Overseas it was out to conquer new continents. On the other hand the outlook for Roman Catholicism in Europe would have dismayed a pope far more deeply versed in mundane affairs than Pius V. During his reign the progress of Calvinism in France had been frighteningly rapid; Catholics and Huguenots were equally balanced and seemed to be condemned to chronic civil war. The same state of affairs prevailed in the Spanish Netherlands where King Philip's armies struggled in vain to crush the Dutch Calvinists. England and Scotland were apparently lost to the Church and in Germany the Emperor Maximilian II was betraying a regrettable sympathy for Lutheranism. Only Philip stood firm, but even he, though doctrinally unimpeachable, tended to arrogate Catholic leadership to himself to the detriment of papal authority. For the moment Pius could do little but pray for better things. When he took the initiative by declaring Queen Elizabeth to be deposed he only made things worse by splitting the loyalties of the English Catholics. The sole ray of light in the world outside Italy was the signal victory of the combined fleets of Spain, Venice and the papacy over the Turks at Lepanto (1571).

Whether or not Pius V deserved his eventual canonization in 1712, his successors, Gregory XIII (1572–85) and Sixtus V (1585–90), were better qualified than he to cope with the problems of the Counter-Reformation. Both were gifted men of broad outlook, enterprising and imaginative, though Sixtus was by far the more dynamic and masterful of the two. The energy with which they pursued a firm and consistent policy filled the Church with new vigour and confidence.

Ugo Boncompagni was a Bolognese, 70 years of age but still very active. As a jurist he had played a useful part at Trent. When the Council was over Pius IV made him a Cardinal and legate in Spain, where he gained the good graces of King Philip. Conscientious, hard-working and unostentatiously devout, he was almost exclusively preoccupied with the fight against Protestantism and the mobilization of all the Church's resources—spiritual, intellectual and diplomatic—for that purpose. Fortunately for him he had no trouble in Italy or Rome. He was well aware that while Catholic theologians had been arguing among themselves at Trent about definitions of doctrine and details of reform, Protestant propagandists were having it their own way among the peoples of Europe. The papacy had been slow and ill-equipped to counter their activity. The Jesuits, organized for exactly that mission, had been alternately encouraged and discouraged by the Vatican. Gregory, however, gave a real impulse to their educational work, and to that of the clergy in general, by his foundation of colleges and seminaries. He greatly developed the Jesuit college in Rome, the creation of Julius III, which soon came to be known as the Gregorian University. The same was the case with the German college, which Julius had also entrusted to the Jesuits. Its pupils provided a welcome reinforcement for the harassed Catholic clergy in Germany, and their influence was so effective in stemming the further advance of Protestantism that more colleges were set up at Vienna, Prague, Fulda and other cities of the Empire. At Rome similar establishments catered for the Hungarians, Greeks, Armenians and Maronites. The English college, founded by the future Cardinal William Allen at Douai and transferred by the Pope to Rome, had a more tragic destiny as a source of martyrs in a lost cause.

By way of complement to missionary work Gregory reorganized the papal diplomatic service. From then on nuncios regularly accredited to foreign courts began to take over the functions of legates assigned to special missions, thus assuming ecclesiastical and pastoral responsibilities in their countries of residence. Largely as a result of all his endeavours the religious frontiers in Germany became stabilized. Although north and much of central Germany had been irretrievably lost, Bavaria, the Tyrol, the rest of Austria (after much wobbling) and Franconia remained Catholic. So did the Rhineland, but Cologne was rescued only with difficulty when its Archbishop seceded. Further to the east Poland opted for Catholicism. To the north the Pope despatched a persuasive Jesuit, Antonio Possevino, on a somewhat forlorn mission to Sweden and Russia. He found the Swedish monarch not unwilling to respond to his blandishments, but the conditions he set for a return to Rome (Mass in Swedish, communion of both kinds for the laity and married clergy) were not acceptable to the Holy See. As for the Czar, Ivan the Terrible, he flew into one of his rages and the nuncio narrowly escaped with his life.

Gregory's touch was less sure when he was faced with situations that obstinately eluded papal control. By nature mild and uninquisitorial, he was exasperated by the poor performance of Catholic reaction in France and the Netherlands, to say nothing of its total failure in England. Since he only became Pope in May 1572 it is unlikely that he was personally associated with the Medici Queen Mother in planning the St Bartholomew's Day massacre of Huguenots, which occurred in August of that year. On the contrary it seems to have taken even the nuncio in Paris by surprise. When however the news reached him he ordered a *Te Deum* to be sung and attended a thanksgiving service at the French church of St Louis. He may have assumed that the Huguenot challenge had been decisively checked. In fact it revived at once and the French religious issue remained as uncertain as ever during the whole of his pontificate. Nor did the military and diplomatic prowess of Alessandro Farnese, Duke of Parma and King Philip's viceroy in the Netherlands, or the murder of the Protestant leader William of Orange, avail to recover the Dutch United Provinces for Spain and the Catholic faith. As regards England, Gregory came to the conclusion that there was no way of removing Elizabeth, the 'Jezebel of the North', except by a Spanish invasion or by assassination, an act which, he declared, would rank as God's work. Yet his character was unsuited to the encouragement of violence and treason in furtherance of religious ends.

Although some of its fruits were not immediately apparent, his diligence as a Counter-Reformer was rewarded in the long term. If he had not been born into an age of intense religious strife he would have no doubt concentrated happily on intellectual interests. Ever since he had taught canon law at Bologna there had been a donnish flavour about him. When the Roman catacombs were rediscovered and their wealth of early Christian remains brought to light, he ensured that they were scientifically studied. He gave his name to both the Gregorian University and the Gregorian Calendar. His reform of the old Julian Calendar (introduced in 46 BC) was announced in a Bull of 1582, but its acceptance was at first confined to Catholic countries. Such division on confessional lines caused enormous confusions, especially in Germany. It was not until 1752 that England and its American colonies were grudgingly reconciled to the loss of their eleven days, while the Orthodox Church waited until the twentieth century before submitting to the change.

For the next five years the papal chair was occupied by the imperious Sixtus V (1585–90). Felice Peretti was the son of a poor farming family in the March of Ancona. When a small boy he herded his father's pigs, but at the age of 12 he was accepted as a novice by the neighbouring Franciscan friary of Montalto. While still in his twenties he established throughout Italy a reputation as an itinerant preacher. Paul IV, who saw in him a kindred spirit, sent him to Venice to reform the convent of the Frari and subsequently as Inquisitor. However his zeal and fiery eloquence were not altogether to the taste of the Venetian authorities, who procured his recall to Rome. There his austere style commended itself to Pius V; he was made Vicar-General of his Order, Grand Inquisitor and Cardinal.

So far his advancement had been very rapid. He was clearly destined to be an outstanding leader of the Counter-Reformation. Nevertheless the Cardinal of Montalto, as he called himself, stayed in retirement, partly enforced and partly voluntary, during the whole of Gregory XIII's reign. The two men had similar aims but were divided by personal antipathy and sharply contrasting temperaments and had quarrelled seriously in the course of a joint legation in Spain. For a man of his impatient energy and consuming sense of mission such prolonged inactivity was hard to bear, but there was no question of his being admitted to the Pope's inner counsels. He spent his time adding to his already profound erudition and cultivating the society of artists and architects. His self-control during the period was admirable. It was severely tested when his nephew, the husband of a Roman beauty named Vittoria Accaramboni, was murdered by an Orsini, the Duke of Bracciano, who had fallen in love with the lady. Instead of resorting to violent reprisals he humbly declared his confidence in the Pope's justice, and when that was not forthcoming he attracted much public sympathy to himself. At the same time he was quietly building up a fund of support within the Sacred College in anticipation of the next Conclave, which resulted in his unanimous election.

His first move was to demonstrate the severity and efficiency of his government in the most striking possible manner. He did this by his exterminating the bandits who infested the papal state. They were said to number 27,000; one of their chiefs, Guercino, was known as the King of Campagna. They frequently operated in collusion with local nobles who gave them asylum and shared in the spoils. The hawk-faced Pope, the most ungentle of Franciscans, showed no mercy to the robbers or to their protectors. 7,000 malefactors were executed and, as Sixtus remarked to the French Ambassador, Cardinal de Joyeuse, he wished that he had done away with more than 20,000. In any event the purge was very welcome to the population as well as to travellers and pilgrims. Its success was celebrated by the striking of a medal with the inscription *Perfecta Securitas*.

Concurrently with public order Sixtus tackled the public finances, and to such good effect that in five years he accumulated a reserve of over 4 million gold crowns (*scudi*). This was achieved partly by economies but mainly through the sale of offices (not ecclesiastical but bureaucratic) in the state administration, which brought in 300,000 *scudi* yearly. Naturally the officials, having purchased their jobs, fleeced the taxpayers, but the central government became financially independent. Money was also raised by state loans at a high rate of interest. Not all these funds were allowed to lie idle. They were used to set up rural industries (wool and silk), to build bridges and roads and to drain part of the Pontine marshes for agriculture. Rome received a new aqueduct, the *Acqua Felice*, which brought water from Palestrina 20 miles away. A vast programme of renovation and embellishment employed thousands of workmen in the city. Renaissance Popes had mostly concentrated their building projects on the right bank of the Tiber and in those left bank districts which lay opposite the Vatican. Although Gregory XIII had given a lead, Sixtus was the real founder of the baroque city on the left bank which, after so many centuries of desolation, revived the dignity of ancient Rome. New avenues now connected the principal basilicas; the hills—the Esquiline on which he had already built himself a villa, the Quirinal on which he finished his predecessor's palace—were again covered with houses and gardens. The Pope's favourite architect, Domenico Fontana, worked furiously. He designed a new and imposing Lateran Palace, built a new papal residence within the Vatican, reconstructed the Vatican Library on a grand scale and helped Giacomo della Porta to bring the cupola of St Peter's near to a long delayed completion. But what chiefly astonished the Romans was his engineering feat in razing and re-erecting in the piazza of St Peter's the immense obelisk that had once stood in Nero's Circus. Three others were sited in front of the Lateran basilica, Santa Maria Maggiore and Santa Maria del Popolo. Many more ancient and mediaeval monuments, including the last columns of the Septizonium, were swept away in this orgy of creation and reconversion. Tumbledown Rome, the scene of endless unruliness and discord, was given a new face; it became majestic, staid and well-policed.

Less spectacular, but of lasting importance, was the Pope's reorganization of the Curia, in which the needs of the Counter-Reformation had made the weight of business too heavy for the old system of Church government. He began at the top, fixing the number of Cardinals at a maximum of 70, 6 Cardinal-bishops, 50 Cardinal-priests and 14 Cardinal-deacons. Among his new creations was his 15-year-old nephew, but luckily the second Cardinal di Montalto turned out as competent as he was devout. Hitherto important affairs had been dealt with by the Consistory presided over by the Pope and composed of Cardinals resident in Rome. It resembled an advisory council rather than a Cabinet in the modern sense. Individual Cardinals presided over subordinate organs such as the Chancery, the Camera (finance) and the Rota (the papal court of law), while others might be appointed to chair committees set up for special purposes. Sixtus regularized the system by instituting 15 separate and permanent Congregations, only one of which, the Holy Office, was already in existence. The new bodies were concerned with the administration of both Church and state, with questions of faith, doctrine and rite, with clergy and friars, with the execution of the Council of Trent, with security (the Congregation of the Navy), with finance, public works, supply and public order. They came into effect by a Bull of 1588 and endured in their essentials until the twentieth century.

One Congregation was charged with the revival of the University, another with the operations of the Vatican printing press. Sixtus took a lively interest in the revision and publication of sacred texts. While still a Cardinal he had sponsored new editions of St Ambrose, St Gregory and St Bonaventura, to which was added the Greek text of the Septuagint. That prepared the way for a more ambitious project, a revised text of the whole Latin Bible, the Vulgate. He entrusted the task to a Cardinals' committee, but it worked so slowly that he plunged into it himself. Printing was finished by 1590 and the new edition was proclaimed by a Bull to be the authentic text. However it aroused a storm of protest from scholars and traditionalists. It was withdrawn after his death, reworked and issued under his name by Clement VIII.

The interaction of religious and political strife between and within the three great powers of Western Europe, Spain, France and England, presented Sixtus with peculiar difficulties. He was unable to sustain his ideal role of impartial arbiter between the Catholic Kingdoms. France, distracted by the undecided conflict between the Catholics of the Holy League and the Huguenots who pinned their faith on Henry of Navarre, was inevitably the weaker of the two. While Sixtus longed for a Catholic victory, he very strongly disliked the prospect of its being won by the League led by the Duke of Guise and bolstered by Spanish power. He had no wish to see the childless King of France, Henry III, reduced to the status of a Spanish puppet. As he was aware, many French Catholics loyal to the king were more anti-Spanish than anti-Huguenot. He would have liked to see them all united, preferably without Spanish assistance, against Henry of Navarre and the Huguenots, but he came to realize that they could never so combine. A solution was made possible only by two murders, the first of the Duke of Guise by Henry III and the second of Henry himself by a fanatical Dominican. It was also facilitated by the dead King's nomination of Henry of Navarre as his successor. The Pope found it hard to credit the latter's profession that he would uphold the rights of the Catholic Church and was at first tempted to enter into an alliance against him with the League and Spain. Dissuaded from that course by the Duke of Luxemburg, who came to Rome as the emissary of Henry of Navarre's Catholic supporters, he stood firm in a stern diplomatic battle with Olivares, Philip II's Ambassador. His resolution was fully justified when, three years after Sixtus's death, Henry reverted to the Catholic faith.

Thus, while France remained predominantly Catholic, the balance of power had been preserved without an open breach between Spain and the papacy. Meanwhile Sixtus fully approved Philip's attempted conquest of England. Indeed he was prepared to finance it to the tune of a million gold ducats, half of which would be paid as soon as the Armada had succeeded in landing a Spanish force. His disappointment with its defeat was perhaps tempered by the consequent damage to Spanish over-confidence at the height of his controversy with Philip over France. In his reign there was never any danger of the papacy degenerating into an adjunct of the Spanish empire.

Sixtus succumbed to malaria. So, after a reign of 12 days, did Urban VII, the Genoese Giambattista Castagna. Gregory XIV (Niccolo Sfondrati), a Milanese and therefore a subject of King Philip, lasted for 10 months. Both owed their election to heavy Spanish pressure, and Gregory obediently sent money and troops to aid the League in France. He was followed for two months by Innocent IX (the Bolognese Giovanni Antonio Facchinetti), an elderly invalid whose only act was to contribute another 36,000 ducats to the League's funds. After four Popes had been lost in less than 18 months it looked as if they would shortly be joined by a fifth, for the Conclave's next choice, Cardinal Ippolito Aldobrandini, a Florentine, was also known to be sickly. Nevertheless Clement VIII (1591–1605) enjoyed a long and calm pontificate. For many Romans it was a welcome respite from the atmosphere of feverish change to which Sixtus had accustomed them.

Clement, a jurist by training and a successful legate in Poland, was distinguished by his deep piety and by the extreme circumspection with which he approached religious and political problems. He spent long hours in devotional exercises, fasting rigorously, confessing daily, officiating personally at all important Church functions and visiting the seven Roman pilgrimage churches fifteen times a year. His austerities did not improve his health; he was often obliged to take to his bed or change his place of residence. His Cardinals were apt to complain that his absences affected the conduct of business. Nevertheless he liked to maintain a dignified and expensive court. Two Cardinal-nephews, Cinzio and Pietro, relieved him of the burden of affairs. Both were lavish spenders, as Pietro showed in particular by building his magnificent villa at Frascati, but they are chiefly remembered for

A sword protects Justinian and the civil law, while Clement V and the canon law have a more peaceful protectress

Probably Pope Clement V with the Emperor Henry VII, Philip the Fair and others

The Palais des Papes, Avignon

Martin V consecrating the church and hospital of Santa Maria Nuova

Detail from the 'Giovanni Dalmata' baluster in the Sistine Chapel

Portrait of Alexander VI, the second Borgia Pope, flanked by the emblems of his worldly family

A meeting of temporal and spiritual authority: *left* François I and *right* Clement VII

having given shelter in the Vatican to the poet Tasso towards the end of his life.

It was inevitable that Clement should become involved in the fierce theological controversy that broke out during his pontificate on the relation between divine grace and human free will. It arose from the publication of a work in which the Spanish Jesuit Luis de Molina sought to establish a 'concord' between the two concepts. The book was attacked by the Dominicans as a revival of Pelagianism while the Jesuits, rallying to its defence, accused its opponents of Calvinist leanings. Apart from theological intricacies, Clement shared his predecessor's view that the Jesuits were becoming too influential and their General, Acquaviva, too autocratic. Without taking sides, however, he appointed a committee to examine Molina's writings. When it recommended that they should be prohibited and 61 propositions of their author condemned, the Pope hesitated and referred the whole matter to a conference of theologians. Immersed in subtleties, they failed to reach a conclusion. Clement then recalled the committee, whose debates continued until it had repeated its recommendation for the fourth time. But he still havered; he knew that Molinism commanded wide support in the Church and did not want to force the issue. Reluctantly he agreed to preside personally over yet another conference. It held 68 sessions but he still declined to adjudicate. The Jesuit Cardinal Bellarmine told him that he might be a good lawyer but he was no theologian; he would never be capable of reaching a decision and had better let the matter drop. Bellarmine was banished from the Curia for his indiscretion but proved to be right. By the time Clement died in 1605 he had made no pronouncement. Two years later Paul V put an end to the dispute; both the opposing opinions were to be permitted but public discussion of the issue was banned without leave from the Inquisition.

In politics the Pope was equally cautious. So far as France was concerned his mind was made up for him by the course of events. His own inclination was to follow Gregory XIV's example and prop up the faltering League. Thus he remained cool towards Henry IV even after the King had declared his wish to be received into the Catholic Church and sought papal absolution. But in 1594 Henry was crowned at Chartres by the French Catholic hierarchy and the Pope's legate advised Clement to accede to his request. This he did at a solemn ceremony in St Peter's in September 1595. He felt it safe to ignore protests from Spain, which was now at war with a united France. In 1598, just before King Philip's death, he fostered a peace between the kingdoms neither of which was more powerful than the other or capable of imposing its will on the papacy. He was not pleased however, when Henry's Edict of Nantes guaranteed to the Huguenots freedom of conscience and the practice of their religion.

In succession to Clement the Sacred College found it prudent to elect a pontiff who would be agreeable to Henry IV. Such was Leo XI, who as Cardinal Alessandro de' Medici had served as Clement's legate in France. But he died after a month and was replaced by a Roman, Camillo Borghese. Owing to careful promotions by recent Popes the College was largely staffed at this period by responsible and intellectually eminent churchmen, as opposed to personal favourites and political appointees. Outstanding examples were Roberto Bellarmine, the imposing Jesuit theologian and controversialist, and Cesare Baronio, author of the *Annales Ecclesiastici*, a twelve-volume history of the Church up to 1198. Either might have made a great Pope if his very prominence had not worked against him.

Borghese, who took the name of Paul V (1605–21, had hitherto pursued a rather humdrum career in the Curia. Like all Popes of the Counter-Reformation he was deeply devout and conscientious, the patron of new Orders such as the Oratorians and of Jesuit missions overseas. He also took a very hard line in defending the absolute authority of the Church in ecclesiastical affairs against encroachment by secular governments. His intransigence on this issue of principle immediately brought him into sharp conflict with Venice. He was outraged by the Republic's imprisonment of two clerics for alleged moral offences and complained strongly of a law that prohibited the building of new churches and monasteries, the establishment of new Orders in Venetian territory and transfers of property into ecclesiastical hands, without prior permission from the Senate. When his protests were ignored he imposed a ban on Doge and Senate and placed the whole Republic under an interdict.

The Signoria, while professing to disregard these mediaeval sanctions as null and void, reacted violently. It forbade their publication on pain of death. It expelled the Jesuits and other Orders faithful to the Pope. It also mounted an intense propaganda campaign against papal intervention in Venetian affairs of state. As its director it appointed Father Paolo Sarpi, a Servite monk, gifted polymath and fanatical anti-papalist. The Pope's spokesmen, orchestrated by Bellarmine, replied in kind and it seemed for a time that hostilities might break out between the powers taking one side or the other in the war of words. French mediation, however, defused the conflict. Cardinal de Joyeuse persuaded papacy and Republic to accept a compromise which in fact favoured the latter. The two clerics were released, but the objectionable laws remained in force and the Jesuits were barred from Venice for the next fifty years. The Cardinal withdrew the interdict, whose very existence the Senate had affected to deny.

If the episode proved anything, it was that the employment of spiritual weapons against the post-mediaeval state was ineffective. In fact it was never again essayed. But the echoes of the dispute continued to embarrass the Pope. When Sarpi narrowly escaped assassination he and the Jesuits were accused of the attempt. There was an outburst of international polemics between those who still upheld the theory of papal supremacy and those who advocated the claims of absolute secular sovereignty. James I of England, no mean theologian, attacked Bellarmine for maintaining that a pope might absolve a king's subjects from their allegiance. Sarpi himself summed up his anti-papalist views in his history of the Council of Trent, published in London under a pseudonym. While James had the Gunpowder Plot (1605) in mind, some Frenchmen assumed that the Jesuits had inspired the murder of Henry IV by Ravaillac (1610); Philippe du Plessis-Mornay wrote a history of the papacy in which the pontiff figured as Antichrist. The Venetian stand also encouraged the underlying Gallican tendencies in French Catholicism. In 1614, when the States-General met for the last time in 1789, the Third Estate rejected the clergy's overdue proposal to introduce the Tridentine reforms into France. The Pope was much disturbed by this agitation and relieved when the clergy subsequently got its way.

Paul was second only to Sixtus V in his zeal for the renovation of Rome. His crowning achievement in this sphere was the completion of St Peter's, after so many decades of hesitation between the plans of successive architects, by the addition of Carlo Maderna's façade. The work involved the final demolition of what remained of Constantine's ancient basilica. Thanks to the intervention of the antiquarian Cardinal Baronio, some of its monuments were saved and deposited in the crypt of the new building, and the tomb of the Apostle received the attention due to it. Another laborious and costly enterprise was the rebuilding of Trajan's aqueduct, renamed the *Acqua Paola*, to supply the right-bank quarters of the city and Maderna's fountains in the piazza of St Peter. Meanwhile the Cardinal-nephew, Scipione Caffarelli, who assumed his uncle's surname, was erecting the celebrated Villa Borghese outside the Porta del Popolo. The Pope's own modest style of living contrasted with his public munificence and his open-handedness towards his family. Scipione in particular received benefices that brought him an income of 140,000 *scudi*; he used it for subsidizing the arts and putting together grand collections of painting and sculpture. His enrichment caused no surprise or scandal. The promotion of nephews to the Cardinalate, a habit which had been grossly abused in Renaissance times, had subsisted throughout the Counter-Reform and had become virtually institutionalized. So long as the nephew stuck to his role—of confidential adviser, right-hand man or simply patron of the arts—and refrained from excesses, no reproach need any longer attach to him.

The role of the individual Pontiff during the Counter-Reformation was all-important. Without a very clear lead from the centre the Catholic Church might have faltered, progressively lost its hold and even finally disintegrated. Most of what had been a uniformly Catholic Europe was in a state of religious uncertainty during the middle years of the sixteenth century. Despite the political compromise reached between Catholic and Protestant Princes within the empire regarding the religious allegiance of their subjects the outlook was still undecided. There was a real risk that Rome would forfeit its claim to universality. But the Popes remained calm. With Germany and France divided, England, Scotland and the Netherlands in secession, Protestantism everywhere on the upsurge, and Italy and the Iberian peninsula the only parts of Europe where Catholicism was still firmly entrenched, they showed no signs of dismay, pursuing a consistent programme of internal reform and of defence against external pressures.

Personally these men of diverse abilities shared a common characteristic intense seriousness and imperturbability. They gathered together and successfully deployed the existing resources and latent energies of the Church. They were by no means well supported by Catholic Soveriegns. Until the ineffective Valois kings of France were succeeded by the Bourbon Henry IV, a convert from Calvinism, they received little effective help from that quarter. Meanwhile the Habsburg realm had split into two. The German lands, under Ferdinand II, were riddled with Protestantism while the Spanish Monarchy of Philip II, though frantically loyal to the Church, was apt to display its devotion in so bigoted a fashion as to render it counter productive. Bigotry and the burning of heretics were unhappily as rife at Rome as anywhere else on either side. There is not much to choose between the immolation of Michael Servetus by the Calvinists of Geneva and that of Giordano Bruno by the Roman Inquisition. One may only observe that the examination of Bruno, whose religious and philosophical ideas were of the utmost obscurity and complication, lasted on and off for eight years before his eventual execution. Unlike Protestants caught by the Spanish Inquisition or Jesuits apprehended by Queen Elizabeth's agents, he was given every chance to elude the stake.

18

ROME OF THE BAROQUE

(1621–1721)

The Thirty Years' War, that calamitous series of conflicts which was to ruin half Europe, first broke out towards the end of Paul V's pontificate. He had watched with alarm the tightening of political and religious tensions in Germany, but there was little that any pope could do to relax them. The differences between Catholics and Protestants had been exacerbated by the Counter-Reformation, while Lutherans and Calvanists were at loggerheads within the Protestant camp. The Habsburg Emperors had lost all real authority over the princes, grouped as they were in a Catholic League and a Protestant Union. Hostilities began when the Protestants of Bohemia rose against the Habsburgs and called Frederick, the Elector Palatine of the Rhine, to the throne of Prague. Thereupon Pope Paul, who had hitherto striven for peace and kept the League at arm's length, threw his weight on the side of the new Emperor, Ferdinand II. Between 1618 and 1620 he contributed 625,000 florins to the Catholic cause which triumphed in the latter year at the battle of the White Mountain.

The Bohemian campaign, however, was only the prelude to continuous war in Germany. Gregory XV (1621–23) more than doubled his predecessor's subventions to the Emperor and to the League's champion, Maximilian of Bavaria. His diplomatic efforts to keep the Catholic powers united were largely successful, with the result that during the twenties the German Protestants were in full retreat. When Maximilian conquered the Palatinate and captured Heidelberg he presented the whole of the famous Palatine library, fifty waggon-loads of books, to the Pope for incorporation into the library of the Vatican.

Gregory (Alessandro Ludovisi) was yet another Bolognese, but he had been educated by Jesuits at Rome. When elected he was Archbishop of his native city. Although himself able and active for his age (he was 67), he immediately raised his nephew Ludovico to the Cardinalate and made him his co-adjutor in all papal business. They made a good combination, for Ludovico was equally competent and hard-working, but it goes without saying that he was just as liberally provided with benefices as Scipione Borghese. His income was calculated at 200,000 *scudi*. He too built a splendid villa and gallery of antique sculpture. Apart from politics the main achievements of this pontificate were a reform of the procedure for papal elections and the stimulation of mission work through the new Congregation *De Propaganda Fide*.

The electoral regulations, which remained unaltered until 1904, were designed to ensure the inviolability of the Conclave and the secrecy of its ballots. They also laid down the detailed and elaborate ceremonial. It was recognized that no election could be entirely safeguarded from political pressures, but in an attempt to reduce them it was established that the Emperor, as well as the Kings of France and Spain, should possess the right to veto an individual candidate. It was exercised for the last time in the Conclave of 1904, when the Emperor Francis Joseph vetoed the candidature of Cardinal Rampolla.

The foundation of the Congregation for the Propagation of the Faith affected the whole mission field, both in countries which had lapsed from Catholicism and in the vast regions overseas which had now become accessible. Such action was already somewhat overdue. It was not that previous Popes had neglected missions. Paul III, for instance, had issued two Bulls in 1537 insisting, to the dismay of Spanish settlers, that the Indians of the Americas were moral and rational beings and thus entitled to whatever blessing Christianity might bring them. In the course of the sixteenth century a full ecclesiastical hierarchy had been established throughout Spanish and Portuguese America and specific tasks of conversion and education allotted to various Orders. The problem was not at all so simple in the Far East, especially in the Chinese Empire with which Christian missionaries were in contact via Portuguese India and the Spanish Philippines. It was doubtful whether they would be able to make any headway there at all in face of ancient religions and an exclusive literate civilization. The Jesuit Matteo Ricci, who arrived in China during the pontificate of Gregory XIII, strove to overcome the obstacles gradually by conforming outwardly to Confucian habits and teaching European science and techniques. This was successful up to a point; by the early seventeenth century several Jesuits were working discreetly in China and enjoyed favours at the imperial court. Nevertheless direct proselytism was still risky and Rome was suspicious of any accommodation on their part with Chinese ancestral beliefs. Clement VIII had appointed a short-lived Committee to study the diffusion of the faith. Gregory XV now decided that problems of conversion, including rivalry between missionary Orders, could only be tackled by strict control from the centre. So the Congregation was established, endowed with funds and strengthened by a training college, while a spiritual impulse was given to missionary movement by the canonization of Ignatius of Loyola and Francis Xavier.

Urban VIII (1623–44) was a characteristic figure of the baroque age in Italy. He moved in a setting of ornate grandeur which the uneven fortunes of his long pontificate failed seriously to tarnish. But his extravagance, wild nepotism and political misjudgements spoiled his reputation and damaged the prestige of the papacy.

Matteo Barberini was a Florentine of no particular distinction as a churchman, but his performance as nuncio in Paris had earned him the commendation of Paul V and promotion to the Cardinalate. He liked the French and was rather too confident of his ability to deal with them. On the other hand he detested Spain without sufficiently grasping that its power was on the decline. He enjoyed the society of literary folk and composed elaborate poems in Latin and Italian. As Pope he diverted himself by decking out the ancient hymns of the Church with baroque conceits. Apart from these trifles, he wished to make sure that the Barberini would leave a more indelible mark on Rome than any previous papal family. The enrichment of his kinsmen and the embellishment of the city were complementary. One brother, Antonio, and two nephews, Francesco and Antonio, were promptly made Cardinals. Enormous sums of money were channelled from the papal revenues into their coffers and those of their lay relatives, another brother, Carlo, and his son Taddeo. Carlo and Francesco were said to have received a total of 105 million *scudi* between them, while only half the benefices granted to one of the Antonios brought in an annual income of 4 million. The family also accumulated lands, castles, palaces and villas; in 1630 the Pope bought the principality of Palestrina for Taddeo for 725,000. Whether or not these figures are to be trusted, it is certain that two decades of prodigality ruined the finances of the papal state. Between 1620 and 1658 (under Alexander VII) the debt rose from 12 to nearly 40 million *scudi*. Nepotism had run riot, but the Holy See was so constituted that nobody except the Pope was in a position to call a halt.

It must be admitted that the fruits of this reckless spending spree were remarkable. The Barberini were highly cultured and discriminating builders and collectors. They employed Bernini and Borromini, Pietro da Cortona and Nicholas Poussin. It was the age of Domenichino, Guido Reni and Guercino, of countless painters and sculptors busily decorating the new baroque churches and palaces. Rome was a paradise for both patrons and artists. In 1626 the new St Peter's was at last consecrated and work was soon started on the colonnade of the piazza. A huge family palace arose on the side of the Quirinal. Francesco Barberini was also a great bibliophile; the library which he amassed was second in importance only to that of the Vatican.

Urban's policy in the Thirty Years War was to stand back from the conflict, while modestly subsidizing the Catholic cause, and to work for a negotiated peace. It made good sense so long as the Catholics were winning, and for some years the imperial generals, Tilly and Wallenstein, carried all before them. But after 1630 the Catholics lost ground. Their military progress was cut short by the victories of Gustavus Adolphus, while their political cohesion was undermined by the cynical and effective diplomacy of Richelieu. This Cardinal of the Roman Church and chief minister of the Catholic King of France had recently quelled a dangerous Huguenot revolt in his own country. Nevertheless he had no scruples about allying it, for purely national reasons, with the Protestant Swedes and as many German rulers, Protestant or Catholic, as he could muster in a coalition against the Habsburgs of Catholic Austria and Catholic Spain. The Pope, who simply desired peace, as opposed to political combinations likely to perpetuate war—a war not of religion but between naked national interests—was no match for Richelieu's clever opportunism. His efforts to detach France from Sweden were fruitless. So were his well-meant offers of mediation in Vienna and Madrid. But he persevered doggedly with a plan to bring the three great Catholic powers to a peace conference at Cologne. His legate, Cardinal Ginetti, proceeded there in 1636 and waited vainly for four years. To Urban's intense disappointment no French representatives appeared and the conference never got under way. The truth is that no Pope, however sincere and strong-minded, was any longer capable of influencing the brutally selfish policies of the powers. Urban's lack of personal authority, either spiritual or temporal, was sadly revealed.

He also suffered two minor but painful humiliations. The first was when a papal force which Gregory XV had sent to occupy the Valtellina, in order to forestall a clash between France and Spain, was unceremoniously hustled out of the region. The political and religious situation in the Valtellina was almost indescribably complicated, but the point to bear in mind is that this sub-Alpine valley was of high strategic importance. Its passes controlled the routes linking Spanish north Italy with the Habsburg lands and with the Spanish Netherlands, and those same routes were also the channel by which the French Crown, by agreement with the communities of the Swiss Grisons, had been accustomed to send troops into Italy for the support of its allies. The presence of the papal contingent at first prevented war, but, as it seemed to Richelieu, it was not strong enough to keep the Spaniards and Austrians out of the Valtellina indefinitely. He therefore sent in a French army, thus brusquely putting an end to this short papal essay in peace-keeping. This incident, which occurred in 1624, was an ominous indication of the Cardinal's off-hand attitude towards the papacy.

The second blow to Urban's pride was his failure to win a futile and expensive little war of his own. Without a shadow of justification he tried to browbeat the Duke of Parma, Odoardo Farnese, into surrendering his secondary duchy of Castro and Ronciglione, which he held as a papal fief, to the Barberini. When the Duke refused, the Pope excommunicated him and invaded his duchy. But the papal force was ignominiously repulsed and the Duke's men, reinforced by Venice and other independent Italian states, counter-attacked and ravaged papal territory. Hostilities lasted for two years (1642–4) at the cost of 6 million *scudi*. At one moment it was feared that the confederates might penetrate as far as Rome. The city walls were hurriedly repaired with materials robbed from ancient buildings and the bronze ceilings of the Pantheon used for casting cannon. This act of vandalism prompted the famous quip, '*quod non fecerunt barbari fecerunt Barberini.*' The sneer may not have been deserved, but the whole incident exposed the temporal power as a sham.

As a result of these frustrations Urban seems to have undergone a mild crisis of conscience. He knew that his failures, combined with his nepotism and extravagance, had ruined his popularity. He deputed a special commission of clerics to consider to what extent a pope could fully spend the revenues of the Holy See and what proportion of them he could properly devote to his own personal needs. The commissioners found their terms of reference embarrassing and understandably hedged. They ruled that the Pope was juridically entitled to dispose of the revenues more or less at will, but two of them, including Urban's own confessor, dissented on the moral issue. He told them all to think again and come back with a more precise answer, whereupon the majority decided that he might dispose of one quarter of the regular revenue as well as the whole income from saleable offices.

Much blame has been directed at Urban for the Inquisition's condemnation of Galileo and the prohibition of his *Dialogue on the Great World Systems*. In fact he cannot reasonably be reproached for his attitude towards the affair, which was always one of studious moderation. When, in 1615, Galileo first got into trouble for his advocacy of the Copernican system, we find Matteo Barberini, at that time a Cardinal, declaring his admiration for the great mathematician but warning him not to fall foul of the theologians. It was partly owing to his intervention with Paul V that the Holy Office's decree of 1616 denouncing the heliocentric theory was followed, so far as Galileo was concerned, by a new admonition from Cardinal Bellarmine. Otherwise he was not punished. There was never any danger of his being sent to the stake like that earlier victim of Bellarmine, Giordano Bruno. But Bruno, the apostate Dominican whose free-thinking philosophy cut at the roots of Catholic doctrine, was in a very different category from the astronomer who, in Barberini's view, was doing no worse than propounding a brilliant hypothesis. Urban's friendship with Galileo survived the admonition. In 1633, when Galileo was hauled before the Inquisition for the second time, the Pope took the utmost care to ensure that he was leniently treated, that he was not put in prison and that his trial and abjuration were so managed as to allow him to stay unharassed and in comfortable retirement for the remaining nine years of his life. Urban's nephew, Cardinal Francesco Barberini, pointedly abstained from subscribing to his sentence.

The list of seventeenth-century Popes reads like a register of noble Roman families. Borghese, Ludovisi, Pamfili, Chigi, Rospigliosi, Odescalchi, Ottoboni—all these names evoke memories of Rome. Most of them, however, originated from other parts of Italy and only settled in the city after an eminent member had occupied the papal chair. In the second half of the century the papacy was deeply concerned with problems arising from the preponderance of the French monarchy, the peculiar claims of the Gallican Church and the sharp differences of religious outlook between French Catholics.

Innocent X (1644–55) was a genuine Roman. He was seventy years of age at his election, which he owed to the Spanish veto of a rival candidate. Since he himself was reputed to be pro-Spanish, Cardinal Mazarin, the new chief minister of Louis XIII, decided to use the French right of veto to exclude him, but his instructions did not reach the Conclave in time. Giambattista Pamfili was hardly an inspiring figure and nothing in his humdrum career seemed to justify his elevation. His sly and suspicious nature is reflected in his unflattering portrait by Velasquez, but he had enough humour to comment 'all too true' when the picture was shown to him. In order to curry favour he set up a commission of enquiry into the financial malpractices of his predecessor. At first it caused a great flutter among the Barberini Cardinals, one of whom, Antonio, fled the country. They all complained to Mazarin and thanks to his intervention the proceedings were dropped.

While practising careful economy in his household and administration Innocent provided more than adequately for his relatives. The chief beneficiary was his imperious sister-in-law, the widow Donna Olimpia Maidalotini, who cast an uncanny and altogether deplorable spell over the old man. Besides accumulating a very large fortune, especially by cornering the markets during two years of scarcity, she influenced Innocent's decisions and upset his judgement of men and affairs. The satirists called her the 'Papresa'. Whatever the exact nature of their relationship the Pope could refuse her nothing and she tightly controlled his patronage. Despite this incubus his pontificate ran a fairly tranquil course. He was not a great builder but all the work that he sponsored was of the highest quality. We owe to him the Piazza Navona with Bernini's fountain and the baroque transformation of the Lateran basilica by Borromini. Inevitably, too, a Villa Pamfili was added to the already numerous resorts of papal families.

The Thirty Years War, in which some regions of Germany lost two-thirds of their inhabitants, was nearing its end. Innocent sent Fabio Chigi, his nuncio at Cologne, to Münster, where negotiations for the Peace of Westphalia (1648) were taking place, with instructions to minimize any concessions which might be offered to the Protestants in the religious field. Such an attitude was unrealistic. All the belligerents, and especially the Emperor Ferdinand III, were desperate for peace. Moreover they knew that it could only be secured by the exercise of some degree of mutual toleration and the acceptance of the principle of equality of rights between Catholics and Protestants in the Empire. When the terms were eventually agreed the Pope denounced them as a betrayal of the Catholic cause. In a thunderous Bull he declared them to be 'null and void, accursed and without any validity or effect for the past, present and future'. His protest, however, was no more than a formal expression of disapproval. No one knew better than Innocent that it was incapable of undoing a *fait accompli*. There would be no point in accusing him of wishing to prolong the bloodshed and devastation. Nevertheless the Emperor forbade the publication of the Bull in his dominions.

Papal pronouncements could still have an impact in the seventeenth century when their content was strictly theological. Such was the Bull by which, in 1653, Innocent condemned five propositions from the *Augustinus*, a huge treatise on grace, free will and predestination composed by Cornelius Jansen, once professor of theology at Louvain and bishop of Ypres. Jansen died in 1638, but the politico-religious storm aroused by his writing rumbled on in France for a hundred years and worried several Popes of the period. It was only to be expected that the Curia would take exception to the strong Calvinist tinge in Jansen's exposition of the teachings of St Augustine. Indeed the Jesuits had long been campaigning bitterly against him. Previous Popes, notably Paul V and Urban VIII, had tried to stifle this dangerous controversy by forbidding the publication either of the *Augustinus* or of the Jesuit writings which attacked it, but their prohibitions only sharpened the argument. Jansenism had plenty of support among churchmen and intellectuals.

Innocent's Bull was a severe blow to the Jansenists. They tried to soften it by maintaining that although the propositions in themselves deserved condemnation, Jansen could not be proved to have held them; in other words the Church was infallible in its doctrinal judgements but could never penetrate into the ultimate and personal beliefs of an individual writer on doctrine. The distinction was thin enough, but it enabled the Jansenists to continue the fight with Pascal's devastating attack on his Jesuit opponents in the *Lettres Provinciales*. Nevertheless the new Pope, Alexander VII (1655–67), firmly reiterated that the five propositions represented Jansen's personal convictions and had been condemned as such. All French clerics were subsequently required to sign a declaration to that effect. From that moment the government of Louis XIV came to the Pope's support by applying heavy pressure to the Jansenists.

In most other fields, however, the France of the Sun King more than upheld the country's reputation as a fractious daughter of the Church. It was not Alexander's fault that the papacy's relations with France grew steadily worse. Fabio Chigi, a Sienese, had been Innocent's Secretary of State. He was the most unprovocative of men, pacific, pious, highly cultivated and an experienced diplomatist. He equally disliked Jansenism and Jesuit casuistry. Unfortunately for him his resistance to French aims at the Münster peace conference had displeased Mazarin, who managed to block his election for eighty days. Mazarin was also annoyed because Alexander gave asylum at Rome to Cardinal de Retz, his opponent during the civil strife of the Fronde. For the latter reason he recalled the French Chargé d'Affaires from the Vatican and began to subject the papacy to a series of humiliating pinpricks and rebuffs. The worst of these was the exclusion of the Holy See from the negotiations leading to the Peace of the Pyrenees of 1659 between France and Spain. It was a snub deliberately designed to show the world that there was no room for papal influence in a Europe composed of national monarchies and dominated by France.

When Louis XIV subsequently decided to send an Ambassador to Rome he appointed the arrogant Duc de Crequy. This magnate proceeded to pick a quarrel with the papal government by claiming diplomatic immunity not only for his residence, the Farnese palace, but for the whole quarter surrounding it. For reasons of public order as well as of principle this could not be granted. The Pope might well have won the battle of protocol if it had not been for a brawl between Crequy's retainers and some Corsican soldiers of the papal guard, as a result of which other Corsicans attacked the embassy and insulted the royal envoy. Crequy rejected all apologies and withdrew his mission. That was the signal for violent French reprisals. The nuncio was expelled from Paris, Avignon and the Comtat Venaissin were occupied by royal troops and preparations made to invade the papal state. If only because he was technically in the wrong Alexander climbed down. He sent his nephew, Cardinal Flavio Chigi, and Cardinal Imperiali, the governor of Rome, to beg the King's pardon. He undertook to exclude Corsicans from his service and to erect a 'pyramid' opposite their former barracks with an inscription recording concessions in favour of Parma and Modena, both Italian satellites of France. After this assertion of power, in a style not unparalleled in past centuries and to be more brutally copied by Napoleon, Louis graciously handed back Avignon and the Comtat.

Such incidents, symptomatic of France's well-advertised disrespect for the papacy, foreshadowed the more serious conflict which broke out twenty years later, during the pontificate of Innocent XI, over the whole relationship between Rome and the Gallican Church. In other respects Alexander's reign was uneventful. He was pleased when the Archduke Leopold was elected Emperor against the wishes of Marazin, who had been intriguing in favour of a non-Habsburg. He also ended Paul V's old quarrel with Venice; the Jesuits were again allowed to enter the Republic and the Holy See contributed a large sum towards its heroic but fruitless defence of Crete against the Turks. Alexander was sometimes troubled, but on the whole gratified, by the presence in Rome of Christina, the former Queen of Sweden and daughter of the Protestant paladin Gustavus Adolphus. Her recent conversion to Catholicism, preceded by renunciation of the throne, was greeted as a moral victory for the Church. She entered the city in triumphal procession and was received by the Pope in a special consistory. Her eccentricities of dress, language and behaviour, her demands on the papal finances and the critical views which she sometimes expressed about aspects of her new religion, were apt to cause him anxiety, but intellectually they were in close accord. They both loved the arts and collected books. The Queen founded her own Academy of learned men while the Pope, a poet in his youth, was the greatest of all Bernini's patrons; it was in this reign that his colonnades were finished, together with his sculptural masterpieces of St Peter's and Santa Maria del Popolo.

Alexander's humiliation by Louis XIV has tended to obscure his very real virtues. His two successors were men of much the same stamp but luckier in that they were not subjected to similar treatment. Both took the name of Clement and both were paragons of discretion. It would almost be true to say that nothing occurred during their pontificates to disturb the papacy's dignified calm. Clement IX (1667–69) hailed from Pistoia and was named Giulio Rospigliosi; like his predecessor he had been Secretary of State under the previous pontiff. He was personally devout, patient in the conduct of affairs and adroit in staving off trouble. Unhappily, like so many excellent Popes, he did not long survive. He succeeded, however, in averting a new clash with the Jansenists. By tactfully ignoring the reservations four obstinate French bishops were known to feel about subscribing to Alexander's formula of submission, he obtained their signatures and satisfied the royal government, which by this time was sick of the controversy.

Clement X (1670–76) had a longer but even smoother passage. Emilio Altieri, a Roman, was nearly 80 when the first Clement made him a Cardinal, and was only elected because two less obscure candidates had been excluded by French and Spanish vetos. Louis XIV's preoccupation with the Dutch war left this mild old man unharassed.

Innocent XI (1676–89) was of an altogether higher calibre. A very strict churchman, he tolerated no laxity in doctrine or morals. In the teeth of Louis XIV at his most powerful he vigorously reasserted the prestige, if not the leadership, of the Holy See in international affairs. As regards the Gallican Church, he resolutely defended papal rights against royal encroachments and the servility of the French clergy towards the Crown. He stood equally firm when Louis tried to intimidate him by the same tactics as he had employed against Alexander VII.

A native of Como, the Odescalchi Pope was known as an efficient administrator and a thrifty head of the financial department (*camera apostolica*). In the hard times of the forties his charitable work in the papal state had earned him the title of 'Father of the Poor'. He continued in the same way as Pope; the expenses of his court and curia were severely cut and there was no hint of nepotism in his establishment.

In a Europe again agitated by war, papal diplomacy had to contend with an intransigent France at the height of her power. By the Peace of Nymegen (1679) Louis emerged stronger than ever from his struggle with the Empire, the Dutch Republic and Spain. His ambitions had if anything been amplified, for he was thought to be aiming to secure the imperial throne for himself or his son on the death of the Habsburg Leopold I. For the Pope the most serious aspect of the King's basic hostility to the Habsburgs was his opposition to any league of Christian states being formed against the Turks. This, a major object of papal aspirations since before the fall of Constantinople, had been frustrated many times in the past by French alliances or understandings with the Sultans. Now Louis had been doing his best to deter the King of Poland, John Sobieski, from forming an anti-Turkish front with the Emperor, while at the same time fomenting a Hungarian revolt against the latter. It was therefore a great triumph for Innocent's persistence and political skill that he succeeded in detaching Sobieski from his French connexion in time for him to lead his army to the famous Austro-Polish victory over the Turks under the walls of Vienna (1683). The subsequent Christian counter-offensive, in the course of which Buda and Belgrade were recovered, and the Morea too wrested from the Ottomans by Venice, afforded immense satisfaction to the Pope, and there was nothing that Louis could do to stop the tide turning.

Innocent's clash with the King in the religious field had already taken place, but with inconclusive results. Gallicanism, in the extreme form which it was now assuming, stemmed from two main sources, the French clergy's dislike of any control by the Roman Curia and the incompatibility of any exercise of papal sovereignty with the national absolutism to which France had become accustomed under Louis XIV. All Frenchmen who were not Huguenots considered themselves to be good and sincere Catholics; once more they justified their claim by their passionate interest in religious discussion and the arguments of their favourite preachers. Few of them, however, cherished a Roman form of devotion and papalist loyalties. While a fervent minority adhered to Jansenism, the great majority consisted of those who professed an Erastian form of Catholicism in which the doctrinal authority of the Pope took second place to the overriding divine right of the King in all other matters. Under the Concordat of 1516 the King's rights in Church matters included that of appointment to all bishoprics and abbeys. In a great many cases he had also come to exercise the *jus régale*, that of the disposal of benefices in vacant sees. When the royal government decided, in 1673, to enforce that valuable prerogative throughout the whole Kingdom only two bishops (both incidentally Jansenists and former non-subscribers) had the courage to protest. As their own Archbishops took the King's side, they eventually appealed to the Pope over the heads of their superiors.

Although the *régale* had to a large extent been already conceded in practice Innocent decided, after long hesitations, to treat the issue as one of principle. He gave his full support to the bishops and summoned the King to revoke his order. Recriminations flew back and forth. His threat to excommunicate one of the Archbishops was denounced as a violation of Gallican liberties dating back to the Middle Ages and beyond. Louis took the opportunity to convoke a General Assembly of the French clergy. It obediently endorsed not only the extension of the *régale* but four articles drawn up by Bossuet, the great preacher and spokesman of official French Catholicism. These asserted that the Pope had no jurisdiction over sovereigns in temporal matters, that in spiritual matters he was subject to the authority of a General Council and that he could not usurp royal rights or the liberties of the Gallican Church; in matters of doctrine the Pope was indeed the arbiter, but his judgement was not 'unalterable', that is not infallible, without the agreement of the Church as a whole. When Innocent was informed of these proceedings he declared those relating to the *régale* to be invalid. Nevertheless, while scathingly rebuking the French hierarchy he did not commit himself to a full-scale condemnation of the four articles, doubtless hoping that a compromise by way of interpretation might be worked out in a calmer atmosphere. For the moment he refused to accept any candidates for bishoprics put forward by the King. In the following year (1685), when the Huguenots were proscribed by the revocation of the Edict of Nantes, he contented himself with praising the royal action in itself while expressing disapproval of the cruelty with which it was carried out.

As he approached the end of his reign, Innocent could be sure that his policy of steady resistance to French pressures had paid off. The Holy See was in a far stronger position than at any time since the Thirty Years' War. Yet, as he had made clear to the King's special envoy, he was by no means disinclined to look for a reasonable accommodation with France, if it would ensure peace and stability in Europe. Their talks relieved the tension for a while. Unfortunately the old dispute about diplomatic immunity flared up again and spoiled the atmosphere. The Pope had persuaded other foreign missions, as well as the incalculable Queen Christina, to abandon their claim for immunity covering a whole district, a system which afforded asylum to half the criminal population of the city. However a new French Ambassador, the Marquis de Lavardin, would hear none of it. Entering Rome with an armed retinue, he truculently demanded 'freedom of the quarter'. Innocent responded sharply by excommunicating the envoy and slapping an interdict on the French church of St Louis. The King was of course deeply offended, and even more when the Pope vetoed the pro-French candidate for the strategically situated Archbishopric of Cologne. Just as he had reacted in the time of Alexander VII, he put the nuncio under detention, occupied Avignon and the Comtat and threatened an invasion of the papal state. If his attention had not been distracted by the Glorious Revolution in England there might well have been question of a schism. As it was, relations between France and the Holy See had simply deadlocked in the year preceding Innocent's death.

Innocent was sternly devoted to his duties. He had little taste for Baroque pomps, for literature or for the fine arts. Although his efforts to reform Roman morals were predictably unpopular and passively resisted, he was esteemed for his charity and for the integrity of his government. In any case the old Roman unruliness, the bane of the papacy for so many centuries, had at last been tamed by the Counter-Reformation. A straightforward Christian himself, he was intolerant of what he considered to be dangerous trends in contemporary Catholicism. He was particularly suspicious of 'probabilism', or the casuistical arguments which Jesuit confessers employed to justify lenience towards their penitents. He warned their General that he would not countenance any such relativism in morals. More questionably he condemned Quietism, the mystical and self-annihilating path to holiness which the Spanish priest Molinos outlined in his *Spiritual Guide* and which attracted many prominent devotees in Italy and France. The movement at first enjoyed his favour, but he suddenly changed his mind and instructed the Holy Office to suppress it. Molinos was imprisoned for the rest of his life, while a senior bishop and intimate friend of the Pope was only saved from investigation by his promotion to the Sacred College.

In sheer ability and strength of character Innocent surpassed all other Popes of his century. When he died his difficulties with France had not been resolved but looked less daunting. He left the Holy See inviolate, confident in its mission and, what is more, comfortably solvent. It is not surprising either that his successors in the eighteenth century should have sought to canonize him or that French influence should have been exerted to block the process. It was not in fact completed until 1956, in the pontificate of Pius XII.

The last two Popes of the seventeenth century were very old men. Alexander VIII (1689–91) succeeded at 79, Innocent XII (1691–1700) at 76. Neither, however, was unequal to his task, and both sensibly followed in the steps of Innocent XI. The former, Pietro Ottoboni, was a Venetian who had been a Cardinal for 37 years. His aim in international affairs was to take the steam out of the papacy's dispute with France without yielding on any point of principle. He found Louis, who was now facing a Grand Alliance of the principal European powers, in a less overbearing mood, ready to restore Avignon and the Comtat for the second time and to forget about the 'freedom of the quarter'. Since, however, no agreement could be reached on the four Gallican articles or the extension of the *régale*, the Pope prepared a Bull denouncing both as invalid, but refrained from publishing it until he was on his deathbed.

After six months' stalemate in the Conclave between the friends and enemies of France the choice fell on the Neapolitan prince Antonio Pignatelli, Cardinal-Archbishop of his native city. Like Innocent XI he was deeply pious and earnestly reformist. Indeed his first act, and one of lasting significance, was to issue a Bull designed to do away for ever with nepotism. He was moved to do so by Alexander VIII's elevation of a young nephew to the Cardinalate, a procedure which was considered both tactless and anachronistic. It was now laid down that if a Pope's kinsman was taken into the College on merit, his revenues should not exceed 12,000 *scudi*; his poor relatives would have to be treated like other needy people and no longer endowed with offices and sinecures. It was a striking indication of the change of moral climate that this revolution in papal manners should have been brought about so suddenly and effectively.

Wherever possible Innocent XII tried to keep religious controversy to a minimum. Further disputations about Jansenism he forbade altogether, but he was reluctantly forced to adjudicate in a confrontation between two major figures in the French Church, Bossuet and Fenelon, over the latter's espousal of Quietism. Fortunately Fenelon accepted his judgement and there were no serious repercussions. But the most notable achievement of his policy of religious pacification was to reach a working compromise with King Louis. While nothing could induce the

King to back down over the *régale*, he was willing to assure the Pope that he would no longer insist on the clergy adhering unconditionally to the Gallican articles. Innocent could have had no illusions about the continuing strength of Gallicanism; it was enough for him that the King had formally given ground and thus safeguarded his prestige.

In 1697 the war between France and the Grand Alliance, of which the Pope had remained an impotent spectator, came to an end. Only three years later, however, the balance between the powers was more profoundly unsettled by the death of Charles II, the feeble-witted and childless King of Spain. Innocent, who himself died a month before Charles, had been considering whether it would be more likely and desirable that the vast Spanish inheritance in Europe and the Indies should pass undivided to an Austrian Habsburg or a French Bourbon. The Emperor Leopold was urging the claims of his second son, the Archduke Charles, Louis XIV those of his grandson, Philip Duke of Anjou. Neither rival would give way, but the Spanish Crown Council declared unanimously for Philip and for the maintenance intact of the Spanish realm. Despite his differences with Louis, Innocent preferred that solution and Clement XI (1700–21) also took the Bourbon side. He thus resigned himself to an armed struggle between the Bourbons and the Empire, supported by England and Holland. The papacy could not have avoided an unpalatable dilemma; it had to choose between an Italy dominated, as in past epochs, by the Empire or by a Spain inevitably subjected to French influence. Although neither prospect looked promising, the Holy See had become accustomed to a Spanish presence which had gradually grown less burdensome. Innocent had therefore concluded that, in the long run at least, it would be less irksome to have the Bourbons in Milan and Naples than the Habsburgs; and Clement, who was not politically-minded, did not dissent. Gian Francesco Albani, a youngish Cardinal from Urbino, owed his election at the age of 51 to the Zelanti, that is the party in the Sacred College which was more interested in religious concord than political alignments. An enthusiast for his apostolic mission, he was appalled by the likelihood of Italy becoming a battle-ground. That is exactly what happened. First the French seized Milan, but in 1706 they were expelled altogether from north Italy by the great captain Prince Eugene. Imperial encroachments on papal territory led in 1708 to a formal state of war between the Empire and the Holy See. However, since the papal forces were in no condition to undertake serious hostilities, a peace was soon concluded by which the Austrians gained access to Naples and the Pope promised to recognize the Archduke Charles as King of Spain.

Clement had chosen the wrong side, at least from a military point of view. In 1711 Charles succeeded to the Empire, despite impotent protests from Rome, and in 1713 the Treaty of Utrecht, while giving Spain to the Bourbon Philip V, made him master of Milan and Naples. He was not however disposed to be too awkward a neighbour to the papal state, preferring to regard Clement leniently as the victim of his own miscalculations. As the Pope's feudal overlordships in the rest of Italy were being disregarded right and left under the new territorial arrangements, he might count himself lucky to keep the papal state itself. He loyally supported the Emperor in a new war with the Turks (1714–18), but even here his best-meant initiative went wrong. Alberoni, the intriguing Italian minister at the court of Spain, had given him to understand that in return for the Cardinalate he would make the Spanish fleet available, but as soon as he had been admitted to the College he used the ships to seize Sardinia from the Austrians. It was the worst possible issue of Clement's lack of judgement.

During all these years the Pope was being nagged by further disputes over Jansenism, a movement which seemed fated never to die down. They caused more distress to his conscientious but indecisive nature than all the vicissitudes of the Spanish Succession. A new prophet, Pasquier Quesnel, had revived Jansenist spirits before the turn of the century. Then controversy broke out afresh when the doctors of the Sorbonne ruled, in answer to an apparently innocent question, that a Catholic might properly hear Jansen's propositions condemned 'in respectful silence', in other words without expressly assenting to their condemnation. The Pope, when he heard of it, duly rebuked the doctors but King Louis, who was thoroughly irritated by Jansenism, insisted on his publishing a Bull (*Vineam Domini*, 1705) laying down that silence was not enough; the offending propositions must be rejected with both heart and voice. The effect of this injunction was the opposite of what the King had intended. Frenchmen of all kinds, both religious dissidents and those who simply bore a grudge against the government in the difficult war years, rallied to the Jansenists. When the lawyers of the Parlement of Paris refused to recognize the papal ban on Quesnel's writings, they were supported by the Archbishop of Paris himself, the aristocrat Cardinal de Noailles. Louis XIV then lost patience. Through his Ambassador in Rome he called upon the Pope to produce a second and more crushingly comprehensive indictment of Jansenism. This was soon forthcoming in the famous Bull *Unigenitus* (1713), which French anti-clericals were to use as a stick to belabour the papacy for the rest of the eighteenth century. But Noailles, in defiance of the old king, would still not acknowledge its authority, and there was talk of calling a national Council of the Gallican Church.

The King died in 1715. The Duke of Orleans, who took over the government, was irreligious, dissolute and anxious to damp down what seemed to him to be an absurd and inconvenient quarrel. At first he favoured Noailles and the enemies of *Unigenitus*, but on realizing that its friends, grouped round another noble Archbishop, Cardinal de Rohan, were equally capable of causing a fuss, he forbade all discussion of the Bull until the Pope had found a way out of the impasse. This time Clement acted firmly and consistently. His answer was a third Bull (*Pastoralis Offici*) excommunicating all those who might disobey *Unigenitus*. Although Noailles, several bishops, the Parlements and the Sorbonne all rejected it out of hand the free-thinking Regent, once the buck had been passed back to him, decided otherwise. Tired of the eternal wrangling, he prohibited all public criticism of the papal pronouncements and curtly commanded the Parlements to register his order. But by that time Clement was on the point of death.

It would be too harsh to hold him personally to blame for the setback which the Church's eastern missions suffered during his pontificate. The Jesuit outposts in South India and China had prospered steadily for more than a century. Their progress continued to be based on a scrupulous respect for local customs and traditions, including the Chinese cult of ancestors, languages and religious terminology. Under K'ang Hsi, the second Emperor of the Manchu dynasty, the Jesuits in Peking experienced some anxious moments. The most eminent among them, the astronomer Adam Schall, who had initially been appointed head of the Imperial Observatory, was arrested and jailed with several of his fellow priests and Chinese converts. But the Son of Heaven later relented, and in 1692 issued an edict of toleration in favour of the Christians. By the end of the century they numbered about 300,000.

The Jesuits were facing a more dangerous threat from within their own Church. The Mendicant Orders in particular strongly objected to the latitude the Jesuits granted to local usages. They accused them of condoning heathen practices, and bombarded the Inquisition with complaints. As from mid-century the Holy See issued a stream of warnings and decrees attempting to define which practices counted as religious, and therefore noxious, and which as civil, and therefore harmless. Although the Fathers were adept at repelling such attacks, and the unwelcome visits of papal emissaries, Clement, under pressure from more conventional advisers, called them sharply to order. But when, in 1704, he sent the Patriarch of Antioch, Maillard de Tournon, as his legate to India and China with instructions to enforce the ban on local rites, K'ang Hsi not unnaturally deported him to Macao and began to make things difficult for the missions. The old atmosphere of confidence was now spoiled. A fierce Bull of 1715 restated the prohibitions and the Emperor retorted by formally banning further proselytism. Nevertheless the missions were not barred from China altogether, while the Jesuits continued to argue for a more flexible approach to conversion until the dissolution of their Order fifty years later. Meanwhile the Chinese Christians dwindled by a third in the course of the eighteenth century.

PART SIX

THE POPES
AT BAY

19

THE AGE OF REASON
(1721–1799)

We think of eighteenth-century Rome as basking in a mellow calm, a paradise for antiquaries, the goal of every gentleman's Grand Tour. But for the seven Popes who reigned between 1721 and the outbreak of the French Revolution the age was not free from anxiety. Although spared the rougher kind of troubles, the Church had to contend with the cold scepticism of the intellectuals, the often bitter anti-clericalism of the governing élites and the absolutism of 'enlightened' monarchs. The intense religious controversies of the immediate past had lost their meaning in a new atmosphere of indifference and philosophical fashions. It was these more insidious dangers that were sapping the foundations of the faith. The papacy, however, was slow to take up the challenge, if only because the enemy had not yet come fully into the open. In 1721 Voltaire was only 27 and Rousseau still a young boy. Moreover the next three Popes were elderly, feeble and incapable of rising to an occasion.

The best that can be said of Michel Angelo Conti, who reigned as Innocent XIII (1721–4) is that he retained the good will of the Regent Orleans by making the Abbé Dubois, his minister, a Cardinal and helping him to keep Jansenism suitably repressed. His successor, the 76-year-old Benedict XIII (1724–30), was an Orsini but hardly a typical member of that imperious clan. Sophisticated foreign travellers ridiculed him as a pious bumbler absurdly intent on banning Roman lotteries and forbidding his Cardinals to wear wigs. His real fault was to have outlived his usefulness. His previous pastoral record had been admirable. A Dominican by training, ascetic by nature, a zealous and popular Archbishop of Benevento, he might have made an excellent Pope if he had been young enough to adapt himself to curial and wider political affairs. But he made no such effort. Senile or not, he saw himself wholly as priest and not at all as administrator. He concentrated on the cure of souls and the punctilious performance of his purely spiritual and ecclesiastical duties, even carrying out long visitations of his former diocese. Meanwhile he handed over the business of the papal state to an unworthy factotum named Niccolò Coscia, who had served him in an inferior capacity at Benevento. Raised to the Cardinalate over the protests of the College, this creature proved corrupt and incompetent, demoralizing the Curia, emptying the treasury and committing a row of blunders in foreign affairs. Luckily no external crisis occurred during this pontificate, but so long as the Pope lived he would hear nothing against Coscia. When his patron died the mob sacked his house in the old Roman way.

Under Clement XII (1730–40) the papacy slid further downhill. After five months' bickering and vetoing in the Conclave an even more infirm pontiff was elected at the age of 79. Lorenzo Corsini, a Florentine, went totally blind in the second year of his reign and spent most of his time in bed. It was as if the Cardinals had conspired to render the papacy impotent; it can only be supposed that they did not expect him to linger on for ten years. Coscia was arrested, imprisoned in Sant' Angelo, fined 100,000 *scudi* and stripped of his benefices but his punishment was almost the only positive act of the reign. Public affairs were entrusted to a nephew, Cardinal Neri Corsini, an amiable art-lover with no flair for diplomacy or administration.

While stagnation prevailed at Rome, the Holy See watched in impotent alarm the dynastic changes occurring in the rest of Italy. They demonstrated that it had lost all its power to influence the behaviour of Catholic sovereigns towards the papacy and each other. The political balance in the peninsula had been upset by the deaths of the last male representatives of the Medici in Tuscany and of the Farnese in Parma. Elizabeth Farnese, the wife of Philip V of Spain, had so intrigued that her son, Don Carlos, might succeed to both the Grand Duchy of Tuscany and the duchies of Parma and Piacenza. This revival of Bourbon power in Italy was more than Austria could stomach. As a result of the complicated hostilities and negotiations that followed, Don Carlos obtained the kingdom of Naples and Sicily whereas Austria was compensated for the loss of Naples with Parma and Piacenza. As for Tuscany, it fell to Francis of Lorraine, husband of Maria Theresia, the sole child and heiress of the Emperor Charles VI. These arrangements brought no comfort to the papacy. Indeed they had been planned with cynical disregard for its rights and sentiments. When engaged in conquering and swapping territories the politicians of Madrid, Naples, Turin and Vienna paid no attention to the fact that Naples and Sicily, Parma and Sardinia were legally and traditionally fiefs in which their rulers needed to be invested by the Pope. Still less did Spanish and Austrian armies scruple to traverse, pillage and occupy papal lands in the course of their campaigns. In short the Pope's temporal authority completely lost credit in Italy and in the wider sphere of Europe. Tanucci, the Tuscan lawyer who became the King's all-powerful minister at Naples, was distinguished by the peculiar virulence with which he attacked the Curia and curtailed the Church's privileges in the southern Kingdom.

While the temporal power of the papacy, and to a lesser extent its spiritual and moral vigour, were in decline, Rome as a cultural attraction was supreme. In the intervals between the frequent but not very destructive wars of the eighteenth century, illustrious, learned or merely fashionable personages flocked to the city from all over Europe. Although the Holy See was sadly short of funds the Corsini spent much of their considerable private fortune on buildings (their family palace, the Consulta, the Fontana di Trevi, a new façade for the Lateran Basilica), libraries and galleries. As patrons of the arts and sciences, however, they were eclipsed by Benedict XIV (1740-58). It was not long before the numerous cultural pilgrims discovered that this Pope was not merely a Maecenas in the Renaissance tradition but a very rare, forceful and dedicated personality engaged in bringing a new inspiration to his office. Looking back on his pontificate, Macaulay called him the best and wisest of the two hundred and fifty successors of the Apostles. His own contemporaries— Christians, anti-clericals, even atheists—were unanimous in eulogizing him. The dry Horace Walpole wrote, 'he was loved by Papists, esteemed by Protestants; a priest without insolence or interest, a prince without favourites, a Pope without nephews, a writer without vanity—the best of the Bishops of Rome.' In dedicating his tragedy *Mahomet* to the Pope Voltaire deftly praised his 'infallibility in the

decisions of literature'. Of all the monuments of Rome admired by visitors the
Pope himself came first.

Cardinal Prospero Lambertini was 65 when elected. A very erudite canonist, he
had served the Church as Archbishop of Ancona and of his native Bologna.
Renowed as he was for the depth and breadth of his intellectual interests, he was not
considered *papabile* until the College had wrangled inconclusively for yet another five
months. At last it found exactly the right man for what was needed, the wafting of a
current of fresh air through the Vatican. For this eminent scholar, historian and
jurist was the most direct and unconventional of clerics. Witty and affable, humane
and accessible, he had time for everybody and never spared himself, but his real
concern with people did not prejudice his strict attention to business and to his
liturgical and ceremonial role. Unostentatiously pious, he lived simply and cultivated the informal touch, frequently walking about the city by himself and chatting
with all sorts of persons. His subtle brilliance was hidden under a mask of bonhomie.
In his easy-going manner, his sincerely liberal outlook and the tight discipline of his
working programme he anticipated the style of a pope of our times.

Benedict worked patiently to restore the Holy See's dignity and influence in
Europe. There was nothing, however, that he could do to prevent the long War of the
Austrian Succession (1741–8), which involved most of the powers and in the course
of which papal sovereignty was again repeatedly violated by Austrian and Spanish
armies. As he himself put it, the State of the Church suffered the 'martyrdom of
neutrality'. He disbanded the papal troops and waited for the storm to pass.
Meanwhile by a policy of calculated pragmatism and judicious concessions, he
succeeded in repairing a number of unnecessarily broken fences. Concordats or
other agreements were negotiated with Spain, Naples, Savoy, Sardinia and Portugal, all Catholic kingdoms which had been squeezing a weakened papacy. He saw
that it was useless to antagonize their absolutist governments by insisting on
historical rights which had become outdated or indefensible. Although he was
criticized for his flexibility, he had so far improved the papacy's posture that he was
able to play a useful and impartial role in the election of Francis I, Maria Theresia's
husband, as Emperor, against the wishes of France and Spain, and in the subsequent
Peace of Aix-la-Chapelle. He needed all his diplomatic skill to deal with Frederick II
of Prussia, who by his conquest of Silesia from Maria Theresia had acquired a
massive block of Catholic subjects. Frederick's idea was to remove the Cardinal-
bishop of Breslau to Berlin in the capacity of Vicar-General of all the Catholics in his
realm, thus bringing him under his own very authoritarian control. As a sop to the
Pope he agreed to convert the Catholic chapel in Berlin into a Cathedral. But
Benedict would not even consider the proposal; he would allow of no barrier between
himself and the primate. It says much for his strength of character that Frederick
backed down. He respected an opponent as firm as himself and did not want a
confessional split within his Kingdom. And Benedict had been careful to address
him as King as opposed to a mere heretic Margrave of Brandenburg.

The war years seriously strained Benedict's capacity for conciliation, his
equanimity and celebrated sense of humour. He wore out, he said, three secretaries
by continuous dictation. The long-standing deficit in the papal finances was a
perpetual source of worry; he reduced it by drastic economies but the depradations
of foreign armies did not make his task any more popular. Somehow he found time to
overhaul Church practices, liturgy and ritual. He directed a commission to consider
a thorough reform of the Roman Breviary, with a view to eliminate material not
derived from the Bible and the early Fathers or based on 'apocryphal or doubtful

facts'. The work was, however, never completed to his satisfaction. He also ordered a suitable reduction in the number of feast days. A further disposition regularized mixed marriages; yet another enjoined that there should be no interference with the rites of Eastern Christians in communion with Rome; it was essential, he declared, that they should all be Catholics but not necessarily Latins. He laid down more precise and liberal regulations for the examination of books by the Congregation of the Index, and its officers were instructed not to display excessive zeal in banning them. At the same time he did not hesitate to take a firm line when necessary, to proscribe the works of his admirer Voltaire and to reiterate his predecessor's condemnation of the rapidly proliferating Freemasonry. Rather less sternly he warned the French Jansenists and their supporters in the Parlements that the rules of *Unigenitus* were still in force and must be observed. While respecting the sincerity of genuine Jansenists, he was aware that anti-clerical enthusiasm for the movement was largely tactical and political. A more radically dangerous assault on the Church was already being launched by the deists and unbelievers of the *Encyclopédie*, publication of which began in 1751 and continued until 1780.

The Rome of Benedict XIV aspired to be the intellectual capital of Catholic Europe, the rival of free-thinking Paris and heretic London. His lively example, and the forty years of peace that Italy and the papal state were to enjoy from 1748 onwards, gave a very real impulse to scholarship and the arts. The Pope lavished special care on the universities of Rome and Bologna. At the former he founded chairs of mathematics, physics and chemistry; in the latter he established a chair of surgery and an institute of anatomy, as well as two professorships, of mathematics and philosophy, to which he appointed women. Finally he endowed it with his own splendid library. He greatly expanded the Vatican Library and brought in a company of distinguished scholars to catalogue the manuscripts and arrange the archives. Among them was Muratori, the former Ambrosian librarian from Milan and Italy's leading scientific historian. He enriched the Capitoline Museum with classical sculpture and founded a new academy and gallery for the encouragement of contemporary art. In this atmosphere Winckelmann began to write his history of ancient art, and before long Gibbon was to conceive his equally monumental work.

Benedict died at 83, genial and witty to the last. In the words of a German Catholic historian, he was a 'great, harmonious Christian personality'. But although he had rescued the Church from collapse new and grave dangers were building up. In the last years of his pontificate the anti-clerical guns were already trained on the Society of Jesus, and both Clement XIII (1758–69) and Clement XIV (1769–74) were to be deeply involved in the crisis that led to its disbandment. As the most vocal champions of the Church and its most skilful controversialists, the Jesuits should have been able to rely on the fullest measure of papal protection, but ever since its foundation the Society's air of intellectual superiority and independent exclusiveness had aroused the jealousy of other Orders and of secular churchmen. It had also irritated various pontiffs. More recently the supposed relativity of its moral teachings had exposed it to sarcastic criticism from laymen and clergy alike. Benedict had been uneasily watching the growth of this antagonism, which was needless to say, sedulously fostered by anti-Catholic writers and sympathizers with Jansenism.

Strangely enough the storm which swept away the Jesuits broke in staunchly devout Portugal and was provoked by events in far-away Paraguay. The Jesuit 'reductions' among the Guarani Indians were a brilliantly successful example, in social and economic terms, of what missionary endeavour ought to be. It so happened, however, that as a result of frontier modifications between Spanish Paraguay and Portuguese Brazil a number of prosperous Indian settlements controlled by the Jesuits and carefully guarded by them against exploitation were uprooted by the Portuguese. When the Indians resisted expulsion into the jungle the Jesuits were accused of inciting them to rebellion. Alternatively they were charged with squeezing excessive profits out of their colonial plantations. In the hope of disarming these attacks Benedict appointed Cardinal Saldanha to carry out a Visitation of the Jesuits in Portugal. This was a mistake, because this Portuguese prelate combined with Pombal, the King's minister and the most rabid anti-papalist of all the servants of contemporary absolutisms, to hound the Society out of the country altogether. By that time Benedict was dead and Clement XIII (1758–69) had become Pope. He was a well-meaning Venetian called Carlo della Torre Rezzonico, Bishop of Padua. Although resolute in his defence of the Jesuits, he did not possess the same personal authority or statecraft as Benedict. Nor could he avoid a damaging head-on clash with Pombal. The minister took advantage of an attempt to assassinate his sovereign to blame it on the Jesuits. Indicted for conspiracy, they were all imprisoned or expelled and their property confiscated. When the Nuncio protested he too was expelled. With revolting hypocrisy Pombal had one Jesuit father burned for heresy.

It would have been impossible in such conditions for Clement to sustain Benedict's policy of flexible response even if he had so wished. The provocation was too gross. Moreover he was too honest simply to throw the Jesuits to the wolves. He was therefore forced to endure a long series of humiliations for which there was no remedy. One after another the Bourbon monarchies joined, some gleefully, in the game of Pope-bating. France, which was full of grudges against the Order, led the way. Free-thinkers resented its influence in education and the Parlements affected to regard it as a state within the state. Such straightforward issues were brought to a head by a complicated and typically French politico-financial *affaire* which caused much excitement. Father Lavalette, procurator of Jesuit missions in the West Indies, had been running a lucrative plantation business as a sideline. It was however ruined by British naval operations during the Seven Years War (1756–63) and went bankrupt to the tune of 1½ million *livres*. When the competent courts pronounced the Society as a whole responsible for his debts it refused to pay on the ground that Lavalette had been expelled from its ranks for improper conduct. The Jesuits then imprudently appealed to the Parlement of Paris, which not only endorsed the judgement and declared the Order's assets to be liable to confiscation, but forbade it to teach and to accept novices pending a review of its constitutions. A compromise proposed by the royal government, according to which the Order in France would be directed by a Vicar-General independently of Rome, was rejected by the Pope in the phrase '*Sint ut sunt aut non sint*' (let them be as they are or not at all). The government did not therefore object when the Parlement, in 1762, declared the Order to be dissolved and banished from France. It predictably ignored the Pope's rejoinder nullifying its acts, and two years later the government formally ratified them. Clement's response was a Bull stiffly denouncing all attacks on the Society and extolling its merits, which only served to irritate its enemies still further. Even his intimate advisers said that he might have been wiser to appoint his own apostolic commission of enquiry into its purposes and activities, a measure which could conceivably have stopped the rot.

As it was the next blow was struck in 1767 by Charles III of Spain (formerly of Naples) and his minister Aranda, a statesman of the same persuasion as Pombal and Tanucci. On the trumped-up charge that they had provoked a riot in Madrid, the Jesuits were rounded up and deported to Italy. Similar action was taken against them throughout the Spanish Empire. In 1768 King Ferdinand of Naples and Tanucci followed suit, and so did the Duke of Parma (the King of Spain's nephew) and his French minister du Tillot. Thus all the Bourbon princes, whether impelled by their own absolutism or by the prejudices of their advisers, had joined in slighting the Holy See in the most high-handed fashion. By this time Clement had become thoroughly rattled and in his distress committed several errors. One was to delay the admission of the Jesuit exiles to papal territory until they suffered severe hardships at sea or from being dumped in Corsica. A worse misjudgement was to threaten the clergy and people of Parma with excommunication if they carried out du Tillot's orders. This gave the Bourbon powers a pretext for united action. Not for the first time the French occupied Avignon and the Comtat, the Neapolitans Benevento and Pontecorvo. Finally they presented a joint note to the Pope flatly demanding the dissolution of the entire Jesuit Order. This final humiliation was too much for Clement; he died of a stroke on 2 February 1769.

Whatever view is taken of Jesuit shortcomings, the Pope had been undoubtedly treated with outrageous lack of consideration by the absolutist monarchies, all of which were destined to collapse in the next generation. Clement XIV (1769-74) inherited a dispiriting situation. The Conclave which elected him met under heavy pressure from the Bourbon envoys. It was also attended, however, by no less a potentate than Joseph II, since 1765 Emperor and co-regent with his mother Maria Theresa. Though himself a doctrinaire and even archetypal enlightened despot, he had been shocked by the crude bullying to which Clement XIII had been subjected. Nevertheless he sought to secure by tactful lobbying that the next Pope would adopt a less unbending attitude towards the sovereigns over the future of the Jesuits and the problems of Church-State relations. He was satisfied when the choice fell on Cardinal Lorenzo Ganganelli, but there are no grounds for supposing that, as has sometimes been alleged, the latter was persuaded to give a written undertaking that he would abolish the Society of Jesus.

Ganganelli was a comparatively obscure member of the Sacred College. The son of a doctor from Rimini, he had entered the Franciscan Order at an early age and spent most of his life either teaching or as a consultor of the Inquisition. He was unversed in politics and had taken no part in the battles waged for or against the Jesuits. Since he kept his own counsel in a Rome humming with intrigue, he was accused of being secretive and devious. His hesitations, which he spun out for over three years, are more likely to have been due to inexperience and honest perplexity. As a Franciscan he was not in principle well-disposed towards the Jesuits, but he was not prepared to bow to demands for their condemnation before making up his own mind whether they deserved it. Meanwhile he refused either to think aloud or to be frightened by the unremitting pressure from the Bourbon courts, cleverly orchestrated by the French Ambassador, Cardinal de Bernis. In order to placate the sovereigns he made them minor concessions, corresponded with them personally and sanctioned a number of measures restricting Jesuit operations in the few regions from which they had not already been excluded. Despite furious threats from Spain he was still temporizing at the end of 1772. At last he declared himself ready to consider a draft Brief for the suppression of the Society, but he was unwilling to proceed further unless Maria Theresia agreed that it should apply to her dominions.

Only when the Empress tossed the responsibility back to him, saying that she would not object if he believed that such action would be salutary, did he consent to sign the Brief with every sign of distaste. It was dated 21 July 1773.

The document, *Dominus ac Redemptor*, was a Brief, not a Bull; in other words a simple disciplinary measure. Even so, as befitting a decision affecting the lives of 20,000 men, it contained a long moral and historical apologia making it clear that Clement was acting with deep regret and misgiving. It explained that the Society, which had rendered such splendid services in the past and particularly in the Counter-Reformation, had outlived its usefulness and become a source of discord between Catholics. The time had now come for it to disappear, in the same way as other Orders had been suppressed in the past. Although it was true that Jesuit activities had lately been crippled by State action, these excuses failed to conceal the fact that the dissolution of the Society was a notable triumph for an Enlightenment which was consciously or unconsciously undermining not only religion but monarchy. It was the severest possible defeat for the papacy and was interpreted as such. As for the ex-Jesuits, they were scattered or went to ground. Some became ordinary priests, others were absorbed into civil life. A few favoured ones were given employment by the Protestant King of Prussia and the Orthodox Empress of Russia. In the papal state they were badly treated. Their former General, Ricci, was incarcerated in Sant' Angelo till his death in 1775. They revenged themselves by spreading slander and ridicule about the Pope. He himself died a year before the General, possibly from the effects of mercury in a medicine he took for a skin disease. Naturally many Romans assumed that the Jesuits had poisoned him.

The two Clements had been hounded into the grave by the Bourbons. In the course of the longest pontificate in history since that of St Peter their successor Pius VI (1775–99) suffered similar but more directly brutal treatment at the hands of French republicans. For the first fourteen years of his reign, however, until the French Revolution struck, Rome enjoyed an Indian summer. The smooth tenor of the Pope's life, so rudely disturbed by the Jesuit crisis, was resumed on the election of Cardinal Gianangelo Braschi, a genial nobleman from Cesena in the Romagna. The new pontiff was no outstanding churchman. Yet his piety, tact and undoubted devotion to his office attracted the sympathy of all for whom the papacy's charisma transcended its recent rebuffs. He presided with urbane dignity over the ceremonial functions of the Roman year. The city overflowed as never before with distinguished visitors eager to catch a glimpse of the Pope or receive a benevolent word from him. Goethe, who saw him officiating in the Palatine chapel in 1786, remarked on his imposing presence. Artistic activity, typified by Canova and Piranesi, had never been so lively in the pre-revolutionary period. Pius built the sacristy of St Peter's and completed the Vatican Museum which his predecessor, undeterred by his political tribulations, had somehow found time to inaugurate. He re-erected three more Egyptian obelisks. As a temporal sovereign he busied himself with draining the Pontine marshes, a project which had baffled engineers since the time of the Caesars, and with improving the roads in the papal state.

He could do nothing to ease the numbing grip which the Bourbon sovereigns had fastened on the national churches of the Latin countries, and it was but a small consolation that their troops were removed from papal territory. A parallel anxiety was the secularizing policy pursued by the Emperor Joseph II after the death of his mother in 1780. Joseph had a very clear conception of the future role of the Church in his hereditary lands. He was not anti-religious nor inspired by an aversion for the Church as such, but he was sure that the authority of the State, as represented by his enlightened self, must in no way be hampered by interference from Rome. He resented papal control of the episcopate through nuncios and considered that the whole ecclesiastical establishment ought to be thinned and reformed. It had indeed become torpid and top-heavy, especially in the sense that the monasteries were grossly overmanned. He proposed to get rid of the contemplative Orders altogether and as a start 1,300 out of 2,000 religious houses were dissolved. As for the secular clergy, his idea was that young priests should be trained in a restricted number of seminaries supervised by the State and offering a modern, liberal education as well as studies in theology and canon law. He proceeded to put these principles into effect. What is more, he issued in 1781 a Patent of Tolerance which, while safeguarding the privileged position of the Roman Catholic Church, extended limited freedom of worship and civic opportunity to his Protestant and Orthodox subjects.

Joseph had probably been stimulated by a challenge to papal authority from another quarter. It was contained in a book published in 1763, under the pseudonym of Febronius, by Nicholas von Hontheim, auxiliary bishop of Trier. In terms which harked back to the Council of Constance, the author attacked the monarchical element in papal rule. He argued that the Pope's primacy was only an honorary distinction and the symbol of Christian unity, whereas the reality of power, as in the early Church, properly belonged to the General Council. If the Pope would abandon his plenitude of power he would open the way to the Protestant return to the fold. He advocated the formation of national episcopal synods—and particularly of one or more for Germany—which would draw up a statute explicitly limiting the Pope's powers. The work was immediately condemned by Clement XIII, but by the time it had been disavowed by Hontheim himself under pressure from Pius, his views had attracted wide support for a system of national churches loosely presided over by the Bishop of Rome. Their appeal, as well as Joseph's secularizing measures, were very much in the Pope's mind when, in 1782, he decided to travel to Vienna and thrash out these crucial questions with the Emperor.

Such an initiative had no precedent in recent times. In the Middle Ages and earlier many Popes had undertaken the arduous crossing of the Alps. They had also moved restlessly about Italy, especially when Rome had become too hot for them. From time to time they had been obliged to flee for their lives from the city. Then came the period of exile and return. But since the Reformation no Pope had left Italy and journeys outside Rome, except to nearby summer retreats, had become very rare. Surprised by the Pope's decision, Joseph sent his Vice-Chancellor, Cobenzl, to escort him on his journey and to find out, if possible, what he expected to achieve by it. While determined not to abandon any part of his programme he himself hoped to convince Pius of his devotion to the Catholic faith and of his sincere belief that the Church stood to benefit from his reforms in the long run. The Pope arrived in Vienna just before Easter. He was received with the utmost deference and lodged splendidly in the Hofburg. His long private talks with the Emperor alternated with gorgeous Masses and public ceremonies in which his impressive stature and bearing aroused huge enthusiasm among the tens of thousands who thronged to see him. There was no doubt of the veneration that ordinary Austrians, and to an even greater extent Hungarians, felt for his person. But it was soon evident that he would not be able to extract any real concessions from Joseph and his ministers. Although he may have concluded that reform would not be allowed to grow more radical, there was obviously no possibility of reconciling his basic principle with the Emperor's. No pontiff could admit the right of the State to direct the religious life of a Catholic people and in Joseph's State no activity, religious or otherwise, could be allowed to elude secular direction. Thus, after weeks of solemn fencing, the two parted amid assurances of mutual esteem.

Pius did not return immediately to Rome. He went on to Bavaria at the instance of its ruler, the Elector Charles-Theodore. There his visit turned into a triumphal progress. Popular fervour exceeded that already manifested in Austria; evidently the religious indifference affected by the upper and intellectual classes throughout Europe was not echoed by the German peasantry. Loyalty to Rome was more conspicuous by the Danube than in the Latin countries, and the Pope was therefore not entirely disheartened by the impressions gained on his tour. In December 1783 he received a formal return visit from the Emperor. No serious business was transacted and their relations remained on a basis of wary friendship. The Pope's reaction against the Febronian offensive seemed to have had some effect. The following years passed quietly enough at Rome, but not without occasional pin-pricks from the same quarter. Scipione Ricci, bishop of Pistoia and nephew of the defunct General of the Jesuits, promoted a local synod in Tuscany under the protection of its Grand Duke Leopold, the Emperor's brother, for the purpose of spreading anti-papal prejudice in Italy, but the populace repudiated him and burned his palace. Then, at a congress held at Ems in 1786, four leading German Archbishops drew up resolutions which, if not forgotten in the turmoil of the French Revolution, might have resulted in the creation of a German national Catholic Church in virtual independence of Rome. But such skirmishes lost interest when, in May 1789, the States General of France were summoned to meet at Versailles.

Pius VI, perhaps the most exalted victim of the Revolution, was done to death by slow stages. His murder took ten years to accomplish, but was murder just the same and a cynical crime. Incongruously enough, the Revolution began with a Mass and a religious procession through the streets of Versailles. When the three Estates comprising the States General of the Kingdom met separately in May 1789, the representatives of the clergy numbered 308, of whom one third were bishops and abbots, as against 285 noblemen and 621 delegates of the Third Estate. By early July, however, they were merged willy-nilly in one National Assembly. From that moment the historical Gallican Church was rapidly reduced to ruin. First the episcopate, under heavy pressure, renounced its feudal privileges; then the Church was deprived of its tithes, that is to say of two-fifths of its income; thirdly, on the proposal of Talleyrand, bishop of Autun, the Assembly voted to nationalize all Church lands and to sell them for the benefit of the nation, subject to provision being made for the maintenance of the clergy. These measures had been put into force by the end of 1789. Early in 1790 the religious Orders were totally suppressed and the secular clergy reduced to the level of one priest for 6,000 persons. Finally the Civil Constitution of the clergy, voted in July 1790 and approved with the utmost reluctance by King Louis XVI, traced the future form of a new national French Church, dependent on the State and removed, so far as its organization and discipline were concerned, from the authority of Rome. It received a new and stiffly logical structure; there were to be ten metropolitans for the whole country and one bishop for each civil department; all bishops and priests were to be chosen by the lay electorate and paid out of a public fund. As for their relationship to the Pope, it was to be confined to a mere declaration of loyalty to the Catholic faith, to its doctrines and forms of worship.

The Constitution was the work of inveterate anti-clericals and extreme Jansenists. It effectively abolished the papal rights guaranteed by the Concordat of 1515 and for that reason alone was anathema to the Holy See. Of course it had further and more sinister implications. Yet the Pope did not immediately denounce it publicly. For the time being he simply warned the anguished King that in sanctioning it he risked leading France into error and heresy. The Curia judged, correctly as it turned out, that so artificial a creation would not work; it would not be accepted by the French clergy and people and might well collapse without any intervention from Rome. In fact the clergy protested vehemently against the Constitution and riots broke out in the south. The assembly then demanded that all ecclesiastics should take an oath to uphold it and the King was forced to sign a decree compelling them to do so. The result was confusion and schism. Only six bishops (Talleyrand, three other holders of sees and two *in partibus infidelium* consented to take the oath and 128 were deprived of their sees. 55 per cent of the lower clergy had refused the oath even before two papal Briefs, issued in March and April 1791, had condemned the Constitution as schismatic. Priests started to emigrate *en masse* and such non-jurors as remained lost their livings. In short the Gallican Church had split in two, the official Church sponsored by free-thinkers and an unofficial, much larger but persecuted body of believers operating in semi-clandestine conditions. True Catholics could give no allegiance to an episcopate whose new members had to be consecrated in droves by the loose-living sceptic Talleyrand and which was headed, as Archbishop of Paris, by the obscure Gobel, formerly Bishop *in partibus* of Lydda. When they went to Mass it was to one celebrated privately by a non-juring priest; the churches, now state property, tended to be bare of faithful.

The Pope was right in thinking that the grotesque Church invented by the agnostics would soon founder. But he was mistaken if he supposed that its failure would lead to a restoration of something like the old order. No one at Rome or anywhere in Europe foresaw that the disappearance of royal and ecclesiastical authority would quickly result in the eclipse of civilized values in France, or that it would be soon followed by a dictatorial reign of terror and twenty years of almost continuous war. Even when the Republic was set up in 1792 the most prescient of observers could hardly have imagined that it would come close to abolishing religion altogether in its homeland or that it would shortly impose its irreligious rule by force of arms at the very heart of the papacy.

The Pope remained a horrified spectator of the excesses that marked the first years of the first French Republic. They included the butchery of priests, the plunder and desecration of churches and their use for the ridiculous festivals of Reason and of Robespierre's Supreme Being. Persecution was eased after Robespierre's fall in 1794 but very sharply renewed between 1797 and 1799. Meanwhile Pius, in his role of temporal sovereign, was the most prominent survivor of the Catholic rulers of the old eighteenth-century Europe. The Bourbons were dead or in their dotage. Of the Habsburgs, Joseph II had died in 1790 and his brother, Leopold II, in 1792; and now that Austria was locked in a seemingly interminable war with the French Republic Josephite ideas on Church matters had lost their appeal. In such circumstances it was inevitable that the Holy See should give moral and political, if not military, support to any European coalition formed against France and of which Austria was the centrepiece. Thus the papal government became a natural target for French enmity, and as from 1792 Rome was troubled by subversive republican agitation. This was by no means well received by the populace. In 1793, Bassville, a secretary of the French embassy, lost his life in a riot. His government demanded compensation, but it was still unpaid in 1796 when Napoleon Bonaparte, the general of the French Directory, launched his series of shattering campaigns against the Austrians in Lombardy.

As soon as he had wrested Milan from the Austrians he held the papal state at his mercy. His orders from the Directory were to liquidate the 'centre of fanaticism', but so long as there was still an Austrian army in Lombardy he preferred, for sound military reasons, merely to seize the Legations (Ravenna, Bologna and Ferrara) and to conclude a highly advantageous armistice with the Holy See. It gave him the right to retain the Legations, to place a garrison in Ancona and to make use of the other papal ports. It also extracted from the papal government an indemnity of 21 million *scudi*, together with five hundred ancient manuscripts and one hundred choice works of art from the papal collections. Barefaced pillage was an avowed aim of the republican liberators. When the expulsion of the Austrians had been completed a few months later, Bonaparte dictated to the Pope the Treaty of Tolentino (February 1797). Pius was required to cede Avignon and the Comtat to France and the Legations to the French-sponsored Cisalpine Republic, to pay another 15 million *scudi* and to submit to the removal of further cargoes of artistic treasures. His brother Joseph was sent to Rome as Ambassador with instructions to prepare for the extinction of papal rule and its replacement by a satellite Roman Republic.

At the end of the year Joseph and his prospective brother-in-law, General Duphot, were ready to provoke the necessary incident. It did not, however, work out exactly as planned. While Duphot was encouraging pro-French demonstrators to proclaim a Republic, they were fired on by papal troops and Duphot was killed. Brushing aside the Curia's apologies, Joseph Bonaparte left Rome and General Berthier, Napoleon's future Chief of Staff, was ordered to occupy the city, to remove the Pope and to set up a Republic. On 15 February, the twenty-third anniversary of Pius's election, the French marched in and installed their puppet government. A tree of liberty was triumphantly planted on the Capitol. The few Cardinals who had been present at the Mass of celebration in St Peter's were placed under arrest.

The Pope was first told that he might stay in Rome as its Bishop but not as temporal ruler; later, on 17 February, General Haller, the officer deputed to deal with him, informed him brusquely that he must leave for Tuscany within three days. When he replied that he would neither abandon Rome nor the Church, Haller resorted to threats and crude intimidation. Pius calmly kept him at bay, refusing to hand over the Fisherman's Ring which the General tried to snatch. His bearing was so courageous that even the Spanish Ambassador Azarea, an atheist who had consistently played the French game, expressed admiration for his behaviour. He managed to appoint a special Congregation headed by Cardinal Antonelli, to exercise his powers during his absence. But before dawn on 20 February the half-paralysed octogenarian, accompanied by only two junior clerics and a doctor, was hustled into a travelling carriage and escorted by dragoons as far as the highway to Siena. Crowds were already kneeling in the rain to watch him pass.

The journey to Siena (in the territory of the Grand Duchy of Tuscany) took five days. Heavy snow was falling on the road. At each stage the exhausted Pope had to be lifted painfully from his carriage. On arrival he was received by the Archbishop, Zondadari, and lodged in the Augustinian convent. It had originally been assumed that he would stay at Florence, but the Grand-Duke Ferdinand, who quite rightly suspected that the French were looking for an excuse to depose him, was anxious to keep the controversial person of the Pope at a distance from his capital. At Siena, where he remained for over three months, his health gradually improved and he was able to organize, under the noses of French spies, a correspondence with Antonelli and other dispersed members of the Sacred College and the Curia. Several Cardinals came to visit him and he was soon the centre of a small but lively court. Every day he drove out, accompanied by the Archbishop, and showed himself to the people. The news that reached him from Rome was shocking; it was being systematically pillaged and vandalized, just as Greece had been treated in ancient times by Roman republican generals. Loads of treasures stolen from the Vatican, the churches, the museums, private palaces and libraries, were being despatched by French commissioners to Paris. He was also worried by the problem of the next papal election; he could not expect to live much longer and there did not seem to be any place in Italy where a Conclave could assemble in freedom from French interference.

His sojourn in Siena was interrupted, at the end of May, by a succession of alarming earthquakes. They occurred when the French were already hoping to relegate him to Sardinia, and there was also a less unattractive proposal to convey him to Spain. But as his health had taken a turn for the worse, he was transferred only as far as the Carthusian monastery at Florence. There he found himself under much stricter supervision. During the winter of 1798 he became so weak that he frequently seemed at the point of death. Nevertheless the Directory continued to insist that he should be sent to Sardinia and the order for his departure was only averted for a short time by the objections of his doctors. But in the spring of 1799 the French domination of Italy was seriously threatened. Bonaparte was far away in Egypt; anti-republican revolts, largely instigated by Archbishop Zondadari, broke out in central Italy and the French hold on Rome and Naples (where a 'Parthenopean' republic had been temporarily installed) seemed very precarious. Austria was again the field, this time supported by Russia. The Directory decided that the Pope must again be moved, if necessary to France. So at the end of March, when French troops seized Florence and suppressed the Grand Duchy, Pius was ordered to travel to an unknown destination.

His last journey to his death was an excruciating ordeal, recalling that of Pope Vigilius after his summons from Rome to Constantinople. It must be supposed that the Directory genuinely feared that, if left in Italy, he would serve as a rallying point for political reaction and anti-French nationalism. Otherwise it is hard to account for their consistently inhuman treatment of this mild and cultured old gentleman. He bore his sufferings and humiliations with exemplary fortitude, uncomplaining forbearance and all the dignity of a pontiff. He was very ill when he left Florence on 28 March; his paralysis was becoming general and he was conveyed across the Apennines in a state of coma. At Bologna he recovered sufficiently to be transported through Modena, where he was insulted by republicans, and Reggio to Parma, where vast crowds acclaimed him. But he was not permitted to rest there for long, as the French were yielding to the Austro-Russian thrust. He was made to leave Parma on 14 April and to spend another exhausting fortnight on the road, among floods and military alarms, before reaching the French frontier. He passed through Piacenza, Alessandria and Turin. At Susa he was told that his destination would not be Grenoble, as he had hoped, but the bleak Alpine townlet of Briançon. In order to reach it he had to cross the very rough pass of the Mont-Genèvre, which was partly blocked by snow and in any case impassable for wheeled traffic. Semi-conscious, in the freezing cold, he was carried in a litter by relays of bearers. Various Popes had crossed the Alps in troublous times, but none in such ghastly conditions.

From Briançon the small band of ecclesiastics who had accompanied Pius from Italy was separated from him and sent to Grenoble. Only his confessor, a physician and two servants were left. At the beginning of June, however, the authorities relented and he was able to rejoin his suite. The *citoyen pape* was even allowed to stay with a ci-devant aristocrat in her château. Finally, on 14 July he reached Valence on the Rhône, his last resting place. There he was lodged under strict guard in a commodious but rather tumbledown building called the Hôtel du Gouvernement. He was now effectively cut off from the Catholic world and prevented from attending to Church business. Although he was obviously dying, the authorities would not leave him in peace; they were constantly threatening to remove him to Dijon. He survived for six weeks, agonizing but lucid. Labrador, the former Spanish Ambassador at Rome, who was with him all the time, testified that he retained his faculties to the end, praising his 'superhuman constancy' and 'unchangeable serenity'.

20

REACTION AND REVOLUTION
(1800–1846)

When the moment at last came to elect a successor to Pius VI the French had been driven out of Italy. The Cardinals were nevertheless unwilling to hold the Conclave in Rome. It had suffered too much from the French and was now occupied by the Neopolitans. Some members of the College had already taken refuge in Venice which, together with the Legations, was in Austrian hands. Indeed the Venetian Republic, recently suppressed by Bonaparte, would never be revived. Venice was the obvious meeting place and it was there that, with the blessing of the Emperor Francis II, thirty-four Cardinals assembled in November 1799 at the island monastery of San Giorgio.

It was a difficult Conclave. The Austrians were anxious to secure the elevation of a Pope who would not oppose their political and military plans for northern Italy. In particular they wished to keep the Legations, which Pius VI had been obliged to cede to the puppet Cisalpine Republic, and not to give them back to the Holy See. Most of the Cardinals, on the other hand, still regarded them as an integral and all-important part of the papal state. They therefore blocked the choice of any candidate likely to prove subservient to Vienna. Eventually the requisite majority was obtained for Barnaba Chiaramonti, Bishop of Imola. He could, it was hoped, be relied upon to defend the vital interests, both spiritual and temporal, of the papacy without needlessly irritating the Austrians. In the former respect they were not disappointed, although it was Napoleon, and not the colourless Francis, whom the new Pope was fated to confront. But his first act was to refuse an invitation to Vienna. The Emperor manifested his annoyance by denying him the use of St Mark's for his coronation, which accordingly took place in the cramped precincts of San Giorgio Maggiore, and by packing him off to the Adriatic port of Pesaro on a leaky and ill-provisioned frigate. He and his suite were storm-tossed for twelve days. Such pinpricks, however, he could afford to ignore.

Pius VII (1800–1823) came like his predecessor from Cesena and they had for long been close friends. He was neither quarrelsome nor intransigent. At Imola he had tried to collaborate with the Cisalpine government on the assumption that a man could not be a good democrat without first being a good Catholic. On the contrary he was gentle, patient and imperturbable, but when he came to uphold the basic claims and rights of the Church against Napoleon, he did so with rare fortitude and determination. Although he could make bad mistakes under pressure and when deprived of the help of advisers, he displayed considerable diplomatic skill. He was sustained through years of difficulties and hardships by his simple and profound piety.

Before reaching Rome and establishing himself in the Quirinal palace he heard that Bonaparte, now Consul of the Republic and master of France by the *coup d'état* of Brumaire, had crushed the Austrians at Marengo. The French were once again the overlords of Italy and he faced, like Pius VI, the prospect of deposition and exile. But when Bonaparte took the initiative it was directed towards a settlement. Very soon the Pope received through the Cardinal-bishop of Vercelli a message informing him that the First Consul would welcome negotiations for a new Concordat and hinting that if agreement could be reached the Holy See might recover its lost territories. It also sketched terms which might form the basis of such agreement.

Pius felt immensely relieved by this news, although his joy was tempered with caution. Instead of being bullied he was being invited to negotiate as an equal and offered a real chance of reuniting France with the Church. After discussion with his Secretary of State, Cardinal Consalvi, he appointed Monsignor Spina, one of the ecclesiastics who had accompanied Pius VI on his last journey, as his negotiator and sent him off to Vercelli. As soon as he arrived there Bonaparte summoned him to Paris.

The First Consul's overtures were of course inspired by his own Caesar-like ambitions. If he was to be the sole ruler of France, he needed the allegiance of the silent mass of French people who had never ceased to be Catholics and were sick of the official republican godlessness affected by the Directory. He sensed that the country was in sympathy with the reaction that was about to be so eloquently voiced in Chateaubriand's *Génie du christianisme*. He knew that the Constitutional Church was incapable of fulfilling the popular need. At the same time he was resolved that the settlement should leave the State, as represented, by himself, in unchallenged control. In brief, his conception of the proper relationship between the French revolutionary State, soon to be converted into an autocracy, and a revived Gallican Church was an advanced form of Josephism.

The substantive negotiations were conducted between Spina and the Abbé Bernier, a former non-juring priest won over to republicanism. They lasted for many weeks in the winter of 1801–2 and an agreed draft was not ready for consideration until the end of February. Some of the issues proved very vexatious. From the papal point of view it was heartening that Roman Catholicism should be proclaimed as the official, or at least the semi-official, religion of France; on the other hand it was irksome to recognize the confiscation of Church lands as irrevocable. It sounded perfectly logical that all existing bishops, both constitutionalists on the spot and absent traditionalists, should resign their sees at the Pope's or the government's request, pending the redrawing of dioceses, the nomination of their occupants by the State and their investment by the Pope; but what kind of successors would Bonaparte select? The Curia was deeply worried by these and other questions. In June, when papal acceptance of the draft was still not forthcoming, the First Consul threatened military action unless it was given within five days. He also convoked a national convention of constitutional clergy. But the French envoy in Rome, Cacault, averted a crisis by insisting that Consalvi should hurry to Paris and resume discussions. The Cardinal proved to be a supremely able diplomat. Unruffled by pressure from the First Consul and Talleyrand, he managed to secure a redraft which he was confident that Pius and the Sacred College would accept. The Concordat was accordingly signed on 15 July and Consalvi rushed back to Rome to obtain the Pope's ratification. This done, Bonaparte ratified too on 8 September.

So far Pius was well pleased, but he had hardly issued all the necessary Bulls when Bonaparte gave him a shock by publishing 77 'Organic Articles' by which the

The coronation of Charles V by Pope Clement VII

Bronze bust of Clement VII, from the façade of the cathedral at Ferrara

The Lateran Palace

Inside the Basilica of St John Lateran

The Pantheon, plundered by the Barberini

The Council of Trent (1545)

Sant' Angelo, originally Hadrian's mausoleum

concessions made to the Church were unilaterally circumscribed and to some extent negated by detailed police regulations. In the Pope's estimation he stood convicted of bad faith. Nevertheless it would have been far too risky for Pius to denounce the Concordat. Instead he swallowed his disappointment and reluctantly concluded another with Bonaparte's Italian satellite, the Cisalpine Republic. Again, after agreement had been reached on a fairly satisfactory text, it was disadvantageously modified by a unilateral decree of Cisalpine government. It was also galling that for the purposes of the Concordat the Republic was held to include the Legations, which the Holy See continued to claim as part of the papal state. Many points of friction still troubled the relationship between Pope and First Consul when it was suddenly announced, in May 1804, that the latter had been transformed into Napoleon, Emperor of the French. Consequentially and according to mediaeval precedent he was due to become King of Italy as well.

It was at once intimated to the Pope through Cardinal Caprara, his weak and not very intelligent legate in Paris, and Cardinal Fesch, Napoleon's uncle and envoy in Rome, that he was expected to crown the new Emperor in Notre Dame. Although the demand was fraught with potential embarrassments, Pius felt that he could hardly refuse it. So did the majority of the Sacred College, despite objections that compliance would give intolerable offence to Austria. Some thought that the Pope should insist on real concessions in return. But no such assurance accompanied Napoleon's official invitation when it was received in September and Pius accepted it without demur. As if to emphasize the contrast between his own progress and that of Pius VI, he set out in considerable state. Escorted by six Cardinals, one of whom died en route, he crossed the Alps by the Mont Cenis. Historically minded persons recalled that over a thousand years had passed since Pope Stephen II had undertaken a similar journey to crown Pepin, the father of Charlemagne.

Napoleon, for his part, had made up his mind to treat the Pope with respect but without excessive deference. He intended to demonstrate to his subjects that he, the Emperor, was superior to the Pope, and that the latter was performing, at his behest, the function of an exalted chaplain. As the Pope's cortège approached Fontaine-bleau he was surprised to encounter Napoleon, who explained that he happened to be hunting in the forest. But unlike the Bourbons he was not a devotee of the chase. He merely wished not to be seen in public greeting the Pope in a manner suggesting that he was according him precedence. They drove together to Paris in the Pope's coach, with the latter sitting in the place of honour, but as they arrived at the Tuileries after dark this nuance went unperceived. When it transpired, however, that the pair had never been married in church he refused to crown Josephine unless they first went through a religious ceremony. Much to Napoleon's irritation, it had to be performed in a hurry by Fesch on the night before the coronation. On 2 December he snubbed the Pope in Notre Dame first by making him wait for an hour and then by placing the crowns himself on his own and his wife's head. In David's painting of the occasion the seated Pius wears an expression of tired irony.

Napoleon would now have liked to get rid of his visitor, but he stayed in Paris for another four months. They were not entirely wasted, for although he failed to obtain satisfaction over such crucial problems as the future of the Legations or a revision of the 'Organic Articles' he attracted much sympathy among the Parisians. He showed himself constantly in public and blessed happy throngs in the streets. His presence, which added stimulus to a growing Catholic revival, began to annoy the Emperor just as he was planning the invasion of England. At last he was edged out of Paris and returned to an anxious Curia. The Emperor followed him in May as far as Milan, where he had himself crowned by Caprara with the historic iron crown of Lombardy. The enactments which he then proceeded to make for the Italian Kingdom were uniformly disagreeable to the Holy See. One of them, the legalization of divorce according to the French Civil Code, was especially obnoxious. Papal protests, however, were contemptuously disregarded. The already uneasy relationship between Emperor and Pope steadily worsened, and the former's intentions were revealed by the policy of strangulation which he applied to the State of the Church.

First Ancona was seized on the grounds of military necessity. Next, after the battle of Austerlitz, Venice and Tuscany were added to the Kingdom of Italy and Joseph Bonaparte became King of Naples. Thus the shrunken papal territory was totally hemmed in by satellite states of the French Empire. Pius and his able Secretary of State, Consalvi, opposed a stiff but vain resistance to further encroachments, which included the occupation of Civita Vecchia and even Ostia. Neither side minced words. 'All Italy will be under my law,' wrote Napoleon, 'Your Holiness is sovereign of Rome but I am the Emperor.' Pius replied, 'You have been elected Emperor of the French, not of Rome. There exists no Emperor of Rome.' As a sop to Napoleon he removed Consalvi from office, but the Emperor responded by replacing Fesch by a virulent ex-republican called Alquier.

The extinction of the Pope's temporal power was delayed by Napoleon's preoccupation with his campaigns against Prussia and Russia and in Spain. However, Alquier continued to urge the Pope to accept for his remaining territory the status of a minor principality within a French dominated federation. His pressure was backed up by the annexation of Umbria and the Marches and finally, in February 1808, by the occupation of the city of Rome by General Miollis. Nevertheless the Pope told Alquier that the French might hack him to pieces or skin him alive without getting him to agree to any diminution of his sovereign rights.

For the next year and more the situation in Rome was extremely confused. The Pope, together with what was left of the Curia, had his seat in the Quirinal. Until 10 June 1809 he was still recognized as the nominal sovereign of the Patrimony of St Peter. His flag flew on Sant' Angelo, but it had become the French commander's headquarters. All papal troops, including the Swiss Guard, had been disbanded. The Cardinals had been forcibly dispersed; only a handful, headed by the new Secretary of State, Cardinal Pacca, remained at the Pope's side. But as from 10 June the Patrimony was annexed, Rome was declared a 'free imperial city' and the tricolour hoisted over Sant' Angelo. Pius, as Bishop of Rome, was isolated on sufferance in the Quirinal. As soon as the French coup had been completed he drew up a Bull excommunicating all those responsible for the sacrilege and Pacca, a fearless and devoted personality, caused copies to be affixed to the doors of the three great Roman basilicas. Miollis, who deplored theatrical interventions, sought to play down the crisis, but his deputy, General Radet, persuaded him that, pending precise orders from the Emperor, the Pope and Pacca should be arrested and removed temporarily to Florence. During the night of 5 July Radet staged a comic opera abduction. While he waited below in a coach with a cavalry escort, his men set scaling ladders against the walls of the Quirinal. They rushed in on the Pope as he was sitting fully robed in conference with Pacca and other clerics. He and the Cardinal were given half an hour to get ready. Then they were bundled, still robed, into Radet's coach and driven towards Tuscany. Pius VII was in no doubt that he was being intentionally handled in the same fashion as Pius VI.

His journey was not without incident. At Poggibonsi the coach was overturned and Radet was hurled into the road. Pius was unhurt, but his adventures during the next five years were to be nerve-wracking enough and at one point he nearly succumbed. So far as his immediate future was concerned the Emperor had given no instructions, but it was assumed that he should be taken to France. The authorities along the northward route were so fearful of imperial reactions that they refused to incur responsibility for harbouring the Pope. As it happened they included two of Napoleon's sisters, Elisa the Grand Duchess of Tuscany and Pauline who was married to Camillo Borghese, governor of the French departments that had once been Genoa and Piedmont. At Florence Pius was separated from Pacca, woken up at four o'clock in the morning and sped on his way. He was smuggled in the utmost secrecy past Genoa and Turin and over the Mont Cenis to Grenoble.

Napoleon was furious with Miollis and Radet. He would have much preferred to keep the Pope at Rome until he could bring him to submit to the role of chief bishop of a Napoleonic Church. Above all he did not want another martyr on his hands. After much hesitation he decided not to send him back to Rome, which would have been a confession of weakness, but to place him quickly out of reach of embarrassments at Savona. So, like a piece of luggage, Pius was deposited in this small town on the Italian riviera. It was no small consolation to him that on the road his former subjects of Avignon greeted him with fervid enthusiasm.

He was comfortably lodged and courteously treated by the local prefect. But he was at the same time totally isolated from the Church and the outside world. He had neither secretary nor confessor. Any letters he wrote had to be smuggled out by his valet and eventually he was deprived of paper and ink. Napoleon had decided to let him stew in his own juice. Meanwhile the papal establishment in Rome had been virtually liquidated. All members of the Sacred College, the heads of Orders, the papal archives, the pontifical seal and the Fisherman's Ring had been transferred to Paris. Rome, no longer a free imperial city, was reduced to an unimportant municipality in the French Empire.

Nevertheless Napoleon's problems were unsolved. How was he to govern a headless Church? How was he, an excommunicate, to obtain his freedom to marry Marie Louise, daughter of the Catholic Emperor of Austria? What if the Pope continued to refuse investiture of the new bishops nominated by himself? In the hope of getting round such difficulties he appointed an advisory committee composed of the more compliant ecclesiastics. Its answers, however, were not wholly palatable. While maintaining that the excommunication was not valid in France, and that the Pope was not justified in withholding investitures indefinitely, it also called for his liberation and recommended that the current impasse should be discussed by a national or, if necessary, a General Council of the Church. The Emperor thereupon dismissed his committee. An obedient ecclesiastical court agreed to annul his marriage to Josephine, but the twelve Cardinals faithful to the Pope pointedly absented themselves from his wedding to Marie Louise. At Savona Pius remained obstinately unmoved on two crucial matters; he would neither institute new bishops nor come to Paris as the head of a Napoleonic national Church. Through 1810 various emissaries vainly urged him to relax his intransigence.

In 1811, however, it seemed that his resistance was breaking down. His long confinement, his separation from Consalvi and Pacca and his declining health were affecting his judgement if not his resolution. Napoleon resumed his offensive by appointing a new committee. It also advocated a national Council. It further suggested that the latter should approve a new procedure by which, if the Pope withheld an investiture for over six months, the right to grant it should pass to the Metropolitan concerned. A deputation of three bishops presented this proposal to the Pope at Savona, and he hesitantly agreed to it, though not signing the paper in which it was set out. Consequently the Council, the members of which came from both France and Italy, declined to endorse it. They said that they needed evidence of its acceptance by the Pope, to whom they reaffirmed their loyalty. Momentarily baffled, Napoleon threw three of the recalcitrant bishops into prison and set to work to cajole or intimidate the rest. The result was that they held a final session in which they agreed to the proposal, now contained in a decree of the Council, subject to the Pope's approval. Another deputation descended on Savona and this time Pius gave in. He signed a Brief on the lines of the decree but excepting the bishoprics of the former papal state from the procedure. To the general surprise Napoleon objected to his proviso and as the Pope stubbornly insisted on it negotiations were broken off. While the Emperor prepared to invade Russia, Pius was granted an unexpected respite.

Before the Grand Army marched, however, the Emperor ordered the Pope's transfer to Fontainebleau. He was to travel with the utmost speed and in strict secrecy, disguised as a simple priest and passing through major towns at night. After two and a half days of arduous jolting he was put to bed, completely exhausted, in the Benedictine monastery on the Mont Cenis pass. Apart from fatigue he was very ill indeed with a urinary blockage. His escort, a Captain Lagorse, besought the Minister of Police by telegraph to allow him to rest and receive proper medical attention. But his arguments gained only three days. When the Minister insisted that he should continue his journey immediately the Pope called for the last sacrament. It was indeed a miracle that he survived the next four days of frenzied driving across France with no sleep. Fortunately a competent doctor was at his side. On arrival at Fontainebleau he retired to bed for many weeks and partly recovered his health.

Napoleon had evidently reckoned that after a quick and sensational victory in Russia he would be free to return promptly and tackle the captive Pope. In the event he did not reach Paris until December 1812 and another month went by before he appeared at Fontainebleau. Pius had already been living there for seven months, still segregated from all contacts except with the so-called 'Red' Cardinals (those whom the Emperor had won over) and French prelates who advised him to settle on Napoleon's terms. He was kept purposely in ignorance of the extent of the disasters the French had suffered in Russia. But Napoleon's determination to bend the Pope to his will had not been abated by his loss of half a million soldiers. Acting as his own negotiator and trading on the Pope's sense of abandonment, he manoeuvred him into accepting the main lines of yet another Concordat. The details remained to be worked out, but its principal features were the Pope's renunciation of his temporal power over Rome and his agreement to the investiture of his bishops by a Metropolitan after a six months' deadlock.

Napoleon was jubilant. As he prepared for the critical campaigns of 1813 he announced that he had the Pope on his side. But at the same time he imprudently relaxed the arrangements for his seclusion. Consequently the 'Black' Cardinals—Consalvi, Pacca and those who had consistently counselled resistance to Napoleon—established themselves in the palace of Fontainebleau and prevailed on Pius to revoke what he had conceded. They got him to write a letter to Napoleon pointing out that he had not signed a formal agreement but only the heads of articles which the Emperor had disingenuously published as a full-blown Concordat. He had acted, he said, out of human frailty and because he had been 'dragged to the table' by certain Cardinals.

The Emperor, locked in losing battles with the Allies, was in no position to react. His subsequent defeats led to the Pope's liberation. As soon as Pius was convinced that he was finished he avoided any further overtures. He was rewarded when, in January 1814, Lagorse was told to take him southwards on the first stage of what was to be his return to Rome and the resumption of all his spiritual and temporal authority. He accomplished his journey in comfort, at a leisurely pace and amid the acclamations of the populace wherever he passed. By February he had reached Savona. On his way through Italy, escorted by Austrian cavalry, he paused to give a gracious reception to Napoleon's dispossessed relatives, his mother, his brother Joseph, his uncle the Cardinal and his sister Elisa of Tuscany. On 24 March he entered Rome in triumph and paid his humble thanks to St Peter.

Pius's tenacious adherence to the principles of his office, his fortitude in standing up to Napoleon and the patient humility with which he had endured his sufferings had both enhanced his own prestige and greatly encouraged the current Catholic revival throughout Europe. In 1814, however, his position was not yet secure. Italy was in chaos. Much of it was controlled by Murat, Napoleon's cavalry leader and brother-in-law and King of Naples, and its future political shape was still under discussion at the Congress of Vienna. It was there that Consalvi, as Secretary of State, was fighting for the restoration of the temporal power. During the Hundred Days, when Napoleon regained France and Murat occupied Rome and all central Italy, the Pope was obliged to retire to Genoa. But by May 1815 Murat had been routed by the Austrians and Pius was back in the Quirinal. Meanwhile Consalvi's negotiating ability at Vienna had ensured the virtually complete reconstitution of the papal state, including the territory of the Legations south of the Po. All that he had to cede was Avignon with the Comtat.

That was indeed a notable success. Moreover it was achieved without subordinating the papacy to a resurgent Habsburg monarchy in firm possession of Lombardy-Venetia. The Holy See, which had recently witnessed with equanimity the extinction of the Holy Roman Empire, had no intention of associating itself with Metternich's Holy Alliance. While approving in general of the principle of legitimacy, it did not wish to be identified with a particular political system. So far as international groupings were concerned it remained uncommitted and wary of Austrian hegemony.

The Pope and his advisers were less inspired when dealing with the delicate problems posed by the re-imposition of ecclesiastical authority in the papal state. These were particularly acute in the Legations, where the French Civil Code had been in force since 1797 and the inhabitants did not take too kindly to the rule of priests. Consalvi introduced a centralized and partly secularized form of government which satisfied neither the extreme reactionaries in the Curia nor the local liberals or 'Jacobins' who had flourished under the previous regime. Consequently attitudes became polarized. Reawakened Catholic loyalties were being countered in turn by liberal distaste for the renewal of the old order. Reaction and counter-reaction assumed an ugly guise when organized Catholic partisans clashed with anti-clerical activists, members of secret societies. For the purposes of administration the whole papal state with its population of three million was divided into twenty-one districts, each governed by a Cardinal-legate or a delegate, also a churchman, and all former municipal and feudal liberties were abolished. It was thus ruled by a mainly clerical bureaucracy, which in the ensuing years was to

become increasingly incompetent and corrupt; the active despotism of Napoleon
was replaced by an inert but no less stifling form of oppression. So long as Pius lived
and Consalvi remained Secretary of State some effort was made to revive the
economy, but it was hampered by lack of capital, the decline in revenue from abroad
and the need to pay compensation for Church properties confiscated under the
French regime. Through the initiative of Pacca the Society of Jesus was restored,
while the Holy Office and the Index resumed their activities.

The 'good man and good priest', as Napoleon once described the Pope in a
moment of benevolence, and the 'great Cardinal' Consalvi worked in total harmony,
although their temperaments were quite different. But at the end of Pius's pontificate they had both outrun their strength. The Pope was 81 and the Secretary was
exhausted by the strain of making new Concordats with the powers and by the sterile
opposition of his reactionary colleagues, the Zelanti, to the modest element of reform
in his internal policies. Pius was of course more than simply good. He was a great
man whose steadfastness had inspired millions in the struggle against Bonapartist
dictatorship. When he died from the effects of a broken leg his trusted Consalvi
survived him by only six months, and the choice of the next Pope was determined by
the Zelanti. Their candidate, Cardinal Annibale della Genga, had already fallen out
with Consalvi in 1814 over the terms of the French Corcordat. As Leo XII (1823–9)
he consulted him at length but did not accept his advice; he demoted him to Prefect
of Propaganda.

Leo was a weak personality and leaned on the intransigent ultra-clericals. It was
during his reign that the papal government acquired its unwholesome reputation of
a repressive police state, the sphere of Baron Scarpia and his minions. It is easy to
argue that at this point of history the temporal power should have been allowed to
lapse. Undoubtedly it was an anachronism. It served no good purpose and inhibited
the Holy See from fulfilling its spiritual mission. It fatally spoiled the Church's
image in the eyes of all liberally minded persons. The papal state had come into
being gradually and almost accidentally, after the collapse of the ancient civilization, because it afforded a measure of protection for the Romans and some other
Italians in an age of chaos. In the absence of a unitary Italian Kingdom (last
experienced under Theodoric the Ostrogoth) it continued to exercise this function,
however imperfectly, for a great many centuries. If the Holy See had been situated in
France, its temporal role would soon have been terminated, but in the still
fragmented Italy of the early nineteenth century what kind of civil authority could
have superseded it, or indeed might have been allowed to do so in Metternich's
Europe? The Italian radicals, Mazzini at their head, were dreaming prematurely of
an Italian republic, but the country was still partitioned between various sovereigns
and the disparate provinces forming the papal domain could not have been held
together by any authority but the Pope's. And for Leo and his two immediate
successors the renunciation of their temporal power would have seemed the betrayal
of a trust received from God.

Leo's energies, such as they were, were expended in strengthening theocratic rule
and forcibly suppressing the opposition. His legate at Ravenna, Cardinal Rivarola,
used the papalist partisans (*Sanfedisti*) to strike at their liberal counterparts (*Carbo-
nari*). Some of the latter were executed and many imprisoned. Such severities quickly
grew into a reign of terror in the Legations, Umbria and the Marches. Meanwhile
Rome and the Patrimony received a dose of bigotry and austerity. A heavy
censorship was imposed, the Jews were once more confined to their ghetto,
educational opportunities were narrowed and morality enforced by niggling regula-

tions. This policy of intolerance alienated the sympathies of a populace which had cherished an affectionate loyalty to Pius VII. Sedition was already widespread when Leo died and was succeeded by Cardinal Francesco Castiglione, an elderly stop-gap who took the name of Pius VIII (1829–30). It was further fanned by the July Revolution in France and the subsequent rising of the Poles against the Tsar. Revolt in the papal state broke out early in 1831 while the Conclave summoned to elect a successor to Pius VIII was still in session. It began at Bologna and spread rapidly towards the south. As the pontifical troops were quite incapable of quelling it, the new Pope immediately called in the Austrians. The latter were only too ready to move in and did so with crushing effect.

But that was only the beginning of a long crisis. It is conceivable that Pius VIII, a sensible and fair-minded man, might have pacified the liberals for a while by offering a much greater share in the administration to laymen. The revolutionaries of 1831 were no wild subversives; the provisional government which they tried to form at Bologna was mainly composed of members of the professions and contained four Counts and a Marquis. Unfortunately Gregory XVI set his face against the slightest compromise and his Secretary of State, Cardinal Bernetti, stiffly disapproved of any significant change. Helpful suggestions for reform were put forward by a conference of foreign Ambassadors to the Holy See but few if any were adopted. The Austrian troops, having done their work, were withdrawn from the Legations. As soon as they were gone, however, the insurrection flared up again and Bernetti recalled them. This time the French government of King Louis-Philippe took umbrage. In order to counter-balance the Austrians it sent a sea-borne force to occupy Ancona. Both contingents remained glowering at each other until 1838.

Gregory XVI (1831–46) was called Mauro Cappellari and came from Belluno in Venetia. A monk and theologian, he had served as Prefect of Propaganda. By disposition he was a hard-line absolutist. Abroad his convictions took the form of a pedantic legitimism; for instance he counselled the Catholic Poles to submit to the Orthodox Tsar and the Catholic Belgians to the Protestant King of Holland. At home he authorized Bernetti to tighten repression. The *Sanfedisti* irregulars, or 'Centurions', were dressed in uniform and renamed Papal Volunteers, but earned a bad name for indiscipline and brutality. The Swiss regiments in papal employ were also vastly unpopular.

Gregory's great defect was that there was no room in his simplistic philosophy for any form of liberal Catholicism. For him the theory that sovereignty resided in the people, as opposed to being derived directly from God by legitimate rulers, was nonsensical and repulsive. It was especially unacceptable to a Pope, the theocratic ruler par excellence, and no concessions to democracy could be envisaged within the territory governed by him, although they might regrettably have to be tolerated elsewhere. But it was awkward, to say the least, that at the moment when he most needed Catholic support from outside Italy he should have forfeited the sympathy of the cleverest of his potential supporters. These were the intellectuals who had spear-headed the very real Catholic revival in France and argued persuasively in favour of unconditional acceptance of papal supremacy as against the Gallican tradition inherited by the restored French monarchy. Their leader, Lamennais, had come to the conclusion that the Church, under its consecrated Head, ought to put its trust in democracy rather than legitimacy. Only by relying on the people could it break away from subjection to or dependence on the State, especially if the latter took a Josephite or worse form. Religion should ally itself not to the throne but to the people and should identify itself with liberty.

While advocating the separation of Church and State elsewhere, Lamennais did not suggest that the Pope should renounce his temporal power; he should merely adopt liberalism for his own. Small wonder that when he visited Gregory in 1831, in company with his associates Lacordaire and Montalembert, they received a dusty answer and returned to France in distress. Furthermore, the Pope went on to condemn their cherished liberties in two scathing encyclicals. Lamennais for his part denounced curial Rome as 'the most hideous cloaca that has ever soiled the human eye'. From that moment all liberals, Catholic or otherwise, Italians or foreigners, were aligned against a papacy conducted as Gregory was conducting it. Until the end of his pontificate it was condemned to chronic disaffection, stagnation and decay.

Giovanni Maria Mastai-Ferretti, Archbishop of Spoleto and then Bishop of Imola, was one of the few higher Italian clerics who were deeply disturbed by curial intransigence and torpor. He realized that if the existing system was to survive it would have to be drastically reformed but that it would be useless to air any scheme likely to please even Catholic liberals during Gregory's lifetime. Previously a sensible and detailed plan, insisting on the need to separate the spiritual and temporal powers, had been laid before Pius VII on two occasions by the enlightened Cardinal Sala, only to be shelved in face of curial opposition. Several more radical proposals were being floated by laymen such as Massimo d'Azeglio and bold-thinking priests like Gioberti and Rosmini. Although he might think them too radical or impracticable, Mastai-Ferretti stored them in his mind. He knew that there would have to be changes but could not see how and when they could be brought about. Meanwhile he was horrified by the severity of the legates and by the excesses of their subordinates. He did his best to shield their victims and recommended many to mercy. In 1845 there was another insurrection at Rimini. It was quelled by Cardinal Lambruschini, Bernetti's successor, but its leaders made a great stir in Italy and abroad by publishing a fiery manifesto demanding the widest possible reforms. They would allow the Pope to retain his full spiritual authority and make him sovereign of one of the most liberally governed states in Europe. Such was the atmosphere when Gregory died on 1 July 1846.

21

PIUS IX
(1846–1870)

Cardinal Mastai's high character, his proven humanity, tolerance and moderation, as well as his connexions with Italian Liberalism and distaste for Austria, made him a potentially strong contender for the papal chair. On the other hand he was not one of the more prominent members of the Sacred College; the Romans knew little about his personality or his beneficial activities in the Legations. Only his intimates were aware that his epilepsy when a youth had led to nervous instability. His career in the Church had been unusual. Born in 1792, he took Orders in 1816 and was immediately sent on a mission to Chile, his only experience of the world outside Italy. On his return he remained in obscurity until 1825. Yet, two years later, Leo XII thought so highly of his abilities as to appoint him Archbishop of Spoleto, while it was Gregory XVI who transferred him, despite his liberal tendencies, in 1832 to the important see of Imola and made him a Cardinal in 1840. He was undoubtedly a favourite with the inhabitants of the Legations and adept at damping down political trouble in that unruly area. There was general surprise, however, that the Conclave that elected him should have lasted for only 48 hours, and that his supporters should have so soon prevailed over the conservative stalwarts in the College. Some thought that he was lucky to have escaped an Austrian veto. When his election was announced on 17 July 1846 he took the name of Pius IX in memory of Pius VII, the heroic opponent of Napoleon and also a former Bishop of Imola.

The start of his pontificate, which was to achieve a span of over 31 years, was altogether felicitous. He swiftly charmed the Romans. He was only 54, handsome and affable, abounding in energy and goodwill. All the omens pointed to a long and fruitful reign. Moreover the fact that a dove had perched on the roof of his carriage as it approached the city was interpreted by the populace as a clear sign that the Holy Spirit favoured his election; he was destined to be the *Papa Angelico*. Suddenly he encountered a surge of public enthusiasm and began to arouse boundless expectations.

On 17 July, a month after his election, the Pope delighted his admirers by declaring a general amnesty for political prisoners and exiles, embracing upwards of two thousand persons. This measure, carefully conceived by the pontiff with the assistance of a small committee of Cardinals, both conservatives and liberals, attracted general acclaim but, as Metternich pointed out, gave a dangerous impulse to nationalist and revolutionary agitation in the whole of Italy at a time when similar movements were coming to a head in other European countries. Nothing daunted, Pius went ahead with further sweeping reforms in the papal state. Helped by his liberal Secretary of State, Cardinal Gizzi, he launched a programme ranging from the introduction of railways and gas-lighting to the foundation of an agricultural institute, reviews of tariffs and criminal procedures and the establishment of a free press (subject to a mild degree of censorship). Far more significant, however, was his move to transform papal theocracy into a constitutional monarchy.

The advance was made by rapid stages, each of which was greeted with extravagant joy by the Romans. It fostered the impression either that the Pope and his advisers were not sure how far they meant to go or that they might be relied upon to yield to further popular demands. The first modest step towards constitutionalism was taken in June 1847, when the government of the papal state was recast in the form of a Council of Ministers. Although no provision was made for any of them to be laymen, the Pope proceeded to announce in October that the government would in future be assisted by a Consultative Assembly (*Consulta*) of twenty-four elected members drawn from the whole state. They might all be laymen but their president was to be a Cardinal. This very important political reform was shortly followed by two more. The first was the reshaping of the Roman municipality as a body of a hundred councillors, ninety-six of whom were to be laymen, the second a measure by which the Council of Ministers might become, with the exception of the Cardinal Secretary of State, completely laicized.

At this point Pius took alarm and decided that he could not afford to make any further concessions to liberalism. He suspected that he had gone too far already. His Secretary of State, Gizzi, had resigned because he objected to the formation, with the Pope's approval, of a Roman Civic Guard. He argued unsuccessfully that such a force might all too easily be manipulated by demagogues for revolutionary ends. The Pope replaced him by his own kinsman, Cardinal Ferretti, while the formidably efficient Cardinal Antonelli assumed the presidency of the *Consulta*.

During 1847 the liberal Pope attained the zenith of his popularity. The Romans acclaimed him frenetically whenever he appeared in public at the Quirinal or drove through the streets. In the other Italian states—Naples, Tuscany, Piedmont, Parma and Modena—pressure on their rulers to follow the Holy Father's example and grant constitutions was becoming irresistible. For the radical nationalists political freedoms could not but lead to Italian unity and the long-sought opportunity to expel the Austrians from Lombardy and Venetia. Everywhere excitement was rising to the highest pitch. In September 1847 Mazzini, the radicals' spokesman, was stirred to address a passionate open letter to the Pope exhorting him to assume the leadership of Italy in the crisis of its destiny. Meanwhile Metternich, watching the situation from Vienna, was redoubling his warnings to Pius regarding the fatal danger of trafficking with revolutionaries and lending himself to the promotion of their designs. He regarded papal policy as rash to the point of insanity and its author as 'warm of heart and weak of intellect'. His admonitions were given point by Field-Marshal Radetzky, the octogenarian commander at Milan, who chose the moment to assert Austria's right under the Vienna settlement to reinforce its garrison in papal Ferrara. Pius, supported by the full weight of Italian public opinion, denounced his action so effectively through diplomatic channels that the status quo in Romagna was restored by the end of the year. But it was a barren triumph for the position was past stabilizing. In 1848 revolution took charge and wrecked any hopes which the Pope or other rulers may have entertained of controlling the march of events.

Early in that year the governments at Paris and Vienna were overturned by popular uprisings. Both Germany and Italy were in turmoil. Milan and Venice burst into revolt against Austria while Naples, Tuscany and Piedmont all extracted constitutions from their sovereigns. The Pope's reaction to this perilously fluid situation was twofold. Faced with a real prospect of the papal state being swept away altogether by a torrent of Italian nationalism, he issued a declaration intended to deter enthusiastic patriots from tampering with the Holy See. Its wording, however, which included the famous invocation 'O Lord God, bless Italy,' was ambiguous enough for it to be represented as a call for Italian unity and a holy war against Austria. It therefore failed in its purpose, and in the prevailing confusion of spirits his second initiative, the grant of a definitive Roman constitution providing two Chambers with full competence in civil and political (but not religious) matters, passed almost unnoticed. In fact war was already imminent when the constitution was published on 15 March. A few days later Radetzky was driven from Milan and Piedmont declared war on Austria. Simultaneously a small pontifical army marched northwards with the ostensible aim of guarding the papal frontiers against Austrian incursions.

Pius was unable to forbid the despatch of this force, but his insistence that it should be used for defence only was ignored by its commander, the Piedmontese Durando, who was determined to link up with the Piedmontese royal army in its campaign against Radetzky. So was a separate and larger contingent of anti-Austrian volunteers from papal territory. When the Pope realized that his directions would be disregarded he decided that his attitude as Head of the Church towards the impending conflict must be publicly clarified. He was shocked by the idea that he, the Holy Father, should be counted a partisan, wherever his sympathies as an Italian might lie, in a war involving Catholics on both sides. So, on 29 April, he delivered an Allocution stating unequivocally that for religious reasons he was unable to associate himself with a secular crusade against Austria. While taking credit for his far-reaching reforms in papal territory he firmly dashed any hopes that he might assume the leadership of a united Italian alliance. His own preference would have been for a league of Italian sovereigns, including himself, in an Italy free from external domination. He utterly abhorred any tendency to republicanism.

His declaration, courageous as it was in the circumstances, had a chilling effect and his popularity, formerly so high, plummeted disastrously. He was condemned not so much for dragging his feet but for betraying the sacred national cause. Mamiani, his very liberal chief Minister under the new constitution, with difficulty staved off an anti-papal coup in Rome. But patriotic indignation was somewhat damped by Radetzky's signal victory at Custozza over the Piedmontese and their papal auxiliaries. With Austrian troops re-established in Ferrara and Rome full of frustrated patriots, the Pope found it hard to keep a Minister. Mamiani resigned, as did his successor, Fabbri, and it was not until September that a more remarkable personality, Count Pellegrino Rossi, agreed to take over the government.

A former radical exile from Italy who had subsequently risen to be a member of the French House of Peers and Ambassador to the Holy See, Rossi enjoyed a reputation for stern efficiency. Had he survived he might conceivably have kept the revolutionary republicans and the Roman mob at bay. But after two months of office he was assassinated as he arrived for the opening of the Roman Chamber of Deputies on 15 November. The man who stabbed him to death was the son of the mob's leader Angelo Brunetti, nicknamed 'Little Cicero' (*Ciceruacchio*), whose specialities were mass demonstrations and inflammatory harangues. The moderate liberals had by now lost all influence and the Pope, so recently the idol of the populace, found himself from one moment to the other helpless, isolated and intimidated. Only Cardinal Antonelli stood stoutly by him. It proved impossible to form a new government of loyal laymen. The extremists, for their part, set up a Committee of Public Safety and presented him with a list of unacceptable demands. They included the abolition of the temporal power, the designation of Rome as the capital of an all-Italian republic and the convocation there of an all-Italian Constituent Assembly. When he rejected them all out of hand he was besieged in the Quirinal by menacing crowds of armed men. Firing broke out and a bishop in his entourage was killed by a bullet. Only the presence of a few members of the diplomatic corps saved him from physical violence.

For nine days after Rossi's murder the Pope remained a prisoner in the Quirinal, closely watched by Civic Guards. Not so carefully, however, as to prevent his escape in what was to be the last in the historic series of papal flights from Rome. The chief authors of the evasion were two diplomats, Count Spaur the Bavarian Minister and the Ambassador of France, the Duc d'Harcourt. Their plan was simple and neatly executed. When the French envoy paid a formal call on the pontiff, he gave any listener at the door of the audience chamber the impression of a lengthy interview by reading out aloud passages from the newspaper. Meanwhile the Pope, aided by his valet, was changing into an ordinary priest's dress and while Harcourt was still droning away the pair slipped down a back passage into the courtyard, entered an unobtrusive carriage and drove to a prearranged rendezvous with the Bavarian. They then quietly left Rome by the Lateran Gate before changing into a larger conveyance in the Alban hills and continuing their journey undisturbed as far as Gaeta in Neapolitan territory. There the Pope was joined by Antonelli and a small staff of clerics. King Ferdinand hastened to install them in his local palace, where a miniature Curia was effectively operating, before the end of the year.

Rome was dumbfounded by the Pope's disappearance, but it enabled the revolutionaries to press on faster with the erection of their republic. A Constituent Assembly, chosen by universal suffrage but in reality by a rather poor proportion of the electors, met in February, pronounced the abolition of the temporal power and formally brought the Roman Republic into existence. Non-Roman sympathizers, among them Garibaldi was prominent, flocked to the city. In March they were joined by Mazzini, the father-figure of Italian popular democracy, who was promptly elected head of the new government with the title of Chief Triumvir. These developments were publicly denounced by the Pope in the most uncompromising terms. Possessed of a new rigour, and shedding all traces of the uncertainty with which he had trodden the path of concession during 1848, he condemned the new regime as sacrilegious and treasonable. He refused to recognize the authority of the Assembly or the existence of the Republic, stressing that all who impugned his temporal sovereignty automatically incurred the penalty of excommunication. Meanwhile Antonelli drafted for him an appeal to the principal Catholic powers—Austria, France, Spain and Naples—to intervene and re-establish his rule. He refrained from including Piedmont, whose territorial ambitions in Italy he understandably distrusted.

In invoking armed aid from abroad Pius was presenting the powers with an awkward problem. Spain was remote and Naples ineffective, but Austria and France were jealous rivals for influence in Italy and unlikely to act in unison. From an Italian point of view it was preferable that France should act alone and the French Republic, which had taken a sharp turn to the right under the Prince-President Louis Napoleon, was disposed to act on the Pope's behalf. On the other hand it was reluctant to risk a direct clash with Austria. It only decided to comply with Pius's request when King Charles-Albert of Piedmont rashly attacked the Austrians in Lombardy for the second time and sustained a second resounding defeat at the battle of Novara. In order to deter Austria from exercising a completely free hand in the peninsula Napoleon ordered a small French army under General Oudinot to land at Civita Vecchia and occupy Rome.

It was not until 30 June that Oudinot, who had begun his attack on 30 April, overcame the obstinate republican resistance with the aid of considerable reinforcements. Prodigies of valour were performed on both sides over the prostrate bodies of the Romans and at the cost of much damage to some districts of the city. Many Romans fought in the republican ranks but many more did not. The real strength of the defence resided in Garibaldi's legionaries, Piedmontese Bersaglieri and volunteers from various parts of northern Italy and foreign countries, notably Poland. The populace, bred in the tradition of a love-hate relationship with its Popes but profoundly Catholic in sentiment, had been offended by the anti-clerical excesses, including the murder of priests and the discouragement of religious observances, of some of its defenders. On the whole it was glad to see the last of Mazzini and Garibaldi and looked forward to its pontiff's return.

Pius, however, was in no hurry. He needed time to think while conditions in Rome reverted to something like normality. The imposition of order, together with such repressive measures as might prove necessary, he left to a commission of three Cardinals. His most delicate problem was that of his relationship with the French, to whom he owed his restoration and on whom his future security depended. He was under no illusions regarding the dangers which the ensuing years might disclose and was glad that the Prince-President had agreed to leave a French garrison indefinitely in the neighbourhood of Rome, while Austrian troops were also available to protect the Legations. At the same time he was resolved not to allow the French to lay down conditions as the price of their continued presence. He insisted on retaining sole authority in political as well as ecclesiastical matters. In particular he declined to reintroduce the ill-fated Constitution of 1848. All he would promise was a limited amnesty, from which persons prominently associated with the republican regime were excluded, a new State Council and Consultative Assembly and partly elective local councils, in other words a theocracy but not a priestly despotism. He of course failed to satisfy liberal opinion in France and still less in Great Britain, but he was right in thinking that Napoleon's government would not demand further constitutional concessions for the papal state. Thus, having got their own way, the Pope and Antonelli re-entered Rome on 12 April 1850 among the plaudits of the citizens. This time Pius decided to live in the Vatican instead of the Quirinal, scene of his own unpleasant experience as well as of the humiliations suffered by two of his predecessors.

His firmness and quiet confidence were to a large extent derived from the support given to him by Antonelli, one of the few clerical members of his government. The Secretary of State has frequently been portrayed as a noxious schemer who held Pius under his thumb, a minor but less attractive Talleyrand unscrupulously playing politics behind his master's back and systematically obstructing the progress of the Risorgimento. In fact he was a discreet and adroit diplomatist who loyally carried out the Pope's wishes and thanks to whom, for better or for worse, the temporal power was kept in being for another twenty years. His private life was admittedly open to reproach and that is no doubt the reason why, after being created Cardinal-deacon in 1847, he remained in minor Orders. He certainly used his position in order to enrich himself and his numerous family of former peasants, to which he bequeathed a fortune of over 1½ million pounds. Notwithstanding these defects his talents procured for the papacy a comparatively peaceful interlude during the fifties, the period when Piedmontese ambitions for the hegemony in Italy were being developed by King Victor Emmanuel and Cavour. A decade of tranquillity preceded one of exceptional storminess. Anglo-Saxon visitors to Rome, nourished on stories of papal tyranny, were amazed to observe signs of public contentment and economic progress. The Pope, when touring his domain, was less surprised but equally gratified.

Pius was deeply convinced that his spiritual and temporal powers were inseparable; he could not effectively fulfil his mission as Head of the Church unless he could at the same time act as an independent territorial sovereign. It was not enough for the Pope to be Bishop of Rome. In order to stand up to the world's pressures and to deal on equal terms with such rulers as Napoleon III he needed to have a temporal base of his own. It is hardly a valid criticism of his belief to assert that it has been disproved by the experience of the last century; in 1850 it was confirmed by recent and searing experience. Pius's isolation and helplessness under Mazzini's regime, and the latter's almost contemptuous disregard for the interests of religion, had left an ineffaceable scar on his mind. Moreover the continuing threat to the Church's position was illustrated by the long and unavailing tussle in which he was engaged after 1850 with the government of Piedmont, which had adopted a provocatively anti-clerical policy involving, among other measures, the suppression of many religious Orders. Bishops who refused to comply with it were arrested. Neither the warm personal friendship he maintained with Victor-Emmanuel nor the Vatican's official protests to Cavour prevented the passage of legislation which, to the detriment of the Church, was eventually to be extended to the whole of the new Kingdom of Italy.

Meanwhile Cavour's plans for the creation of that Kingdom were maturing and the Pope, who was not ill-informed, could not fail to grasp that they would very soon pose a new threat to his sovereignty. From the moment when Cavour gratuitously contributed a Piedmontese contingent to the Crimean War, thus ingratiating himself with the two major western powers, the fate of the papal territories was sealed, although it may have taken longer than the Piedmontese expected to extinguish the temporal power. Napoleon, who was committed to guaranteeing the papal state's neutrality through the presence there of a French garrison, met Cavour at Plombières in 1858. They reached an understanding by which France (for the price of Victor Emmanuel's homeland, Savoy and Nice) undertook to help Piedmont to expel the Austrians from northern Italy and annex Lombardy and Venetia. It would also obtain the papal Legations. Central Italy, comprising Tuscany, Umbria and the Marches, would form another State. The Pope would be left with only the Patrimony of St Peter, but he would be consoled by assuming the presidency of an Italian Confederation. But after the frightful carnage of the Franco-Austrian war in the summer of 1859, and in view of the growing Catholic feeling in France in favour of the Pope, the plan was modified at the armistice of Villafranca so as to leave Venetia to Austria and the former papal boundaries intact.

The difficulty was that papal authority in the Legations had disappeared. As soon as the war began they had been taken over by nationalist partisans in the interests of Piedmont and there was no practical prospect of their recovery. Pius, while ready to accept Napoleon's proposal for a congress to discuss the political settlement of Italy, refused to allow Antonelli to attend it when the French publicly proposed that the

Legations should be assumed to have seceded from the papal state. His unwilling-ness to acquiesce either in the absorption of the Legations by Piedmont or in Napoleon's elaborate territorial plans irritated the Emperor and soon led to the loss of Umbria and the Marches as well. Pius's advisers estimated, correctly as it turned out, that the French guaranteeing force would be instructed not to oppose a Piedmontese attempt to subvert, if not openly to occupy, the two provinces. Since he no longer possessed an army, apart from a small corps of Swiss, they were virtually defenceless. In his predicament he turned to Monsignor Xavier de Mérode, a papal Chamberlain of Belgian nationality who had served with distinction in the French army. This unusual cleric suggested that the Pope should launch an appeal for volunteers from the principal Catholic nations. What is more he persuaded a former friend and fellow soldier in France's Algerian campaigns, General Lamoricière, to take command of them.

Antonelli was doubtful but the Pope accepted the proposal. Appointed Minister of War, Mérode applied himself vigorously and with surprising success to the task of recruitment. By the summer of 1860 he had raised about fifteen thousand men. One third of them were Austrians and there were contingents from Belgium, Switzerland, Ireland, France and other European countries. Full of enthusiasm but deficient in arms and training, they were stationed at various points in the threatened provinces, while Napoleon's garrison was confined to the Patrimony.

1860 was a year of vast upheaval in Italy. Garibaldi was in process of demolishing the Neapolitan kingdom, the Piedmontese army hovered on the papal frontier and small revolutionary bands roamed the papal state. In September Cavour decided that the moment had come to unleash the royal troops. Their rapid advance, preceded by an ultimatum to which Antonelli was given no time to reply, caught Lamoricière unprepared and his units dispersed. His main body was easily defeated, after a brave but useless resistance, at Castelfidardo and the port of Ancona yielded to a bombardment by Victor Emmanuel's fleet. Only the presence of French troops at Rome saved the Patrimony from invasion and the temporal power from immedi-ate extinction. Much as he disapproved of Lamoricière and the French volunteers under the papal flag, Napoleon would not risk offending the strong and vocal ultramontane sentiments of a large section of his subjects.

It is a wonder, however, that papal sovereignty in the Patrimony should have lasted for another decade, hemmed in on all sides by a new Kingdom of Italy which desperately desired to secure Rome as its capital. Before Cavour died in June 1861 he made a speech recommending the advantages of 'a free Church in a free State', that is of a system under which the Pope would lay down his temporal power in return for strict safeguards for the Church's independence in the religious sphere. He had already floated the idea confidentially at Rome but his overtures had encountered brusque discouragement. Pius, who had not failed to notice that the obnoxious Piedmontese anti-clerical legislation had at once been stringently enforced in Naples and other recently annexed territories, was totally sceptical of Cavour's sincerity. In his opinion an independent Church and an anti-clerical state could find no basis for fruitful co-existence.

Consequently he and Antonelli were engaged during the sixties in a prolonged fencing match with both Napoleon and Cavour's successors. Much as the Emperor would have liked to find a solution to the Italian problem, on the basis of an understanding between Rome and Turin, it continued to elude and embarrass him.

In his own country he was uncomfortably poised between the Catholics, on whom he increasingly depended for political support, and the militant anti-clericals who looked backwards (and forwards) to a republic. He therefore vacillated between conciliating the Pope and encouraging Italian irredentism. Victor Emmanuel was equally fearful of radicalism as represented by Mazzini and Garibaldi and would have preferred an accommodation with the papacy. In 1862 Garibaldi, raising the slogan 'Rome or death', tried to force the issue and was incarcerated by the royal government. The situation was temporarily stabilized, though not to the Pope's satisfaction, in 1864 by the so-called September Convention between France and Italy, providing for the withdrawal of the French force in Rome within two years. The Italian Government, which was shortly to move to Florence, one stage nearer to Rome, undertook to abstain from aggression against the papal state, but Pius regarded the arrangement as a most unreliable compromise. In 1867, when the French had actually withdrawn, Garibaldi tried again. Breaking out of his island exile at Caprera, he put himself at the head of a scratch revolutionary force and invaded the Patrimony. There, at Mentana, he clashed with the reconstituted papal army. The issue of the battle was still uncertain when French troops, hastily recalled as a result of the incursion, struck the decisive blow. As the French commander reported to Napoleon, the *chassepots* (a new type of rifle) had worked marvels. Thereafter the Emperor's garrison, installed for an indefinite period, protected the Patrimony for three further vital years.

They were vital because they witnessed the fruition of the Pope's aims in the sphere of religion. It would be a great mistake to suppose that he was uniquely and obsessively occupied with the defence of his temporal power against the encroachments of Italian nationalism. His sovereignty was only one of the bulwarks of the faith, though of much importance in his eyes. Of much closer concern to him was the spiritual and intellectual health of the Church. He felt an urgent need to define its attitudes towards modern ideas, to guide its reactions to the onset of scientific materialism and to control possible divisions within its own ranks.

It was not that he was dissatisfied with the condition of the Church as a whole, for its expansion during the nineteenth century was spectacular. Even in such citadels of Protestantism as England and Holland the number of Roman Catholics was increasing so satisfactorily that he decided to re-establish the Catholic hierarchy in both countries. Unfortunately the year chosen for this act, 1850, coincided with his condemnation by the British public as an oppressive reactionary and there was a short but furious outcry of 'No Popery'. At the same time he was preparing another act which, popular as it was among the Catholic faithful, was calculated to encounter incomprehension or excite sarcasm among non-Catholics and unbelievers. This was the proclamation in 1854 of the dogma of the Immaculate Conception of the Virgin Mary. The belief that Mary was exempt from original sin did not of course spring from the Pope's head; it was derived from a very ancient tradition and Pius had received strong requests, especially from France, for it to be defined in dogmatic form. His pronouncement was attributed to Jesuit inspiration and interpreted as a challenge to the nineteenth century spirit of scepticism, but its impact was minimal as compared with that of the publication, ten years later, of the 'Syllabus of Errors'.

It had long been the Pope's intention to compile, for the guidance of the Church but not necessarily for general consumption, a list of modern 'errors and false doctrines' to be condemned and refuted. Eventually it was attached to the encyclical *Quanta Cura*, which was issued in anticipation of the Jubilee Year of 1865, and directed to the episcopate as a summary of previous pontifical declarations on the subject. The decision to make the list public seems to have been prompted by Pius's irritation with Napoleon's jibe that the papacy was not in step with the enlightened conceptions of the nineteenth century. No less than eighty propositions, religious, philosophical, ethical, social and political, were condemned outright, but they were all summed up by the eightieth, which read 'The Roman Pontiff can and should reconcile and compound himself with progress, liberalism and recent civilization.'

As an exposition of what the papacy regarded as the extravagances of European liberalism and deviations from true Christian doctrine the 'Syllabus' was a masterly document. But its tone was stiff if not truculent. Inevitably it ran into a storm of criticism and alienated many whom it had been designed to rally. Even before its publication liberal Catholics in France, Germany and elsewhere (Montalembert, Dupanloup, Döllinger, Acton) had been voicing their anxiety regarding the Pope's evident disapproval of tolerance and freedom of expression. Now they were shocked by the sharpness with which he dissociated himself from current assumptions and their dismay gave rise to much anguished and embittered controversy with the strict ultramontanes. He himself, however, appeared unruffled by the disturbances which the Syllabus had caused or by the threat of disunity in the Church. On the contrary his confidence was growing and his energies were in full flood. In 1862 and again in 1867 he held huge assemblies of bishops and clergy at Rome to which tens of thousands of pilgrims were also invited. On the second occasion he announced his decision to summon a General Council for 1869; it was to meet on 8 December, the Feast of the Immaculate Conception.

This Vatican Council was intended to be the crowning event of what was already an exceptionally long and difficult pontificate. The largest in history, it was calculated to counteract the political setbacks the papacy had undergone in the past twenty years. It was attended by about seven hundred bishops drawn from all five continents. One hundred and twenty of them, including a strong contingent from North America, were English-speaking. Heads of States, however, were not invited to send representatives as in former times.

The agenda had been carefully prepared. It was envisaged that the drafts submitted by theologians should, after consideration by committees of participating bishops, take shape as two Constitutions, that of the Faith and that of the Church. The former, which dealt with the defence of religion against scepticism and unbelief, presented no great difficulty and was unanimously agreed after due debate. The latter was concerned with more delicate material such as the nature and function of the Church, its relationship to the State and the authority and primacy of its Head. It was not originally conceived that a dogmatic definition of papal Infallibility should be the main issue to be debated, but as the discussions proceeded it assumed an increasing importance. An insistent demand for a definition from the majority of bishops was countered by an equally determined resistance from the minority. In fact the disagreement created a cleavage which was exacerbated by the impassioned campaign waged inside and outside the Council by liberal Catholics on the minority's behalf. Those who were opposed to a dogmatic pronouncement did not necessarily reject infallibility as such; they questioned the wisdom of defining it publicly because it would excite objections from governments and lay opinion generally and offend Christians of other denominations. Although the Pope did not intervene personally in the debates he was thought to be identifying himself too openly with the majority and it was in accordance with his wishes that the question of infallibility was promoted to a higher place on the agenda.

After very lively discussions the issue came to a head on 18 July. The formula to be voted on declared that the Roman Pontiff is infallible 'when he speaks *ex cathedra*, that is when in the exercise of his office as pastor and teacher of all Christians he defines by virtue of his supreme apostolic authority doctrine concerning faith or morals to be held by the Universal Church'. In the final reckoning 533 bishops voted in favour and only two (Cajazzo in Campania and Little Rock, Arkansas) against, but they too fell on their knees and submitted. The remaining dissentients, who out of respect for the Pope had withdrawn before the vote was taken, announced their adherence within the next few weeks or months. Thus both the proposed Constitutions, the second of which contained the dogma of Infallibility, received the Council's approval.

The Council was a striking manifestation of Church unity, an endorsement of Pius's thinking and actions and a tribute to the qualities of a man once criticized for being weak in intellect. Its dénouement was dramatic enough, but its sequel was as sensational as it was unexpected. Three days before the adoption of the dogma Napoleon declared war on Prussia, thus ensuring his own downfall. After early French defeats had brought about the withdrawal of his garrison from Rome it became clear that Victor Emmanuel would not miss this opportunity to invade the Patrimony, occupy the city and bring temporal power to an end. As soon as Napoleon, a prisoner of the Prussians, had announced his abdication the Italian government brusquely informed the Pope of its immediate intention to send troops into the Patrimony on the pretext, scornfully refuted by Pius, of maintaining order. But he instructed his own army, which numbered thirteen thousand, not to oppose the invading force of sixty thousand men. Although a French warship was waiting at Civita Vecchia in case he might decide to make a second escape, he rejected the idea of flight and calmly awaited the arrival of the Italian commander, General Cadorna. He showed himself publicly in the city for the last time on 19 September before retiring into the precincts of the Vatican. On the next day, Cadorna, finding the gates of Rome closed against him, started a futile bombardment. It ended when the Pope, having put up a show of resistance and delivered a formal protest to the Ambassadors accredited to him, authorized his own commander to conclude an armistice. Nevertheless Cadorna's men had already gone through the farce of breaching the wall at the Porta Pia and storming the undefended defences. A few casualties were incurred before the papal troops were grouped together, ready for disbandment.

PART SEVEN

MODERN
TIMES

22

BACK TO THE WALL
(1870–1922)

The crisis that abolished papal sovereignty was played out at dizzy speed. All of a sudden Pius found himself confined to the Vatican. It is true that he was also allowed to keep St John Lateran and Castelgandolfo, but he was mortified by losing the Quirinal, destined to become the royal palace. 'Here I am at last,' exclaimed Victor-Emmanuel, *Finalment i sum* in Piedmontese dialect, on his arrival there. His dynasty was to last a mere seventy-six years before it was sent packing.

To do it justice the royal government tried hard to reduce the bitterness of the transition. Pius would have no direct dealings with it, but it soon spontaneously inspired a Law of Guarantees whereby he retained some important attributes of sovereignty. He was to enjoy complete personal immunity. Somewhat illogically a diplomatic corps continued to be accredited to the Holy See. He kept his Guard and his Court. The curial organization of the Church remained undisturbed and its communications with the outside world were safeguarded by an independent Vatican post office. While the State claimed ownership of the buildings which the Pope was permitted to use it proposed to compensate him for his lost lands by yearly payments of 3,225,000 *lire*. Not unnaturally he refused to accept them. Nor was he impressed by the published result of a plebiscite in the Patrimony in which the electors were alleged to have approved its incorporation into the Italian kingdom by 133,000 votes to 1,500. Despite the alleviations granted to him, the eight years epilogue to the longest pontificate in history was full of trials and sadness.

A cause of deep anxiety was the *Kulturkampf*, the process by which the Chancellor, Bismarck, hoped to achieve the subordination of Church to State in the new Imperial Germany. His campaign was inaugurated by the May Laws of 1873 and was pursued with drastic vigour until Pius's death in 1878. It first took the form of interference with the education of seminarists and with ecclesiastical appointments in general. When the clergy, including several bishops, refused to comply with the new regulations and were punished with prison or exile, the Pope issued an encyclical pronouncing the laws to be null and void. The State retaliated with fresh legislation affecting Church property and revenues and suppressing the activities of religious Orders. As for the Jesuits, they had already been expelled from Germany. But in the end the moral and political damage his regime was incurring obliged Bismarck to call off the conflict.

Though bereft of its sovereign status, the papacy weathered the German storm without too much difficulty. The next serious trouble arose in Italy. The government, which had so far inclined to the right, had not responded to Bismarck's suggestions that the Law of Guarantees was far too favourable to the Pope and ought to be modified. It still hoped for a peaceful co-existence with the papacy but was disappointed when Pius turned a deaf ear to its conciliatory gestures. In his eyes all Italian governments were equally damned for their offences against God's Church. He could not forgive the application of Turin's anti-clerical legislation to all Italy. But in 1876 the country acquired a left-wing administration, headed by the Freemason Depretis, which was not so much anti-clerical as frankly anti-religious in sentiment. It proceeded to enforce existing legislation more rigorously and to devise new measures of harassment. These were particularly directed against such religious Orders as had managed to continue their activities. Luckily for the Pope, the Italian Senate killed a bill which would have prohibited any openly expressed opposition by the clergy to State policy, but there was no escape from the fact that the official Italian attitude towards the Holy See was changing from benevolent neutrality to nagging hostility.

Pio Nono died on 8 February. One of his last acts had been to send a priest to the bedside of the dying Victor-Emmanuel with authority to remove the ban which would have prevented the King from receiving the last sacraments. A child of the eighteenth century, he remained tolerant and broad-minded throughout youth and middle age until revolutionary liberalism drove him to take a less kindly view of human nature. After he became Pope he equated liberalism with modernism and regarded them both, unless restrained by religion, as essentially destructive forces. It was not an attitude which could be indefinitely sustained in the century of Darwin and Huxley, Marx and Engels, Renoir and Strauss. On the other hand he left the Church in a far healthier condition than in the earlier half of the century. It was no longer stumbling nor stagnating. Largely owing to his own courageous intransigence in matters of principle and in spite of the battering it had endured, it had recovered its favour and self-confidence at a time when its phenomenal expansion in the world as a whole was amply justifying its claim to universalism. He bequeathed to his successor the unsolved puzzle of adapting itself to a rapidly changing social environment.

This task was imposed, after another very short conclave, on a frail sixty-eight-year-old aristocrat, Vincenzo Gioacchino Pecci, who reigned as Leo XIII (1878 –1903). He had previously distinguished himself as an administrator in the papal state and nuncio in Belgium under Gregory XVI and as Bishop of Perugia under Pius IX, who raised him to the Cardinalate. He was on bad terms with Antonelli, who thought him too ready for compromise with the new Italy, but Antonelli had died before Pius. Nobody expected him to live for another twenty-five years or to rule the Church with such energy. Firm, patient and conciliatory, he possessed the right qualities for a pontiff in a very tricky period. They served him well in the two spheres where they were most needed, that of the Church's involvement in social problems and that of its difficulties with the leading nations of Catholic Europe. It seemed as if the greater the number of Catholics those countries contained the deeper the lack of understanding between their governments and the Vatican.

In Germany the new Pope's overtures were gratefully received by Bismarck, who was already looking for an excuse to moderate, if not to abandon, his anti-clerical policy without loss of face. Negotiations with the Vatican were lengthy, but concluded to the satisfaction of both sides. By 1885 good relations were fully restored. The Iron Chancellor even asked the Pope to arbitrate in an obscure dispute between Germany and Spain over the ownership of the Caroline Islands in the Pacific. Leo conferred high papal decorations on him and after 1888 the Kaiser was a frequent visitor to Rome and the Vatican.

Leo's experience of his own country was less fortunate. Throughout his pontificate left-wing governments under Depretis and Crispi continued to harass the Holy See by administrative pinpricks and legislation which infringed the Law of Guarantees. They were egged on by Masonic and other anti-clerical groups which often resorted to crude provocations. The worst of these was the riot which interrupted the solemn transfer of the remains of Pius IX, in accordance with the latter's wishes, from St Peter's to the basilica of San Lorenzo Fuori le Mura. Stones and mud were hurled at the procession and priests were insulted or assaulted. The Pope, while complaining that he was being 'robbed of his lawful rights and hindered in the performance of his supreme duties in a thousand ways', did not allow himself to be discouraged or manoeuvred into dangerous confrontations. He felt that his enemies would over-reach themselves sooner or later and that there would be a popular reaction in his favour. His hope, as expressed in his own words was to 'bring Italy to recognize that the papacy is a great glory to her and that she will be the more glorious and powerful the closer and stronger the ties binding her to the Pope.'

Nevertheless the tension did not slacken, nor did the pressure on the Church. Episcopal appointments were held up; the clergy, edged out of educational and even charitable activities, were deprived of their tithes and subjected to discrimination in a new penal code. The very numerous Catholics who resented the government's anti-clerical bias and fretted under their own political impotence pressed Leo to permit the formation of a Catholic parliamentary party, but he was adamant in refusing his sanction for any proposal which would drag the Church directly into the political arena. The furthest he would go was to urge Catholics to use their votes in local and municipal elections. Although this policy ensured the eclipse of conservatism in Italy it prevented the Church from necessarily being identified with the political Right. However he found other means of countering attacks on the Church and on himself. Remarkably spry and articulate despite his advanced age, he stated his case forcefully but without rancour in a stream of eloquent Encyclicals and Allocutions and usually had the better of the argument. He also made sure that although he might be confined to the Vatican Catholics from all countries should be afforded an opportunity to pay homage to its prisoner. He celebrated no less than three Jubilees, occasions which attracted quantities of pilgrims to Rome and caused much displeasure to Italian anti-papalists.

A similar and perhaps more dangerous attack was launched against the Church's position in France and was sustained until, in the year of Leo's death, it resulted in the separation of Church and State. By the time of his accession the conservative and monarchist reaction which had followed the defeat of France in 1870, to say nothing of the nightmarish Paris Commune in which the Archbishop of Paris had met his death, had spent itself. A royalist restoration was no longer on the cards. In subsequent years successive governments veered to the left. Taking their cue from Gambetta, coiner of the slogan '*Le cléricalisme, voila l'ennemi,*' they pursued an increasingly anti-clerical policy. The campaign opened when Jules Ferry, the Minister of Public Instruction, introduced legislation sharply restricting the freedom of religious institutions in the field of higher and secondary education. The Republicans could not stomach the fact that in many respects the independent education available in Catholic colleges was superior to that provided by the State system and was attracting the best pupils. One of Ferry's bills contained an article forbidding members of 'unauthorized religious Orders' to teach in either State or private schools. When it was thrown out by the Senate the government overrode the veto by decree. One decree ordered the closure of all Jesuit schools and houses of residence; a second obliged all other congregations to apply for official authorization.

The Pope's attitude towards political shifts in France was clear enough. So long as the Church's freedoms, as specified by Concordats or previously unchallenged, were respected by the State the Holy See would hope to have good relations with governments of any complexion, royalists, bonapartist or republican. There was nothing illegitimate or immoral in republicanism as such. But he was obliged to protest vigorously through his nuncio against the execution of the decrees. The Jesuit houses were dissolved forthwith. When the other Orders affected declined to apply for registration the Pope tried to avert a crisis by negotiating a compromise whereby the government would not compel congregations to register in return for a declaration of their strict neutrality in political life. Unfortunately news of the negotiation leaked out and the government reverted to intransigence. The result was that many congregations preferred forcible dispersion to submission to the decree. Although most of them were permitted to return to their religious houses before long a scandal had been created and the Holy See had suffered a severe rebuff. Moreover, from the radical viewpoint, the Catholic establishment was now fair game. A fresh law secularized primary education. The ministries in power during the early eighties promoted a long list of anti-clerical measures such as the reduction of churchmen's stipends and of general expenditure for religious purposes, the legalization of divorce and the obligation of military service for seminarists. Once more Leo protested in an outspoken Encyclical (*Nobilissima gens Gallorum*) and a personal letter to President Grevy; once more his remonstrances were ignored.

Nevertheless he continued to strive doggedly for reconciliation, but political opinion in France was so fragmented that it was impossible to bring about an understanding between Catholics and the less doctrinaire Republicans. It was also a period of intense political confusion, that of General Boulanger's bid for dictatorship, of a variety of resounding scandals and finally of the sinister *Affaire Dreyfus*. Allegiances were subdivided and energies dissipated in impassioned enmities. The Republicans began to feel that the very foundations of the State were being sapped by clerical intrigue. While the hierarchy loyally supported Leo's efforts for peace, there was a lamentable lack of cohesion among the Catholic laity. The zealots posed as more Catholic than the Pope. For instance they were furious when the Archbishop of Algiers, Cardinal Lavigerie, a picturesque prelate who had endeared himself to the Vatican by his missionary endeavours in French Africa and his successful campaigns against the slave trade, proposed what sounded like a toast to the Republic on the occasion of a fleet visit to the capital of his diocese. The Pope, however, backed Lavigerie and issued a fresh Encyclical (*Inter innumeras sollicitudines*) explaining why French Catholics, while in duty bound to oppose laws discriminating against religion, must at the same time respect the legitimate authority of a government, republican or otherwise. It was a distinction that did not appeal to many Catholics or induce them to rally to the Republic. The old controversies thus smouldered on until, towards the end of the century, anti-religious agitation received a new and decisive impulse.

French Catholics as a whole put themselves morally and tactically in the wrong by allying themselves with the anti-Dreyfus lobby and attacking the Dreyfusards with exaggerated malignity. In the forefront of their assault was the Assumptionist Order with its newspaper *La Croix*. Its excesses prompted the radical Prime Minister, Waldeck-Rousseau, to bring in a law concerning freedom of association by which all bodies were granted such freedom except the religious Congregations. The latter were again required to seek special permission and those who failed to obtain it were made liable to dissolution and the expropriation of their property. Again the Pope protested, but his intervention stood no chance against the verdict of the 1902 elections, which produced a majority inclining still further to the left. Waldeck-Rousseau then gave way to Combes, a former trainee for the priesthood. Having apostatized, he was fanatically bent on bringing the church to its knees, annulling the Concordat and achieving the complete separation of Church from State. Former politicians had been content with adjourning separation to an opportune moment. The opportunity had now arrived, and Combes proceeded to put the first stage of his programme into effect. The enforcement of the law, involving the use of troops, gave rise to much unrest and distress, but all those Congregations not prepared to request authorization (which was generally denied) either dissolved themselves or were forcibly expelled. These events occurred when the Pope, aged 93, was on his death-bed; the formal divorce between State and Church followed in his successor's pontificate.

The value of Leo's work should not be measured by the setbacks and disappointments that he suffered while resisting secular pressures in the old Catholic countries. It is of far greater significance that he was the first Pope to turn the Church's attention towards the social problems of the industrial age. Pius IX, in his preoccupation with doctrine and politics, had lost sight of the fact that the influence of religion among the working class of the cities was in steep decline. Leo, on the other hand, fully grasped the importance of arresting this process, even if it was too late to reverse it.

When still Cardinal-bishop of Perugia he had been fascinated by the achievements of Don Bosco, the founder of the Salesian Order, who was pioneering technical education and the organization of social welfare among young Italian workers. As Pope he gave a mighty impetus to the Order's expansion. His difficulty was to decide how to give expression to his social concern. On the plane of theory his condemnation of international Socialism was absolute. In an early Encyclical he denounced it as a 'murderous pestilence creeping through the innermost organs of human society'. He spurned it as a monstrous aberration born of crass materialism and a spurious doctrine of equality. It was, he proclaimed, inconsistent with the spirit of Christian charity and conducive to the oppression of the individual by the godless State. He knew, however, that such fulminations would be pointless until justified by programmes of social action inspired by the Church and spontaneously implemented, so far as possible, by Catholic organizations. Such groups were already active in France, Germany and Austria. In Leo's time they also proliferated in Italy until they constituted an impressive and effective social force. Prominent among them was the *Opera dei Congressi e dei Comitati Cattolici*, a co-ordinating body which sponsored fourteen congresses during his pontificate. The next step was the formation of Catholic Trade Unions; initiated under Leo XIII, they were to be abolished in Italy by Mussolini, by Hitler in Germany. The Pope enjoyed greeting workers' pilgrimages to Rome. Stimulated by non-Italian Cardinals such as the American Gibbons and the British Manning (a former Anglican Archdeacon who had become a hard-line theological conservative and a favourite of Pius IX) he grew increasingly sensitive to the just complaints of the workers, to the evils of pauperism and overwork, squalour and ignorance.

It remained for him to set out in Christian terms the intellectual and moral basis of his social policy. This he did, after many years of reflection, in the most celebrated of his many Encyclicals, *Rerum Novarum*. Once he had made up his own mind, he drove his draftsmen hard until he was satisfied with the outcome. Described by Pope John XXIII as the 'great charter' of Catholic social doctrine, it insisted on the worker's right to a just wage. While refuting the Marxist concept of the class war, it castigated the callous behaviour of contemporary capitalism. 'The conflict now raging', he asserted in the preamble, derives from 'the vast expansion of industrial pursuits and the marvellous discoveries of science; the changed relations between masters and workmen; the enormous fortunes of some few individuals and the utter poverty of the masses; the increased self-reliance and closer mutual combination of the working classes; as also, finally, the prevailing moral degeneracy.'

After this crisp summing up of the problem he emphasized that the State could never hope to solve it by means of the simple transfer of property from private individuals to the community. 'There is no need to bring in the State. Man precedes the State and possesses, prior to the formation of the State, the right of providing for the sustenance of his body.' Private property is inviolate. The State must therefore not concern itself with the distribution of goods but must limit its intervention to ensuring by law that contracts between employers and workers are strictly respected and to regulating such matters as factory hours and safety measures. The Pope denied absolutely that social evils could be eliminated through the enforcement of unnatural equality by political and economic means. Justice and harmony, he insisted, could only be achieved through the recognition of the principles of Christian charity by employers and workpeople alike and through their observance in day-to-day industrial relations. Religion is the only sure guide to industrial peace. The Encyclical goes on to define the essential rights and duties of both sides and to stress that workers' associations for the protection of their rights are permissible and desirable.

Leo could not fail to be gratified by the warm welcome accorded to his Encyclical. Its message was of course rejected by those for whom religion was irrelevant to social development. Among Catholics there was a tendency to request further definitions. What exactly, for instance, constituted a just wage, and was there any limit to private riches? In the remaining years of his pontificate a division was discernible between those who thought that the Pope had gone far enough to satisfy the social conscience of Christians and those who hoped for further progress towards a Christian corporate society. In 1901 he published a further Encyclical with the intention of clarifying his thoughts on social matters and of indicating where the line should be drawn between conservatism and Christian democracy. If, on balance, he came down on the side of the latter, he was pointing towards fruitful evolution in the future, and not only in Italy.

On reaching the age of 93 the Pope was still completely lucid and his stamina seemed unimpaired. His versatility and open-mindedness had increased with his years. There was no sphere of intellectual activity in which he was interested— literature (he was a great Dante scholar and himself wrote poetry), theology, philosophy, science and the arts. He was a competent financier and left the papacy much more soundly endowed than in the era of temporal power. Inured as he was to political shocks, he was distressed by his exclusion, at the instance of the Italian government, from the Hague Peace Conference of 1899, and horrified by the assassinations, one after the other, of King Umberto of Italy, President McKinley of the United States, President Carnot of France and the Empress Elizabeth of Austria. These outrages seemed to have justified his worst forebodings about the dangers of godless anarchy. And his death coincided with the heightening of the religious crisis in France.

The ensuing Conclave produced a surprise when the Emperor Francis Joseph's veto was used to exclude one of the most likely candidates. Cardinal Rampolla, Leo's capable and trusted Secretary of State, had offended the Austro-Hungarian government by his too evident distaste for the Triple Alliance between the German Empire, the Habsburg Monarchy and Italy, and by his desire that it should be counter-balanced by the current *rapprochement* between France and Russia. The imperial prohibition was conveyed to Rome by the Polish Cardinal Przyna, Archbishop of Cracow. It was received with indignation, but Rampolla not only failed to be elected Pope but was replaced as Secretary of State under the new pontiff by the Spanish Cardinal Merry dal Val. At the seventh ballot the choice fell on Giuseppe Sarto, Cardinal Patriarch of Venice.

Pius X (1903–14) was the son of a country postman. His whole ecclesiastical life had been spent in his native Venetia and as Bishop of Mantua. He was not a man of the world and, although a kindly and gentle pastor of souls, did not possess his predecessor's gift of handling people and getting the best out of them. In his public attitudes he was deeply conservative and suspicious of modernism. He also lacked the confident energy which had inspired Leo's social initiatives. When he fell back into a defensive posture papal leadership faltered and lost its momentum.

The Pope's outlook was soured from the beginning by his humiliating impotence in face of the French government's anti-religious offensive. During 1904 and 1905 Combes and his followers were preparing the Law of Separation which was to annul Napoleon's Concordat. Its terms, as framed by Aristide Briand, the future Prime Minister, were both comprehensive and severe. The Church was stripped of its properties and forfeited its revenues. Nevertheless the government was careful not to incur the charge of subjecting Catholics to an ordeal comparable to that which they had undergone in the Revolution. There was to be no overt persecution. It was accordingly specified that property rights in respect of buildings and other ecclesiastical assets should be exercised by '*associations culturelles*' composed of Catholic laymen in each locality, who would also administer the cult's finances. This attempt at a compromise did not of course appease the Pope. He denounced it in an Encyclical issued early in 1906, particularly objecting to the ideas that control of public worship should be removed from a divinely ordained institution and handed over to the laity. More generally he lamented the end of the age-long connexion between the Holy See and France, the elder daughter of the Church. Separation involved a severance of diplomatic relations lasting until 1921, when they were renewed by the same Briand.

Since the Catholics of France, in obedience to papal wishes, would not agree to form the desired associations, the government handed over the legal ownership of Church property to the local communes. Luckily this did not mean that the clergy were denied the use of church buildings; they retained it on sufferance. But the episcopate, supported by a strong section of the laity, refused to regard separation as a total disaster. They argued that in the long run it would probably prove a blessing and that a free and revitalized Church would benefit from the independence thrust upon it. Their contention, though frowned on by the Vatican, was justified more quickly than they expected. In the short run the Church suffered from penury and a shortage of priests, but it soon gained in zeal, unity and reliance on its own resources. Also the old Gallican tendency gave way to a new loyalty to Rome.

It was however a French cleric, the Abbé Loisy, who was a main target of Pius's anti-modernist Encyclical (*Pascendi*) of 1907. The term 'modernism' eludes definition, for the Catholic modernists of the early twentieth century—Loisy in France, Tyrrell in England, Murri in Italy—were not so much a concerted movement as a group of brilliant intellectuals expressing individual points of view. They bore a certain resemblance to advanced theologians such as Küng and Schillebekkx who are causing so much trouble to Pope John Paul II. Basing themselves on recent biblical research, an activity encouraged by Leo XIII, and on critical studies of the historical origins of Christianity, they rebelled against the literal acceptance of Scripture and tradition. They also urged that Christian philosophy need no longer be rooted in mediaeval scholasticism. But Pius had no use for watered down versions of Catholicism which either made light of the supernatural or took refuge in personal mysticism. Harking back to the 'Syllabus of Errors', he branded such developments as 'insane' and at least potentially heretical. In order to combat them he devised a new system of censorship of modern ideas among the clergy. Bishops were required on oath to report cases of deviation. Simultaneously, however, he was founding an institute in Rome for the promotion of biblical scholarship and the training of priests in up-to-date intellectual methods and scientific techniques.

St Peter's chair had been filled for well over half a century by two imposing personalities, Pius IX and Leo XIII. The issues in which they had played a leading part had commanded the widest attention; their pronouncements had echoed through the Victorian world and further afield. They had inspired fervent support and encountered vehement opposition. It was otherwise with Pius X. He was a secondary figure and his pontificate an anti-climax. Pleasure-loving Edwardian Europe was not primarily interested in his anxieties about modernism or, for example, in the parochial question of the extent to which the Christian Social movement should involve itself, and necessarily the Vatican, in Italian politics. Moreover serious minds were occupied with exciting adventures in physics or, on the political plane, with the alarming international tensions of the period preceding the First World War. The mainstream of history seemed to be leaving the papacy high and dry, absorbed in irrelevant controversies. It was not that Pius was inactive. After 1908 he devoted himself to a much needed reorganization of the Curia and entrusted to Cardinal Gasparri the enormous task of recodifying Canon Law. He foresaw with perfect clarity that a European war was impending in which Catholic nations would be involved on both sides with calamitious results, but realized equally well that it could not be prevented by prior warnings and exhortations from the Holy See. Nor did he make any secret of his fatalism. Even so, when war finally came, its suddenness appalled him and certainly hastened his death on 20 August 1914.

It was soon felt that his exceptional piety and humility, his simple beauty of character, amounted to sanctity and merited canonization. Stories were also sprouting about miracles of healing performed by him or by his intercession. The Church, however, moved with its customary caution. The preliminary process of beatification was initiated by Pius XII in 1943 and completed in 1953. Two of the miracles attributed to Pius X were selected for examination and declared to be genuine. Canonization duly followed two years later. It was the first time that such an honour had been conferred on a pontiff since 1712, when it was tardily bestowed on Pius V, the Pope of Lepanto.

How ought the Holy See to react to murderous conflict in which Catholic

Austria-Hungary and partly-Catholic Germany stood initially opposed to an alliance of Catholic, but officially irreligious France, with Orthodox Russia and Protestant Great Britain? That was the problem, shortly to be complicated by Italy's entry into the war, which confronted Benedict XV (1914–22). Elected on the sixteenth ballot, Giacomo della Chiese was a Genoese nobleman, a bird-like little man of insignificant appearance. He was nicknamed 'il piccoletto' by the people of Bologna—the notoriously difficult see that he had occupied for seven years—being created a Cardinal only two months before the conclave. But before his appointment as archbishop he had worked for many years under Rampolla in the Secretariat of State and was reputed to be the most acutely intelligent diplomat in the service of the Church. By reason of his forced concentration on the war and its immediate aftermath he must rank, with Pius X, as a transitional Pope, a judgement which implies no disparagement of the courage and sagacity with which he faced the crisis.

He adopted a rigidly neutral position between the belligerents. While denouncing the war as a crime against religion, humanity and civilization, he blamed both sides equally for allowing it to happen and to continue. Neither appreciated his attitude or responded to his exhortations. The British misinterpreted his impartiality as pro-Germanism; the French, aware that he disapproved of Italy joining the Allies, were only too ready to assume papal complicity with Germanic imperialism; the Austrians tended to distrust him as Rampolla's former assistant. It was true that thanks to his very able nuncio in Bavaria, Monsignor Eugenio Pacelli, the Holy See enjoyed what the Allies regarded as too easy a relationship with the government of Berlin. It may be that Benedict personally believed that the Central Powers had better prospects of winning and that their victory was likely to be used in a manner more acceptable to the papacy than the outcome of an Allied triumph. Nevertheless he was upset and embarrassed by the current assumption in Germany and Austria that he favoured their cause. He told both German and French bishops that it was wrong for them to engage in nationalistic propaganda and assured Cardinal Mercier of Belgium that he deplored the violation of his country's neutrality. So far as Italy was concerned, he was shocked by the cynical opportunism with which its government was prepared to barter Italian lives for territorial gains at the expense of Austria-Hungary. Worse still, it later transpired that one of Italy's conditions for entering the war was the exclusion of the Holy See from an eventual peace conference.

He himself strove imperturbably for a negotiated as opposed to a dictated peace. A succession of appeals to the belligerents, urging them to put an end to the 'degrading slaughter', led up to his detailed peace plan of August 1917. It comprised provisions for freedom of the seas, progressive disarmament and an international tribunal of arbitration for the settlement of disputes. But in the heated atmosphere of 1917, when Allied resolve had been hardened by the American declaration of war, the plan proved too theoretical and idealistic to gain their acceptance, even as a basis of negotiation. The Allies objected that its proposals for reciprocity of treatment ignored the distinction between aggressors and victims. They also believed that any peace which left the imperial regimes of Central Europe intact would not be worth concluding; it would only result in another war sooner or later. Nothing would satisfy them but the surrender and consequent penalization of the Central Powers. The Kaiser, to whom Pacelli presented the papal scheme, did not categorically turn it down. He temporized by suggesting that a start might be made by a negotiation between Austria and Italy. His Chancellor, Bethmann-Hollweg, appeared more receptive. However he was soon replaced by Michaelis who joined with the German generals in counselling rejection. So the Pope's initiative for peace shared the fate of that attempted in the same year by the young Austrian Emperor Charles and finally wrecked by Italian intransigence. The simple truth was that neither Germany nor the Allies were seriously interested in negotiations on the basis of agreed principles so long as there seemed to be a chance of outright victory.

The Pope bore his disappointments calmly. His resentment with having been barred from the Paris peace conference of 1919 caused him to stigmatize the Treaty of Versailles, not unfairly, as a 'consecration of hatred' and a 'perpetuation of war'. But he was already immersed in more practical activities. Already in 1918, when it seemed clear that an independent Catholic Poland would emerge from the war, he sent Monsignor Achille Ratti to reorganize the Polish Church in the territories formerly partitioned between Germany and Austria. He even cherished hopes that the eclipse of the Russian Orthodox Church might open the way to Catholic proselytism in the Soviet Union. He set up a very large fund for relief to young people in all countries ravaged by the war and as far removed as Russia and China.

More particularly he turned his attention to Italy. While its government was absorbed in territorial aggrandizement the country was being crippled by economic disruption and social unrest. It was also menaced with political anarchy. Encouraged by the success of the Russian Soviets, the Communists were taking over industrial plants and installing their own agrarian committees in the villages. Law and order were vanishing, especially in the north, where the Communists skirmished with Mussolini's Fascists and with the Socialists, now the largest legal party. At that time all three factions were militantly anti-religious. Prospects were so bad that the Pope wisely rescinded the ban (*'non expedit'*) that Leo XIII and Pius X had imposed on Catholic participation in Italian national elections and decided to sponsor the Catholic Popular Party recently founded by Don Luigi Sturzo, a Sicilian priest. It immediately attracted massive support and by the year of Benedict's death had risen to be the second largest group in parliament. Had the organized Catholic vote been allowed to grow unchecked it would probably have provided the much-needed stabilizing force in the centre of the political field. It was, tragically, Benedict's successor Pius XI who cut short its development, thus committing Italy to twenty years of Fascist rule.

23

THE AGE OF
UNREASON
(1922–1958)

The Pope who reversed Benedict's policy was the Monsignor Ratti to whom he had entrusted the mission to Poland. Subsequently he was appointed to the see of Milan, where he stayed for seven months only, and raised to the Cardinalate. His was the first of the five deeply significant pontificates that have succeeded one another over the past sixty years. Despite the upheavals caused by the rise of the dictatorships and the Second World War, the impact of Communism and the prevalence in Christian countries of unbelief, agnosticism and self-satisfied materialism, the present century has paradoxically witnessed a steady rise in the prestige of the papacy and of its influence in international affairs. Strong criticism of the policies and actions of individual pontiffs has scarcely diminished the increasing esteem and respect which the institution, no longer disregarded as an archaic survival, now generally commands. There is no question of its being dismissed as irrelevant to the modern age and relegated to the sidelines, as might have been predicted in the early nineteen-hundreds. All five Popes have contributed in different ways to the vigorous reassertion of its universal authority, subject to the obvious limitations. Each has had a part to play in the *aggiornamento*, or adaptation of the Church's mission to the needs of today's world, which has been principally and rightly associated with the work of John XXIII.

Pius XI (1922–39) was 65 at his accession. Until he went to Poland he had devoted his life to scholarship as an active and innovating Prefect of the Ambrosian (Milan) and Vatican libraries. As the world was repeatedly reminded he was also a skilled alpinist. Schoolmasterish in appearance, as a British diplomat reported, he was middle class, learned, exact and authoritarian. He did not lean heavily on advisers, but it was noted that he broke with precedent in retaining his predecessor's Secretary of State, Cardinal Gasparri. It was to prove, from his own point of view, a shrewd decision.

His pontificate had not lasted for nine months when Mussolini seized power and was accepted as the King's Prime Minister. The outrages committed by the Blackshirts did not spare Catholic institutions. Nevertheless their leader was not yet a dictator. He did indeed suppress the Communists, but the Socialist and Catholic Popular parties together outnumbered the Fascists in parliament and their combined strength would still have been capable of thwarting Mussolini's plans. Such an alliance, however, was impossible to bring about. Don Sturzo, whose men were fighting the Fascists constitutionally in parliament and militantly in the streets, was not averse to it, but the Pope rejected it utterly as an unthinkable compromise with the powers of evil. The advanced social and economic tendencies of the Christian populists had already aroused his apprehension. He accordingly made it clear to Don Sturzo that he regarded his political activity as incompatible with his priestly status. Thus disavowed, Sturzo obediently resigned his leadership of the party and withdrew into exile, leaving the way open to Mussolini to impose his dictatorship. In 1924 the whole potential opposition was swept away. Christian democracy did not of course disappear overnight, but without overt Vatican support it lost its *raison d'être* and went into the wilderness. It could not work effectively without being linked in some way to the Holy See, and in any case no clear distinction could be drawn between spiritual and moral inspiration and straightforward political direction.

If the Pope's behaviour seems incomprehensible today, we should recall the climate of the early twenties when not only the Catholic hierarchy but moderate as well as conservative opinion in Europe and America was terrified of Bolshevism. Had it not narrowly failed to triumph in Germany, Poland and Hungary? In the circumstances any overtures to the Italian Left would have struck the Pope and the Curia as sheer lunacy. Pius thought that the Church's cause in Italy would be better served by a non-political Catholic body with influence in all branches of the national life. Hence he fostered and expanded Catholic Action, a movement designed to associate the laity more closely with papal aims. It soon acquired a very large membership, especially in the professions and the universities, while running its own charitable and youth organizations, a powerful confessional complex invulnerable to political attack. Pius foresaw correctly that it was well suited to coexist with Fascism and eventually to outlast it.

For the next five years the Vatican maintained an uneasy but gradually improving relationship with the one-party Fascist state. As soon as Mussolini had taken over the royal government and begun to enlist conservative support he found it prudent to drop his once provocatively anti-religious posture. He tried out a number of conciliatory gestures calculated to assure Catholics that he could at least behave more graciously towards them than the extinct Liberals and Socialists. For instance religious education was reintroduced into the State schools and crucifixes were displayed in the law courts. More bluntly he announced that 'the religious policy of the Italian State has to be reconstructed on a completely new basis.' The suggestion was plain; there was no contradiction between the corporate State and the papacy and it only remained to regulate their future relations within an Italian and an international framework. Yet the Pope was not easily to be drawn. Although he considered that a general settlement would be salutary for both domestic and international reasons, he was warned by the government's totalitarian pretensions and especially by its inroads on family life and the formation of young people. For tactical reasons he decided not to take the initiative and waited for an approach from the Fascist side.

This came, after many preliminary soundings, in 1927. When discussions started Pius was represented by Gasparri, a hard and sly negotiator who could be relied upon to extract the best possible terms from the government. The Pope and he believed that in the short run the State might stand to gain more than the Church from a formal agreement but if, as was probable, Fascism would not last very long the Church would emerge as the winner. The talks, the details of which were kept secret, continued until both sides were satisfied that no further advantages could be obtained by prolonging them. At last, on 11 February 1929, Gasparri and Mussolini met at the Lateran Palace, on the site of the hall where Leo III had greeted Charlemagne, and signed two agreements, a Treaty and a Concordat. When they had done so the Pope appeared on the balcony and blessed the crowds kneeling in St

Peter's square, thus symbolically ending his and his predecessors' seclusion in the Vatican. It was the first time that a pontiff had shown himself in public since 1870.

Under the Treaty the Pope re-entered the ranks of independent sovereign rulers. His Vatican dominion of 10 acres was recognized as the juridical equal of the Italian Kingdom and he acknowledged Rome to be the latter's capital. In return for his renunciation of his claim to the former papal state he received a cash payment of 750 million *lire* and 1,000 million *lire* in State securities, the whole amounting at the time to about £21 million. Thus the papacy acquired a very substantial interest in the prosperity of the Kingdom, together with a certain degree of dependence upon it. The Concordat was on the face of it extraordinarily favourable to the Holy See. Not only was Catholicism declared to be the official religion of the State but other cults incurred disabilities. Marriage in church was given civil effect and divorce was made subject to the restrictions of canon law. Defrocked priests were excluded from public employment. Above all Catholic Action was granted freedom for all its activities so long as they conformed to directives from the Holy See.

The papacy was back on the map of Europe and the world. Its diplomatic achievement, however, was sourly regarded outside Italy. It was given little credit for its resilience and its power of weathering the crisis of rationalism and prejudice. Foreign opinion tended to view the settlement as a betrayal of Italian democracy. In France, where Fascism was disliked for ideological reasons and Italy was suspect as a rival in the Mediterranean and Africa, criticism of the Pope was especially severe. Moreover it was thought to be justified when the Duce, regretting that he had gone so far along the path of conciliation, again abused the Church in public statements and encouraged his followers in their anti-clerical antics. Once again recriminations centred round the Fascist insistence on monopolizing the training of youth against which Pius protested in a stiff encyclical. Three years passed from the signature of the Concordat until differences were sufficiently patched up for him to receive Mussolini in ceremonial audience.

The Vatican's activity need not be measured by its output, but the sheer volume of work accomplished during this pontificate cannot fail to impress. The Pope's industry seemed equal to all demands and he inspired his collaborators, whom he drove very hard without giving them much freedom of action, with his own confident energy. He negotiated as many as eighteen Concordats and took his stand on vital problems in three ringing encyclicals. The Duce's fluctuating attitudes were the least of his worries. In the troubled post-war world the Church's anxieties multiplied and, as the thirties advanced, some of its difficulties grew so horrific as to appear insoluble. The disastrous decade which followed the papacy's recovery of its ancient status was that of the great economic depression, the triumph of Stalinist Communism, the rise of Nazi Germany and the Civil War in Spain.

His socio-economic encyclical, *Quadragesimo Anno* (1931), attacked the excesses of capitalism in the strongest terms. Its purpose was to commemorate the fortieth anniversary of Leo XIII's *Rerum Novarum* and to place where it belonged the blame for the workers' sufferings in the depression. The whole economic regime, he declared, had become 'hard, cruel and relentless' as a result of unchecked individualism. The remedy did not lie in Socialism, either in the 'pure' Marxist variety which was undistinguishable from 'impious and nefarious' Communism, or in 'moderate' Socialism which was less harmful but incompatible with a religious way of life. In recommending a corporate system within which capital and labour could

Detail from David's famous depiction of the Coronation of Napoleon, with the Pope a powerless onlooker

The People's Gate, Rome

Pope Pius VII, engraving by Ronjat

Swiss Guards in Holy Year, 1950

Previous page: Pope Pius XII's Jubilee, 1949

Pope Pius XII with his pet 'Gretel'

live in prosperity and harmony he stressed, in a clear reference to Italy, that it must not serve political ends as an instrument of State control. The message was that Capitalism and Communism were equally productive of misery.

In some countries governments behaved obstructively; in others Catholics underwent harassment or real persecution. Firmness and patience were required in dealing with these various situations. The regime of independent Czechoslovakia, for example, began by striking an anti-Roman attitude ostentatiously harking back to the age of John Hus. It drew up anti-clerical legislation on French lines and at the same time attempted to revive the national Bohemian Church founded by the mediaeval reformer. But the policy did not work. Not only was it abhorrent to the strongly Catholic Slovaks, but the government was soon forced to seek help from the Catholic Christian Social party in order to counteract the influence of the Sudeten Germans. So Benes, the Prime Minister, was sent scurrying to Rome for the pupose of mending its fences with the Vatican. Gasparri, for his part, was delighted to receive this anti-clerical statesman in the role of a suppliant and had no difficulty in securing the necessary concessions from him. Curiously enough the Pope found it impossible to avoid a sharp clash with profoundly Catholic Poland over the treatment of the large Orthodox minority in the eastern part of the new State. Its Head, Marshal Pilsudski, would have been content to leave the Orthodox Ukrainian Church undisturbed so long as it remained independent of a Moscow Patriarchate under Soviet influence. Pius, on the other hand, insisted that its members should be urged to join the Uniate Church, a body professing allegiance to the Roman Pope but using the Orthodox rite in its devotions. He confided the task of persuasion to the Jesuits, whose mission was impeded at every turn by the Polish authorities. Both the Pope and Pilsudski were autocrats. Neither would give way and the difference was still unresolved when, after the latter's death, Polish independence was again extinguished by Hitler and Stalin. In a third Slav country, Yugoslavia, agreement on a Concordat was frustrated by the irreconcilable enmity between Orthodox Serbs and Catholic Croats.

If Pius had shown himself testily intransigent in the Polish affair, he handled his relations with France tactfully and delicately. The 1914 war was the turning point in French official and public feeling on religious matters. Even the most ideological of anti-clericals had been obliged to admire the impeccable patriotism of Catholics in face of the enemy; indeed over five thousand priests had fallen in battle. The atmosphere had utterly changed since the Combes era when the Carthusians could be violently ejected from their historic monastery between ranks of infantrymen with fixed bayonets. After the 'Union Sacrée' of the war such a scene could never have been repeated. Moreover the government had grasped how deeply the national prestige throughout the world was indebted to the work of Catholic intellectuals, missions and cultural organizations. These considerations moved Briand to restore diplomatic relations with the Holy See in 1921. When they were again broken off three years later by the doctrinare left-winger Herriot the Pope, realizing that French anti-clericalism was no longer so potent a force, did not take this rearguard action too seriously. He was rewarded when Herriot's government fell in its turn and his successor, Painlevé, not only sent the French Ambassador back to the Vatican but took discreet steps to scale down, if not to abrogate, previous anti-clerical laws.

The time had come for Pius to reciprocate. He did so by denouncing the *Action Française*, the movement and newspaper founded by Charles Maurras, which had been a thorn in the side of the Third Republic since the beginning of the century. Ostensibly Catholic and monarchist, he at first attracted favourable attention from

Pius X and from the French bishops. After the war, however, it became evident that his Catholicism merely masked a nasty form of extreme nationalism. His own writings revealed that he was intellectually a positivist and was using religion for disreputable political ends. In 1926 he was waging a particularly virulent campaign against the Locarno Treaty, of which the Pope approved heartily as a step towards reconciliation between Germany and its former enemies. The papal condemnation was expressed in an oblique manner, first through an article by the Archbishop of Bordeaux in his own diocesan magazine and secondly through an open letter from the Pope himself supporting the prelate. When Maurras refused to bow to censure, his books, together with the *Action Française*, were placed on the Index of forbidden publications. From that moment, although he continued to howl and fume, his movement slowly withered, while relations between the Republic and the Vatican advanced from correct to cordial.

In a very different situation Pius employed a still heavier weapon from his armoury. He was gravely disturbed by the plight of Catholics in distant Mexico. Founded after the Spanish conquest by dedicated friars, the Mexican Church had eventually grown rich and sluggish. As a result of the Liberal victory in the bitter civil conflicts of the mid-nineteenth century it was stripped of its treasures and lands, but it survived in a weakened state because Catholicism, tinged with the residue of indigenous cults, was deeply rooted in the people. A modest revival was checked by the long drawn-out Mexican Revolution of 1911 and the imposition of harsh anti-clerical laws by the Constitution of 1917. Even so, in the interests of national harmony, they were not strictly enforced for a decade. But in 1926 the dictator of the moment, Calles, clamped down on religious life with a severity which seemed designed to terminate it altogether. Finding their remonstrances ignored, the Mexican bishops appealed to Rome. The Pope's answer was to lay the country under an interdict, that most formidable of mediaeval sanctions. Priests were ordered to abandon their churches, to cease administering the sacraments and to take no part in religious ceremonies.

With the government as obdurate as the hierarchy, the former was faced by rebellion in the solidly Catholic rural areas. For the next three years the army was engaging the Catholic armed bands, known as the *Cristeros*, who at one moment numbered 40,000. Deaths in battle ran into thousands and were swelled by the atrocities committed on both sides. Thus the interdict inflicted further sufferings on the faithful, while Pius was upset by the reluctance of foreign powers to arraign the Mexican government for the inhuman treatment of its own nationals. Nevertheless Calles, brutal tyrant as he was, was sufficiently impressed by the stubborn Catholicism of his own countrymen to listen to proposals for mediation from the American Ambassador, Dwight Morrow. Thanks to him a wary compromise was arranged allowing the clergy, with the consent of Rome, to return to their duties. It could not properly be represented as a climb-down by either side, but the fact that public worship could now be resumed was interpreted by the Catholics as a victory for themselves. On the other hand most of the irksome restrictions on religious observance remained temporarily in force and even today clerical dress cannot be worn on the streets of Mexico. The number of priests whom the authorities allowed to be registered, on the recommendation of the bishops, was reduced to a few score, so that in most of the villages the Indian peasants conducted their own services. In more than one province the governor persisted in demolishing churches, executing priests and decimating their flocks with machine guns. But the situation slowly improved until President Cardenas (1934–40), himself an atheist, ended the persecution and sent Calles into exile. His successor, Avila Camacho, stood up and announced 'I am a believer.' Whether the Pope was right or wrong in ordering the interdict the Church emerged the stronger for its trials. It would not be correct to assume, as one eminent writer has done, that 'the whole episode greatly weakened its hold on Mexican minds.' As the recent visit of John Paul II to Mexico has demonstrated, the contrary is the case.

In the twenties, before Pius's reign was bedevilled by the rise of Nazism, Russia was much in his mind. He was patiently hoping to reach a practical understanding with the Bolshevik regime. Even if the Vatican were barred from exploiting Russia as a mission field it might, he thought, be possible to secure a measure of protection for Catholics in the exercise of their religion. It would help if the Soviet government agreed to receive an Apostolic Delegate. Lengthy talks were in fact held in Berlin between the nuncio, Pacelli, and Soviet officials, but they eventually told him that Moscow was no longer interested in a Concordat or any form of bilateral agreement. The Pope at last understood that with Stalin in power there could be no question of any relationship between Moscow and Rome but one of bitter hostility. But it was only in 1930 that he personally and openly protested against the anti-religious excesses of the Soviet regime and ordered a Mass of expiation in St Peter's. He also waited until March 1937 before condemning atheistic Communism root and branch in his encyclical *Divini Redemptoris*. 'Communism is intrinsically wrong,' he declared, 'and no one who would save Christian civilization may collaborate with it in any field whatsoever.' In that same month he delivered an overdue counterblast to Nazism in *Mit brennender Sorge*.

Germany gave him no cause for alarm in the early years of his pontificate. The Church's interests were effectively safeguarded by the existence of the strong Catholic Centre Party in the Reichstag and the country. Although he did not in principle approve the active part played in it by individual clerics, he did not forbid it. Guided by Pacelli, he concluded separate Concordats with Bavaria, Baden and Prussia, where the majority of Catholics lived. The first warning signal was hoisted when the Nazis made very substantial gains in the autumn elections of 1931, and from that moment it was only a step towards Hitler's accession to office in January 1933. Pius, however, received the news with equanimity. Whether or not he had studied *Mein Kampf*, he observed that Hitler's early public statements as Chancellor were not unfriendly to the Church and stoutly hostile to Communism. Again counselled by Pacelli, Cardinal and Secretary of State since 1930, he decided that he must have a Concordat with the Reich as a whole, just as he already had with Italy. He felt no serious qualms on learning that the success of the negotiation, which he undertook at the Führer's suggestion, would probably depend on his readiness to throw the Centre Party to the wolves in the same way as he had treated the Italian Popular Party. He had convinced himself that German Catholic freedoms could be more effectively defended by the terms of the Concordat than by parliamentary action. Consequently he consented to the inclusion of the clause which ensured the total eclipse of the Centre Party, already weakened in the elections of March 1933, and Hitler's assumption of dictatorial power. The ground had been so well prepared that the final discussions, which were held in Rome between the Pope, assisted by Pacelli, and von Papen, took only eight days, and the Concordat was signed on 20 July.

To be fair to Pius, it must be added that leading members of the German episcopate also thought it preferable to have a Concordat on the terms agreed than no Concordat at all. But any optimism which Pope and hierarchy may have felt about the future was dispelled as reports poured in of breaches of the Concordat, both in letter and in spirit. The Nazis employed a variety of methods to make it a dead letter—the regimentation and political indoctrination of youth, the intimidation of parents who sent their children to Catholic schools, the suppression of Catholic associations and trades unions. These pressures were so effective that the Vatican reluctantly realized that the legal guarantees provided by the Concordat were proving worthless. Moreover they were being aggravated by crude physical violence against Catholics and a scurrilous propaganda campaign orchestrated by Goebbels and Streicher against religion as such, the papacy and the person of the Pope. Persecution of recalcitrant Catholics was coming to resemble that of the Jews. Numerous protests from the German bishops and from Pacelli through the nuncio were scornfully rejected or simply disregarded. Early in 1936 Pius himself remonstrated angrily with the German Ambassador, but his intervention was of no avail whatever.

Despite the failure of these representations Pacelli was still advising against a public confrontation. The Pope, however, was losing patience. In January 1937 he received five leaders of the German hierarchy. After their talk Cardinal Faulhaber of Munich, the most outspoken enemy of the regime, was invited to draft an encyclical in the German language expressing the Church's repugnance to Nazism and castigating its outrages in the most forceful terms. The result was the encyclical *Mit brennender Sorge*. This brilliant polemic was conveyed secretly to Germany, printed and distributed under the noses of the authorities and read out in the churches on Palm Sunday. No epithets were omitted in its excoriation of Nazism, Hitler himself being described as 'mad prophet possessed of repulsive arrogance'. Although the government prevented the circulation of the text in Germany, it was enthusiastically welcomed abroad and effaced the unfavourable impression left by the Concordat. Pacelli, for his part, sharply rebuffed German protests. It was hardly to be expected that the Führer, when paying a State visit to Italy, would comply with the routine procedure of requesting an audience with the Pope, but the latter showed his aversion to him by retiring to Castelgandolfo. In reply to abusive Nazi propaganda he repeated unequivocally that Germany was suffering a full scale religious persecution.

He was much afflicted when the persecution was extended to Austria by its incorporation into the German Reich. This was especially grievous to him because the country, with the exception of Socialist Vienna, had been governed for many years on Catholic principles, first by a priest, Monsignor Seipel, and subsequently by Dollfuss, a devout layman. He considered Seipel so indispensable that he waived on his behalf his own objections to clerics in Parliamentary life. After Seipel's death, however, Dollfuss did away with parliamentary democracy. Having suppressed the Viennese Socialists by armed force he imposed a new constitution on corporative lines based on Pius's *Quadragesimo Anno* and enshrining the terms of a Concordat signed in 1933. The Pope was therefore dismayed by Dollfuss's assassination at Nazi hands a year later and, in 1938, by Austria's disappearance from the map. All he could do was to send for the Archbishop of Vienna, Cardinal Innitzer, who had been unwise enough to declare his loyalty to the Reich, and to dress him down thoroughly.

While the tension with Germany was at its peak an agonizing civil war was raging in Spain. Aversion for the defunct Franco regime should not be allowed to conceal the stark fact that Catholics underwent a savage persecution before and during the conflict in the regions dominated by the Republicans. In Catalonia the practice of religion was virtually eliminated. Twelve bishops and thousands of priests, friars, monks and nuns were murdered; churches, monasteries and ecclesiastical properties of all kinds were destroyed. Admittedly the Spanish Church had suffered from grave defects in pre-republican times; it had been reactionary, obscurantist and all too powerful, but it did not deserve so grim an ordeal. When the Monarchy was abolished in 1931 and the Republic decreed the separation of Church and State the Vatican reacted calmly, emphasizing its desire to establish correct relations with the new regime. The survival of Catholicism was not bound up with that of the Monarchy and if the Republic could guarantee religious liberties there would be nothing to fear. In 1933 a government of the Right took office and soon began to negotiate a Concordat, but before it could be concluded the Left was swept back into power. That was the signal for an outburst of anti-religious atrocities and for political anarchy leading to military rebellion in July 1936.

In view of the wrongs done to Catholics it would have been unnatural for the Pope not to hope for a rebel victory. Nevertheless it was embarrassing, to say the least of it, that the victory was being achieved with the help of two dictators, one of whom was throughly inimical to him and the other he was at pains to keep at arm's length. Furthermore Spanish Falangism had acquired some of the worst traits of Fascism and Nazism and was perpetrating the same excesses. The same leaders of the Spanish hierarchy as had narrowly escaped martyrdom at the hands of the Reds were now protesting against the totalitarian behaviour of their enemies. However Pius's death preceded the final triumph of the Nationalists by a few months.

Guilty as Pius may have been of miscalculation in his handling of Mussolini and Hitler, his opposition to their acts and ideology was more vigorous and consistent than that displayed by any one State or combination of States. Incidentally he had little confidence in the capacity of the League of Nations to restrain aggressors. His own anti-totalitarian stand grew firmer with advancing years, so that his stature was never higher than at the end of his life. In 1938 he was very ill and had to spend six months quietly at Castelgandolfo, but he recovered sufficiently to make a moving appeal for peace during the Munich crisis. In his last days he was working on an address to the Italian episcopate in which he proposed to mark the tenth anniversary of the Concordat by an indictment of Fascism. He urged his doctors to keep him alive at all costs for the occasion. But that was not to be, and the speech was never delivered.

It was generally expected that, in accordance with Pius XI's wishes, he would be succeeded by his Secretary of State, Eugenio Pacelli, and in the event the Sacred College took only one day to elect him. He obtained the necessary majority at the second ballot, but surprised his colleagues by requesting their confirmation in a third before embarking on his nineteen-year pontificate (1939–58).

Pius XII's family came from Latium. His grandfather, Marcantonio, moved to Rome in 1819 and entered the service of the Holy See. He was promoted by Pius IX to the post of Under Secretary of the Interior in the papal state and held it until 1870. In that capacity he helped to set up the papal newspaper, the *Osservatore Romano*. His father, Filippo, was a distinguished Vatican lawyer. His brother, Francesco, followed the same profession and, as Cardinal Gasparri's assistant, performed the spadework in the negotiation of the Concordat with Italy. As a young priest Eugenio was also trained in canon law and worked with Gasparri in its codification. But law was for him only a sideline. At the age of twenty-five he was assigned to the Secretariat of State and there he stayed, serving in Rome or abroad, until he became Pope.

Originally a reluctant diplomat, he was soon thoroughly versed in the techniques of the trade and over the years he acquired unusually wide experience of the world outside the Vatican. He knew Paris and London, which he visited as a member of the papal mission to the coronation of George V. His nunciature in Germany, which lasted from 1917 to 1929, coloured his future approach to European problems. After his appointment as Secretary of State, he travelled extensively overseas, to Argentina, Uruguay and Brazil and finally to the United States in 1936, when he met President Roosevelt. He was back in London for a second coronation in 1937 and in the next year represented the Pope in a Eucharistic Congress at Budapest.

From the start of his pontificate he faced the difficulty which Pius XI and he himself had so far failed to resolve. Was there any possibility of a compromise between totalitarianism and religion? From a diplomatic point of view transactions, however impermanent, may be preferable to dangerous confrontations, and that was the principle to which Pacelli had always adhered. To Soviet Russia, however, it was now plainly inapplicable. In Italy, on the other hand, millions of Catholics were not disposed to regard their religion as incompatible with Fascism. Even bishops had applauded Mussolini's invasion of Abyssinia as a victory over barbarism and an opportunity to substitute the Catholic for the Coptic Church in that country. Similar sentiments were voiced when he grabbed Albania shortly after the new Pope's accession. In spite of his intimate acquaintance with Germany he was slow to grasp that Nazism presented a more immediate and explosive menace than Communism to all that the Holy See stood for. However that may be there was nothing he could personally do in the first six months of his reign to preserve peace except to convey repeated and well publicized warnings to the dictators. His last eloquent appeal, the nearest he got to an outright condemnation of the imminent rape of Poland, was broadcast on the signature of Hitler's pact with Stalin, but its effect was spoiled by his subsequent suggestion that it might be bought off by Polish concessions. Again, after Poland had already been overwhelmed, he issued an encyclical (*Summi Pontificatus*) expressing his love for its people, 'whose faith in the service of Christian civilization' was 'written in ineffaceable letters in the Book of History'. But as he well knew such rhetoric, to which he was addicted, could not save Poland itself from effacement. Just as Benedict XV had avoided designating imperial Germany as the aggressor when condoling with Belgium, he too was careful not to compromise his neutrality by naming the Germany of Hitler. Nevertheless his meaning was plain enough. A little later he authorized Vatican Radio to censure Nazi oppression of the conquered Poles in much more outspoken terms. In reply to his expostulations the German Ambassador was blandly reminded that the broadcasting station was run by the Jesuits as an independent concern with which the Pope did not propose to interfere.

Throughout the 'phoney' war he continued to sponsor or support peace initiatives. He was delighted when President Roosevelt appointed Mr Myron Taylor to represent him personally at the Vatican for that very purpose. His own annual Christmas message set out the principles, each time listed under five heads, which ought to inspire a just international peace. Such generalities, however impeccable, had no influence on the course of hostilities. His silent disapproval of Italy's entry into the war contrasted with the strident enthusiasm of many Italian bishops; it was only too obvious that so long as Fascism was on the winning side Italian Catholics would not disavow it. Not expecting the British government to persist in its belligerency after the fall of France, he directed the Apostolic Delegate in London to urge it discreetly to take advantage of Hitler's much advertised peace offer. He failed to understand why his suggestion was immediately spurned. Great Britain, he thought, must bear a load of blame for the continuation of the war.

For a whole year Pius retired behind the curtain of his neutrality. With Europe dominated by the Axis Powers he felt isolated and insecure. His ability to protect its Catholic peoples against totalitarian abuses had been sadly impaired and neither the Axis nor the British would accept him as a mediator. When Hitler's invasion of Russia added a new dimension to the war the official Vatican view was summed up by the Assistant Secretary of State, Monsignor Tardini, in the words 'one devil chasing out the other'. It was also recalled that whereas the papacy had never wavered in its abhorrence of Communism Hitler had not scrupled to join Stalin in an aggressive conspiracy. For that reason alone there could be no question of the Pope blessing his attack on Russia as a holy crusade. Privately, however, Pius favoured a German victory. Apart from the fact that he liked the German people and thought that he understood them, he was tempted to speculate that Soviet Communism might forever be shattered by the blow. Alternatively both Communism and Nazism might be so gravely weakened that the Western nations might be able to reassert themselves, do away with both forms of totalitarianism and create a new international balance in Europe. In the meantime, however, he gave some comfort to the Axis by referring, in a broadcast, to the exploits of its armies, as 'magnanimous acts of valour which now defend the foundations of Christian culture'.

This was hardly an impartial statement and implied some confusion of mind. The Holy See was on firmer ground in warning the British, and later the American, governments that the ultimate aims of Soviet Communism, including the extirpation of religion, had not changed just because Stalin had formed an alliance of necessity with the western democracies. The latter should not naively mistake his propagandist manoeuvres for a change of heart. Nevertheless the Pope, under discreet pressure from his old friend Roosevelt, slowly came round to the view that Hitlerism was a worse menace, at least in the short term, than Stalinism, and that Hitler's opponents were justified in co-operating with Stalin in order to defeat the common enemy in the field. His own uncertainties regarding the outcome of the war were dispelled in the course of 1942. First he was appraised of a peace feeler put forward by von Papen, then German Ambassador to Turkey, to the nuncio Monsignor Roncalli (the future Pope John XXIII). His suggestion that the Holy See might sound out the Western Powers seemed to indicate a loss of confidence in Berlin. Secondly, Mr Taylor presented to the Pope on 20 September a message of transcendent importance from the President. It announced the irrevocable determination of America to 'obliterate' Hitlerism and to do so in concert with Soviet Russia. Furthermore the Allies had decided to impose the eventual peace and the Holy See must cease to entertain any idea of a negotiated settlement. The effect of this overpoweringly convincing declaration of intent was enhanced by a series of Allied victories in Africa and successful counter-offensives in Russia.

Pius could now foresee that Germany would lose the war, although he looked forward with dread to the prospect of Soviet Communism filling the void left by the disappearance of the Nazi New Order. His public utterances, and particularly his Christmas allocution of 1942, acquired a more strongly anti-totalitarian tone and evoked violent German protests. He was even threatened with 'physical retaliation'. At that stage the danger was not great, for the Italian government would not have wished to commit a breach of the Concordat, for instance by interfering with the Vatican's services, supplies and communications. But it became very real in the late summer of 1943, when Mussolini was overthrown and the Germans took control of Rome. If Hitler had so willed he could at any moment have sequestered the Pope, whisked him away across the Alps and dissolved the whole Vatican establishment, thus depriving the Church of its Head and central administration. The Holy See, in short, would have ceased to exist.

For the Pope this was the bleakest period of the war. Fortunately his links with the world outside the Axis were regularly maintained through somewhat overloaded diplomatic channels. Those with the hierarchy in the Axis-dominated countries, though not immune from tampering, were not seriously interrupted. Points of friction with the Western Allies were not lacking. The Americans were annoyed with the Vatican for establishing diplomatic relations with Japan in 1942, but the Secretary of State, Cardinal Maglione, logically replied it could hardly not do so when the Asian territories overrun by Japan contained eighteen million Catholics. The Holy See was equally incensed because the British expelled or incarcerated Italian clerics in the Middle East and Abyssinia who were convicted or suspected of un-clerical activities. Finally the Pope was dismayed when Rome was twice raided by Allied aircraft in July and August 1943 and the church of San Lorenzo Fuori le Mura seriously damaged. Subsequently, however, while not recognizing Rome as an open city, the Allies in fact treated it as such although it was under German occupation. The origin of a single aircraft which dropped bombs on the Vatican City itself later in the same year, luckily without killing anyone, has never been elucidated.

These disputes and incidents were not of prime importance when measured against the appalling evidences of persecution and atrocity that poured into the Vatican from Hitler's Europe. The purpose of the Führer's anti-religious policy, as applied in Germany, was quite simple: Catholicism must be eliminated but not until the war was won. Meanwhile awkward episcopal pronouncements should be stifled or ignored. While no frontal attack on the Church should be attempted for fear of outraging the millions of Catholic Germans fighting in the ranks and engaged in the war effort, it should be assiduously undermined by propaganda and administrative pressure. In these conditions certain German bishops courageously denounced concentration camps, mass deportations, the organized euthanasia of the infirm, the confiscation of Church properties and the corruption of youth by semi-pagan teachings. The news from the occupied lands—Poland, Czechoslovakia, the Low Countries was worse but the behaviour of the clergy and faithful grew if anything more staunch as the abuses multiplied. In France, where the majority of Catholics at first welcomed the Pétain regime and its readiness to compound with Germany, it was not long before the bishops were protesting to the Marshal against his tolerance of the same aberrations, and their attitude stiffened when the whole country was occupied. Despite difficulties of communication and differences of national outlook the Catholic reaction to totalitarianism was on the whole admirably uniform and well co-ordinated.

Yet the resources of the inadequately staffed Secretariat of State were strained to the utmost. It sometimes failed to keep track of events. That is the only charitable but quite unsatisfying explanation of the Vatican's obtuseness in face of the extermination of the Orthodox Serb minority in the newly created Fascist State of

Croatia. According to one estimate seven hundred thousand persons were slaughtered in a series of massacres which seem never to have disturbed the world's conscience to the same extent as Hitler's parallel attempt to wipe out the Jews of eastern Europe. The Church cannot convincingly deny its deep though indirect implication in this ghastly operation. Local Franciscan friars joined joyfully in it. The Croatian dictator and former terrorist, Pavelic, who initiated it, was an obstentatiously zealous Catholic and his regime was at first hailed with enthusiasm by Archbishop Stepinac of Zagreb. The Orthodox victims were nominally offered a choice between death and conversion to Catholicism, but it appears that remarkably few of them were able to avail themselves of the option. When the Archbishop fully realized what was happening he changed his tune, thereby incurring the enmity of the dictator. However it was too late to save the Serbs. As for the Pope, he remained silent, although he must have been made aware of the facts by some of the numerous Italian clerics, officials and soldiers then active in Croatia.

Much ink has been spilled by those who argue the question whether the Pope could or could not, through some dramatic intervention, have saved the Jews, or some of them, from Hitler's gas ovens, and no doubt this obstinate controversy will be pursued until the last document has been exhumed from the relevant archives and the last contemporary observer of the tragedy has died. Passionate and occasionally envenomed attacks have been made on Pius XII for his alleged passivity and reluctance to denounce genocide. Some of the adverse criticisms have been inspired by a sincere conviction that papal action could have achieved the desired result, others by an obvious anti-religious or anti-Catholic bias. The second category is exemplified by Herr Hochhuth's famous play, *The Representative*, which, effective as it is on the stage, caricatures the Pope instead of trying to portray him as he really was.

It may be that an inborn prejudice against the Jews still lurked in the recesses of the Curia, but if so it affected neither Pius XI nor Pius XII. The former, speaking in September 1938, expressly warned his hearers that anti-Semitism was incompatible with Christianity. 'Spiritually', he declared, 'we are all Semites.' As soon as the outbreak of war swelled the flood of Jewish fugitives, the Church sheltered, fed and subsidized them on a very extensive scale. It goes without saying that in most cases such help had to be given as unobtrusively as possible. According to one Jewish source 'the Catholic Church saved some four hundred thousand Jews from certain death;' it 'saved more Jewish lives than all other Churches, religious institutions and rescue organizations put together'. Many other authorities have borne witness to the Pope's personal interest in the work and to his general concern with the sufferings of the Jews.

We may assume that he and his advisers were not the last to hear about the gas chambers in Poland. Certainly they were slow to credit the first horrific reports. But when these were confirmed why did he not broadcast a flaming indictment of Hitler and his henchmen? Would it not have provoked so wide and deep a revulsion in the civilized world and in Germany itself that the Führer would have felt obliged to halt the programme of extermination? There is no doubt that a public fulmination from the Holy See would have caused an immense stir in the world and exonerated the Pope from future charges of indifference. But if we ask whether it would have brought the massacres to a halt, or even slowed them down, we have to confess that the question is unanswerable. We simply cannot judge whether it would have eased or aggravated, if that were possible, the plight of the victims. It is equally hard to guess to what extent open papal intervention on behalf of the Jews would have resulted in retaliation against German Catholics by an enraged and paranoiac Führer. It may well be that both Pius and the German bishops with whom he was in correspondence were inclined to exaggerate this risk and that the nuncio allowed himself to be unnecessarily impressed by the violence with which Hitler reacted when, under instructions from Rome, he raised the Jewish question with him. But it was sinister enough that the outspoken protest in their favour from the Archbishop of Utrecht was followed immediately by the despatch of all baptized Catholics of Jewish origin in his diocese to the Polish ovens.

After the bloodless liberation of Rome by the Allied armies Pius's pontificate still had fifteen years to run. It pained him deeply that the disappearance of Fascism and Nazism, those twin founts of violence and error, should have involved the penetration of Soviet armies into eastern and central Europe and the imposition of Communist regimes on several of the countries concerned. The emergence of strong Communist parties jockeying for power in Italy and France was equally worrying. The peril seemed to be acute on both the ideological and the political fronts. It was therefore, in his view, the Church's duty to proclaim and conduct a campaign of total opposition to atheistic Communism in every possible field while frowning on any tendency to appeasement or compromise. In international affairs the political task might safely be left to the Western governments under American leadership, but in order to repel the ideological enemy the papacy needed to strengthen and reshape its own defences. Pius XI had made a good start in expanding and internationalizing the Church by creating fifty-seven new bishoprics, forty-five of them in America and Asia. In 1946 Pius XII raised the membership of the Sacred College from thirty-eight to seventy, with the result that the non-Italians well outnumbered the Italians, and added another twenty-four in 1953. This reform was most salutary, especially in the longer term.

He showed less than his usual prudence, however, in issuing a decree forbidding Catholics in all countries, under pain of excommunication, to vote for Communist parties or to co-operate with them in any way. He did this in 1949, the year after the Christian Democrats had won a decisive success in the Italian elections. Their leader, de Gasperi, who had won his victory with clerical support but without clerical direction, was embarrassed by this prohibition. It clearly violated the principles of liberal democracy. It was also easy for nominal Catholic voters to ignore it if they wished, as it was indeed ignored in Catholic countries outside Italy. The Pope's relationship with Christian Democrats remained uneasy until the end of his pontificate. It was particularly strained in 1952–3 when he and the president of Catholic Action, Professor Gedda, made an ill-judged attempt to propel the Christian Democracy into an alliance with the neo-Fascists. If it had succeeded it would have wrecked the prospects of Christian Democracy as a solid centre party of government. Its dilemma was that while it needed the Church's support for electoral purposes it was impatient of Vatican control, and after de Gasperi's death its left-centrist element gradually prevailed. For Pius, on the other hand, the rejection of Communism and of alliances on the left was not so much a political necessity as a religious obligation. Peace had been the constant theme of his allocutions, but was it compatible with an unbending attitude towards Communism which seemed to preclude any useful dialogue? In the light of the Church's depressing experience of Stalinist and Titoist Communism in Europe, and of the total eclipse of Catholicism in the once promising mission field of China, it would be hard to fault him. And the brutal suppression of the Hungarian uprising, which evoked three encyclicals from the Holy See, took place five years after Stalin's death. Evidently no softening could be expected on the Soviet side.

When the war was over Pius reigned in a style recalling the grand centuries of the papacy. Ascetic and solitary by temperament, frail and spiritual in appearance, he nevertheless took pleasure in the traditional splendours of his office. He retained all the decorative paraphernalia of the papal court. A ceremonial figure of ethereal dignity, he was also the most humanly accessible of pontiffs. He multiplied both mass and private audiences, delighting in being seen and heard by as many people as possible. His peculiar gift for mastering abstruse subjects at short notice astounded specialist groups of scholars, scientists and technicians. Like his predecessor, he had a limitless capacity for hard work, although he spent far too much time in polishing and repolishing the ornate eloquence of his own compositions. While he readily adapted himself to minor features of modern life, such as the use of the typewriter and the telephone, and kept abreast of major developments, his attitudes hardened with advancing age. He felt himself to be spiritually and intellectually self-sufficent. After the death of Cardinal Maglione in 1944 he acted as his own Secretary of State, aided by Monsignor Tardini and his equally talented alternate Monsignor Montini, the future Pope Paul VI. He had few intimates outside his own family, and malicious writers depicted him as tending his canaries, fussed over by his housekeeper, the formidable German nun Sister Pasqualina, and unduly influenced by his disagreeable physician, Dr Galeazzi Lisi.

He survived until 1958. In his later years he did not supplement his early encyclicals which from *Summi Pontificatus* onwards had been distinguished by their philosophic and theological excellence, by pronouncements of equal value on social and other pressing problems of the post-war period, contenting himself with announcing the dogma of the bodily Assumption of the Virgin. It seemed as if he had nothing new to say. Yet his successor, John XXIII, was to declare that in his pontificate 'we are witnessing the unmistakable opening of new horizons.' In other words, Pius, the last and very impressive Pope of the old order, prepared the way for a sudden and fruitful unfolding of the new.

24

AGGIORNAMENTO
(1958–1978)

The reign of John XXIII (1958–63) is commonly thought to have been a turning point, if not a revolution, in the life of the Church. A cynic might see his *aggiornamento* as a bold but probably unsuccessful attempt to secure the future of Catholicism in a society which is becoming increasingly irreligious and materialistic. According to that view the Church has chosen to adapt itself to the demands of the modern world in the hope that timely concessions will guarantee its survival. But it would be more true to history to regard the changes of outlook and direction that have resulted from John's pontificate and the Second Vatican Council as a necessary stage in the Church's evolution and even of the same order of significance as the great conciliar movements of the past, from Nicaea to Trent. It may still be too early to assess John's aims and accomplishments. What is certain is that while the Church had been hoping to escape from the immobilism and rigidity of thought that had characterized Pius XII's later years, it did not suspect that the reign of the former Patriarch of Venice, Cardinal Angelo Roncalli, aged 77, had any great surprise in store.

The clever child of poor peasants at Sotto il Monte, near Bergamo, Roncalli received an excellent education as a seminarist but his early record, though intellectually distinguished, was not such as to attract much notice. At Bergamo he taught history and theology and served as secretary to its bishop, whose biography he later wrote. He composed a learned monograph on Caesar Baronius, the sixteenth-century historian of the early Church, and his researches into the Life of St Charles Borromeo brought him into touch with Monsignor Ratti at the Ambrosian Library. In the First World War he was called up into the army. It was not until 1920 that he left Bergamo for the Congregation of Propaganda, the organizing body for foreign missions, at Rome. Five years later Pius XII appointed him Apostolic Visitor to Bulgaria.

That was the start of a diplomatic career which lasted for twenty-eight years, nineteen of which he spent in Bulgaria, Greece and Turkey. It was not an easy job. At Athens and Sofia, and in the Patriarchate of Istanbul, he encounted the full force of the traditional Orthodox distaste for Rome. Catholic communities were scanty and dispersed. During the war Turkey seethed with international intrigue, while Greece was crushed under a harsh Axis occupation. Roncalli's experiences, however, filled him with a vast enthusiasm for the reunion of the Churches. He also fulfilled his tasks so efficiently and discreetly that in 1944 he was given a more important and delicate assignment, that of nuncio in liberated Paris. There he stayed for another nine years before being raised to the Cardinalate as Patriarch of Venice. His genial personality and tactful handling of affairs won him the esteem of successive French governments. The first difficulty he surmounted was General de Gaulle's demand that thirty-three bishops should be deprived of their sees for having supported the Vichy regime. He managed to whittle down this number to three, thus avoiding what might have been a serious rift between France and the Vatican. Another cause of friction was the latter's attitude towards the worker-priest movement which had been launched during the war under the auspices of the Archbishop of Paris, Cardinal Suhard. Some members of the national hierarchy were convinced that the assignment of priests to the shop floor and their identification with the life and interests of the workers would be of real help in checking the almost total divorce of the French industrial working class from the Church. The concept, however, did not commend itself to Pius XII, who felt that the experiment would have little impact and would probably infect the priests themselves with revolutionary ideas. Roncalli thought that it should at least be tried out and arranged for French bishops to discuss it personally with the Pope. In the event it proved impossible to reconcile the sacerdotal functions of the worker-priests with their industrial duties, union obligations and, in some cases, their strongly expressed left-wing political sympathies. The movement, distracted by quarrels and restricted in its activity by papal order, lingered unhappily on until it fell to Roncalli, as Pope, to dissolve it altogether.

Roncalli expected to die in Venice. His patriarchal office, though highly honorific and ornamental, offered little scope for initiative. He occupied himself with pastoral work, especially among the poor of the city's industrial hinterland, and with dispensing wit and charm to those who attended the many international gatherings held in the city. When Pius XII died there was no obvious successor for the Conclave to elect, and three days of balloting went by before its choice descended on Roncalli. It did not do so because he was a neutral compromise candidate who would give the papacy a short breathing space, but by reason of his positive qualities, his exemplary piety, his loyalty to a pontiff whose philosophy he was known not fully to have shared, his talent for conciliation and his immense experience of diplomacy. Whereas no startling innovations were expected of him, there was some uncertainty about his handling of the Curia, given the fact that it was thirty-three years since he had held a post at Rome. It is unlikely that his colleagues in the Sacred College drew the wrong conclusions from his apparent simplicity of character, the product of his peasant origins, for his career had obviously taught him to be an acute judge of men and events. What they had evidently not reckoned upon was the capacity of this old man, in terms of will and energy, to set in motion a project of the first magnitude.

John's first Secretary of State, Cardinal Tardini, is said to have confessed that when the Pope first mentioned to him his intention to summon a General Council he thought that he must be out of his mind. Apocryphal or not, the story indicates that the idea that a Council might be opportune and salutary had not entered the heads of senior churchmen at Rome; nor had it occurred to them that John was likely to figure as more than an amiable stop-gap, a *papa di passaggio*. According to the first public announcement of the conciliar plan, which was made, oddly enough, in the *Osservatore Romano* of 26 January 1959, the general purpose would be to enhance 'the spiritual welfare' of Christians. Moreover the Council would afford an opportunity for the 'separated communities' to advance towards the goal of unity. A possible assumption was that John was inviting Orthodox, Protestant and other non-Catholic Christians to a meeting on the lines of the fifteenth century Councils of Ferrara and Florence. But he waited until Whitsun to explain that attendance would be confined to the bishops of the Roman Communion. He stressed that the work of preparation would be arduous and hinted mysteriously that the outcome of the

Council would 'shake the heavens and the earth'. There was no reference, however, to a sweeping programme of renovation.

The preparation was to occupy nearly three and a half years. First a commission of Cardinals was set up under Tardini's chairmanship to receive proposals for an agenda from a variety of ecclesiastical and academic sources. The process took a whole year to complete and a further six months passed before a batch of preparatory commissions, each presided over by a curial Cardinal, was ready to start ploughing through the mass of material submitted and drafting the 'schemas' that composed the actual agenda. This phase lasted for another whole year. At last, on 11 October 1962, all was ready for the Pope to inaugurate the Council in St Peter's, where two thousand five hundred Fathers were assembled.

Unable to speed the process of preparation, John had worked strenuously during the interval in order to exert the strongest possible influence on the Council's eventual deliberations. He knew that it would need the personal inspiration and guidance which could not be derived from formal schemes emanating from the commissions and reflecting the conservative views of the curial Cardinals. Hence his decision to issue, in the first place, a statement of the same import as Leo XIII's *Rerum Novarum* and Pius XI's *Quadragesimo Anno*. Published in May 1961, on the anniversary of Leo's encyclical, his own *Mater et Magistra* was intended to replace rather than to confirm, as he modestly put it, the social and economic teachings of his two predecessors. Indeed both these pontiffs would have considered his approach to social problems as scandalously radical, for it endorsed without demur the welfare philosophy of the post-war years. Papal blessing was unhesitatingly conferred on the increased role of the State in the social sphere. Yet John was careful to justify State intervention in terms of assisting the individual to assert his natural rights, that is his rights as divinely sanctioned, and the latter were specifically extended by John to embrace health, education, housing and leisure in accordance with the principles of democratic socialism, Christian or otherwise. While admitting that such intervention might give rise to bureaucratic abuses, he held that they could be limited, if not eliminated, by observance of Christian morality. But the Head of the Church seemed to be concerning himself very closely with the relationship between the State and the individual, and less with the duty of society as a whole to God. Like Pius XI he stressed the importance of autonomous administrative bodies paid for but not controlled by the State. In industry too he preferred the small to the giant enterprise. Taxation and credit, prices and wages, transport and the media all received attention, but the most detailed analysis of modern economic problems was reserved for agriculture and the need for its revival. He was clearly moved by his family's experience of small farming in the Bergamo countryside.

John was already thinking of a second encyclical which would deal with the primary themes of world order and peace. Meanwhile the lack of initial response to his call for Christian unity was causing him disappointment. In order to reaffirm that this was a principal aim of the Council he created a special secretariat headed by Cardinal Augustin Bea, a German Jesuit. An indefatigable traveller, Bea promoted the Pope's aspirations in many places throughout 1961 and 1962. He persuaded the World Council of Churches to send observers, and Anglicans were encouraged by John's cordial reception of Dr Fisher, the Archbishop of Canterbury, at the Vatican. The Orthodox Churches, on the other hand, were more than hesitant. The Patriarch of Constantinople, Athenagoras, to whom John addressed himself in the first instance, was an enthusiast for ecumenism, but he was not authorized to answer on behalf of the 'autocephalous' (self-governing) eastern Churches. He was therefore obliged to refer the papal invitation to those bodies at Moscow, Athens and elsewhere. In the worst tradition of Orthodox stickiness, they first complained that they had not been approached directly. Then, after Athens had turned down the invitation, the Patriarch had to inform the Holy See that in the absence of unanimity he would be unable to send a representative of his own. Finally the Russian Patriarch, whose reply depended on the whim of the Soviet Government, cabled at the very last moment that he was prepared to send observers. Two priests duly arrived, but they missed the opening ceremony.

This was of course of grandiose spectacle. The massed hierarchy of the Roman Church, together with its guests and diplomatic envoys from eighty-six countries, numbered three thousand persons, and the event was covered by an equal number of journalists. After a service lasting four hours John treated his audience to a discourse in Latin. The continued use of that language in the liturgy, as well as its employment in the Council's debates, was a subject on which he took a strong traditionalist line, but some of the Fathers, and especially those who came from the newer countries, were embarrassed by their lack of proficiency. Only forty per cent of those present hailed from Europe; Africa and Asia each sent two hundred and fifty and Latin America six hundred.

John then left the Fathers to their discussions, which he watched on closed-circuit television whenever he felt so inclined. But his public utterances were designed to leave them in no doubt that the Council was no mere routine procedure, albeit on a grand scale, for the examination of schemes prepared under the supervision of conservatively minded curial Cardinals. Although it could never have been organized without the help of the curial machinery, he expected the bishops to exercise their own initiative and think independently. He urged them to concentrate on a renewal of the Church's duty to take the lead in promoting peace, unity (not only of Christians but of all mankind) and social concord. Above all its role must be seen as positive and not defensive. In his inaugural address he went out of his way to attack the 'prophets of doom' who 'in the existing state of society see nothing but ruin and calamity'. He besought the Council to take a more cheerful view of the future, to rid itself of the ideas of the Church as an embattled fortress and of the Pope as its castellan fighting behind the last ditch against communism, modernity and error.

As a result of these exhortations the bishops grew impatient of curial direction. They insisted on deciding for themselves who would compose and preside over the ten committees that replaced the preparatory bodies, and they threw out one of the original schemas (on Divine Revelation) altogether. That was a good beginning, but on the whole very little progress was made during their first session, which ended before Christmas 1962. Before they adjourned John reminded them that they would need to do a lot of homework if they wished to live up to his ideal of making the Church a determining factor in world affairs. And, as he reminded the diplomatic observers, the international balance was unsteady in the extreme. The opening of the Council had indeed coincided with the Cuban missile crisis. Luckily Khrushchev, conscious that war had been so narrowly avoided, was glad to take advantage of his appeals for peace and of his friendly gestures towards the Moscow Patriarchate. He reciprocated by releasing Monsignor Slipyi, the Uniate Archbishop of Lvov in the Ukraine, who had been relegated to a Siberian Labour camp for the last eleven years. At his request, too, John agreed to receive his son-in-law Alexis Adjubei, the editor of *Izvestia*, as a member of a group of journalists congratulating him on the award of a peace prize. In April 1963, only two months before his death, he issued *Pacem in Terris*, the encyclical which was designed to complement the exposition of his social doctrine in *Mater et Magistra*. Beginning where the latter broke off and addressed to 'all men of good will', his new message summed up in striking language what he believed to be the right solutions for the world's politico-economic ills. It seemed important enough to be reproduced in full in the *New York Times*.

The encyclical had much to say about the natural and God-given rights of human beings and the manifest duty of governments to respect and foster them. John's own concept of those rights, religious, cultural, political and economic, was comprehensive and while not condemning other political systems out of hand he made no secret of his preference for democracy as the surest guarantee of individual freedoms. He was also inclined to pin responsibility for the advancement of poorer nations squarely and rather uncritically on the more economically developed world. Their problems would be solved through charity and co-operation. He condemned the colonial system, at that time undergoing liquidation, for its defects, without giving it any credit for its past positive qualities. It seemed that the Holy See, suddenly awakened from its preoccupation with Europe, and responding to the insistence of its overseas episcopate, was bestowing a premature blessing on a nationalism which in many cases violated the principles of political liberalism and social justice. But the Pope was apparently not disturbed by the fragmentation of the developing world into a multitude of quarrelling States biting the hand that fed them and invoking aid from sources that were patently not disinterested. Nevertheless his idealism was hardly out of place in the early post-colonial phase when the wind of change blew sweetly, and in most of the countries concerned the Church survives and flourishes as a stabilizing force. In a few, notably in South-East Asia, it has been swept away or underground.

John keenly approved the work of the United Nations and its agencies, as well as all negotiations for disarmament. In his view the prohibition of nuclear weapons was the first requisite, the second the introduction of disarmament by stages. There was nothing very original about his espousal of modern thinking about nationalism, the world economy and war, and its lofty tone risked irritating those dealing with such issues from day to day on a more mundane level. What was novel was the concentration of the papal attitudes into one trenchant declaration and the spelling out of an entirely fresh and pragmatic approach to Communism. Essentially it distinguished between the philosophy of Marxism, which Catholics should continue to regard as detestable, and the adoption by Communist governments and parties of specific programmes with laudable purposes. The encyclical explained that there would be no objection to Catholics joining them in pursuit of such limited aims, and of course of the vital aim of peace. The way was thus cleared for mutually beneficial dialogues with Communism. In the Catholic world as a whole this partial rejection of Pius XII's uncompromising posture did not seem too revolutionary, but it had an unsettling effect in Italy, where the publication of *Pacem in Terris* narrowly preceded national elections and the new line was interpreted as a licence for Catholics to vote for the Communist party if they so wished. In the event the Christian Democrats lost support at the polls and the Pope was exposed to bitter reproaches in their press.

His health was now failing fast and on 3 June he died, amid a great surge of sympathy and regret, of incurable cancer. He could rest content that his work could hardly have been carried further at that stage had he remained alive for some while. As he put it, his bags were already packed. He could only pray that the constitutions which the Council was due to frame during its remaining sessions, whether they were concerned with the clarification of doctrine, the future structure of Church government, the reform of the liturgy, the morals of society or contemporary politics and economics, would respect the guidelines he had so boldly traced. He himself had launched the Council; it would be his successor's difficult task to accommodate the papacy to conciliar decisions.

Cardinal Giovanni Battista Montini, Paul VI (1963–78) was another northerner. Born near Brescia in 1898, he belonged to a well educated and established Catholic family .vith strong political connexions. After entering the priesthood he spent virtually all his life up to 1954 in the Secretariat of State. He proved extremely able and when Pius XII dispensed with a ranking Secretary of State he was promoted to the post of alternate to the Under-Secretary, Tardini. For some years the pair worked successfully in harness but in 1954 they fell out; it was assumed that Montini was becoming too progressive for his colleague's conservative inclinations. Pius solved the difficulty by removing Montini but compensated him with the prestigious archbishopric of Milan. There he remained for the next nine years, and John XXIII rather tardily made him a Cardinal. By contrast with Tardini's sceptical reception of the conciliar plan, Montini at once assured the Pope that 'the Council will make Rome the spiritual capital of the world whence the light will spread over those places and institutions where men are working for the poor, for progress, justice and liberty.' His conception of the Holy See's social mission clearly corresponded with his predecessor's.

Elected on 21 June, Paul had three months to instal himself before the second session of the Council and to make up his mind, if he had not already done so, about the great causes with which John had identified himself in his encyclicals. Even more delicate were the questions of curial reform and of the extent to which the Church might expect to be governed in future by the episcopate acting as a collegial body. What place was the Pope, 'the Servant of the servants of God', to occupy under a new collegial system? And how was his scriptural mandate to rule the Church and restore its unity to be properly fulfilled? Before the Council reopened, Paul warned the Curia of impending changes and began to broaden curial appointments by bringing more clerics into it from outside Italy. Until it was concluded, however, his hands were largely tied.

He enjoyed greater freedom as regards the outside world. In his role of universal pastor and ecumenical pioneer, or as he preferred to say, of a pilgrim, he took ardently to overseas travel and showed a weakness for dramatic gestures. He met and embraced the Patriarch Athenagoras three times, twice in Palestine and once in Constantinople. At Ephesus, that ancient home of the faith, he prayed in the legendary house of the Virgin and in the ruins of the huge cathedral of St John. He was the first Pope to address the United Nations. Until 1971, when his journeys came to an end, he was continually on the move, photographed as he stepped in or out of an aeroplane. He visited Africa, South America, India and the Philippines, where he was stabbed by a madman but not seriously hurt. In all the continents he spoke to gatherings of bishops and nuncios. Such initiatives were striking and praiseworthy, but his decision to attend the celebrations at the shrine of Fatima, the site of the Virgin's alleged appearance fifty years earlier to three Portuguese children, incurred severe criticism, first because the miracle itself was considered dubious by many Catholics and secondly because liberal opinion frowned on Portugal's struggle to retain colonial Angola. He was advised not to go and, when he persisted, rightly censured for a diplomatic blunder. On the other hand, he attracted sympathy when the Communist government of Poland refused to let him participate in the ceremonies to be held at the far more ancient shrine of Czestochowa for the millennium of the Polish Church.

He was also a tireless host. He granted audiences to no fewer than ninety State visitors, a bizarre procession of sovereigns and presidents, dictators, democrats and Communists, black and white, Christian and Jewish, Moslem and heathen. These attentions had more than a formal significance. They seemed to indicate that only a hundred years after the Holy See had been confined, in the progressive view, to the museum, it was fast regaining its long lost reputation among rulers and statesmen as a source of mature wisdom and of moral reassurance against disorder. In fact that upturn in its international prestige started with Pius XI and continued, despite doubts and setbacks, during the reign of Pius XII. Accelerated by Pope John's dynamism, it might have lost momentum if Paul had failed to carry through to the best of his ability, and at the same time to keep under control, the changes that John had set in motion. That was the arduous task to which Paul dedicated himself with very fair success. If he has been accused of hesitancy and uncertainty of touch, it is because the twin purposes were peculiarly hard to combine and reconcile.

Paul did not lack a sense of urgency; he moved as fast as circumstances allowed. So far as ecumenism was concerned progress was unimpressive. His own overtures to the Orthodox Churches produced little result beyond a lessening of friction, while there was also a limit to what he could achieve with the Anglicans. In 1966 he solemnly greeted Dr Ramsey, the Archbishop of Canterbury, in the Sistine Chapel, and they together attended a service of thanksgiving in San Paolo Fuori le Mura. As a result of their meeting a joint theological commission was set up, but apart from identifying the really obstinate issues in the most charitable spirit it did not encourage optimistic expectations. Perhaps there were few of these to be discerned on the Roman side. Nevertheless the theme of Christian unity had pervaded the Council's debates and found expression in a decree on ecumenism and a declaration on religious liberty. The presence of the separated brethren in the background was seldom out of the Fathers' minds.

Pope John had thoroughly approved their action in so promptly removing the direction of the Council from the hands of the Curia. Pope Paul, for his part, equally welcomed their adoption of the principle of collegiality as spelled out in the constitution De Ecclesia. They were at pains to convince themselves and all Catholics that the new system under which the Pope would govern the Church in concert with the whole episcopate would not involve any derogation from his historic supremacy. On the contrary, it was likely to strengthen an authority apt to became unduly circumscribed by the curial bureaucrats. Admittedly the concept of the episcopate as one vast college seemed vague and clumsy. The Church was familiar with local and regional conferences of bishops, but some new machinery was obviously needed at the top. The Pope accordingly called into being, at the Council's suggestion, the Synod of Bishops, a partly consultative, partly deliberative body to be summoned at his own discretion if he should require advice or information. That he regarded this innovation as more than window-dressing is proved by his convocation of five Synods from 1967 onwards, all of them concerned with the most vital problems. Consistent with his promotion of the collegial idea was his further expansion, internationalization and rejuvenation of the original Sacred College. John had increased its membership to eighty-five; Paul raised it to one hundred and eleven, fifty-six Europeans and fifty-five from overseas. Heads of Congregations were urged to retire from the Curia at seventy-five and more non-Italians were brought into curial posts. Finally stringent regulations for the conduct of future conclaves disqualified octogenarian Cardinals from taking part in the ballot. This measure caused very hard feelings. Cardinal Ottaviani, aged 89, a worker's son from Trastevere and the doyen of the conservatives in the College, enquired sarcastically why in that event an octogenarian should still be considered capable of filling St Peter's Chair.

Paul also gave his support, although with some heart-searching, to the Council's liturgical reforms. His predecessor had hardly spoken out in favour of Latin as the common language of the Church, and indeed signed a constitution enjoining its continued use, then found himself sponsoring significant changes in the rite and the introduction of the vernacular on the widest scale. This was an issue on which a great many Catholics, especially in Europe, could be expected to feel strongly, and it duly brought traditionalists and innovators into sharp conflict. But it was inevitable that the former would have to resign themselves with the best possible grace to the changes adopted by the Council, for both Pope and hierarcy recognized the overriding need to make the liturgy intelligible to the mass of overseas Catholics, to say nothing of the non-Latinist Europeans, in their own numerous languages. At the same time it was understood that major papal pronouncements and conciliar decisions too should continue to be framed in Latin. If Paul was disconcerted by the force and eloquence, combined with the shrewd use of publicity, with which Archbishop Lefebvre championed the Tridentine rite from his stronghold at Ecône, he did not perhaps lack understanding of the Frenchman's forlorn stand against the whole conciliar approach to the Church's future. In the hope that the dissident could be talked over he invited him to a meeting but failed to break his intransigence. Subsequently the Holy See has left Lefebvre unharrassed, confident that his movement will peter out and not produce a real schism.

Paul undoubtedly showed a sure touch in steering the Council towards a successful outcome. His own contribution to its various achievements is hard to assess. He did not for instance direct the drafting of its pastoral and dogmatic constitutions which Dr Edward Norman, the eminent Anglican theologian, considers to be 'two of the most important religious documents of the twentieth century'. By standing back from the debates he avoided irritating the progressives or offending the conservatives. He did not try to hurry the Fathers and when he applied the brake he did so gently. Although the progressives were not fully satisfied with its results, the Second Vatican Council ended in an atmosphere of harmony and confidence. It was a far cry from the agonies and frustrations which marred the concluding stages of the First. The lines on which the Church's pastoral mission was to be exercised in future had been traced and the collegial system had clearly come to stay. What was not clear was the extent to which it might inhibit a Pope's personal authority and restrict his initiatives. How would his primacy be expressed during his remaining years and by his successors, especially if they were to be men of powerful character and intellect?

One important sphere in which Paul was resolved to remain his own master was that of diplomacy. Schooled in its techniques under Pius XI and Pius XII, he inherited and developed the policies of John XXIII. While his nominal Secretaries of State were employed on other tasks he personally took charge of their execution. Nuncio and Apostolic Delegates had never been kept busier. He soon became profoundly worried by the war in Vietnam, where flourishing dioceses of the Catholic Church were being ruined in a struggle involving rival super-powers and irreconcilable ideologies. His public appeal for peace, repeated at the United Nations and reinforced in his own letters to the leaders of the states chiefly concerned, including the United States, the Soviet Union and China, did indeed bring about a short truce, but his intervention, despite the praise it evoked at the time, made no further progress and failed to save the Church in South-East Asia. Nevertheless he persisted, more than once urging that Mao's China, which had well nigh eradicated all forms of Christianity, should be admitted to the United Nations.

It was too much to expect that papal influence could check the fatal course of events in the Far East. In eastern Europe, however, it worked effectively enough in favour of détente. Paul's first encyclical *Ecclesiam Suam*, echoed John's view that while Communism itself was hateful the Church did not despair of entering into 'a more positive dialogue' with individual Communist regimes. His itinerant envoy, Monsignor Casaroli, was encouraged to make contact with them. In Yugoslavia he secured a formal agreement safeguarding the interests of Catholics in Croatia and Slovenia. In the wholly or partly Catholic countries of the Soviet bloc the policy stemming from *Pacem in Terris* was making life easier for the national Churches. The harassments and discrimination from which Catholics had suffered at Communist hands since 1945, and which had amounted during the Stalinist period to real persecution were sensibly diminishing. If the alleviations continued they might, so it seemed, very gradually lead to the restoration of full religious liberty. Nevertheless, when Paul became Pope, the primates of Hungary and Czechoslovakia were still imprisoned or prevented from exercising their functions. Whereas the newly repaired churches in those two countries might be filled to overflowing by the faithful, the heavy hand of Communism confined other essential religious activity within narrow limits. But Paul's patient efforts procured the release of a recalcitrant Cardinal Mindszenty and a consenting Archbishop Beran, thus opening the way, if the regimes displayed a modicum of goodwill, for a progressive relaxation of their harsh and restrictive measures.

There was no prospect of the Holy See reaching a satisfactory agreement with either the Hungarian or Czechoslovak government. In Poland, however, the national episcopate was strong enough to deal with the regime on equal terms and without the Vatican being associated with the negotiations. It was the indomitable Cardinal Wyszinski, Archbishop of Warsaw, who twice, in 1950 and 1956, came to terms with Gomulka, the Communist leader, thus safeguarding religious freedoms in return for the Church's support of the government's national policies and social aims. Pius XII, while not taking kindly to such displays of episcopal independence, could not but be pleased by the results of the bargain, and John XXIII reserved an especially warm welcome for the Polish bishops, headed by Wyszinski, when they arrived at Rome for the Council. Among them was the Auxiliary Bishop of Cracow, Karol Wojtyla. Unhappily the Polish Church made too much of its emancipation. The government took umbrage and retaliated, as soon as the Council was wound up, by forbidding Paul's presence at the Czestochowa celebrations. Its pretext was the Pope's reluctance to nominate Polish bishops, as opposed to provisional administrators, to the dioceses in the former German territories annexed to Poland in 1945. And when, in the following year, the President of Poland paid a State visit to Italy, he offended the Vatican by pointedly omitting to seek, as protocol required, an audience with the Pontiff. But such irritations were superficial. The important fact was that the Communist Party and the Catholic hierarchy were left balancing one another within Poland. It is only recently that they have been joined by a third power in the shape of Solidarity, the free Trade Unions.

The Pope earned much applause by his efforts for peace and by his insistence on the obligation of the richer nations to provide for the economic and social welfare of the Third World. His concern for the developing countries was expressed in the encyclical *Populorum Progressio* (1967). Not a very inspiring document, it contained the ritual condemnation of colonialism and was unkindly criticized by the *Wall Street Journal* as souped up Marxism'. Papal solicitude for Asia and Africa is wholly beneficial and takes many forms, but whatever influence the Catholic Church may bring to bear in those largely non-Christian continents is bound to be marginal. The needs of Latin America, where the rapidly multiplying peoples are at least nominally Catholic, are even more urgent. Its nations can hardly be classed as 'emergent', for they emerged early in the nineteenth century and have kept their identity, but in terms of political stability, uniform economic advancement and social cohesion they have remained disappointingly backward. Here was a field in which the Church, understaffed and somnolent, had failed to rise to the occasion.

The Holy See was slow to grasp the gravity of the situation, but shortly before Paul's accession it made amends by setting up a Pontifical Commission for Latin America with a mandate to revivify the local hierarchy and to organize Catholic aid of all kinds for the sub-continent. While the Council was still in session he told the Latin American bishops very clearly that it was their duty to accelerate social change, and there was even a hint in *Populorum Progressio* that in extreme cases the Church might approve revolution against an impossibly tyrannical regime. The hierarchy was not slow to follow the Pope's lead, which indeed suited its own inclinations. In a very few years it ceased to be regarded as a mainstay of reaction and acquired a reputation for radicalism. Its principle of support for the underdog, publicly proclaimed when it met in 1968 at Medellin in Colombia, led to a deterioration in the relations between Church and State in several countries and by 1970 the Pope himself was obliquely denouncing the use of torture by the dictatorial government of Brazil, the largest of them all. As the seventies advanced it began to be felt at Rome that the Latin American Church was becoming over-committed politically.

It was hard to fault a pope so wise, tolerant and compassionate, so full of energy and goodwill, as Paul VI in the early years of his pontificate. His reputation for liberalism seemed unassailable. Yet critics looking for a chink in his armour thought they had found it in his attitude toward problems affecting the intimate lives of priests and laymen, and which the Pope regarded as so delicate that he excluded them from the competence of the Council, thus taking the heavy load of responsibility for their treatment on his own conscience. He tackled the vexed questions of clerical celibacy and birth-control in two encyclicals, *Sacerdotalis Coelibatus* (1967) and *Humanae Vitae* (1968), both of which precluded any relaxation of the rules prohibiting the marriage of priests and the use of contraceptives by married persons. It was the second which caused the greater stir. Liberals within and outside the Church were worried because papal thinking on the subject did not seem to have advanced since Pius XI's total condemnation of contraception in his encyclical *Casti Connubii* of 1930. They also professed to be scandalized because Paul had rejected the majority report drawn up by a commission of experts appointed by himself and endorsed by the majority of a panel of bishops. It recommended a change of principle and suggested ways of reconciling it with traditional doctrine. But the Pope not only put it aside when it was submitted to him in 1966 but followed up his rejection with an uncompromising encyclical. The furthest he would go was to sanction the so-called rhythm method. He was thereupon variously berated for indecision, timidity or sheer unreceptiveness to up-to-date ideas and values. It was alleged that he was succumbing to the fatigue and pessimism of old age. The relative inactivity of his later years may rightly be attributed to natural causes, but it should not be forgotten that Pope John Paul II's stand on birth-control and other such controversial issues has been just as explicit and even more forthrightly expressed.

Paul died quietly at Castelgandolfo on 6 August 1978. His distinguished pontificate complemented the seminal work of John XXIII and the two reigns, considered as a whole, braced and refreshed the Church for its future tasks. These Popes left it fortified by conciliar reforms and capable of a more perceptive approach to the modern world. Their successors could now be sure that the liveliest and most deferential attention would thenceforth be paid to the papacy as a source of moral inspiration and an impartial and stabilizing factor in the affairs of the nations.

EPILOGUE

25

THE POPE FROM POLAND

No Pope of the twentieth century is likely to turn out a nonentity. More than any other modern institution of world-wide scope and influence, the papacy depends on the personality of its head. He cannot afford to be colourless or indecisive; he has to lead all the time and to be seen to be leading. Despite the present ascendancy of the collegial idea, the Church cannot operate without the firmest control and the most vivid inspiration from the top. In no other field is the leader so capable of marking history with his own personal stamp and of commanding such instant, universal and respectful attention for his pronouncements, irrespective of their subject. John Paul II, now in the fourth year of his pontificate, has caught and held public imagination to an unusual degree. He is both attractively human and supremely dignified. He evokes esteem and affection on a scale which no President of the United States, no successor to Stalin or Mao, no Secretary-General of the United Nations, no transient competitor for the allegiance of Islam, is likely to attain in the foreseeable future. His fortunate—some would say miraculous—escape from assassination has further emphasized the power of his personality and the universal character of his ministry.

In a sense Karol Wojtyla is Pope by accident, for it could not have been foreseen that his predecessor, John Paul I, would die after 33 days. If Albino Luciani, Patriarch of Venice, was envisaged as a *papa di passaggio* or stop-gap, there was every possibility that the *passaggio* would be a long one. Nobody could predict how Luciani, a sympathetic but hardly imposing personality, might develop in the normal course of events. His frank and simple manner endeared him to the populace and his only public statement promised faithful adherence to the principles of John XXIII and Paul VI. While Paul had disbanded his Noble Guard John Paul I will no doubt be remembered for having rejected other appurtenances of papal sovereignty such as the tiara and the *sedia gestatoria* (portable throne). It will remain something of a mystery why the Sacred College elected a prelate whose qualities stemmed so exclusively from his upbringing and career in the Venetian hinterland and who possessed so little knowledge of the outside world. When he died so unexpectedly the Cardinals chose a man of a very different mould. There could be no doubt about Wojtyla's exceptional strength of character and versatility of intellect. He had also been trained and tested in an altogether rougher and more exacting school than that of Venetia.

Volùmes have already been written about the Polish background of the first non-Italian Pope for 455 years. His origins, though humble enough, were not exactly working class. At the time of his birth in 1920 his father was serving as a minor clerical officer attached to the newly created Polish army. He received an excellent education in his native town of Wadowice and in 1938 began to study literature at the University of Cracow. This was the beginning of twenty years of intense intellectual activity doggedly pursued throughout the strains and dangers of the war and of post-war Communism. After the dissolution of the university by the Germans he joined a company of clandestine actors, wrote poetry and scraped a living by work in a quarry and a chemical factory. This precarious and half bohemian existence ended in 1942 when his growing vocation for the priesthood brought him under the tutelage of Cardinal Sapieha, Archbishop of Cracow, the descendant of princes and a hero of war-time Poland. For the remainder of the war he lived in the archiepisco-pal palace, studying theology in equally clandestine conditions. At last, in 1946, he was ordained and immediately sent to complete his studies in Rome. The Cardinal had clearly recognized his potential and decided to bring him forward. His stay at the Roman *Collegium Angelicum* gave him a broader view of Christian culture than that which he had gained in his own country. Also, he found his way about the Vatican and acquired an adequate knowledge of Italian and French. Subsequently, he became fluent in several more languages.

Back in Poland, his pastoral duties soon yielded place to academic appointments. Until he was made auxiliary bishop of Cracow in 1958 he was almost wholly absorbed in philosophical and theological study and teaching, principally at the Catholic university of Lublin. The chief influence on his development as a moral philosopher was Max Scheler, a German opponent of Marxists and utilitarians who emphasized the divine origin of human values. But his life was by no means confined to the classroom and seminar. He was on easy terms with all sorts and conditions of men, an active skier in the Tatra mountains and a poet who continued to publish under a pseudonym. During those years he was not directly involved in the current confrontations between the Polish Church, under the leadership of Cardinal Wyszinski, and the Communist government. His nomination as auxiliary bishop was followed six years later by his promotion to Archbishop of the same ancient see, and in 1967 he was made a Cardinal. Between 1962 and 1965 he had taken a very active part in the debates of the Vatican Council. His contributions enhanced his reputation as a theologian, while his experience of communist ideology and practice was of great help in the preparation of the Council's constitution *Gaudium et Spes* (The Church in the Modern World). But it was his subsequent work in the Synod of Bishops that made him a likely future choice for the papacy although, strangely enough, his candidacy does not seem to have been seriously mooted at the conclave that elected John Paul I. His enthusiasm for the collegial system was demonstrated at successive meetings of the Synod. He served on its permanent council and became identified with the more dynamic element in the Sacred College and the episcopate in general.

His frequent absences from Poland on synodical business did not interfere with his pastoral work in his own diocese or with his defence, when necessary, of the religious and human rights of his compatriots against pressure from the communist regime. The twin pillars of the Polish Church were its primate, Wyszinski of Warsaw, and Wojtyla of Cracow. The former's approach to Poland's problems was the more astringent and challenging, the latter's the more subtle but no less effective. Wojtyla was affable, patient and tactful, but fearless when he thought that a clash with the authorities was unavoidable. Together the two prelates stage-managed the millen-nial celebrations at Czestochowa to which Paul VI was denied access, and it was the

Cardinal of Cracow who, in the face of every kind of official discouragement, carried through the building and consecration of the vast new church in Nowa Huta, Cracow's satellite steel-producing city which the regime had planned as a centre of godless industrialism. Later in the same year (1977) President Gierek thought it advisable to appease national sentiment by seeking an audience with Paul VI at the Vatican.

Thus, by 1978, Wojtyla was at the height of his powers and of his prestige at Rome as well as in Poland. Nevertheless it was ironical that a quirk of fate, in the shape of Albino Luciani's sudden death, should have been necessary to make him Pope. Nor is it likely that he would have been elected unless the possible Italian contenders had eliminated each other by their own rivalries. Once they had done so, however, Wojtyla was the obvious non-Italian choice, and it was well received in Italy.

The Polish Pope lost no time in asserting himself. He did so primarily by demonstrating through his own physical presence in many quarters of the globe the paramount importance he attached to the papacy's worldwide mission. Wherever he went and addressed mass gatherings he drove home the lesson that the Head of the Church is not a remote and unknowable monarch but an immediately present and familiar leader and friend. All Catholics may expect to see him some time in the flesh and always, thanks to modern media of communication, on the screen, and to enjoy his gift of stirring eloquence in many languages. In a sense he is visible and audible at any time. It was the same message that Paul VI had tried to proclaim in the early stage of his pontificate, but John Paul II put it across with much greater force and credibility. He very soon set out on his travels. Some of them, especially his triumphal progress through his own country, have been spectacularly successful. In Poland he may well have changed the direction of its social and political development. By his visit to the Orthodox Patriarch at Istanbul he exhibited his faith in ecumenism. His voyages have already taken him to Mexico and Brazil, to Ireland and the United States, to France and Germany, to Africa and the Indian sub-continent, to the Philippines and Japan. Others are planned, subject to his state of health. Critics have affected to regard him as fascinated by movement for its own sake and by the acclaim of enthusiastic crowds, but it is evident that each journey, apart from the comfort it brings to Catholics in the countries concerned, is undertaken for a specific purpose.

The need for the Pope's presence in Latin America was especially obvious and urgent. Over the past two or three decades the bishops of that region, formerly notorious for their neglect of social problems, had swung to the opposite extreme. They now included in their ranks some of the most radically inclined Catholic churchmen. There was much confusion of mind among them regarding the right application of the principles of *Populorum Progressio* in the Third World. According to the proponents of 'liberation theology', it was the Church's duty not only to oppose economic exploitation and to speed social change, but to identify or ally itself with political movements, even if they were subversive or basically irreligious, which sought to achieve change if necessary by non-peaceful means. In addressing the assembled Latin American bishops at Puebla in Mexico, a country where the Church, once heavily persecuted, had reasserted its role in the national life, John Paul made it clear that the episcopate must continue to devote itself to the elimination of social and economic injustices. He stressed that capitalism and Marxism were equally responsible for those evils. But he also insisted that the Church must dissociate itself from revolutionary activism ostensibly pursuing similar aims but in fact committed to a society totally incompatible with religious freedom.

Another striking feature of John Paul's pontificate has been his disapproval of doctrinal innovations. His allegedly inflexible conservatism in this respect has been under fire from several quarters, from avant-garde theologians, Jesuits and ex-Jesuits, Dominicans and others. The most outspoken among them, the Swiss Hans Küng and the Dutchman Edward Schillebeeckx, have incurred strictures from the Congregation of the Doctrine of the Faith at Rome. Himself a formidable theologian, the Pope has little sympathy with subjectivists for whom the value of Catholic dogma resides rather in the intentions of the believer than in its relation to objective reality. He requires academic theologians calling themselves Catholics not to deviate publicly from the collegial line which represents the collective thinking of the Church. His ruling on the subject was plainly expressed in the words of his first encyclical, *Redemptor Hominis*, 'nobody may treat theology as if it consisted simply of explaining his personal ideas.' Evidently the concept of human rights, which Wojtyla so vehemently defends in the case of oppressed workers and peasants, does not shield dissident theologians engaged in undermining the foundations of the faith in the name of subjective truth. Nevertheless the reproofs and prohibitions the dissidents have suffered hardly amount, as is sometimes suggested, to a new version of the Inquisition.

At the same time widespread anxiety, mingled with irritation, has been felt and expressed over the Pope's disinclination to compromise with contemporary attitudes towards questions of discipline and morals, as affecting both clergy and laity. His humanity, accessibility and understanding of human nature are contrasted with his rigid views on such controversial and lively issues as clerical marriage, the admission of women to the priesthood, the release of clerics from their vows, divorce, contraception, abortion and homosexuality. He is attacked for imposing his personal authority and for cutting short collegial discussion on these matters, as happened at the 1980 synod on the family. He is accused of closing his mind to the realities of the modern world, as exemplified by the menace of over-population, and of ignoring the advice of scientists and economists. It is further claimed that his intransigent conservatism is driving Catholics to disregard *en masse* the Church's teaching as no longer relevant to their private lives and to the upbringing of their children. The Rome correspondent of *The Times* has called this tendency a 'silent revolution'. The Pope is urged to stop vainly trying to block the march of progress and to conduct instead a thorough review of the theological position and of the Church's duties to humanity.

Such grave charges, not easily to be dismissed as expressions of impatience and ill-humour, have not outwardly disturbed a pope who no doubt thinks in centuries and not in accordance with the urges of the moment. But while it might be an exaggeration to picture the Catholic laity as unanimously kicking against the restraints imposed by a backward-looking pontiff, it is clear that the *Aggiornamento* has so far failed to solve many of the personal and social problems that are worrying twentieth-century Catholics. Paul VI, in his encyclical *Humanae Vitae*, sought without success to damp down popular hopes of a more elastic papal attitude towards birth control, and John Paul II has caused outspoken, if not widespread, disappointment by showing himself equally immovable on this issue. Indeed, as lately as 18 May 1981, only five days after his narrow escape from death, the Italians demonstrated their feelings by decisively rejecting, through a national referendum, a proposal put forward by the 'Right to Life' movement, and warmly supported by himself, for the repeal of the existing liberal law on abortion in favour of something much more restrictive. However, despite the evidently prevailing impression among Catholics everywhere that a progressive Church must necessarily become more permissive, there would seem to be little prospect of the present Pope travelling along the same road. On the contrary, he is likely to refuse all concessions which in his view might lead to chaos in the Church. For him the individual Catholic is no more entitled to moral autonomy than to a personal theology.

Thus these issues were still very much pending when, on 13 May 1981, John Paul was shot and seriously wounded by a Turkish gunman in the course of his general audience in St Peter's Square. The virtual impossibility of guaranteeing his security on such popular occasions enabled the assailant to edge so close to his intended victim that it was a wonder that he was not killed instantly. As it was he was struck by three pistol bullets, two of which inflicted merely superficial wounds in his right arm and the index finger of his left hand. The third, however, perforated his intestines and narrowly missed his spine. Luckily his personal staff kept their heads: they rushed him through the horrified crowds to the Gemelli hospital, where an emergency operation was at once performed.

The would-be assassin, Mehmet Ali Agca, was seized on the spot. At his subsequent interrogation and trial he gave nothing away. Forgiven by the Pope, he was condemned to life imprisonment. Presumably he was not acting on his own but as the agent of some terrorist organization with international links, the motives of which are still obscure. It appears that after escaping from a Turkish maximum security prison, where he was serving a long sentence, he spent many months moving from one country to another in both eastern and western Europe and was maintained between his flittings in comfortable surroundings. Why the unknown employers of this professional hit-man should have chosen May 1981 for his attack on the Pope is still a matter of guesswork. At present there appears to be no sound reason for connecting the crime, as some journalists have been tempted to do, with a critical stage in the Polish situation, coinciding as it did with the illness and death of Cardinal Wyszinski and following upon the Pope's reception of Lech Walesa, leader of the Solidarity movement, at the Vatican.

The immediate public reaction to this outrage from both admirers and critics of John Paul was an immense surge of affectionate sympathy. Open challenges to his attitudes were at least temporarily stilled. It was recalled how often and forcefully he had expressed his feelings of anxiety and frustration over the persistence of terrorism in the world at large, and particularly in the Middle East, Latin America and Northern Ireland. Naturally enough there was a burst of speculation as to the extent to which his injuries might affect his stamina, inhibit his activities and oblige him to modify his style of vigorous populism. His health suddenly became a matter of high historic drama. In the immediate future, would he still be capable of defusing the dangerous confrontation that had developed in his homeland? It was supposed that he had recently urged caution on Walesa in his dealings with the communist regime.

Early reports on John Paul's progress were fairly optimistic. No serious doubts were entertained of his eventual recovery. Nevertheless it was forecast that his convalescence might be a long one. It therefore came as a surprise when he emerged from hospital on 7 June in order to attend the celebration in St Peter's of the anniversary of the Councils of Constantinople (381) and Ephesus (431). This was a grand affair, attended by over 50 Cardinals and 350 bishops, and was designed as a reaffirmation of the ecumenical idea. But shortly afterwards the Pope suffered a marked setback due to a virus infection. Re-admitted to hospital on 20 June, he underwent a secondary operation on 5 August 'to ensure the normal functioning of his intestines'. In the intervening weeks he endured recurrent bouts of fever, remained very much an invalid and was unable to attend to any but the most essential business. Only on 14 August was he allowed to return to the Vatican. After blessing the crowds in St Peter's Square on the following day, the Feast of the Assumption, he retired on 16 August to Castelgandolfo.

During his illness the daily conduct of Vatican affairs was left in the capable hands of the Secretary of State, Cardinal Casaroli. As was inevitable, however, the pace slowed down, initiatives were halted and an awkward backlog of business began to accumulate. Projected papal journeys to Spain and Switzerland were cancelled. On the other hand plans for a visit to the United Kingdom, a territory never previously trodden by a Pope, were actively pursued with the full co-operation of the Church of England. One of Casaroli's more important tasks was to preside over a council of fifteen Cardinals (eleven of them drawn from outside Italy) to discuss deficits in the Vatican's budget estimated at £15–17 million. It was certainly embarrassing that two lay financial advisers to the Holy See had recently been arrested for fraud. Rumours concerning the precarious condition of the papal finances, linked with insinuations about the allegedly dubious sources of papal income, have of course long been part of the stock in trade of international journalism, but unlike some of his Italian predecessors the present Pope has not been content simply to ignore them. He has insisted on the maintenance of order in the finances and on the probity of those who handle them. Meanwhile the Holy See was quick to dissociate itself from any connexion with the prominent Christian Socialists implicated in the so-called P2 scandal through their membership of a Masonic Lodge.

On 26 August John Paul resumed his general audiences at Castelgandolfo, where he was soon speeding up his rhythm of work, and by 4 October he was back in Rome presiding over a ceremony of beatification. Three days later he appeared in St Peter's Square for his first general audience there since the attempt on his life, using the car in which he had been shot. After he had given his address the elaborate precautions taken for his safety did not deter him from greeting the crowds on foot.

The occasion demonstrated in striking fashion that the Pope was back at the helm. But on 16 September, while still at Castelgandolfo, he had already made public his 24,000 word encyclical *Laborem Exercens* on the value and dignity of human labour. Written, as the world was assured, in hospital, and aptly timed to appear ninety years after Leo XIII's *Rerum Novarum* and half a century after Pius XI's *Quadragesimo Anno* it was presumably designed to mark a further advance in papal thinking about the rights of workers. In fact it said nothing very new or startling. In the words of the religious correspondent of *The Times*, John Paul's purpose was 'not to make novel comments on contemporary industrial relations but to apply fundamental beliefs and human nature to a range of particular circumstances'. However that may be, he declared that there was a 'need for new movements of solidarity of the workers and with the workers' and that the Church must seek to justify its claim to be the Church of the Poor.

The word 'solidarity' occurred in more than one passage of the encyclical. While it was being composed the already long drawn out political crisis in Poland was becoming more acute. There was no doubt that the beliefs and aspirations of the vast majority of John Paul's compatriots were represented by the Roman Catholic

Church and by Solidarity, the independent trade union movement headed by Lech Walesa, loyalty to the latter being perfectly compatible with devotion to the former. On 20 September the Polish episcopate, headed by its new Primate, Archbishop Glemp, issued a pastoral letter supporting Solidarity's claim for free access to the media; it was unacceptable, the bishops asserted, that only one social group and only one ideological outlook (the Communist) should enjoy a monopoly. And on the same day the Pope himself declared that Poland should have the right to solve its own problems without interference from outside and risk of bloodshed; 'a nation that has paid so high a price for its independence has a right to make independent decisions.'

These were strong words, reflecting the feelings of all lovers of freedom. At the same time the Polish hierarchy has constantly sought to promote some form of understanding and cooperation between Solidarity and the Communist regime, a vital aim if economic collapse and Soviet intervention are to be forestalled. It has striven, for some time successfully if by narrow margins, to prevent fatal confrontations. John Paul's direction of their endeavours to avert disaster and to achieve a measure of national harmony has undoubtedly been very close, although it may well be a long time before the full extent of his personal involvement can be disclosed. His choice of the tactful Glemp to succeed Wyszinski was a wise one, and it was a hopeful sign that envoys from the Church and Solidarity were able to pass freely between Poland and the Vatican. Indeed, the Pope had real grounds for optimism before the imposition of martial law in mid-December threatened to ruin his patient work for peace.

Amid these alarms John Paul, apparently restored to health and full of energy, was also turning his mind to the internal problems of the Church. On 28 October, for instance, he had received from Cardinal Felice the text of Canon Law as revised by a Commission set up by John XXIII fourteen years earlier. This was a stupendous work of scholarship and legal expertise, but progressive critics were already hinting that its whole approach was disappointingly conservative. It will be the Pope's onerous duty to approve or reject this new version of the Church's basic law. Equally delicate were the perennial difficulties of the Society of Jesus, its dwindling membership and the penchant of many of its remaining members for 'liberation' theology and radical politics. Since its General, the Spaniard Father Arrupe, was incurably crippled by thrombosis, it was being administered by an American Vicar-General, Father O'Keefe. But at the end of October O'Keefe was abruptly dismissed by the Pope, who replaced him by a 'personal delegate', the Italian Father Dezza. The latter is charged with preparing a general congregation of the Society under close papal superintendence, and once again critics have tended to interpret John Paul's action as an anti-liberal move.

It would be rash to speculate about the future course of a possibly long pontificate. No doubt John Paul's temporary removal from the centre of affairs has done far less harm than was once forecast either to the Church or to his own standing. In some ways his authority and charisma have been enhanced. On the whole the world approves of a Pope who, according to an English newspaper, 'behaves like a Pope and who does not forever steer or trim towards fashionable beliefs', who, while pursuing his own way, tries to avoid clashing with either reactionaries or progressives, and who does not encourage those who hold that the survival of Church and papacy must depend on their identification with advanced socio-political thinking, an elastic attitude towards moral questions and the replacement of traditional theology by something much less explicit. Will he eventually be remembered for his vain resistance to the march of ideas, or for his steadfast defence of the faith, his deep intelligence, true liberalism and work in the cause of peace?

DECEMBER 1981

Pope John Paul I

Overleaf: John Paul II saying Mass with an Irish congregation of over a million

John Paul II announcing an international visit

John Paul II meeting the crowd in St Peter's Square

——Bibliographical Note——

Papal biography began with the official *Liber Pontificalis*. But since this jejune chronicle petered out before the end of the Dark Ages countless books have been written about the Popes and the papacy. No historian of the subject could fail to be intimidated by the sheer bulk of published works in many languages (to say nothing of unpublished material) devoted either to the Holy See as an institution or to the careers and personalities of the pontiffs themselves. They have of course multiplied at an increasing rate over the two thousand years during which the papacy has formed successively an integral element of the Roman Empire, of Europe and of the world as a whole. The approach of any writer who has the temerity to cover the whole field from 64 to 1981 AD in a short book must therefore be very strictly selective, and I have inevitably confined myself to secondary sources. Substantial bibliographies are attached to most if not all the works mentioned below.

The massive general histories of the papacy produced in the nineteenth and early twentieth centuries are still eminently worth exploring. Such are L. von Ranke's *History of the Popes in the 16th and 17th centuries* (London 1847), L. von Pastor's *History of the Popes from the close of the Middle Ages* (London 1891 onwards), Horace K. Mann's *The Lives of the Popes in the Early Middle Ages* (London 1902), H. Grisar's *History of Rome and the Popes in the Middle Ages* (London 1911–12), Mandell Creighton's *History of the Papacy from the Great Schism to the Sack of Rome* (London 1903 onwards) and F. Gregorovius's monumental *History of the City of Rome in the Middle Ages* (London 1895). The recent work of F. X. Seppelt, *Geschichte der Päpste von den Anfängen bis zur Mitte des 20ᵗⁿ Jahrhunderts* (Munich 1954 onwards) is more immediately useful. So are Paul Johnson's *A History of Christianity* (London 1976) and the relevant chapters in the Cambridge Mediaeval and Modern Histories.

Records of individual Popes in the period preceding the triumph of Christianity are scanty, but they are well summarized in P. Carrington's *The Early Christian Church* (Cambridge 1957). The ensuing centuries are much better documented, although the leading Christian personalities in the West—Jerome, Ambrose, Augustine—were not Popes. Much attention, on the other hand, has been lavished on Pope Gregory I. His classic biography in English is by F. Holmes Dudden (London 1905), while Jeffrey Richards, in his *The Popes and the Papacy in the Early Middle Ages* (London 1979) gives an excellent modern assessment of his and other pontificates. Also indispensable are two classic histories of the Later Roman Empire, those of J. B. Bury (London 1889), which carries the story down to 802, and A. H. M. Jones (Oxford 1964), which terminates two centuries earlier.

Among the multitude of modern works dealing with the mediaeval papacy, I have especially relied on G. Barraclough's *The Mediaeval Papacy* (London 1968) and on three studies by Walter Ullmann, *The Growth of Papal Government in the Middle Ages* (London 1962), *Mediaeval Political Thought* (London 1965) and *A Short History of the Papacy in the Middle Ages* (London 1972). Much significant material has been gathered from S. Runciman's *History of the Crusades* (Cambridge 1951–4), *The Eastern Schism* (Oxford 1955) and *The Sicilian Vespers* (London 1958). The same applies to the biographies of Frederick II of Hohenstaufen by E. Kantorowicz (London 1931) and Georgina Masson (London 1957) and J. J. Norwich's *The Normans in Sicily* and *The Kingdom in the Sun* (London 1967 and 1970).

The period of the Avignon papacy and of the Great Schism is very well covered by G. Mollat's *The Popes at Avignon* (London 1963), Yves Renouard's *The Avignon Papacy 1305–1403* (London 1970), M. Bishop's *Petrarch and His World* (London 1964), W. Ullmann's *The Origins of the Great Schism* (London 1948) and J. Holland Smith's *The Great Schism, 1378* (London 1970).

By contrast with the vast wealth of background material for the Middle Ages available to the historian, papal biography as such is a disappointing branch of literature for this or any period. When it degenerates into mere hagiography it is historically useless, just as the addiction of many later writers to papal vices rather than papal virtues is equally misleading. An example of the latter tendency is E. R. Chamberlin's *The Bad Popes* (London 1970). Not even the great and good Popes of the past have always been served by good biographers. Gregory I was fortunate in that respect, and as for Leo I, T. Jalland's *St Leo the Great* (London 1941), is very useful, but curiously enough there seems to be no classic life of Gregory VII, for instance, or of Urban II. Innocent III, on the other hand, has earned six volumes from A. Luchaire (Paris 1907), as well as a study by C. H. C. Pirie-Gordon (London 1907).

When we arrive at the Renaissance and the Reformation, the task of assessing the role of individual Popes amid the religious, political and cultural developments of the period becomes even more complicated. The literary field is almost infinite, but the biographies are neither numerous (with the exception of those devoted to the Borgias) nor reliable. It is necessary to seek enlightenment from general works and modern studies such as Jacob Burckhardt's *The Civilization of the Renaissance in Italy* (London 1900–1910), Owen Chadwick's *The Reformation* (London 1968), R. H. Bainton's *Erasmus and Christendom* (London 1970) and H. Jedin's *History of the Council of Trent* (London 1957). G. Mattingley's *Renaissance Diplomacy* (London 1963) provides a sure guide to papal involvement in contemporary inter-state politics.

The prominent role of the Popes of the Counter-Reformation in the politico-religious conflicts of the period is well brought out in Pastor's *History*. It is also powerfully stressed throughout F. Brundel's *The Mediterranean* (London 1970). It emerges in all books about contemporary Venice eg. in J. J. Norwich's *Venice. The Greatness and the Fall* (London 1981). As regards the three illustrious dissidents who caused the Popes so much trouble, Norwich contributes an interesting passage on Paolo Sarpi. On Giordano Bruno I would recommend J. Lewis McIntyre's study (London 1903) of the man and his philosophy, while the drama of Galileo is brilliantly presented in Arthur Koestler's *The Sleepwalkers* (London 1959). C. V. Wedgwood's *The Thirty Years War* (London 1968) paints the gloomy background against which baroque Rome flourished.

During the second half of the seventeenth century the papacy was undermined by Jansenism and by the aggressive Gallicanism of Louis XIV; in the eighteenth century it was outmatched by the militant scepticism of the Enlightenment as well as scorned by Catholic sovereigns. These movements originated in France and the best sources for the period are consequently French. They are also copious; for example Sainte-Beuve's *Port-Royal* (Paris 1882) fills six volumes and E. Michaud's *Louis XIV et Innocent XI* (also Paris 1882) runs to form. The eighteenth-century Popes have found few apologists: indeed Paul Johnson dismisses them summarily as nonentities, a view disputed by R. Hayes in *Benedict XIV, Philosopher King* (London 1970). On the Church's enemies see T. Besterman's *Voltaire* (London 1969), also G. R. Cragg's *The Church in the Age of Reason* (London 1960). Among recent works on the Jesuits and the dissolution of their Order by Clement XIV I would mention David Mitchell's *The Jesuits* (London 1980).

The revolutionary avalanche of 1789 threatened to overwhelm the papacy altogether. That it failed to do so was due to the steadfastness in adversity of Pius VI and Pius VII. The story of their struggle with republican and imperial France, as well as of its prelude and aftermath, is admirably told by E. E. Y. Hales in his *Revolution and Papacy 1769–1846* (London 1960). He also deals judiciously with the period following Napoleon's fall during which the Popes earned a bad name for reaction. His earlier work *Pio Nono* (London 1954) is an impressive appraisal of the pontificate and personality of Pius IX.

So far as I am aware, the long reign of Leo XIII, author of the first papal encyclical dealing with workers' rights, still lacks a really objective biographer. Historians have tended to condemn his innate conservatism and defensive outlook, a charge which can justly be levelled at his successor Pius X. Leo's life by E. Soderini (London 1934–5) is instructive but at the same time adulatory.

The role of the Popes in the era of great wars, world upheavals and radical ideas has attracted a host of writers, good and bad, who have dissected their characters and policies. Pius XI has been heavily attacked for his transactions with the dictators, and just as strenuously defended for his services to peace and to the well-being of the Church. Pius XII has been bitterly arraigned for his failure to protect the Jews, and this charge has been just as hotly denied. These controversies are likely to echo for many years before a balanced view prevails. Meanwhile readers must make up their own minds. In his *The Vatican in the Age of Dictators* (London 1973) Anthony Rhodes puts the case for the two above-mentioned Popes clearly and persuasively; others, to put it mildly, are less kind. Two books by Peter Nichols, *The Politics of the Vatican* (London 1968) and *The Pope's Divisions* (London 1981), offer a comprehensive survey, both critical and sympathetic, of the problems confronting the modern papacy and of the different approaches of recent Popes towards them. *Pope John and his Revolution* by E. E. Y. Hales (London 1965) illuminates this pontificate and the Second Vatican Council; so does Paul Johnson's *Pope John XXIII* (London 1974). See also Peter Hebblethwaite's *The Runaway Church* (London 1975). A spate of books about John Paul II is no doubt pouring from the presses.

The Popes

A CHRONOLOGICAL LIST

64 (?)	Linus	366–384	Damasus I
79–90 (?)	Anencletus (Anacletus)	366–367	Ursinus, anti-pope
90–99	Clement I	384–399	Siricius
99–107 (?)	Evaristus	399–401	Anastasius I
107–116	Alexander I	401–417	Innocent I
116–125	Sixtus (Xystus) I	417–418	Zosimus
125–136	Telesphorus	418–422	Boniface I
136–140	Hyginus	418–419	Eulalius, anti-pope
140–155	Pius I	422–432	Celestine I
155–166	Anicetus	432–440	Sixtus III
166–174	Soter	440–461	Leo I
174–189	Eleutherus	461–468	Hilarus
189–198	Victor I	468–483	Simplicius
198–217	Zephyrinus	483–492	Felix II
217–222	Callistus (Calixtus) I	492–496	Gelasius I
		496–498	Anastasius II
217–235	Hippolytus, anti-pope	498–514	Symmachus
		498–505	Laurentius, anti-pope
222–230	Urban I		
230–235	Pontianus	514–523	Hormisdas
235–236	Anterus	523–526	John I
236–250	Fabianus	526–530	Felix III
251–253	Cornelius	530	Dioscurus
251–258	Novatian, anti-pope	530–532	Boniface II
		533–535	John II
253–254	Lucius I	535–536	Agapetus I
254–257	Stephen I	536–537	Silverius
257–258	Sixtus II	537–555	Vigilius
260–267	Dionysius	556–561	Pelagius I
269–273	Felix I	561–574	John III
275–283	Eutychianus	575–579	Benedict I
283–296	Caius	579–590	Pelagius II
296–304	Marcellinus	590–604	Gregory I
307–309	Marcellus I	604–606	Sabinian
309	Eusebius	607	Boniface III
310–314	Miltiades	608–615	Boniface IV
314–335	Silvester I	615–618	Deusdedit I
336	Marcus	619–625	Boniface V
337–352	Julius I	625–638	Honorius I
352–366	Liberius	640	Severinus
355–365	Felix, anti-pope	640–642	John IV
		642–649	Theodore I

649–655	Martin I	913–914	Lando
655–657	Eugenius I	914–928	John X
657–672	Vitalian	928	Leo VI
672–676	Deusdedit II	929–931	Stephen VII
676–678	Donus	931–935	John XI
678–681	Agatho	936–939	Leo VII
681–683	Leo II	939–942	Stephen VIII
684–685	Benedict II	942–946	Marinus II
685–686	John V	946–955	Agapetus II
686–687	Conon	955–964	John XII
687–701	Sergius I	964	Benedict V
701–705	John VI	964–965	Leo V
705–707	John VII	965–972	John XIII
708	Sisinnius	973–974	Benedict VI
708–715	Constantine I	974	Boniface VII
715–731	Gregory II		(Franko)
731–741	Gregory III	974–983	Benedict VII
741–752	Zacharias	983–984	John XIV
752–757	Stephen II	984–985	Boniface VII
757–767	Paul I	985–996	John XV
757–767	Constantine II,	996–999	Gregory V
	anti-pope	997–998	John XVI,
768–773	Stephen III		anti-pope
772–795	Hadrian I	999–1003	Silvester II
795–816	Leo III	1003	John XVII
816–817	Stephen IV	1003–1009	John XVIII
817–824	Paschal I	1009–1012	Sergius IV
824–827	Eugenius II	1012–1024	Benedict VIII
827	Valentinus I	1024–1032	John XIX
827–844	Gregory IV	1032–1044	Benedict IX
844–847	Sergius II	1045	Silvester III
847–855	Leo IV	1045–1046	Gregory VI
855–858	Benedict III	1046–1047	Clement II
858–867	Nicholas I	1048	Damasus II
867–872	Hadrian II	1049–1054	Leo IX
872–882	John VIII	1055–1057	Victor II
882–884	Marinus I	1057–1058	Stephen IX
884–885	Hadrian III	1058–1059	Benedict X
885–891	Stephen V	1059–1061	Nicholas II
891–896	Formosus	1061–1073	Alexander II
896	Boniface VI	1061–1072	Honorius II,
896–897	Stephen VI		anti-pope
897	Romanus	1073–1085	Gregory VII
897	Theodore II	1084–1100	Clement III,
898–900	John IX		anti-pope
900–903	Benedict IV	1086–1087	Victor III
903	Leo V	1088–1099	Urban II
903–904	Christophorus	1099–1118	Paschal II
904–911	Sergius III	1100–1102	Theodorich,
911–912	Anastasius III		anti-pope

1100	Albert, anti-pope	1294	Celestine V
1105–1111	Silvester IV, anti-pope	1294–1303	Boniface VIII
		1303–1304	Benedict XI
1118–1119	Gelasius II	1305–1314	Clement V (Avignon)
1118–1121	Gregory VIII, anti-pope	1316–1334	John XXII (Avignon)
1119–1124	Calixtus II		
1124–1130	Honorius II	1334–1342	Benedict XII (Avignon)
1124	Celestine II, anti-pope	1342–1352	Clement VI (Avignon)
1130–1143	Innocent II		
1130–1138	Anacletus II, anti-pope	1352–1362	Innocent VI (Avignon)
1138	Victor IV, anti-pope	1362–1370	Urban V (Avignon)
1143–1144	Celestine II	1370–1378	Gregory XI (Rome)
1144–1145	Lucius II		
1145–1153	Eugenius III		
1153–1154	Anastasius IV		
1154–1159	Hadrian IV		

The Great Schism

1159–1181	Alexander III	1378–1389	Urban VI (Rome)
1159–1164	Victor IV, anti-pope	1378–1394	Clement VII (Avignon)
1164–1168	Paschalis III, anti-pope	1389–1404	Boniface IX (Rome)
1168–1179	Calixtus III, anti-pope	1394–1423	Benedict XIII (Avignon to 1417, Spain)
1179–1180	Innocent III, anti-pope	1404–1406	Innocent VII (Rome)
1181–1185	Lucius III		
1185–1187	Urban III		
1187	Gregory VIII		
1187–1191	Clement III	1406–1415	Gregory XII
1191–1198	Celestine III	1409–1410	Alexander V
1198–1216	Innocent III	1410–1415	John XXIII
1216–1227	Honorius III	1417–1431	Martin V
1227–1241	Gregory IX	1423–1429	Clement VIII, anti-pope
1241	Celestine IV		
1243–1254	Innocent IV	1425	Benedict XIV, anti-pope
1254–1261	Alexander IV		
1261–1264	Urban IV	1431–1447	Eugenius IV
1265–1268	Clement IV	1439–1449	Felix V, anti-pope
1271–1276	Gregory X	1447–1455	Nicholas V
1276	Innocent V	1455–1458	Calixtus III
1276	Hadrian V	1458–1464	Pius II
1276–1277	John XXI	1464–1471	Paul II
1277–1280	Nicholas III	1471–1484	Sixtus IV
1281–1288	Martin IV	1484–1492	Innocent VIII
1285–1287	Honorius IV	1492–1503	Alexander VI
1288–1292	Nicholas IV		

1503	Pius III		1676–1689	Innocent XI
1503–1513	Julius II		1689–1691	Alexander VIII
1513–1521	Leo X		1691–1700	Innocent XII
1522–1523	Hadrian VI		1700–1721	Clement XI
1523–1534	Clement VII		1721–1724	Innocent XIII
1534–1549	Paul III		1724–1730	Benedict XIV
1550–1555	Julius III		1730–1740	Clement XII
1555	Marcellus II		1740–1758	Benedict XIII
1555–1559	Paul IV		1758–1769	Clement XIII
1559–1565	Pius IV		1769–1774	Clement XIV
1566–1572	Pius V		1775–1799	Pius VI
1572–1585	Gregory XIII		1800–1823	Pius VII
1585–1590	Sixtus V		1823–1829	Leo XII
1590	Urban VII		1829–1830	Pius VIII
1590–1591	Gregory XIV		1831–1846	Gregory XVI
1591	Innocent IX		1846–1878	Pius IX
1592–1605	Clement VIII		1878–1903	Leo XIII
1605	Leo XI		1903–1914	Pius X
1605–1621	Paul V		1914–1922	Benedict XV
1621–1623	Gregory XV		1922–1939	Pius XI
1623–1644	Urban VIII		1939–1958	Pius XII
1644–1655	Innocent X		1958–1963	John XXIII
1655–1667	Alexander VII		1963–1978	Paul VI
1667–1669	Clement IX		1978	John Paul I
1670–1676	Clement X		1978–	John Paul II

Index